RUTHERFORD B. HAYES

Rutherford Birchard Hayes

RUTHERFORD B. HAYES
Warrior and President

Ari Hoogenboom

University Press of Kansas

Published by the University Press of Kansas (Lawrence, Kansas 66049), which was organized by the Kansas Board of Regents and is operated and funded by Emporia State University, Fort Hays State University, Kansas State University, Pittsburg State University, the University of Kansas, and Wichita State University

Library of Congress Cataloging-in-Publication Data

Hoogenboom, Ari Arthur, 1927–
Rutherford B. Hayes : warrior and president / Ari Hoogenboom.
p.   cm.
Includes index.
ISBN 0–7006–0641–6 (cloth)
1. Hayes, Rutherford Birchard, 1822–1893.   2. Presidents—United States—Biography.   3. United States—Politics and government—1877–1881.   I. Title.
E682.H78   1995
973.8′3′092—dc20

[B]   94-5274

British Library Cataloguing in Publication Data is available.

Printed in the United States of America

10 9 8 7 6 5 4 3 2 1

For
Clara Johanna Behn Hoogenboom
(1900–1971)
and
Clara Helen Hoogenboom

CONTENTS

ILLUSTRATIONS

ACKNOWLEDGMENTS

My debts are many. Director Roger Bridges and former Director Leslie H. Fishel, Jr., of the Hayes Presidential Center have facilitated my research in ways far beyond what any visiting scholar—even one who has become a warm personal friend—could reasonably expect. Their staff members—particularly Archivist Thomas J. Culbertson and Assistant Director and Head of Research Thomas A. Smith—have been unusually helpful in alerting me to materials and in solving knotty problems, while Culbertson and Head of Photographic Resources Gilbert Gonzalez were collaborators in the selection of illustrations. Curator James B. Snider has generously shared his knowledge of Hayes memorabilia. Other staff members at the Hayes Presidential Center—Caroline Rinebolt, Janice Haas, Nan Card, Rebecca Hill, and Barbara Paff—have ferreted out obscure evidence and have made pleasant my extended stays in Fremont, Ohio.

The late Professor Hoyt Landon Warner of Kenyon College, historian and friend, introduced me to Kenyon College in a most gracious manner. The late Thomas Greenslade, curator of what is now called the Greenslade Special Collections of Kenyon College and Jami Peelle, special collections librarian of Kenyon College, provided information on Kenyon as Hayes knew it, and Peter Norling, Kenyon alumnus, lawyer, and friend instructed me in matters of Kenyon and legal lore. I am also indebted to the overworked reference librarians at Brooklyn College, to the patient staff of the University of Göttingen Library, and to all who have made, and still make, the New York Public Library and the Library of Congress incomparable institutions. Grants from the Research Foundation of the City University of New York facilitated my work at the Hayes Presidential Center and the Library of Congress and reduced the price of the book. Wang Chi Wong, manager of the Academic Computing Center at Brooklyn College and his staff, especially Eddie Valentin and Ramez Mekhail, have guided me on many occasions when I was stumped by my word processor.

I owe much to fellow historians. Brooks D. Simpson of Arizona State University read the entire manuscript, as did Leslie H. Fishel, Jr., and I am grateful for their innumerable sound suggestions. Old friends Jerome Sternstein of Brooklyn College, Robert V. Bruce of Boston University, and Irwin

Unger of New York University read and criticized sections of the manuscript. Clifford Nelson of the U.S. Geological Survey has helped me in geological matters, and John F. Coleman of St. Francis College, Loretto, Pennsylvania, has indentified several obscure individuals. I am grateful to Marie Luise Frings, Hermann Wellenreuther, Ursula and Karl Tilman Winkler, and Thomas J. Müller, colleagues at Göttingen who facilitated my research and writing during my year in Germany. I wish to thank Fred M. Woodward, director of the University Press of Kansas, for his patience and advice and also his staff members, Susan Schott, Susan McRory, Megan Schoeck, and Dorothea Anderson for their generous help. In addition I want to acknowledge the sensitive copyediting of this book by Linda Lotz and the indexing by Doug Easton.

My greatest debts are to members of my own family. Both my daughter Lynn and my son Ari, Jr.—experienced editors with a grasp of history that does their father proud—have gone over this manuscript with a fine-tooth comb, and their sister Jan has shared in our many discussions. Finally, their mother and my wife, Olive, has interrupted her own scholarly pursuits to read and reread this biography in all of its stages.

I have dedicated this book to my mother and sister, who share the name Clara. Thanks to the public schools and public libraries in Brooklyn, my mother loved to read, enjoyed history, and inclined me in that direction. But it was the example of my sister, an early graduate of Queens College and a history teacher, that inspired me to go to college, teach, and become a historian. I am grateful to them both.

Ari Hoogenboom

Brooklyn College of the City University of New York
Brooklyn, New York
1 February 1994

INTRODUCTION

"Garfield, Arthur, Harrison, and Hayes," Thomas Wolfe intoned, "were the lost Americans: their gravely vacant and bewhiskered faces mixed, melted, swam together in the sea-depths of a past intangible, immeasurable, and un-knowable. . . . Which had the whiskers, which the burnsides: which was which?"[1]

Wolfe's vague impression of unshaven, indistinguishable, interchangeable presidential faces endures in the late twentieth century. Historians have looked past the Gilded Age White House to the steel mills of Pittsburgh, the oil refineries of Cleveland, and the boardrooms of New York for the domi-nant figures of that era. They have not only argued that captains of industry orchestrated national policies but also claimed that presidents played second fiddle to powerful congressional leaders such as James G. Blaine and Roscoe Conkling.

Contrary to this overriding theme and interpretation of the Gilded Age, Rutherford B. Hayes was not an agent of "big business" and was not under the thumb of the congressional leadership. He was remarkable for both his independence and his savvy. Concerned more with results than with postur-ing, he often preferred to remain in the background, where he could skill-fully pull the right strings to achieve his ends. Take the way he handled the disputed presidential election of 1876. Hayes remained behind the scenes in Ohio during the entire four-month dispute. From this vantage point, he shrewdly encouraged his Republican supporters and any possible Demo-cratic defectors while setting parameters for behind-the-scenes negotiators and allowing his Ohio allies to speak for him unofficially. Concerning the paramount issue of southern policy, Hayes reiterated the position he had stated in his letter accepting the nomination. He would favor home rule for the South when the civil and political rights of blacks and whites were re-spected, and he hoped that the South would be conciliated on that basis. Keeping a clear eye on the prize and promising nothing beyond this pub-lished formula for reconciliation, Hayes's strategy succeeded when he was declared president after the Democrats ended their filibuster three days be-fore the inauguration.

If Hayes's shrewd political behavior during this election has been disregarded by modern historians, so has his long-term commitment to civil rights and to an egalitarian society. Late-twentieth-century historians have failed to appreciate Hayes's restrained response to the Great Strike of 1877 as well as the compelling reasons for his abandonment of military Reconstruction. Similarly, his role in shaping the modern presidency has been ignored, despite the fact that he succeeded in reclaiming long-lost presidential powers in his relations with Congress and took steps toward establishing a modern bureaucracy.

Hayes's earlier renown as the "statesman of reunion" has been transformed by the present generation of historians into contemptible notoriety for "appeasing" white-supremacy Democrats—an ironic and inaccurate portrayal. Far from aiding and abetting the triumph of white supremacy in the South, Hayes was painfully aware of the political and social realities in 1877 America, which had strong racist propensities, and he was practical enough to realize that he had to work within those limits. He was, above all, a pragmatic reformer, as his southern policy showed.[2]

When Hayes took office in March 1877, military Reconstruction—with a precarious foothold only in the capitals of South Carolina and Louisiana—was doomed. It was widely perceived as a failed policy that had unwittingly promoted white supremacy. Hayes, who had earlier supported radical Reconstruction measures, agreed that the "bayonet policy" was counterproductive. Furthermore, to restore Republican control in South Carolina and Louisiana, it would have been necessary to deploy more troops throughout those states. This action would have been unpopular in the best of times but was impossible with the nation suffering from a severe depression. Indeed, the Democratic House of Representatives had already blocked appropriations for the army because its troops were upholding Republican governments in the South. The question Hayes faced was not whether to withdraw the troops but when to withdraw them and what concessions he could gain before the soldiers were forced out. Despite his poor bargaining position, he extracted promises from South Carolina and Louisiana Democrats that the civil and political rights of black and white Republicans would be respected. The promises were empty, but nothing was given up that had not already been lost.

Critics have contrasted Hayes's unwillingness to use troops to protect blacks in the South with his supposed kowtowing to corporations and the rich by dispatching the army to suppress striking railroad workers. But contrary to this widely accepted assumption, Hayes neither did the bidding of railroad managers nor broke the Great Strike. He responded with federal troops only when they were properly requested by local or state authorities who had exhausted their means of stopping the rioting, looting, and burning; and he specifically ordered troops—at St. Louis, for example—not to "quell the strikers or run the trains" but to protect public property.[3]

An egalitarian, Hayes revered the Declaration of Independence, the Northwest Ordinance of 1787, and the Constitution with its Reconstruction amendments. He often spoke of how these documents fostered political and legal equality as well as universal education and suffrage; and he often repeated Abraham Lincoln's view that everyone should "have a fair start and an equal chance in the race of life." Hayes, consequently, distrusted plutocrats and monopolists, favored railroad regulation, and consistently advocated federal legislation to achieve equal voting, educational, and economic opportunities for all Americans. Although he was practical enough to recognize that his high ideals were unachievable in his lifetime, Hayes worked to build a society that eventually would be as level as the topography of his section of Ohio.[4]

The disputed election, the inauguration of a new southern policy, and the Great Strike—all notable issues that have received a good deal of attention—obscured the steps Hayes took toward establishing a modern presidency. By introducing civil-service reform into major federal offices, Hayes laid the foundation for the modern American bureaucracy. He also checked the long-term erosion of executive power at the hands of an aggressive Congress, even though hostile Republicans and Democrats dominated the Senate and hostile Democrats dominated the House of Representatives. Hayes regained the appointing power of presidents by defeating "senatorial courtesy"—the notion that senators controlled federal civil-service appointments in their states. He also preserved his constitutional power to approve legislation by vetoing appropriations bills to which Democrats had attached riders designed to destroy voting-rights laws. Hayes shrewdly sensed that these vetoes would rally public opinion to his side and force the Democratic Congress to yield.

Ironically, Hayes has frequently been labeled an inept politician, a tag for which he is partly responsible, having cultivated an image of being above the political fray. In fact, he was an astute political analyst and strategist who often masked his calculated political moves with a cloak of principle. His ban on liquor in the White House—for which Lucy Hayes was unfairly ridiculed—resulted only in part from his aversion to congressmen in their cups: He realized that this symbolic ban would prevent Prohibition-minded Republicans from drifting into a third party. Although Hayes wished to conciliate the South, he was not above appealing to northern voters' antipathies by "waving the bloody shirt." And to gain votes for his party, he stressed the anti–Catholic school issue.

Hayes embraced the politics of reform by exploiting issues—rather than patronage—in his battle to control the nation's affairs. By bypassing party bosses, he anticipated twentieth-century presidents and used his office as a "bully pulpit" to preach the virtues of honest money, honest government, and honest elections. During his unprecedented wide travels, "Rutherford the Rover" took his policies directly to the people, mobilizing public opinion by exercising moral leadership. To parry criticism of his travels, he explained that it was important for presidents to periodically take a "popular bath," and he boasted that he and Lucy could "travel longer . . . without losing our spirits than almost any persons we ever met." Throughout his political career, Hayes was phenomenally successful at winning elections, and James A. Garfield succeeded him in large part because Hayes had united the Republican party and convinced the public that his policies had produced prosperity. When Hayes left the White House, Henry Adams declared that he had been a "most successful" president.[5]

But for Hayes, the presidency was only the most significant phase of a long and admirable career. He kept the White House years in their proper context when he perceived: "The first half [of] my active political life was . . . to resist the increase of slavery and . . . to destroy it. . . . The second half . . . has been to rebuild, and to get rid of the despotic and corrupting tendencies and the animosities of the war, and the other legacies of slavery."[6] In these lifelong endeavors, Hayes was a warrior who fought intelligently and successfully.

The evolution of Hayes from an antiabolitionist youth into a defender of runaway slaves in Cincinnati typified the change that came over many inhabitants of the Old Northwest. Hayes's life illustrates the arousal of antislavery sentiment and the rise of the Republican party in the 1850s. He went off to fight in the Civil War because he loved the Union, but Hayes quickly realized that for it to survive, slavery must be destroyed. Wounded five times, he was a good colonel, beloved by the volunteer soldiers he led into battle. "His conduct on the field," Gen. Ulysses S. Grant wrote, "was marked by conspicuous gallantry as well as the display of qualities of a higher order than that of mere personal daring."[7] After the war, Hayes was a radical congressman and a three-time governor of Ohio before ascending to the presidency. As governor, he introduced nonpartisanship into the administration of reform and charitable institutions and was responsible for the establishment of Ohio State University and for Ohio's ratification of the Fifteenth

Amendment to the Constitution, guaranteeing the vote for people of all races.

In his significant postpresidential career—which, among his successors, only Jimmy Carter has emulated—Hayes energetically worked for people in need. He urged larger pensions for Union veterans, prison reform for even the most incorrigible convicts, and education for the children of the poor of all races. Because he had faith that education would ultimately cure society's ills, he made it his "hobby." He believed that manual training—on all levels and for all students, rich as well as poor—would promote understanding, alleviate hostility between capital and labor, and provide everyone with a trade to fall back on. To help erase the legacy of slavery, Hayes was a conscientious trustee of the Peabody Fund, which promoted the education of southern children. He also worked diligently as the first president of the board of trustees of the Slater Fund, established to educate African Americans. "Especially grateful" to Hayes for his "tireless energy and singleheartedness for the interests" of the black race, W. E. B. DuBois pledged to "strive that these efforts shall not be . . . without results."[8]

Although many Gilded Age politicians destroyed their papers, Hayes saved his correspondence and kept a diary. This vast record tells us not only about Hayes but also about life in an imperfectly perceived era of American history. Hayes recorded his travels by barge on the Erie Canal; by stagecoach on runners through snow and on wheels through mud; by sumptuous steamboats on lake, river, and coastal waters; and by rail on a handcar, in the cab of a locomotive in Utah's Echo Canyon, and in a palatial Pullman car. He commented on lectures by Ralph Waldo Emerson and on Thomas Edison's middle-of-the-night White House demonstration of his phonograph. Hayes proclaimed his pleasure in western informality and unpretentiousness at the White House, where his wife's vivacious friends helped out at receptions. He described the pain of his war wounds as well as the maddening itch of poison ivy as it reached the "last place" on his person. The life of Hayes both spanned and shaped the maturing years of the adolescent nation. Growing up, he associated with pioneers; in old age, he damned the Standard Oil monopoly and was inspired by the twentieth-century urban vision of Chicago's Columbian Exhibition. Hayes's papers afford a rare opportunity to view a swiftly changing world through the eyes of a sensitive observer who was also the president of the United States.[9]

Mark Twain "arrived at the verdict that" Hayes's presidency, in "its quiet & unostentatious, but real & substantial greatness, would steadily rise into higher & higher prominence, as time & distance give it a right perspective, until at last it would stand out against the horizon of history in its true proportions."[10] I have undertaken this biography in the hope of fulfilling Twain's prediction and to give Rutherford Birchard Hayes's extraordinary life the "right perspective" so that it can be viewed "in its true proportions."

OHIO AND NEW ENGLAND

Thirty-year-old Sophia Birchard Hayes had experienced great sorrow when, on 4 October 1822, she gave birth to a sickly son, whom she named Rutherford Birchard Hayes. Two and a half months earlier, her thirty-five-year-old husband, Rutherford Hayes, Jr., had died of typhus. A year before, death had snatched Sophia's four-year-old daughter, Sarah. Sophia's maiden years in Vermont had also been filled with grief. When she was thirteen, her father, Roger Birchard, had died of tuberculosis, leaving his wife and children in straitened circumstances. Sophia's mother, Drusilla, remarried four years later, but that marriage failed and she was divorced the next year. Worse yet, in the following year, Sophia's brother Lorenzo and sister Arabella died of typhus, as did her mother in 1813, just before Sophia's twenty-first birthday. An older sister and three younger brothers survived.[1]

At the time of her mother's death, Sophia Birchard had already fallen in love with Rutherford Hayes, Jr., the handsome, redheaded son of a nearby Brattleboro, Vermont, blacksmith, tavern keeper, and farmer. The attractive young woman with rosy red cheeks had earlier been sent to New York City to spend a winter with her uncle Daniel Austin—to get her away from Hayes. On the streets of New York, she had cried when a meddling woman had pointed at her vibrant face and exclaimed, "Oh, see the paint." "The lass with the roseate cheeks" had already resolved that, if she married anyone, it would be "the lad with the rubicund hair." When a still-determined Sophia returned to Vermont, however, opposition to the match had ceased. On 19 September 1813, six months after her mother's death, Sophia and Hayes were married by the justice of the peace in Wilmington, Vermont, her birthplace.

At the time of his marriage, Hayes had a thriving store in nearby Dummerston. His partner was his brother-in-law John Noyes, who would be elected to the U.S. Congress the next year. Although the Hayeses' first child was stillborn, another child, Lorenzo Birchard, was born on 9 June 1815. Two years later—with slack trade following the War of 1812 and another baby coming—Hayes scouted opportunities in Ohio and decided to settle among other Vermonters in the village of Delaware. There he rented a house and, on 21 July, purchased a 125-acre farm located two miles north of the town. When he returned to Vermont for his family, he found that on 10 July a daughter, Sarah Sophia, had been born.[2]

The young family departed for Ohio on 10 September 1817. Accompanying them in "their emigrant wagons" on the forty-nine-day trip were Sardis, Sophia's "wild" sixteen-year-old brother, and her cousin, Arcena Smith, whose family had been wiped out by typhus. Optimistically investing their capital, the Hayeses purchased "wild lands" on the Sandusky Plains near Bucyrus and property in Delaware. They also operated a distillery (with Dr. Reuben Lamb) near a sulphur spring that is now on the campus of Ohio Wesleyan University. Another daughter, Fanny Arabella, was born on 25 January 1820, and the Hayeses had begun building a brick home in Delaware when tragedy struck again. First Sarah died, then, on 20 July 1822, her father, leaving Sophia a pregnant widow with two young children.[3]

Sophia was still weak from a "dreadful fever" when her contractions began on the gloomy and chilly evening of 4 October. Arcena was sick and unable to help, but Mrs. Smith, "a most excellent nurse," took her place. Sardis ran for Dr. Lamb, who, between nine and ten o'clock, delivered Sophia's fifth child, a feeble little boy. The fee was $3.50.[4]

For two years—filled with "hopeless desolation"—Sophia despaired of her son's life, but Rutherford Birchard Hayes survived. As his health improved, Sophia began to rejoice in her children. She reported in 1824 that nine-year-old "Lorenzo splits our wood, gets the cows, goes to school [and] is a good boy" and that four-year-old Fanny "learns very well" in school. Sophia also related that on Saturday, 25 September, Fanny "wanted a pillowcase to sew. I fixed it for her and then I had no peace till I had given Rutherford a needle and thread with a piece of cloth."[5]

The relief that accompanied Rutherford's improved health was shattered a few months later when Lorenzo drowned while ice-skating. Lorenzo's death, heaped on her other sorrows, made Sophia take refuge in the Presbyterian faith, which she had embraced at Rutherford's christening. She also became extremely protective of her surviving children. Isolating them from other children, she kept Fanny and Rud, as her son was called, at home much of the time. Still, Rud had mishaps. "I fell into the coals on the memorable occasion of putting on my first pair of pants," he later recalled. Using Lorenzo's books, Sophia taught Rud to read, write, and spell. He had become a handsome, large-headed, blue-eyed, auburn-haired boy who enjoyed playing with Fanny's dolls before he was given toy soldiers. Lest he overtax his once-delicate constitution, Sophia refused to let Rud do household chores. He was seven before she allowed him to play with other children and nine before she permitted him to participate in strenuous sports.[6]

Constant playmates, Rud and Fanny shared an exceptionally strong bond. Fanny was "my protector and nurse when I was a sickly, feeble boy, three or four years old," Hayes later remembered. "She would lead me carefully about the garden and barnyard and on short visits to the nearest neighbors." When she was seven and recovering from dysentery, Rud returned the favor. "I daily gave her little rides," he recalled, "upon a small hand-sled which, with great difficulty, I hauled on the grass about the garden." They would also "curl dandelion stems & hang them on their ears, string 'four o'clocks' on long straws of timothy or dig mimic wells & fill them with water"; they would "lie down in the shade of great old cherry trees, with their books." Fanny had read all of Shakespeare's plays by the time she was twelve and, with the help of Rud, dramatized Sir Walter Scott's "The Lady of the Lake," which she knew by heart. Then, repairing to the kitchen, they would admire "the strength & speed with which" Sophia thrust "the long handed iron shovel . . . in & out of the glowing oven till every nook was filled with savory pies."[7]

Neither Rud nor Fanny seemed adversely affected by their mother's overprotectiveness. They were friendly, outgoing children who impressed adults, got along with their peers, and loved the outdoor life. On Saturday afternoons in autumn, they often tramped noisily through the woods looking for nuts, and on snowy winter mornings they "scampered off to the 'run' to slide until breakfast time." Neighbors found Fanny's tomboyish exploits shocking; she played boys' games and was a superb rifle shot. Rud became expert at "hunting, fishing, rowing, sailing, swimming, skating, riding and the like."[8]

Rud and Fanny shared a tendency to be irreverent in their puns and jokes, which their pious mother tolerated but did not encourage. They also fought with each other when their play got out of hand. Fanny made fun of Rud, who could not match her sharp wit, and between the ages of nine and twelve he often responded with his fists. He later marveled at how hatefully they behaved while loving "each other dearly."[9]

Although his mother and sister were the core of his family, Rud did have the companionship of other adults. Sardis, the youngest brother of Sophia, "became the head and main stay of the family," and Sophia's cousin Arcena Smith remained as a household helper. Fanny was devoted to "Aunt" Arcena, and Rud particularly admired Uncle Sardis. Two lodgers rounded out the household: "Uncle" Sam Rheem, a mason with strong antislavery views, and Thomas Wasson, who owned a tannery and later married Arcena.[10]

Sophia needed the lodgers to make ends meet. The $8,000 that she and her husband had brought to Ohio was invested mostly in land, which had dropped in value following the panic of 1819. Had she yielded to her impulse to return to Vermont after Lorenzo died, Sophia would have had to sell her Ohio lands at a great loss. Even though their house, which was completed in 1828, was as nice as any house in Delaware, Hayes recalled that the family's resources were so limited that furniture was in scanty supply. "A new bureau and stand . . . and plain wood-bottomed chairs, a gilt-framed looking-glass, a good carpet, and cheap window curtains furnished the parlor." Nevertheless, Rud and Fanny were content. The only possessions of their peers that they envied were "the picture and story books which Mr. [A. H.] Pettibone, the leading lawyer of the village, gave his children."

Young and attractive, Sophia was "grand company" and talked "a perfect hailstorm, faster and faster, and never was tired." She had suitors who might have eased her burden, but, perhaps remembering her mother's disastrous second marriage, Sophia hesitated. Her income (apart from her lodgers) came from the farm, whose tenants paid her a third of the crops and half of the fruit produced on it.[11]

"The great events of our childhood were connected with this farm," Hayes recalled. Three or four times a year, Sophia, Fanny, and Rud would make a day-long excursion to the farm on the east bank of the Olentangy, or the Whetstone, as the displaced Vermonters called it, after the tributary that flowed into the Connecticut River at Brattleboro. Usually they walked together and used a canoe to cross the river a short distance below the farm. "Sugar-making, cider-making, cherry time, and gathering hickory nuts and walnuts were the occasions of these long looked for and delightful trips. . . . Fanny and I were always favorites with the tenants," Hayes remembered nostalgically. "They gave us colored eggs filled with sugar at Easter, pet birds, squirrels, rabbits, quail's eggs, turtle's eggs, and similar gifts easily got in the country at that time." In warm weather, when they were older, Rud and Fanny took weekly walks to the farm, pausing to rest in the shade and to bathe their feet in the brook, where they spotted minnows and gathered pebbles.[12]

Within a few years, Sardis gave the family financial security, but not before causing Sophia considerable anxiety. When he had first come to live with her, Sardis had been "a slender, delicate sickly boy, wayward and fond of wild sports and wild company." In Ohio, he worked hard and was usually dependable, but his wild streak was still discernible even after he became the guardian of Sophia's children. When Rud was two, Sardis set off with a friend and a jug of brandy to return a buggy that Sophia had borrowed in

Sophia Birchard Hayes

Portland (later Sandusky), Ohio. He tarried along the way and got uproari-
ously drunk. Sardis then sailed to Detroit, got sick in Michigan, and finally
made it back to Delaware after walking for a week from Portland. But soon
after his memorable trip to Detroit, Sardis earned $500 when he and a friend
drove five hundred wild hogs from Delaware to Baltimore. Traveling on the

Sardis Birchard

National Road, Sardis met Sen. Andrew Jackson, who was on his way to Washington. The hogs impeded the carriage that Jackson was escorting on horseback. (At that moment [1824], Jackson was the leading candidate for the presidency but would soon lose the election in the House of Representatives to John Quincy Adams.) Although he had supported Henry Clay, Sardis was impressed by Jackson, who helped clear the road for the carriage and then graciously paused to discuss "the market for hogs" with the twenty-three-year-old uncle of a future president.[13]

Sardis's heavy work and hard drinking taxed his constitution. In the summer of 1825, he was "housed up sick" with consumption after overexerting himself mowing hay. Discouraged by the Ohio "fevers and agues" that had afflicted her family, Sophia again thought of returning to Vermont. During the long winter, she despaired of Sardis's life, but it was a glorious time for three-year-old Rud, who listened avidly to his uncle's tales of adventure. When, in the spring of 1826, Sardis was able to travel to Vermont for the summer, Rud sorely missed him and complained, "How can we eat breakfast [when] all the folks are gone?"[14]

Sardis disappointed Rud and his family by not returning to their home. After wintering in Georgia, Sardis settled in Lower Sandusky in 1827. There, at the scene of his spectacular binge three years earlier, he began to prosper as a merchant by dint of hard work, fair dealing, and good luck. A year after he moved there, the Seneca Indians—recognizing Sardis's honesty with his policy of one firm, low price for all—deposited their annual gold payment from the state of New York with him and drew on it when making purchases. Sardis was also fortunate in his partners, who were able and energetic, and in his land speculations, which were enormously profitable. When the panic of 1837 struck, he was not overextended and emerged from the ensuing depression with large, choice real-estate holdings. To the Seneca Indians, Sardis was "An-Se-Queg, the Man Who Owns Most of the Land."

Wealth brought Sardis prominence in northwestern Ohio. He was a founder of the Whig party in Sandusky County, and his network of friends included Ohio Supreme Court Justice Ebenezer Lane of Norwalk and Morrison R. Waite, an able young lawyer in Maumee. As Sardis rose in political and financial circles, he shared his fortune with his sister and her children. He was their "protector and adviser in every trouble," visiting them frequently, and acting as a father to Fanny and Rud.[15]

To Sophia, Sardis—whom she had mothered since he was orphaned—was both a son and a brother. If he needed her, she was willing to leave her children in the care of others to be with him. In the fall of 1830, she departed "in a great hurry" for Lower Sandusky—which, she was convinced, was "as sickly as New Orleans"—to nurse Sardis, who had a severe attack of "bilious fever." Upon seeing him, she "lost all hopes of his recovery," but a month of her nursing restored Sardis to "his normal state" of "very poor" health.[16]

Rud and Fanny missed their mother dreadfully during her absence. They stayed with Arcena, who had recently married Thomas Wasson. "We had never before known," Hayes recalled, "how much we loved her, nor how necessary she was to our happiness." During that time, their "old family puss," who had been with them as long as they could remember, wandered off to die. Upon finding her body under a neighbor's apple tree, Rud and Fanny imagined that she had been stoned to death and "were inconsolable [for] several days."

Most trying, however, for these sensitive children was the opening of a public-supported district school for pupils ranging in size from eight-year-old Rud to grown young men. Rud thought that the schoolmaster Daniel Granger, who "flogged great strapping fellows," was "a demon of ferocity." When he threw a large jackknife into the wall just beyond the head of a boy who was whispering near Rud, the children feared for their lives and tearfully begged Wasson to take them out of school. But he refused, insisting that Granger was "a kind-hearted little man." Their only hope for escape from Granger's schoolroom was their mother's return, and they longed for it passionately. When they heard that she had arrived on a "dismal rainy" November morning after a five-day journey on horseback, Rud and Fanny flew home "with a joy rarely experienced even in childhood." Later, ignoring his frightening, shortlived experience with Granger, Rud called Joan Hills Murray, who ran a private grade school he attended in Delaware, his "first school-teacher."[17]

As he grew older, Rud displayed remarkable self-assurance, whether as a student, a lawyer, a soldier, or a politician. His confidence in himself was almost certainly the result of the secure atmosphere that Sophia had created, with significant help from Sardis and Arcena. Once he had carefully made up his mind, Rud did not waver or have second thoughts. Nurturing his self-confidence may have had a negative effect, however, as far as Sophia was concerned, for her son never experienced a religious conversion. Convinced of his worthiness, he never felt the need to be born again in Christ and did not join a church, although he attended services regularly and liberally supported organized religion.

Rud never rejected, however, the moral principles instilled in him by Sophia and reinforced by the Presbyterian church they attended in Delaware. He obeyed the spirit as well as the letter of the Ten Commandments and seldom failed to treat others as he wanted to be treated. He learned to value the gentlemanly virtues of honesty, fairness, kindness, generosity, and decency— all of which were relatively easy to embrace, because Uncle Sardis had made the Hayes family economically secure. Growing up in a household of women also pushed Rud into a leadership role that augmented his self-assurance. As he grew into adolescence, Rud began to act as the head of the house, and his relationship with Sophia changed. She still scolded him for a variety of offenses (he was "too loud," and his manners were bad), but she also deferred to him in ways that gave him new responsibilities and maturity.[18]

Rud became intensely patriotic. He gloried in the history of the young republic of which he was a citizen, and he loved the even younger state in which he resided. George Washington was his hero, and while playing with his toy soldiers, Rud dreamed that he too would become a hero on the battlefield and a leader of his country. Encouraged by Fanny, he memorized parts of patriotic speeches by Patrick Henry, Daniel Webster, and Henry Clay, and at the slightest provocation he would deliver them at the top of his lungs. His favorite was Webster's "Reply to Robert Y. Hayne," with its stirring peroration: "Liberty and Union, now and forever, one and inseparable." Rud appreciated his New England heritage and New Englanders like Webster, but he was a westerner through and through and was especially proud to be a "Buckeye."[19]

Rud was also ambitious. Thanks to the prodding of Sophia, Sardis, and Fanny, his friendliness was not allowed to slip into complacency. With Sophia often reminding him of the virtues of the father and brother he never knew, Rud felt challenged to emulate them. Lorenzo, he learned, was "kind and good-natured, prompt, energetic and courageous," in short, an ideal boy. Rud tried hard to be like Lorenzo and to deserve the kind of praise heaped on his dead brother. He was also aware of his larger-than-life father, remembered by family, friends, and neighbors. This father was strong, hardworking, good-humored, tolerant, and generous: He had refused to join an abortive attempt to lynch a local physician for lewd behavior; he had listened to a variety of preachers interpret the scriptures and had contributed to several Delaware churches. His most memorable offering with the most tangible results had been seventeen gallons of whiskey to cheer the laborers who raised the Methodist church steeple.

To the inspiration of Rud's father and brother were added the expectations of Sardis and Fanny. Both uncle and sister lived vicariously through Rud. An undereducated, self-made man, Sardis never married and thought of Rud as his own boy, for whom he wanted an excellent education and a distinguished career, preferably in law and public service. Rud did his best to fulfill his uncle's dreams. For him, Sardis was a surrogate father on whom he modeled his mannerisms and much of his behavior. For her part, Fanny was a brilliant student in Delaware and at the Female Seminary at Putnam, Ohio. Realizing that a leadership career was closed to her, even in egalitarian Ohio, she resolved to taste success through her beloved brother. Like it or not, and at times he did not, Rud Hayes was being groomed for an extraordinary life.[20]

At about four o'clock on the morning of 4 June 1834, Rud and his family "huddled . . . into the crowded stage" and left Delaware for a five-month visit to New England relatives in the Connecticut River Valley. Rud's account of this journey marked his first attempt at what later became a lifelong habit of keeping a journal. The trip not only introduced him to the technological innovations that were revolutionizing transportation but also acquainted him with his Hayes grandparents and numerous uncles, aunts, and cousins. Before this trip, Rud had met only one cousin and had never traveled outside of Delaware, Ohio. That summer spent in the bosom of his extensive family, in the valley of his ancestors, was the beginning of his great interest in his kinfolk and forebears. "You know," he confessed to an uncle in 1874, "I am given to antiquarian and genealogical pursuits. An old family letter is a delight to my eyes. I can prowl in the old trunks of letters by the day with undiminished zeal."[21]

The trip was an adventure for eleven-year-old Rud. The first leg of the journey—on which Sardis was with them—was an arduous sixteen-hour stagecoach ride from Delaware to Lower Sandusky, where they stayed for a few days. Then on Sunday, 8 June, they went down the Sandusky River to Portland, where on Monday evening, Rud, Fanny, and Sophia boarded the steamboat *Henry Clay* and "had a pleasant passage down Lake Erie to Buffalo." Taking an Erie Canal boat, they disembarked five days later at Schenectady and rode a short distance on the recently completed railroad to Saratoga, New York. At Saratoga the little family visited the grave of Rud's maternal grandfather, Roger Birchard, and the springs whose waters had failed to cure the tuberculosis that had brought him there twenty-nine years earlier. Although the family liked to think of Roger Birchard as a man "of uncommon business capacity," his death at age forty-seven had exposed his improvidence, which left his wife and children poor.[22]

Continuing by stagecoach, Rud and his family stopped at Wilmington, the town where Sophia had been born on 15 April 1792. Moving on to the "pleasant village" of West Brattleboro, they spent a week with Rud and Fanny's grandparents. Their grandfather, Rutherford Hayes, Sr., a Connecticut native, had migrated as a young man up the Connecticut River to Vermont, where he worked as a blacksmith and later kept a tavern and farmed. When Rud and Fanny first saw him, he was nearly seventy-eight and content with his possessions and his life. He was short and lively and was fastidious about his appearance, brushing his coat, collar, and vest, adjusting his new wig, and often washing his "remarkably white" hands. He had "less intellect, ambition and industry" than their grandmother, Chloe Smith Hayes, and the contrast between them helped inspire Rud's later belief that Hayes women were superior to Hayes men. While Grandfather Hayes washed away the evidence of his earlier manual labor, his wife continued to work hard and was bothered by her husband's aversion to getting his hands dirty. When Rud and his family visited, his grandmother was seventy-one, and although her husband would die in two years, she would live to be eighty-four, and Rud would see and admire her on subsequent visits.[23]

Rud and his family also visited his uncle Austin Birchard for two weeks in Fayetteville (now Newfane). There, on the Fourth of July, while Rud and his cousin Charley Birchard were firing a small cannon on the square, an old man cut his own throat. Hurrying to the scene, they were horrified by his "heaving and groaning," and Rud thought that he would "never again desire to witness the glories of a battlefield." When the dying man was out of sight, however, Rud, with a bravado laugh, tried to mask the tenderness that was the core of his being. Playing with Charley was fun, but associating with his mother's brother Austin — who had risen above the adversity of deafness to become a successful merchant and local political leader — was inspirational. "If Uncle could accomplish so much with so little encouragement, and held back by his infirmity," Rud reflected, "what ought I not to accomplish with so great assistance and motive as I have always had?" Rud was less impressed by his uncle Roger Birchard, who was a successful though eccentric merchant.[24]

Sophia also took her children to Putney to visit their paternal aunt Polly and her husband, John Noyes, who had been a member of Congress and Rud's father's partner in the Dummerston store. Ever since John Noyes had left Vermont a sober man and returned from Washington a drunkard, Sophia had regarded politics as a degrading profession, and whatever ambitions Sardis and Fanny harbored in their hearts for Rud, Sophia did not want him to have a political career. About that visit, though, Rud chiefly remembered that he "had lots of fun . . . breaking up bumblebees' nests" with his cousin George W. Noyes. Rud did not meet George's oldest brother, John Humphrey Noyes, who had recently been expelled from Yale for announcing that his heart had attained a state of pure, sinless perfection. But his cousin's rejection of the Calvinistic doctrine of human depravity had neither disturbed the family nor as yet ruffled the calm of the village.[25]

Rud and his family also traveled to Chesterfield, New Hampshire, to visit his cousin Mary Jane, the eldest sister of John Humphrey Noyes, and her lawyer husband, Larkin Goldsmith Mead. The Mead family was both unusually good company and unusually talented. At the time of Rud's visit, Mary and Larkin Mead had begun their family of nine children, among whom would be a sculptor who bore his father's name; industrialist Charles Levi Mead; architect William Rutherford Mead; and artist Elinor Mead, who married novelist William Dean Howells.[26]

Although the Hayeses visited relatives and went sightseeing in New Hampshire and western Massachusetts, they concentrated on Vermont. Rud saw Dummerston, where his parents had lived and worked before migrating to Ohio. On the south side of the common was the little store in which Rud's father had started his business, and adjacent to it was the house where Rud's parents had settled after their marriage.[27]

Toward the end of his New England visit, Rud met his nineteen-year-old cousin Horatio Noyes, a student at Yale College, who took him under his wing. On Sunday morning, 28 September 1834, Rud and Horatio were in West Brattleboro and had a particularly enjoyable day. Fanny, who at fourteen and a half was no longer a child, generally associated with her female cousins rather than Rud, but on this Sunday afternoon she accompanied him and Horatio down to the river. Despite, or perhaps because of, the Yale man's presence, she waded in with her old tomboyish enthusiasm. "We sent Fanny in after sticks," Rud reported; then they put a board across Whetstone Brook and climbed up the rocks. They "went down to where the river [ran] in a very narrow place and [was] so swift" that boats were reeled up by turning a large log to which a towrope had been tied. Having inspected the ingenious reel, they stopped at the local iron furnace and "saw all the moulds for making stoves, kettles, boilers, and every kind [of] iron ware." They finished their adventure by watching a steam-powered sawmill in operation.[28]

After a tea on Wednesday, 1 October, that was attended by nearby relatives, Sophia and her children prepared to return to Ohio. She had planned to go back with Sardis, but when he did not come, she feared that he was "sick at Sandusky" and hastened her departure. On Rud's twelfth birthday, Saturday, 4 October 1834, Grandfather Hayes and cousin John Pease took the departing trio to Wilmington. They remained there until Monday morning, when they met the westbound stagecoach. As they were about to board it, Sophia received a letter from Sardis, who had arrived in Brattleboro. They got on the stagecoach anyway, and Sophia later offered to wait for Sardis until 15 October in Auburn, New York, where they would visit other relatives. But Rud had apparently tired of keeping a journal and did not say whether Sardis joined them on the way home.[29]

The New England journey was enormously important for Rud. He learned about the world beyond Delaware, Ohio, and met relatives whom he cherished. His grandparents, his uncle Austin Birchard, and the Mead family particularly impressed him, and close contact with college student Horatio Noyes inspired him. Years later, Rud recalled Uncle Austin Birchard watching Fanny (and presumably Rud as well) "with his bright face and eyes beaming with love and delight." After being isolated from most of their relatives all their lives, Rud and Fanny found themselves part of an elaborate network of beckoning hearthstones in the Connecticut Valley. Rud had also had fun playing with and confiding in his cousins Charley Birchard, George Noyes, and John Pease, and he would see a great deal of Pease in the future.

During the trip, Rud experienced the technology of the age. He inspected a paper mill, a sawmill, and an ironworks; he watched Erie Canal locks open and close; and he rode on a steamboat and behind a steam locomotive less than six years after work had begun on the first American passenger railroad. Rud and Fanny had become such experienced travelers that Sophia let them go by stagecoach from Delaware to Lower Sandusky to visit Sardis for three weeks in the spring of 1835. They traveled with Gen. Otto Hinton of Delaware, "the great stage man," and the innkeepers along the route knew Sardis and looked out for "his little folks." Nevertheless, the trip, which included overnight stops at Marion and Tiffin, reinforced twelve-year-old Rud's self-confidence.[30]

Rud was a good student. His account of his New England journey was an essay of which any twelve-year-old could be proud. Studying Lorenzo's books, associating with his precocious sister, and the training he received in Joan Hills Murray's school in Delaware equipped Rud with a good basic education. He was a champion speller, and when he completed his studies with Murray, she chose him as her outstanding boy scholar, an honor that included an award. To Sardis's amusement and to Sophia and Fanny's disgust, Rud chose as his prize a Jew's harp rather than a book. He was thirteen, and despite their efforts, he had no burning desire to attend college. Was not Uncle Sardis a self-made man?[31]

Realizing his own limitations, however, Sardis was determined that his nephew would become a scholar and a gentleman. And Sophia, also regretting "that our education was totally neglected after the death of our Father," was determined that her children should "have no such cause of complaint." But as yet, there were no good preparatory schools in Delaware, and she could not think of being separated from both her children. Plans for her to accompany Rud and Fanny to Granville, Ohio, where the schools were "very good," fell through because of sickness there. Although both children were disappointed, Sophia was more concerned about Rud. "You know," she reminded Sardis, "that when boys are interrupted in their studies at his age they are apt to lose their ambition—and think it is not very important that they should improve their time." In a quandary, she asked Sardis for his advice.[32]

Sardis suggested that thirteen-year-old Rud should attend the Norwalk Seminary run by Rev. Jonathan E. Chaplin in Norwalk, Ohio. Sardis chose this Methodist preparatory school because it was only thirty miles from his home in Lower Sandusky, was next door to the home of his good friend Judge Ebenezer Lane, and was the school that Lane's son William attended. Sardis admired Judge Lane, a cultivated and humane man, and felt that in educating Rud they could do no better than to follow the course Lane had chosen for his own son. Shortly after Sophia's request for advice, Rud began attending the Norwalk Seminary. "I do not think I shall have to go home because I am homesick," he wrote with some pride to Sardis on 21 June 1836. "I like staying here better than any other school in Ohio." Rud wrote Sophia "a very good long letter" in which he assured her that he studied from "five in the morning till five at night." Despite his brave talk of no homesickness, he was as eager to visit home between terms as Sophia and Fanny were to see him.[33]

Sophia managed her resources carefully, but she also knew that she could depend on Sardis, particularly when it came to meeting the needs connected with her children's education. When Rud completed the term—which stretched almost through the summer—he went home for a visit. There he "was attacked with the fever," Sophia reported, "but we succeeded in throwing his off by medicine." By 11 September, he was feeling fine and was eager to get back to school. When he returned to Norwalk on 18 September, Chaplin demanded the tuition before the term began. To Sophia's chagrin, Rud asked Sardis for the money. Sophia had also been ill and thought that she might need her cash on hand, so she had not sent Rud's tuition with him. But she had corn to sell and knew that she could pay the tuition by October. When Fanny enrolled in the Female Seminary at Putnam later that month, Sardis not only picked the school and paid the tuition but also insisted that Sophia keep Fanny company for a couple of months. Since both Fanny and Rud were content to be away at school and Sophia missed them terribly, it was his sister's welfare that Sardis had in mind.[34]

Fanny excelled at Putnam, and Rud did well at Norwalk. Along with routine studies concentrating on the classics, the Norwalk curriculum emphasized speaking and writing. In October, Rud wrote a composition on the subject of liberty and did "tolerably well" in his maiden speech on William Pitt. "I was not scared as much as the most of the boys are the first time they speak," he assured Sophia. Contemporary politics fascinated Rud even more than history. Eighteen thirty-six was a presidential election year, and his hero was William Henry Harrison, the Whig candidate of the Northwest. Harrison lost the election, but the Whigs triumphed in Ohio, and Rud begged his mother to let him know who won the offices in Delaware County.[35]

Two months after his fourteenth birthday, Rud told his skeptical mother that he would be ready for college in four months. Although she had presumed that he was "getting along pretty well," Sophia did not think that he was "quite so near the end of his preparatory studies." Rud was making progress, but Sophia decided that when the term ended in March, he would study at home until Fanny returned from the Female Seminary. Sophia was lonely and reasoned that because of his youth, Rud would not be hurt by this interruption in his formal schooling. Besides, she added, "he is very steady and a very good boy and I cannot spare him till Fanny comes."[36]

Once home, however, rather than fulfill his mother's hopes, Rud fulfilled her earlier prophecy about boys who interrupt their studies. He lost ambition for further education. He went sledding on what snow remained "not so much for the fun as to say I had slid downhill on the 4th of April." He wished that Fanny were home so they could make lots of maple sugar wax candy together. For clearing the grass near the fences on their town property, Sophia paid Rud two dollars. With these earnings, he got a subscription to the Philadelphia *Saturday Courier*, which he promised to share with Fanny if she would bring home the issues he sent to her. "I have not studied any yet nor shall," he happily reported, rejoicing to be "free from the musty crusty fusty rules" of such "antiquated fools" as John Locke and Francis Bacon.

Sophia quickly realized her mistake. She had to nag Rud to write even the few lines he sent to Fanny and observed, "He is just as lazy about studying as ever." Rud argued that "all the plow joggers are happier than students." A discouraged Sophia thought that perhaps she should make a farmer out of him, but she realized that although he was slow to study at home he was a fast learner at school. Consequently, she urged Fanny to come home so they could send Rud off to school again.[37]

Fanny, who reveled in her studies at Putnam, was "upset extremely" by Rud's attitude, which threatened her own education. She had nothing but contempt for his romantic notion that "the ignorant farmer boy is happier than the student" and emphatically told him that "the literary man has a thousand sources of enjoyment that the rustic never has." Lest he forget the luck and responsibility that his sex gave him, she combined envy and resignation in her reminder: "Many is the time this winter I have wished myself in your place so I could go to college."[38]

Although Sophia thought it "quite a lecture," Fanny's admonitions had little effect on Rud. Sophia asked Sardis what he thought of sending Rud to Kenyon College at Gambier, an Episcopal school with an excellent moral climate. Meanwhile, in late May 1837, she engaged Sherman Finch, a local lawyer who had been a tutor at Yale, to instruct Rud in Greek and Latin. At first, Rud did "very well," but he failed to regain momentum after Finch returned from a sudden brief visit to New York. When Fanny came home in July, she studied the same texts and reinforced Rud's lessons by reciting to him after his sessions with Finch.[39]

Even with the participation of Fanny, who also taught him French, Rud did not study diligently. By July, however, he once more looked forward to college. "Rutherford," Fanny told Sardis, "reads considerable, studies some, and plays *a little occasionally for variety*; he is anxious to go to Gambier in the Fall." Since he did not strain himself studying, Rud had what amounted to a long vacation. The considerable reading he did was primarily novels, every one of which, to his surprise, Fanny had already read. Making himself useful around the house, he was "splendiferously happy" whitewashing walls and cleaning out the cistern. Besides hunting with his friends, Rud dropped in on Arcena Wasson and her family and on his other Delaware cousins Sarah and Harriet Moody (their mother Clarissa was Rud's father's sister). He also had "lively frolics" in the evenings with Sarah Bell, one of two young women students who now boarded with Sophia. She came from Lower Sandusky and was living with Sophia at Sardis's "urgent request." Sarah was, Rud later confessed, his "earliest lady friend." After months of unfocused activities, however, the time had come for him, in his mother's words, to "be at something of more importance."[40]

Although Sophia agreed with Rud that he was ready for Kenyon College, Sardis thought differently. Her "eyes filled with tears" when she learned in August that Sardis, after consulting with Judge Lane, planned to send Rud to Isaac Webb's Preparatory School in Middletown, Connecticut, where Lane's boy Will was enrolled. But after a visit from Judge Lane, Sophia agreed with her brother's decision. Reflecting on Rud's aversion to studying at home and his prowess as a hunter, she told Sardis, "I have more hopes of him when I think his taste and habits are much like yours when a boy." Nevertheless, she confessed that she was "not free from anxiety" lest "the same habits might continue when a man." When Rud first heard of Sardis's plans, he said, "I will not say I wont go—but I dont wish to go." He immediately agreed to go, however, when Sophia told him that Will Lane was at Middletown and wanted his company.[41]

With Sardis, Rud made the long journey to Connecticut in October 1837. A former Yale tutor, Isaac Webb accepted only twenty diligent boys of good character into his school, where the principles of "thorough study, faithful instruction, and steady discipline" prevailed. Ever fearful that Rud's morals might be corrupted in the pursuit of an education, Sophia was reassured by Webb's objectives. "Habits, principles, feelings, and tastes were to be assiduously cultivated; truth, justice, honor, and religion to be regarded as the cardinal points of character." The total cost of tuition, room, and board at Webb's school was $250 a year, which Sardis paid.[42]

When Sardis was hurt by Rud's "apparent want of feeling" at their parting, Sophia tried to excuse her son. She stressed that both of her children had a "contented disposition," and although they were happy at home, they did not mind leaving their loved ones and being among strangers. "I do not think," she also perceived, "it is a want of affection for their Friends but a determination not to discover their feelings." It was not Rud's affection but his direction that Sophia was anxious about. With his all-consuming interest in politics, she worried to Sardis, "I dont know what we shall make of him."[43]

Webb's school turned out to be exactly what Rud needed. "I like this school very much indeed," he wrote to Sardis in December. Both pleasant and "not to be trifled with," Webb knew how "to take care of a parcel of boys." Even though Rud had missed the summer term, he caught up with Will Lane and his other classmates. Webb found Rud to be "dutiful and respectful in his deportment" and "faithful and industrious," as well as becoming "more thorough and investigating" in his "habits of study." With school in session from nine to twelve noon, one to four, and six to nine, Rud observed, "I study only nine hours and I learn the fastest I ever did in my life."[44]

But all was not work. Rud and his chums organized a secret society, aptly called "The Cobwebbs," and assumed nicknames from Charles Dickens's *Oliver Twist*, which was appearing in serial form. A cheerful, laughing companion, Rud was appropriately called "Charley Bates." Saturday was a day of leisure, and Sunday was a day of rest, although attendance was required at interminable church services. Some of Rud's incidental expenses included charges for a black ball, $.06; a ball club or bat, $.10; two broken windows, $.37¹/₂; repairing skates, $.37¹/₂; a sleigh ride, $.43; jujube paste (a confection), $.18¹/₂; suspenders, $.38; a haircut, $.12¹/₂; repairing boots, $.37¹/₂ and $.75; and a seat in church, $1.[45]

Rud liked New England. On Saturday afternoons, he and his friends trotted eight miles to a mountain from which they viewed Hartford, New Haven, Saybrook, and ten or eleven small villages. Webb's Thanksgiving dinner "beat everything all hollow," and when summer came, the students ate from Webb's garden all the cherries and strawberries they could hold. After witnessing a grand Fourth of July celebration in which Connecticut and New York City troops participated, Rud maintained, "The common soldiers were dressed better than the general officers out our way." Rud also spent a relaxing month visiting Vermont relatives (resisting with glee John and Polly Noyes's efforts to make him an abolitionist) but was glad to get back to Webb's school, because "it seems like home here more than anywhere else."[46]

Although fond of his Yankee relatives and of New England, Rud remained a staunch Buckeye. Rather than yield to his pleasant surroundings, he became aggressive in upholding the honor of his section and state and acknowledged his "aversion to the Yankees." Church services were not as interesting as in Ohio. "We have to go to meeting twice every Sunday," he complained. "The priest prays thirty minutes; everything else in proportion." He liked his Buckeye friends Will Lane of Norwalk and Converse Goddard of Zanesville "a little 'taller' than anybody else in Connecticut" and was at a loss to explain Webb's virtues until he found that Webb was fond "of the Queen of the West" and "a real Buckeye in every sense of the word." Rud also believed that westerners had more stamina than New Englanders. After he, his Ohio friends, and an Alabamian walked thirty miles in six hours, he boasted, "Quite Pedestrians, the Buckeyes!" Often indulging in hyperbole, Rud kept his Ohio chauvinism on a playful level. "I've had one sleigh-ride," he wrote to his cousin Harriet Moody, "but give me a Buckeye ride in mud two feet deep than a Yankee one in snow the same depth." And when he imagined a coat of arms, Rud identified himself with Ohio and its land by placing a scythe, rake, pitchfork, and haycock above "R. B. H., Buckeye."[47]

In the spring of 1838, Isaac Webb thought that Rud, who was still fifteen, was too young for college and urged that he return to Middletown for another year of preparation before entering Yale. Sardis agreed, and Rud was tempted (talking "werry" loud with Will Lane of walking to Ohio some vacation), but he thought that an extra year of preparation was unnecessary. He also realized that both Sophia and Fanny wanted him in Ohio; he was afraid they might think that he did not wish to see them and that he "thought more of the Yankees than of them." Sophia wanted Rud to start college in Ohio and told Sardis, "If we think best he can spend his last year in an eastern College." Sardis protested and consulted with Judge Lane, but

Sophia was adamant, declaring, "If Rd. lives he is to be a Western man." In August, she decided that Rud would enter Kenyon College at Gambier that fall.[48]

Sophia got her boy back to Ohio, and Sardis, though disappointed, graciously gave up his dream of making his nephew a Yale man. Despite Yale's attraction, Rud was happy to start college immediately and was delighted to be attending a Buckeye school. He left Middletown at the end of September, having "grown 'werry tall' " and matured considerably at Webb's school. On 4 October 1838, his sixteenth birthday, Rud was on board the steamboat *Columbus* on Lake Erie. That afternoon he arrived in Sandusky City, spent the next day on a stagecoach, and arrived home at eight o'clock on the morning of 6 October. After a year's absence, home was "quite natural," Rud reported. He was met not only by a loving, thankful mother but also by a "beautiful and joyous" sister. The following day he "spent loping about, seeing the folks." Apart from his interest in the election on 9 October, he hunted and loafed the rest of the month. "There never was so good a time for small game," Rud claimed, as that dry, pleasant fall. "Those slaughtered by me," he boasted, "were 60 or 70 squirrels 1 porcupine 1 skunk 2 turkies 3 ducks 3 pheasants & a crow the wounded were 1 deer & some other beasts of prey. I saw one bear & a blue bird."[49]

Years later, Rud recalled that time apart at school had changed his and Fanny's relationship. After he returned from Norwalk and she from Putnam, they "had one renewal of our former quarrels," he remembered, "which we laughed ourselves out of before it was fairly begun, and from that time we were loving sister and brother." When he returned from Webb's school, Rud found that the "rather plain-looking" playmate, who loved to go sledding and willingly waded into the river after sticks, had been replaced by a mature, beautiful young woman of eighteen. Fanny, who had always been intelligent, well informed, and sensible, had built on her training at Putnam and continued to grow intellectually. She had organized her friends into a reading and debating club, called the Union, and made the Hayes home the cultural center of Delaware. In addition, Rud's home had become a social center, since, as Sophia complained, "Young Ladies of Fannys acquaintance" from as far off as Columbus brought their brothers to meet Fanny.[50]

Rud was growing up, but his boyish high spirits remained, and his behavior confirmed Sophia's prejudices concerning an eastern education. "I presume," she dourly wrote to Sardis the day Rud came home, that he "has acquired considerable book knowledge but he is just as unpolished as ever. I see no great improvement as to manners." Rud irreverently, facetiously, and arbitrarily accounted his year at Middletown a profitable one. He entered in his notebook the cost of his tuition, room, board, and "needfuls" as three hundred dollars, then estimated the "present worth of what I've learned" at five hundred dollars, declared a "profit in one year" of two hundred dollars, and concluded: "WERRY GOOD THAT! HAH! HAH!"[51]

Despite his mother's observations, Rud had matured. Although still playful, he had studied so well at Middletown that Isaac Webb regretted his departure "for my own sake as well as that of his companions and himself." Aware of the differing expectations that Sophia, Sardis, and Fanny had for him, Rud adjusted to them. With his placid, good-natured personality, he was willing to fulfill the plans of Webb and Sardis or the wishes of Sophia and Fanny. But when it came to choosing a college, Rud sensed that his mother's mind was made up, and he cheerfully fell in with her plans.[52]

KENYON AND HARVARD

After a month at home, Rud left for Kenyon College on 31 October 1838. Reflecting her practical view that "he must have but few clothes while growing so fast," Sophia outfitted him meagerly and mostly from material provided by Sardis. His wardrobe consisted of a "roundabout and pantaloons," some shirts and stockings, and a coat. Rud arrived at Gambier on 1 November, and two days later, before being admitted to the freshman class, he was examined in Latin, Greek, mathematics, grammar, and elementary knowledge. Since Isaac Webb had done his work well, Rud passed "without any trouble." He named Sardis as the person who was sending him, but Sophia—who preferred being financially independent and had sold her farm—paid his bills. While informing him that she had "no money for unnecessary things," she told her son that she would "cheerfully" pay for apples and crackers to keep him "happy and comfortable" during long evenings of study.[1]

Rud was content at Kenyon College, just as he had been at Norwalk and Middletown. Compared to the grinding nine-hour days at Webb's school, Kenyon College was a lark. After three weeks, he wrote to Will Lane, who was still at Webb's school, that he was having "werry easy times so far" with his studies and "lots of fun" in his room where—in violation of college rules—"we can roast taters parch corn etc." A week after writing to Lane, Rud went skating with friends and broke through the ice where the water was eight feet deep. He was helped out "without much trouble" and claimed that he "was not scared much" and could have gotten out "without any help." His calm response was remarkable; his brother had died in a similar mishap, and Rud was fighting a "tendency to nervousness." Aware of the mental illness of "a number of near relatives" on both sides of his family, he had resolved "to maintain steady nerves . . . under the most trying circumstances." Whatever the ratio between self-confidence and bravado, his cool reaction to his skating mishap was an exercise in self-discipline.[2]

At four in the morning on 21 December, Rud and three friends began the long walk home. Twelve hours and forty miles later, and "not much fatigued," Rud arrived in Delaware. The next day he "went skating as usual." A week later, he stayed overnight with a friend's family en route back to Kenyon and continued his journey even though it "was very stormy and the snow was three or four inches deep." Tired and lame, he arrived at Gambier at 4 P.M. and decided to begin the year "happily" without studying for his New Year's Day classes.[3]

By February, however, Rud was unhappy and contemplated changing schools. Neither his tutors nor their assignments challenged him, and Kenyon regulations irked him. When a friend was caught making a custard for three in his room, a sharp-nosed tutor "jawed" the chef and routed the guests out of the closet and from under the bed. Rud was most outraged when the principal of the preparatory division, who dismissed an unrepentant student for refusing to call the roll, was backed by the Kenyon faculty. These faculty "tyrants," Rud complained, "give a student a fair trial, they say, but do not allow him to say a thing for himself."[4]

Disturbed by Rud's rebelliousness, Sophia and Fanny urged him to like his teachers. "Well," Rud responded to Fanny, "I do like them—a great ways off." Rud greeted Sophia's other admonitions—to write, to guard his health, to wear dry clothes—with similar rejoinders. Having in brash adolescent fashion told Fanny and Sophia to stop nagging him, Rud described in a carefree vein his first visit to the library, which he discovered was filled with gigantic Bibles in every language. In closing he asked for forty dollars and acknowledged that the "dreaded examination comes on in six weeks and I verily fear that about a dozen of us will have to study in vacation."[5]

Rud's letter delighted Fanny and neither moved nor offended Sophia, who ignored the constant banter of her children. She continued to admonish Rud to brush his shoes and teeth and to keep his nails and hair cut short. Fanny shrewdly complimented him for "scientifically" dissecting her letter and flattered him that he had the makings of "a first rate reviewer." By March, Rud had calmed down. He was happy to receive a good letter from Sophia and Fanny containing the forty dollars he had requested. To his mother's defense of the college's disciplinary actions, he asserted that when he got home he would convince her that the "dismissions" were unjust, but that he was in no danger.[6]

Rud never faced dismissal; indeed, he noted that his tutors were biased in his favor. He broke rules and got caught, but just as he sensed how much sass his mother would take, he avoided offending the college authorities to the breaking point. Although it was against the rules to hunt, he kept two guns, regularly hunted, and cooked the game in his room. Vice President William Sparrow, Rud later remarked, "could smell a cooking rabbit further than any mortal." But Rud's innate caution kept his rebelliousness under control, and he settled into a moderately defiant position that could do him no lasting damage. He reckoned that at the end of the session "old Sparrow . . . will say I am a tolerable good boy, considering my birthplace." By the following year, Rud had earned the reputation of having "not only the levelist but the oldest head in college." Rud was alone among his peers in urging Stanley Matthews to escape dismissal by apologizing for an infraction. Matthews, a senior, followed his advice, graduated, and was eternally grateful.[7]

Following the term break, Rud no longer desired to change colleges and even conceded that "hard necessity" compelled the faculty to act "tyrannically." The bursting spring seemed all the more glorious because playing ball from seven to nine each morning was "all the fashion." Although at the beginning of the summer term his studies were tolerably hard, he soon got his lessons very easily and did not skip any recitation that session.[8]

The Fourth of July celebration at Kenyon confirmed Rud's decision to remain. Flag raising at 4 A.M. was followed by prayers and "the poorest breakfast you ever saw." But the music, speeches, lemonade toasts, and above all "the best dinner" he "ever saw"—seven varieties of meat, ice cream, and twenty-nine kinds of cake—made that Fourth, Rud exclaimed, "the happiest day I ever spent." The rival northern and southern literary societies, however, came close to blows when a "noble warm-hearted Kentuckian" objected to the remarks of the day's orator, and sectional feelings were aroused. A brawl was averted when two students suggested that they all march together to the tune of "Yankee Doodle," reminding Hayes and other "combatants" that they were all Americans. "I trust," Rud added in retrospect, that "all other sectional divisions and disputes may always be as fortunately ended as this."[9]

The summer of 1839 at Kenyon College was also memorable for a religious revival in which the entire student body was converted except for Rud and nine other holdouts. Although his best friends had originally had less respect for religion than Rud, all of them were "gone," as they called conversion. He missed them but remained unmoved, even after attending all the meetings and reading all the books urged upon him.[10]

Rud's sense of well-being was shattered in late July when Fanny became engaged. Although her fiance had been calling for over a year, Rud was shocked by, what seemed to him, her sudden decision to marry someone he did not know. Fanny, realizing that she had done nothing to prepare him for a brother-in-law, expected him to be "quite angry." After all, she and Sophia were the stable core of his family, a core he had always taken for granted. Sophia was unhappy as well. Her 20 July 1839 letter to Rud, announcing

Fanny's engagement to William Augustus Platt, a prosperous thirty-year-old jeweler from Columbus, was a catalog of woes. After reminding her son that "seventeen years this day . . . your dear Father left this world of pain and sorrow," Sophia lamented that Sardis's health "will never be restored" and that Rud would be away until his education was completed. She then added that "Fanny intends to leave her Mothers House and go to Columbus"; that Rud "must reconcile" himself to her marriage to Will Platt, who was as "under size" as she was, and must "try to like him well enough for a brother"; and that, if he needed them, Rud should "get pantaloons." Without skipping a beat, Sophia had shifted from the "tragic" to the mundane.[11]

Two days later, Fanny softened the blow for Rud by lampooning Sophia's letter. At her playful best, Fanny referred to the "base ingratitude of a daughter leaving her Mother's house, a proper good brick one too, & going to that vicious place Columbus," to live with Will Platt, whose bulk did not bring to mind "the Pyramids of Egypt." Fanny consoled Rud with the thought that *"trying"* to like Platt was all that was required of him.[12]

Fanny knew that her clever letter would challenge Rud to respond in kind. It was two weeks, however, before he wrote to Fanny, and then his effort was more heavy-handed than lighthearted. Without spelling out the words *engagement*, *married*, or *husband*, he proceeded with half-facetious, half-serious, and half-truthful arguments against the marriage. He did not wish "to bust" her feelings, but he was "very sorry" that she was to be married on her account, on her husband's account, on his own account (knowing that he would be "lord of the house no longer"), and on Delaware's account. He feared that the place would lapse into "barbarism" and that the "glorious 'Union'"—a club in which Fanny was the moving spirit—would disappear or move to Columbus. But if Platt were a Whig and had "plenty of guns," Rud declared, he could like him "without 'trying.'" In his parting pun, Rud declared, "I am for the Union in every sense of the word."[13]

Rud not only adjusted to Fanny and Platt's union—which took place on 2 September 1839, during his vacation—but also gained in the "good graces" of Sardis, who still remembered Rud's failure to show affection when they had parted at Webb's school two years earlier. Suffering from chills and a fever, Sardis remained in Delaware for weeks after the wedding, and a more mature Rud impressed him with his "good sense," which strengthened the bond between them. After Sardis left, Rud saw the newlyweds before returning to Kenyon in October. The following spring, he spent a "pleasant" vacation with them in Columbus and looked forward to returning there in the summer. He was "much pleased with William's plan of fixing his house," which would also be Rud and Sophia's new home.[14]

Fanny Arabella Hayes Platt

By the fall of 1839, when Rud entered his sophomore year, he was not only fond of Kenyon College but also diligent in his studies and engaged in stimulating extracurricular pursuits. As a result of courses in Latin, Greek, biblical literature, natural philosophy, and mathematics, he had grown intellectually. Perhaps most important, he had sharpened his wits in the Philomathesian Society. In this club's activities—in debates in which he participated, in orations he delivered, and in compositions he presented—Rud staked out positions, honed his thinking, polished his rhetoric, and collected apt quotations. He was fond of Russian proverbs, and although he was not sympathetic with abolitionists (whom Sardis despised), he copied four antislavery verses on the American "Starred and striped banner," including Thomas Campbell's:

> The White Man's liberty in types
> Stands blazoned by your stars
> But what's the meaning of your stripes?
> They mean your negroes' scars.

The notes Rud took during debates reveal his belief that war could be justifiable, that property qualifications should not restrict the right of suffrage, and that there are limits to social improvements.[15]

Rud's most spirited description—one that Fanny enjoyed enormously—was of a trial held in Gambier in June 1840. Attending it were "*all* the students," who whooped, laughed, and cheered as the spirit moved them. The case involved "Master Thomas Jefferson Haywood, a little imp of Satan," who had tried to whip his district schoolteacher. The teacher's superior, Mr. Sawyer, was on trial because he had "whipt the boy slightly." The star of the occasion was Mrs. Haywood, "a perfect virago," whose enactment of her rescue of her "*o o o nly* son" provided good theater. Grabbing a broom, she had seized Sawyer's arm and in a loud voice threatened, "give me my child or I'll split you to the floor!" The courthouse erupted with "a roar of laughter, cheers, & cries of well done," and when the justice and others called for order they were drowned out by every student screaming "*order* at the top of his voice."[16]

The 1840 presidential campaign fascinated Rud. Like Sardis, he was an ardent Whig and an admirer of that party's nominee William Henry Harrison; he despised Martin Van Buren and the Democrats. So intense was Rud's interest that beginning on 25 June 1840 he wrote a partisan history of the campaign, stressing that Democratic banking policies had produced cohesion among the Whigs. He gleefully detailed the Whig mass meeting of 20,000 held at Columbus on 22 February (with its "Log cabins, hard cider, canoes, boats, [and] thousands of mottoes"), which proved to be the first of the "great conventions for which," he predicted, "this campaign will be remarkable." In November, Rud jubilantly concluded, "The 'whirlwind' has swept over the land and General Harrison is undoubtedly elected President. I never was more elated by anything in my life."[17]

For Rud, his junior year at Kenyon College brought a "full share of content and happiness." Besides Harrison's victory, the birth of Fanny's daughter Sarah made him an uncle; he was also the treasurer of the Philomathesian Society and was reciting to Bishop Charles Pettit McIlvaine, the ex officio president of the college, whom he liked. Rud was also fond of his "high, dry, and healthy" room with a "bull's eye" window, on the top floor of "Old Kenyon," where he cooked most of his meals. "I have risen (prepare for a thunderstroke!)," he warned his mother, "at the first bell. I have never before felt like applying myself to my studies with such hearty good-will." An avid reader of newspapers, Rud had always been well informed about politics, but in his last two years at Kenyon, he became a serious scholar.[18]

The school year passed rapidly. Apart from his regular schoolwork, Rud was more involved than ever with the "Old Philo," debating subjects that ranged from the virtues of medieval monasteries to federal power versus states' rights. He began to wonder about his future. In February, midway through his junior year, Rud confided in Sophia that if he had good land, he "would love to be a farmer," but failing that he would spend every cent he could on "a *good* and *complete* education, and . . . practice law in some little dirty hole out West." Sensing that Fanny and Sardis's desire to live vicariously through him clouded their judgment, Rud asked Sophia to say nothing to them, because "there is no *mother* among them."

Rud also worked to perfect his writing. "Do not be frightened that I should so soon write again," he teased Sophia, "nothing serious has happened, only I have turned over a new leaf about writing letters." Having been struck by a remark in a rhetoric lesson "that nothing but exercise could make a good epistolary writer" and knowing "no one upon whom I can more properly *inflict* a few letters than my mother," Rud told Sophia to brace herself for a series. "If you knew," Sophia responded, "how much we prize your letters you would not fear writing too often." For his own amusement, Rud completed short, frank sketches of several classmates. His most elaborate one was of "talented, energetic, honorable" Lorin Andrews, who later became president of Kenyon, but he also noted that his "warm and constant friend," Guy M. Bryan of Texas, was "a real gentleman . . . though not a good scholar" and that R. B. Hayes was "remarkable for self-esteem."[19]

In June 1841, Rud again decided to keep a diary and, despite lapses, remained faithful to his resolve. Like with his letter-writing binge, his purpose was self-improvement. "I find great difficulty in putting my thoughts upon paper in a clear and satisfactory manner," he confessed. "Even when I sit down to write a letter the ideas which I had previously collected suddenly vanish, leaving me to twirl my pen and thump my head in a vain attempt to recover them." Rud also thought that his conversation and his informal speeches could be more coherent. Recording his good resolutions, he decided, would force him to keep them, and he hoped in later life to be amused by his "youthful anticipations, broken resolves, and strange desires."[20]

In his second diary entry, Rud rated his "very good opinion of himself"— his most salient character trait—a plus. Without self-esteem, he decided, he would not deserve the respect of others. Yet Rud claimed that no one was more anxious than he to conceal his good opinion of himself. His pride, he insisted, was in his common sense—"a sound practical judgment of what is correct in the common affairs of life"—for which he was often commended and which he thought was a family trait. Closely related to self-esteem was Rud's susceptibility to flattery, which he claimed to detest while frankly admitting that he seemed "like quite another being while under its agreeable influence." Acknowledging his ambition, Rud insisted that his common sense held it in check by reminding him that "an undeserved reputation is of more injury than benefit."[21]

Finding an individual without decisiveness a "pitiable atom," Rud concluded that this was the most important character feature. "There have been times when I exercised considerable firmness and decision, apparently without exertion," he noted. "At other times, after making the best of resolutions, I find the strenuous will to carry them into effect almost entirely wanting." Knowing that he was no more deficient in these qualities than his college friends, Rud nevertheless was "determined . . . to use what means I have to acquire a character distinguished for energy, firmness, and perseverance."[22]

In the spirit of his vow to be decisive, Rud outlined his plans for the future. To make himself "a tolerable debater," he wished to stay at Kenyon an additional year after graduation to master "logic and rhetoric and to obtain a good knowledge of history." Beyond the profession of law, he had idealistic "hopes and designs" for a political career, not for power or as a stepping-stone for wealth, but to serve the people. Whatever his ability or station, he was determined to "preserve a reputation for honesty and benevolence" and to "never do anything inconsistent with the character of a true friend and good citizen. To become such a man," Rud realized, "I shall necessarily have to live in accordance with the precepts of the Bible, which I firmly believe, although I have never made them strictly the 'rule of my conduct.' "[23]

The day after Rud committed these resolutions to paper, his eight-month-old niece died suddenly. Full of "mirth and glee" that morning, little Sarah was dead before the sun went down. "Great as my sorrow is," Rud wrote, "I almost forget it when I think of the anguish of the fond and doting parents." In her letter informing her brother of her child's death, Fanny spoke of Sarah in the present tense, as though she were alive. She requested that Rud "not say more of this melancholy event" and ended with the hope that "time will heal the wound." Stating in his response that he must not be excluded "from the common bereavement," Rud added, "One word of advice and I am done. Do not permit yourself to brood over any apparent error in your treatment of her; it will only add poignancy to your grief without cause, and open another source of unavailing regret." Although the death of Arcena and Thomas Wasson's son John had been a blow to the family two years earlier, this was the first time that Rud grieved for the loss of one so close and so loved.[24]

Rud did not dwell on his grief, but little Sarah's death, coming at a time of self-examination, reinforced his desire for self-improvement. Plunging back into his schoolwork and the activities of the Philomathesian Society, he wrote in his diary for his own amusement a scathing review of a poem presented by a sophomore "on the decline of the Indian race," which had "neither wit, sense, nor rhyme." But having skewered his fellow Philo with the brashness and unkindness with which he and Fanny often judged others, Rud felt uneasy and feared that he had violated his resolution to govern his tongue. Lest he get in the habit of slandering his acquaintances, he resolved to follow Francis Bacon's advice to talk of things rather than of persons. "My love of fun is so great," Rud acknowledged, "and my perception of the ludicrous so quick, that I laugh at everything witty, and say all I can to add to the general mirth. Now, this [is] agreeable enough at times, but the tendency to carry it to extremes is so great that I shall stop it entirely in the future, if I can."[25]

In his junior year, Rud emerged as a leader at Kenyon College. At the end of that year, on 28 July 1841, he was elected president of the Philomathesian Society. During the next year, he presided over society meetings each Wednesday evening and decided whether the affirmative or negative side of the debated question deserved the honors of the evening. These questions ranged from "Is animal magnetism true?" and "Is Lord Byron deserving of the censure he received?" to "Should the teetotal pledge be adopted by the Temperance Society?" and "Should Texas be admitted into the Union?" With a few exceptions, debated subjects were rooted in recent history or in current politics. Shortly after John Tyler vetoed proposals for a fiscal bank in August and September 1841, the Philomathesian Society debated whether or not the president should possess the veto power.[26]

As president of the thriving Philomathesian Society, Rud generously worked to strengthen its rival, which had fallen on hard times. During the nullification controversy in 1832, the southern students at Kenyon had seceded from the Philomathesian Society and established Nu Pi Kappa (NPK), whose members were drawn from slaveholding states. In time, intense passions subsided—although they revived briefly on 4 July 1839—and close friendships (such as that of Rud and Guy Bryan) were made, despite sectionalism. With fewer students from slave states coming to Kenyon, NPK had withered while its rival had flourished. Working to reestablish two strong literary societies, Rud and Bryan proposed that potential members be divided by lot rather than by section. Convinced that he and his fellows were forming "opinions . . . which will remain with us through life," Rud argued that integrated societies would reduce sectional prejudices on campus and promote nationalistic sentiment for the Union. At the 4 May 1842 meeting of his society, Rud's plan was adopted and became part of the "Act of Agreement" between the two societies.[27]

In 1842, Rud journeyed to a mass meeting at Dayton to see his hero, the great compromiser, Henry Clay. After Clay had spoken for an hour and a quarter to "perhaps fifty thousand," he withdrew to a nearby house, where Rud and a classmate "were kindly greeted by the great Kentuckian, who was resting on a lounge." The occasion was made even more memorable for Rud when Alfred Kelley, a leader of the Ohio Whigs—"a vain, pompous man without tact" and the father of Helen Kelley, with whom Rud would fall in love—chided Clay for overtaxing himself by speaking so long and so loud. Delighting those present, Clay with a wave of his hand invited Kelley to "attribute this indiscretion of which you speak to my youth and inexperience."[28]

Fired by his belief that his destiny depended on his own exertions, Rud worked to make his senior year at Kenyon an unqualified success. His decision to study law had hardened into a desire to become an eminent lawyer, and he was convinced that he had to acquire the habit of enduring and intense application. His future would be as happy as it would be laborious, Rud exhorted himself, if he utilized to the utmost his current opportunities.[29]

Although he had become a diligent student as a junior, Rud attacked his

Kenyon friends for life: Hayes, Guy M. Bryan, and Stanley Matthews

studies even more purposefully as a senior. His class studied mathematics, chemistry, and "mental philosophy," which concentrated on "eminently practical" subjects, particularly the "habits of study and reflection." Ruminations on controlling his own destiny made his goals seem possible, if he were properly disciplined. As far back as he could remember, the desire for fame had been uppermost in Rud's thoughts, and Fanny had helped keep it there.[30]

Rud read history and biography, fiction and poetry. He took more books out of the Philomathesian library than any of his classmates. He enjoyed the "strong good sense" in the poetry of Chaucer and in Edmund Spenser's *Faerie Queene*. After reading Sir Walter Scott's *The Lord of the Isles*, he longed for the poetic power to immortalize "our Revolutionary sires" and to celebrate America. "What a country we have; what mountains, what lakes, what rivers, what plains, what cataracts, to inspire the poet and arouse poetic fire! What great deeds of valor and patriotism are to be described; what men are to be painted to life!" Would that some Shakespeare might do justice to the American Revolution and the men who made it.[31]

Rud and his closest friends met in his room and organized a fraternity. Calling it the Phi Zeta Club and choosing the motto *Philia Zoe* (friendship for life), they procured matching silver-headed canes from his jeweler brother-in-law and twirled them "in a perfect ecstasy of boyish glee." The jealousy and hostility aroused by the club's exclusiveness was soon channeled into the founding of a rival club. Besides strutting with their canes, Rud and his cohorts read and criticized one another's essays.[32]

Although serious about studying, Rud remained a fun-loving, light-hearted young man. He regaled Fanny with humorous descriptions of his voracious appetite, less-than-elegant manners, and tattered appearance: "A fly in a pot of honey, 'a pig in the clover,' a toad in a gutter, — O pshaw, out with it, — Hayes at the dinner table!" "I feel a good deal 'stuck up' today," he reported, "for I have got my hair cut, my peaked-toed boots blacked, and my t'other *new* brindle-colored pants on. And, what is still more surprising, I have my face washed and a clean collar on. It is a hard matter for me to 'slick up' here for everybody notices it." His old pants were missing so many buttons that it was "quite miraculous that they should be induced to stay on."[33]

Rud often used humor to parry his mother's constant thrusts. Although he had left home with a cough, he assured her that it was entirely gone, but added that Dr. Case had told him that he would have to stop drinking, regulate his diet, keep out of the cold, and entirely abstain from laughing. He could quit laughing and eating sugar and sweet potatoes, but to give up gin was "too much. . . . Do you recollect how soundly I slept in the morning when I was at home?" he asked Sophia. "You didn't know it was hock [wine], good old hock, that made me sleep so late."[34]

Sophia knew that her son was teasing her. She realized that "Doctor" Douglass Case was a member of Phi Zeta who planned to study medicine. Nevertheless, Rud's banter about drink made her nervous. She went to two or three temperance meetings a week, including "a *Martha Washington sewing Temperance Meeting*, where," Fanny explained, "the ladies sew up the gapes in elbows of the reformed drunkards." Try as Sophia might, she could not erase the memory of Sardis's old binges, and she worried because Rud was not a total abstainer. In a letter to Fanny, Rud ridiculed temperance by linking it with other fads of the day. "I heard," he wrote, "that you have all turned animal magnetizers. Well, I was some astonished to hear you had become temperate, but to hear of your believing in such a humbug is quite amusing, quite, I assure you." He mentioned approvingly that a fellow student, who apparently had a taste for strong drink, had joined the teetotaling Washingtonian Society, but, confident of his own self-control, Rud added, "I shall not."[35]

For Rud, even as a young man, moderation was the key. He was temperate in religious matters, in consuming beverages, and in reacting to discipline. After several students were censured or dismissed for "spreeing and other refined amusements," the seniors skipped their chemistry examination. "Many of my classmates were so excited," he reported to Fanny, "that they really supposed they were resisting a most unwarrantable oppression. I, of course, was in the matter up to my eyes, but I wasn't blinded." Rud found the whole affair laughable, but his mother was not amused. "I can bear to see you come home shabby—but to have you dismissed and sent home—I should feel that your mind and heart were as much disordered as your apparel."

Rud was not sent home. The seniors were censured and punished "a little," but as Rud explained, the faculty lacked the nerve to dismiss "every mother's son of us." As a student, Rud tested authority but expected his challenges to be met and himself to be disciplined. He did not question the legitimacy of authority, and when he was in a position to use it, he did not hesitate to act.[36]

Even while criticizing their courage, Rud declared that the Kenyon faculty was composed of fine men, and they reciprocated in their evaluation of him. Prior to his final term and after the senior rebellion, Sophia received a flattering evaluation of her son. The Kenyon faculty found that in his studies Rud had "evinced the possession of intellectual powers of a superior order. For strength of mind, clearness of perception, soundness of judgment, he is surpassed by none among us. In all his studies he has attained the highest grade." Apart from the recent "misunderstanding, . . . his conduct has been most gentlemanly and exemplary." The report concluded: "In the opinion of all who know him, he bids fair to become a bright ornament to society."[37]

Rud's final term at Kenyon was one of academic triumph. On 20 April he retired as president of the Philomathesian Society, argued in debate that evening that Americans had nothing to fear from Roman Catholics, and was appointed to a committee to help select the class poet and commencement orator. He was named valedictorian. His chum Bryan said that, although his classmates "were all satisfied that he deserved it," Rud did not expect the honor, because "it was always given to a member of the church."[38]

Just as the term began, however, Rud heard that Fanny was desperately ill. While he had been home between terms, she had given birth to a second daughter, Laura Arabella. Both mother and daughter were doing fine when Rud returned to Kenyon, but on the night after his departure, Fanny became "mentally deranged." Her psychiatrist, Dr. William M. Awl of the Ohio Lunatic Asylum in Columbus, blamed her condition on "too great mental excitement for the strength of the body." She had been unable to sleep for two or three nights in succession, and "her mind gradually gave way through excessive fatigue." Fanny apparently was afflicted with postpartum psychosis, perhaps exacerbated by unresolved grief over little Sarah's death. After four days with no improvement, Platt decided, on 17 April, to tell Rud before he heard an exaggerated version of Fanny's illness from someone else. "Dr. Awl," he wrote, "thinks the symptoms in her case are favorable for a speedy recovery so do not allow yourself to be unnecessarily alarmed—you shall hear from us often."[39]

When Fanny, who had become violent, did not improve, Dr. Awl concluded that she had to be hospitalized. The longer she remained at home, he insisted, the longer it would take "to effect a cure & the greater the risk of making the derangement permanent." Exhausted and feeling "more crazy than sane" himself, Platt accepted Awl's advice and placed "Fanny the life & soul of us all . . . in the Lunatic Asylum. This will startle you my dear Brother," Platt wrote to Rud, "& pierce your very soul but severe as it is you must know the truth." Even before Fanny was hospitalized Platt had told Rud, "Do not think of coming home. . . . You can be of no assistance to us." Now Fanny was allowed no visitors. Platt agreed to that rule with reluctance when Awl insisted that it was a "most beneficial" regulation.[40]

As Platt had feared, the hard truth of Fanny's condition riddled Rud with anxieties. Worried that his sister's "feeble constitution" would not stand the strain, he begged for news but took hope from the knowledge that everything possible was being done. Luckily, Fanny's psychiatrist was a leading exponent of "moral treatment," a humane, optimistic, sympathetic therapy that often yielded positive results. Before committing Fanny, Platt visited the asylum. "The hall from which her room opens is very pleasantly ornamented with ever greens," he told Rud, and "is furnished with a swing & has in all respects the air of comfort & cheerfulness."[41]

Both Platt and Sophia sensed that it was difficult for Rud to confront Fanny's illness. He was devoted to Fanny, but her condition confirmed his fear that the family was susceptible to insanity. "If her state was *different*," he wrote to his brother-in-law on 25 April, "I would wish to be with her; as it is I could not bear to see her—I have *now* no desire to come home on her account." Rud was devastated in early May when Sophia wrote to him that Fanny had continually inquired after him during her first days of illness and had refused to believe that he had returned to Gambier. Telling her mother that she had "always thought Rutherford was almost perfection," Fanny had insisted that she must see him. But by the time Rud heard of her entreaties, Fanny was in the asylum and it was impossible for him to see her. "I cannot tell you," Sophia wrote, "how I long to see you tho I do not wish you to come home. I know you could not be happy here."[42]

Rud buried himself in his studies. Even though Platt informed him often "of our dear Fanny's situation," it was a month before Rud wrote again. He then explained his long delay by stating, "I try to keep melancholy thoughts out of my mind, but when writing home I can't." After comparing Fanny's absence in his thoughts to her absence from Platt's home, Rud reversed himself, saying, "No, she is not absent from my thoughts, but there is a feeling of emptiness which continually reminds me that she is gone." By mid-June reports of Fanny's progress—"precisely as Dr. Awl anticipated"—made Rud hopeful of her speedy recovery and of her presence at his graduation in August. He was also pleased that his mother still intended to come. "She needs something to restore her spirits," he told Platt, "if possible, after so great anxiety." But Rud did not go to Columbus for the big Fourth of July celebration, although Guy Bryan and Douglass Case did. They called on Sophia and Platt, giving them the good news that Rud had won highest honors as well as his excuse that he "was too busy writing his addresses &c to wish to come."[43]

Although recovering, Fanny had setbacks and could not attend the commencement. She had a relapse in late July, and although Rud had been assured that he would be informed of any interruption in her recovery, he was not told. Sophia and Sardis were at Gambier on 5 August 1842 to hear their boy deliver the valedictory. For both of them as well as for the absent Fanny, it was the realization of nearly two decades of dreams: Rud had grown up to be a slim, handsome, auburn-haired young man who had excelled in college and was ambitious for a career in law and public service.[44]

Rud, too, remained anxious about Fanny, but hearing only of her steady improvement, he thoroughly enjoyed commencement. In the two weeks before it, he polished his speeches and, with examinations over, rambled "about the country . . . hunting and fishing." He wrote to a friend that during commencement week "came parties, and at the parties we had silly ladies and weak lemonade—admirably adopted to each other, but ill calculated to enliven the spirits of this 'cod-fish' of Kenyon." The women, of course, were no more silly than their hosts were callow. However well Kenyon trained its young men intellectually, it left them ill at ease in the society of young women. "Like most youngsters whose time has been spent at school where we have little society of any kind, and none of the ladies," Rud admitted in his diary, "I am quite bashful when in company, and of course very awkward." Sophia also perceived that her son, who had a "happy faculty of communicating" news and yarns to his family circle, was "quite too *mum*" when strangers were present. While striving to overcome his awkwardness, Rud made "it a subject of sport," both for himself and for those who observed it.

After the parties "came commencement day—that great day for which all other days were made." Members of the graduating class wore Kentucky blue jean coats with black velvet collars, white waistcoats, and white linen trousers. The exercises lasted from morning till night, and Rud, who was extremely busy, had only a few moments with Sophia and Sardis. But for the three of them it was a day of rejoicing and thankfulness, a day of triumph.[45]

Rud gave his oration and a separate valedictory (literally a farewell address) after the orations of his eight classmates, two poems, and eight pieces of music. His oration on "College Life" stressed that it should not develop in the student "overweening self-esteem and insufferable arrogance" but the realization of "how weak and limited are his powers." By mortifying the inexperienced beginner who neglects his studies, college discipline converts him from "the thoughtless idler" to "the industrious persevering aspiring student," teaching him that "patient labor is the condition of success." With new lessons reinforced by new friends, the successful student "labors to become a useful member of the society in which he lives and thus prepares himself to deserve the only reputation which is valuable and lasting." In his valedictory, Rud thanked the faculty for being the graduates' "parents, instructors and friends." He assured the president that the senior class appreciated his good intentions and concern for its welfare during the recent controversy. He urged the remaining students to eschew the superficially brilliant and "to master what is profound and difficult" and "substantial" through disciplined study. In his two speeches, Rud summed up his hopes and what, to a large degree, Kenyon College had done for him.[46]

Rud tried not to take his graduation too seriously. That day of days came "and it went," he reflected. "And that night I felt of myself all over, and to my astonishment I found I was 'the same old Rud' not a single cubit added to my stature, nor a hairs breadth to my girth, on the contrary if anything I felt more lank & gaunt than common, much as if a load were off my stomach." He would always be Rud or Uncle Ruddy to friends and relatives, but commencement had introduced him to the world as Rutherford B. Hayes.[47]

Hayes and a couple of friends—if their plan materialized—hired "an old apple-cart" a week after commencement to carry them and their gear to Columbus. After spending a week at home, Hayes visited his friend Rowland Trowbridge in Birmingham, Michigan. "Old Trow" had graduated from Kenyon the year before, and as they talked of shared events during four days of riding and hunting, Hayes discovered that "old times, like old wine" had improved vastly with age.

On the way from Michigan back to Columbus, Hayes visited Sardis in Lower Sandusky, who was filled with pride and admiration following Hayes's triumphant commencement. "He is a sound Boy," he assured his brother Austin, "has got good hard *sense like a Horse!*" With Sardis, Hayes discussed his plans for a law career and decided that for a year he would study with a lawyer in Columbus. But Sardis also resolved, "I shal send Rud East next fall to Cambridge Law scholl."

While Hayes was visiting Sardis, they heard the good and unexpectedly early news that Fanny would probably come home on 30 August. Overjoyed but apprehensive, since he would not see Fanny "until the day she returns," Platt planned a trip east to celebrate her recovery and to renew their intimate ties. They had been separated for four and a half months under the most trying circumstances, and Dr. Awl agreed that travel would benefit Fanny. Platt urged Hayes to cut his visit short and return on 29 August, but Hayes tarried with Sardis, making Sophia "much concerned" over his delay.[48]

With Hayes finally back, Fanny and Platt embarked on their trip, leaving him and Sophia in charge of their six-month-old daughter and household. When the couple returned in mid-October, Fanny had gained weight and a new wardrobe. Having acquired a calf and a canary, the family's menagerie approached completion, especially since Hayes thought that Fanny could substitute for a walrus, and she thought that he would make an admirable baboon. With Hayes and Fanny verbally slugging it out as they had in the past, he cheerfully reported that "family matters are remarkably well conditioned at this present writing." Fanny loved having Hayes in her home, remarking that "he seems just such a happy appendage to a household as every family ought to have to preserve the pleasant equilibrium of social life."[49]

In mid-September, while Fanny and Platt were gone and Hayes was helping his mother manage their home, he began "studying a little." Reviewing some of his college courses, he hoped to start German in about two weeks and reading law a week later. Like most law students in 1842, Hayes planned to study under the supervision of an established lawyer. In seeking a mentor, he followed the advice of an "eminent writer," who declared that the chosen instructor must be accessible, affable, and communicative. He must have neither too large a law practice nor too many students. Hayes settled on Thomas Sparrow, the younger brother of the former head of Kenyon, whom Hayes had admired for his "nerve and decision."

Although his Platt in-laws did not like Sparrow, Hayes began to study with him on 17 October 1842. "He is not so learned or experienced as many others," Hayes explained, "but he gives me more instruction than law students usually receive so . . . I have a better opportunity to learn than I shall have with an older and abler man." For Hayes, being at Sparrow's office became even more pleasant when his classmate and fellow Phi Zeta member Leander Comstock joined him there. Their tuition was doing odd jobs around Sparrow's office, but the German lessons, which Hayes hoped would enable him in two or three years to read Schiller, cost twelve dollars a quarter.[50]

As was the custom, Hayes commenced his legal studies with Sir William Blackstone's four-volume *Commentaries on the Laws of England* (1765–69). He realized that mastering the law would unlock "the passport which is to conduct me to all that I am destined to receive in life." He believed that "my chiefest obstacles are within myself. If I *knew* and could *master myself*, all other difficulties would vanish." After a month of study, Hayes attempted an impartial evaluation of his accomplishments and was satisfied with the quantity of his work but not with its quality. As he began Blackstone's second volume, he determined to read "with more attention." But, as might be expected, Columbus was filled with distractions for a young man of twenty. Politics, which had always fascinated him, was not simply a pastime in this state capital, it was an industry. Then too, Sparrow's office was situated above an attractive book store and a coffeehouse was in the same building as Platt's shop. Steeling himself against temptation, Hayes resolved to read no newspapers, rise at seven, read Blackstone for six hours and record his difficulties with him, then study reasoning and logic for two hours, German for two hours, and retire at ten.[51]

For ten "vexatious and tedious" months, Hayes read law under Sparrow's direction. Thirty-five years later, Hayes recalled this first year out of college, with its loss of companionship, "as the doleful period of my life." Although Sparrow was helpful, Hayes was convinced that the progress he was making was not enough; he wanted to attend Harvard Law School. He knew that formal instruction at Cambridge would better prepare him for his goals, and Sophia and Fanny reluctantly agreed. Fanny realized that, "in the intellectual atmosphere of Boston," Hayes would "have better opportunities for becoming more & more what I desire my dear, my adored brother to be."

Sardis wanted to send Hayes to Harvard. "The money that has been spent for his Education will be well laid out," he declared. Hayes, however, was not completely dependent on Sardis, for whom it was "hard to convert Landed property into money at present." Acting for Sophia and himself, Hayes sold their Marion County property in June for $2,300. Sophia was encouraged that "he succeeded so well" in this, "his first business," and told Sardis that since Rutherford's share was $1,600 in silver (which he lent to Platt at 10 percent interest), "you will not be obliged to raise any for him unless you please." Sardis kindly preserved Hayes's new nest egg for him by paying his expenses beyond the interest it earned.[52]

In addition to his uncle's stated preference, Hayes was attracted to Harvard by its professors. He wanted to be instructed by "those eminent jurists and teachers" Justice Joseph Story of the U.S. Supreme Court and Simon Greenleaf, author of the authoritative *Treatise on the Law of Evidence* (1842). Armed with a letter from Sparrow stating that he had "with great diligence regularly prosecuted the study of the law" and attesting that he was "a young man of good moral character," Hayes entered Harvard Law School's middle class in August 1843. Among the students were eight Buckeyes whom he knew and three of Webb's "Middletown lads."[53]

Both Story and Greenleaf combined illustrations and explanations with student recitations. Hayes thought that their approach had "all the advantages of recitations and lectures . . . without their disadvantages." Greenleaf was "searching and logical in examination," making it "impossible for one who has not faithfully studied the text to escape exposing his ignorance." He kept "the subject constantly in view, never stepping out of his way for the purpose of introducing his own experience." In contrast, Story was "very fond of digressions to introduce amusing anecdotes, high-wrought eulogies of the sages of the law, and fragments of his own experience."[54]

Story was also a font of good sense, high ideals, and intense patriotism. He advised his students to "keep out of politics till you are forty" and mature enough to "direct your course." But he also recognized that "ambition and confidence . . . are proper inmates for the youthful breast," and he did not want his advice to nip in the bud a student's desire to live a life that would benefit his age and country. Since "law is the perfection of human reason, the wisdom of all ages . . . precedents must not be slavishly followed," Story insisted, "but in every case reason and justice should prevail." Story's lecture "on the duty of American citizens to adhere honestly and implicitly to the Constitution"—"the most eloquent" Hayes had ever heard—attacked abolitionists as madmen. If people, "in the name of conscience, liberty, or the rights of man," disregarded Article IV, Section 2, of the Constitution, enabling a slaveholder to reclaim a fugitive slave from a free state, Story stressed that the South "may refuse to obey that part which seems to bear hard upon its interests." If this should happen, the Union would become a "rope of sand" and the Constitution a source of "discord and civil war," with anarchy or despotism the result.[55]

Moot court was as important for Hayes as reading and lectures. As a regular practice, Story would hear arguments in moot court on cases appealed to the U.S. Circuit Court, over which he presided. And when he and Greenleaf were referred knotty legal questions, they allowed their students to argue them in moot court. The moot court, Story said, was "the high-court of appeals for the whole world."[56]

Besides reading Blackstone and studying David Hoffman's two-volume *Course of Legal Studies* (2d edition, 1836), Hayes read Cicero and Aristotle. But he was more influenced in ethics and morality, philosophy and psychology, by three modern authors—James Beattie, William Paley, and John Locke. A leader in the Scottish school of "common-sense philosophy," Beattie believed that certain truths, principles, and laws were self-evident and that people were innately rational and moral. Declaring that Beattie was plain and practical and that his great merits were good sense and good intention, Hayes read him on psychology, moral philosophy, theology, and politics. Hayes rejected Paley's Christian utilitarianism and refused to believe that "expediency is the test of the morality of actions, or that an act is therefore right, which conduces to the greatest happiness." Locke's *Essay Concerning Human Understanding* (1690) contradicted Hayes's notion of an innate faculty that led humans "to believe there is a moral quality in actions." Although he was unwilling to accept Locke's view that people were born without ideas and acquired them through sensory perception, Hayes admitted, "I cannot discover its weak points." Locke's persuasive ideas were also

congenial with Hayes's belief that the conscience could be molded by training and society's ills cured by education.[57]

Hayes did not neglect languages and literature. He continued to study
German and took up French. He also heard rather dry lectures by Henry
Wadsworth Longfellow on Anglo-Saxon literature and on modern languages
and literature. Longfellow's remarks on Goethe forced Hayes to confront the
presence of what he considered immorality in literature. He decided that
Goethe would have preferred to write nothing immoral, but sacrificed "virtue . . . to literary excellence." After attending the theater and seeing the English tragedian William Charles Macready play Hamlet and Junius Brutus
Booth in another Shakespearean play, Hayes decided that, since the charm
of their acting was destroyed by fumbling stock players, he would as soon
read a play as see it.[58]

Hayes reacted to Boston with the same ambivalence he had to its theater.
"Boston is certainly the finest city in the world," he wrote to Fanny after two
months' experience, but "all is seeming, false, and hollow." His negative reactions, based primarily on observations made while attending elegant
church services, smacked of his Buckeye chauvinism. He had not heard a sermon "better than Mr. Dobb usually delivers" in Columbus. He had heard
the reputedly excellent choral singing of "three shrill, piercing female voices,
assisted by the harsh croaking of two cracked bass ones," and listened to the
ten-thousand-dollar Trinity Church organ, which gave forth leaden tones.
He had seen fashionable men, all wearing the same kind of cravat, coat, and
whiskers, with their "hair brushed sleek and smooth and glossy behind,
carefully coaxed up (often contrariwise of nature) in front," and demure,
self-satisfied expressions on their faces. He had seen proud, pious women,
but "as for beauty," he had "yet to see the girl who could be a belle in Columbus."[59]

Although these hypercritical remarks about fashionable Bostonians were
typical of Hayes and Fanny, they suggest an unease, a self-consciousness,
and a sense of loneliness felt by Hayes—a westerner and a stranger. He betrayed his longing for feminine companionship by making some lighthearted
bets about marriage. Typical of these was a twenty-five-dollar bet that he
would be married in four years. Hayes, however, made no attempt to meet
young people of the area. Although Fanny entreated him to tell her "something of the Boston ladies," she sensed correctly that he was "not very susceptible" to their charms. Rather than make social contacts or meld into his
New England surroundings by acquiring the requisite cravat, coat, and hair-
style, Hayes remained a Buckeye who associated primarily with other Buckeyes.[60]

When he was not trying to entertain Fanny and reaffirm his Buckeye persuasion, Hayes enjoyed Boston. He saw Bunker Hill, the Boston Navy Yard, and Mount Auburn Cemetery. He heard Jared Sparks lecture on colonial learning, religion, and authors; heard an eloquent Irishman talk on the plight of the Irish and their brave leader Daniel O'Connell, the founder of the Catholic Association; and heard Richard Henry Dana, Jr., define patriotism as loving the country but not necessarily its institutions and government.[61]

Despite deriding Boston's ministers, Hayes soon found in Dr. James Walker—professor of natural religion, moral philosophy, and civil polity—a superior preacher whom he often listened to twice on Sundays in the college chapel. A conservative Unitarian (as distinct from the radical Theodore Parker), Walker, who would become president of Harvard in 1853, was "a powerful reasoner," and his sermons provided logical grounds for views that Hayes found congenial. He liked Walker's warning to radicals that the consequences of acting upon one's principles might be mischievous for others and "may render bad that which by our theory is good." Walker's concept of Christ—that of a moderate social reformer—pleased Hayes, with his strong Union and antiabolition bias. "Evils are to be removed as He would have removed them; not by fanaticism, by violence and bloodshed, but quietly, persuasively, with passionless serenity."[62]

Hayes also enjoyed listening to speeches at political rallies. Despite his own bias toward Whigs, he found that the Democrat and historian George Bancroft had "an elegant flow of language, a chaste style, and a well stored mind." Among his own party, Hayes considered Congressman Robert C. Winthrop "agreeable and effective" and Sen. Rufus Choate "impulsive, ardent, able." At first, Hayes was impressed by his childhood hero Daniel Webster, who in 1843 had resigned from Tyler's cabinet. "In speaking, he betrays no passion, no warmth, but all is cold and clear. . . . Yet there is a charm about the greatness of his intellect and grandeur of his mien which holds one suspended upon his lips." Six months later, Hayes was more critical. He called Webster's 1844 Faneuil Hall address, ratifying Henry Clay's nomination for the presidency, a "poor" speech and decided that, by remaining Tyler's secretary of state so long, Webster had injured his reputation.[63]

Hearing John Quincy Adams did not change Hayes's "opinion of the venerable but deluded old man," since his speech contained "much abolitionism" that Hayes thought was "unreasonable and very unfair." But Hayes acknowledged Adams's power. "I do not wonder that he is regarded as a dangerous adversary in a mere personal encounter. He is quick, sharp, fearless, and full of the wit and learning of the ages."[64]

Between terms, in early February 1844, Hayes visited his grandmother and other New England relatives. Although almost eighty, Chloe Smith Hayes impressed her grandson with her penetrating queries about his habits and principles, to which Hayes "sounded the trumpet" in what he considered to be "the right Key." He spent most of his vacation with Uncle Austin Birchard, whose talent and industry in overcoming deafness continued to excite Hayes's admiration, and his wife, whom Hayes had "never liked at all." Hayes dismissed their daughter Mary—by whom he had been quite taken when at Webb's school—as "a doll-baby beauty" with a "*rather blank*" mind, "silly airs," and a bad temper, but he liked their large, handsome, and intelligent younger daughter Charlotte and their son Charles. Most lamentably, however, Charles had been made into a recluse by his father, who thought that his son's health was worse than it was, and by his mother, who constantly told him that he was "a bashful booby." Appreciating his old playmate Charley's good mind, Hayes wished that he could be "placed where his defects . . . would not constantly [be] dinned in his ears."[65]

Hayes was caught up in the excitement of the times during the spring term at Harvard. "Every few weeks some great stir is made to keep us from suffering from the blues," he explained. Not only did southern law students and college seniors skirmish, but there were also Texas meetings opposing annexation, Whig meetings ratifying Henry Clay's nomination for the presidency, "Loco-foco" (Democratic) attempts to excite enthusiasm for James K. Polk, and statewide abolitionist and temperance meetings. Hayes "had a grand good time" at the Washingtonians' temperance celebration. He was particularly amused by "the spirit of one crowd of little girls, the eldest not above twelve," walking behind a banner carried by two seven-year-olds and inscribed, "Temperance Men or no Husbands." Although Hayes enjoyed the theater, his real diversion in the spring of 1844 was playing ball. "I consider one game of ball worth about ten plays," he told Sardis, who was concerned that he was studying too hard. "I am now quite lame, from scuffling, and all my fingers stiffened by playing ball. Pretty business for a law student. Yes, pretty enough; why not? Good exercise and great sport."[66]

By this point in his life, Hayes had become a dedicated student. Although he intended to stay at Harvard but one year, he soon recognized that an extra year, or at least an additional term, would be advantageous. Sardis did not want Hayes to stay beyond the year originally agreed upon, but Fanny, Sophia, and Will Platt—as much as they wanted Hayes home—urged an extra term. Since Sardis admired the business acumen of Platt, Sophia shrewdly relayed his opinion to Sardis. "William thinks that Rutherford ought by all means to stay at Cambridge another term. he says he will have no time for study after he commences practice. he says he is so young that he need not be in any hurry about it."[67]

As Hayes delved deeper into his studies, he became more critical of Story and appreciative of Greenleaf. "Judge Story," he told Sardis in April 1844, "has returned from Washington and is again in full blast. Great as he is on the bench . . . he is too prolix — too garrulous — to loose — to be close and accurate." In May, with about two months left in the term, Hayes dropped all of Story's courses except Conflict of Laws to study with Greenleaf — a more profitable instructor by "many degrees" — and to prepare cases for argument before the Marshall Club. Hayes also had an Ohio connection with Greenleaf and his wife Hannah. Their daughter had married a Kenyon College professor, and Hayes regaled them with tales "which would surprise people in Ohio." After making them wonder "how people could live in such a country," Hayes then "took the other tack and expiated on the beauty of our forests, spring, indian summer, and discoursed of wonders even greater than the stories of mud; before I left Mrs G only wished she lived in such a mild and healthful climate and said she should certainly visit her daughter some time."[68]

In 1844, Hayes spent parts of July and August in Columbus. When he left to return to Cambridge, Sardis, who was going to Vermont, accompanied him. Together they enjoyed Niagara Falls and visited the Thousand Islands and Montreal, where they saw "the great Cathedral — the nunnery . . . and best of all the race ground where the games were in progress." Hayes once again teased his mother with a letter hinting that her dear son and much-loved brother might become racetrack touts.[69]

During his last term at Harvard in the fall of 1844, Hayes declared, "I hardly have time to think of politics." But he could not completely ignore the 1844 presidential contest between Clay and Polk. In late September, Hayes and Sardis, who had come down to Boston, enjoyed a huge Clay rally, "marched . . . with the Buckeye delegation," for which Hayes made and carried a "rude banner," "cheered the ladies — and did all other acts to such occasions appertaining. . . . Altogether the Buckeyes," Hayes told Sophia, "were quite as noisy and crazy as any other set of men I had the pleasure of seeing among the hundred thousand who assembled . . . on Boston Common."[70]

Hayes, who cast his first vote for Henry Clay, would have cheerfully started in the world "without a penny" if such a sacrifice could have made Clay president. Yet for Hayes, Clay's loss had one advantage. Despite Judge Story's solemn warning that the man who wagered on an election might corrupt that election, Hayes had bet on Polk. "I have won about $20 worth of books on the election," he told Will Platt. "I generally bet on the Loco side in order to have some consolation for the defeat." When an aroused Sophia chastised him for gambling, Hayes told Fanny, "Do tell Mother to be easy on the subject of my bets. I have compromised most of them. . . . By taking theatre-tickets!!!" After the election Hayes resolved to withdraw his "thoughts from party politics" and apply himself "patiently, earnestly, constantly to the law till I leave the Law School."[71]

A few weeks later, however, Hayes could not resist commenting on the Texas issue. He had argued against the admission of Texas into the Union on constitutional grounds, but after the Whigs lost the election, and with Clay "not to be affected by the question," Hayes began "to view the annexation of Texas quite favorably. I don't think," he told Sardis, "I would howl if it were admitted on fair terms, as it probably will be, if admitted at all." The fact that his dear friend Guy Bryan was from Texas most certainly encouraged Hayes to lean toward expansion, even though Texas would be a slave state.[72]

Hayes worked to make his last days in Cambridge worthwhile, but he and his old friend Will Lane, who started at Harvard Law that term, also had some fun. Since the "barbarous result" of the election kept Hayes in tickets, he assured Sardis that "the only dissipation we venture upon is Theater-going which you know is the entrance to all other vicious habits." During these final days, Hayes concentrated his reading on works that would be difficult to find elsewhere. For his own library, he purchased approximately $175 worth of books, all from the list that Lane's father, the judge, considered "absolutely necessary for an Ohio practitioner."[73]

With less than three weeks of law school left, Hayes told himself on New Year's Day 1845 that he would soon "begin *to live*. Heretofore I have been getting ready to live. . . . My labors have been to cultivate and store my mind." In the coming year, he resolved, "*I will strive to become in manners, morals, and feelings a true gentleman.*" At the age of twenty-two, Hayes realized, "The rudeness of a student must be laid off, and the quiet, manly deportment of a gentleman put on." In making this New Year's resolution, Hayes's self-confidence again manifested itself. "I believe I know what true gentility, genuine good breeding, is. Let me but live out what is within, and . . . little of what is important would be found wanting."[74]

LOWER SANDUSKY

To Sophia and Fanny's dismay, Hayes decided to practice law in Lower Sandusky. He made his decision, unshaken by their conviction that its moral,
social, and physical climate was perilous for personal and professional reasons. Living in Lower Sandusky would enable him to be reasonably close to
Sophia and Fanny yet not in the same town. Hayes apparently felt that at
twenty-two he needed to be on his own. But with Sardis and John R. Pease, a
favorite cousin, in Lower Sandusky, Hayes was not abandoning his family as
much as escaping from the immediate influence of the two strong-willed
women he loved.

Hayes's professional reasons also appeared sound. Sardis, the area's leading businessman, and Pease, also in business, could be counted on to steer
clients to him as well as use his services themselves. Even without these connections, Lower Sandusky seemed right. Professor Greenleaf had convinced
Hayes "that the young man who goes into a large place, unless under circumstances peculiarly favorable, commits a great error. If he settled in an
obscure place where he is sure of some business he is much more likely to
reach the ultimate object of his desires." Dreading the plunge into his profession, Hayes concluded that in Lower Sandusky he could "get into practice
soonest, and consequently learn soonest to overcome the difficulties of practice."[1]

Before leaving the East Coast, Hayes visited Washington. "The public
buildings, and situation of the City" exceeded his expectations, and he
found that he had more acquaintances in the capital than he had time to
visit. With the joint resolution to annex Texas under consideration, the
House of Representatives "was in a riotous state," with more than a score of
congressmen constantly contending for the floor. Hayes proudly wrote that
Dr. Alexander Duncan, Whig congressman from Cincinnati, "was the only
man who could be heard. In contrast, the Senate "was dignified and grand."
With Dr. Edson Baldwin Olds, a Democratic member of the Ohio state legislature, for a traveling companion (Uncle Austin had introduced Hayes to
Olds's brother in Vermont), the journey home from Washington was pleasant.[2]

By the beginning of February, Hayes was back in Columbus, where he studied for a month before journeying by stagecoach and steamboat to Marietta. There, Gen. C. B. Goddard, the father of Hayes's fellow "Cobwebb" Converse Goddard, introduced and "puffed" Hayes to several members of the bar and got a committee appointed to examine him. On 10 March 1845, Hayes was declared fit to practice law in Ohio. Having fielded questions from this committee for an hour or two, Hayes told his friend Will Lane, "The only 'dead' I made was on some simple matter in bailments," which ironically had been stressed at Harvard, "and about which I knew more than any other." After lingering in Marietta to hear some cases, Hayes returned home via Cincinnati, the Queen City of the West, where he enjoyed the theater and loved the "glorious" views from its hills.³

Back in Columbus by mid-March, Hayes delayed his departure to Lower Sandusky until the weather became "settled and the roads good." Killing time while the Ohio mud solidified, he gathered gossip for Lane's benefit, including the news that Dud Rhodes "had given up Miss Perkins," a young woman to whom Hayes would become strongly attracted. Leaving for Lower Sandusky near the beginning of April, he stopped off at Gambier to visit his old haunts. After his nearly two-year absence, Kenyon College impressed him as "really a splendid place," but he worried that the nasty controversy between the college trustees and the recently sacked President David Bates Douglass—which hampered fund-raising efforts—would endanger Kenyon's future.⁴

By 12 April 1845, Hayes had settled in Lower Sandusky. Even before his books arrived, he found a convenient little fifteen-foot-square office and planned his studies—Latin, German, French, a little Francis Bacon and Edmund Burke, some logic at night, and poetry and light literature on Sunday. He realized that his work would be "mostly in the practical matters of the law," of which he was "totally ignorant," so he decided to review Greenleaf's *Evidence* (1842) and Story's *Agency* (1839) and to master each week a new case in John William Smith's two-volume *A Selection of Leading Cases on Various Branches of the Law* (1838–40). Claiming the motto "Business first always," he planned to adjust his studies to the needs of his clients. By Sunday, 20 April 1845, Hayes, who had tried his first case, reported triumphantly to Fanny, "I . . . have hopes of becoming quite a pettifogger." He noted that his prospects were better than those of "most young lawyers. . . . I have but little competition, . . . for with one exception (R. P. Buckland) those of our lawyers who are responsible or honest are not industrious, and *vice versa*."⁵

Although Hayes did "not suffer for want of company," he had no trusted crony his own age. He shared a room in the Thompson House, formerly called the Blue Bull Tavern, with his older cousin John Pease, an ardent Democrat, whose wife of two years had recently died. Hayes bragged to Fanny that they showered every morning in a "washing machine" they had rigged up. To Pease's young half sister, Janette Elliot—who would not scold him—Hayes admitted that they lived "like 'pigs in clover.'" In their room "everything like order and neatness is banished from our presence as a nuisance—old letters and old boots and shoes, duds clean and duds dirty, books and newspapers, tooth-brushes, shoe-brushes, and clothes-brushes, all heaped together on chairs, settees, etc., in dusty and 'most admired confusion.'"[6]

Hayes had no illusions about society and culture in Lower Sandusky. At Cambridge, he had heard sophisticated sermons, experienced the theater, appreciated music, and enjoyed art; in Lower Sandusky, he could only read about these interests. Hayes attended the Episcopal church, but his speculations about religion were those of a deist rather than an orthodox Christian. "Providence interferes no more in the greatest affairs of men than in the smallest," he stated, "and . . . neither individuals nor nations are any more the objects of a special interposition of the Divine Ruler than the inanimate things of the world." He also realized that Lower Sandusky left something to be desired in the eyes of most beholders. When his cousin Charlotte visited, the rude and crude appearance of "this little mud-village," which Sardis had described glowingly, "disappointed her sadly."[7]

Lower Sandusky certainly did not fit into Fanny's professional or social plans for her brother. "You are too ambitious in your anticipations concerning my fortunes," Hayes warned Fanny. "That I shall not 'make an ill figure' in the world, I feel confident, because I think I have a pretty perfect knowledge of my own ability. . . . Beyond this my wishes do not go." Fanny was even more anxious for an appropriate sister-in-law. Although Hayes kept at arm's length the "little squad of girls . . . trying to get acquainted with" him and even told their messenger that he "was engaged to a girl in Columbus," Fanny was not reassured. "Do *not* fall in love with any of the Sandusky beauties," she commanded, "do not marry a wife you will blush for any where."[8]

Hayes also informed his mother that he wished to live his own life. Sophia was chagrined that her son had turned down an invitation to deliver the Master's Oration at Kenyon College on Commencement Day 1845. Planning to attend the ceremony, she had arranged for some eligible Columbus girls to accompany her to Gambier, where they could meet her son. Since she had neither told him of her plans nor urged him earlier to make the speech, Hayes told her that she herself was to blame for her frustration. He further chided her for the "mournful strain" and the scolding in her letter and announced he would only "visit Columbus twice a year, making a good stay each time."[9]

Hayes, who had attracted a few clients and was beginning to be noticed, claimed to be "contented as a clam." Lower Sandusky was on a judicial circuit, with a periodic court week to try cases beyond the authority of local justices of the peace. In addition, the Ohio Supreme Court progressed through the state and would be in session in Lower Sandusky on 20 August 1845. Just as Hayes had journeyed to Marietta earlier that year to catch that court, he urged Will Lane to apply for admission to the Ohio bar at Lower Sandusky. "You must have a head full of gossip about my friends and acquaintances at Cambridge," he told Lane, "besides lots of new notions about law and your general reading which I would like to hear. Do come, no committee who could be appointed here would be disposed to pester you with an ugly examination." Lane did not come, but Stanley Matthews did, and Hayes was appointed to the committee to examine him. With a mix of modesty and honesty, Hayes declared Matthews "beyond dispute a better lawyer than any of the examining committee. The good lawyers were all too busy in court to be sent off on such sham service."[10]

Hayes was enjoying his new profession. On Sunday, 12 October 1845, court week had just closed and he wrote to his mother, "I had often been told when I was studying law that the *study* was very pleasant, but the *practice* dry and tedious. I have thus far found the contrary nearer true." Wrestling with problems, such as figuring out the water rights conveyed by an imperfectly drawn deed, pleased Hayes. To convince his mother of the merits of Lower Sandusky, Hayes wrote: "Judge [M. H.] Tilden and Judge Lane both told me this court [week] that I deserved success for the wisdom I [had] shown, in spite of appearances, in selecting my location." On the personal side, however, Hayes had little social life in Lower Sandusky, and despite his good intentions, he had "not read an astonishing deal."[11]

Hayes was home in Columbus for Christmas in 1845 and remained there through January. He loved his mother's excellent sweet potatoes and Fanny's children, Laura and Willie. In addition to gadding about with his male friends, Hayes visited several young women, among them Caroline Willis, whom Fanny approved of, and Mary Sisson, whom Fanny disparaged. Hayes was in Columbus for the state conventions of both the Democrats and the Whigs. With the Democrats struggling among themselves over the hard-money issue, he was optimistic that the Whigs, led by William Bebb, would win the governorship in 1846.[12]

On 5 February 1846, the day after Bebb had been nominated at the Whig convention, Hayes started for Lower Sandusky on a Toledo-bound stagecoach, accompanied by Sardis's friend Morrison R. Waite of Maumee. Following the old "Mud Pike," a primitive road made worse by heavy rains and the January thaw, the stagecoach made slow progress from Columbus through Delaware, Marion, Upper Sandusky, and Tiffin. To lighten the load for the horses, the male passengers walked for miles at a time, frequently far ahead of the coach. At Worthington, three or four of them went to a sugar camp half a mile off the road, enjoyed a taffy pull, and then caught up with the coach. By midnight they arrived at Delaware (twenty-four miles), had "a capital supper," and then pushed on in the dark, but before they had gone a mile, the coach tipped over. It took two hours to right and repair it and to get a surgeon to sew up the scalp of an injured passenger. With such progress, Hayes spent three days traveling to Lower Sandusky, a distance of 105 miles.[13]

To Hayes's delight, cold weather and snow soon brought sleigh rides. On Friday night, 27 February, he remained out sleighing until just before daylight, and on Saturday a heavy snow ensured "another lively week. . . . We see nearly a hundred sleighs in our streets," Hayes boasted. He had enjoyed two sleigh rides with a large mixed group and, without disparaging Lower Sandusky girls, he told Fanny "that if Miss W[illis], or even one or two younger girls of your acquaintance, had been of the party, I should have been quite as much delighted with the whole affair."[14]

Caroline Willis, however, was annoyed with Hayes. When he had failed to call, as expected, one afternoon while he was in Columbus, she had spied him "promenading with Mary Sisson & 'little Nell' entirely *oblivious*" of his appointment with her. And when he had not met her, as planned, at a party that evening, she knew "where he was '*detained*' till eleven o'clock." She would never speak to him again, she told Fanny, unless to quarrel with him to relieve "the weariness of travelling." Calling her anger preposterous, Hayes claimed that she had no reason to "snarl or bite" and told Fanny "that if I do happen to meet her this summer in any car, stage, or steamboat, and there is no one else . . . no books or papers to read, and the weather is gloomy . . . *perhaps*, to while away the time, I'll speak to her."

Having disposed of Caroline Willis, Hayes told Fanny that he would "probably pick up a figure nearer home though you may keep an eye to 'em." Fanny became less critical of the young women Hayes liked, but concluded, "I have done with selecting a wife for you brother—the more I look about the more I am convinced I shall never find one perfect as you deserve, . . . so suit *yourself* & I'll be suited, reserving . . . the privilege of putting in a word before the bargain is made."[15]

The spring thaw put an end to sleigh rides and brought Hayes back to a routine existence. His clients usually came with minor problems, often involving debt collection or land titles. Those who presented him cases involving large interests asked him to consult with an established lawyer such as Ebenezer Lane. On 1 April 1846, Hayes entered into a partnership with Ralph Buckland, "a sound lawyer, without ostentation or brilliancy; of excellent principles, strict integrity; an inveterate politician, Whig (of course); every way an estimable man, but with a slight infirmity of temper which makes him enemies, but which has never been exhibited towards me." Sensing in May that her son was not his usual cheerful self, Sophia wondered if the partnership were a good idea, but Hayes assured her that it was. As the junior partner in Buckland & Hayes, "Land & Collecting Agents," he had "a little more labor than before" and found "it much pleasanter than being alone."[16]

The summer of 1846 was very hot, with more sickness "than any year . . . since the early settlement." After sickness and the weather, the main topics of conversation were politics and the Mexican War, which had begun in May. As both a Whig and an expansionist, Hayes had the same trouble dealing with the war as he had dealing with the annexation of Texas. Although he referred to the "blackguard Mexican War" as "one of Polk's blunders," he rejoiced that Gen. Zachary Taylor, a Whig and "a first rate leader," had "flogged the Mexicans." In Ohio, Hayes observed, "Whigs enlisted to show that they were not tories and Locos enlisted because the Whigs called them cowards."

While rooting for Taylor, Hayes was critical of the administration's conduct of the war. Without adequate supplies, volunteers were sent by the thousands down the Mississippi "to spend the dog days under the tropic" sun. The war was enormously expensive, and the new Walker tariff, which reduced rates that summer, failed to meet even peacetime expenses. Hayes chortled that with the Mexican War, Polk "got too much pork for a shilling" (more than he bargained for) and remarked derisively that without a fight he had given Britain "five degrees of our 'clear and indisputable' territory in Oregon," settling for a northern border at the forty-ninth parallel.[17]

With the war, Hayes noted, "the feeling against slavery & slave holders is increasing with astonishing rapidity. The Northern Democrats heretofore the silent willing tools of the South are growing mutinous." Only two months had elapsed since Representative David Wilmot, a Pennsylvania Democrat, had added a proviso to an appropriations bill preventing slavery in any territory acquired from Mexico. Hayes predicted "that all parties will soon take the ground in the North — no more slave holding presidents — Slave territory or Slave States." Yet he believed that politics, not principles, explained the revolt of the "Dough faces" (northern Democrats) against the Polk administration. Polk had vetoed a pork barrel bill to improve rivers and harbors, which was "the favorite measure of the North West"; Polk's friends had killed a land graduation bill that would have lowered the price of public land in proportion to its time on the market; and Polk had failed to expand in the Pacific Northwest to "Fifty Four Forty." Then there was the patronage grievance, which Hayes termed "the real home thrust": Polk had excluded "Northern Democrats from high station." But despite their disarray on the national level, the Democrats had triumphed over Bebb in the Ohio gubernatorial race by opposing the tax equalization law, recently passed by the Whigs, and attacking Bebb, who had advocated repealing Ohio's racist "Black Laws."[18]

Neither war nor politics was Hayes's main concern. By the summer and autumn of 1846, everyone, including his grandmother in Brattleboro, was urging him "to get a good principled wife." He ostensibly agreed with them, but in the summer heat he was indecisive and apathetic and did his best to avoid matrimony. Despite his family's prodding, Hayes was neither economically nor emotionally ready for marriage. When Caroline Willis visited nearby Sandusky, Hayes stayed put in Lower Sandusky and admitted to his sister, "this is not the first sin of the kind I've committed." Both Judge Lane and Hayes's friend Jacob A. Camp, who had graduated as valedictorian from Kenyon in 1845, puffed Will Lane's pretty cousin, Fanny Griswold Perkins, who was visiting the Lanes at Sandusky. Hayes finally promised to visit her, but suspecting that she was Will Lane's girl, he wrote to him first to "find out the truth of the matter!" When at last Hayes saw her, he "resolved to see her again and as often as possible." But sickness in his partner's family kept Hayes away from Sandusky for a month. Meanwhile, Jacob Camp had fallen in love with Fanny. With Camp "being in," Hayes "drew off," not wishing to be a rival. "Had I visited her sooner," a tentatively wistful Hayes thought, "or repeated the visits oftener, I might have perhaps warmed in the pursuit . . . and been disposed to finish the chase."[19]

Hayes was adrift. He still made good resolutions and broke them "as of old," but his verve and intensity were eroding. "I've studied less, trifled more, been changeable, fickle-minded, and heedless in many things," he admitted. Although he claimed that matrimony was "uppermost" in his mind as he marked his twenty-fourth birthday, the "two fine girls" he had previously had in his sights were either gone or no longer triggered his desires. Fanny Perkins had returned to New London, Connecticut, and was, Hayes feared, engaged to Camp. Caroline Willis failed to attract him when he saw her later on a business trip to Columbus.[20]

After his return to Lower Sandusky, business was slow, and Hayes was overwhelmed by ennui. He clearly articulated his incapacity to focus his love but did not ascribe his emotional immaturity to growing up without a father in a home dominated by his mother and sister. "I feel the strong longing," he acknowledged, "but not the *fixed* attachment which belongs to the true love." He sensed that the lack of willpower to cut his way out of his funk rendered him "almost wholly worthless." Marriage, he believed, was the core and the cure of his condition, but if he failed to overcome his reluctance to fall in love, he despaired of making "a respectable figure in life." For the present, he worried: "I must be in the chrysalis state, neither a boy nor a man; not in love and yet not whole of heart. Well, I hope I shall be safely delivered soon, for if I am not, woe to the future!"[21]

Hayes compromised his conflicting feelings for and against matrimony by challenging Camp for Fanny Perkins's affections. When he had last seen Perkins, Hayes had wagered twelve pair of gloves "that she would be *engaged* before she reached home." Having heard "nothing of it" by December 3, he "merrily & sillily" asked her, "how about those gloves?" In response, she asked him not to write again. Although he denied to his sister that he was "dead gone," he asked her if, possibly, as in Shakespeare, "my girl means 'aye' when she says 'no.'" Should he "'blab it out,'" he wanted to know, "in 'a foxy style' that will take with her if she is ready to be taken?" When Fanny advised that he write to Perkins, Hayes sent her the letter to address and mail from Columbus to allay gossip at both Lower Sandusky and New London. Although Perkins's reply gave Hayes no encouragement, an "*understanding*" of their virtually nonexistent relationship emerged from their exchange of letters, and that understanding seemed to free Hayes from his "murky mood" and "troublesome thoughts."[22]

With the marriage question postponed, Hayes's morale picked up as the winter progressed. He went on some rowdy sleigh rides. "If I thought it would be interesting," he teased his mother, "I might try to describe to you the eating, kissing, playing button and blindhood, screaming, giggling, singing, and the other elegant diversions, which were resorted to." By 22 March, he had attended "a good many soirées" and "a most glorious Irish supper [raising $250 for famine relief] got up by the ladies at the court-house" on St. Patrick's Day. Hayes and the rest of Lower Sandusky were also entertained when the wife of a minister sued for divorce. Hayes took richly detailed depositions, complete with "ses I" and "ses she" from "all the pious old Presbyterian ladies," including one who was so hilarious that Hayes and "three *young* ladies present" could not control themselves and "burst out into a most boisterous and unanimous laugh."[23]

Because he did not much care for the religion that the hapless clergyman shared with Sophia, Hayes was especially amused by the divorce. He thought that his mother illustrated the tendency of Presbyterianism, as well as of Methodism, "to cultivate the horrible in religion as distinguished from the lovely." He also continued in his high-spirited way to tease his mother about temperance, but he assured her that he would vote "right" if the issue came up in Lower Sandusky. He then told her that his vote would only be "for the looks and name of the thing," because it did not matter "whether spirituous liquor is sold *legally* in consequence of *lax* laws, as is now the case, or *illegally* in consequence of *lax* officers as would probably be the case (at least hereabouts) if no licenses were granted."[24]

Hayes was not as lighthearted as he appeared. Although he claimed in April 1847 to be in one of his "most unsentimentally jolly moods," he was troubled. More serious than his broken heart or his "prostrated" mind was his "sore throat," which had begun to bleed. By the end of May, he felt compelled to tell his mother about his illness, which presumably had been brought on by confinement to his office. When "applications" brought only temporary relief and the bleeding began again, his physician—apparently suspecting tuberculosis (from which both Sardis and Pease suffered)—told Hayes that "an entire change of habits of life, diet, climate" for a year or two would "effect a perfect cure."[25]

Hayes refused to admit that he was seriously ill. After consulting with friends and physicians, he decided, against their advice, to go to war in Mexico for therapeutic as well as patriotic reasons. If he could secure an officer's commission, Hayes reasoned, he would avoid "the drudgery and hardships of a common soldier," change his mode of living, benefit from a warmer climate, and be occupied in mind and body. If he were to travel, he could not think of a better "way of playing the Vagabond." He was afraid, however, that it might be too late to get a commission or that Dr. Reuben D. Mussey, professor of surgery in the Medical College of Ohio—whose advice Hayes had promised to take—would not prescribe campaigning in Mexico. He admitted to Judge Lane, but not to his family, that he was very weak.[26]

Hayes realized that his ideas about the Mexican War were contradictory. As a northern Whig, he agreed with Ohio's Sen. Thomas Corwin that the war was unjust, yet he longed to be a part of it. "Whatever doubts," he observed, "I might otherwise have of the morality of this feeling are entirely *swamped* in the love of enterprise, etc., etc., which I share in common with other young men of my age." In addition, Hayes felt a "satiety" from years of studying and of systematic efforts to improve himself and declared, "I must sow my wild oats. . . . Had I married, as I wish I had, a year ago, I am persuaded this would not have occurred. My health might have been safe and myself a well-behaved civilian instead of a rough volunteer."[27]

Dreams of wild oats, military exploits, and a Mexican convalescence evaporated in Cincinnati when Dr. Mussey and a colleague spoke "very discouragingly of the proposed trip to Mexico." Mussey impressed Hayes with the seriousness of his sore throat and predicted "debility and danger" if he were exposed to the "extreme heats of the South." He prescribed "daily potations" of cod-liver oil, snakeroot, and whiskey; exercise in the open air; and cold water and bathing. He assured Hayes that "a few months of *starvation* and outdoor loafing will set all to rights." Hayes, who was already drilling in Cincinnati with a Lower Sandusky company of volunteers that had not yet been mustered into service, reluctantly abandoned soldiering. A kind, warm letter from Judge Lane helped reconcile him to the doctors' decision.[28]

Hayes gave up the "wild scheme of going to Mexico," and his family rejoiced that the doctors had decided in their favor. Fanny had grown "pale and poor" with worry and guilt. Her ambitions for her brother, she feared, were in part responsible for his illness. Sophia, however, had remained calm. Her naive faith that God, the "Father to the fatherless," would continue to guide her boy was combined with her shrewd conviction that only an insane physician would encourage a sick man to go soldiering in a hot climate in the summer.[29]

Hayes returned to Fanny's home in Columbus to convalesce. He had planned a leisurely visit from Cincinnati to Mammoth Cave in Kentucky, but Dr. Mussey would not allow it and advised that, when Hayes was able to travel, he should go north. Moderate exercise, reserpine (a tranquilizer) in the snakeroot, vitamins A and D in the cod-liver oil, and whiskey (whose medicinal value Mussey did not doubt, even though he was a total abstainer) began to have a salutary effect. "The throat," Hayes reported on 1 July, "is healed a good deal; not bled any for almost a week."[30]

Hayes hoped to take a trip east that summer with John Pease, but he warned Pease not to tell the Yankee cousins about his illness, lest he be bored with making explanations. On 6 July, he felt strong enough to accompany his mother and niece, Laura Platt, on a visit to his hometown. Remaining two days in Delaware, Hayes attended a Sons of Temperance celebration, dined with a convivial family who, to Sophia's disgust, urged wine on him, and "visited Miss Lucy Webb." Sophia was fond of Lucy's mother, Maria Cook Webb, who lived with her family in Delaware. Hayes first encountered

Lucy, who was almost sixteen, at the sulphur spring on the campus of Ohio Wesleyan. She impressed him as "a bright, sunny-hearted *little* girl, not quite old enough to fall in love with," which—given his procrastination concerning matrimony—was an advantage. Before departing for the East from Lower Sandusky, he wrote to his sister that he would court Fanny Perkins if encouraged, but bantered: "Mother and Mrs. Lamb selected a clever little schoolgirl named Webb for me at Delaware and it would not do to defeat their plan by seeking another sweetheart in New England."[31]

When Hayes left Lower Sandusky with Pease on 20 July 1847, he felt improved and optimistic. He planned to return to work in the fall and had enjoyed a good visit with Will Lane, who had recently come back from a stay in Germany. Besides promoting his full recovery, the trip east would enable him to visit Yankee relations, tour New England, and quest for the heart of Fanny Perkins. Traveling by steamboat downriver to Sandusky City and by another steamer to Buffalo, Hayes and Pease then took the railroad to Troy and stagecoaches from there to Brattleboro. It was a delightful five-day trip, although Hayes "quarreled with a crusty old codger about the right to a seat" on the train.[32]

Hayes enjoyed seeing his relatives but was annoyed that Sophia had written to them about his illness. "I find your monstrous story of my sickness has gone everywhere. I deny its truth *in toto*. I shall be careful not to tell such facts again." Judging by the rapid pace at which he and Pease visited aunts, uncles, and cousins, Hayes had regained much of his strength. Apart from Uncle Austin Birchard, Hayes found that "our Yankee relatives by marriage are nearer kin than our blood relatives," and concluded, "I like them better than any of the rest."[33]

Hayes visited Aunt Polly Hayes Noyes at Putney and spent the evening with his cousin George Noyes and his new wife, Helen Campbell. But Hayes apparently did not see his controversial cousin John Humphrey Noyes. He and his Bible Communists, the Perfectionists, had already begun to scandalize their Putney neighbors by practicing "complex marriage" (marriages were not monogamous, since all his male followers were married to all his female followers). Expecting the worst, Hayes told his mother: "I was agreeably disappointed at Putney. There are more sincerity, charity, and refinement there than in any family exclusively given up to religion that I have been in. George Noyes was married a short time ago to one of the converts at Putney. Mrs. Noyes (aunt) said that 'reasons of state' (perfectionism) were at the bottom of it; but when I saw his intelligent and beautiful bride, I could easily believe that other 'reasons' had quite as much to do with the match." The following year, John Humphrey Noyes and his followers would be harassed out

Lucy Webb at sixteen

of Vermont as promiscuous adulterers and would organize the Oneida Community in New York.[34]

After parting with Pease, Hayes pretended to concentrate on seeing sights and friends, but his primary objective was to "hot foot" it to New London and Fanny Perkins. She seemed pleased to see him on 3 August, and he found her as attractive as ever. He was impressed by the air of things about her home, liked her family, and found her mother "a splendid looking woman — pious, amiable and apparently of great sensibility." In Perkins's company, Hayes called on four other families to whom she was related and found them to be "decidedly agreeable people."

A few days with Perkins convinced Hayes that she had "as good character as could be desired." She was enough of a Puritan to please his mother, enough of an aristocrat to please his sister, and her "half frolicksome, half poetical" disposition, her "decided taste for reading and music," and her sincerity were enough to please him. Although he had said nothing of love, "leaving it to be taken for granted," he was optimistic when he left town for a couple of days on Saturday, 7 August. "She would not . . . wish to leave home at present," he noted, "and I am very sure I do not wish to marry for some time, so that there will probably be no disagreement between us on this point."[35]

Perkins's cousin, Will Lane, had warned Hayes that it would be difficult to obtain the consent of her mother and older sister "to an engagement which would take her so far from home." Nevertheless, her mother gave Hayes the impression that her consent could be obtained. When Hayes returned to New London and called the following Tuesday, Perkins's sister — who had recently married a New York merchant — was home, and there was a change in the household. The mother, who had appeared amiable and sensible a week earlier, was "looking quite unhappy" and, Hayes discovered, was "quite nervous & subject to fits of melancholy." Realizing that he was the cause of the unhappiness, he told Perkins that he would call again in about three weeks.[36]

In the meantime, Hayes gadded about New England and New York, visiting relatives and scenic and historic attractions and mulling over his cool reception in New London. In the White Mountains — which he declared were "some pumpkins" — he passively concluded "that if the mother's consent could not be had, the matter better be dropped." When Hayes returned to New London in early September, he found things worse. He was chagrined to learn that his failure to visit Perkins a year earlier, after he had first met her (allowing Jake Camp to get his "foot in"), had been a mistake. "She told me she might have been engaged then without difficulty in the family as her sister was still at home and not engaged." Hayes, who was adamant about living in Ohio, refused to hurt her mother's feelings or cause trouble within her family by trying to persuade Perkins to buck their views. Will Lane, who knew his cousin well, thought that Hayes was right, "for the reason that her mother's complaints would make her an unhappy wife for a Western man." Realizing that they had reached an impasse, Hayes and Perkins frankly discussed their irreconcilable differences with feeling, then "joked & laughed as usual." Telling her that he "hoped she would select the best of the five or six that her mother & sister had chosen for her," Hayes promised to "call & see her some day." She responded that "she would be glad to pay her respects to Mrs. Hayes. . . . And so," Hayes reported to his sister, "we parted. Queer wasn't it?"[37]

Sister Fanny, who had been eager for Fanny Perkins to be her sister-in-law, emphatically agreed. "It *is* queer . . . the way you both acted your parts" and observed that their course was "rather unloverlike . . . for a youth & a maiden" and more becoming "to a couple on their crutches." Noting that her brother already had a wrinkle on his brow, Fanny advised, "if you *can* find another one as desirable to fall in love with — do so with all your heart before 'old bachelor' is fixed upon you."[38]

By 26 September 1847, Hayes was back in Lower Sandusky, even though he planned to move from there. He still talked of marriage, but he had "resolved not to bring a wife to Lower Sandusky." His sister was aware of this resolution, and during the past June, while he was seeing physicians in Cincinnati, she had hoped that he would "become quite enamoured" of that city and told him that she dreamed of eating "strawberries with yourself & charming wife every month of May in some lovely cottage thereabouts."[39]

Remembering his disappointment in Connecticut, Hayes did very little "squinting toward gallantry" in Lower Sandusky and teased Sophia about what Fanny called her "descant upon the charms of Lucy Webb." Facetiously remarking that he needed a wife to correspond with friends and relations, Hayes hoped that Sophia and "Mother Lamb will see to it that Lucy Webb is properly instructed in this particular. I am not a-going to take a wife on recommendation unless her sponsors will fulfil to the utmost what they assume." When Fanny dismissed Lucy as "truly a fine girl but too young for you," Hayes countered, "Youth, however, is a defect that she is fast getting away from and may perhaps be entirely rid of before I shall want her." Lucy had been attending classes at Ohio Wesleyan in Delaware, but her mother, fearing that she would be snatched up by a graduating ministerial student, had sent her "to Cincinnati to stay in school for two years."[40]

After a rather busy fall, Hayes spent Christmas and early January in Columbus. As she watched him laugh and romp with her children, Fanny was delighted to see that he was "truly *well*," with spirits "as buoyant as a schoolboy's." Although he "danced attendance on the fair ones" morning, noon, and night and "had half a mind to fall in love with two or three," he returned to Lower Sandusky without any serious attachments. Fanny's current favorite was Helen Kelley, who "pouted right prettily" because Hayes did not bid her good-bye.[41]

During 1848, Hayes did not become involved with any woman. He liked Kelley and "that pretty brunette" Margaret Johnson, but he did nothing. Hoping to arouse her brother, Fanny described both Kelley's virtues and those of the youthful Lucy Webb, who had a wonderful disposition, was "so frank so joyous, . . . remarkably intelligent," and "very much improved in manner since you have seen her." She "would be handsome," Fanny insisted, "only that she freckles." Noting that Sophia had converted Fanny to her good opinion of Lucy, Hayes assured his mother that freckles were of no moment, that he was not concerned "about faults only *skin-deep*."[42]

Although Hayes was "still busy pettifogging," other interests also claimed his time. He joined the Sons of Temperance (quipping that he enjoyed "as good health as could be expected — seeing how recently I broke off using liquor!"); campaigned "like a trooper" for Zachary Taylor; read, among other things, Charles Darwin's *Voyage of a Naturalist*; and decided that he would like to settle in Cincinnati, if an attorney of his "years and calibre" could get enough business to pay office rent. Accepting Guy Bryan's invitation, Hayes also planned a winter "ramble into the wilds of Texas."[43]

Zachary Taylor's 1848 election pleased Hayes, but he was disappointed that defections to the Free-Soil party had prevented Taylor from carrying Ohio and the Whigs from electing a senator. Hayes, nevertheless, was sufficiently antislavery to be pleased when the new legislature deadlocked and then elected Salmon P. Chase, the Free-Soil candidate, to the Senate. Chase differed from Whigs in many particulars and was "as ultra as Calhoun," but Hayes predicted that he would "rank among the first men in the Senate" and would "find no master" on questions connected with slavery.[44]

Two weeks after the election, Hayes left Lower Sandusky on the first leg of his journey to Texas. After tarrying at Columbus, he and Sardis, who was traveling with him, arrived in Cincinnati on 8 December. While in that city, Hayes heard a "lunacy case" argued at the old courthouse, attended the theater with his Kenyon College friend George W. Jones, observed "all Fourth Street swarming with the fashion," made no attempt to see Lucy Webb, but had Sunday dinner with "Miss Maggie (what a nickname) Johnson," who was keeping house for her father. After a delightful little gathering with Maggie and her family, Hayes recorded, "How exquisitely she looked!" He also "visited the slaughter-houses and witnessed the whole business of converting a drove of hogs into mess pork, keg-lard, stearine candles, glue, and bristles. . . . It's a bloody, brutish business and is all done in less time than it would require to tell it."[45]

Booking passage for New Orleans on the steamboat *Moro Castle*, Hayes and Sardis left Cincinnati on 13 December. Whether gamblers, merchants, or planters, the passengers were conventional except for "a loud-talking, boastful youngster (a Jew, Moses, of Cincinnati), whose garb and gab alike," Hayes noted, "proclaim a volunteer officer." On the fifth day out, Hayes participated in "a mock trial of a young Jew for smoking in the cabin; our sport marred by the Jew's anxiety to escape the penalty." Although Lieutenant Moses (if indeed he was the "young Jew" in question, since there was a substantial Jewish community in Cincinnati) endured harassment for his misdemeanor, he would not tolerate being cheated. The same evening that he smoked in a nonsmoking area, there was, Hayes reported, "a bit of a row at one of the gaming tables. A small, villainous-looking professional gent accused by Lieutenant Moses of cheating; the lie given; pistols cocked. No blood shed but gambling probably done for."[46]

The ever-changing river was even more fascinating than the passengers. Shooting the rapids of the Ohio at Louisville, Kentucky, was highly exhilarating, as was watching the "many flatboats, loaded with coal, hay, flour, whisky, etc., of all shapes and dimensions" passing through the rapids every few moments. Hayes noted that the water changed from the bright yellow of the Ohio to the deeper dark of the Mississippi and that the weather changed from cold and cloudy to warm and sunny. Below Memphis, the river overflowed its banks, its channel appeared imperceptible, and, with its "bayous, chutes, and bends," it resembled "a great lake full of islands. . . . Pretty little white cottages and an occasional grand edifice for the planters, and rows of neat, whitewashed cabins for the negroes are always in sight." He and Sardis were particularly pleased to see the "neat, one-story, long cottage — porch all round — on a pleasant hill" that belonged to their hero Zachary Taylor, and they thought they saw Old Whitey, the general's famous warhorse, "quietly feeding near the house."[47]

After being on the river for a little over a week, the *Moro Castle* tied up at New Orleans on 21 December, and Hayes was overwhelmed. It was, he discovered, "a city of ships, steamers, flatboats, rafts, mud, fog, filth, stench, and a mixture of races and tongues." It also had "a sprinkling of cholera," and Hayes and Sardis determined to catch the first boat for Galveston. Their miserable accommodations at the Planters' Hotel seemed worse when Hayes got "desperately sick of an acclimating fever" the evening of the day they arrived, reminding him that one should "never get caught in a cheap tavern in a strange city." After Hayes tossed and rolled all night, the quinine administered by a local physician had "good effect" and the fever subsided. Cholera, however, was on the increase, and the "alarm and excitement [were] too great" for a tourist to enjoy New Orleans while waiting for the Galveston boat.[48]

Hayes and Sardis boarded the "fine ocean steamer *Galveston*" at nine o'clock Sunday morning, 24 December. "Loaded with passengers running away from the cholera," the steamer had on board Gen. William Worth, commander of the Department of Texas, who, despite an acrimonious controversy with Gen. Winfield Scott, was "exceedingly agreeable . . . affable and easy in his manners." In a few months, he would die from cholera. Christmas Day on the Gulf of Mexico was notable for a number of discussions between "some *pro*- and some *anti*-slavery" passengers.[49]

Hayes and Sardis arrived in Galveston the next day and found it to be "a dry, healthy, pleasant town" built on a high, sandy island. "What a glorious contrast," Hayes exclaimed, "to the disease and filth of New Orleans!" In addition, their "most noble hotel, the Tremont House," was one of the best he had encountered. The next day, 27 December, he and Sardis went up the Brazos River, seeing "wild prairie, low grassy banks, chocolate-colored water, cattle, and buzzards." They arrived after dark that evening at Guy Bryan's home in Gulf Prairie on the Brazos. They were "met by a bushy-headed, fine-looking boy" whom Hayes mistook for Guy's brother Stephen because of the strong resemblance, and he "shook him heartily by the hand." Hayes had quite literally come to grips with slavery.[50]

This firsthand contact with slavery did not keep Hayes from enjoying his visit. Guy's mother, brothers, stepfather, and stepsister, as well as neighbors and friends, were most hospitable. Two days after Hayes and Sardis arrived, Guy's family threw a party in their honor. "Gentlemen and ladies," Hayes reported, rode "on horseback, through mud and rain, ten, fifteen, or twenty miles. An exceedingly agreeable, gay, and polished company. The ladies particularly noticeable for the possession of the winning qualities. Merriment and dancing until 4:30 A.M. . . . Sleeping arrangements for all got up in all manner of ways, but comfortable." The next morning, the guests breakfasted at ten and were gone by noon.[51]

Texans and their customs fascinated Hayes. They "are essentially *carnivorous*," he noted. "Pork ribs, pigs' feet, veal, beef (grand), chickens, venison, and dried meat frequently seen on the table at once. Two little black girls for waiters pass everything possible around, and take the plates of the guests to the carvers, *never failing to get the right name*." At dinner, there were in addition to the "seven or eight kinds of meat, sweet potatoes in two or three shapes, half a dozen kinds of preserves, and pastry in any quantity. It is quite surprising," Hayes told Fanny, "to find the refinement one meets everywhere in a country newer in appearance than any part of Ohio you ever visited. Every place you find the planters ready for company and 'seemingly' expecting you."[52]

The "large and beautiful flower-garden . . . trimmed and cultivated under the watchful eye" of Bryan's mother sharply contrasted with the "wildness of the country." When he and Stephen Bryan called one afternoon on Major Lewis's young and agreeable daughters, Louisa, Cora, and Stella, Hayes was delighted by "music, singing, and dancing, city refinement and amusements in a log cabin on the banks of the Brazos, where only yesterday the steam whistle of the steamboat was mistaken for a panther!" Besides cougars (panthers) there were jaguars (leopards), and Sardis killed a young one. The country also abounded with fowl and deer. While fishing, Hayes was impressed by the fossil remains on the bottom of the Brazos and by the "clouds of mosquitoes thicker than the . . . locusts of Egypt." He found it exciting to watch Gus, a slave cowboy, at the "somewhat perilous" task of lassoing a wild cow. The pictures in their old geography book of this feat in Argentina were graphic and true, he assured Fanny.[53]

After a few weeks, though, Hayes became more critical of Texas and Texans. Although there were "many finely improved sugar plantations" along the Brazos, the white men on them were "generally dissolute and intemperate," and there were "few villages, no mechanics, no public improvements." He visited a "shrewd, intelligent, cynical old bachelor" on his plantation and concluded that his way of life had affected his character. "The haughty and imperious part of a man develops rapidly on one of these lonely sugar plantations, where the owner rarely meets with any except his slaves and minions." Hayes doubted (quite naively) "whether a person of Northern education could so far forget his home-bred notions and feelings as ever to be thoroughly Southern on the subject of slavery." He was particularly critical of the inefficiency of slave labor. He observed that Bryan's mother had as much vexation in dealing with her help as did his mother, whom he accused of "changing 'girls' once a fortnight." In addition, Bryan's mother (who was weak from the ravages of tuberculosis), "instead of having to care for one family, is the nurse, physician, and spiritual adviser to a whole settlement of careless slaves. . . . To have anything done," he told his mother, "requires all time. It may be I am mistaken, but I don't think Job was ever 'tried' by a gang of genuine 'Sambos!'"[54]

On 7 February, Hayes, Sardis, and Bryan began a month-long trip to Austin and San Antonio, an arduous seven-hundred-mile journey. They rode over "boundless prairie"—even witnessing it on fire one evening—and through thick canebrake. They stayed with planters, who ranged from a delightful, incessant talker to a "laughing joker" of a horse racer to a pious Baptist. Hayes found Austin, with its modest frame capitol and log cabins for the governor's office and judges' chambers, "an inconsiderable village" with "large expectations." Its diverse population—"armed to the teeth," sporting "fierce whiskers, [and] gaming and drinking" everywhere—made Austin unlike any town Hayes had ever visited.

San Antonio seemed proud to be "the scene of more bloody fights than any other [town] on the continent." It was, Hayes noted, "peopled by Spanish Mexicans with all their vices, amusements, and worship." Attending mass, he appreciatively observed "Mexican girls of all colors, with no bonnets, but shawls gracefully thrown over their shoulders, kneeling reverently on the ground floor." He also looked in on two fandangos, or dance halls, where a dime purchased "a figure [dance] and refreshments for your doxy, who instead of eating prudently stores her cakes, etc., in a basket to be taken home for the family." The preparations being made in both Austin and San Antonio by those bound overland for California goldfields intrigued Hayes, who had been touched but not consumed by the "California fever." He was surprised to find at the Alamo "a party of California emigrants cooking in the room where Crockett fell." Although they had encountered horse thieves, temperance advocates, and smallpox and had endured abominable sleeping quarters, Hayes declared the trip "most delightful."[55]

Hayes and Sardis would have pushed on for Ohio almost immediately, but Guy's sister-in-law, Mrs. Joel Bryan, and her daughter and her nurse decided to accompany them as far as Kentucky and needed time to get ready. While waiting, Hayes—with Guy and Sardis—visited Houston, a "fine town on a muddy flat," with an "academical style of architecture prevailing." After several days of sentimental good-byes, they left Galveston with their charges on 25 March. Even though Guy, who had felt depressed to the point of "*derangement*," insisted that he had not been a sociable host, Hayes had found the Texas visit most enjoyable and instructive. Augmenting his earlier travels in the East, it brought Hayes into contact with southerners and slaves and the vast West and its wild inhabitants.[56]

Cholera still raged in New Orleans, so the travelers took the first available steamer (the *General Scott*) up the Mississippi. They were accompanied by "cholera and alarm," with "several dying" on board. Once they cleared Memphis, however, there was "fun aplenty." Reaching Cincinnati at noon on 6 April 1849, Sardis headed for Lower Sandusky, but Hayes spent three days in the city that he had already decided would be his new home. He again looked up his friend George Jones and called on the lovely Maggie Johnson. On 10 April, he went by train and stagecoach to Columbus, where he spent a couple of weeks with his family before returning to Lower Sandusky to wind up his affairs.[57]

The cholera epidemic soon arrived in Ohio, causing a "general stampede" into the countryside and altering Hayes's plans. In Lower Sandusky, he dissolved his partnership and settled his accounts with Ralph Buckland, but the cholera in Cincinnati kept him from moving there. In late June, he was shocked to hear that Maggie Johnson had died. He imagined her as he had seen her only a few weeks earlier, "healthful and happy, and with such capacity for shedding happiness around her"; he could "hardly believe" he would never see her again. Hayes urged his mother to visit Delaware, observing, "Nothing about the cholera is more certain than that it does not visit the farmhouses." He himself spent August "flitting about the country." Before the summer was over, however, the cholera had even entered Delaware and Mount Vernon, the "cities of refuge."[58]

By September, the cholera scare was over, and Hayes was "winding up affairs preparatory to leaving for Cincinnati." One of his last acts in Lower Sandusky was to present the petition of its nearly unanimous citizens to the Court of Common Pleas to change the town's name to Fremont. Their main objective was to eliminate the confusion caused by five neighboring post offices with "Sandusky" in their names. They would have preferred an easily spelled, nice-sounding Indian name, but they could find none with local significance; their next thought was to immortalize the local hero George Croghan, but if his name were pronounced correctly ("Krawn"), no one could spell it, and if it were spelled correctly, no one could pronounce it. "Hence," Hayes explained, "we took refuge in the *then* romantic and *nonpartisan* name, Fremont," after John Charles Frémont, the pathfinder of the West and a future Republican candidate for president.[59]

Before leaving Fremont, Hayes helped Sardis divide the lands that he had owned jointly with his deceased partner, Rodolphus Dickinson. The task was complicated by a suit contesting some of their land titles, which were defective. Called the Boswell case, it had been appealed to the U.S. Supreme Court. To win that case and to secure incontrovertible titles, Sardis had employed Judge Lane as well as Hayes, but they were opposed by Secretary of the Interior Thomas Ewing, in whose department the federal Land Office was lodged.[60]

On 10 November, Hayes left Fremont but stopped for over a month at Columbus, where—after a bout with tonsillitis—he worked on the Boswell case. After studying disputed land titles in nearby counties, he was certain that they would win in the Supreme Court, especially since Ohio courts had recently upheld an "ancient" though faulty land entry. Based on his legwork, Hayes and Judge Lane printed a "short but good" argument and sent it to Washington, where Henry Stanbery—a future U.S. attorney general whom Sardis had also engaged—planned to argue the case during the Court's January term. Having done all that he could to ensure a satisfactory conclusion of the case, Hayes left on Christmas Eve to begin a new life in Cincinnati.[61]

CINCINNATI

Hayes left Columbus on Christmas Eve to avoid escorting Helen Kelley (despite her request) to the celebrated widowers' party. He feared that the inevitable publicity in the *Ohio State Journal* would herald him as her "accepted and intended," when no acceptance was intended by either of them. He claimed that their once-blooming flirtation had dwindled to "pretty much sham," but Hayes—still ambivalent in matters of love—sent her an anonymous New Year's gift, knowing that she would guess its source.

Although he arrived in Cincinnati unattached, when he engaged a room at the Pearl Street House at 9:30 on that cold, clear night, Hayes had numerous friends and acquaintances in the city. Indeed, he had journeyed there with Judge M. H. Tilden and then had Christmas dinner with him. During his first week in town, he was with Judge Tilden and Judge Lane a good deal. "All speak," Hayes recorded, "encouragingly of my new move if I can but have the patience to hold on until the tide brings my turn around."[1]

Sophia was afraid that Hayes might become apprehensive before the tide brought his "turn around." She urged him not to be discouraged even if he had "no business of importance the first year or two. . . . I fear," she perceived, "you have not been thrown quite enough upon your own resources in early life, to launch your Barque alone—in so large a sea, without some anxiety to yourself." Admitting that the family had sheltered Hayes too much, Sophia again regretted that he had not "been blessed with a Fathers counsel in business matters."[2]

"*Health* and *stimulus*" were, Hayes stated, his "principal motives" for moving to Cincinnati. He had come around to his mother's opinion that Fremont's lake climate was unhealthy, and he realized that Fremont did not challenge his legal talents. After a month in Cincinnati, he lamented, "Oh, the waste of those five precious years at Sandusky!" But he believed that he could recover what he had lost and, after two months "in an atmosphere grim and dark with coal smoke," claimed that his health had never been better.[3]

Cincinnati was stimulating professionally, intellectually, and socially. On 8 January 1850, Hayes rented an office "with John W. Herron, not as a partner but as a mere office chum." The two men worked and lived in their office. In a twelve-foot-square, partitioned-off corner of the room, they had "two husk mattresses on bunks . . . , a washstand, a bureau, and divers pegs on which hang divers dusty garments." Hayes quickly settled into a routine. At five each morning, an Irishman arrived to build a fire; at seven, the newsboy brought the paper and Hayes scratched open his eyes, read the news, and went out to breakfast, while the Irishman and his wife cleaned the office. "If anything interesting" was going on, Hayes spent the morning in court; otherwise, he "read law student-fashion." After an excellent one o'clock dinner—enjoyed at a respectable boarding house operated by a Presbyterian widow—Hayes remained at his desk until about four and spent nearly half his evenings reading in his office.[4]

As expected, lawyering in Cincinnati did not begin profitably. Will Platt helped Hayes meet his monthly expenses of about thirty dollars. On 14 February, he received his first Cincinnati retainer (five dollars) to defend a coal dealer. Hayes was also collecting debts owed to his friend George W. Jones, a prosperous wholesale dry-goods merchant. He hoped to earn twenty-five dollars from the case and about a hundred dollars from the debt collections.[5]

From the start, Hayes's social life was full. At about half-past five he met friends to exercise for an hour at a nearby gymnasium. He also spent "one or two evenings a week with the ladies, and one or two at lectures." On New Year's Eve, he attended "a small gentlemen's gathering," where he sipped wine and feasted on "oysters and quails." Although he considered the "conversation no great shakes," he met, "among other notorious persons," the militant Kentucky abolitionist Cassius M. Clay. Hayes was surprised to find him not only agreeable but *unobtrusive and modest*." Hayes attended the Episcopal church, joined the Eagle Lodge of the International Order of Odd Fellows, and heard lectures at the Sons of Temperance and the Young Men's Mercantile Library Association.

Hayes's favorite social activity was attending the newly formed Cincinnati Literary Society. It was, Hayes said, "a delightful little club, composed of lawyers, artists, merchants, teachers, which meets once a week—has debates, conversations, . . . essays, and oysters." Club members apparently washed down the oysters with "liberal amounts of the local Catawba wine," and "exuberant members often adjourned to Gleissner's in the Over-the-Rhine area for some German lager." Hayes later testified that "no one part of my education was so useful to me as the years . . . in the club."[6]

One of Hayes's first moves after arriving in Cincinnati was to call at Wesleyan Female College for Lucy Webb, who, unfortunately, had gone home for the Christmas recess. On Saturday evening, 5 January, he found her in and had "fun a plenty." Lucy, Hayes wrote home, "had so far forgotten me as not to recognize me, although I laughed and chatted with her a long while before I relieved her curiosity by telling her my name." Through George Jones, Hayes had met "more than one charming damsel," but he admitted that "for a country-bred boy, it's pleasanter to meet the natural gaiety of" a Lucy Webb "than any of the artificial attractions of your city belles." Two weeks after renewing his acquaintance with Lucy, Hayes had "enjoyed the light of her gleesome smile and merry talk times not a few nor far between."[7]

Lucy was fun, but, despite his protests to the contrary, the city-bred belles attracted Hayes. An additional set of young women, including Helen Kelley, rode into town on 28 February on the first train from Columbus (Kelley's father was president of the railroad) to celebrate the new rail link and stayed three weeks. Fanny and Will Platt also came on the first train, and, this being Fanny's "first visit to the City of Pigs," they "strolled up and down Fourth Street gaping at the windows of shops and houses" before returning to Columbus the next day.[8]

Once again—apparently even more ambivalent about Hayes than he was about her—Kelley turned her charms on and off, enthralling, baffling, and frustrating him. "She loves and don't love," he complained. On 11 March, he found "nothing to dampen or discourage" his ardor, although she asked for her letters back while wanting to keep his. "As long as there is a hope," Hayes confessed, "my love is so blindly strong I must cling to it, though my pride prompts decision." When pride no longer tolerated oscillating between bliss and desolation, Hayes resolved, "I'll talk again with her—probe her yet again."[9]

Probing Kelley was not satisfactory, and from then on Hayes's comments about their relationship became more rational than emotional. He accompanied her back to Columbus on 20 March, and the next day while "chatting lovingly" with her before departing, he returned the letters she had requested. Away from her, he claimed that his feelings were "midway between love and entire indifference," but he confessed that at the sight of her handwriting on an envelope "my blood was sent leaping hotly through my veins." By July, he could declare with some honesty that "she is no longer my charmer," and after a "good old-times talk" with her, he declared, "It all went off with a laugh, and now I am again at my ease with any lady; can converse with my ancient glibness."[10]

Yet neither Hayes nor Kelley could laugh away their relationship. While visiting Columbus in January 1851, he remained with her after "a merry party . . . until 3:30 A.M.(!!) talking over and finally disposing of a long dream of mingled happiness and pain. . . . Everything was called up, errors and misconstructions corrected, apologies, confessions, and repentances exchanged, until all was clear again." Kelley told Hayes, with "both hands clasped warmly over" his "and a tearful eye and husky voice," that no other man was "so *liked*" by her, but it "was no longer love."[11]

During Hayes's first year in Cincinnati, business picked up slowly. He pursued claims in the commercial court, examined land titles, drew up legal papers, and observed the arguments and behavior of seasoned lawyers. The Boswell suit, concerning the title to two large tracts of land owned by Sardis and his late partner, was still his most important case. It had gone well with a favorable decision in the Ohio Supreme Court, but despite the brief he and Judge Lane had prepared and Henry Stanbery's argument (which did not go beyond the brief), the U.S. Supreme Court ruled in April 1850 against Sardis and his partner's heirs. Although Sardis felt the loss keenly, he could still "laugh & enjoy a joke as well as ever," and the rest of the family took the decision in stride. Fanny even thought that it removed "a stumbling block" to Hayes's progress, since, without "a fortune to fall back upon," he had to rely on his "own energy."[12]

After studying Justice John McLean's opinion, Hayes thought that there was "ground for hope." The opinion applied to only one tract and dodged, but did not overrule, the Ohio decision. The matter could still be contested, with prolonged litigation "see-sawing between the state and federal courts" for years. "The rascals," Hayes observed, "will soon get tired of it and want to compromise. Ewing is always pinched for money, and you know how it is with the others." Sardis went ahead with his suit in the fall term of the U.S. Circuit Court at Columbus, over which McLean presided. Although Hayes spent "considerable time writing and looking over the Boswell papers" (Sophia called his effort "something like locking the stable after the horse is stole"), Sardis continued to use the more experienced and fee-greedy Stanbery in the courtroom.[13]

Hayes's daring tactics worked. In a desperate move similar to the way in which "a drowning man catches a straw" Stanbery, "*acting under instructions*, coolly told the court" that Sardis "had a *perfectly good* tax title" to the property. When the circuit court rejected Stanbery's assertion, he "*appeared so astonished*" that the court postponed the proceedings until the following spring. By then, Hayes's prediction that the "rascals" would settle came true. He wrote to the opposing lawyer, alluding "to the probability of a protracted litigation," pointing out that the fight was ruining the property for all sides, and stating "that a part *now* is better than the whole *hereafter*." Sardis's antagonists agreed, and in June 1851 Hayes met their designee, compromised, and settled his "Uncle's interminable lawsuit." Sardis was pleased with his nephew's work.[14]

With his practice making limited demands on his time, Hayes indulged more in intellectual and romantic pursuits than in politics. The Compromise of 1850 aroused his interest but not his passion. He regretted Daniel Webster's efforts to conciliate southerners (by supporting the fugitive slave bill), and he copied in his diary John Greenleaf Whittier's scathing denunciation of Webster: "When faith is lost, when honor dies, / The man is dead." Webster's willingness to sacrifice the freedom of runaway slaves to save the Union seemed unnecessary to Hayes, because he did not take the threat of secession seriously. "The cry of disunion," he wrote to Guy Bryan in June, "is shown to be impossible. The border States will not permit it. . . . It may be a good hobby further South *and off North* but where the division line is to be run, the feeling is in opposition to it."[15]

Apart from practicing law, Hayes attended literary club meetings, read widely, saw plays, and heard lectures. He enjoyed reading *The Works of Lord Byron*, Shakespeare's comedies, and Charles Dickens's latest novel *David Copperfield* and seeing Charlotte Cushman's portrayal of Meg Merrilies in the stage adaptation of Sir Walter Scott's novel *Guy Mannering*. Hayes made his first speech to the literary club on 2 March 1850 and called it *"ratherish good*, considering."[16]

For Hayes, the literary high point of 1850 occurred during the last ten days of May, when Ralph Waldo Emerson was in Cincinnati. With his literary club colleagues Isaac C. Collins and Ainsworth Rand Spofford, Hayes invited Emerson to meet with the club for a "free confab on literary men and matters." He found Emerson awkward in his movements, agreeable in his manners, and quaint in his talk. Although Hayes later avowed that he worshipped Emerson, this half-hour chat left him feeling that Emerson shared the common fault of the transcendentalists, "thinking that the hearty, earnest, sincere benevolence in the world is centered in themselves; that all others . . . 'have too little *pluck* to avow'" the truth. At the club, Emerson conversed for "two and a half hours on all matters from letters to raising corn and pigs" to immortality, emphasizing that Platonism rather than transcendentalism described the views of the "self-trusting, self-relying, earnest" people like himself, who believe that "there is something more than this narrow scene in which we are to act." Hayes found that Emerson avoided "a connected chain of reasoning" in his lectures. They seemed "but a bead-string of suggestions, fancies, ideas, anecdotes, and illustrations having no connection with each other except that they are upon the same subject." Hayes found Emerson's "misty notions on religion"—stressing the "magnetism or divinity" possessed by all people—intriguing but frustrating, because he *"intimates* or walks around about what he *would* say but *don't* say."[17]

Although critical of Emerson's imprecise religious views, Hayes had rejected the dogmatic assertions of conventional Christianity. Orthodox tenets did not comfort him when, in October 1850, his cousin Sarah Wasson suddenly died. Her parents had always been a part of his life; she was the first newborn baby he had seen, and he had tasted wine for the first time on the day he first saw her. Only a few weeks before her death, he had called on her at Delaware "and found a beau who seemed confused at being seen with her." Feeling roguish, Hayes had given "her a smacking buss, knowing she would relish the joke if not the kiss." And now she was gone. "The mystery of our existence — I have no faith in any attempted explanation of it," Hayes confessed. "It is all a dark, unfathomed profound."[18]

As his ties with Helen Kelley weakened, Hayes found himself taking Lucy Webb more seriously. Since she was only eighteen when he arrived in Cincinnati and was nine years his junior, he had not thought of her as an immediate candidate for matrimony; and since she was not a coquette, he did not flirt with her. Relaxing and not playing games in her company, he found her small-town ingenuousness a delightful change from the sophistication of the numerous belles he called on in the spring of 1850. On Friday, 3 May, he spent the evening "with that charming, sweet girl" and became aware that Lucy Webb aroused deep feelings, even though he still felt unready to marry. "Must keep a guard on my susceptibles," he warned himself, "or I shall be in beyond my depth."[19]

Hayes's "susceptibles" were safe over the summer, since Lucy graduated from Wesleyan Female College in June and left town. When in July he disentangled himself from Helen Kelley (who was a coquette), he resolved that the next time he fell in love it would be "with another sort of person." On 24 September, his "susceptibles" were considerably aroused at the wedding of John Little, his boyhood chum, and Carrie Williams. Lucy was a bridesmaid and Hayes a groomsman in the wedding party. Seeing "the old acquaintances of boyhood" put Hayes in a "peculiar" mood, but, as he confessed, "another peculiar feeling was awakened too by the bright eyes and merry smiles of that lovely girl whose image is now so often in my thoughts." When the wedding cake was cut, Hayes discovered a gold ring in his slice, which he, "of course," gave to "the bridesmaid, Miss Lucy Webb." Masking his feelings, he playfully said that he "was to be hers, if she was of the same mind, or ever became so," but Lucy, although enjoying the attention, did not take his declaration seriously.[20]

As she began to fill his thoughts, Lucy outshined Hayes's old flames.

When word came in November that Jacob Camp and Fanny Perkins were to wed, Hayes was relieved that his "affair" with her had gone no further. He told himself that even three years earlier (and "*now*" even "*more so*") he preferred the sweet smile of the " 'bonnie' schoolgirl of sixteen" to the charms of the "blooming woman of twenty-two or upwards." That same month, he welcomed the news that Lucy would be back in Cincinnati (her mother was moving there) with the comment, "I shall see somebody soon." Later, in January 1851, even as he mourned his "*dead passion*" for Helen Kelley, he was glad that it was dead, for the "bright vision" of Lucy had been before him for months.[21]

With the possibility of sharing the future with Lucy, Hayes became more concerned about his health and wealth. To marry, he needed an income and had to increase his practice. "I have got me a sign," Hayes told Fanny, "newer, larger, showier and more richly gilt than any other on the front of the Law Building. . . . I don't think," he explained, "modesty 'pays' " in making either money or reputation. Beginning to blow his "own trumpet," Hayes spoke before church groups on temperance (but not total abstinence) and to various lodges of the Odd Fellows. While his business picked up slowly, he speculated in Cincinnati real estate and Virginia coal lands (the latter primarily to make legal contacts). He realized that to succeed in Cincinnati he must "*push, labor, shove.* . . . Two years must find me with a *living* and *increasing* business, or I quit the city and probably the profession."[22]

Hayes's anxiety over earning a living was exacerbated by his anxiety over his health. Awakening on 21 November 1850 with his old complaint, a sore throat, Hayes admitted to "many fears that it will be my ruin if not my death." His main complaint, however, was "cholera morbus" or diarrhea. "On the lake shore, colds and sore throat were my enemies, now it is disease of the bowels that disturbs my peace." A worried Fanny urged him to watch his diet, to exercise, to "bathe regularly in the *morning*," and to ventilate his room and air his bed daily. Hayes's morale suffered. "I find," he wrote in March 1851, "that with me low spirits and feeble health come and go together. The last two or three months I have had frequent attacks of the blues. They generally are upon me or within me when I am somewhat out of order in bowels, throat, or head." The death in January of Fanny's six-year-old boy from the croup devastated Hayes, and the suicide a few months later of Linton Pettibone, a boyhood and college friend (who, like Hayes and Lucy, had been part of the recent wedding party), further disturbed him.[23]

Still, the blues did not completely conquer Hayes, who had a full social calendar. He called on friends, attended lectures, spent Wednesday evenings with the Odd Fellows, Thursdays with the Sons of Temperance, and, best of all, Saturday nights with the literary club. He saw Gen. Winfield Scott and thought, "*He'll do for President*"; heard Jenny Lind sing but was not thrilled by her excellent voice; and found Thomas De Quincey's "Essays" amusing and good but not wholesome. He considered Ik Marvel's *Reveries of a Bachelor* appropriate for his condition.[24]

Hayes also listened to Louis Agassiz lecture on the egg as "the type of all animal and vegetable matter." Although he thought the lecture interesting, Hayes was intrigued by "a fine face—black hair and eyes" belonging to the young woman seated in front of him. She was in black, as was the woman with her, whom Hayes presumed was her sister, and they were accompanied by a "gent." Hayes had the trio followed in the rain to a house alongside a coal yard on the north side of Third Street but did not learn the young woman's name or marital status. "I must," he resolved, "look her up," but a glance at her house the next day disenchanted him. "Worst symptom," he wrote in his diary, "is a dirty faded window curtain in 2nd story window. . . . Romance fading fast away—can stand poverty but not dirt."[25]

Hayes also fought off the blues by calling on Lucy Webb. His roving eye during the Agassiz lecture and his fascination with the woman in black made him examine his feelings for Lucy. He acknowledged less than a week later that he loved her and admitted that he had "suspected it for some time." Then he confessed, "it grows on me," and enumerated her physical, spiritual, and intellectual qualities in a stereotypical Victorian manner. "Her low sweet voice is very winning, her soft rich eye not often equalled; a heart as true as steel, I know." Despite his unorthodox religious views, he valued her deep spirituality. "Intellect, she has, too, a quick sprightly one, rather than a reflective, profound one. She sees at a glance what others study upon, but will not, perhaps, study out what she is unable to see at a flash. She is a genuine woman, right from instinct and impulse rather than judgment and reflection." This inventory of Lucy's body, heart, and mind led Hayes to exclaim, "It is no use doubting or rolling it over in my thoughts. By George! I am in love with her!"[26]

Three weeks later, on his "lucky" Friday the thirteenth of June 1851, Lucy made Hayes " 'happy as a king,' 'a lark,' 'a clam.' " The evening started auspiciously, while he walked on Race Street near the corner of Longworth in the direction of Lucy's house. Suddenly he saw "a magnificent horse plunging and leaping like mad, with a buggy at his heels, along the sidewalk," bearing down on him and a "respectably dressed, apparently . . . married lady." Hayes threw his arms around the woman and pushed her into the doorway of the engine house on the corner. Despite her alarm, she readily accepted his apology for grabbing her so unceremoniously and thanked him for his gallantry. Hayes went on his way "an inch taller for this feat—*of arms.*"

Feeling like a conquering hero, he was soon chatting gaily with his "cheerful, truthful, trusting, loving, and lovable girl," whom he compared, on this occasion, with Nathaniel Hawthorne's Phoebe, the sunbeam in *The House of the Seven Gables.* A relaxed Hayes became sleepy and mesmerized by Lucy's soft, low voice and by her eyes, matchless for their "tenderness and goodness." Suddenly an "unthought of, unmeditated, involuntary" impulse seized him:

> I grasped her hand hastily in my own [he wrote in his diary] and with a smile, but earnestly and in quick accents said, "I love you." . . . She was not startled—no fluttering; but a puzzled expression of pleasure and surprise stole over her fine features. She grew more lovely every breath, returned the pressure of my hand. I *knew* it was as I wished, but I waited, . . . until she said, "I must confess, I like you very well." A queer, soft, lovely tone, it stole to the very heart, and I, without loosing her hand took a seat by her side, and— — —, and the faith was plighted for life![27]

Once the decision was made, both Hayes and Lucy were ecstatically happy. With warmly clasped hands, they had sealed their engagement with their first kiss. Lucy gave Hayes the ring he had given her from the cake at John and Carrie Little's wedding, and he wore it the rest of his life. Lucy, who felt that she might be dreaming, modestly told him, "I thought I was too light and trifling for you." Actually, she was a bright, vivacious, unpretentious woman whose strong beliefs in Methodism, total abstinence, and abolition made her anything but "light and trifling." She coupled her ardent commitments with a tolerance for Hayes's unorthodox Christianity, his temperate use of alcoholic beverages, and his considerably more moderate anti-slavery attitude. Hayes wondered what Lucy's mother would think, and Lucy wondered what his sister would think. As a matchmaker, Sophia had been an unqualified success, since Hayes concluded that her plans coincided with those of the Almighty. "Truly," he told Lucy, "I always had a presentiment that Fate or Fortune, or Heaven had linked our destinies together."[28]

Hayes and Lucy, who did not plan to marry for some time, kept their engagement secret. When Hayes was in Columbus a week or so later, Fanny spotted the wedding-cake ring on his finger, found out where he had gotten it, and "replied, smiling archly, 'I thought it meant something.'" He also saw his old flame Helen Kelley, who surmised that the ring had special significance. He "stoutly denied" it, but deception was not one of his talents. Friends suspected, but Lucy told John Herron a "white lie," and Hayes admitted nothing.[29]

His engagement inspired Hayes to become more romantic and more resolute. He was a classic swain, falling in love with love, as he pined to hear Lucy play her guitar and sing her sweet songs and rhapsodized about her big gray eyes. His love moved to a deeper level as Lucy became the "be-all and end-all" of his "hopes, thoughts, affections, . . . existence." Lucy, he felt, would make him not only happy but also a success. "The truth is," he confessed to her, "I never did half try to be anything, or to do anything . . . and so I have lived, not an *idle*, but a *useless* sort of life." But now, with Lucy depending on him, Hayes told her, "I shall have purpose and steadiness to keep ever *doing*, looking to your happiness and approval as my best reward."

Hayes wanted to communicate fully with Lucy. "Hereafter," he told her, "*with you* I mean to *think aloud* and I wish you to do the same with me. If we are to spend our lives *with* and *for* each other, the more intimately and thoroughly we understand each other the better each will be able to please the other." Hayes believed that he and Lucy could improve each other. He realized that her "thoughts and tastes" might help remove some of his "deficiencies and faults," but he also knew that they both had imperfections that could not be gotten rid of and that, as "sensible people," they must learn to tolerate. Although Hayes believed that Lucy's principles were almost perfection, he thought that her mind—while cultivated—could be "*finished* by the better training of voluntary reading, conversation, and writing. . . . To point such a charming pupil to the right path," he decided, "is certainly no unpleasant task, *possibly* not a useless one. In *such* company the search after intelligence and cultivation is 'Like a journey in the path to heaven.' "[30]

Hayes returned to Cincinnati in early July and poured out his thoughts and feelings to Lucy until 28 July, when she left for an extended visit to family members in Chillicothe, Ohio. While she was out of town, he discovered that Lucy had an annoying shortcoming—she hated to write letters. Ironically, four years earlier he had facetiously instructed his mother to teach Lucy the art of letter writing. While he waited over three weeks for her first letter, he alternated between being vexed and amused by his " 'perverse' little angel." But when it did arrive, despite "her modesty and trembling," the letter proved a good one—indeed, "a spirit-rouser." Hayes realized that neither lack of energy nor lack of interest accounted for Lucy's aversion to letter writing. "If you have any failing," he told her, "it is the *lack of a rational self-confidence in small matters*." Lucy's fears that her letters were inadequate were "moonshine," according to Hayes, but he understood that "the *feeling* which you have is a substantial reality." He told Lucy to do "the thing you dread to do until the feeling leaves you" and suggested that she write to him often, "hit or miss," carelessly, without effort, and without dread "of ill-natured or even good-natured criticism." Lucy, however, never became a good correspondent. Hayes understood her diffidence and, having preached tolerance to ingrained shortcomings, resigned himself to being the chief correspondent of their household.[31]

When not pleading for letters, protesting his love, or lawyering, Hayes read Laurence Sterne's *Tristram Shandy* and *A Sentimental Journey* "to drive dull care away." Like Henry Fielding's *Tom Jones*, these "bawdy" novels were, for Hayes, amusing and even instructive (Tristram Shandy, for example, was much like Sardis in his droll and "whimsical way of arguing for absurdities," which began in jest but ended in earnest), but he professed not to like them. He perceived that Sterne, an eighteenth-century clergyman whose "witty and shrewd" observations of the "worst parts of human nature" had delighted his own age, would not be tolerated by decent nineteenth-century society. Hayes heralded this progress, albeit slow, toward decency and wished to support "the good projects of the age." Starting with himself, he decided that it was "useless, vulgar, inexcusable, and perhaps . . . wicked" to use profanity. "I must stop it," he resolved.[32]

As an antidote to "bawdy" novels, Hayes read William Henry Channing's three-volume *Life of William Ellery Channing* (1848), the great Unitarian clergyman. "If ever I am made a Christian," he wrote Lucy, "it will be under the influence of views like his. He says the test of Christianity is the state of the heart and affections, not the state of a man's intellectual belief. . . . The half of the orthodox creeds, I don't understand and can't fully believe." Even more skeptical in his diary, Hayes declared that "most of the notions — which orthodox people have of the divinity of the Bible, I disbelieve. I am so nearly infidel in all my views, that . . . in *spite* of my wishes . . . none but the most liberal doctrines can command my assent."[33]

When in November 1852 "the notorious Christian infidel, Theodore Parker, of Boston," lectured and preached for three days in Cincinnati, Hayes was all ears. Parker was witty and conversational but bold and sincere, knowledgeable to the point of omniscience on his topics and "fond of giving collateral stabs at opinions, characters, and parties." His sermon on the evolution of ideas about God was "*the talk* of all." He began with the "absurd" ideas entertained by early heathen peoples, then proved, Hayes thought, that the God of the Old Testament was "partial, revengeful, hating and loving without just cause, unmerciful, etc." He continued by arguing that the God of the New Testament, although more just, was still imperfect in love and goodness and furthermore created evil, the devil, hell, and endless punishment, which compelled God to suffer the crucifixion of Jesus to save his creatures. Parker thought that even the authors of the best concepts of God found in recent literature—including Emanuel Swedenborg and Channing, both of whom Hayes admired—were "tinged with a *fear, an apprehension*" of a wrathful God. "But," Parker concluded, "the true idea now beginning to struggle with the popular theology is that God is a *perfect being* in love, justice, mercy, power, etc."[34]

Although 1852 began "rather prosperously" for Hayes, with money, clients, friends, and a "loved one," that year failed to meet his expectations. His growing professional reputation as a defense attorney added little to his income. Unless he earned more, he could not marry Lucy. Also, his throat problems had kept him from speaking outdoors in the fall political campaign, and the Whig party's loss of Ohio in the October state election presaged the defeat in November of its presidential nominee Winfield Scott. Initially, Hayes thought, " 'Old Lundy' is bound to win," but with neither party inclined to disturb the status quo following the Compromise of 1850, "thinking men" had little interest in the ensuing campaign. With no principle apparently at stake, Hayes asked, "Who cares?" when Franklin Pierce defeated Scott. Although labeling Scott "a true patriot," Hayes knew that he was also "an exceedingly vain, weak man in many points." Unless Pierce revived northern Whigs by attempting to enhance the slave power with the annexation of Cuba, Hayes perceived that the Compromise of 1850 had ended the disruptive political controversies that had plagued the nation during most of his life. "Politics is no longer *the topic* of this country. Its important questions are settled—both on the construction of the Constitution and the fundamental principles which underlie all constitutions. . . . The people's progress, progress of every sort, no longer depends on government. But enough of politics. Henceforth I am out more than ever."[35]

Although Hayes was soured on politics and neither as healthy nor as wealthy in 1852 as he wished to be, he was more in love with Lucy than ever. He called on her constantly and when out of town wrote affectionately to his "Gympsey," a name he called her "in sport." While he was visiting Sardis in Fremont that summer, Fanny and her daughter Laura joined them. He reported to Lucy, "We had the subject of matrimony, the prospect of my *ever* marrying, whether I was engaged and what sort of a damsel Lucy Webb was, up for discussion." Mrs. Valette, Sardis's landlady, exclaimed that she had not believed the rumors that Hayes was engaged but now "had no doubt of it," and he "needn't deny it," because "there was something indescribable" in his manner. Everyone realized that Hayes and Lucy had an understanding.

Upon his arrival a few weeks earlier, Hayes had stayed up after midnight talking with Sardis about "Gympsey." Hayes also reported to Lucy that Sardis "says if I will promise to spend here two or three months in the hot weather, or to send my wife here, he will build me" a "pretty little summer retreat . . . in a pleasant grove. . . . How say you? Shall I promise? I feel like doing it."[36]

No longer ambivalent about love and matrimony, Hayes told Lucy that he did not want to go through another summer without being married to her. They had delayed their wedding because Maria Cook Webb was in no hurry to lose her daughter, and because Hayes feared that his income was inadequate for marriage. Once again Sardis came through, assuring Hayes of his willingness to aid him financially. "In regard to the matter of marrying," Hayes assured him, "I am of your way of thinking. I don't like to be too dependent, but . . . I should not feel any delicacy in calling on you in case of need." Attending Helen Kelley's wedding in October further sharpened Hayes's desire to be married, but unfortunately, Lucy's brother James was seriously ill. Hayes told Sardis that as soon as Jim's fate was resolved, "*I shall see that your 'suggestion' is adopted on short notice.*" Lucy and her mother nursed Jim back to health that fall. Although on 19 November Hayes wrote to a friend, "Matrimonially nothing new—shall probably wife somebody at a convenient season," he decided the next morning, "I *shall fix the day tomorrow.*"[37]

Lucy agreed to marry around New Year's Day, and they settled on Thursday, 30 December 1852. Hayes's family was overjoyed, for Lucy appeared in "every way fitted to make him happy." Sardis made plans to come, but Sophia neither felt well enough to travel to Cincinnati in the winter nor wanted to be away from Fanny's younger children while their mother and sister were gone. Sophia told Hayes what he had known from the start, that "your choice is mine, I shall welcome her to my heart as a beloved daughter." Hayes suddenly became so busy in his law practice that he had little time to think about his approaching wedding. "Ought a man to have a wedding ring?" he asked Fanny. She thought so and procured a suitably engraved one, which he said that he would pay for if "ever able."[38]

The modest wedding received a brief notice in the press. "December 30th, by Prof. L. D. McCabe, of the Ohio W. [Wesleyan] University, R. B. Hayes, Esq., to Miss Lucy W. Webb, all of this city." Fanny called it "one of the most *interesting* weddings I ever attended," and her daughter Laura was especially gratified to have participated in the ceremony; Lucy followed the Kentucky "fashion of having the bride hold a little girl by the hand." Hayes elaborated on the newspaper clipping: "Thursday afternoon, about 2

Rutherford and Lucy Hayes at the time of their wedding

o'clock, at the residence of Lucy's mother on the south side of Sixth street, between Race and Elm (No. 141) Cincinnati, Ohio. Present, sister Fanny and her daughter Laura, Uncle Birchard, [William K.] Rogers and [Richard C.] Anderson (Phi Zetas), Lucy's mother [and] two brothers, Uncle Isaac Cook, Aunt Lucy [Cook], and [Cousin] Will Scott, together with about thirty friends. Took the cars same evening to Columbus; remained there in brother Platt's family four weeks. A delightful honeymoon."[39]

FIVE

LAW AND FAMILY

While on his honeymoon at Columbus in January 1853, Hayes had "the greatest triumph" of his professional life. He argued his "first case *orally* in the Supreme Court of the state — 'State of Ohio *v.* James Summons'" (who was accused of poisoning his family), and it was included in the *Ohio Reports*. Hayes proudly told Sardis that he had defended Summons "in a very satisfactory style," with "a large audience of lawyers" present. Hayes later learned that the most distinguished of these lawyers, Thomas Ewing, had commented, "That young man will, I predict, make his mark in the State."[1]

The triumph had its origin almost a year earlier when Hayes made his "maiden effort in the Criminal Court" with a "sensible, energetic," but futile speech on behalf of a client guilty of grand larceny. Impressed, the court appointed Hayes to help defend Nancy Farrer, "the poisoner of two families." Her case, Hayes exulted, "is *the* criminal case of the term." Since Farrer was so homely that many described her as deformed, Hayes thought that "probably from this misfortune has grown her malignity." He planned to show how her constitution, early training, and associations could diminish responsibility. He also wished to study medical jurisprudence on poisons and to improve his style through reading good speeches and poetry.[2]

Although Nancy Farrer allegedly murdered two women and three children with arsenic, she was indicted only for the murder of eight-year-old James Wesley Forest. The trial in the Hamilton County Court of Common Pleas got under way on 18 February 1852, with Hayes, the "leading counsel in Defence," striving to establish Farrer's mental incompetence and to play upon the all-male jury's sympathies. Catering to the prejudices of the day, which elevated women and degraded blacks and Native Americans, Hayes observed: "No white woman has ever yet, I believe, been executed in Ohio, and if this idiotic girl is to be the first, I feel sure that the court will see that she is not sacrificed by a violation of any" rules of law guarding every man and woman's life and rights.

Personally aware of "the calamity of insanity," which in "its thousand forms" could carry "grief and agony unspeakable" into every home, Hayes wished that there were additional "rules" regarding insanity that "would satisfy an intelligent man if, instead of this friendless girl, his own sister or his own daughter were on trial." As he cross-examined witnesses and argued for Nancy, Hayes was pleased that he had overcome a tendency to be nervous and could control himself in the excitement of the crowded courtroom. After nine days of testimony and arguments and sixty-three hours of deliberation, the jury returned the verdict of guilty. Hayes's motion for a new trial "gained some laurels" but was unsuccessful, because the judge was anxious to "*shine* . . . before the assembled crowd."[3]

Following the Farrer case closely, Sophia wondered whether what was happening was not "degrading to the female sex." Noting that "Nancy Farrer is sentenced to be hung, and that if the Governor pardons her it will be because she is a *woman*," Sophia wanted her son "to give her a good reason why a woman should be acquitted, when the same crime would condemn a man. They are as capable of knowing right and wrong as any man," she insisted, "and they should be as severely punished."[4]

Deterred by neither the hanging judge nor his egalitarian mother, Hayes — doing his best to save Farrer from the gallows — sued out a writ of error to secure a new trial. He carefully prepared a sixty-page bill of exception, which, to his surprise, the judge "signed without crossing a 't' or grumbling." Hayes claimed that the court had committed six errors, including allowing testimony about another murder Nancy had allegedly committed but for which she was not being tried and "giving the Jury the form of a verdict they were to render" after they had been deadlocked for three days. The writ also cited the behavior of the jury, which included drinking intoxicating beverages, conversing from the windows with persons outside, reading newspapers covering the trial, and using in its deliberations the "partial and imperfect notes" taken by a member. Hayes argued his writ before the district court (one of the judges was his college chum Stanley Matthews) on 21 April 1852, but that court neither set aside nor affirmed Farrer's conviction and reserved the decision for the Ohio Supreme Court. Hayes was pleased. He had maximized his "best opportunity to 'show off,'" and Farrer, who had been scheduled to be hanged on 25 June 1852, had been temporarily spared.[5]

Because of his performance in Nancy Farrer's trial, Hayes was asked to defend the notorious James Summons, accused of poisoning his family in July 1849. Although his parents survived the arsenic in their tea, two other family members died. After three hung juries, Summons was convicted in April 1852 and sentenced to be hanged on 3 February 1853 (with the jury recommending executive clemency). Summons's lawyer, Judge Nathaniel C. Read — who, Hayes said, mixed godlike qualities with beastly propensities — was "too drunk," and Summons's other lawyer, F. Chambers, "was too unwell," so Hayes (although not doubting that Summons was guilty) got up the bill of exceptions. Objecting particularly that the crucial testimony of a now-deceased witness had been repeated by a legally incompetent individual, Hayes successfully argued at the district court for a new trial. Delighted "to blow off in two murder cases instead of one," Hayes chortled, "I've evidently hit upon a good lead."[6]

In May 1852, he was appointed to help defend Henry Lecount, another accused murderer. Hayes could not save Lecount, who had smashed the skull of his wife's lover with a dray pin. Even though he merely assisted in the defense, his sense of duty compelled Hayes to be present at Lecount's execution on 26 November 1852. It was Hamilton County's first hanging in many years and aroused "extraordinary interest," with one spectator nearly getting killed when he fell from a tree beyond the jail yard. After witnessing the "shattering" execution, with Lecount seeming "hardly conscious of what was passing," Hayes was even more determined to save Nancy Farrer and James Summons.[7]

Hayes prepared prodigiously for these courtroom appearances. Adopting a relatively new defense strategy based on the mental incompetence of his clients, he studied recent relevant murder trials, including William Henry Seward's classic defense of William Freeman. Because of his sister's earlier illness and the mental problems of his cousin Charles Birchard, Hayes had seen firsthand the difficulties of the mentally ill and sympathized with them. Within his family, he had insisted that he "would as soon think of finding fault with a person . . . sick of a fever" as with Charles, who could not control his delusions.[8]

The Summons case came up before the state supreme court just after Hayes married. "Taking my wifing, the Summons case and all," he observed, "this has been the luckiest period of my life." While noting for the court that "occasional fits of *delirium tremens* and repeated attacks of epilepsy" reduced Summons "almost to imbecility," Hayes argued that the issue at stake was the fundamental rules governing admissible testimony at trials. Hayes insisted that Summons should not go to the gallows because of what a witness who could not be cross-examined had purportedly said. When Hayes heard a few days later that he had persuaded a majority to reverse the lower court's guilty verdict, he revealed how deeply the case had affected him. "Previously," Fanny noted, "he had appeared careless & indifferent, said very little about it—but when he returned from court & attempted to tell us of his triumph in the same cool manner, . . . he sank into a chair in a tremor of excitement & actually wept with joy."[9]

The report that Summons was to be spared was premature. State supreme court justice Allen G. Thurman, who had presided over the Summons trial on the district-court level and had admitted the remembered testimony of a dead witness, fought to uphold the conviction. After arguing for two weeks, Thurman changed a colleague's mind and by dividing the court postponed a final decision. For several years, the court remained deadlocked, with Hayes periodically rearguing his position and doubting that the case could be resolved with Thurman still on the bench. "The hardest task a man can have," Hayes thought, after arguing the Summons case three times, is to do better with "the zest of novelty gone, and conscious that the part of your audience you are most desirous to convince were unconvinced by your former argument." Finally, in February 1857, the court upheld the death sentence against Summons, but as Hayes had predicted, the governor commuted the sentence to life imprisonment.[10]

Because Thurman delayed the court's decision in January 1853, Hayes and Lucy remained in Columbus four weeks, enjoying an extended honeymoon. Within a few days, Lucy relaxed sufficiently among her new relations to reveal "the world of fun that is in her." Lucy, Fanny decided, was "a precious gift from Heaven. She is not the least beautiful but her expression is so charming that she is sometimes called so. She has a most happy disposition, more free from morbid feeling than any *woman* I ever saw, — full of joyousness & mirth which make her a most agreeable home companion." Her new nieces adored Lucy, for, as Laura pointed out, "When she tells a thing it sounds better than it is." Fanny tried to shield Hayes and Lucy from "a perfect rush of calls & invitations" until she found that "Lucy thought visiting was very fine sport." Fanny then accepted for all but Hayes, whom she "excused on the score of business," but when, as Fanny reported, he "saw his wife arrayed in 'the good clothes' (as he called her elegant wardrobe) & all radiant with joyous excitement he was proud to accompany her & there was no keeping him at home, so to dinner parties, tea drinkings & evening fandangos they went with unremitted zeal."[11]

Although Hayes had expected to argue both the Summons and the Farrer cases before the state supreme court in early 1853, the Farrer case was postponed until December 1853. For Nancy Farrer, Hayes had resolved to make "the best effort of my life," and he had stronger arguments for setting aside the verdict in her case than in the Summons case. The admission of evidence indicating that she had poisoned a person not named in the indictment was questionable, and the conduct of the jury was inexcusable. Primarily because of jury misconduct, the Ohio Supreme Court reversed the guilty verdict, remanding the case for a new trial.[12]

Hayes's next tactic in the Farrer case was to secure an inquest of lunacy, beginning on 7 December 1854, before Judge J. B. Warren of the probate court. Convinced that Farrer was unable either to give an accurate account of herself or to provide needed information for her defense, Hayes insisted that she was so lacking in intelligence that she was not responsible for her actions. She was deprived by both heredity and environment; her mother was a monomaniacal Mormon who thought that she was the wife of Jesus Christ, and her father was a drunkard who had attempted suicide. Farrer's "silly expression" during the inquest and her abnormal face and apparent love for her victims buttressed Hayes's interpretation, but the "shrewdness and cunning in the execution of her designs, and the concealment of her agency" in her murders, were "difficult to reconcile with an insane, and particularly with an imbecile mind." Furthermore, even though she looked foolish, Farrer understood what witnesses said and disputed their testimony. Physicians and nonmedical witnesses claimed with equal authority that she was sane or insane. Virtually every witness agreed that she at first appeared to be an imbecile or an idiot, but when they had become better acquainted with her, several thought that she knew right from wrong.

After deliberating for eighteen hours, the jury declared "Nancy Farrer to be of unsound mind." Hayes had saved her from the gallows. "It has been a pet case with me," he remarked, "has caused me much anxiety, given me some prominence in my profession, and indeed was the first case which brought me practice in the city. It has turned out fortunately for me, . . . and I am greatly gratified that it is so." Nancy was committed to an asylum and, theoretically, she could be released if the attending physician certified that she had regained her reason. Farrer was not released and either died in custody or wandered off, depending on which account is believed.[13]

Defending celebrated murderers brought Hayes considerable publicity and some business, but he and Lucy did not feel prosperous enough to have their own home. They avoided extra expenses by settling "down pleasantly in Mother Webb's family." Hayes told Sardis: "No boarding-house would be so agreeable as an abiding place, nor so *homelike*. Besides, it is preferred by all parties interested." They had at least one item of furniture. Dr. McCabe presented Lucy with a desk, purchased with the two gold eagles Hayes had given him for marrying them.[14]

The newlyweds were very happy and full of resolutions to make their marriage a success. Their "little differences" were "readily adjusted." Lucy put up with his "innocent peculiarities" and provided for his "little wants," because she was determined to "make home dear to him!" Hayes appreciated her efforts and resolved to be "loving, kind, and thoughtful" and, realizing that Lucy was sensitive, to keep in check his passion to improve those he loved. They hid little from each other. She had access to his diary, in which she expressed her sense of inadequacy and her annoyance when he spent Saturday nights with his literary club. "Ruddy has gone to the club. I did think I had become reconciled to it, but when the evening comes, all the feeling is revived. . . . I know his desire that I should improve. Why do I not exert myself more. Dear Rutherford, love me with all my faults. —Lu."[15]

Lucy did not nag Hayes about religion, total abstinence, slavery, or anything else. But she influenced him. He adopted her antislavery views; in time, he attended church with her regularly; and ultimately, he abstained from using alcohol. Stressing good works more than blind faith, Lucy knew that her husband was a decent man with impeccable morals. She was not perturbed that he read the Bible as he did "Shakespeare, for illustration and language, for its true pictures of man and woman nature, for its early historical record."[16]

At the time of his marriage, Hayes was involved in a railroad case that concerned Sardis. With heavy real-estate investments in and around Fremont as well as an emotional attachment to the place, Sardis had committed himself to developing rail connections there. He was dismayed when, to achieve a more direct route between Cleveland and Toledo and points north and west, the Junction Railroad planned to bridge Sandusky Bay rather than cross the Sandusky River at Fremont, as demanded in its charter. Sardis and his Fremont allies sought an injunction preventing the railroad from crossing the bay. To build their case they relied on Hayes, who argued that the railroad bridge would violate the Junction Railroad charter and obstruct navigation. Thomas Ewing, who was hired to bolster the Fremont cause, pronounced Hayes's brief *"perfect"* and predicted that, in the U.S. District Court, Justice John "McLean will at once grant the injunction." Hayes, however, warned Sardis that, with the importance of navigable streams as compared to railroads diminishing daily, the case was less certain than it would have been earlier.[17]

Sardis's nephew was a better prophet than Ewing. Hayes made his "first *oral* argument" in a federal court in April 1853 when, along with Ewing and George E. Pugh, he presented Fremont's case before McLean. They were opposed by Judge Lane, who was a prime mover and chief council for the Junction Railroad. Not only did Sardis and Judge Lane break over the issue, but the friendship of Hayes and Will Lane was strained by the case. Hayes felt reasonably confident of success, but McLean did not issue a sweeping injunction forbidding the construction of the bay bridge as a hazard to navigation; instead, he prohibited the bridge because it was not contemplated by the railroad's charter. Since the Junction Railroad people had moved to consolidate with the Cleveland, Norwalk, & Toledo Railroad to secure a charter enabling them to bridge the bay, Hayes advised building a *"strong case on the obstruction to navigation"* and urged collecting affidavits from sailing-vessel masters to prove that freight rates above the proposed bridge would be higher than those below it. After the two railroads consolidated as the Cleveland & Toledo Railroad, the new company offered to build a railroad from Fort Wayne, Indiana, to Fremont—connecting there with railroads to Norwalk and Sandusky City—if the Fremont interests would cease objecting to the bay bridge.[18]

Hayes advised Sardis and his friends to compromise. Even if they could prevent the bridge, the railroad would probably be built, since "a ferry will answer their purpose across the Bay." Furthermore, although Hayes agreed that the bridge would be a nuisance, he admitted, "I have not been so sure that it would be such a serious injury to the town of Fremont as many have supposed. The injury, in my opinion, is not at all to be compared with the benefit to be derived from another railroad." In mid-June, Sardis met with the railroad people at Norwalk and struck a deal favorable to Fremont's interests. Indeed, the town's future appeared so bright that Hayes asked Sardis to "look out a bargain or two for me."[19]

By the fall of 1853, hard times had increased "the pickings" for Hayes. "Failures, assignments, and attachments" had brought him more business, and his success was assured with the establishment, the day after Christmas, of Corwine, Hayes & Rogers. Richard M. Corwine was "an easy clever fellow" who had been practicing with R. S. Holt and Caleb B. Smith (a prominent Whig who later served in Abraham Lincoln's cabinet); he brought to the new partnership a large and lucrative business. William K. Rogers, a fellow Phi Zeta from Kenyon College, brought little beyond devotion to Hayes. Together with Rogers, Hayes agreed to pay Smith and Holt $600 each and arranged with Corwine to divide the first year's profits among Corwine, Hayes, and Rogers on a one-half, one-third, one-sixth basis, respectively. Not overly fond of Corwine, who was easily diverted by politics, Hayes recognized that he and Rogers would have to do most of the work, but he also realized that Corwine excelled "in beating the bush for game." The work for Hayes would be pleasant. "I am to do no more drudgery—am not to search the records or to do ordinary office work. The Court House and the legitimate lawyers work is all I am to attend to."[20]

Besides being gratified by his professional success, Hayes was ecstatic about his personal life. He and Lucy visited Fremont and Niagara Falls during the summer of 1853. Lucy had a "glorious voice" and, while singing on the veranda where Sardis lived, she not only delighted those seated around her but also, Hayes learned, the neighbors a half-mile away, who heard her perfectly. When they pushed on to the falls, Hayes declared that he had "never enjoyed a trip better." Lucy was pregnant, and her condition seemed to enhance her merry and happy spirits. It was a marvelous summer, and Hayes observed, "Its real enjoyment embraces many special things. I know my Lucy far better than before. We have been alone together among strangers, and I can't express how much deeper my love for her is." When on 4 November 1853 his son Birchard was born, Hayes's love for Lucy and the meaning of his own life took on more dimensions. "The new feeling is more 'home-felt,' quiet, substantial, and satisfying," he observed, noting that with his son's birth he was experiencing "the beginning of a new life." That beginning made Hayes particularly aware of his responsibility to children. Remembering his own joyous childhood, he felt that grown-ups should "study the feelings and preferences of little people so as [to] be able to make them happy."[21]

Hayes rejoiced that Lucy was "safe from her peril," looked charming, and was "sharing his joy." The delivery had been uncomplicated; she had been attended by two doctors, including her brother Joe, and four women, including her mother and a longtime family servant, Lavina, whom Hayes referred to as the "culled pusson." On Saturday, 3 December 1854, a month after Birch was born, Hayes went to Columbus to argue the Nancy Farrer case before the state supreme court. He thought that he could leave his family for a week because the baby, after a slow and anxious start, had begun to "*Nuss* . . . savagely" and was obviously doing well.

Lavina and Topsy, an adolescent who looked after little Birch, were the first blacks Hayes had close contact with, apart from those he had encountered in Texas. In contrast, Lucy had always been around blacks. Her father, Dr. James Webb of Chillicothe, Ohio, was a native southerner. When Lucy was two years old, he died of cholera in Kentucky, where he had gone to free and colonize in Liberia some fifteen to twenty slaves he had inherited. Lucy's mother, left with three children "in straitened circumstances" at her husband's death, was advised to sell the slaves (who had not yet been manumitted). "*Before I will sell a slave*," she replied, "*I will take in washing to support my family.*" The Webb family freed its slaves, kept in touch with them, and often employed them and their children as house servants. Lavina as well as Topsy's parents almost certainly had belonged to the Webb family.[22]

Growing prosperity and the presence of little Birch convinced Hayes and Lucy that they should acquire better quarters. In the spring of 1854, he began looking for a suitable house to bid on at the 8 May sheriff's sale of buildings condemned for nonpayment of taxes and successfully bid $4,500 for "No.

383 Sixth Street; south side, west of Mound." Following the advice of his mother and Will Platt, Hayes made the necessary repairs on the newly acquired three-story, red brick, attached house before moving in. Paying for his bargain by borrowing $500 from his mother and $4,000 from Sardis, Hayes spent an additional $1,000 on improvements and furnishings. Just before moving day, he was offered $6,000 "*cash in hand*" for the house and, when he refused, the bid was raised to $6,500 (which Hayes considered the house's true value).[23]

On 4 September 1854, Hayes and Lucy, along with her mother and brothers, began their move. "A muss," exclaimed Hayes, "all sorts of laughing over our loads of furniture, a good deal of it Lucy's mother's when she went into housekeeping—good, but old; a great sending of it back and forth for cleaning, varnishing, making as good as new; but finally all settled comfortably, pleasantly." When they sat down to their first meal in their new house, they found that they had forgotten spoons, knives, and forks and had to use Birch's little silver knife and fork and an old spoon he had picked up "for a plaything."[24]

Christmas 1854 was particularly merry for Hayes. He had just saved Nancy Farrer's life and he was prosperous and pleased with his wife and son. "Five years ago today," he wrote, "I awoke to my first day's residence in Cincinnati. . . . I told Uncle before I came . . . that in five years . . . he and every other friend I had would be glad that I had gone to Cincinnati. It is enough to fill me with pleasant feeling, that I am sure that my hope has been realized." Hayes's busyness caused his mother to exclaim that it was a good thing Lucy had brothers to pay her some attention, since "Rutherford has not time to provide any thing but money for his family."[25]

At the time, Hayes was not deeply involved in politics. He opposed the 1854 Kansas-Nebraska Act, which opened those territories to slavery. He observed with pleasure the defections from the Democratic party, with equanimity the disintegration of the Whig party now that its "idols" Clay and Webster were gone, and with gladness the "new divisions by which men of all opinions will be willing to join us in honoring their memories." But he regretted the rise of the nativist Know-Nothing party, noting: "How people do hate Catholics, and what a happiness it was to thousands to have a chance to show it in what seemed a lawful and patriotic manner."[26]

In the first year of his marriage, Hayes had begun to defend the freedom of blacks. "My services," he later wrote, "were always freely given to the slave and his friends in all cases arising under the Fugitive Slave Law." He did not seek publicity for these acts, lest his practice suffer in a city that bordered on Kentucky and was filled with southern sympathizers. He was outraged when

Judge Jacob Flinn, who relished sending runaway slaves back to slavery, "got into greater odium than ever by assaulting Mr. Jolliffe while passing [in] the street in company with his wife." John Jolliffe, Cincinnati's most conspicuous defender of fugitive slaves, had advocated that Flinn be impeached. A few days after the attack on Jolliffe, Hayes offered him his services in the defense of fugitive slaves. Although Lucy had sensitized Hayes on the slavery issue, she was out of town when Jolliffe was attacked, and Hayes decided on his own to volunteer. A few weeks later he defended Louis, a young runaway slave who slipped out of the courtroom to freedom while judge and lawyers were engrossed in a passionate argument over his fate.[27]

Hayes's emerging antislavery credentials were enhanced when, with Sen. Salmon P. Chase and Judge Timothy Walker, he defended Rosetta Armstead, a young girl who was allegedly a runaway slave. Henry M. Dennison, the Louisville, Kentucky, clergyman who was her owner, had placed her in the charge of a man traveling to Richmond, Virginia. Having left an Ohio River steamboat at Cincinnati, they were traveling by rail through Columbus when alert antislavery activists had them detained. There, the probate court freed Rosetta Armstead on a writ of habeas corpus and, since she was a minor, appointed Lewis G. Van Slyke as her guardian. At Columbus, in the presence of Van Slyke and others, Dennison asked Armstead to choose between going with him and remaining free. When she chose freedom, he said good-bye after warning her that she would probably never see him again. Later changing his mind, Dennison procured a warrant for Armstead's arrest as a runaway slave from U.S. Commissioner John L. Pendery of Cincinnati. She was brought to Cincinnati, where her guardian sought a writ of habeas corpus from Judge James Parker of the Court of Common Pleas of Hamilton County. Because of Hayes's "clear head and good heart," Van Slyke wanted him as well as Chase and Walker to represent his charge.[28]

The Rosetta case, as it was called, attracted enormous attention. Not only was the slavery or freedom of a human being at stake, but intriguing legal questions were also involved. Did a slave who was not a runaway become free upon touching Ohio soil? Did Dennison, by allowing Rosetta Armstead, a minor, to choose freedom and then acquiescing before witnesses, legally manumit her? If the Ohio court entered into a conflict with a federal commissioner over the writ of habeas corpus, who would prevail? Judge Parker ordered that Armstead be set free. He declared that "under the constitution of Ohio the alleged right of transit with slave property through the State did not exist," and he ruled that on a writ of habeas corpus, a state court could determine the legality of the imprisonment of anyone by a U.S. marshal.[29]

U.S. Commissioner Pendery would not let Parker's challenge to federal authority go unanswered; Rosetta Armstead was rearrested by a federal marshal. Before a packed courtroom, Pendery conducted a hearing at which Hayes made the major argument for the defense and, in Chase's words, "acquitted himself with great distinction." Hayes attacked Dennison for "despising his pledged word" by trying to reenslave Armstead after freeing her; he argued that even if she were not manumitted, she was free because the fugitive slave law did not apply to her case. Armstead did not run away; Dennison's agent had brought her to Ohio. When Hayes finished, the courtroom burst into applause, and fellow lawyers crowded about to congratulate him. "You may be proud of your *boy*," Fanny wrote to Sardis. "Rutherford has made the best speech in the 'Rosetta case'—won Laurels from his legal brethren & every one that heard him." After mulling over his decision for nearly a week, Pendery declared that Rosetta Armstead was free under U.S. law as well as Ohio law. Van Slyke and others credited the outcome to Hayes's "eloquent and masterly closing speech."[30]

Hayes had come a long way from the sentiments of his childhood. Although not an abolitionist, his antislavery views were in advance of those of his community and of other family members. Sardis, for example, did not want Lucy to bring her black servants when she visited his home. And although both Fanny and Sophia were proud of Hayes's triumph in the Rosetta case, they remained cool to the plight of slaves. Fanny noted that her brother "had been 'speaking beautifully for the innocent' again," but wondered "if he can be so eloquent over Nancy & Rosetta what would he be with nobler subjects." Normally so perceptive, Fanny failed to realize that there could be no greater inspiration than to save one young woman from the gallows and another from slavery. Sophia equated the property rights of the slaveholder with the right of the abolitionist to free speech, but she was blind to a slave's right to liberty. She lamented that a person could not travel through Ohio with a slave without having it "coaxed away," nor pass through the South expressing abolitionist views without being "mobbed and abused" and concluded, "The North and South must reform."[31]

Although Hayes was committed to the antislavery cause by 1855, he, along with most other opponents of slavery, regarded blacks with a condescending, amused detachment. Neither contemptuous nor hostile, Hayes simply failed to take blacks seriously. Contributing to this attitude was his tendency to poke fun at everyone and everything. "Uncle Ruddy," Fanny wrote to her daughter Laura, "is in fine health & spirits—romps with his boy & turns the whole of life into a joke." Three months after arguing for Armstead's freedom, Hayes joined Lucy, her mother, and Birch at the mansion of Lucy's great-uncle, Thompson Scott. He was a banker in Lexington, Kentucky, where people seemed "to live for the sake of living more than in most places." For Fanny, Hayes described the large, high-ceilinged, well-ventilated rooms that were teeming with Lucy's cousins, some of whom were wild, some well-bred, "and lots of niggers." Hayes's report of the meeting between Lucy and her mother and their former slaves reveals further condescension: "Today we have been receiving calls from our 'people.' They all have complaints to make. We send them away with kind words and a dollar apiece. One chuckle-headed Cudjoe said to Lucy: 'Why, Miss Lucy, I'm so glad you have got such a pretty man!' "[32]

His condescending attitude toward blacks notwithstanding, Hayes opposed the extension of slavery and in 1855 helped mold the disparate opposition to the Democrats into the Ohio Republican party. "In the political circles of the Fusion party," he observed, "the chief difficulty seems to be to distribute the proceeds among the principal lien holders's viz Old Whigs, Old Democrats, Free Soilers and K[now] N[othing]s." For attorney general of Ohio, Hayes pushed Corwine, the senior partner of his law firm, who, like Hayes, was an old Whig. "It will be an advantage to *the firm* and to *ME*," Hayes acknowledged, while lining up support for Corwine. Intense rivalry among "Sams" and "Sambos," Whigs and "Locos" made the Cincinnati convention to select state convention delegates "very squally." Although Hayes, his brother-in-law Joe Webb, his partner Billy Rogers, and his friend John Herron were all delegates, Free-Soilers would not balance the ticket by nominating Corwine for attorney general after their man Chase was named for governor.[33]

Years later, Hayes recalled, "I was an earnest and active Republican 'from the start' and aided in the organization of the party in Ohio in 1855." Actually, because the new party snubbed the old Whig element, Hayes was less ardent in the 1855 campaign than he remembered. On 7 October of that year, he commented that Ohio was "in the midst of one of our periodical election excitements, but [I am] not engaged in it; therefore reasonably indifferent of results." When Chase won, Hayes suspected that he "will answer our purposes so far as state affairs go very well," but by April 1856 Hayes was still an unenthusiastic Republican. "I don't yet belong to your party," he wrote to Guy Bryan, who would be attending the June 1856 Democratic National Convention in Cincinnati, "but my opposition to it this fall will be hearty or otherwise according to your candidate. Not being a K. N. [Know-Nothing] I am left as a sort of waif on the political sea with symptoms of a mild sort towards Black Republicanism."[34]

On 20 March 1856, the birth of a second son, Webb Cook Hayes, gave

Hayes another reason to remain aloof from politics. Lucy's brother Joe arrived just in time to deliver the baby. Webb "was fatter than Birtie; darker, hair apparently black, eyes dark," although in a few weeks his hair turned lighter, even threatening "to become *red*." Both Lucy and the baby were fine, and after almost three months, Hayes reported that Lucy was blooming and that " 'Samson,' as she calls the little boy, is nearly over his colic, and behaves and thrives admirably."[35]

Hayes, however, was apprehensive about his sister Fanny, who, weakened by several hemorrhages, feared that her approaching confinement would be fatal. On 16 June, she gave birth to twin girls who did not survive. Fanny hemorrhaged severely during and after labor and suffered from an "inflammation of the womb." She "remained in a critical situation" and was purged with "a tolerably large dose of magnesia." The medication was "entirely uncalled for" according to Dr. Joe Webb, who insisted that Fanny's psychiatrist, Dr. Awl, was not up on obstetrics, having been "too long in the asylum." Fanny improved slightly after discharging pus from her infection, only to sink again and die on 16 July.[36]

Hayes was devastated. "My dear only sister, my beloved Fanny, is dead! The dearest friend of childhood, . . . the confidante of all my life, the one I loved best, is gone." In pouring his heart out to Bryan, Hayes exclaimed: "I can recall no happiness in the past which was not brightened either by her participation in it or the thought of her joy when she knew of it. All plans for the future, all visions of success, have embraced her. . . . For many years my mother's family consisted of but three — Mother, Sister dear, and myself. Oh, what associations now broken cling around those tender early days! And such a sister! . . . My heart bleeds and the tears flow as I write."[37]

SIX

POLITICS

Fanny's death hit Hayes hard, but Lucy and their "fine little boys," as well as his profession and a newly kindled interest in politics, assuaged his grief. The day after Hayes returned from Fanny's funeral in Columbus, Birch "ran off and was not found for over two hours—not until the bell-man and police had been sent for, but before the crier started fortunately. He was found a long distance off happy as a lark." Hayes had an ambrotype taken of the runaway and reflected on how dear Birch was to him and Lucy.

Without the excitement of politics, Hayes confessed, he could not have endured Fanny's death. During her last illness, John Charles Frémont had been nominated for president on a platform opposed to the extension of slavery. Despite Hayes's earlier equivocation, Frémont's nomination committed him irrevocably to the Republican party. A week after Fanny died, Hayes pasted a woodcut in his diary and noted: "Colonel Fremont. Not a good picture, but will do to indicate my politics this year. For free States and against new slave States."[1]

A leader among Cincinnati Republicans of Whig extraction, Hayes was nominated by the local Hamilton County convention for judge of the court of common pleas. He declined, knowing that the hostility of the Know-Nothings (who were running Millard Fillmore for president) made his election impossible. Not having to maintain the dignified silence of a judicial candidate, Hayes was able to be an enthusiastic campaigner. "We had," he reported in late August, "a glorious meeting at Fremont. Men women, children and dogs, banners, cannon, and music beyond anything I saw in 1840." In early September, Hayes spoke "over the Rhine" in Cincinnati, where the Germans "yelled and bellowed" for Frémont. Later that month, Hayes was speaking every night and enjoying it. Proud of the Republican party, he noted after a "great torch-light" parade: "Ours was peculiar—first, for the great number of quiet people who turned out in it—second for the outrageous and amusing manner in which it was assailed by Fillmore and Buchanan rowdies; and third, for the 'burly confidence' with which the procession pushed on in spite of the interruptions," such as when a stone struck one of his friends on the arm.[2]

Democratic victories in the October elections in Pennsylvania and Indiana forecast the triumph of James Buchanan. Hayes was downcast but, encouraged by the antislavery sentiment that had been created, was determined "to aid in forming a public opinion . . . which will 'mitigate and finally eradicate the evil.'" Although prepared for the worst, Hayes and his Republican cohorts in Cincinnati enjoyed the national election on 4 November. "Our wards came in well. Any news that was not outrageous we . . . cheered. . . . Although beaten, our majorities are so prodigious and Fremonts electoral vote so respectable that the . . . Democrats do not crow over much." Reading about the lives of British antislavery leaders and reliving their triumph over the slave trade and slavery gave Hayes confidence that "right" would prevail and enabled him to endure Frémont's defeat in "the first pitched battle." To Hayes, who had become a warrior, the imagery was reality. "However fares the cause," he declared, "I am enlisted for the war."[3]

As 1856 ended, Hayes called it the "most eventful, longest, and saddest year in its one great affliction that I have ever known. The void still remains. The wound does not heal." Even while enjoying himself at the literary club or speaking for Frémont at the hustings, the loss of Fanny crowded his thoughts. Hayes envied people like his law partner Billy Rogers, who had a "beautiful faith" that Fanny had already joined her son Willie in a hereafter. "If there are any Mansions of the blessed," Hayes told Rogers, "she I know is there and I shall again be with her. But the agonizing doubt or disbelief leaves me with a 'rooted sorrow' which will remain."[4]

With the new year, Hayes found more time for reading and socializing, but both pastimes reinforced his antislavery feeling. The emphasis of his reading was on exploration, expansion, and slavery in America, and his social life revolved around his literary club—most of whose members had campaigned for Frémont. At the club he met, for example, the thoughtful young Rev. Moncure D. Conway, who "was driven from a Unitarian Church in Washington D.C. because he thought and spoke heresy on the Slavery issue." Currently ministering to Cincinnati Unitarians, Conway admired radicals and read and talked progressively on religious, literary, and social questions.[5]

With acquaintances like Conway, Hayes was less inclined than ever to be moved by Guy Bryan's proslavery views. Neither Hayes nor Bryan allowed their irreconcilable differences on this one issue to affect their friendship, but they continued to express their beliefs. More diplomatic than Bryan, Hayes had hoped that if Frémont were elected, the country's bitter division would end, with the South recognizing that event as a first step toward the ultimate eradication of slavery. "You are wrong," Bryan told him, declaring, "I am a *freeman*." He wanted the South to present the North with an "ultimatum" to place slavery "beyond Congressional interference, or *dissolve*" the Union. In explanation, he insisted, "With us of the South slavery is a *practical question* — it enters into all the ramifications of society. With us it is a *life and death* question. With you it is an *abstract* one."[6]

Attempting to be as conciliatory as possible, Hayes did not attack Bryan's passionate but self-serving belief that as a free man he could deny freedom to others. He admitted that Bryan was probably correct about the temper of the South and, ignoring the ultimatum, encouraged Bryan to cast about for a true remedy and suggested that he might agree to a formula that would, as Bryan desired, "remove the whole subject from Congress." Ironically, Hayes soon discovered on a visit to Kenyon that their college efforts to make peace between the two literary societies had unraveled in the fractious environment of the late 1850s. "All the bad passions belonging to the larger politics of the world are exhibited in miniature," he told Bryan. "You would have enjoyed looking on as I did." Despite their political differences, Hayes rejoiced in the spring of 1857 when Bryan was nominated for Congress (which was tantamount to election) and urged him to meet the "two able, honorable gentlemen," George Hunt Pendleton and William S. Groesbeck, representing Cincinnati. "My only objection to them is," Hayes added, "that they agree with you in general politics."[7]

While Bryan's political career advanced, Hayes still could not afford public service; his steadily improving practice brought in barely enough to support his growing family, but he was very happy. He rejoiced in Lucy's ready laughter and in the enthusiastic way she " 'jumped up and down' with delight," and together they enjoyed the antics of their little boys. An indulgent parent, Hayes advised his mother, who was caring for Fanny's children, "to overlook most things, and not to be too solicitous about perfection." The "little peculiarities, which with your older judgment do not seem favorable," he assured her, "will gradually disappear as they get older." With parents who enjoyed their shouting, Birch and Webb were noisy. Hayes proudly told Sardis how one night during the recent presidential campaign Birch "recited in his most excited manner and at the top of his voice all the scraps of nursery rhymes he knew and finally began to hurrah for Buchanan and the other candidates — giving his loudest shout for 'Uncle Birchards Fremont.' "[8]

The legal profession partly insulated Hayes from the wild swings of the business cycle. When the panic of 1857 struck, he reported that Cincinnati's "3d Street swarms with excited Bankers and Bankrupts" and that the latter were so respectable that they gave bankruptcy "character." Lest she worry, he assured Sophia, "The scarcity of money does not affect people of my profession very seriously, and while I feel a good deal of anxiety for friends, I am tolerably free from difficulties of my own." Hayes was concerned in particular about Sardis, who in late September asked him to raise $3,000 to help prevent his Fremont bank from suspending payments. Hayes owed $1,000 on a note that was due, but he was willing to stave off his good-natured creditor (and even risk a "protest") to send Sardis cash. Assuring his uncle that his bank would not fail, Hayes tried to secure a loan of "$3 or $5000 at 12 per cent on Mortgage on my real estate." He also arranged with Will Platt to raise funds, if needed, and curiously—in view of his later belief—argued "the necessity for a general suspension of specie payments with as much zeal as if it was a legal or political question." Sardis did not need these heroic measures, but as the crisis passed, Hayes urged him, without success, to get out of the banking business "at the earliest possible moment. It is too hazardous and annoying," he protested, "for your ill health."[9]

With Sardis avoiding bankruptcy and Hayes "getting on very pleasantly and prosperously in business," 1857 ended on a positive note. Leaving the boys at home, he and Lucy went to Columbus to "take a Thanksgiving dinner" with his mother and the Platts. Hayes quickly returned to Cincinnati, but Lucy remained three weeks with Fanny's children. Will Platt wrote to Sardis that since Fanny's death "our house has at no time . . . been so free from a feeling of loneliness." A week before Christmas, Lucy returned to her tumultuous household. A new kitten had joined their dog Nellie Bly, and Birch was suffering from whooping cough. Despite a siege of colds added to the whooping cough, which Webb quickly caught, Hayes could recall no holidays filled with as "much amusement and happiness." He hung up Christmas stockings and blew on a tin trumpet to attract the attention of Kriss Kringle and reported to Sardis that "our boys are happy with drum, trumpet, firecrackers . . . cake, candies and eatables."[10]

The brightening fortunes of the Republican party also cheered Hayes. Although it initially seemed certain that Chase would not be reelected governor in 1857, Hayes predicted correctly that "Chase's luck" would prevail. Hayes closely followed the struggle between proslavery and free-soil forces in Kansas and the attempts by the Buchanan administration to resolve that struggle. Recognizing that the new president had made a disastrous mistake in his first annual message by advocating the admission of Kansas into the Union as a slave state, Hayes gleefully chortled, "Farewell, Mr. Buchanan." Hayes was further delighted when Stephen A. Douglas, the leading western Democrat, broke with Buchanan because of his obvious rejection of popular sovereignty. Admiring Douglas for his stand, Hayes congratulated him on his "noble speech." After several months of debate, however, Hayes declared Kansas a "doleful subject" that had been "squeezed dry."[11]

While economic conditions improved and Hayes prospered, another "great awakening" revived Cincinnati spiritually. Intrigued, Hayes attended "quiet, unobtrusive, decorous" prayer meetings ("no indecent excitement about them"), and although he thought that they would have a "permanently useful" result on believers, he was not moved. When in June 1858 his niece Laura graduated as valedictorian from the Esther Institute in Columbus, Hayes again grieved over Fanny's absence and regretted that "I cannot feel the satisfaction some . . . do in the reflection that her eyes beheld the scene from the other world."[12]

Lucy did not accompany Hayes to Laura's graduation because she was "patiently waiting for her troubles"—the birth of their third child. That spring, besides nursing the boys through the whooping cough, she had nursed Hayes through a severe cold and a cough that had hung on for an additional six weeks. Although concerned, he had taken nothing for it "except a few swallows of whiskey at night to stop the cough." Preparations for the new baby were simplified when Lucy's mother gave her a sewing machine in March 1858. "It works wonders," Hayes marveled and proudly recorded that in one afternoon Lucy did the work of several days without tiring herself "so much as sewing in the old way."[13]

The child for whom much of that sewing was intended arrived on 24 June 1858 and was named Rutherford Platt Hayes. He was large and fat, had very little hair, and resembled his Uncle Joe Webb. As she had in her previous confinements, Lucy did well, but a few evenings later she took a chill. First, Hayes reported, "she had severe pains in her breasts; and for ten days . . . had rheumatism creeping over her from one place to another, giving her great pain." In August, when she had recovered enough to travel, Hayes took Lucy and the boys to her Uncle Moses Boggs's home at Elmwood, near Circleville, Ohio, before accompanying Sardis, his cousin Pease, and niece Laura to New England.[14]

When Hayes returned to Cincinnati, Lucy and the boys were still away and the 1858 political campaign had already begun. Had he wished, he could have been nominated to Congress. He was pleased that the Democratic Cincinnati *Enquirer* had feared his nomination as a formidable candidate, but he was not ready for the financial and personal sacrifices that public life demanded. The state of Hayes's clothes and Lucy's constant sewing indicated their level of affluence. On his return from his eastern trip, his best suit was so worn that it had to be patched. He wrote to Lucy, who was visiting in Columbus, "I have ordered a new suit of clothes—plain black frock coat and black pants. So we can go out without trouble about the patch you laughed so much about."[15]

Although Hayes was not yet prepared to run for Congress himself, he wholeheartedly campaigned for a thoroughly aroused Republican party. "I have never seen," he told Lucy, "such large meetings as we are now having. Processions and gatherings every night. Very lucky that it is so short a canvass. If it was a month I should want to run away. As it is I enjoy it vastly." On his thirty-sixth birthday, he made a campaign speech in Walnut Hills and reported that the "most prodigious political excitement" continued. "The like has not been seen within the memory of the oldest inhabitant. Meetings, torchlight processions, cannonading, bonfires, singing, and illuminations every night, 'Sundays excepted.' " Hayes's optimistic predictions were borne out when the Republicans defeated incumbent Congressman Groesbeck.[16]

After the political campaign ended on 12 October, "the hurry of the first opening of Courts" failed to foretell the "unusually quiet times" that followed. Despite a building boom, the law business, Hayes discovered, was "not nearly so good" as he had anticipated. Furthermore, he was unhappy with his partnership. Billy Rogers, whom Hayes loved like a brother, had moved to Minnesota, and Corwine's political ambitions continued to hamper his practice of law. Hayes was careful not to offend Corwine—making only veiled references to his annoyance in his correspondence with Sardis—but he wanted to find a graceful way to terminate their partnership. When in late November 1858 a vacancy on the Cincinnati common pleas bench was anticipated, the bar, with substantial unanimity, recommended Hayes as an interim appointee. Two years earlier, in the face of certain defeat, Hayes had declined to run for that bench. Circumstances had changed, however, and the pay made the judgeship attractive. But before Governor Chase could appoint him, an even more attractive opportunity beckoned.[17]

In early December, the city solicitor of Cincinnati was killed by a locomotive, and the thirty-four-member city council had to fill his office. The Republicans and Know-Nothings together controlled seventeen votes, as did the Democrats, but eighteen votes were needed for election. It was, as Hayes said, "the best lawyer's office in Cincinnati," and seven men were nominated, including Caleb Smith and Hayes. On the first ballot, Smith had twelve votes and Hayes four, but on subsequent ballots Hayes's votes increased while Smith's went down. Because he had offended both the radical German followers of Friedrich Hassaurek and the Know-Nothings five years earlier, when he had defended the police who broke up an anti-Catholic parade, Smith lost support. Hayes was not sympathetic to the Know-Nothings, but he had offended neither them nor the Germans. By the seventh ballot, Hayes had seventeen votes. His partner Corwine convinced R. M. Bishop, the nonvoting president of the council, that Hayes would "make a good solicitor"; Bishop, in turn, talked Dennis J. Toohy, a young Irish lawyer, into voting for Hayes on the thirteenth ballot on the night of 8 December.[18]

William Disney, a rival for the post, later wrote, "So it was that Hayes was taken from private life, and without his solicitation was placed in his first public office. His luck followed him to the end of his days." In time, Hayes's luck became an axiom for Ohio political pundits, but it was neither blind nor dumb. Hayes never appeared to be seeking office, but by instinctively and deliberately enhancing his availability, he created conditions conducive to good luck. Eschewing extreme positions, he made himself acceptable to a wide spectrum of voters. Genuinely decent and kind, he was careful not to take his friends for granted nor to offend his rivals. Corwine, for example, from whom Hayes wished to disengage himself, played a key role in securing the one Democratic vote needed for the city solicitor job, and that vote could be secured because Hayes had not alienated that Democrat. His reputation for fairness and integrity made Hayes acceptable to many with whom he was not in agreement.[19]

Hayes was overjoyed to be city solicitor. "The berth," he told Sardis, "is a good one. Salary three thousand five hundred dollars per year and duties agreeable. . . . This is much better than the judgeship. Besides, I discovered that the judge appointed by the Governor only gets fifteen hundred dollars." Hayes elaborated on what was expected of him. "The duties of my new office are all in the line of my profession. The suits of the city, advice to all its officers in legal matters, etc., etc., occupy my attention. The litigation of a city like this is very important and of a great variety." Hayes was pleased to be "well spoken of by all" the Cincinnati newspapers. All in all, the solicitorship came "at a time of life when one's first office tastes sweet in the mouth."[20]

The solicitorship of a growing metropolis was no sinecure. Government officials and agencies and private citizens relied on Hayes for readings and interpretations of the charter and ordinances of Cincinnati, and he represented the city in court. For example, in his greatest triumph as solicitor, he won for the city a $250,000 verdict from a railroad. Still, most of his work was routine rather than spectacular. He told Mayor N. W. Thomas that city council members could legally buy property sold under a resolution passed by the city council, and he informed a coal dealer, at his request, that the standard bushel of stove coal in Cincinnati was *five pecks.*"[21]

Some of Hayes's opinions facilitated the development of Cincinnati. He asserted that the city council could borrow money and lease property for an additional reservoir. He also determined that since the city council had created the Board of City Improvements, the council, if it chose, could ignore or bypass the board and legislate improvements. Several of Hayes's opinions involved conflicting claims of the city and property owners over streets that had not been formally designated streets. Hayes tended to be pragmatic. He observed that if litigation were resorted to, its outcome would be determined by the length of time and nature of the private claimant's use of the property as opposed to how long it had been used as a street. In instances in which long-term use as a street could be established through oral testimony, he was confident that the city's title could be maintained.[22]

The way Hayes conducted the office led to his election to the post in April 1859. Running ahead of the ticket, he was jubilant and teased his mother, who was fearful of the temptations that public office might throw in his way. "I hope you are not cast down about the election here," Hayes playfully told Sophia. "It will, I hope, not prove my ruin." Far from spelling ruin, the new income enabled Hayes and Lucy to pay off, within a year, the $554 remaining on their mortgage and to add a new brick kitchen and three stories to the rear of their house.[23]

While Hayes and Lucy were enlarging their Cincinnati home, Sardis, to attract them to Fremont, was building a home among the huge old trees he called Spiegel Grove. He had named it that because the pools of water reflected the trees and because the German word for mirror conjured up images of *"good spirits."* Depending on Sardis's mood, good spirits meant that the shades of dead friends were hovering about, that it was the "home of cheerfulness and happiness," or that he always had "the best of *spirits* to warm the inner man." While visiting Hayes and Lucy during the winter and spring of 1859, Sardis had vowed to start building the house he had long dreamed of, the one he hoped they would occupy someday.[24]

When Sardis got back to Fremont, he began planning the new house in earnest. Hayes was enthusiastic about a summer home where his boys could learn "to ride, drive, and do all sorts of things that country boys do." Beginning in April, Sardis consulted frequently with Hayes and Lucy, and house plans were the main reason that Hayes and Birch visited Sardis in early July. After returning to Cincinnati, Hayes sent Sardis a sketch. Hayes, who did not want excessive outside ornamentation, particularly valued a wide porch for summer living, while Lucy insisted on a passageway between the kitchen and dining room. When Sardis gave Hayes the option of a brick or frame structure, Hayes chose brick, after finding that it would not cost a great deal more. Nevertheless, as the house went up, Hayes feared that Sardis was "building a much more expensive house" than he had intended. It was "large and very handsome," but "not too large." It was "just such a house" as Hayes "would prefer to live in," and "Lucy was very much taken with it."[25]

During this otherwise happy period, Hayes was saddened by the illness of John Pease, his cousin and former roommate, who was dying of tuberculosis. Quite possibly, Pease's condition caused Hayes to worry anew about his own health in October 1859. He recalled that in early 1852, during the Nancy Farrer case, he had had a severe cold, which he believed had injured his lungs, particularly his right lung. Occasionally since then he had "felt a weakness . . . under the lower ribs on the right side" when speaking. The "same weakness increased after long writing," with his right side touching the desk. Uneasy because this trouble recurred, Hayes resolved to speak without exerting his voice, to write facing the desk or with his left side touching it, and to quit either task if he felt the weakness coming on.[26]

As winter arrived, Hayes found more time for reading biographies and studying the all-engulfing question of slavery. Admiring "the doers rather than the talkers of the world," he appreciated Thomas Carlyle's *Life and Letters of Oliver Cromwell* (1845) and the first two volumes of his *History of Frederick the Great* (1858). Hayes wished to investigate further Alexis de Tocqueville's charge that sixteenth-century Christians "brought back slavery into the world" after Christianity had abolished it for a thousand years. While groping for a solution, Hayes found Dr. Nathan Lewis Rice's formulation of the slavery question useful: "What is the true method of treating slavery . . . to mitigate its evil, whilst it continues, and . . . most speedily and safely to abolish it?" Rice's *Lectures on Slavery* (1860) also impressed Sophia, who wanted Sardis to read it and "be sound on that question!" Even Sophia and Sardis seemed to be abandoning their antiabolitionist biases.[27]

In briefing Abraham Lincoln, who was campaigning for William Dennison in the 1859 Ohio governor's race, Hayes described the delicate combination of Republicans and nativist Know-Nothing Americans in Cincinnati politics. He suggested that Lincoln "not give a too strictly partisan cast to his address." If Lincoln, "an old Clay Whig, of Kentucky parentage, . . . with a wholesome dislike of Locofocoism," were cautious "as to our peculiar position," Hayes thought, he would make a fine impression.[28]

Lincoln appeared grateful for Hayes's advice. When he came to Cincinnati, Hayes showed him to his hotel room and, at his behest, remained for "a chat." They had met previously in 1855 when Lincoln was in Cincinnati for the famous McCormick reaper patent case. Renewing their acquaintance, Lincoln "very dramatically" described his debates with Stephen A. Douglas during the 1858 campaign. Although Lincoln did not replace Douglas as a senator from Illinois, he became a national figure. Years later, Hayes remembered "that the presidential bee had already begun to buzz around" Lincoln's head and that everything he said pointed to himself as "the logical" candidate for the Republican party.[29]

That evening, Hayes attended the Lincoln meeting in the Fifth Street Market. When he heard Lincoln speak, Hayes later recalled that he thought, "Here is Henry Clay over again." But his contemporary reaction invoked the image of another Kentuckian, John J. Crittenden, in "his truth and candor," although Lincoln spoke with "greater logical force, greater warmth of feeling." Ungainly in his appearance, undemonstrative in his delivery, Lincoln was nevertheless "an orator of great merit" because of the substance of his remarks. With Lincoln's help, the Ohio Republicans elected Dennison governor, and their majority in the forthcoming legislature ensured that Chase would represent Ohio in the Senate. "So far so good," exulted Hayes.[30]

The fall was packed with political activity; the rest of the year, Hayes, who was not overworked as city solicitor, was engrossed with family activities. "I am in the boy business chiefly these days," he told his niece Laura in the spring of 1860: "Playing with the boys, scolding the boys. Telling the boys how it used to be when I was a little boy. Lecturing the boys on the folly of being boys; and the likes which my father and all other fathers have done since the boy business was inaugurated by Adam and Eve a number of thousand years ago." Laura had already begun to replace her mother in Hayes's heart and mind; in time, he told her that she filled Fanny's role "so well" that "I can hardly feel sometimes that she is gone."[31]

While Lucy, Birch, and Ruddy were in Columbus with Fanny's children on the Fourth of July 1860, Hayes set off firecrackers and torpedoes all day with Webb and then spent "a jolly, sensible" evening at the literary club, returning "home sober at 1:45." Lonely and pensive, he "ruminated how loving and confidential" he would be if Lucy were with him and confessed to her by letter that there was a hidden side of his nature that he suspected she did not know about. He was sensitive to "saddening influences"—like meeting old friends when "dear ones" were "absent, possibly dead," or "the occurrence of happy or sad anniversaries"—which aroused strong emotions. The happy Fourth of July paradoxically had triggered such feelings: Lucy was away, he saw old friends at the club, and he remembered that four years earlier he had been "all day with Fanny, hardly expecting her to live out the day."[32]

Hayes and Lucy also broke their routine in August, when they took a month-long vacation to visit relatives and see sights. "For a civilized being," the worst part of the twenty-five hundred miles they traveled by rail was the three nights spent in sleeping cars. While on steamboats, they lost an anchor, spent two to three days in fog, ran on a rock, and endured two storms, but, Hayes insisted, "I had rather risk a shipwreck than a sleeping car." In Vermont, Hayes was particularly gratified to be given Grandfather Hayes's old clock, which he planned to put into working order, and a letter written by his father in 1820 and one written by his mother at about the same time. "You know," he explained to Sophia, "I am prone to keep old letters and relics and value them more than most people do." By the time they reached New York on 25 August, Lucy was eager to get back to their boys, but Hayes wanted her to "see more of this city & Phila[delphia]." After they enjoyed "a cool bright Sunset, and beautiful views" at Brooklyn's Green-Wood Cemetery, Lucy insisted on returning home. "Our trip," Hayes wrote on 2 September, "was in every respect a fortunate one but we had enough of it."[33]

In the early months of the 1860 presidential campaign, Hayes was curiously detached. Ohio had supported Chase for the nomination, but when the convention named Lincoln, Hayes commented to Sardis, "You are, of course, pleased," and added, "He takes well here." Sardis probably preferred Lincoln because he was a former Whig and a less radical antislavery man than Chase. By late June, after the Democratic party split, there were three other presidential candidates. Southern Democrats nominated John C. Breckinridge, northern Democrats named Douglas, and a remnant of the Whig and American (Know-Nothing) parties nominated John Bell on a Constitutional Union ticket. Hayes thought that Lincoln's chances were the best, "but not a moral certainty." He feared that no candidate would secure a majority of electoral votes and that the election would be decided in the House of Representatives, where Bell or Breckinridge might win. In late September, anti-Lincoln fusion movements in New Jersey and Pennsylvania made Hayes less optimistic than many of his fellow Republicans. Although he had delivered a "few little speeches" and planned to make a few more, he confessed, "I cannot get up much interest in the contest." His "chief feeling" was a "wholesome contempt for Douglas, on account of his recent demagoguery," attacking Republicans as disunionists. In September, Hayes seemed as interested in observing the Prince of Wales passing beneath his windows as in any political procession, and he was more excited about the Mechanics Fair in Cincinnati than in any political meeting.[34]

But in October, Hayes spoke of the "pleasant, lively little election canvass. . . . Our meetings are prodigious; but for the American element, we would carry this county easily; as it is, we shall do well." Indeed, enthusiasm permeated the entire household. "Our boys," he told Laura, "have red Wide Awake Captains caps and torches and have processions these pleasant evenings, which are quite as grand in their eyes as the exhibitions of the bigger boys." After the state and local elections on 9 October foretold a Republican victory in the national election, Hayes exclaimed, "We have had jolly good times rejoicing over the elections." The Republicans kept up the relentless pressure and had "a great Wide Awake doing"—a lantern and torchlight parade—on Friday night, the second of November.[35]

Since "the October elections settled Pennsylvania and the other doubtful states," Hayes concluded on election day, "All now depends on New York." He wondered, however, if the "ultra South," specifically South Carolina and two or three other slave states, would carry out the threat of disunion if Lincoln were elected and, if so, what would happen. Neither Guy Bryan's warning that the South was willing to break up the Union nor subsequent events changed Hayes's opinion that the moderate states of the upper South and lower North (his beloved Ohio Valley) would hold the Union together. But Hayes was not afraid to confront threats of secession: "I feel as if the time had come to test this question. If the threats are meant, then it is time the Union was dissolved or the traitors crushed out."[36]

SEVEN

WAR

Lincoln was elected, and South Carolina moved rapidly toward secession. Disunion sentiment also proved strong in the upper South and even in the border slave states. In the four months between the election and inauguration, Buchanan did nothing and Lincoln said nothing to impede secession. Without leadership, various northerners either advocated coercion or compromise to save the Union or acquiesced in its demise. Although the Union was collapsing in what Hayes called "these squally times," he was against concessions and appeared content to be rid of bad neighbors. "The approaching dissolution of the Union don't alarm me a bit," he assured Sardis in late December.[1]

A staunch Republican, Hayes opposed abandonment of the free-soil principle that had triumphed in the 1860 election. He rejected Sen. John J. Crittenden's proposals to entice the secessionists back into the Union by giving them a stronger fugitive slave law and an unamendable amendment protecting slavery where it existed and in the territories south of the southern border of Kansas. Hayes feared a compromise that would perpetrate slavery more than he feared disunion and civil war, arguing, "We can recover from them." Twenty free states "in the temperate zone, stretching from the Atlantic to the Pacific," and their twenty million people—vigorous, inventive, educated, moral, and, "above all, free" will form "a glorious nation," he predicted, that will be "scarcely inferior in real power to the unfortunate Union of thirty-three States which we had on the first of November."[2]

On 12 January, Hayes believed, as did many Americans—both northern and southern—that two nations were inevitable. For the present, he thought that the federal government should continue to collect the revenue and defend the forts in the seceded states (possibly as bargaining chips) and should go to war only if necessary "to give us a good boundary. If Maryland attempts to go off, suppress her in order to save the Potomac and the District of Columbia. Cut a piece off of western Virginia and keep Missouri and all the territories." A war to round out boundaries, he thought, would be neither long nor expensive if it were energetically pursued, but an attempt to conquer the South "would leave us loaded with debt and would certainly fail."[3]

"Let them go," Hayes reiterated later that month, after six states had seceded. But he insisted that the breakup of the Union did not mean that "the experiment of popular government" had failed. It was successful in all free states and in most, if not all, slaveholding states. Disunion, Hayes concluded, probably demonstrated that there was an "irrepressible conflict" between freedom and slavery, that perhaps it was impossible for them to exist side by side under the same popular government, and that "our new relations may as well be formed with that as an *admitted* fact."[4]

Further contact with the president-elect made Hayes his unabashed admirer. With Lucy and "a jolly party of friends," Hayes went to Indianapolis on Monday, 11 February, and "returned on the Presidential train to Cincinnati, seeing all the doings here and on the road." They talked with Lincoln and heard him "make several of his good speeches." On his birthday the next day, Cincinnati gave Lincoln a "most impressive" reception, which Hayes and his family viewed from the windows and steps of their house. It was simple and "in keeping with the nobility of this typical American." Hayes thought that Lincoln was "homely" but "by no means ill looking," and Sophia, who found character in his face, was "glad to see him so good a looking man." Hayes was amused by Lincoln's "awkward look when he bows. It cant be caricatured. . . . His chin rises—his body breaks in two at the hips—there is a bend of the knees at a queer angle." More important, Lincoln was "in good health; not a hair gray or gone; in his prime and fit for service, mentally and physically. Great hopes may well be felt."[5]

Hayes was impressed by what Lincoln left out of his speeches and put into his conversations. In his public utterances, "Lincoln was wary at all times" and said nothing anyone could find fault with. When the German turnvereiners, who were radically antislavery and wished to make it an issue of war, serenaded him and attempted "to draw from him some expression in sympathy with their own views," Lincoln's response left them baffled. "In private conversation," however, "he was discreet but frank" and revealed his belief "in a policy of kindness, of delay to give time for passions to cool, but not in a compromise to extend the power and the deadly influence of the slave system." Finding "great satisfaction" in this approach, Hayes abandoned his "let them go" attitude. He also perceived that Lincoln "undoubtedly is shrewd, able, and possesses strength in reserve" and realized that these virtues would soon be tested.[6]

Despite radical "German Turners" and the reception Lincoln received in Cincinnati, that city wanted neither war nor the rumor of war. The Democrats and Know-Nothings united in March, the month Lincoln was inaugurated, and threatened to sweep Republicans out of local offices in the election of 1 April "as a means of saving the Union," Hayes quipped. "I shall go under with the rest," he predicted, "but expect to run ahead of the ticket." He preferred not to be beaten but rationalized that he had derived all the reputation and experience he could from his office and, if turned out, "shall be referred to as the best, or one of the best solicitors, the city has had." Vexed by a rumor that the Lincoln administration had decided to give up Fort Sumter at Charleston, South Carolina, Hayes insisted, "I would give up the prospect of office, if it would save the fort."[7]

In Cincinnati, the "Union-saving avalanche" overtook Republican office-holders, as Hayes had predicted, and his "little potato patch went down with the rest." Although he had enough cash on hand for a year, Hayes moved immediately into a new partnership, lest Sardis try to talk him into returning to Fremont. Vacating the solicitor's office on 9 April, he tried a case that very day. His new partner was Leopold Markbreit, who was the half brother and former partner of Friedrich Hassaurek, the leader of the German radicals in Cincinnati.[8]

The new partnership was short-lived. Three days after Hayes resumed private practice, South Carolina forces opened fire on Fort Sumter; on 15 April, Lincoln called for 75,000 volunteers. Hayes proudly noted that after drifting for four months, the people responded with "wild and joyous excitement" and "unbounded enthusiasm. How relieved we were to have a Government again!" A great meeting in Cincinnati unanimously adopted Hayes's resolutions upholding the Union against the rebels in disloyal states. "We are all for war," Hayes told Sardis. "The few dissentients have to run like quarter-horses. A great change for two weeks to produce." Welcoming the war, Hayes simply stated, "I like it. Anything is better than the state of things we have had the last few months."[9]

Individual members of Hayes's household reacted differently toward the war. "Mother," Hayes reported to Sardis, "thinks we are to be punished for our sinfulness, and reads the Old Testament vigorously. Mother Webb quietly grieves over it. Lucy enjoys it and wishes she had been in Fort Sumter with a garrison of women. Dr. Joe is for flames, slaughter, and a rising of slaves. All the boys are soldiers." Typically, Hayes was amused by the radical shifts in opinion the war had produced. "A great state of things for a Christian people," he chided Sardis, the antiabolitionist model of his youth, "and then to have old gentlemen say, as you do, 'I am glad we have got to fighting at last.' Judge Swan and Mr. Andrews and the whole Methodist clergy all say the same. Shocking!"[10]

Actually, Hayes was equally enthusiastic, but he assured Sardis, "I would not think of going into this first movement." He helped his brother-in-law

Dr. James Webb get appointed assistant surgeon in the Second Regiment of Ohio Volunteers and saw him off to the East on 19 April, but Hayes doubted his own military capacity or that the war would last. Even so, the next day, to learn how to "eyes right and left," Hayes joined the Burnet Rifles. It was a "volunteer home company" composed chiefly of literary club friends, who picked him as their captain. Hayes took the honor seriously and drilled on Sunday morning, despite the clergymen in his company. In Cincinnati, the immediate concern was whether Kentucky would follow the upper South and secede. All in all, Hayes found the "first ten days of the war . . . as jolly and as exciting as you could wish."[11]

War seemed less of a lark when "a long friendly secession letter" from Guy Bryan forced Hayes to contemplate what a war could accomplish. Hayes had to admit that Bryan's oft-repeated prediction that "the agitation of slavery" would break up the Union seemed to be coming true. He had clung to a weakening hope that "we could live together notwithstanding slavery," but on 8 May 1861 he had "next to no hope of a restoration of the old Union," and "no hope whatever" if Guy were correct. Hayes still doubted that the South could be conquered, and he still doubted "the expediency of doing it even if it were practicable." He did "not think it wise or desirable" to force any slave state to remain if that state's "settled and final judgment" were "that she cannot live in the Union."[12]

If the war were one of conquest, Hayes would oppose it, but, he told Bryan, "the war is forced on us." The Confederacy of seceded slave states "has not by its *acts* sought a *peaceful* separation" but has assailed the federal government, taken its property, defied its authority, and "undoubtedly" planned the capture of Washington. Although in "the cotton-growing States, a decided and controlling public judgment" might favor disunion, Hayes believed that "rebellious citizens" in the upper South were "bent on forcing out of the Union States whose people are not in favor of secession." He would not predict what the ultimate objective of the war would be, but he trusted that it would "not be merely the conquest of unwilling peoples." Having implied that the destruction of slavery might become a war objective, Hayes noted that the war currently aimed "to defend the rights of the Union, and to strengthen the Union men in the doubtful States" and that such a war was "necessary, wise, and just."

Rather than feeling repelled by the thought of fratricidal war, Hayes embraced it as an ennobling experience for both northerners and southerners. "People forget self. The virtues of magnanimity, courage, patriotism, etc., etc., are called into life. People are more generous, more sympathetic, better, than when engaged in the more selfish pursuits of peace. The same exhibition of virtue," he continued to Bryan, "is witnessed on your side. May there be as much of this, the better side of war, enjoyed on both sides, and as little of the horrors of war suffered, as possible, and may we soon have an honorable and enduring peace!"[13]

Although Hayes told Bryan that he would probably take no active part in the war, thinking through Bryan's letter and his response had the opposite effect. A week later, Hayes and their mutual Kenyon friend Stanley Matthews, having discussed Bryan's letter, agreed that a war to save the upper South for the Union was "just and necessary" and would demand all the power of the country. They determined that they should go to war together. On 15 May, Hayes declared, "*I would prefer to go into it if I knew I was to die or be killed in the course of it, than to live through and after it without taking any part in it.*"[14]

Hayes and Matthews found it difficult, however, to carry out their decision. Although Hayes had claimed that there were a thousand men in Cincinnati who wanted them for their officers, they had to go to Columbus "to lay ropes for a regiment." Failing there, they pulled strings in Washington until, by the end of May, they were encouraged by Treasury Secretary Salmon P. Chase. By then, the eastern counties of Virginia had overwhelmingly approved secession, and, as Hayes observed, nothing indicated "an early termination of the war." On 5 June, they heard from Washington that unless Ohio authorities interfered they would get their regiment. Ordered to Columbus five days later, Hayes learned that Governor Dennison had made him a major in the Twenty-third Regiment of Ohio Volunteers and Matthews a lieutenant colonel. They would serve under Col. William S. Rosecrans.[15]

Hayes was "vastly" pleased. "You know how I love you; how I love the family all," Hayes explained, "but Lucy, I am much happier in this business than I could be fretting away in the old office near the courthouse. It is living." Hayes's commission was dated 7 June, he began serving on 10 June at Camp Jackson—soon renamed Camp Chase—a converted racetrack four miles west of Columbus, and was sworn in on 12 June. Rosecrans, "a West Pointer and intimate friend of Billy Rogers, and a capital officer," was "energetic . . . very cheerful and sensible."[16]

From the first day, Hayes was proud of the Twenty-third, which was the first three-year regiment organized in Ohio and, according to him, the best of the four in camp. The Twenty-third was also the first Ohio regiment that did not elect its own field officers. Because Governor Dennison had selected officers from one part of the state to lead men recruited in another, Hayes and Matthews feared that they would be resented by the men and their cap-

tains. They also were embarrassed having to tell Cincinnati friends and relations that they could not serve with them. Hayes felt particularly awkward
explaining the situation to his brother-in-law Dr. Joseph T. Webb, who
wished to be his surgeon, and to his literary club crony Manning F. Force,
who had raised a company. When the captains of the Twenty-third did protest, the governor's only response was to transfer two of them, with their
companies, to another regiment. "Our captains," Hayes remarked after the
crisis had blown over, "impress me, as a body, most favorably." There was
Captain McIlrath, the former chief of police of Cleveland, six feet three and
a half inches tall, whose company was "the best of any in camp"; Captain
Giddings (the son of Joshua R. Giddings, the abolitionist congressman), "a
pleasant gentleman" at the head of "a capital company"; Captain Skiles,
who had served in Mexico and was a church member of fine character; Captain Moore, a shrewd and trusty New England farmer type; and Captain
Zimmerman, a "conscientious, amiable, industrious" man who led a "stout
set of men from the iron region," among whom was Pvt. William McKinley.[17]

Camp Jackson was "higgledy-piggledy," and Hayes and Matthews worked
to bring order out of chaos. Without quarters, Hayes slept at Platt's home
until 12 June, when he had his first "cool but refreshing" sleep "under canvas." Without a uniform, he ordered one "*very loose* about the legs"; without a horse, he searched for a "small or medium-sized animal of good sense,
hardy and kind, good looking enough, but not showy." When Rosecrans
was absent, Matthews and Hayes were in charge. "What we don't know, we
guess at," Hayes reported, "and you may be sure we are kept pretty busy
guessing." He enjoyed it all "as much as a boy does a Fourth of July."[18]

Moving and acting in concert, the regiment aroused Hayes's emotions.
The "spirit and enthusiasm" with which the men took the oath excited him.
Rather than feeling embarrassed by these inexperienced, ununiformed, and
unarmed volunteers on parade, Hayes—who thought "the long line looked
well" and the regimental band sounded good—was possessed by "a swelling
of the heart." His skilled and resourceful men, Hayes boasted, were "fully
equal to the famous Massachusetts men in a mechanical way. They build
quarters, ditches, roads, traps; dig wells, catch fish, kill squirrels." He discovered "a new sensation" in "the affection and pride" he felt for a body of
men.[19]

On Sunday, 16 June, Hayes was left in command of the entire camp of almost 3,000 men. It was "an odd position for a novice, so ignorant of all military things." When the officer of the day, a young West Point–trained captain, stumped Hayes by asking for his orders, Hayes put into practice his

Major Hayes

motto: "When you don't know what to say, say nothing." Noting that nothing appeared to need special attention, Hayes promised to issue an order if anything out of the ordinary occurred. He began that Sunday seated at a table in his tent, with an orderly on his right to run errands, an adjutant on his left to help "*guess*," and a clerk to write orders. Out front, a pacing sentinel told those who entered to take off their hats. Hayes issued routine guard-duty orders, gave permits to swim in the Scioto River, read and corrected morning reports, and settled disputes between soldiers and, more troublesome, difficulties "between soldiers and the carpenters whose tools disappear mysteriously, and farmers in the neighborhood who go to bed with roosts of barnyard fowl and wake up . . . fowlless." Later that morning, Hayes, along with 1,000 men, waited in vain for a preacher. The Twenty-third, Hayes assured his mother, was "strictly a temperance camp" (to the dismay of some visitors) "and ratherish a religious camp," with a Methodist chaplain and several "glee clubs and choirs" that sang Hayes and other tired officers and soldiers asleep each night.[20]

Hayes's usual day involved less responsibility and more work. At 5 A.M. a gun was fired and reveille sounded, bringing everyone to roll call, where each captain reported on the condition of his men. Most of the day was taken up with drilling and training, interrupted by the ceremonial mounting of the guard at 9 A.M., dinner at noon, and supper at 6 P.M. After a parade with a band at 7 P.M. — "a decidedly imposing affair" — came the finale at 10 P.M. Above all, Hayes enjoyed the evenings: "The music and hum, the cool air in the tent, and open-air exercise during the day, make the sleeping superb." Although Hayes had been too ill to serve in the Mexican War, he declared, "I enjoy this life, and it is going to be healthy for me. I shall hardly be more exposed to cold than in a very open tent the two cold nights a few days ago; but I am gaining in strength and spirits."[21]

After actively commanding the Twenty-third for only a few days, Rosecrans was promoted to brigadier general and ordered into western Virginia. Since Matthews was too inexperienced to command the regiment, the governor appointed Eliakim Parker Scammon colonel. Hayes found him "amiable and social" but "deficient in physical health and energy" and lacking "a happy way of hitting the humors of the men."[22]

Hayes was more concerned over the regiment's surgeon than its colonel. He had not given up on Dr. Joe Webb's appointment, and, after lobbying for two weeks with the governor and the colonel, he succeeded in having Joe attached to the Twenty-third as his equal in rank. Hayes was fond of his brother-in-law, and Joe was a competent medical doctor, who would be a pleasant addition to a congenial field officers' mess consisting of Scammon,

Matthews, and Hayes. Having removed not only himself but also Joe from the household in Cincinnati, Hayes apologized to Lucy. "I am sorry you are to be left with so much responsibility," Hayes told her, "but, with your mother's advice, do what you both agree is best and it will perfectly satisfy me." A few days after Joe's appointment, Matthews happened to meet the "green, ignorant young doctor" who had been intended for the Twenty-third and commented (prophetically for Hayes), "What an escape we have made."[23]

By late June, everyone in camp was annoyed; they had not been paid and were neither armed nor equipped. The complaint, Hayes told Secretary Chase, was "that the State Government ought to have armed and equipped all who have enlisted . . . trusting to the justice of the General Government . . . to reimburse the State." The chief ambition of the men of the Twenty-third was to be armed with "rifles or rifled muskets," since many of them were excellent marksmen. Exasperated with Governor Dennison, Hayes told Chase, "if you were our Governor Ohio Soldiers would have fared differently. . . . The good things done at Washington people are disposed to place to your credit." When obsolete smoothbore muskets arrived, the men—in a state of virtual mutiny (which Scammon exacerbated)—refused them until a stirring speech by Hayes, promising better weapons and arousing their patriotic fervor, calmed them down. By mid-July, the regiment, at last uniformed and equipped (but not with rifled arms), expected to move to western Virginia or Tennessee.[24]

Hayes enjoyed his introduction to military life at Camp Chase. He worked hard at whipping both the regiment and himself into shape. He learned as much as he could from Scammon and particularly from Col. Jacob Ammen of the Twenty-fourth, a West Pointer who had been in the army and had taught mathematics in several colleges. Ammen had "seen all sorts of life" and was "a capital instructor in military things." Finding Matthews and Hayes "fond of his talk," he took to them warmly. Camp life was made easier by the closeness of Hayes's relatives in Columbus and by visits from Lucy, the boys, Sophia, and the Platts. Birch and Webb were in the camp a great deal and sometimes spent the night with their father. The Fourth of July, which was like a Sunday for the Twenty-third, marked the only break from daily routine. "Matthews and I," Hayes reported, "formed the regiment into a hollow square (rather oblong, in fact). I read the Declaration and he made a short pithy speech and wound up with cheers for the Union; and no more duty during the day. In the evening there were fire-balls and a few fireworks."[25]

Any lingering hope that the war would be a lark, however, was swept away on 22 July, when "news of a dreadful defeat at Manassas," or Bull Run, reached Camp Chase. "What a calamity!" Hayes exclaimed. He feared for the safety of Washington and that "secession fever" might sweep the border states out of the Union. Thinking that the Twenty-third would be sent to Washington, he lamented his lack of military knowledge and experience and resolved to do his "utmost . . . to promote the efficiency of our regiment." Scammon's calm reaction to the defeat (he reminisced about school days with an old West Point buddy while Hayes agonized over Bull Run) confirmed Hayes's view that Scammon was "somewhat deficient in . . . vigor of nerve" and "not well fitted for volunteer command." Meditating and dreaming about "the great disaster," Hayes slept miserably, but the next day's news was somewhat reassuring. Despite the panic, the loss was "not very heavy," and the army was again in position. While acknowledging that the "lesson is a severe one," Hayes hoped that it would prove "useful." He believed that "raw troops should not be sent to attack an enemy entrenched on its own ground unless under most peculiar circumstances. Gradual approach with fortifications as they proceeded would have won the day."[26]

After receiving orders to move into western Virginia and chatting with Gen. John C. Frémont, Hayes's spirits brightened. "He is a hero," Hayes exclaimed. "All his words and acts inspire enthusiasm and confidence" as well as "affection in the masses of people! . . . He is a romantic, rather perhaps than a great, character," Hayes realized. "But he is loyal, brave, and persevering beyond all compare." On 24 July, Frémont and Dennison reviewed the Twenty-third; with Lucy, Laura, and friends present, "It was a stirring scene."

The drama was enhanced by the knowledge that the Twenty-third would depart the next morning at 5 A.M. to join Rosecrans's force. That evening, Hayes went into Columbus to say good-bye to his family. Sophia feared that she would never see her son again, and Lucy, who "showed more emotion" than she had in the past over his departure, decided to spend the night with him at Camp Chase. They went out together and "passed a happy evening going around among the men gathered in picturesque groups, cooking rations for three days." Early the next morning, Lucy returned to town by hack to fetch her mother so that they could both watch the Twenty-third— with husband and brother, son and son-in-law—leave camp. "I marched in with the men afoot," Hayes wrote in his diary, "a gallant show they made as they marched up High Street to the depot. Lucy and Mother Webb remained several hours until we left. I saw them watching me as I stood on the platform at the rear of the last car as long as they could see me. Their eyes swam. I kept my emotion under control enough not to melt into tears."[27]

This first movement of the Twenty-third illustrates the degree to which the steam engine had revolutionized troop movements. Apart from the short march to the train station, the Twenty-third steamed off to war, proceeding by rail to Bellaire, Ohio, and then into northwestern Virginia. During the 130 miles to Clarksburg, the Twenty-third was "greeted by shouts and demonstrations of joy" by Union men, who had feared that they would be abandoned after Bull Run. "Our men," Hayes told Lucy, "enjoyed it beyond measure. Many had never seen a mountain; none had ever seen such a reception. They stood on top of the cars and danced and shouted with delight." Arriving at 2 A.M. on 27 July (forty-five hours after leaving Camp Chase), Hayes was surrounded by confusion and "worked like a Turk in the rain all the morning laying out a camp and getting it up, on a fine hill with a pretty scene before us."[28]

They did not enjoy the pretty scene for long. That evening, Rosecrans ordered the Twenty-third to march early the next morning "up the mountains" to Weston, on the west fork of the Monongahela. Up at 4 A.M. that Sunday morning, the men of the Twenty-third began striking tents and packing baggage, which proved to be "enormous and extra," causing a "great stew," before it was loaded on their 103 wagons. Instead of 7 A.M., they departed at 11 A.M. "in a great shower," but the sun soon came out, burning Hayes's nose and face. After marching fourteen miles on a good road lined with blackberries, they camped in a meadow. Too weary to put up tents, many of the soldiers threw themselves on the ground and slept through a rainstorm while Hayes "got wet . . . trying to get them sheltered." Since they were in "the enemy's country," many of the men "fancied threatening dangers in all novel sights." A nine-mile march the next day brought them to Weston shortly after noon.[29]

Situated on a hill overlooking a fine large village, the camp was "surrounded by lovely hills, almost mountains, covered with forest or rich greensward. . . . We are a great grown-up armed blackberry party," Hayes confessed, "and we gather untold quantities." There were about as many secessionists in the neighborhood as Union supporters. Fearing no reprisals, secessionist women openly avowed their beliefs, but the men were "prudently quiet." It was at Weston that the Twenty-third suffered its first casualty. A loaded gun was thrown from a stack by a careless sentinel, went off, and tore a great hole through the foot of Lt. John E. Jewett of Zanesville. At best he would be crippled, and he ran the risk of losing his foot and even his life. No doctor, not even a clever one like Joe Webb, knew antiseptic procedures.[30]

Hayes and the left wing of the Twenty-third spent three weeks at Weston,

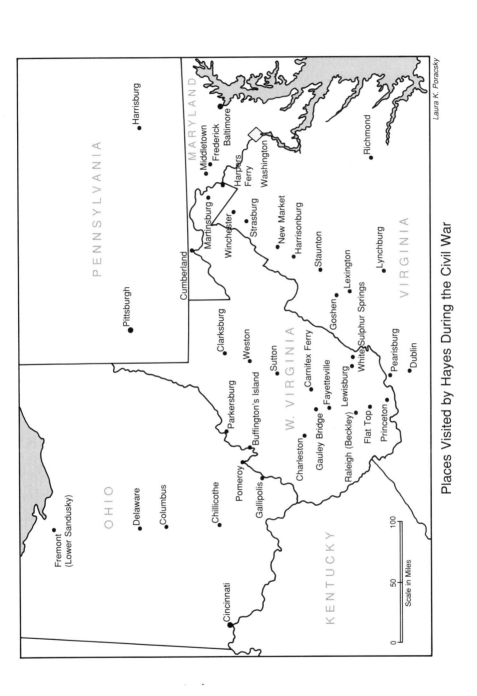

Places Visited by Hayes During the Civil War

Laura K. Poracsky

while its right wing under Matthews pushed further south to Sutton. With the Confederates, under Gen. Henry Alexander Wise, abandoning western Virginia, the Twenty-third's main function was to encourage Unionist sentiment. In the absence of civil authority, he and Dr. Joe "held a sort of police court" to settle disputes between citizens, whom Hayes found, "in these irregular times . . . more pugnacious than usual." He called on local lawyers and politicians (mostly Union men) in search of maps and information, and he visited Jewett and others in the makeshift hospital in the courthouse. Although "divers humane old ladies" furnished the hospital with knickknacks, Hayes longed for a Florence Nightingale. His attempt to get his niece Laura to play that part failed. Hayes also practiced shooting and found himself a poor shot with his pistol, a good one at a hundred yards with an Enfield rifle, but only "tolerable" at three hundred yards.[31]

On 17 August, Hayes called the increasing number of guerrilla attacks "a general rising among the Rebels. They rob and murder the Union men, and the latter come to us for help. . . . We have out all the time from two to six parties of from ten to seventy-five or one hundred men on scouting duty." A brush with guerrillas wounded three men and gave the Twenty-third its first battle casualties. The guerrillas, whom the men called bushwhackers, so infested the region that Matthews, to the disgust of Scammon, deemed it too unsafe to return to Weston with the right wing of the Twenty-third, as ordered. Hayes agreed that Matthews was mistaken but admitted that the numerous guerrillas could be part of Wise's army returning to reclaim western Virginia. "There are some bloody deeds done in these hills, and not," Hayes admitted, "all on one side." A squad of the Tenth Regiment brought in the body of one of "the wild men of the mountains," who had been shooting at them. "He wore neither hat nor shoes," Hayes reported, "was of gigantic size—weighing two hundred and thirty pounds; had long hooked toes, fitted to climb—a very monster. They probably killed him after taking him prisoner in cold blood—perhaps after a sort of trial. They say he was attempting to escape." A few days later, upon hearing that a captain in another regiment had allegedly ordered his men to kill three prisoners, Hayes vowed, "If any of my men kill prisoners, I'll kill them."[32]

After reports on 18 August that the enemy was coming through the mountains to the southeast, the left wing of the Twenty-third at Weston was ordered to cook three days' rations, gather forty rounds of ammunition, and be ready to march. Although suspecting that the information was just another rumor about guerrilla activity, Hayes was excited by the thought of combat and confronted the possibility of death. "I feel no apprehension—no presentiment of evil," he assured Lucy, "but at any rate you know how I love you and the dear boys and Grandma and all will take care that I am not forgotten." The next evening, the Twenty-third was ordered at midnight to pack quietly and march sixteen miles east to Buckhannon. "After a world of confusion, aggravated by an incompetent quartermaster," the half regiment got off at daylight. Over the next two weeks, the left wing shed luggage and marched strenuously via Buckhannon, Beverly, and French Creek to Sutton. Hayes thrived while on the march and declared to Lucy, "I never enjoyed any business or mode of life as much as I do this."[33]

On 5 September, the wings of the Twenty-third were reunited at Sutton, where Rosecrans concentrated 6,000 to 8,000 troops. The army camps, on high hills on both sides of the Elk River, were connected by "a beautiful suspension bridge." Hayes could imagine the humorist Artemus Ward calling the scene "gay and festive," especially at sundown, when three or four rival regimental bands played. Newly acquired dogs added interest to camp life, as did two young boys—pets of the Twenty-third. One, who was from Cleveland, had been with the regiment from the start, and the other was a runaway from Norwalk who, after trying out two other regiments, became " 'a boy of the Twenty-third.' He drills, plays officer, soldier, or errand boy, and is a curiosity in camp." The troops also "realized" horses and mules "from Secessionists," until most captains had horses.[34]

Although Hayes's letters to Lucy stress the idyllic side of army life, his diary records some of its more vicious aspects. By Scammon's order, Hayes had to drum three youngsters, who were "probably confirmed thieves," out of the regiment, and although the men approved, it made him sick. While separated from the rest of the regiment, the Twenty-third's right wing had had some serious problems—"one man shot resisting a corporal, two men in irons for a rape, and one man arrested for sleeping on post (third offense penalty death)." A bit later, when Union "pickets killed a colonel or lieutenant-colonel of the enemy who rode among them," Hayes exclaimed, "All wrong and cruel. This is too like murder. Shooting pickets . . . ought to be put down."[35]

On Saturday, 7 September, the army moved south to Birch River. As officer of the day on Sunday, Hayes crossed that river thirty to forty times and rode back and forth fifty to sixty miles for nineteen hours as the army moved upstream. The next day, it crossed Powell Mountain, camped eight miles above Summersville, and, with the enemy near, anticipated a battle. On 10 September, Rosecrans advanced. The Union forces drove the Confederate pickets out of Summersville and followed them nine miles to Carnifex Ferry on the Gauley River. There, Hayes estimated that 3,000 to 6,000 Confederates, commanded by Gen. John B. Floyd (who a year earlier had been Buchanan's secretary of war), were "entrenched on a hill, high, steep, and hidden by bushes." Rosecrans attacked at about 3 P.M. with his first two brigades but held in reserve his third brigade, of which the Twenty-third was a part. While listening to the cannon and musketry and awaiting his turn, Hayes felt as he did before beginning an important lawsuit. He joked with his fellow officers and with privates and observed that "all were jolly and excited by turns."

Finally, Rosecrans ordered Hayes to take four companies to the extreme left and advance while searching out the enemy's right flank. The companies marched over a hill, through a cornfield, down a steep, rocky hill, and through a dense thicket of laurel. It was late by the time they reached the foot of a precipice, where the enemy was entrenched. On the way up, Hayes, who was on the right of his detachment, came close to shooting at his recent associate Markbreit, who was on the left of the Twenty-eighth Ohio, and both "had a jolly laugh and introductions to surrounding officers as partners."

Coming under fire from the enemy, only two of Hayes's men were wounded. While fighting in the dusk, they rarely saw the enemy but fired "at bushes and log and earth barricades" until dark, when all firing ceased and they were ordered back to their regiment. The next morning, after a sleepless night, Hayes was delighted to hear "great cheering near the fort." Union forces had discovered that during the night the "enemy had run away in a panic." Rosecrans complimented Hayes and his men and in part attributed the hasty retreat of the Confederates to their belief that their rear and flank had been uncovered by Hayes's detachment.[36]

Pleased by the way Hayes had handled his independent command, Rosecrans entrusted him with a larger detachment and sent him back to Birch River to head off Confederate reinforcements. At Hughes Ferry, Hayes and two men, who were mounted and ahead of his troops, were attacked but not hit by "guerrillas concealed in rocks." Until the guerrillas were driven off, Hayes was in far greater danger than at Carnifex Ferry, and he knew that his mettle had been tested. "You need have no fear of my behaviour in fight," he assured Lucy, "I know somewhat of my capacity. It is all right."[37]

Hayes correctly gauged his own nerve in battle but underestimated the mettle of the enemy. "The truth is," he wrote to Lucy, "our enemy is very industrious and ingenious in contriving ambuscades and surprises and entrenchments but they lack pluck." And to Sardis he boasted that they "are no match for us in fair fighting. They feel it and so do our men." Letters and diaries left behind by Floyd's army at Carnifex Ferry, Hayes claimed, showed that the situation of the South was desperate and that thousands in its army were "heartily sick of the whole business." Those of the upper class were kindhearted, good-natured, and courageous but had "no endurance, enterprise, or energy," while those of the lower class were "cowardly, cunning, and lazy," with ambition only "to shoot a Yankee from some place of safety." Hayes thought that the rebels in western Virginia were without "heart enough to make a stiff battle."[38]

Hayes had enjoyed his independent command for only a few days when Rosecrans, on 19 September, appointed him judge advocate of the Army of Western Virginia. "It is," he told Lucy, "a laborious and painful business" that he hoped to "get out of . . . somehow." Hayes found, however, that the new assignment had some advantages. He hobnobbed with Generals Rosecrans, Jacob D. Cox, and Robert C. Schenck and with Donn Piatt, a journalist who was on Schenck's staff. It was pleasant to "go with the generals on all reconnaissances, see all that is to be seen, and fare as well as anybody." He thought that he might see Lucy sooner than otherwise, and since he was now attached to headquarters, he could be in touch with her in an hour by telegraph. He had a clerk to help with his paperwork, a talented orderly who had been a sailor, a hostler, and a cook to take care of his routine needs, plus "an escort of cavalry and a couple of wagons with tents and grub" when on "an extensive tour of court-martial." Hayes also was the most independent officer he knew, since as a staff officer he was excused from duty as major of the Twenty-third, but as an officer of the Twenty-third he was "free to come and go" as he pleased.[39]

By early October, it was clear that the campaign in western Virginia was winding down. Rosecrans began to march his troops back from their advanced position up the Gauley River on Mount Sewell to more suitable winter quarters at Mountain Cove, Gauley Bridge, and Summersville. For the sick, the move in "road-wagons in rain and mud" was severe; Hayes was all pity, while Dr. Joe was "up to his eyes in hard work." Since only a skeleton force would be needed to hold the new positions, Hayes hoped that he and the Twenty-third (a "capital" regiment) would be ordered to Kentucky, where they could see some action. Through Will Platt, he tried to influence Governor Dennison to effect a transfer, but to no avail.[40]

Hayes tried to cheer up Lucy, who was expecting another child in December and was discouraged with the progress and condition of the Union armies. Her courage was not helped by Sardis, who anticipated that she and the children would be driven out of Cincinnati by the war and was rushing to get the new house in Fremont ready for them. "Don't worry about the war," Hayes counseled, reminding her that they were doing their best and predicting that they would "get through with it safely." Hayes, however, did con-

cede on 7 October that the "South may not be conquered, but we shall secure to the Nation the best part of it." Eleven days later, he was feeling more
optimistic. "For a first campaign by a green people, we have done well. The
Rebellion," he predicted, "will be crushed even at this rate by the time our
three years are up."[41]

Fearing that Lucy was "among croakers and grumblers, people who do
more mischief than avowed enemies to the country," Hayes wrote again the
next day. He told her not to worry about "suffering soldiers" and not "to
give up [on] President Lincoln," who, though "not all that we could wish,"
was "honest, patriotic, cool-headed, and safe." Realizing that his family admired Frémont (Sardis—thoroughly radicalized by the war—wanted the
government "to take Fremonts plan & declair the Slaves of the Rebels free"),
Hayes emphasized that he preferred neither him nor anyone else to Lincoln.
Furthermore, Hayes believed that, despite poor transportation, bad roads,
faithless contractors, and negligent or fraudulent officials, *"our army is better fed, better clad, and better sheltered than any other army in the world."*
He told Lucy to save her sympathy for "the poor families at home," especially "the poor women and children of Cincinnati." Upon reflection, Hayes
still thought that the tales of neglect were exaggerated, but he admitted that
some soldiers were in need and that their suffering would increase in the
coming winter. Nevertheless, he argued that responsibility was widely
shared and that the chief culprits were in the army, from generals on down
to privates. He asked Lucy and Sardis to encourage sewing societies to send
the army warm clothing, particularly blankets, since the government allow-
ance was inadequate for soldiers in the Virginia mountains.[42]

With campaigning virtually over until spring, Hayes reflected on his half
year's experience. He no longer considered a West Point education "requisite
for this business" and believed that "good sense and energy are the qualities
required." Some of his superiors, Hayes believed, lacked these qualities. He
exclaimed that one "blunder" was "Stupid! Stupid!"; and a proposed "folly"
led him to ask, "Why don't these generals have common sense?" Scammon,
who was genial but absentminded, neglected his duty while talking by the
hour "of West Point, of General Scott, of genteel and aristocratic people." If
Scammon had known something about "men and rough life," he would have
gotten on better with the regiment. Although Hayes believed that "accident
largely" determined the outcome of battles, he did not despair, because Union soldiers excelled in the "steady work, such as finally determines all great
wars." Ambuscades might delay but would not prevent "success if our
people at home will pay the taxes and not tire of it."[43]

Hayes had gained confidence in his own military capacity. On 2 November, he learned of his promotion to lieutenant colonel of the Twenty-third, was relieved of his duties as judge advocate, and, after all his months of service, was finally paid (although only up to 31 August). Although he had been sorry to lose a talented, "witty, cheerful, and intelligent" companion when Matthews left to command a new regiment, Hayes welcomed his own promotion, confessing that he was "prejudiced" against the title "Major," not only because doctors were majors but also because his old partner Corwine was one. Despite having two months' back pay still due him, Hayes was able to send Lucy $700. To provide "a fair start" for his family, he had been frugal in his expenditures. Hayes realized that his new position entailed more than usual responsibilities. "I must learn all the duties of colonel, see that Colonel Scammon does not forget or omit anything."[44]

The last move in the fall campaign was also instructive for Hayes. On 13 November, the Third Brigade of Rosecrans's army (of which the Twenty-third was a part) crossed the New River in pursuit of Floyd's men. Despite hard marching (even at night) and camping for five days without tents in mud, rain, and snow, they failed to catch Floyd, who ran "like a quarter-horse." Hayes learned from this experience that night marches did not pay, that men marched further from dawn to dusk and were less tired than when aroused at midnight and forced to march until the next night.[45]

Ordered to the beautiful village of Fayetteville, Hayes and the Twenty-third went into winter quarters, where Hayes discovered that he could cope with hardships better than he could manage luxurious living. Two days after visiting Rosecrans's headquarters on 22 November, he began "to pay for 'pickled oysters and mixed drinks.'" After suffering several days from diarrhea, he "took opium powders" and recovered, only to relapse from apples or "perhaps too much fresh meat." Hayes had reason to be careful. In early November, about 250 men (or almost a third of the regiment) were sick; approximately a hundred of these had typhoid fever, and five of them died. Among them were the "industrious, faithful" Captain Woodward of Cleveland and "Bony" Seaman, a "noble, true" soldier from Logan County, who reminded Hayes of Birch.[46]

War and death were on his mind when Hayes thought of the Cincinnati Literary Club on its twelfth anniversary. He was proud of the roles its members were playing in the war, from Salmon P. Chase, "the power (brain and soul) of the Administration," and Gen. John Pope on down to people like himself. Witnessing death around him, Hayes wondered what happens after "we fret our little hour, are happy and pass away." Although "an unbeliever," he imagined that he would drift toward Christianity in his "closing years on the down-hill side of life." But, for the present, the war had become a crusade for Hayes and fighting in it his religion. "My belief in this war," he affirmed, "is as deep as any faith can be."[47]

EIGHT

WAR IN EARNEST

With Colonel Scammon in charge of all troops wintering at Fayetteville in western Virginia, Lieutenant Colonel Hayes commanded the Twenty-third. After the secessionists fled, the officers were comfortably housed in the village, with its "pretty gardens, fruit, flowers, and pleasant homes," while they drilled the men and supervised the preparation of their quarters and the building of two small forts. Supplies came by wagon and pack mule "over a road remarkable for the beauty and sublimity of its scenery, the depth of its mud," and precipices so "dizzy," Hayes told his niece Laura, that when the lead horse of a bread wagon "hawed when he ought to have geed," it left the road, fell seventy feet, and landed in the top of a ninety-foot tree.[1]

With time on his hands, Hayes resolved to improve the regiment and himself with "regular lessons and drills." He read Henry Halleck's *Elements of Military Art and Science* and thought it "goodish" and asked Lucy to send two or three additional "good reading" military books. At the first meeting of regimental officers on 4 December, Hayes went over guard duty in the "Regulations" and thought that he and the others "learned something." On 7 December, he met with the sergeants to instruct them. Along with the lessons, drills, and parades, the men worked steadily building the forts.[2]

With study and experience, Hayes became less critical of his superiors. After a "long confidential talk" with Scammon, Hayes realized that he was "best liked when best known." Although the men thought otherwise, Hayes believed that Scammon was a "warm-hearted, kindly gentleman" and resolved "to give them just ideas of him." A proposed "folly" (crossing the New River) that had caused Hayes to ask why the generals lacked "common sense" a month earlier now, upon reconnoitering and reconsideration, appeared as though it would have succeeded if it had not been prevented by sudden rising waters. "The bold enterprises" that he had thought reckless he now decided were "the successful ones."[3]

Problems relieved some of the tedium of camp life. A foolish country boy came into camp to sell a cartload of apples, pies, bread, and tobacco. He tried to get ten cents a dozen for the apples and twenty cents for each pie, but the soldiers, thinking the prices exorbitant, "got mad and robbed the apple cart in the streets." Ashamed of his men, Hayes gave the boy five dollars and persuaded another officer to do the same. More serious were morale problems stemming from promotions. Appointing a new major to succeed Hayes proved difficult. To the annoyance of Captain McIlrath of Company A (who was thought to be first in line), Scammon recommended Captain Drake of Company H; then Ohio's governor made everyone angry—particularly Drake—by appointing an outsider, James M. Comly. Hayes found Comly to be "diligent, gentlemanly," reasonable, and able, but after six weeks his appointment was still so resented that Capt. R. B. Moore advised Hayes "that he and most of the officers will resign." Scammon exacerbated matters by passing over all the lieutenants to make Sergeant Haven the captain of Company G.[4]

As Christmas approached, Hayes worried because Lucy was "looking for her troubles to be over soon." Feeling more secure if Dr. Joe were attending her, Hayes arranged for him to be at her side. Along with Lucy, Hayes hoped for a girl, but on 21 December she gave birth to another boy, whom she and her boys called Joe. Hayes was anxious for news about Lucy, the new boy, and "all the boys," but, with Lucy recovering, busy, and averse to writing, he heard first from Dr. Joe. All was well, and Hayes was amused that Birch was indignant that little Joe was not big enough to drill. With Scammon sick and other officers and Dr. Joe on leave, Hayes could not get away until February. He believed that leaves of absences were abused and was "a little embarrassed" that, with Lucy no longer needing his services, Dr. Joe was among the abusers. Hayes would not leave the regiment unless "plenty of officers" remained.[5]

While aching to get home, Hayes noticed in the Richmond *News* of 30 November that James D. Bulloch, a "whole-hearted, generous fellow" he had known at Webb's school, was now a captain in the Confederate navy and had recently run the blockade in the *Fingal*. Hayes did not realize that Bulloch had already arranged for the construction in England of Confederate commerce destroyers, of which the *Alabama* was the most famous. Hayes especially appreciated Bulloch's opinion—cited in the *News*—that the seizure, from the British vessel *Trent*, of Confederate agents James Mason and John Slidell by Union Capt. Charles Wilkes would not lead to war. "It will blow over," Hayes agreed. "First bluster and high words, then correspondence and diplomacy, finally peace." If war with England came, Hayes predicted, it would be "a severe and dreadful trial of our stuff. We shall suffer, but we will stand it. . . . We are in the right and must prevail."[6]

For Hayes, the war had already become a crusade against slavery. On Forefathers' or Pilgrim Day, 22 December 1861, he declared, "We are at the same high call here today—freedom, freedom for all. We all know that is the essence of this contest." With the new year, Hayes believed—as did everyone else in Rosecrans's army—that the runaway slaves of rebels ("contrabands") should not be returned to their masters, who had repudiated their rights under the fugitive slave law and the Constitution. But they reluctantly conceded that undoubted Union men were legally entitled to their runaway slaves. Hayes did not want Congress to meddle with slavery because the war, "in a way consistent with eternal principles of justice," was dealing it "death-blows" and it was perishing.[7]

Several contrabands remained with the Twenty-third, employed as cooks and servants; others went to Ohio. They avoided Cincinnati, however, where they might be recognized and sent back to slavery. Hayes employed "a bright fellow" named Daniel Husk, who had escaped by traveling a hundred miles through the mountains by night, and urged Sardis to employ or find work for a contraband couple whom Hayes had urged to settle in Fremont. "Faithful, intelligent, and industrious," Allen would make an ideal house servant, while his "neat and orderly wife" was a cook. Hayes found contrabands more intelligent than the "unenterprising, lazy, narrow, listless, and ignorant" poor whites of western Virginia. He blamed their sorry condition on slavery. Under it, one class is "well-bred, brave, high-spirited. The rest are serfs."[8]

In February, Hayes finally got leave. Since other officers had been gone as long as two months, Rosecrans annoyed him when he asked "if thirty days isn't too long for these times?" Resolving to obey orders "without demur," Hayes got twenty-eight days after all, with a three-day grace period. Fearing that General Schenck, whose return from a two-month leave was imminent, might object to his absence, Hayes hurriedly left Fayetteville on 1 February in "mud indescribable and unfathomable." Along with some fellow officers, he was accompanied by "Thomas, the gay, dramatic colored servant of Dr. Webb," who was helping the house servant of a Fayetteville resident to freedom by passing her off as his wife on the steamer down the Kanawha River. At Charleston, Hayes had "a good talk" with General Cox, whom he wished commanded "our brigade." At Gallipolis on the Ohio, he spent seven hours over "oysters, eggs, and ale" while waiting for a Cincinnati boat. He finally arrived home on 4 February "as the clock finished striking 12 midnight."[9]

The husband and father that Lucy and the boys joyously greeted had changed in appearance. Not having shaved since he had arrived in Virginia six months earlier, Hayes—like so many of his army fellows—had a full beard. Furthermore, the urbane lawyer, who before the war had lived comfortably in a warm, pleasant home, had grown stronger and healthier as a

Officers' mess in western Virginia in early 1862: Hayes, Dr. Joseph Webb, Old Gray (orderly), Carlos A. Sperry, Thomas (orderly), and M. P. Avery

soldier, despite sleeping "a half dozen times on the ground without shelter, once on the snow," and for weeks at a time in all his clothes.[10]

It was "perfectly splendid" to be home. After a week, Hayes visited Will Platt and his children and then went on to see Sophia, who was living with her cousin Arcena Wasson. "*Old* Delaware is gone," Hayes reported to Lucy, who was home with the boys, but "old times come up to me — Sister Fanny and I trudging down to the tanyard with our little basket after kindling. All strange; you are Sister Fanny to me now, dearest." Hayes then saw Sardis in Fremont and made arrangements for Lucy and the boys to move there for the duration of the war. On the way back to them in Cincinnati after a week's absence, Hayes heard of Ulysses S. Grant's victory at Fort Donelson (following his earlier success at Fort Henry). Observing the "crowds of happy people everywhere," Hayes noted that these victories convinced "everybody that the Rebellion can be conquered," but with his experience he did not expect "a sudden wind-up."[11]

Parting was difficult after their few weeks together following long months of separation. When Hayes returned to camp, he wrote, "I never loved you more than I do as I think of you on my late visit, and," realizing the work and anxiety his absence caused, "I never *admired* you so much." But his return to camp was another homecoming, with his men greeting him as warmly as his little boys had. A few days later, there was "real gloom" when his soldiers heard that he was to be named colonel of the Sixth Regiment of Ohio Volunteers. Hayes, however, did not wish to be separated from his men. "How I love the Twenty-third," he said. "I would rather command it as lieutenant-colonel than to command another regiment as colonel." To Lucy he bragged, "The men were never in finer condition. You would enjoy seeing the Twenty-third now; well dressed, bravely looking, and soldier-like."[12]

Hayes's enthusiasm for his command was matched by a more highly pitched, radical fervor for the war. He was encouraged in January when he heard the rumor that Secretary of War Simon Cameron (true) and Secretary of the Navy Gideon Welles (false) had resigned and hoped that they would be replaced by Edwin M. Stanton (realized) and Joseph Holt (unfulfilled). When McClellan was relieved as general-in-chief on 11 March (but left in command of the Army of the Potomac), Hayes was pleased, especially since Frémont, whom he admired, was named commander of the Mountain Department in which Hayes served. Hayes thought McClellan dilatory and did not like his views on slavery, but he expected to move rapidly under the command of Frémont, a man whose hostility to slavery was unquestioned.[13]

By the end of March, Hayes was "gradually drifting to the opinion that this Rebellion can only be crushed finally by either the execution of all the traitors or the abolition of slavery. Crushed, I mean, so as to remove all danger of its breaking out again in the future." Since the execution of all traitors was out of the question, Hayes advocated that the slaves of rebels be set free in "the disloyal States," but he would allow the loyal border state governments to "dispose of slavery in their own way." He predicted that abolition would come "if it is found that a stubborn and prolonged resistance is likely to be made in the cotton States." Hayes thought that Lincoln's recent efforts on behalf of gradual compensated emancipation indicated the administration's recognition that slavery would have to be abolished to suppress the rebellion. "I hope," Hayes concluded, "it is so."[14]

Hayes's humane nature, which caused him to drift toward a radical position on slavery and the pursuit of the war, kept him from being vindictive toward the rebels. When the sixteen-year-old son and namesake of Gen. Alfred Beckley was captured carrying dispatches, Hayes, not wanting "one so young packed into a crowded guardhouse," took him into his own quarters and paroled him two days later. When, within two months, General Beckley wished to surrender (because the Confederacy was giving up western Virginia and "his duty" was "to go with his home"), he did so through Hayes.[15]

Excessive spring rains delayed campaigning in early 1862. In early March, Hayes and the Twenty-third moved south from Fayetteville to Raleigh (Beckley) and were mired in its vicinity for about a month and a half. To "keep mirthful" despite the rain and mud, the men sang and played the fiddle and banjo. Hayes whiled away the time by listening to yarns, cracking jokes, and reading books such as Charles J. Lever's *Jack Hinton: The Guardsman*, while others played cards or drank whiskey if they could get it. Hayes was amused when on Easter Sunday Dr. John McCurdy, a Presbyterian, participated by proxy in a poker game and lost fifty cents and a knife, but he was angered one night when he found the sutler selling whiskey and "ordered two hundred bottles poured out." He told Lucy about neither the Easter Sunday poker game nor McCurdy's loss but imparted the more acceptable news that her brother Joe was "in the next tent with Major Comly and Dr. McCurdy singing sacred music." When alone, Hayes would get out his two pictures of Lucy and "have a quiet talk" with her, but he noted, "If we are resting I don't feel like writing; when going, of course I can't."[16]

By late April, Hayes and the Twenty-third moved further south. On 1 May, they marched twenty-two miles in mud and rain to capture Princeton, which the retreating rebels left burning. On the way there, the advance unit repelled an attack by a superior force of Confederates and the "Flat Top Copperheads," a notorious band of local bushwhackers. As Hayes rode up, the men, several of whom "were bloody with wounds," proudly "saluted with a 'present arms.'" He was so choked with emotion that he "could not speak, but a boy said: 'All right, Colonel, we know what you mean.'" On the march, Hayes had "kind words" for several badly wounded rebels but none for two "wealthy scoundrels" who had fled to Princeton with their slaves from Kanawha County after Union soldiers had arrived there. He planned to detain them until Scammon arrived and hoped that he would "put them in the guard-tent." With the Confederates fleeing and local militiamen "coming in glad to take the oath and get home 'to work crops,'" Hayes reported, "This whole region is completely conquered."[17]

Hayes wished to capitalize on the "*scare*" and advance eastward to the Narrows of the New River to capture considerable baggage, which, contrabands assured him, was but lightly defended. "*Do send* the order," he begged Scammon, and also urged him to expedite the arrival of their new long-range rifled muskets, which were sitting at Gauley Bridge. The Twenty-third's experience over "the last few days," Hayes observed, "satisfies everyone that a man who can kill at four hundred yards is worth three or four men with common muskets." Hayes sent three companies and some cavalry under Comly to the Narrows on the morning of 6 May. Finding nothing at that point, they pushed on to Giles Court House (Pearisburg), Virginia, where, behaving in a *"perfectly impudent"* fashion, they captured some prisoners and a large amount of stores, including 250 barrels of flour. Fearing that Comly and his 250 men would be captured, Scammon ordered Hayes and the rest of his command to Giles Court House, where they arrived on 7 May after a fatiguing march of twenty-eight miles through scenic country.[18]

Although at first Hayes assured Scammon "we are perfectly safe," he called for reinforcements because the captured property was *"very* valuable." Furthermore, much additional forage was available, but his force was not large enough to keep it from being spirited away in that land of "Secesh." Anticipating an attack, Hayes called more shrilly for help (particularly artillery) and thought it "a great outrage" and "shameful!" when he received no reinforcements. At 4 A.M. on 10 May, the Confederates attacked the Twenty-third with artillery and superior numbers (Hayes thought 3,000 strong) some three miles south of Pearisburg. Under fire, Hayes was pleased that his horse and "the men were standing it well." His "sole responsibility" made him "insensible to *personal* danger." With the enemy rapidly closing around them, the Twenty-third "behaved gloriously." Giving ground grudgingly, it was driven through the town (to the delight of the inhabitants) and five and a half miles further to the Narrows, "without breaking into confusion or a rout." There the Twenty-third held until Confederate artillery shelled it out of its strong position. The enemy pushed Hayes five miles further, but not through the Narrows.

Hayes's losses were slight: Two men were killed, six were missing (some drunk; others presumed prisoners), and ten were wounded, including Hayes, who "was scratched and torn on the knee by a shell or something." Although he claimed that his injury was not serious, twenty-five years later he acknowledged, "*I feel it yet.*" Hayes thought that his "well-ordered retreat . . . was creditable" and told Lucy, "never was a man prouder of his regiment than I of the Twenty-third." He also told her that the battle was "really jolly," with constant jokes, laughs, and cheers. "I certainly enjoyed . . . fighting our way out of Giles to the Narrows as much as any excitement I ever experienced."[19]

Hayes soon learned that there had not been enough Union troops in the area to reinforce him at Giles Court House. Indeed, Scammon's brigade (the Twenty-third was one of its three regiments) soon had to evacuate a strong position only eleven miles from Giles Court House because a "greatly superior force" had attacked Cox's army at Princeton, and he had sent an urgent call for reinforcements. Ordered to cover the hasty move to Princeton, the men of the Twenty-third were up at 3 A.M. on 17 May; they abandoned their blankets, mess furniture, and tents, which they "slit and tore," and, after a hard march, bivouacked on the ground at Princeton. Although Hayes was able to save his "personal baggage, tent included," he could not use it. To his dismay, he was ordered to retreat farther north.[20]

The troops moved off quietly before daybreak on Sunday morning and again were unmolested as they marched to the Bluestone River. On Monday, 19 May, they finally stopped retreating when, after "a hot dry march—with knapsacks," they arrived at Flat Top Mountain. In reviewing the ten days of falling back, Hayes realized that there had been some narrow escapes; on one occasion, his whole command would have been trapped if he had not had his mounted pickets two miles farther out than usual. Disappointed and angry that they were retreating so far, he was in a foul mood that Monday. He scolded officers who rested their men before rather than after fording a stream that had to be crossed single file and got "mad" at Colonel Scammon for halting the Twenty-third in the sun for half an hour with neither water nor explanation. Before the day was over, Hayes recovered his usual good humor and determined: "Must swear off . . . swearing."[21]

At Flat Top Mountain, Hayes felt "safe as a bug in a rug." He thought that the Confederates were too afraid to attack and that "*some* of us do fear them quite enough." Cox had probably erred in retreating rather than attacking at Princeton, Hayes commented, yet he realized that Cox was probably not strong enough to start offensive operations. The Twenty-third would remain at Flat Top Mountain for almost two months. The camp was twenty miles south of Raleigh and fifty to sixty miles to the rear of the Twenty-third's advanced position at Giles Court House. Flat Top Mountain, Hayes said, "is the boundary line between America and Dixie—between western Virginia, either loyal or subdued, and western Virginia, rebellious and unconquered."[22]

Watching and waiting at Flat Top Mountain was like being in winter quarters again. He read novels and discussed literature with Cox, "a reader of the best books." At division headquarters, Hayes, Cox, and other officers would "gossip over the news, foreign and domestic (all outside of our camps being foreign, the residue domestic)." Above all else, they looked for news of McClellan's progress up the peninsula toward Richmond and Henry Halleck's advance on Corinth, Mississippi. "All will be well," Hayes assured Lucy, "if we carry the pivots at Richmond and Corinth." Anticipating that they would be carried at any moment, he was disappointed when Beauregard slipped out of Halleck's grasp at Corinth and McClellan stalled before Richmond.[23]

Suspecting that McClellan's and Halleck's lack of zeal was rooted in their tolerant attitude toward slavery, Hayes found his fears confirmed by a letter to Cox from Gen. James A. Garfield. Garfield, who was with Halleck, had contempt for him and for West Pointers in general, whom he felt were pro-slavery and halfhearted warriors. Garfield "speaks of the want of sympathy among army officers with the cause of the war," Hayes reported, "that they say Seward, Chase, and Sumner are more to blame than Davis and Toombs! General [William T.] Sherman said he was 'ashamed to acknowledge that he had a brother (Senator John Sherman [of Ohio]) who was one of these damned Black Republicans!' " Convinced that proslavery thought was linked to the caution that paralyzed action, Hayes exclaimed: "These semi-traitors must be watched. . . . The man who thinks that the perpetuity of slavery is essential to the existence of the Union, is unfit to be trusted. The deadliest enemy the Union has is slavery—in fact, its only enemy."[24]

Hayes was frustrated by his "inglorious idleness." The arrival on Sunday, 1 June, of the Twenty-third's "new" weapons (almost a year after the near mutiny to secure them) relieved the tedium. Most of them were old, and many of them were used smoothbore muskets that had been rifled—grooved spirally to make them fire a spinning projectile, which increased accuracy—and "altered from flint-lock to percussion." At target practice that day, one shot in eight would have hit a man at two hundred yards, one in ten at four hundred yards (about a quarter of a mile), and only one in eighty at about seven hundred yards. Despite the rifling, the shooting was "not remarkably accurate," but Hayes thought that the powerful gun was an "excellent arm." Its ball passed through the largest wooden fence rails at four hundred yards and lost little of its impressive force and velocity at half a mile.[25]

When on 7 July warm weather finally came to Flat Top Mountain, the men built "great bowers over their company streets, giving them roomy and airy shelters" to use "in the bayonet exercise and manual of arms" and for recreation. A few days later, on the anniversary of sister Fanny's death, Hayes tried to cheer his mother with a description of their wholesome camp life. He assured her that they were so far from settled country that even the drunkards "regain the healthy complexion of temperate men" and told her that they spent their evenings dancing from a little after sundown until a little after nine o'clock. "Occasionally," Hayes elaborated to amuse Sophia, "the boys who play the female partners in the dances exercise their ingenuity in dressing to look as girlish as possible. In the absence of lady duds they use leaves, and the leaf-clad beauties often look very pretty and always odd enough." Obviously, Hayes detected no homoeroticism in this behavior.[26]

But diversions could not make Hayes content to sit out the war on a mountainside. Discouraged by news of McClellan's defeat in the Seven Days Campaign before Richmond, Hayes called for "courage and clear-headed sagacity. . . . Let slavery be destroyed and this sore disaster may yet do good." Hayes also hoped that "we shall be sent to eastern Virginia." After learning that McClellan had not been routed, that his army was in good condition, confident, not discouraged, and close enough to "forestall foreign intervention," Hayes tried to cheer up Lucy (who was spending the summer at Chillicothe with the boys and her Uncle Scott) by insisting, "Richmond is not so bad as it was. Our men, *certainly*, and our general, *perhaps*, did admirably there." Hayes again counseled Lucy not to worry about the country; even though things go wrong, if "we do our part . . . all will come right. We can't get rid of the crime of centuries without suffering."[27]

Hayes not only wanted to be in on the action at Richmond, he also wanted to be a full colonel. Although commanding a brigade, Scammon was still colonel of the Twenty-third, so Hayes wrote to Platt in an effort to get himself appointed colonel of a new regiment. Hayes hated to leave the Twenty-third and would not leave it if his promotion would lead to inaction. "But," he said, "I certainly wish the command of a regiment before the war closes." Hayes and most of the Twenty-third got a change of scenery on 13 July when they marched ("the happiest gang of men you ever saw") fourteen miles east and down the mountain to Camp Green Meadows, about three miles from the junction of the Bluestone and New rivers. Although the view was not as pretty as the one at Flat Top, it was more exciting. They were nearer the enemy.[28]

Suddenly Hayes's wishes started to come true. On 23 July, he heard that he had been appointed colonel of the Seventy-ninth Regiment, to be recruited from Hamilton, Warren, and Clinton counties in southwestern Ohio. He was in a quandary. When he looked "at the neat, hardy, healthy, contented young fellows" of the Twenty-third and thought of the "mob of raw recruits — dirty, sickly, lawless, and complaining," he thought himself a "great fool" to consider leaving. But he wanted a promotion. He knew that he would "never like another regiment so well" as the Twenty-third, and he would have preferred to stay with it as its colonel, in place of a promoted Scammon. But he also knew that "Scammon is so queer and crotchety that he is always doing something to push aside his chance for a brigadiership." Hoping that the rumors of Scammon's imminent promotion were true, Hayes postponed his decision, all the while aware that he would probably go to the new regiment.[29]

With the Confederates on the other side of the New River, Hayes found some excitement at Camp Green Meadows. In late July, he led a daring raid across the New River; on 6 August, when an alarming number of Confederates fired across the river on a detachment of men under Major Comly at Pack's Ferry, Hayes rushed in reinforcements, shouting to his soldiers, "Fighting battles is like courting the girls: those who make most pretension and are boldest usually win." Before Hayes's yelling troops arrived, accompanied by a blaring band, Comly had unwisely—to Hayes's thinking—destroyed the largest ferryboat. Whether the Confederates left "because they heard our band and reinforcements coming or because *they saw the major had done their work*" was problematical. Ironically, a bolt of lightning following the bloodless battle would have killed eight men had they not been instantly revived by dashing them with cold water.[30]

A couple of days after the Confederate attack on Pack's Ferry, Hayes secured reluctant permission to send 150 men twenty miles into enemy country to destroy the Mercer salt well. Situated in what was otherwise a saltless area, this productive well was needed by the Confederates to preserve meat. Arriving at 2:30 A.M. on Sunday, 10 August, the men of the Twenty-third found and destroyed a "good" pumping engine and two thirty-foot-long boiling pans. Subsequent threats of enemy attacks and secret orders to be prepared to move at half an hour's notice kept Hayes busy over the next few days. Nevertheless, he decided to join the Seventy-ninth (which had been almost filled by volunteers, without resorting to the draft) as soon as he could get a leave. Not only would he get the promotion, but he could see Lucy and the boys while training raw recruits. And he would "get out of these mountains before another winter."[31]

No sooner had Hayes decided to leave the Twenty-third than his literary club acquaintance Gen. John Pope ordered it and most of Cox's division to join him in eastern Virginia. McClellan was being withdrawn from the peninsula, enabling Lee to move his army and press Pope's Army of Virginia on the north bank of the Rappahannock. Hayes left Green Meadows on Friday, 15 August, made "long and rapid" marches four days to the head of navigation on the Kanawha River, went by steamboat down to the Ohio and up it to Parkersburg, and then by Baltimore & Ohio Railroad to the East. No longer eager to join his new regiment, Hayes was of one mind with the Twenty-third. "Our men are delighted with the change. They cheer and laugh, the band plays, and it is a real frolic. During the hot dusty marching, the idea that we were leaving the mountains of west Virginia kept them in good heart." Going up the Ohio, the water was so low that they had to disembark and march around the shoals with the "drums and fifes and band all piping their best." In Meigs County, the "men, women, and children turned out with apples, peaches, pies, melons, pickles . . . in the greatest profusion." The men of the Twenty-third were happy, "behaved like gentlemen, and marched beautifully. Wasn't I proud of them?" Hayes exclaimed.[32]

After ten days of marching and traveling by steam, they arrived at Washington on 25 August, where they remained for two days. There, Hayes found all arrangements connected with military matters "perfect." There were "fine hospitals, good police for arresting stray soldiers; a soldiers retreat, where all lost and sick are lodged and fed well, and a place where all were furnished with cooked rations to carry on marches." All in all, "Washington was a happiness to the Twenty-third." On 27 August, they crossed the Potomac; by 30 August, they had moved to Upton's Hill near Falls Church, where Hayes could hear heavy fighting to the west and southwest, which he correctly presumed to be at Bull Run. He anticipated getting into action and told Lucy that in case of accident, he and Joe would be reported at the Kirkwood House in Washington. He assured her that he felt "a presentiment" that they would not be hurt, but he wanted her to know, "I love you so much," and reminded her of an earlier farewell he had written from western Virginia. Although Scammon and some of his troops were involved on 27 August in a preliminary action at Bull Run Bridge (where he was, to Hayes's surprise, cool, steady, and skillful), Hayes and the Twenty-third missed the battle of Second Bull Run.[33]

On 2 September, Hayes, after sifting through scraps of news, concluded that Pope's army had been defeated but not crushed at Second Bull Run by "superior generalship on the part of the Rebels." When the retreating army heard that McClellan had superseded Pope and was again in command of troops in Virginia and around Washington, "the cheering was hearty and spontaneous." With the numerous camps and the signal corps communicating from height to height by waving lights, Hayes found the scene that evening "wild and glorious." Expecting Upton's Hill to be the first place attacked should the rebels advance on Washington, Hayes slept in his boots and spurs with his horse saddled. He was glad to be with the Twenty-third and hoped to stay with it if Scammon, who had distinguished himself, ever got his elusive promotion.[34]

By the next evening, Hayes was "discouraged—more so than ever before"—by "the conduct of men, officers, generals and all, in the late battles near Bull Run. . . . The Eastern troops don't fight like the Western," he complained. Although he had no idea that Pope would blame his failure on Gen. Fitz John Porter for disobeying orders and on McClellan for delaying vital reinforcements, Hayes sensed that "generalship is our great need." The veterans he spoke with agreed, but they blamed the defeat on Pope and Gen. Irvin McDowell (whom they supposed could have crushed Stonewall Jackson), not on Porter or McClellan. Disappointed by the failures of antislavery generals such as Frémont, McDowell, and especially the *"perfectly sound"* Pope, Hayes reluctantly decided that McClellan was the "only man who can get good fighting out of the Potomac Army."[35]

Observing and listening, Hayes sized up the military situation in the East: The rebels were superior in generalship and officers, cavalry, and infantry (although Union troops from the West were the best of both armies) and, despite the preponderance of Union cannon, were its equal in good artillery. "The result," Hayes concluded, "is we must conquer in land warfare by superior numbers." Although Hayes disparaged the troops from the East that largely made up the Army of the Potomac, he admitted, "There is nothing of the defeated or disheartened among the men. They are vexed and angry—say they ought to have had a great victory, but not at all demoralized." For the moment, the Confederates were assuming the offensive in Kentucky and Maryland, but Hayes realized that they would have to be more successful than they had been at Second Bull Run to win the war. He predicted that "these attempts to carry the war into our territory must recoil heavily on the Rebels," that they would fail "to hold their advanced conquests," and that "they must go back vastly weakened and disheartened."[36]

With the Confederates under Lee crossing the Potomac into Maryland, Cox's six Ohio regiments were pulled out of Virginia on 6 September and assigned to Gen. Jesse L. Reno's corps of Ambrose E. Burnside's army. Since Burnside had a good reputation, Hayes was glad to serve under him. Some of McDowell's "demoralized" men took over the fieldworks at Upton's Hill, while Hayes and his men endured "dust, heat, and thirst" on a two-day march through Georgetown to near Leesboro, some twelve to fifteen miles from the outskirts of Washington, on the road to Frederick. Although he was proud of Cox's division, Hayes was appalled by the "confusion and disorder" among thousands of straggling men in the Army of the Potomac, whose officers left their commands "to rest in the shade" and "to feed on fruit."[37]

Halting after a second day's hard march, the men of the Twenty-third took unthreshed wheat from nearby stacks to feed horses and to lie upon, since they were camping on a stubble field with ridges of hard ground. When Major General Reno, the commander of their corps, saw what they were doing, he flew into "a towering passion," roaring "you damned black sons of bitches," and demanded to see their colonel. Hayes stepped forward, assumed responsibility, and respectfully defended his men, saying that they had always made campfires with fence rails, for example, and that they would pay for what they took. Reno denied both the necessity of helping themselves and their right to do so, emphasizing that they were in Maryland, a loyal state. But as Reno began to find his temper, Hayes began to lose his respect. When Reno asked Hayes his name, he impertinently asked Reno his name, and when Reno lectured him on the evil of pilfering, Hayes remarked, "Well, I trust our generals will exhibit the same energy in dealing with our foes that they do in the treatment of their friends." Reaching for his pistol but not drawing it (while bystanders also handled their arms), Reno demanded to know what Hayes meant by his remark. Realizing that he had gone too far, especially since he had a high opinion of Reno's "gallantry and skill," Hayes replied, "Nothing—at least, I mean nothing disrespectful to you." Still enraged, Reno rode off and was made even more apoplectic by the cheers sounding behind him for the lieutenant colonel of the Twenty-third.[38]

Neither Reno nor the men from Ohio could get the episode out of their minds that evening. Reno talked of putting Hayes in irons, and Reno's abusive language had so offended the Ohio troops that Cox (who told Hayes that he had behaved properly) wanted to get his division transferred. Cox feared that the men would be reluctant to fight under Reno's command. Hayes was "sorry the thing goes so far," tried not to exaggerate the altercation (he made it clear that others, not he, had observed the hands moving toward weapons), and regretted that Reno was bitter against him. Hayes, however, put the affair in perspective and did not worry excessively. "Well," said he, "it's all in a lifetime." He also had faith that, if Reno proved vindictive, "Governor Chase and the President will see justice done . . . to all our Ohio men."[39]

Hayes managed to put the encounter behind him, and apparently so did Reno. In any event, the angry altercation did not get Hayes into trouble, and Cox's division remained in Reno's corps—"always near the front, if not the front" of the Army of the Potomac—as it moved toward Frederick. The weather improved, and Hayes's men marched along in fine fettle. When asked who they were, they responded, "Twenty-third Utah, Twenty-third Bushwhackers, Twenty-third Mississippi, Drafted men, Raw Recruits, Paroled prisoners, Militia going home, Home Guards, Peace Men, Uncle Abe's children, The Lost Tribes," and other witticisms. Since most bands had been mustered out of service, the Twenty-third's band was a novelty and attracted children. Hayes told Lucy he could "see our boys running after the music in many a group of clean, bright-looking, excited little fellows."[40]

On 12 September, after a fourteen-mile march and "a good deal of skirmishing, cannon firing and uproar," but with little fighting, Cox's division retook Frederick, Maryland. Barbara Fritchie was not the only patriot in town. "There was no mistaking the Union feeling and joy of the people,"

"Our Regimental Band"

Hayes wrote to Lucy. "Fine ladies, pretty girls, and children were in all the doors and windows waving flags and clapping hands." Some of them did as Lucy did when excited and " 'jumped up and down' with happiness." Her brother Dr. Joe enjoyed it enormously and "rode up the streets bowing most gracefully." The men of the Twenty-third, so exhausted before the formal entry into the town that they could hardly get up, marched "erect and proud hurrahing the ladies!" Fooled by Stonewall Jackson, who had actually turned southwest, toward Harpers Ferry, the townspeople told the Union troops that the enemy, "in great force, filthy, lousy, and desperate," had headed northwest two days earlier "to ravage Pennsylvania." Hayes anticipated a "most terrific" battle and believed that, with "forty thousand Western troops to give life and heartiness to the fight, we should . . . whip them," but he did not think it a certainty.[41]

The next day, 13 September, Reno's corps moved west along the National Road to Middletown, where McClellan had decided to concentrate his army. He knew that Lee's army was poorly concentrated (it was actually in four segments) to the west of South Mountain but neglected to order Reno to continue marching that evening to occupy Turner's Gap in South Mountain. His procrastination proved costly when, on 14 September, he tried to force Turner's Gap. The terrain was difficult, with poor roads and trails, small clearings, and narrow valleys that tested troop leadership. To secure Turner's Gap, McClellan selected Reno's corps; Reno called on Cox's division to lead, Cox placed Scammon's brigade up front, and Scammon picked Hayes and the Twenty-third to spearhead the assault. Although it might appear that, after their altercation, Hayes was playing Uriah to Reno's King David, it was Scammon, not Reno, who gave Hayes the crucial and dangerous mission.[42]

Moving out at 7 A.M. on 14 September, Hayes and his men were ordered up a mountain path through Fox's Gap to get around the rebel right and take a battery of two guns thought to be posted there. Seeking clarification, Hayes asked Scammon, "If I find six guns and a strong support?" He was told, "Take them anyhow." It was, Hayes realized, "the only safe instruction." Up the hill they went, making contact with a rebel picket at 9 A.M. Soon after, when a strong force came down the hill toward Hayes, the Twenty-third formed a line "hastily in the woods" and "pushed through bushes and rocks over broken ground towards the enemy." Then they "received a heavy volley, wounding and killing some." Fearing confusion, Hayes "exhorted, swore, and threatened," but he admitted to himself, the "men did pretty well." Finding the position untenable, Hayes, with "his eyes shining like a cat's," ordered a charge and shouted: "Now boys, remember you are the Twenty-third, and give them hell. In these woods the Rebels don't know but we are ten thousand; and . . . we are as good as ten thousand, by God." As they "rushed forward with a yell," the "enemy gave way" until the Twenty-third "halted to reform" their line, when "heavy firing resumed." Fearing that his men "could not stand it," Hayes "again ordered a charge"; "the enemy broke," with the Twenty-third driving them "clear out of the woods." Halting "at a fence near the edge of the woods," Hayes and his men "kept up a brisk fire upon the enemy, who were sheltering themselves behind stone walls and fences near the top of the hill, beyond a cornfield in front" of Hayes's position.

Just as Hayes ordered another charge, he "felt a stunning blow." A musket ball had struck his left arm just above the elbow, fracturing but not splintering the bone, leaving a gaping hole, and bruising his ribs. "Fearing that an artery might be cut," he had a soldier tie his handkerchief above the wound and then rallied his men, since the charge had fizzled when his arm was hit. Feeling "weak, faint, and sick at the stomach," he laid down about twenty feet behind his men, who had advanced a short way into the cornfield. They discovered that the Confederates on the crest of the mountain were "a vastly superior force" that they could not dislodge without reinforcements. Hayes was "pretty comfortable" and had "a pretty accurate notion of the way the fight was going. The enemy's fire was occasionally very heavy," he remembered several days later, and "balls passed near my face and hit the ground all around me." Shortly after he lay down, Hayes, "seeing something going wrong and feeling a little easier," got up and began directing his men, but after a few moments he had to lie down again. He saw "wounded men staggering or carried to the rear," and although he was certain that the Twenty-third, now led by Comly, was holding its own, he strained "to hear the approach of reinforcements" and wondered why they did not come.

Despite his wound, Hayes gave occasional commands. When it appeared that the Confederates might flank the Twenty-third on its left, near where Hayes was lying, he called out to Captain Drake "to let his company wheel backward so as to face the threatened attack." Drake fell back about twenty yards to the edge of the woods and the rest of the line gradually followed, leaving Hayes between his troops and the enemy. Comly worked his way out to Hayes and learned that, although he had not wanted them all to fall back, Hayes now recognized that the men needed the cover of the woods, and, if Comly thought best, they should remain there. Pinned down by the fire of his own men as well as that of the Confederates, weakened by loss of blood, passing in and out of consciousness, Hayes could no longer observe or direct his men. Freed of that responsibility, he faced the reality that he might die. He thought of Lucy, the boys, and others in his family and was comforted by three letters he had received from Sardis that morning. Fortunately, there was a wounded Confederate soldier lying nearby with whom he had a "considerable talk" and to whom he gave messages for Lucy, family, and friends. Hayes had just urged his men to "give them hell," but now that he and a wounded enemy approached hell or heaven together, to Hayes's surprise they were "right jolly and friendly," and "it was by no means an unpleasant experience."

After fifteen or twenty minutes, the heavy firing ceased, and Hayes wondered whether the Confederates had disappeared or his own men had fallen back. "Hallo Twenty-third men," he called out, "are you going to leave your colonel here for the enemy?" Several of his men sprang forward to carry him back to their lines, but the Confederates opened fire and once again the battle raged. Hayes ordered his men back to cover, "telling them they would get me shot and themselves too." During the next lull, Lt. Ben W. Jackson did reach Hayes and brought him back to his men. There he was laid behind a big log and revived with a canteen of water. When the battle died down again, Jackson took Hayes to their field hospital, where Dr. Joe dressed the wound. Then Hayes walked about half a mile to Widow Kugler's house, where the wounded gathered to be transported to the rear by ambulance. While waiting for an ambulance, Hayes chatted with an officer from North Carolina or Georgia in a "pleasant, friendly way," with both remarking, "you came a good ways to fight us." In a couple of hours the ambulance came, and Hayes and Captain Skiles of his regiment, whose wound would cost him his arm, bounced for three and a half miles on a poor road to Middletown, Maryland, where a local merchant, Jacob Rudy, and his family took Hayes into their home. The morning after the battle, he dictated telegrams for Lucy, his brother-in-law Will Platt, and his friend John Herron, informing them of his wound.[43]

NINE

WESTERN VIRGINIA INTERLUDE

The Battle of South Mountain was a Union victory, and Hayes was proud of his regiment. After it held its advanced position for an hour, reinforcements arrived. Later the Twenty-third and the rest of Scammon's brigade took the crest of South Mountain on the Union left and did not give it up. It was a costly victory; 130 of Hayes's men were killed or wounded. The remainder of Reno's corps and part of Hooker's corps took the rest of the day to gain the mountain crest on the Union right, and General Reno was among the dead. Scammon's report praised Hayes for his gallantry and skill in leading his troops, and Cox's report praised the Twenty-third for overcoming the vigorous resistance of the enemy on the crest.[1]

Pride in his regiment and interest in the ongoing Antietam campaign helped offset the pain Hayes suffered from his fractured arm and bruised ribs. Although Hayes telegraphed Lucy, Platt, and Herron that he was "seriously wounded," Dr. Joe, who remained at Middletown in charge of a hospital, optimistically wrote Sardis that the wound was not dangerous and that Hayes would not lose his arm. He was "comfortably fixed" with the Rudys, nursed "with the greatest care" by his orderly, Harvey Carrington, and fed "sumptuously" by Mrs. Rudy and her daughters. Although Hayes got some sleep the night he was wounded, Ella Rudy recalled that he "suffered constantly and got little sleep for a week and longer." Nevertheless, he was cheerful and would not let the Rudy family take "any extra trouble . . . on his account," with one exception. He asked that boards be substituted for the cords under his mattress to level it. Propped up in bed the day after he was wounded, Hayes wrote Lucy's mother, who was with the boys, "to show you I am doing well" and quipped that he was with a family "named Rudy—not quite Ruddy." The next day, 16 September, he assured his mother that the "worst period of my wound is now over." He did not write Lucy because he assumed she was on her way to him.[2]

Despite his pain, Hayes focused his attention on the impending battle of Antietam. The Rudy house in Middletown was "flush up to" the National Road, and Charlie Rudy, who was eight or nine, sat by the window and described the scene for Hayes as the troops of the Army of the Potomac passed. All through the night, Hayes "could hear the men singing as they marched." On 17 September, he could hear the "heavy cannonading" of a great battle and paid Charlie and another boy a dollar each to describe the horsemen riding by, to give him an inkling of how the battle was going. Finally, Hayes learned that evening that the Battle of Antietam was "favorable, but not finally decisive," leading him to the conclusion that "the final struggle will occur soon." McClellan, however, did not press his advantage and allowed Lee to cross the Potomac into Virginia unhampered.[3]

Hayes improved gradually, but he looked for Lucy and talked about her more and more. Although he had his worst day on 19 September, Dr. Joe still predicted a "favorable result," and after a good sleep, Hayes was much better the next morning. He had hoped to see Lucy that day, but instead he got a dispatch from Platt that filled him with the fear that Lucy had no idea he was wounded. "This hurts me worse than the bullet did," he wrote in his diary. Hayes was partly right. For days, Lucy had not known he was wounded, and on the twentieth she did not know where he was.[4]

Lucy learned that Hayes was wounded on 18 September, when she received his second telegram: "I am here, come to me. I shall not lose my arm." It reached her near Chillicothe, where she had been staying with relatives, and it appeared to have originated in Washington. Lucy was outraged when she learned that Platt and Herron had received earlier telegrams but that she had not. Because the messenger had had only enough money for two telegrams, he had sent them to the two men rather than to her. She never completely forgave Platt or Herron for not inquiring about her plans after receiving their telegrams, which would have alerted her. Leaving the boys with her mother and other relatives and relying on them to secure a wet nurse for little Joe, Lucy caught a stagecoach for Columbus, where she met Platt, who insisted on accompanying her to Washington.

Arriving in Washington via Baltimore on Sunday, 21 September, Lucy and Platt went to the Kirkwood House, where Hayes had said that he would be in case of an accident. Lucy was stunned not to find him there. She and Platt systematically looked for him in the many military hospitals in the Washington area and could get no information from the surgeon general's office or from Secretary of the Treasury Chase. On Monday, Platt located a copy of the dispatch Lucy had received and found it had originated not in Washington but in Middletown, Maryland. Before leaving for Frederick (the train station nearest Middletown), Lucy went back to the hospital in the Patent Office building, hoping to secure specific information. Upon arriving, she saw "23" on the caps of some wounded soldiers lounging on the steps. Calling "Twenty-third Ohio?" to them, Lucy was relieved when they recognized her and were able to tell her where Hayes could be found in Middletown.

The crowded train that took Lucy and Platt to Frederick was the first one to reach there after the battle. Lucy stood most of the way, and when she finally got a seat it was next to a woman who feared that her husband, who had lost both legs, would be dead by the time she reached his side. Arriving at Frederick, Lucy was overjoyed to see her brother Joe, who for several nights running had driven there in anticipation of her arrival. When they got to the Rudy home late that Tuesday evening, Hayes quipped, "Well, you thought you would visit Washington and Baltimore," but he could not hide from Lucy that she had "found him very anxious." Too subdued to join in the banter, she simply told him she "was glad to see him." Later, after reading Oliver Wendell Holmes's article in the *Atlantic Monthly* describing the terrible time he had finding his wounded son after the Battle of Antietam, Lucy told Hayes to stop laughing at her for searching for him in Washington when he was at Middletown.[5]

After Lucy's arrival, Hayes improved steadily. But just when he thought the "rascally arm" was about well, he would "have a few hours of worse pain than ever." His chief annoyance was the "weariness from lying abed." Since Hayes did not require constant attention, Lucy visited the wounded daily and came back in tears. Then she and Hayes would "take a little refreshment and get over it." By his fortieth birthday on 4 October, Hayes was sufficiently strong to help Lucy hunt up the battlefield "graves of our gallant boys." The next day, he and Lucy left for home via Baltimore, Harrisburg, Cleveland, Fremont, and Columbus.[6]

Before leaving Middletown, Hayes attempted to straighten out his status in the army. At the time of South Mountain, he had been discharged from the Twenty-third to enable him to take command of the Seventy-ninth, and he had not been mustered back into the army as colonel of his new regiment. But with Scammon's promotion assured, Hayes declined the colonelcy of the Seventy-ninth and asked to have his discharge from the Twenty-third revoked. Cox, who hoped Hayes would soon be "in command of the gallant old Twenty-third," approved and forwarded the request to the War Department. On 15 October, Scammon was made brigadier general, enabling three officers and a commissary sergeant in the Twenty-third to move up a notch: Hayes became colonel; Comly became lieutenant colonel; McIlrath of Company A became major; and William McKinley, who had coolly delivered rations while under fire, was made a second lieutenant.[7]

Despite his slow-healing wound and the temptation of political advancement, Hayes resolved to remain in the army. While he was still in Middle-

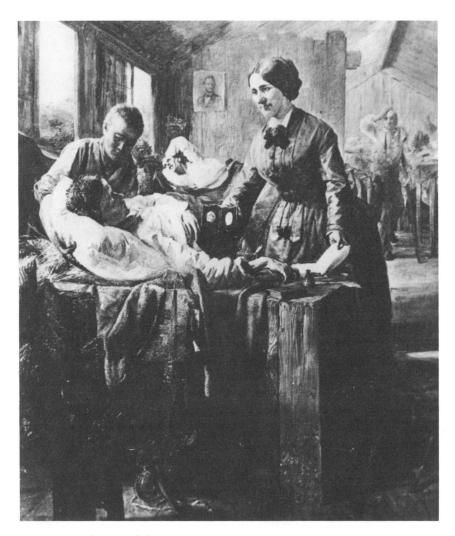

Lucy visiting the wounded

town, the Cincinnati *Commercial* had run a "card" proposing him for Congress and had followed up with an enthusiastic editorial on 1 October, extolling his career at the bar and in the war. It praised him as "a clearsighted, strong, honest man, with deep convictions, earnest purposes, and an unblemished record." Although Hayes's friends John Herron and Reuben H. Stephenson were ready to push his candidacy, Hayes discouraged them. Sardis told him that he had done his share and should stay home, but Hayes countered, "I have nothing to do." Fearful of losing his nephew, who was like a son to him, Sardis shot back, "You dont need to do anything." Still, Hayes felt compelled to continue in the Union army.[8]

Recuperating in October and November with his family in Ohio, Hayes was in a positive frame of mind. He attended the marriage of his niece Laura Platt to Col. John G. Mitchell ("a *capital fellow*," who was "taller than Laura and about as 'chunky'"). Even the Republicans' failure in the political campaign of 1862 did not dampen Hayes's spirits. He perceived that the setbacks invigorated the administration (it replaced the cautious McClellan with the bold Burnside), which more than compensated for "the defeat of a gang of *our* demagogues by the demagogues of the other side." Hayes also reasoned that with success, power, and responsibility, Democrats would be more "warlike."[9]

Getting back to the Twenty-third turned out to be more difficult than Hayes had anticipated. To the disgust of the men, the regiment had been ordered back to western Virginia and was stationed near Gauley Bridge. On Friday, 21 November, Hayes boarded the *Izetta*. When it immediately ran aground, he took the horsecar home and waited for the Ohio River to rise. He said good-bye to his family four times before the *Izetta* finally proceeded upstream on 26 November. When Hayes arrived at camp on the evening of 30 November, "It was like getting home after a long absence." First he greeted his men, then he opened the wine he had brought and had "a jovial festive meeting in" his "shanty of all the officers, twenty-four or twenty-five in number," where they "fought over South Mountain and Antietam, with many anecdotes, much laughter, and enjoyment."[10]

Fortunately for Hayes, it was time to go into winter quarters. He was not entirely well; his arm was weak, easily hurt, and could not be raised above his head. On Sunday, 14 December 1862, "a fine, warm Indian Summer day," Hayes and some companions "went up the mountains just above the falls on the right bank of [the] Kanawha to the rocks, like old ruins, on the summit." He had reason to remember that three months earlier, "on a similar Sunday," he had fought the battle of South Mountain, because, as he wrote in his diary, "My wound grew hot & painful clean through my arm with the severe exertion of climbing." He told Lucy that only one man had beaten him to the top, but he did not mention his pain.[11]

Attending "to the general interests of the regiment" kept Hayes busy. He asked Lieutenant Colonel Comly to drill and discipline the men and Major McIlrath to order supplies. He personally supervised the digging of sinks for sewage and the provisions of drainage in the camp, the making of sand walks, the clearing of a parade ground (a task he delegated to "handsome bright, gallant" William McKinley), and the building of a new log-cabin town to be called Camp Reynolds. The men, among whom were ingenious mechanics and resourceful thieves, were rapidly putting up the log cabins, although they had few nails, no tools, and little sawed lumber. "The knocking about among the men," Hayes wrote Lucy, "getting out lumber, building cabins, ditching and cleaning camp and sich, agrees with me spiritually and physically." He requested a sawmill or ten thousand feet of lumber, a window sash, nails, and a paymaster. He got the sawmill and the promise of a visiting paymaster by 10 January; the last one had been seen in August, when the regiment had been paid only to 30 June.[12]

Although the men were still working on their cabins, the approach of Christmas put all in a holiday mood. Dr. Joe, Comly, and McIlrath were able to go home, leaving Hayes the only field officer on duty. He got into the spirit of the season on Friday evening, 19 December, when he and his lieutenants shared an eggnog, mixed by the visiting father of one of them. After Christmas dinner, which was cooked by his orderly William T. Crump (with whom Hayes would have a long association) and shared with Lucy's four cousins, who were in Company D of the Eighty-ninth, Hayes held a shooting match and awarded a turkey and two bottles of wine to the three best marksmen. Eager to have Lucy and some of his boys visit, he tried to impress her with the amenities of their log-cabin camp life by assuring her that "dancing and merriment" prevailed on New Year's Eve. When Crump visited Cincinnati after Christmas, Hayes invited him to stay in their home and told Lucy, "If you are curious to know how we live, put him in the kitchen a day or two."[13]

As the village neared completion, Hayes indulged in his passion for reading. He devoured books, ranging from Eugene Sue's *Mysteries of Paris* to Adam Smith's *Wealth of Nations*, as well as magazines and newspapers, with their war news. Burnside's defeat at Fredericksburg was a cruel disappointment. Not only was "so much blood shed in vain," but Hayes feared that the loss might provoke foreign intervention and that Lincoln might abandon the policy of emancipation announced on 22 September. In his anguish, he queried, "When will our generals learn not to attack an equal adversary in fortified positions?" Again he concluded that partisanship was no test of generalship. It appeared to Hayes that in so equal a struggle neither eastern army could successfully invade the territory of the other. If the people would "cultivate patience" and "hold out," he was certain that "we shall find the right man after while."

Convinced that "desperate diseases require desperate remedies," Hayes thought the South could not be conquered until the North emancipated the slaves. "I was not in a hurry to wish such a policy adopted," Hayes admitted to Sardis, "but I don't now wish to see it abandoned." As Hayes contemplated the effect of emancipation, he was optimistic that with it "all will yet go well." On 1 January 1863, Lincoln proclaimed freedom for slaves behind Confederate lines. Hayes feared he had expected too much from the Emancipation Proclamation but was "glad it was issued." Two months later, he admitted that the "negro policy doesn't seem to accomplish much. A few negro troops give rise to disturbances where they come in contact with our men and do not as yet worry the enemy a great deal."[14]

Discouraging war news became easier for Hayes to bear after he learned that Lucy and their older boys Birch and Webb would visit him at Camp Reynolds. They arrived on 24 January and remained with him until 21 March. Despite his "open shake roof" that "let the snow through in clouds," Hayes knew they would very much enjoy the log-cabin life. "The boys are especially happy, running about where there is so much new to be seen," he reported. Fearless of the rebels with Hayes so near at hand, Lucy rode horseback four or five miles outside the lines. She also rowed and fished with her boys on the Kanawha. Using live minnows for bait, they caught salmon pike, weighing from three to ten pounds, and rowed soldiers across the "large roaring river."

"Dear boys," Hayes mused, "how I love them!" Webb, "mischievous but kind-hearted and affectionate," was the soldiers' favorite and, Hayes imagined, was like his own brother Lorenzo. "He is to be seen," Hayes wrote of Webb, "driving some soldier's team or riding whenever there is a chance." Birch, a bit older, "more scholarly and more commanding," enjoyed reading books such as *Boy Hunters and Voyageurs*. The boys also "built dams, sailed little ships, played cards, and enjoyed camp life generally." Hayes, who could see through a child's eyes, knew they would "never forget their visit to papa and the Twenty-third," but his mother, who found him and Lucy too indulgent as parents, was dismayed to hear that the boys' beloved Uncle Joe had taught them to play cards.[15]

On 15 March, Hayes and his command moved "out of the wilderness." With Lucy and the boys, he left the log-cabin camp and moved downstream to his new headquarters at Camp White, opposite Charleston, in western Virginia. But soon his family left for home—only fifteen hours away—on the steamboat *Allen Collier*. Since January, Hayes had commanded the First Brigade of the Second Kanawha Division. Although he described it as "rather a small affair," his command included the Twenty-third, the Fifth and Thirteenth Virginia, three companies of cavalry, and "a fine battery." Scattered from Gauley Bridge to the mouth of the Sandy River on the Kentucky border, some of the best and some of the poorest troops in service were under his command. His weak division tempted Confederate raiders; at the end of March, they cut Hayes off from "America" for four or five days before his men repulsed them, killing or capturing seventy men to Hayes's four killed and five wounded. In April and May, Hayes fortified Camp White, "partly to occupy time, partly to be safe." When not building and drilling, the men found time for "boating, ball-playing, and the like."[16]

With vigorous Union prosecution of the war, Hayes's optimism grew in the spring of 1863. Congress passed conscription, banking, and habeas corpus acts, giving "the Government great power and the country more confidence." War Democrats, such as John Van Buren, spoke out against the peace Democrats, whom Hayes thought of as rebel-sympathizing Copperheads and Butternuts. In the meantime, Grant was threatening Vicksburg, whose fall would mean Union control of the entire Mississippi; large sections of the South were occupied; Virginia's western counties had voted to enter the Union as West Virginia and would become a state on 31 December 1863; and the rebels were desperate for provisions. Even after Gen. Joseph Hooker's failure at Chancellorsville in early May, Hayes was willing to "stick" with him. Hadn't the Army of the Potomac under him fulfilled its mission by keeping the "largest and best Rebel army" employed?[17]

By mid-May, Hayes's area was quiet, and he encouraged Lucy to visit again before he was ordered "further out," which was anticipated as soon as Grant captured Vicksburg. Lucy, her mother, and all the boys arrived on 15 June "in good health" for what became a short, disastrous visit. The boys were delighted to be in camp, but after a "few happy days," little Joe, who was eighteen months old, sickened and died. "Teething, dysentery, and brain affected" were the "diseases" blamed for his death. "I have seen so little of him . . . that I do not realize a loss," Hayes confessed, "but his mother, and still more his grandmother, lose their little dear companion, and are very much afflicted." The next day, Hayes detailed a corporal to take little Joe's body to Cincinnati, where Lucy's brother James would bury it. As she watched the boat "bear the lonely little body away," Lucy endured "the bitterest hour" of her life. With her mother and remaining boys, she stayed another week before departing for Chillicothe. Realizing that Hayes, too, might die in the near future, she tried to mask her grief and make the visit pleasant. "Lucy has been cheerful since—remarkably so," Hayes noted on 1 July, "but on leaving today without him she burst into tears on seeing a little child on the boat."[18]

As Lucy and her family embarked on the *Marwood*, the Battle of Gettysburg was beginning. With Lee's invasion of Pennsylvania, Hayes dreaded the news on the one hand, because it seemed that in the Army of the Potomac somebody always behaved badly "at the vital point, where it is ruinous." On the other hand, Hayes expected the army, under its new commander George Gordon Meade, to do better "on our own soil" and counted on Lee's invasion "to prove his ruin" and "do much to unite us." After several days of suspense, news of the victory at Gettysburg sparked a joyous Fourth of July celebration at Camp White, with artillery salutes, "a good deal of drinking but," Hayes assured Lucy, "no harm," and the emptying of the guardhouse. Three days later, on the evening of 7 July, when news arrived that Grant had captured Vicksburg, Hayes and his men "fired one hundred guns and had a good time." Vastly encouraged by the victories and the patience and firmness of the people, he nevertheless realized that a great deal remained to be done.[19]

With the fall of Vicksburg, Hayes was ordered "further out." On 9 July, he went up the Kanawha River; by 11 July, he was at Camp Joe Webb (named for Lucy's brother) near Fayetteville, in western Virginia. From that point, Hayes was ordered to take and destroy rebel installations in Raleigh County. With his weak force, the risk was considerable, and since the objective was unimportant, Hayes did "not fully approve of the enterprise." Anticipating that he might die, yet not wishing to cause anxiety, Hayes wrote a farewell letter in his diary: "Dear boys, darling Lucy, and all, good-bye! We are all in the hands of Providence and need only be solicitous to do our duty here and leave the future to the Great Disposer." Hayes and his men reached Beckley (Raleigh) on 14 July and beyond it "found the enemy strongly fortified at Piney River." Since Hayes deemed a frontal assault unsafe and lacked the time to turn the position, he "resolved to leave without attempting to storm the works." The Confederates also had their qualms. "During the night," Hayes reported, they "kindly relieved us by running away!" Hayes's men quickly destroyed the works, and, rather than the disaster he had feared, the foray into "Dixie" turned out to be a "lively and pleasant raid."[20]

While Hayes was raiding Raleigh County, Confederate Gen. John Hunt Morgan, with over 2,000 cavalry, was raiding Ohio. Upon returning to Fayetteville on 16 July, Hayes learned that Morgan was threatening to destroy supplies and to cross the Ohio at Gallipolis, at the mouth of the Kanawha. Hayes then concocted a plan, to which Scammon reluctantly agreed. With the Twenty-third and the Thirteenth Virginia, Hayes marched overnight from Fayetteville to Loup Creek on the Kanawha, where his troops boarded two steamboats at dawn and arrived at Gallipolis on the morning of 18 July in time to confront Morgan, who was only five miles away. When Morgan decided to head upstream to cross the Ohio River at Pomeroy, Hayes and his men returned to their boats, steamed upriver, and arrived in Pomeroy on Sunday morning, 19 July, before Morgan, who came in force about noon. Skirmishing with Hayes's men informed Morgan that he was opposed by "regulars and not militia," and he "hurried off, with some loss." Had Hayes not been there, Morgan would have crossed the Ohio at Pomeroy and escaped south.

With Morgan heading by an overland shortcut to a river crossing at Buffington Island, Hayes and his men steamed upstream around the long bend of the Ohio River. Morgan got there first, but it was night, and a fortification blocked his path. The dawn brought Hayes and his men as well as Union cavalry under the command of Gen. Henry M. Judah, who had finally caught up with Morgan. Supported by gunboats and Hayes's infantry, the Union cavalry attacked, and Morgan's exhausted army collapsed. "Not much fighting by Rebels, but great confusion, loss of artillery, etc.," Hayes noted. "We got over two hundred prisoners. Everybody got some." Morgan, who had lost about 820 men, escaped with nearly 400, but he was captured a week later near the Ohio-Pennsylvania border. By then Hayes was back at Camp White, calling the pursuit of Morgan "the most successful and jolly little campaign we ever had."[21]

After chasing Morgan, Hayes suspected that he would remain at Charleston for a while. His troops were within striking distance of the Virginia & Tennessee Railroad, and the Confederates had strengthened their posts to protect it. In view of that buildup, Hayes thought that Union forces in the area would be augmented rather than withdrawn. Apart from planning some raids and going on others, he was not overly busy. "I ride about," he wrote Lucy on a hot 15 August, "read novels, newspapers, and military books, and sleep."

With time on his hands, Lucy filled Hayes's thoughts. Grief over their baby's death seemed to activate her feelings of low self-esteem. She feared she was not as good a Christian as her friend Eliza Davis nor as "gentle in her manners" as Comly's bride, who had joined her husband in camp. Hayes strove to assure Lucy of her worth. "Your moralizing on your want of dignity . . . doesn't disturb me," he reassured her. "You'll do for your husband, and I love you so much, darling. Be cheerful and happy." To Lucy's queries about Libby Smith Comly, of whom Lucy claimed to be "not . . . at all jealous," Hayes responded, "She is affable and approachable, but . . . she can't make friends as you do. Your gifts are rare enough in that line."[22]

In late August, Hayes was cheered by "the movements of Rosecrans on Chattanooga, Burnside towards Cumberland Gap," Quincy Adams Gillmore at Charleston, South Carolina, and the resultant "despondency in

Dixie." Hayes allowed himself to dream that if they "are reasonably success-ful, the Rebellion will be nearer its end by the middle of October than I have anticipated." On the evening of 21 September, his hopes were again dashed by news that his friend Rosecrans, whom he considered the best Union gen-eral, had been badly beaten at Chickamauga. With relatives and friends in that vanquished "noble Army of the Cumberland," Hayes anguished, "How these blows strike my heart!" He realized he had to nerve himself, and, after thinking it over and analyzing his reaction, he felt easier. Yet he marveled at the depth of his commitment to the cause of Union and freedom. "I suffer from these blows more than I did from the loss of my sweet little boy. But I suffer less now than I did from Bull Run, or even Fredericksburg. Can Rose-crans hold Chattanooga? Has he lost his army? Will he be driven across the Tennessee?" Hayes's optimism that the end of the war could be near van-ished. Nine days later, while encouraging but not urging the men of the Twenty-third to reenlist, he predicted accurately that, barring foreign inter-vention, the war would end shortly after the presidential inauguration, or about June 1865.[23]

Even though Rosecrans held on to Chattanooga, the reverses in that area kept Hayes stationed at Charleston, in western Virginia, and enabled Lucy to be with him for extended periods. Before Chickamauga, he again urged her to visit because he might be "ordered forward." She arrived at Gallipolis, without the boys, two days after the news of Chickamauga. She enjoyed camp life but missed her children. Birch, who was almost ten, was with Sar-dis in Fremont; seven-year-old Webb and five-year-old Rud were with Lucy's mother at the home of Moses and Margaret Boggs near Circleville, Ohio. Like her husband, Lucy was fond of young William McKinley, who so avidly attended the campfire when she was near it that she called him "Casa-bianca" when chatting with the officers' wives who formed her "pleasant little circle." On 21 October, since it appeared that Hayes's command would not be moved for a while, Lucy went to Ohio to "fix up matters, gather the chickens, and return . . . if all things look well, for the winter."[24]

Shortly before Lucy left, political news from Ohio heartened Hayes. On 13 October, election day, he "went to bed like a Christian at 9 P.M.," but an ex-cited McKinley awakened him at 11 P.M. with the news of a Republican tri-umph. Although "a few traitors" not under his command had voted for Clement L. Vallandigham, the Democratic gubernatorial candidate, Hayes's entire brigade had voted for John Brough, the Republican. With a secret bal-lot unheard of at that time, peer pressure on voters, particularly in the army, was enormous. Hayes pronounced Brough's huge majority of 40,000 or

50,000 votes "equal to a triumph of arms in an important battle. It shows persistent determination, willingness to pay taxes, to wait, to be patient."[25]

Hayes had a cheering autumn and winter. With Grant in command of the western armies, Chattanooga was saved, and the Union again seized the offensive. When Grant was ordered to the East, William T. Sherman was left in command of the West. The job of Hayes's brigade was to prevent nearby rebels from sending reinforcements elsewhere. Raids to harass them proved exhausting. Although Hayes's men were virtually unopposed in early December while raiding Lewisburg, in western Virginia, they returned wet, tired, and shouting, "Show me the damned fool who will reenlist."[26]

With the bitterly cold weather of the new year, the Kanawha froze, and only the cavalry remained intermittently active. Hayes was comfortable and content in his cozy winter quarters—"two tents together on a stockade, making two good little rooms with a coal stove." He was even prouder of the Twenty-third when three hundred of its men, damn fools or not, reenlisted— getting both a bounty and a furlough—making it the first Ohio regiment to enlist as veterans. Hayes was flattered when friends asked if they could push for his promotion to brigadier general. Although the promotion would remove the risk of serving under a "stupid brigadier," Hayes understood that, in an army of volunteers, colonels played a crucial role, mediating between democratic, egalitarian, undisciplined enlisted men and West Point–trained, professional soldiers. "A good colonel makes a good regiment" was an axiom with which he agreed. For the present he "would rather be one of the *good* colonels than one of the *poor* generals."[27]

Lucy, her mother, Webb, and Rud had joined Hayes on 21 November and stayed for most of the winter, while Birch remained with Sardis. In mid-February, when Hayes finally received his furlough, he and Lucy left Webb and Rud in her mother's care and toured Ohio for approximately a month, meeting and liking Sarah Follett Platt, Will's new wife, at Columbus and picking up Birch at Fremont. Upon getting back to Camp White, Hayes exclaimed, "Home again with Lucy and all the boys—well and happy." The boys were delighted to be together again. Although their schooling was irregular that year, they received some instruction at Camp White. While Lucy tutored Birch and a young soldier, Emma H. Ellen, the wife of Hayes's quartermaster, taught Webb and Rud. Like Birch, Rud took "to larnin," but Webb hated books and was "a little backward." Having brought her sewing machine from Cincinnati, Lucy made blue uniforms for her boys. She also earned the eternal gratitude and devotion of the enlisted men by looking after them when they were ill and mothering them in general.[28]

Upon his return, Hayes started preparing for the spring and summer campaigns. With Grant the commander of all Union armies and in immediate command in the East, Hayes knew that his troops would be involved in "severe fighting." It had been difficult to drill and discipline his men, scattered as they were in ten to twelve locations, but by the end of April, his brigade had been pulled together and beefed up to four regiments. Sprinkled among the raw recruits, who needed more training, were "some of the best men in service." Hayes had faith in his men and in himself, and he had confidence in the "skill and good judgment" of his immediate commander, Gen. George Crook.[29]

Campaigning began on 29 April 1864, with Crook's Army of West Virginia marching up the Kanawha. To keep pace with the marching soldiers, whom Birch and Webb—in their uniforms—had joined, Lucy and other army wives chartered a small steamboat. At the head of navigation, Hayes put his boys on board, hastily said good-bye, and watched the boat head downstream, with Lucy standing aft and waving encouragingly. While Hayes was off on an adventure, Lucy was anxiety ridden as she and her children journeyed home. Years later, when he reread the letters she had written during those years, Hayes became fully aware that "every horror of the awful time struck sledge-hammer blows on her very heart." Three days after their parting, Hayes wrote Lucy that her visit had been "the greatest . . . happiness" to him. "I carry with me," he said, "the pleasantest recollections of you dear ones." Again, he said good-bye for what might have been the last time.[30]

THE VALLEYS OF VIRGINIA

George Crook did not disappoint Hayes. Crook's objective in May 1864 was to cut communications between Richmond and the Southwest by destroying the Virginia & Tennessee Railroad bridge over the New River and the track toward Staunton. While Crook aimed at Dublin, Virginia, with his infantry, he ordered his cavalry under Gen. William W. Averell to raid Saltville (to destroy the salt works) and Wytheville, to the southwest on the same railroad. Moving out from Camp White, Crook shrewdly sent a regiment with loud-playing musicians east toward Richmond (by way of Lewisburg and White Sulphur Springs), while his army headed south toward Princeton, West Virginia. Marching in cold rain to Fayetteville and camping in wet snow on 2 May was, as Hayes noted, "a rough opening of our campaign," but by 4 May the army was enjoying "fine, bright weather." Maintaining control over his men, Crook regulated halts and ordered "no rails to be burned" for campfires. Reminded of his clash with Reno, Hayes recorded that some men grumbled, but he did his best to carry out the order. Although the Confederates had blocked the road with trees near Flat Top, thirty or forty axmen quickly chopped them away, and the army was not delayed.[1]

The ruse worked. Arriving at Princeton on 6 May, Crook discovered that the Confederates had left their fortifications and baggage to hurry sixty or seventy miles to Lewisburg to confront him. Were it not for the deception, the substantial entrenchments at Princeton would have delayed Crook. Over the next two days, his army covered forty-four miles, entering Virginia through Rocky Gap and moving on to Poplar Hill. By this time, the Confederates, led by Gen. Albert Gallatin Jenkins (a Democratic congressman before the war), had discovered the ruse and fortified a strong position on Cloyd's Mountain, commanding the road running between Poplar Hill and Dublin Depot.[2]

On the morning of 9 May, Crook's army reached Cloyd's Mountain, and the Confederates greeted it with cannon fire. Discovering that his foes were strongly fortified, Crook ordered Carr B. White's Second Brigade to flank them and Hayes's First Brigade to assault their position frontally. Hayes formed a line at the edge of the woods with the Twenty-third in the lead, followed by the Thirty-sixth Ohio. At the sound of White's guns, Crook, Hayes, and his men charged four hundred yards under heavy fire "on a slow double quick" march across a meadow and through a creek to the base of the steep, wooded hill occupied by the rebel breastworks. Out of the line of fire because of the curve of the hill, they paused to reform their line and catch their breath, and for Crook to shake water out of his boots.

"And then," Hayes recalled, they "charged up the hill, and the moment we passed the curve as fearful a fire met us as I ever faced, a dreadful fire, that killed men and officers terribly. It seemed as if the whole line was falling." But the men made it to the top of the hill and shocked the Confederates by climbing over their fence-rail defenses and attacking them simultaneously from the front and behind. It was a "very desperate . . . rough and tumble fight" lasting only ten minutes, with the Union capturing the cannon. Crook fainted from overexertion, and while his staff revived him, some of his men bayoneted surrendering Confederates before Union officers could stop them.

Hayes instinctively realized that the Union should take advantage of the Confederate rout. With about five hundred men, he "pushed on very rapidly" to a second Confederate line formed by arriving reinforcements commanded by John H. Morgan (Hayes had pursued him in Ohio a year earlier, and he had subsequently escaped from a Union prison). Morgan's men had just repulsed Averell at Wytheville and were coming to support Jenkins. Urging his few men to "yell like devils," Hayes audaciously charged again. Although his troops resembled "a scattered mob," they broke the Confederate line in a "very hot fight" lasting five minutes.

At Cloyd's Mountain, the Federals captured five pieces of artillery and three hundred men and killed and wounded at least as many, including General Jenkins, who was mortally wounded. Hayes estimated the killed and wounded in his brigade at 250; the Twenty-third lost 123. There were 688 Union casualties altogether. Hayes was enormously proud of the Twenty-third, which was "*the* regiment," although he admitted that the Thirty-sixth Ohio would have done as well if it had led. But he had contempt for the Pennsylvania troops of the Potomac Brigade, who "broke and fled."[3]

Having destroyed much of Jenkins's army, Crook struck the railroad at Dublin Depot that evening. There, the Union army found and burned many stores, including "a great quantity of shoes with thick wooden soles," and "at once commenced destroying the railroad." The men tore off the iron rails, heated them on burning ties, and rendered them useless by bending them out of shape. The next day, the remnants of Jenkins's army tried to protect the railroad bridge over the New River, primarily with cannon, but after a two- or three-hour artillery duel, Crook's men burned the bridge. To protect the men setting the fire, Hayes took a detachment to the river's edge and ordered it to take cover, but a member of the Fifth West Virginia Cavalry (who had dismounted) refused to obey as long as Hayes was exposed. Just as Hayes insisted that he be obeyed, an exploding shell fatally wounded the soldier; the men administering first aid were shocked to discover that "he" was a woman. While she died on the riverbank, the victory celebration began. With flags flying, the band of the Twenty-third playing, and soldiers hurrahing, the army watched the spectacle of the burning bridge from the beautiful heights of the New River. It took the Confederates six weeks to get the Virginia & Tennessee Railroad back in operation.[4]

Although he had not achieved all his objectives, Crook concentrated on extricating his command from a hostile country. Grant had wanted him to continue northeast, destroying the railroad and linking up with Gen. Franz Sigel near Staunton for a drive on Lynchburg. But Crook had heard nothing from Sigel (who would be defeated in a few days at New Market) and nothing from Averell (who had failed at Saltville and Wytheville but had destroyed the railroad as far as Christiansburg). In addition, Crook had heard, erroneously, that Lee had defeated Grant in the Wilderness, and he anticipated that Lee would send troops after him. He was separated from his base by 140 miles of bad roads and was short of ammunition and rations. In his train, he had two hundred wounded (150 of the seriously wounded had been left behind), three hundred Confederate prisoners, and between one hundred and two hundred former slaves freed by the Emancipation Proclamation. Crook did not turn away these African Americans, even though they slowed his army and helped consume its dwindling food supplies. Some of them had wagons, but most of them were on foot, carrying their children and a few belongings on their trek to freedom. On 11 May, Crook started back to West Virginia.[5]

The march was difficult. The watching Confederates under Gen. William L. (Mudwall) Jackson were powerless to do anything, but the rain was fierce. Not an advocate of a scorched earth policy, Hayes kept close control of his brigade in the land of the enemy. "I protect all the property in my vicinity. I take food and forage and burn rails, but all pillaging and plundering my brigade is clear from." His contempt for the Pennsylvania troops was confirmed by their "infamous and universal plundering." Continuing rain on 12 May made the muddy uphill road horrible, and Hayes, who was responsible for the wagon train, tried to "force it along." He was particularly affected by "the train of contrabands, old and young, male and female . . . toiling uncomplainingly along after and with the army." After one of the worst days of his life, Hayes got to camp by midnight and "slept on wet ground without blankets."[6]

Over the next week, the army and its caravan pushed on, often in "driving rain over execrable roads" and with little food. They avoided "starvation only . . . by energetic and systematic foraging." After four men were killed while foraging, presumably by bushwhackers, Crook ordered the execution of a bushwhacker who had been captured by the Thirty-sixth Ohio. "This is the fate of all bushwhackers" read the epitaph pinned to his body. After a difficult crossing of the swollen Greenbrier River, the hungry expedition (many of them without shoes) reached Meadow Bluff on 19 May, linked up with Fifth West Virginia troops, and made it safely inside Union lines.[7]

Despite "twenty-one days of constant marching, frequent fighting, and much hardship, and some starvation," Hayes insisted that it was "the most completely successful and by all odds the pleasantest campaign I have ever had." He ecstatically declared it perfect in plan and execution and described Crook as "the best general I have ever known." Hayes thought that Crook's one fault, which was not always a bad fault, was "a too reckless exposure of himself in action and on the march." There was not much food on their arrival, but by that Friday, "rations of coffee, sugar, hard bread, etc. filled our camp with joy." Within a few days, shoes and other supplies followed, and after a week in camp, Crook's army was ready for another campaign. By this time, Hayes was annoyed at newspaper accounts that referred to the recent campaign as "Averell's raid" and griped that "the cavalry part of it was a total failure."[8]

Hayes thought that Crook's army would move on Staunton, by way of White Sulphur Springs. His brigade, consisting of the Twenty-third and Thirty-sixth Ohio and the Fifth and Thirteenth West Virginia, made "a fine body of troops." The Ohio regiments, he felt, were the best to be found, and the West Virginia ones were promising. Hayes expected to get under way as early as 27 May, but they were delayed for four days, in part because Gen. David Hunter had replaced Sigel in command of the Department of West Virginia, but mostly because of rain and a lack of supplies. Hayes assured Lucy—who was pregnant again and had settled with her boys "in a good boarding-house at Chillicothe," close to her Aunt Phebe McKell—that "this is a happy time with us. . . . You must not feel too anxious about me. I shall be among friends."[9]

As Hayes had anticipated, Crook's army passed through White Sulphur Springs, advanced into Virginia, and struck the Virginia Central Railroad at Goshen. Virtually unopposed, Crook's troops destroyed the railroad on 6 June as they marched northeast to Craigsville. Both Hayes and Crook felt lucky that day, since Hayes had spied a new moon over his right shoulder and Crook had found a four-leafed clover. "Funny," Hayes mused, "how a man of sense can think for an instant even of such follies." Leaving the railroad the next day, Crook's army went over North Mountain, entered "the beautiful Valley of Virginia," and heard that on the lucky day before Hunter had "flogged the Rebels badly" and taken Staunton. On 8 June, Crook's army entered Staunton and linked up with Hunter. "All operations in this quarter," Hayes declared, "have been very successful." But he was saddened by the departure—with the band playing "Home Sweet Home"—of 160 men and nine officers of the Twenty-third, whose three-year enlistments had expired. Reenlistees of the Ohio Twelfth would soon replace these men, whose last tasks were to conduct prisoners back to "America" and to present the battle-scarred regimental flag to the governor.

Finding Staunton a "fine town of five thousand inhabitants," Hayes was impressed by its "very extensive hospitals." They were filled with the wounded, a third of whom were Union men. In addition, "the Secesh were friendly and polite," and there was "not the slightest bitterness or unkindness between" Union and Confederate patients. Although Lucy could hardly be cheered by the sentiment, Hayes told her that if he were "to be left in a hospital this is the spot."[10]

At Staunton, Crook's army became a division of Hunter's Army of the Shenandoah and participated in his campaign to capture Lynchburg. With Hayes's brigade in the lead, the army moved southwest down the Valley of Virginia to Lexington, which it captured on 11 June "after an artillery and sharpshooter fight of three hours." It was a very noisy, but not dangerous, affair. Hayes's men suffered almost all the casualties, but they were light. In Lexington, Hayes also found that many of the people were "Union," and the "Secesh" were "not at all bitter." But all that changed when Hunter, to the disgust of the officers in Crook's division, burned the Virginia Military Institute and would have burned Washington College as well if his officers had not dissuaded him. He gave the wife and daughters of Gov. John Letcher of Virginia ten minutes to clear out of their home before sending it up in flames to avenge the burning by bushwhackers of the home of Gov. Francis H. Pierpont of the "restored" state of Virginia (the part controlled by the Union). "Hunter," Hayes predicted, "will be as odious as [Benjamin F.] Butler or Pope to the Rebels and not gain our good opinion either."[11]

As he destroyed Union sentiment in Lexington, Hunter also killed time. He dallied until 14 June before pushing twenty-four miles down the valley to Buchanan; meanwhile, the Confederates rushed troops to Lynchburg. It was "a hot, dusty march," and Hayes cleaned up and cooled off in the James

River. Turning east the next day, the Union forces crossed the Blue Ridge and enjoyed "fine views of Peaks of Otter"; on the south slope of the mountain, they picked rhododendron blossoms, which were growing in profusion, stuck them in their gun barrels, and appeared to be a moving bank of flowers. On 16 June, they were beyond Liberty (Bedford) on the Virginia & Tennessee Railroad and commenced working "on the railroad, tearing up and burning, etc." On the following day, Friday, Carr B. White's brigade of Crook's division "cleaned out Rebels handsomely to three miles of Lynchburg," but Hunter, who arrived late on the field, did not press his advantage. Part of Jubal Early's division reinforced the defenders of Lynchburg during the night. On Saturday, after probing with skirmishers and containing a Confederate assault, Hunter concluded that his army could not take Lynchburg; that evening he backed down the Liberty road.[12]

The remainder of the campaign was neither pleasant nor rewarding, as Hunter hurried over the mountains to West Virginia. Initially harassed by Confederates and then stalked by starvation, the army endured privations for over a week. On 27 June, it met a train of provisions and had "a jolly feeding time." On 1 July, it finally found rest in Charleston; for Hayes, "the hardest month of the war" had ended. "Hungry, sleepy night marches; many skirmishes; two battles," he recorded. "Men worn out and broken down."[13]

The men of Crook's army nursed their sore feet and filled their stomachs for a week. In mulling over the recent "severe and hazardous campaign," Hayes concluded that "a more active and enterprising commander than General Hunter," namely "General Crook, would have taken Lynchburg." Observations that he and other officers had made on the raid convinced Hayes that "the Rebels are now using their last man and last bread. There is absolutely nothing left in reserve. Whip what is now in the field, and the game is ended." After chafing under the vindictive and lethargic Hunter, Hayes was glad to hear that Crook was given command of the Army of the Kanawha, under the direct control of Grant. With a commander like Crook and troops like those in his brigade, Hayes was confident of victory.[14]

Hunter's vindictiveness bothered Hayes, who tried to restrain the viciousness of war. When Lucy complained that Lincoln failed "to protect our unfortunate prisoners by retaliation," Hayes characterized her outburst as "thoughtless." She feared that if he were wounded, Hayes might be left behind and perhaps end up in the Confederate prison at Danville, Virginia, and she worried about the fate of her cousin Willie McKell, who had been captured and would die at Andersonville. But Hayes argued that retaliation—acts like the burning of Letcher's home—was "all a mistake." Just days later, Early's troops underscored Hayes's point. After chasing Hunter,

Crook, and Hayes into West Virginia, they turned north and chased Sigel up the Shenandoah Valley and invaded Maryland. On the outskirts of Washington, they burned the home of Postmaster General Montgomery Blair. Although Early had not ordered its destruction, the act was widely believed to be in retaliation for the burning of the Letcher home.

Hayes lectured his impulsive, spirited wife: "There are enough 'brutal Rebels' no doubt, but we have brutal officers and men too. . . . And there are plenty of humane Rebels. . . . War is a cruel business and there is brutality in it on all sides, but it is very idle to get up anxiety on account of any supposed peculiar cruelty on the part of Rebels. Keepers of prisons in Cincinnati, as well as in Danville, are hard-hearted and cruel."[15]

Hayes had assumed that his men would have two to three weeks to recuperate, but Early's invasion of Maryland had caused enormous political damage in a presidential election year, and Hayes was "ordered to Parkersburg and East" on 7 July. Managing "to slip ahead" of his command, Hayes had "a jolly time" with Lucy and the boys at Chillicothe on Sunday, 10 July, before reaching Parkersburg on Monday. After waiting two days there for his brigade to catch up, he accompanied it to Martinsburg on the Baltimore & Ohio Railroad.[16]

Beginning on 17 July, Hayes and his brigade did a considerable amount of "hard marching and plenty of fighting of a poor sort." From Martinsburg and Harpers Ferry to Winchester, Virginia, they looked for Early. The "Rebel cavalry," Hayes complained after three days of skirmishing, "is very active and efficient, but it don't fight. Our losses are ridiculously small for so much noise." On 22 July, Crook's 12,000-man army entered Winchester, and the next day it skirmished south as far as Kernstown with what appeared to be a "small force of Rebel cavalry." The Union cavalry—the army's eyes—so underestimated Early's strength that Crook assumed that he had gone to Richmond; it also failed to guard the army's flanks, causing Crook to be surprised by the enemy on Sunday, 24 July.[17]

At the battle of Winchester, or Kernstown, Hayes's brigade took the brunt of the Confederate assault. At noon, Crook, unaware of the danger, ordered Hayes's brigade and the division under Col. James A. Mulligan to advance on what they presumed to be a Confederate "reconnaissance in force." As they were about to attack, Dr. Joe, who was "a natural soldier" and "had an eye to take in the situation," rode up to warn them that the enemy was in force on a hill on Hayes's left, just as Mulligan heard that the enemy was also massed on a hill on his right. Virtually surrounded and in a "fix," Mulligan and Hayes decided to go forward but were enveloped in a withering cross fire from the nearby hills. Within five minutes, Mulligan was dead, and it was too noisy for Hayes's men to hear what would have been his obvious command, "about face, run."

Without a command, Hayes recalled, "We broke back pretty soon and we slowly ran out. It so happened there was a pretty rough wall there. We ran to that wall—I dont know what became of Mulligan's men, but my men held on to this and there we formed." While retreating to that wall, Hayes was hit on the shoulder by a spent ball that did little damage (his third wound in the war). His horse was hit, and Hayes must have taken a spill, since his "pocket emptied out map, almanack, and little photographic album." He and his men "charged back ten or twenty yards and got them!" Confederates pressed them "very close and very hard," but they held on to the wall.[18]

But for Hayes's stand at the stone wall, Dr. Joe maintained, "Crook's army would have been captured Bag & Baggage" by Early's 17,000-man force. To enable his army to withdraw in an orderly fashion, Crook ordered Hayes to hold his position until a battery of artillery got safely under way and then to cover the retreat on the road to Martinsburg. For eight miles down the road, Early's men harassed Hayes, but when "they got a little too close," his men "would pitch into them." Upon reaching Martinsburg on Monday, Hayes and his men, supported by cavalry, turned on Early's advance guard and "flogged" it "handsomely," while Crook, with his own stores, evacuated the town. That night, the men endured a "severe, sleepy" march, crossed the Potomac at Williamsport, Maryland, turned south, and camped the next day on Antietam Creek. There, Hayes had time to write to Lucy about his "decided defeat in battle." Although his brigade had suffered the heaviest casualties, he knew that neither he nor his men were responsible for defeat by a superior foe. He also realized that they had helped prevent a disaster. "We are queer beings," he wrote to Lucy. "The camp is now alive with laughter and good feeling; more so than usual. The recoil after so much toil and anxiety."[19]

Hayes and his men did not remain at Antietam Creek, despite their need of rest. After a good night's sleep, they marched for two days, recrossed the Potomac River, joined Hunter's army, and rested for two days near Halltown, Virginia, about five miles south of Harpers Ferry. Although they were "too far from water," the men were "clothed and shod again," and their mood was good. Since Hunter's army was also joined at Halltown by a large force under Gen. Horatio G. Wright, Hayes assumed that they would be moving up the Valley of Virginia again but hoped that the offensive would be delayed long enough for his men "to heal their sore feet." They had endured, he explained, "three months of hard campaigning—marched one thousand to one thousand two hundred miles, besides seven hundred by railroad and steamboat. Much night marching, four or five pitched battles, and skirmishing every other day." Although "bothered with boils from constant riding in hot weather," Hayes pronounced his own health perfect.[20]

Hayes's rest was cut short when Confederate cavalry under John Mc-Causland burned Chambersburg, Pennsylvania, on Saturday, 30 July. Beginning at 4 P.M. that day, Hayes and his men headed back to Maryland, crossed the Potomac again, and, after enduring "night marching, dust, heat & confusion—all very disastrous to men"—passed through Middletown, where Hayes and Dr. Joe breakfasted with the "cordial and kind" Rudy family before camping six miles further on, near Wolfesville. This grueling twenty-four-mile march left the men so exhausted that "only fifty to one hundred men in a regiment came into camp in a body."[21]

Hayes's men finally got their rest. They had "a jolly good time . . . living on the fat of the land" for two days in the Middletown Valley before marching eighteen to twenty miles on Wednesday, 3 August, across Catoctin Ridge and through Frederick to the Monocacy River. There they remained until Saturday, picking berries, swimming, and eating "good bread & pies." While in camp, ninety recruits arrived for the Twenty-third; among them was one named Whitlow who had tempted fate once too often. Earlier in the war, he had deserted the Confederates, joined the Twenty-third, deserted it, and rejoined the Confederates. At Cloyd's Mountain, he was captured by the Twenty-third but had the good fortune to escape. He then made his way to Ohio, where he enlisted again as a substitute for someone about to be conscripted. "By a remarkable providence," Hayes exclaimed, he was sent back to the Twenty-third, "tried and shot within twenty-four hours. . . . We are getting a considerable number of substitutes—many good men, but many who are professional villains."[22]

On Saturday, Hunter's army marched twenty miles in pleasant weather to Sandy Hook, near Harpers Ferry on the Potomac, where it rested until Monday afternoon. While suffering from poison ivy at Sandy Hook, Hayes learned that on Sunday, 7 August, Grant had relieved Hunter and appointed Gen. Philip Sheridan commander of what became the Army of the Shenandoah. It consisted of the Sixth and Nineteenth Corps, each with about 12,000 men, and the Eighth, or Crook's, Corps (to which Hayes was attached) of about 7,000 men. Crook's corps was also called the Army of West Virginia. Sheridan was very young, very short, very profane, and very aggressive. Since Crook was pleased, the change suited Hayes, who anticipated being "engaged in some of the great operations of the autumn" but was unaware of just how hard-driving Sheridan could be. Hayes assured Lucy, "Service in these large armies is by no means as severe as in our raids."[23]

On Monday afternoon, 8 August, Sheridan moved cautiously into the Shenandoah Valley. He was unfamiliar with his new army and overestimated the size of Early's army, but by Friday, having marched "in line of battle" (to avoid surprise) to Cedar Creek, near Strasburg, Sheridan was just three hours behind the rebels, who were also in battle order. The forces skirmished that day but had "no fight"; nor did they fight on Saturday or Sunday, although Union skirmishers determined that the rebels were in force on Fisher's Hill, beyond Strasburg. Sheridan fell back to a strong position on a line between Halltown and Charles Town, and over the next two weeks, he and Early probed at each other, but there was no battle. "Both armies," Hayes observed, "had good positions and both were too prudent to leave them."[24]

While in the vicinity of Charles Town, Hayes rejoiced to hear from Lucy for the first time since he had left her in July. For both patriotic and personal reasons, he was fascinated by news of the 1864 political campaign. Upon hearing that the Democrats had nominated McClellan for the presidency, Hayes feared that he would be elected and, putting the best face on that disturbing probability, reasoned that it would not be "so bad a thing." McClellan would continue to prosecute the war and cause the Democratic party to back it more vigorously. Thanks to Cincinnati friends who had nominated him for Congress, Hayes was also a candidate. In between skirmishes on 24 August, he responded to William Henry Smith's suggestion that he get "a furlough to take the stump." Rejecting it outright, Hayes exclaimed, "An officer fit for duty who at this crisis would abandon his post to electioneer for a seat in Congress ought to be scalped." Both Hayes and Smith realized that this letter written from the front would advance Hayes's political career more effectively than stump-speaking in Cincinnati.[25]

As Sheridan gained confidence in his army's strength, he moved it up the valley again. On Saturday, 3 September, Crook's corps marched eleven miles to Berryville and camped in the path of a division of Early's army that was heading back to Lee at Richmond. Both Crook and the Confederate commander, Richard H. Anderson, were surprised, but Anderson, who was already in motion, attacked, pushing Crook's First Division back. "The Rebels," Hayes reported, "were sure of victory and run at us with the wildest yells." But Duval's Second (Kanawha) Division, to which Hayes's brigade belonged, fired a devastating volley from behind stone walls. Turning "the tide in an instant," the men jumped up and chased the Confederates back to their lines; as darkness came, the rebels rallied and pushed the Union troops partly back into the nearby woods. Neither side wanted to fight in the dark, but since shots were answered, it was difficult to cease. The firing "finally died out absolutely," and within five minutes the surgeons, stretcher bearers, and burying parties "of both armies mingled together right there with lights and lanterns looking for the dead and wounded."[26]

It had been a long, fierce fight in which Hayes's "brigade had the severest fighting," but he was elated that they had "whipped" the enemy. The battle exhilarated him, although he keenly felt the loss of two captains of the Twenty-third and of his color-bearer, Pvt. George Brigdon of Company B. "I suppose," he wrote to Lucy, "I was never in so much danger before, but I enjoyed the excitement more than ever." Then realizing that his exhilaration was Lucy's torment, he assured her that she was always on his mind. "My apprehension and feeling is a thousand times more for you than for myself," he insisted, but even while acknowledging the anxiety that Lucy was enduring, he was loving war more and more.[27]

And Hayes loved his brigade more and more. "We have fought nine times since we entered this valley and have been under fire, when men of my command were killed and wounded, probably thirty or forty times since the campaign opened. I doubt if a brigade in Sherman's army has fought more. None has marched half as much. I started with twenty-four hundred men. I now have less than twelve hundred, and almost none of the loss is stragglers." Since Hayes considered Sherman's army (which had just captured Atlanta and was composed of westerners) the best in the world (with Lee's army second), his opinion of his brigade could not have been higher.[28]

The battle was not renewed on Sunday, and Hayes enjoyed a two-week respite. Anderson's division went to Lee; Early, in a weakened state, moved to Opequon Creek to defend Winchester, but Sheridan did not press his advantage. Thinking politics again, Hayes was pleased by McClellan's acceptance letter, which repudiated the peace plank in the Democratic platform. Hayes was for Lincoln and had contempt for peace Democrats, but he did not want his "innocent little" boys repeating "bitter talk" about McClellan. "He is on a mean platform and is in bad company, but I do not doubt his personal loyalty and he has been a soldier, and what is more a soldier's friend. No man ever treated the private soldier better. No commander was ever more loved by his men." Differing with McClellan primarily over slavery, Hayes felt certain that if the Democrats were responsible for carrying on the war, they would soon realize the necessity of emancipation. After uttering these speculative thoughts, Hayes assured Lucy that "with reasonably good luck in the war, Lincoln will go in."[29]

Noting that Grant had consulted with Sheridan on Saturday, 17 September, and that recruits and convalescents were filling up the ranks, Hayes looked "for an active fall campaign." With a presidential election approaching, Early's 12,000-man army had to be destroyed. Sheridan pushed south and west to Early's line at Opequon Creek and attacked him on Monday morning, 19 September, holding Crook's corps in reserve. The battle went badly for the Union, and at noon the "Rebels were jubilant . . . cheering and rejoicing over the victory." Then Sheridan threw in Crook's men, with Hayes's brigade leading the way against a battery on the rebels' extreme left flank. Initially, Hayes's men walked fast, but just as they were about to "yell and charge at full speed," they came upon a boggy creek—twenty-five yards wide, with high banks. Hayes wrote Lucy:

> The Rebel fire now broke out furiously. . . . To stop was death. To go on was probably the same; but on we started again. My horse plunged in and mired down hopelessly, just as by frantic struggling he reached about the middle of the stream. I jumped off, and down on all fours, succeeded in reaching the Rebel side—but alone. . . . I was about the middle of the brigade and saw nobody else, but hundreds were struggling in the stream. . . . Soon they came flocking, all regiments mixed up—all order gone, no chance of ever reforming, but pell-mell, over the obstructions, went the crowd. Two cannons were captured; the rest run off.

Hayes later confessed, "Perhaps the happiest moment of my life was then, when I saw that our line *didn't* break, and that the enemy's *did*."

Making no attempt to form lines or regiments, Crook's men chased the Confederates to a second line of defense and again came "under a destructive fire." As Hayes told Lucy, "Things began to look dark," but Sheridan's "splendid cavalry . . . with shouts at a gallop charged right into the Rebel lines. We pushed on and away broke the Rebels. The cavalry came back, and an hour later and nearly a mile back, the same scene again; and a third time; and the victory was ours just before sundown." Early had suffered a crushing defeat. Crook's corps had made victory possible, and the cavalry had saved it, but the key decision had been made by Hayes at the slough of Red Bud Run, when he fearlessly plunged into the mire. During the battle, Col. Isaac H. Duval, commander of Crook's Second (Kanawha) Division and Hayes's immediate superior, had been seriously wounded, and Crook appointed Hayes in his place. Sheridan's 5,000 casualties included the serious injury of Hayes's adjutant general, Capt. Russell Hastings, but his legendary horse Old Whitey had escaped injury. A huge horse that had proved too spirited for wagon trains, Old Whitey had been transformed by Hastings into "a capital war horse," surviving nineteen battles to become the mascot of the Twenty-third Ohio.[30]

Fleeing twenty miles up the valley, Early fortified Fisher's Hill, two miles south of Strasburg. On 20 September, Sheridan followed fifteen miles to Cedar Creek, where he camped in the open with his two large corps, keeping Crook's corps (which arrived after dark) hidden in the woods. Early's position was strong, but to take advantage of Confederate demoralization following their rout at Opequon Creek, Sheridan thought that he would attempt a frontal assault. Crook argued that it made more sense to turn Early's left flank, which was anchored at Little North Mountain. Hayes, who accompanied Crook to the council, told Sheridan that a frontal assault "would be simply murder" and assured him that his Kanawha Division, having climbed mountains for three years, could cross Little North Mountain. Hayes later heard that the Confederates had said that "nothing but a crow could go up there."

Adopting Crook's plan, Sheridan positioned his Sixth and Nineteenth Corps for a frontal assault but moved Crook's corps before sunrise on 22 September to Little North Mountain. With Hayes's division in the lead and Hayes, Crook, and their guide, Lt. I. I. Lane of the Pennsylvania cavalry, out front, the Union men picked their way up through underbrush, over rocks, and down ravines until they were to the rear of Early's extreme left. When Crook's corps was in position, Hayes recalled, "We just yelled as we came down at the top of our voices and the enemy were taken with a panic and fled like sheep. We got every gun they had." Hayes's men chased Early's men down the road until dark, "sweeping everything before them." Hayes's division, which was "farther to the front than any other," halted at Woodstock. Hayes believed—and Sheridan concurred—that if Averell's cavalry had done its job, Early and the bulk of his men would not have escaped. Exulting that the Fisher's Hill victory cost so few Union casualties, Hayes boasted, "We have, I think, from the two battles five thousand Rebel prisoners unhurt—three thousand wounded, five hundred killed; twenty-five pieces of artillery." In summing up the victory, Hayes called Sheridan "a whole-souled, brave man," but he especially praised Crook as "the brains of this army."[31]

Over the next few days, in pursuit of Early's "broken army," Sheridan moved up the valley as far as Staunton. Early got away because, as Hayes derisively noted, the "Rebs outran the first Bull Run." After leading the chase on the day of the battle, Hayes and his men played a less active role during the remainder of the campaign. With the cavalry and small scouting parties taking up the pursuit, Hayes went as far as Harrisonburg (a hundred miles south of the Potomac and about thirty miles shy of Staunton), where he and his men rested for several days. Quickly bored by inactivity, he read magazines and, although claiming not to fancy them, "women's novels," including Ellen (Mrs. Henry) Wood's immensely popular romance, *East Lynne* (1861). Hayes had time to write to Lucy, who was approaching confinement, almost daily and to savor the glory of recent victories. He took care to appear modest but was jealous of his reputation and eager for his men and Crook to get credit for their exploits in official reports as well as in unofficial newspaper accounts. When Sheridan's report of Fisher's Hill gave Crook's men "proper credit for once," and the Sixth and Nineteenth Corps of Sheridan's army agreed that Crook's little corps "should have the lion's share of the glory," Hayes was pleased. He was also pleased that Crook valued him as someone who was capable in battle and articulate at headquarters. Although "five or six brigadier-generals, and one or two major-generals sucking their thumbs in offices at Harpers Ferry and elsewhere," wanted Hayes's command, Crook kept Colonel Hayes at the head of his division.[32]

In early October, Hayes hoped that Crook's corps would be ordered north. He was anxious for news about Lucy and wished to be closer to her. After a month of hearing nothing, he finally learned on 12 October that ten days earlier she had given birth to a boy. Sheridan's army did move north, but not before the men "burned all wheat stacks, mills, and barns with grain" and, Hayes reported, drove "in all cattle and horses." He did not relish this kind of warfare but recognized the military necessity of taking or destroying everything edible. There would be "no more supplies to Rebels from this valley," Hayes commented. "No more invasions in great force by this route will be possible."

At this point, Hayes was beginning to lose some of his verve for soldiering. Perhaps the birth of another child heightened his awareness that Lucy and the boys needed him as a live presence, not as a dead memory. Near Fisher's Hill, Confederate cavalry harassed Sheridan's rear, and Hayes, on the evening of 8 October, confessed feeling "a great repugnance to fighting another battle." The next day he was "all right" when Union cavalry, supported by two of his regiments, "flogged the Rebels handsomely." That "signal cavalry victory," it seemed to Hayes, ended a splendid campaign on a high note. He hoped that "Crook's hard-worked command" would have the pleasant "duty of guarding the Baltimore and Ohio Railroad in winter quarters" and that he would "get home by Christmas for a good visit."[33]

But the campaign was not over. On 13 October, having received reinforcements from Longstreet's corps, Early probed at Sheridan, who was camped at Cedar Creek, but discovered that he was too strong to assault. Once again, Early occupied his old position at Fisher's Hill. With little food and forage left at their rear, Hayes assumed that Early and his army would soon be hungry and that "we may fight another battle with him." In the meantime, Hayes kept busy with entrenchments, writing letters, and, since Sherman's capture of Atlanta and Sheridan's defeat of Early had made the Republicans winners, rejoicing over the political news. Hayes had been elected to Congress by a 2,400 majority, one of seventeen Republicans (but only two Democrats) elected to Congress from Ohio. Years later, he learned that the first dispatch Lincoln had received about the October election "contained the welcome intelligence of the election of Rutherford B. Hayes."[34]

In a heavy fog before daylight on 19 October, Early surprised Sheridan's complacent army. Joseph B. Kershaw's division overwhelmed Crook's small First Division, killing its commander, Col. Joseph Thoburn, as he tried to rally his troops. Hayes, commanding the Second or Kanawha Division a mile to the rear, hurriedly got into line. Gen. Horatio G. Wright—commanding in the absence of Sheridan (who was fifteen miles down the valley en route back from Washington)—Crook, and Hayes assumed that the Second Division plus a brigade under Col. J. H. Kitching and troops from the Sixth and Nineteenth Corps could stop Kershaw's attack. Hayes was smugly guaranteeing Kitching that the Second Division would hold when he was horrified to see it break as a Confederate division under Gen. John B. Gordon fell upon it and Kitching's brigade from out of the fog, just as "the fugitives of the First Division" came pouring back.

Although it suffered two surprises and was "flanked out of its position in confusion," the army did not panic, but neither did the men respond to the pleas of their officers to make a stand. A disorganized mass, they were of one mind: to walk, not run, to the rear. Hayes galloped after his troops, but his "fine large black horse was killed instantly, tumbling heels over head and dashing" Hayes "on the ground violently," injuring his ankle and knocking him out. Without checking on his condition, some of his men said that he had been killed, and his death was reported in the press. As Hayes regained consciousness and got to his feet, attacking Confederates ordered him to halt. Despite his injured ankle, he escaped to a nearby woods, caught up with his fleeing troops, and got another horse from Lieutenant Henry of his staff. On the way to his men, he "was also hit fairly in the head by a ball," he told Lucy, "which had lost its force in getting (I suppose) through somebody else! It gave me only a slight shock."

Neither Early nor his men pressed their advantage. He seemed paralyzed by unexpected success; his tired men, who had been up all night, wasted precious time plundering Sheridan's camp. They took "perhaps fifteen hundred prisoners," twenty-five artillery pieces, "and much camp equipage." Hayes lost his horse trappings, saddle, and small pistol. Because the "Rebels failed to push on fast enough," the Union army was able to form a line on a ridge about two and a half miles down the valley near Middletown. The Sixth Corps, which had not been engaged and still functioned as an organized unit, reached the ridge first, but Hayes soon arrived with about sixty men from his division and took a position between the two divisions of the Sixth Corps. Once the line was established, many among the disorganized mass of retreating men found their units. The Nineteenth Corps formed to the right of the Sixth Corps, and some of Thoburn's crushed division lined up behind Hayes's men, who were now approximately twelve hundred strong. The sun also burned off the fog at about 9 A.M., eliminating the major source of confusion. Occupying a strong position and seeing the field before it, Sheridan's riddled army regained its confidence as it awaited another attack by Early.

The attack did not come, but Sheridan did and converted a Union defeat into a stunning victory. The men on the new line heard cheering to their rear and, jumping up, they saw "Little Phil" Sheridan astride a huge galloping black charger waving his hat and shouting. He was followed by erstwhile stragglers returning to fight. Cheers erupted "all along the line. His enthusiasm," Hayes wrote, was "magnetic and contagious." He heard Sheridan yell, "We'll whip 'em yet like hell"; the men believed him and roared back, "Sheridan! Sheridan!"

Sheridan did not launch an immediate counterattack; he was not as impetuous as he sounded. He arrived a little before noon; planned an attack by the Sixth and Nineteenth Corps, with Crook's badly mauled Eighth Corps in reserve; and was ready at about 4 P.M. Even after his careful planning, Sheridan did not realize that Hayes and most of his division were still on the line in the middle of the Sixth Corps. Although his body ached from his fall and his head hurt from the spent bullet, Hayes was ready to join in the attack. At the last moment, Sheridan realized where Hayes was and ordered him to the rear.

Situated on the left of the pike, Hayes had a fine view of the battle. The Union attack surged forward, and the rebels fought poorly and were "awfully whipped" with "cannon and spoils now on our side." It was "glorious." Sheridan, Hayes exulted, "retook all we had lost and utterly ruined Early. . . . The fact is," Hayes concluded, "all the *fight* is out of Early's men. They have been whipped so much that they can't keep a victory after it is gained." And he predicted accurately, "This is the last of fighting on this line."[35]

ELEVEN

THE END OF THE WAR

Cedar Creek was Hayes's last battle. Even before it was fought, he had suspected that Crook's "hard-worked command" would go on garrison duty along the Baltimore & Ohio Railroad, while the Sixth and Nineteenth Corps would return with Sheridan to Grant, before Richmond. Lucy feared that Hayes would be ordered to join Grant. It had been an anxious summer and fall for her. The battles of Opequon and Fisher's Hill had occurred just before the birth of their fifth son, George Crook Hayes, and before he was three weeks old, his father had been wounded twice at Cedar Creek. The Ohio press reported that Hayes had been killed, but fortunately Lucy's uncle, Matthew Scott Cook, with whom she was staying in Chillicothe, kept the newspaper from her. Shortly after the paper arrived, she received a telegram from Capt. Thomas B. Reed, one of Thoburn's staff officers. "The report that your husband was killed this morning is untrue. He was wounded, not dangerously, and is safe." Once again, Hayes had narrowly escaped, but Lucy was afraid that his celebrated luck would run out if he were sent to Grant.[1]

Sheridan's army remained at Cedar Creek for three weeks, apparently to prevent rebel raids before the presidential election. Since the rebels did not show themselves, the officers of the Eighth Corps relived Cedar Creek. "We now talk of our killed and wounded," Hayes told Lucy. "There is however a very happy feeling. Those who escape regret of course the loss of comrades and friends, but their own escape and safety to some extent modifies their feelings." Refighting Cedar Creek put the men of the Eighth Corps on the defensive. Before it, they had taken few pains to hide their high opinion of themselves as the "A No. 1" corps of Sheridan's army. After it, Hayes believed that jealous, "foolish fellows in the Sixth and Nineteenth Corps . . . got the Eastern correspondents to represent the rout of Crook's Corps as worse than theirs." Hayes was incensed and defensive. Minimizing the fact that his men had broken under a crunching Confederate attack, Hayes made the dubious claim that "*I* lost nothing. My division fell back, but brought *everything* we had—our *two cows*, tents, and everything."[2]

At Crook's behest, Hayes had tried to mount a newspaper counterattack, but he soon gave it up. He was not contentious by nature, and after the war he deplored controversies between soldiers over battlefield conduct. He felt better about Cedar Creek after Sheridan's report "restored things gloriously." In fact, Hayes had reason to be proud of his leadership and of his division for the way it had re-formed after its initial rout. With his usual self-confidence, Hayes told Sardis, "People are not agoing to believe that Crook's men behaved badly." Hayes was mollified further by word that Crook (a diffident man whose hurt Hayes had been trying to assuage) had been promoted to major general. Nor was Hayes neglected. Crook and Sheridan recommended his promotion to brigadier general.[3]

Election day, 8 November, continued Hayes's happy mood. With the victories of Sherman in Georgia and Sheridan in the valley, Lincoln's election appeared certain. Hayes went to the polls with Sheridan and Crook:

[At] about nine o'clock . . . five thousand soldiers and two brass bands were on hand. The polling-place was a wagon, and three non-commissioned officers were judges and two young fellows clerks. I said I would vote first, so as to show Crook and Sheridan how it was done. I stepped up and said: "My name is Rutherford B. Hayes; I vote in Hamilton County, Ohio, in the Fifteenth Ward, Cincinnati." . . . Then Sheridan stepped up. He was a little embarrassed under the gaze of all the men. He looked at the judge, the judge stared at him. "Your name, sir!" said the judge, with infinite dignity. Sheridan spoke up, "Philip H. Sheridan." "In what State do you vote?" asked the judge, impressively. "In Ohio." "In what county?" "Perry County." "In what ward or township, sir?" asked the judge, with solemnity. "My father lives in Reading Township," Sheridan replied, in an embarrassed way, for it was all new to him. Then General Crook stepped forward, pulling his mustache nervously, as was his habit. He gave his name, and said he lived in Dayton, Montgomery County. "What ward, sir?" asked the judge. "I don't know," General Crook said; "I always stopped at the Phillips House, though." "Oh, call it the First Ward," I said, and down it went that way. In speaking with Sheridan afterward, he said, with feeling: "This is my first vote: I don't ever expect to vote again, but I did want to vote for Old Abe."

On that same day, in that same place, William McKinley also cast his first ballot in a presidential election. Hayes was delighted to report that, in his division, Lincoln got 575 votes to 98 for McClellan and to hear that Lincoln would carry all but three states.[4]

The day after the election, Sheridan moved eleven miles north from Cedar Creek to the vicinity of Kernstown, where Hayes remained for over a month. On 23 November, Hayes said, it got "colder than any huckleberry pudding I know of!" Bad weather like that made almost everyone "cross and gloomy" and made them growl in "old-soldier style" about the "thin linen tents—almost like a fish seine, the deep mud, the irregular mails, the never-to-be-seen paymasters." But the morrow was a fine day, and Hayes marveled how it "brightens and cheers us all. We people in camp are merely big children, wayward and changeable."[5]

There were things to growl about, but Hayes appreciated the Kernstown location, just four miles south of Winchester. "A number of ladies," he told his mother, "can be seen about the camps—officers' wives, sisters, daughters, and the Union young ladies of Winchester." He visited his wounded friend Hastings (who did not die as predicted) and stopped with McKinley at a local lawyer's office to "read the constitutional provisions as to amendments." Earlier in 1864, the Senate had passed and the House had rejected the Thirteenth Amendment, abolishing slavery. The recent Republican triumph now pointed to the amendment's passage by the House. Hayes also indulged in "oyster and wine suppers and festive times generally." There was "a good deal of horse-racing with tolerably high betting," and he found the races very exciting. "You would enjoy them," he told Lucy, since military discipline and compulsory sobriety rid those spectacles of the rioting and drunkenness that accompanied them in civilian life.[6]

Friday, 9 December, was a gratifying day for Hayes. In the afternoon, Crook entered his tent with the news that Hayes had been promoted to brigadier general and gave him "a pair of his old brigadier-general [shoulder] straps. The stars," Hayes told Lucy, "are somewhat dimmed with hard service, but will correspond pretty well with my rusty old blouse." He realized that "all sorts of small people" had attained and "cheapened [the rank] shamefully," but he felt honored to earn "it at the close of a most bloody campaign on the recommendation of fighting generals like Crook and Sheridan." When the news got around on Saturday, Hayes was "the centre of congratulations in the camp." That evening he celebrated with his friends, who, he reported, "drink poor whiskey with me!"[7]

Despite a storm that dumped eight inches of snow on the Shenandoah Valley and a "fierce northwester" on 12 December that made Hayes fear that the men on the picket line would freeze, their camp was happy and comfortable. On 17 December, taking advantage of a thaw, Hayes inspected his brigade (Duval had recovered and again commanded the Second Division) and pronounced the Twenty-third "the crack regiment," but he noted how few of its original members were left. "I could see only six to ten in a company of the old men. They all smiled as I rode by. But as I passed away I couldn't help dropping a few natural tears. I felt as I did when I saw them mustered in at Camp Chase." The smiles of the old men and the tears Hayes shed acknowledged an unbreakable bond.[8]

On 19 December, Crook's corps left its cozy camp and marched ten miles through mud, snow, and rain to Stephenson's Depot, five miles north of Winchester. The First Division left immediately by rail to join Grant, but the Second Division camped "on a bleak, wet, muddy" hillside while it "snowed, blowed and 'friz agen.'" Although he wanted to get out of Stephenson's Depot and felt an urge "to be present at the taking of Richmond," Hayes preferred the safety of winter quarters. The weather improved, and Hayes and his staff enjoyed a good Christmas dinner of "wine, oysters, turkey, etc." On 30 December, his twelfth wedding anniversary, the army marched seventeen miles to Martinsburg, camped in the snow, and the next day arrived at Cumberland, where it went into winter quarters.[9]

On the Baltimore & Ohio Railroad line and only twenty-four hours from Cincinnati, Cumberland was ideal for Hayes. His troops built huts on a snowy hillside a mile north of the railroad and east of town; Hayes called it Camp Hastings. With his promotion official, he swore his oath of office as brigadier general of volunteers on 3 January 1865. On Tuesday evening, 10 January, Hayes and Dr. Joe left for Ohio with twenty-day leaves in their pockets. After an "icy, slippery" walk to town, they caught a sleeper west to Benwood on the Ohio. The next morning, with the river "full of floating ice," they took the steamboat *Eagle* (filled with western Pennsylvania "petroleum speculators") downriver to Parkersburg; on Thursday, they went by rail to Chillicothe, where Lucy was based.[10]

Since Lucy was "down with rheumatism" and little George was a colicky baby who needed her care, she could not visit relatives and constituents with Hayes. Birch and Webb accompanied him to Columbus, Delaware, and Fremont, where they saw Fanny's children, Sophia, and Sardis. "Laura," Hayes bragged undiplomatically to Lucy, "is a most charming, affectionate mother, and her pretty little girl is a model of . . . all sorts of infantile perfections. Cholic and crying unknown." At Delaware, Sophia gave Hayes her "journal of the family" and of "her early times in Ohio," which Hayes assured her he would "always preserve and prize." In Fremont, Hayes used it to jog Sardis's memory and enjoyed listening to his comments.[11]

Hayes spent the remainder of his leave with Lucy and the boys at Chillicothe, except for a week with his supporters and friends in Cincinnati. Among "mostly strangers," he had a good time at the literary club and was amazed to learn that none of its forty-five members who were in the army had been killed. Patronage questions took up much of Hayes's time; as a congressman-elect, his recommendation was tantamount to appointment to the federal civil-service positions in his district as well as to the military and naval academies. In Chillicothe, with Lucy still "housed up with her rheumatism," Hayes spent much of his time with his beloved boys. Before returning to the army by way of Columbus (and "a fine little visit" with Laura), Hayes declared that George, whom he had thought troublesome a few weeks earlier, "behaves very well, and is very good natured."[12]

As usual, Hayes enjoyed being back with the army. On the evening of 9 February, his first full day back, he commented on the "cold, windy" camp and his "light & flappy" tent but added, "it is *homelike* to me." Sleeping in that tent with its "groans, squeaks, and flaps," Hayes told Lucy, "is not so *comfortable* as in a house these days, but it is more refreshing and invigorating." There was also a merry social whirl in Cumberland, and Hayes was swept up in it as well as in the pleasures accompanying the deep snow. With other officers, including William McKinley and Dr. Joe, he went on a ten-mile sleigh ride to a hospital and had "a great time snowballing."[13]

Hayes soon had additional military responsibilities. Duval went to Cincinnati for medical treatment, leaving Hayes in command of the division. Since most of the Army of West Virginia was with Grant before Richmond, Hayes's men were virtually the only infantry left in Crook's corps. Their round of parties was rudely interrupted on 21 February by a "daring and well executed" Confederate raid that captured Generals Crook and Benjamin Franklin Kelley. The raiders (about fifty strong), Hayes wrote, "inquired for me but on learning that I quartered in camp did not look further." Having taken over Duval's command, Hayes was in town that night, but the Confederates, knowing that Duval was gone, did not call at headquarters.[14]

Hayes blamed no one for the Confederate coup, but it was obvious that Kelley, who commanded the post, should have posted more pickets, and Hayes proceeded to do so. "The truth is," he told Lucy, "that all but 'a feeble few' are taken to the coast from Savannah to Richmond, leaving these posts to take their chances. I think it is wise policy, but at the same time *we* are exposed to surprise and capture at any time." Hayes had "great faith in my troops, my vigilance, and my luck," but he knew that only weakness kept rebels from overwhelming a number of Union posts. He assumed correctly that Crook and Kelly would not suffer in prison and that their loss would be temporary, but he feared that Crook's reputation might suffer and found the ludicrous capture of the generals "mortifying."[15]

Despite the "unfortunate" kidnapping, the war was going "gloriously." Federal manpower needs were met, as Hayes advocated, by conscription and by African American volunteers. Hayes reported to Lucy that in the last year, black troops had been proving themselves to doubters like Crook. "He has become a convert to negro soldiers," Hayes told her. He "thinks them better than a great part of the sort we are now getting." Hayes evaluated armies and their recruits for his old literary club companion Gen. Manning F. Force. Once again, he denigrated the Army of the Potomac as "composed too largely of the scum of the great Cities" and told Force that "officers of good sense in that army who were formerly prejudiced against the negro troops now say that they are the best troops." Convinced, however, that his own men were second to none, Hayes added, "I have no doubt the negroes are better than many of us thought they would be but I am sure they are not better than our good white troops."[16]

The end of the war seemed to be in sight. With Sherman conquering South Carolina and moving north, Lee would soon be caught in a vise between Sherman and Grant. If Lee would evacuate Richmond, it would be "a confession of defeat," and the war would "be substantially over." Although Hayes missed Crook, he liked the new commander of the Department of West Virginia, Winfield Scott Hancock, a "noble-looking man—not less than six feet three inches high"—who was "very fair . . . but nervous, excitable, and hasty." Wisely resisting pressure to disturb Crook's "favorites," Hancock left them in their places.[17]

Hayes had hoped to attend Lincoln's second inaugural. His friend Judge William Johnston of Cincinnati was in Washington and urged him and Lucy to come for "the greatest demonstration the world ever saw." Hayes hoped that Lucy could "drop little George for a fortnight" and visit Washington " 'strictly incog.' Bring on two hundred to three hundred dollars—no care about dress—and we can manage it." Hayes's dream to be a part of the great celebration was not to be. Lucy's rheumatism was so bad that she could not even consider going. Hayes, after the "kidnapping" of the two generals, found it "imperative" to remain on duty at Cumberland until Duval returned.[18]

Although it appeared that Hayes would survive the war without a debilitating injury, he was troubled by Lucy's continuing rheumatism. As he anxiously awaited news, he confronted the possibility that Lucy, who had been so vibrant and lively, might become an invalid. "If you should be so unlucky," he wrote to her, "as to become a cripple, . . . you may be sure I shall be still a loving husband, and we shall make the best of it together. There are a great many worse things than to lose the ability of easy locomotion. Of course, you will have to use philosophy or something higher to keep up your spirits." Hayes also reminded her of her childhood friend, Carrie Williams Little (whose wedding party they had been part of), who no longer could get about on her own but gave "more happiness to her household by her cheerfulness and agreeable ways than most of the walking women" he knew.[19]

Crook's parole and exchange were arranged quickly, but not as smoothly as Hayes had anticipated. When he dispatched an officer to inform Secretary of War Edwin M. Stanton of Crook's capture and to urge his quick exchange, Stanton was furious. He said that Crook and Kelley could rot in prison for their carelessness and threatened to arrest the messenger for being away from his post of duty. Never one to abandon a friend and undeterred by Stanton's wrath, Hayes appealed to Grant, who, Hayes noted to Sardis, "rules matters where he really attempts it." Grant managed the "special and privileged exchange" that Stanton had refused to arrange and requested Crook for his army. But, "to show the public he was not in disfavor," Crook wanted to return to the command of the Department of West Virginia. He came out for a day, received "a regular jolly mass-meeting sort of reception" that Hayes had orchestrated, with two bands, speeches, and "about forty rousing cheers," and then left to join Grant. To Hayes's delight, Crook took command of one of Sheridan's cavalry divisions and fought aggressively and effectively in the Appomattox campaign.[20]

If Hancock's nose was out of joint because of the bizarre coming and going of Crook (and because of Hayes's cheerleading), he did not let it affect his judgment. He gave Hayes considerable responsibility. By mid-March, Hayes's First Brigade of four regiments was at full strength with nearly 4,000 men. As "the only movable column west of Winchester," it was ready to confront all enemy threats. In early April, Hayes was given command of the Second Brigade, which at 5,000 men was "quite a little army," and was ordered to take it "over awful mountain roads, through a destitute country," to Lynchburg, Virginia. Before leaving his old command, Hayes and his men celebrated the fall of Richmond, and his speech on that occasion was, in effect, a farewell address. He also wrote to the officers and men of the First Brigade—some of whom had served with him for almost four years, and all of whom had been with him through the tough and bloody campaigns of 1864—telling them that they would forget neither what they had survived nor one another.[21]

With Lee's surrender to Grant on 9 April, the expedition to Lynchburg was unnecessary. Hayes reveled in the glorious news and "the manner of it too! Our best general vindicated by having the greatest victory. General Crook too. Did you see," Hayes exclaimed to Lucy, "it was his immediate command that captured so much." Since the war was all but over, Hayes planned to resign in June, after he had completed four years in the army. Then he anticipated being with Lucy and the boys "for good!"[22]

At 8 A.M. on 15 April, Hayes's euphoria was shattered by news of Lincoln's assassination. He heard of it just as he was boarding a train at New Creek, West Virginia, where he was stationed. As he traveled to Cumberland, he could think of nothing else. The "possible results in their worst imaginable form" came to mind, until he "began to feel that here was a calamity so extensive that in no direction could be found any . . . glimmer of consolation." There was the personal, uncalled-for calamity that Lincoln had suffered, the "Nation's great joy turned suddenly to a still greater sorrow!" But above all, there was the exchange of Abraham Lincoln, "a ruler tested and proved in every way," for Andrew Johnson, "whose ill-omened beginning" (drunk at his inauguration as vice president) "made the Nation hang its head." And the "work of reconstruction requiring so much statesmanship [had] just begun!" Hayes's mind filled with "images of evil and calamity"; his heart sank as it had "when the defeat of our army at Manassas almost crushed the Nation."

In the depths of his grief, Hayes began to realize, as the train rattled along, that even in "great affliction, one comes to feel that it is not all darkness." He recognized that the catastrophe would have been even greater if it had occurred earlier. Having met and conversed with Lincoln, Hayes knew his worth and accurately prophesied his place in history:

As to Mr. Lincoln's name and fame and memory, — all is safe. His firmness, moderation, goodness of heart; his quaint humor, his perfect honesty and directness of purpose; his logic, his modesty, his sound judgment, and great wisdom; the contrast between his obscure beginnings and the greatness of his subsequent position and achievements; his tragic death, giving him almost the crown of martyrdom, elevate him to a place in history second to none other of ancient or modern times. His success in his great office, his hold upon the confidence and affections of his countrymen, we shall all *say* are only second to Washington's; we shall probably *feel* and *think* that they are not *second* even to his.[23]

With the Lynchburg raid called off, Hayes had little to do beyond paroling guerrillas. All of them, from John S. Mosby on down, seemed "disposed to quit and surrender." If that feeling continued, Hayes predicted on 21 April that "we shall soon have peace throughout Virginia." He was flattered that the Ohio soldiers of his old division had adopted resolutions urging the Union party to nominate him for governor of Ohio, but he did not wish to be a candidate and tried to prevent their publication. "The answer is simply," he told Lucy, "*I have accepted another place*, and that is reason enough for not looking further."[24]

Hayes regarded the surrender of Gen. Joseph E. Johnston to Sherman on 26 April as the end of the war. He celebrated by wearing a white collar for the first time in his four years of service. He did not resign immediately. He wanted to know what was to be done with, as he put it, "my favorite troops. As soon as that is known I quit." In early May, he received a leave and, appropriately for a congressman, visited Washington (although Congress was not in session, his term had begun on 4 March 1865). He stayed with Judge Johnston and saw Postmaster General William Dennison (the former governor) and other Ohio friends. Hayes also had two talks with President Johnson and was more impressed than he had anticipated. "He strikes one," he told Sophia, "as a capable and sincere man—patriotic and with a great deal of experience as a public man." Washington was particularly exciting, with the great armies arriving from the South. As Hayes wrote to a member of his staff, "There is more *visible* here than at New Creek," making it difficult to tear oneself away. Grant and Sheridan were in town by 7 May, Sherman was coming soon, and Hayes determined that neither he nor Lucy would miss the grand army reviews.[25]

Fortunately, Lucy's rheumatism had abated, and she was able to travel. Hayes, who had business to attend to at Marietta, Ohio, on 14 May, continued on to Chillicothe and brought Lucy back to New Creek on the evening of 19 May. The next day he resigned as brigadier general of volunteers (to take effect on 8 June, thus completing four years of service) and arranged to ship his traps and his outfit's mascot—Russell Hastings's horse, Old Whitey—to Sardis at Fremont. Hayes wrote to Hastings, who was still convalescing, about the arrangement, with the hope that he would again be able to ride Old Whitey.[26]

After leaving New Creek, Hayes and Lucy managed to see Crook in Baltimore and still get to Washington on Monday morning, 22 May. The next day, they were in the congressional stand for the grand review of the Army of the Potomac. With the flag at the White House flying at the top of its staff for the first time since Lincoln's assassination, thousands of men marched up Pennsylvania Avenue from the Capitol to the White House, while crowds sang and cheered. On 24 May, Sherman's army, made up mostly of westerners, had its grand review along the same route. For Hayes, "Sherman and his army was the great show." The Army of the Potomac looked and marched wonderfully, but Hayes was prejudiced against it to the end. He preferred Sherman's ragged, imprecise, and rough-cut men. In their parade, they included mules laden with the spoils of war, camp pets, and former slaves who had stayed with the army.[27]

Lucy enjoyed both parades enormously. She borrowed Hayes's field glasses to study Johnson and Grant, who sat in an opposite reviewing stand. She thought that Johnson looked like a man of honesty and sincerity and that Grant appeared noble and unassuming, while his boys leaned on him "with all fondness and love." Lucy rejoiced in the victory and was thankful that her husband had survived, but she did not forget those who were absent. "While my heart filled with joy," she wrote to her mother, "at the thought of our mighty country—its victorious noble army—the sad thoughts of thousands who would never gladden home with their presence made the joyful scene mingled with so much sadness—that I could not shake it off."[28]

After the grand reviews, Hayes and Lucy remained in Washington for a few days. With them were Hayes's niece Laura and her husband, Brig. Gen. John G. Mitchell, who had marched with Sherman's army in the grand review. With passes from General Grant, Hayes and Lucy visited Richmond and Petersburg at the end of May and saw "all of the awful desolation." The trip to Richmond symbolized for them the end of the four-year struggle. Satisfied, they returned to Chillicothe.[29]

On 8 June 1865, Hayes was mustered out of the army and, after his discharge, was breveted major general for "gallant and distinguished services during the campaign of 1864." He had experienced physical hardship, personal danger, and mental strain and had proved a worthy warrior; he had been wounded five times (once badly) and had had four horses shot under him. In battle, he had "displayed personal daring, self-possession, and efficiency." William McKinley recalled, "His whole nature seemed to change when in battle. From the sunny, agreeable, the kind, the generous, the gentle gentleman . . . he was, when the battle was once on . . . intense and ferocious." Although Hayes was pleased with his title, he freely admitted, "I never fought in battle as a general." As a citizen officer who had helped make the army of a free, democratic republic successful, he asserted with pride, "I was one of the good colonels in the great army."[30]

Being a warrior had been hard, but it had given Hayes the experience of a lifetime. When his soldiers were leaving for home, Hayes doubted "that many of them will ever see as happy times again as they have had in the army." As he was about to lose the camaraderie of camp and field, he realized that the four most glorious years of his life were ending. But, if war had been fascinating, he sensed that peace could be enchanting and knew that its time had come. To his mother, Hayes simply wrote, "I am very happy to be through with the war."[31]

TWELVE

CONGRESSMAN

Congress was not scheduled to meet until 4 December, but while he was still in the army, Hayes was busy replying to letters "from divers office-seekers." Since the president and department heads depended on congressmen for advice on appointments, federal job distribution was largely in congressional hands. Congressmen used the appointments at their disposal to build political organizations, but with so many candidates for each significant office, distributing patronage was work and trouble. Hayes discovered that each appointment disappointed old friends and failed to make new ones.[1]

It was difficult for congressmen to choose among applicants, and this difficulty was multiplied for Hayes, who had been away from Cincinnati and out of politics for four years. He had to rely on friends to evaluate a candidate's capacity for a job, ability to help the party, and loyalty to him. Turning to Ohio's Secretary of State William Henry Smith, Hayes asked, "Who am I to look to for the truth when I get to Washington?"[2]

Hayes had doubts about a career in politics. If he were to quit after serving only one term in Congress, he told Lucy, they would have to decide whether to open a law office in Cincinnati or prepare a home in Fremont. "Don't worry over it," he reassured her, "but think of it and when we meet we will confer." They thought and conferred but made no decision. "I suspect," Hayes wrote to Lucy, "we shall final[ly] leave 'events to shape themselves,' as McClellan used to do." In early July, with Lucy still in Chillicothe, Hayes rented a room in Cincinnati, took meals at the Burnett House, and established his headquarters at the office of Reuben H. Stephenson and Edward F. Noyes. He replied to correspondents and listened "to all sorts of applications," but it was hot and he was lonely. He told Lucy that the thought " 'Politics [is] a bad trade' runs in my head often."[3]

By early July, Hayes and Lucy had made some decisions. Lucy would remain in Chillicothe for the summer with the younger boys, and Birch and Webb would join Sardis at Spiegel Grove. In October, the family would return to their old home in Cincinnati and bring Sophia there to live with them for the winter, despite the fact that the noise of the children would get on her nerves, and her melancholia would get on the nerves of Hayes and especially Lucy. After William Platt remarried, Sophia had moved back to Delaware to live with Arcena Wasson; she no longer felt useful without Fanny's children to look after. In August, Arcena's daughter and Sophia's namesake insisted that she leave. Laura, Sophia's oldest granddaughter, and her husband, Gen. John G. Mitchell, then took the old woman to Vermont to spend a few months with her brothers. Although she feared that it would be the death of her, she not only survived the trip but enjoyed better health in Vermont than she had in Ohio.[4]

During the summer of 1865, Hayes heard from his old college friend from Texas for the first time in four years. Guy Bryan wanted a pardon and asked for Hayes's support. "I am ashamed," Hayes responded, "that I have not written to you since the close of the War to say I was ready to do what you wish. The truth is I was not sure how you might feel. . . . *I will make this a personal matter* & have no doubt it will all be as you wish." Hayes urged Bryan to be patient and not to sacrifice his property and was eager to hear about him and his family. "I never saw a Texan soldier," Hayes told him, "that I didn't inquire of you. But I learned next to nothing."[5]

In the fall, Hayes's family and his party competed for his time. Hayes, Lucy, and their older boys spent two weeks together at Spiegel Grove in early September before he plunged into the important state political campaign. Hayes's old comrade in arms Jacob Dolson Cox was running for governor, and the political complexion of the state legislature would determine whether John Sherman would be returned to the U.S. Senate. As a popular war hero and a good speaker, Hayes was in demand and warned his mother that she would get only a few short letters from him. At first, he campaigned primarily in his own district, but in late September and early October, he spoke at meetings throughout the state. The Republicans triumphed, Cox was elected, and Sherman was reelected senator. By 1 November, the family was together in their old home.[6]

Hayes remained with his family scarcely a week before departing east to get his mother. His first stop was Washington, where he engaged modest quarters for the winter and procured a presidential pardon for Guy Bryan and his brothers. Aware that the South's representation in Congress would increase after 1870, since the three-fifths clause of the Constitution was no longer operable (no slaves remained to be computed at three-fifths their number in apportioning representatives), Hayes unrealistically urged the Bryans to accept a further constitutional amendment (beyond abolishing slavery) that would base congressional representation on actual voters. Hayes deemed such an amendment, which had broad Republican support, essential for Reconstruction, since it would increase the South's power in

Congress and in the electoral college if blacks received the vote but would decrease that power if blacks remained disfranchised.[7]

Moving on to Vermont, Hayes picked up his mother. Together they left Brattleboro by rail on 14 November and were in Fremont thirty-two hours later. Sophia was uncharacteristically ecstatic. "We had a delightful time. No one could be more blessed in going and returning than I have been." Learning that Lucy's mother was ill and aware that her son's household was hectic, Sophia was content to remain with Sardis. "I should be happy in this pleasant home," she wrote to Birch, "if I could see my Children now and then coming in."[8]

When Hayes reached Cincinnati, he had only ten days with his family before he left for Washington on 29 November. Among his companions on the train was Representative Samuel McKee of northeastern Kentucky, who "doesn't travel on the Sabbath, plays no cards, neither drinks nor uses tobacco, and is an abolitionist! The war," Hayes marveled, "has done the work of centuries. Five years ago the same constituency would have voted to crucify him." Hayes could not anticipate that, despite peace, Congress would continue to do the work of centuries during the few years he was a member and that he, a moderate by temperament, would become a radical. Arriving on the morning of 30 November, he first went to his rooms at 452 Thirteenth Street and then checked in at the House of Representatives, picking up his official stationery. As a member of the House, he was allowed seventy dollars worth of stationery, fifty dollars for newspapers during that session, twenty-four copies of the current *Congressional Globe*, and a copy of all back numbers.[9]

The "agreeable and harmonious" Ohio Union (Republican) delegation caucused on the evening of 1 December. On the crucial issue of the moment, it "agreed to oppose the admission of any delegate from the Rebel States for the present," rejecting President Andrew Johnson's attempt to reconstruct the Union. Under Johnson's auspices, governments were set up by voters who had been qualified to vote in 1860 and now swore allegiance to the Constitution and acquiesced in the abolition of slavery. These governments appalled Republicans by enacting black codes, which were designed to replace slavery with peonage, and by turning to prominent Confederates for political leadership at home and in Congress, where, if Johnson prevailed, they would resume their prewar seats. Robert C. Schenck announced that he would introduce a constitutional amendment basing representation on actual voters, and all in the caucus seemed to acquiesce. But when Hayes "offered the resolution, with *educational test or condition* added" (at Schenck's suggestion), James M. Ashley and Samuel Shellabarger dissented. In sizing up his colleagues, Hayes recorded his first and lasting impression of James A. Garfield as "a smooth, ready, pleasant man, not very strong."[10]

The following evening, Republican members of the House caucused. Justin S. Morrill, an intelligent Vermont merchant, chaired the meeting, and Thaddeus Stevens of Pennsylvania made "the important motions." But when the caucus took "a test vote" and agreed with the Ohio delegation to back an amendment basing representation on voters instead of population, Stevens angrily resisted it. He "threatened to leave the caucus" and "finally carried his point" that Congress should create a Joint Committee of Fifteen to consider Reconstruction issues, including suffrage and representation. The committee's immediate task, Hayes noted, would be "to report as to the status of the Rebel States and whether they were in a condition to be represented." For the present, the caucus decided to exclude "members from those States" from Congress. The caucus also agreed upon Schuyler Colfax for Speaker and Edward McPherson for clerk of the House.

Two days later, the Republicans organized the House. They were led, Hayes wrote admiringly, by "Thad Stevens, grim-looking, cool, with a ready wit, perfect courage, and the sort of independence which long experience, assured position, and seventy years of age gives an able man." McPherson, who was Stevens's friend, made the crucial move by excluding from the roll those claiming membership from former Confederate states. "We start off here with perfect unanimity," Hayes reported to Warner M. Bateman, a politically astute member of the Ohio legislature, but added, "I have no better means than you have of guessing the future."[11]

After a week in Washington, Hayes was ambivalent about being a congressman. "With my family here, pleasantly homed, I would like it well. As it is, I find nothing very gratifying . . . and nothing decidedly the contrary." His college chum, Representative Rowland E. Trowbridge of Michigan, "came bouncing into" the Ohio caucus to welcome him "in his old jovial way," and, as Hayes told Lucy, they cronied "together a good deal." Hayes also spent time with Ohio friends.[12]

Socializing in the opening days of Congress came to a bittersweet climax on 16 December. That evening, Hayes attended a "very pleasant meeting of Ohio men" at the home of James C. Wetmore, the state's agent in Washington. Chief Justice Salmon P. Chase was there, as was his Supreme Court colleague Justice Noah H. Swayne, Senators Benjamin F. Wade and John Sherman, and many members of the House. The guest Hayes most enjoyed was former Gov. Thomas Corwin, who had been Lincoln's minister to Mexico and was practicing law in Washington. "I saw him standing at some distance from where I was comfortably seated," Hayes recorded in his diary. "I went to him and conducted him to my seat. He was happy, genial, humorous as ever. Late in the evening he was struck with paralysis on the right side, soon became unconscious," and died two days later. "So disappears the finest genius Ohio has ever produced," Hayes noted, "without an equal as a popular orator in this country."[13]

Hayes found the House "more orderly and respectable" than he had expected" and its chamber "very large and beautiful." Describing it for Birch, he noted: "Over the Speaker's chair are two rather small sized American Flags. On his right is a full sized portrait of Washington — on his left LaFayette. Only one other picture in the Hall — Washington bidding farewell to his Generals." Congressmen met at noon and usually adjourned in about two hours, doing most of their work, Hayes explained, "in Committee rooms." To Sophia, who thought that military life was more wholesome than political life, he wrote, "If you could see my associates and could also take a look at camp life as it was, you would very quickly change your notions as to the comparative temptations of my former and my present mode of life."[14]

Hayes told Lucy that "the noticeable men on our side of the house are Thad Stevens, Judge Kelley, and Roscoe Conkling." Hayes liked the "sharp-faced" look of Stevens and remarked: "The only blemish in his puritanical, severe appearance is a brown wig. He is witty, cool, full of and fond of 'sarcasms,' and thoroughly informed and accurate. He has a knack of saying things which turn the laugh on his opponent. When he rises everyone expects something worth hearing, and he has the attention of all. . . . He is radical throughout, except, I am told, he don't believe in hanging." Hayes reported that the frequent short speeches of William D. Kelley of Philadelphia were exceedingly well delivered, and that Conkling from Utica, New York, spoke "in a distinct, clear tone, with great deliberation and in language fitted to print." Loath to admit the superiority of easterners in any endeavor, Hayes proudly added that Columbus Delano of the Ohio delegation was "a good specimen of the lively, earnest style of Western talkers," and later, when Shellabarger spoke energetically, Hayes exclaimed, "Good for Ohio!"[15]

Hayes left his committee assignments "to chance," realistically assuming that the large Republican majority left little hope "for new members on important committees." He got on Land Claims, a "tolerably important" lawyers' committee, and felt "lucky" because of his "bookish" proclivities to be named chairman of the Joint [Senate and House] Committee on the Library, where his colleagues were "all gentlemen and scholars." Anything relating to the fine arts was referred to Hayes's committee, and his chairmanship gave him "control in a great measure of the fine Botanical Garden with its green-

Congressman Hayes

houses, . . . an educated gardener and twelve assistants, with the whole bouquet business. A funny sort of thing for me," Hayes remarked, "but very nice and no labor worth mentioning."[16]

After a two-week break for Christmas, Hayes arrived back in Washington late Saturday night, 6 January 1866. He had been with his family in Cincinnati and visited his mother and uncle in Fremont. Although he had hoped that Lucy would return with him, Birch had a fever and she stayed in Cincinnati. Reconstruction issues made work in the House interesting, but work for constituents kept Hayes running to the War and Treasury Departments and the Patent Office. Late Wednesday night, he wrote to Lucy: "Have been nowhere, seen nobody. President Johnson's first reception last night. Didn't go. The truth is, this being errand boy to one hundred and fifty thousand people tires me so that by night I am ready for bed instead of *soirees*."[17]

Hayes was kept up that night by the Republican caucus, which was considering William D. Kelley's bill that would extend the vote to black males in the District of Columbia. Fearing that the issue of Reconstruction might split the Republican (Union) party, Hayes emphasized, "The first thing is to keep together, united and harmonious." Kelley had supported his bill in Congress with a very effective "offhand brilliant speech," but the caucus, amid "much confusion and some feeling," decided against his bill, preferring "*qualified*" suffrage. An angry Stevens, Hayes reported, "preferred no bill at all!" Although a month earlier Hayes had favored an "*educational test or condition*" for suffrage, Stevens, Kelley, and Shellabarger had changed his mind. "The radical element is right," he declared. "Universal suffrage is sound in principle." But Hayes thought that the leadership was trying to railroad Kelley's bill through and was pleased "that the despotism of the committees and the older members was rebuked." Despite the frayed tempers at the meeting, Hayes was confident that "the signs of harmony are more hopeful."[18]

With Birch recovered, Lucy arrived in Washington on 18 January for a six-week stay. Together they visited "public buildings, courts, and Congress." They also went on an excursion to the naval academy and the old capitol building at Annapolis. At their boarding house, they shared a table with Vice Adm. David G. Farragut, who was very sociable. Lucy sat in the House's diplomatic gallery each day wearing a checkered shawl, which easily caught Hayes's eye. On Sunday, 21 January, they attended services in the House and heard its chaplain, Charles Brandon Boynton of Cincinnati, preach to a large audience. In the same hall, the historian George Bancroft eulogized Lincoln on his birthday before Johnson and "a Multitude of people," including the cabinet, the Supreme Court, both houses of Congress, and military and naval officers.[19]

Despite his claim that "gaiety . . . is simply tedious," Hayes enjoyed party-going. On their second night out, he and Lucy hopped from Gen. Ulysses and Julia Grant's first reception to one given by Sen. John and Margaret Sherman. "I have always wanted to be the first," Hayes told his mother, "the *very* first at a big party. I never heard of anybody who was first. We did it at Grant's. There were a goodly number of ladies and gentlemen in the clothing-rooms all waiting for somebody to break the ice. Lucy and I hurried off our things and got down first. It was right jolly. General and Mrs. Grant, a sister, and a staff officer's wife waiting anxiously for an attack. We charged and had a good merry time of it all to ourselves."[20]

Being together in Washington was like another honeymoon for Hayes and Lucy. They enjoyed what Hayes called "six weeks of real, genuine, old-fashioned love." After Lucy went back to Cincinnati, the sight of her forgotten gloves aroused his desire for her. In letters, he called her "My Darling Baby" and wondered, "What'll become of me." A month after her departure, Hayes confided to her, "I begin to think that I ought to quit a 'biz' which separates me from you so much."[21]

Despite missing Lucy, Hayes made the most of his time in Washington. A few days after her departure, he saw Albert Bierstadt's monumental painting *Storm in the Rocky Mountains, Mt. Rosalie.* Since Hayes was intensely patriotic and prone to exaggerate the virtues of anything western, he responded enthusiastically to the painting's grandiose, romantic vision. "By gaslight the effect is incomprehensible, such brilliancy and light and shade! Mr. Bierstadt says it is better by daylight. I shall see." On the anniversary of Lincoln's death, Hayes visited Washington's Mount Vernon for the first time and loved its setting on the Potomac. Compelled by the time and place to compare the two heroes, Hayes confirmed what he had suspected a year earlier: "The truth is, if it were not sacrilege, I should say Lincoln is overshadowing Washington. Washington is formal, statue-like, a figure for exhibition," but Lincoln is "the highest character." Hayes believed that "neither could have done the other's work, and without the work of both we should have had a different history."[22]

Completing Lincoln's unfinished task of reconstructing the Union was the major concern of Congress. On 31 January, the House passed a proposed constitutional amendment that would base congressional representation on the entire population ("excluding Indians not taxed"), but if a state denied the vote on account of race or color, those persons affected would not be counted in apportioning its representatives. Hayes had "voted with Schenck to make *Voters* the basis" of representation, but the "full debates in the house" changed his mind, and he supported the amendment as passed. It would give Ohio, with its large number of unnaturalized, nonvoting immigrants, one more congressman than would the Schenck proposal.

Hayes insisted, "we can't admit the South until this Amendment is safe." Under it, the South would lose representatives if it continued to deny blacks the vote, and the amendment would prevent northern Democrats and recent rebels from controlling the government. Hayes told his friend Murat Halstead of the Cincinnati *Commercial*, who opposed making this amendment a condition for admitting southern representatives to Congress, that the South would never approve the amendment unless it were made "a condition" for reconstructing the Union. And if the South were admitted with its old political power, Hayes feared that the Democrats would repudiate the federal debt and assume the Confederate debt. Worse yet, the South's power would be augmented in the House and in the electoral college after the 1870 census, when former slaves would be fully counted for representation. Hayes urged Halstead, who was so antiradical that he was in "danger of getting off the track," to recognize the necessity of reducing the political power of those who were against giving blacks the vote.

Hayes also defended the District of Columbia suffrage bill. It was not an issue "between a people like those of Ohio and the negro," he told Ohio legislator Bateman, who was nervous about giving the vote to former slaves; it involved "the people . . . who were more disloyal, and with less excuse than those of any other place, and a loyal negro population. A people who . . . were spies for the Rebels . . . deserve no consideration." Tailoring the argument to fit Bateman's prejudices, Hayes did not claim black suffrage as an inalienable civil right, but viewed it as a punishment for rebels.

Hayes hoped to "get through without a break." His overriding consideration on 31 January was the unity and continued dominance of the Republican party. He did not want to see the fruits of victory frittered away by foolish, conciliatory notions like that of Halstead or by internecine strife among Republicans. "There are dangers all around us," he warned Bateman. "The extremes of both wings—ultra Radicals and ultra Conservatives, *act* as if they *wished* a rupture—the body of the Union men and, I think, the President himself, wish to avoid it." With the House's passage of the proposed amendment, Hayes thought, "Harmony is rather up just now."

Hayes was wrong about harmony. The Senate would not approve the amendment passed by the House, and Johnson—rupture or no rupture with moderate Republicans—would not abandon his plan of Reconstruction. Sen. Charles Sumner opposed any formulation that would allow a state to deny the vote to anyone on the basis of race or color, whatever penalty was contemplated. With Republicans working at cross-purposes, Stevens told Sumner, "if we are to be slain [I hope] it will not be by our friends." But rather than exploit the rift among Republicans, Johnson healed it. He inadvertently united the party and virtually divorced himself from it when he vetoed the Freedmen's Bureau bill on 19 February 1866. That bill, by extending the bureau's life indefinitely, would have enabled its agents to continue to aid former slaves and to build a Republican party in the South. Three days later, Johnson denounced Stevens and Sumner to a group serenading him on Washington's Birthday. "Many of our good men still hope that we may retain the President," Hayes wrote to Sardis, "but it is a very faint hope. . . . The general impression is . . . that Rebel influences are now ruling the White House and that the sooner Johnson is clear over, the better for us."[23]

Yet Hayes was reluctant to write "Andy" off "in a party sense." Hayes realized in early March that "doctrinally, he is against us on many things," but he "seems to feel that he was misled and is really anxious to conciliate." Hayes thought that if Johnson signed the civil rights bill, declaring former slaves to be U.S. citizens who possessed the civil rights of all other U.S. citizens, "a complete rupture will be avoided." Realizing that his "ever hopeful temper" was "a good thing in these perplexing and exciting times," Hayes admitted that he now enjoyed Congress "very much." Johnson, however, again disappointed him when he vetoed the civil rights bill on 27 March.[24]

Hayes defended the actions of Congress to his more conservative Cincinnati friends. When Friedrich Hassaurek, editor of the Cincinnati *Volksblatt*, remonstrated that the civil rights bill was "unpopular in Ohio," Hayes asserted that "it is grossly misrepresented and greatly misunderstood." Halstead's *Commercial* "speaks of it," Hayes explained, "as if it gave unusual and unheard of rights and privileges to negroes—as if it would compel the schools to receive negro children, the Hotels, negro guests"—when "*it undertakes to secure to the negro no right which he has not enjoyed in Ohio ever since the repeal of the Black Laws in 1848–9.*" The object of the bill, Hayes insisted, was to protect "Freedmen and Loyal men generally in the Rebel States. The great danger there, is local oppression—local ruffianism—depriving the individual citizen on account of color or loyalty or both, of the Commonest rights." Quoting Grant, Hayes rejected the "foolish notion of States Rights" that would protect American citizens abroad but not at home. Hayes had no doubt that the bill was constitutional, believing, as he did, in "the maxim that in behalf of the natural rights of the Citizen all provisions are to be construed liberally." Furthermore, its enforcement machinery was "an exact copy" of many penal statutes.[25]

"The truth is," Hayes responded to the complaints of Manning F. Force (who had recently relinquished command of the military district of Mississippi and returned to Cincinnati), "Congress has done next to nothing." But Hayes believed that the position held by the majority was unassailable: "The Rebel States having gone into insurrection and lost their lawful State Governments, it is for the law-making power of the Nation to say when (or whether) such new State Governments have been set up as ought to be recognized. Is not this sound? Granting this, ought we to recognize any State Government which does not *undertake*, at least, to afford adequate protection to Union people and freedmen? And further, is there evidence showing such State Governments except in Tennessee and possibly Arkansas?"[26]

Still, the Republican majority was reluctant to break with Johnson. He and his appointees would administer whatever laws Congress might pass to protect loyal southerners and freedmen, and the civil service, which he headed, contributed funds and party workers for political campaigns. Johnson's power gave even ultraradicals pause before breaking with him, and he had made some conciliatory gestures after Congress passed the Civil Rights Act over his veto in early April 1866. "Both President and Congress feel better," Hayes reported. "After growling at each other a long time, they have come to blows and that being over they are nearer being friends again." Hayes was optimistic that Congress could devise a Reconstruction program to which Johnson could agree. At the same time, Hayes knew that recently freed slaves depended on Congress for protection. "The colored procession celebrating their freedom just passed" with flags and bands, he wrote to Lucy on 19 April. "It was a curious and pretty sight. . . . Their cheering for the House and Senate as they passed the east front [of the Capitol] was peculiarly enthusiastic."[27]

Johnson, however, would not agree to the Joint Committee's plan of Reconstruction, which Stevens reported to the House on 30 April. It proposed a fourteenth amendment to prevent states from depriving any person of life, liberty, and property without due process of law; to reduce the representation of states that denied the vote to any male citizens over twenty-one; to disfranchise all Confederates until 1870 (guaranteeing a Republican victory in the 1868 election); and to repudiate the Confederate debt. The committee also proposed two bills. The first required that the former Confederate states ratify the proposed fourteenth amendment and that it be in effect prior to readmission to the Union, and the second disqualified as federal officeholders high Confederate officers, both civil and military. Among Republicans, the committee's plan had wide support, although the radicals were unhappy that it failed to guarantee blacks the vote and permitted disfranchisement if a state were willing to have its congressional representation reduced. Johnson rebuffed both the radicals and the moderates by insisting that southern states not be required to pass any amendment as a condition for readmission, and he gave his views to the press on 2 May.[28]

Hayes was in Cincinnati when Stevens reported the Joint Committee's plan. With his boys suffering from scarlet fever, he had made a quick trip home, where he remained for about a week until their crises had passed. When he returned to Washington, he remained worried, especially about "thin and feeble" little George, who he feared would not survive the coming summer. Hayes supported the Joint Committee's plan and, after the House passed the proposed fourteenth amendment on 10 May, rejoiced that "there is now almost perfect harmony in the Party here. Negro Suffrage is not to be insisted upon, but difference of opinion over that allowed." He suspected correctly that the Senate would strike out the section disfranchising former Confederates until 1870 (the only section Stevens really liked) and that the House would "adopt it solid."[29]

To achieve party unity, Hayes was willing to lean either to the moderates or to the radicals, but he preferred moderation. He was comfortable with the party's stance on 15 May, leaving "to the States the question of suffrage." In the District of Columbia and the territories, however, where Congress decided, Hayes would deny no one the franchise on account of race or color and insisted that all persons be equal before the law. Upon applying for statehood, the people of a territory should decide when writing their constitution whether blacks could vote or not. His own "decided preference" was: "Suffrage for *all* in the South, colored and white, to depend on education; sooner or later in the North also—say, all *new* voters to be able to write and read."[30]

An ardent but critical Republican, Hayes believed that blacks were oppressed by southern ruffians, and he believed that the allegations by Lucy's cousin, Gen. Joseph S. Fullerton, of corruption in the Freedmen's Bureau were partly true. "I am inclined," Hayes wrote to Lucy, "to think my party friends are more than half *wrong*, and that Fullerton is more than half *right*. The . . . men who are in charge of the freedmen . . . are weak men of small experience, or corrupt men in too many instances." While partisan Republicans either denied or played down the corruption that existed, others—bent on destroying the Freedmen's Bureau and subsequent Republican efforts to extend equal rights to black southerners—exaggerated and embraced corruption as an issue.[31]

When he heard on 16 May that little George was "failing," Hayes left for home the next morning. On 24 May, George was dead. Despite constant nursing by Lucy and her mother, he never regained his strength after his bout with scarlet fever. In his grief for George, Hayes grieved again for his sister Fanny. "His corpse," he noted, "reminds us of hers." Returning to Washington in early June, Hayes worried that Lucy, surrounded by reminders of George, would be overwhelmed by grief. But in trying to help, he revealed his battlefield mentality when he told her, "My chief consolation is . . . thinking of the good ones we have left."[32]

Hayes wanted Lucy to come to Washington. He longed to comfort her and to be comforted by her, with his arm around her waist, drawing her head snugly against his shoulder. When she decided that the boys needed her in Cincinnati, Hayes could not keep from Lucy his need for her. In his disappointment, he declared: "There is nothing in the small ambition of Congressional life, or in the gratified vanity which it sometimes affords, to compensate for separation from you. We must manage to live together hereafter. I can't stand this, and will not. Don't you want to be with me?[33]

As much as he hated to be away from Lucy, Hayes was conscientious about attending Congress. Even during George's final illness, Hayes resolved to be present when the fourteenth amendment came up. The Senate adopted it on 8 June, and the House on 13 June. It was a moderate proposal. The due process clause remained in tact, representation was based on eligible voters, citizenship was defined precisely, the disfranchisement clause was dropped (as Hayes had predicted), but the disqualification for federal office of high civil and military Confederate officers was added, and the federal debt was guaranteed. Hayes proudly told Lucy that "no man elected, or claiming to be, Union, voted against it."

The Ohio Republican congressional delegation was in a moderate, conciliatory mood. Its caucus on the evening of 14 June, at which Hayes had a "goodish time of it," agreed seven to two that states should be admitted as they ratified the proposed fourteenth amendment, and the vote was eight to one against requiring "negro suffrage as a condition of restoration." Congress did not pass enabling legislation before adjourning on 28 July, but by readmitting Tennessee after it adopted the amendment, Congress gave the South a clear signal that accepting the amendment was the path to reunion. Since pro-Johnson newspapers thought the amendment reasonable, hope for reconciliation between Congress and the president (as well as between North and South) once again surfaced. Among the "good indications" for Hayes was the administration's apparent decision not to remove his friends from their federal civil-service jobs in Cincinnati.[34]

Johnson, however, opposed Congress's proposed fourteenth amendment as the basis for restoring Confederate states to the Union. Since, according to his thinking, those states had never legally left the Union, Congress should seat their representatives. On 25 June, Johnson supporters issued a call for a National Union convention to meet in Philadelphia in August to rally support for his policy. Postmaster General William Dennison, Ohio's second most prominent Washington politician, resigned from the cabinet in July over differences with the president, and Hayes ominously told Lucy that "others are going." Johnson's relations with Congress further declined when, on 16 July, he rejected a second Freedmen's Bureau bill and Congress overrode his veto the same day. Hayes had voted for the first Freedmen's Bureau bill, which Johnson had successfully vetoed, and despite his belief that the allegations of corruption in that bureau were more than half true, he would have voted for the second bill had he not been "indisposed."[35]

Enduring the hot days of summer, Hayes longed for Congress to adjourn. "A little cholera wouldn't be bad now," he told Sardis on 7 July. "Anything to get up a scatterment." A recess finally came on Saturday, 28 July, and Hayes was in Fremont with his family on the evening of 30 July, where Lucy and the boys had been spending the summer with Sardis. After two days, Hayes, Lucy, and Rud left for Cincinnati, where Hayes had some political affairs to attend to. On 4 August, the Republican congressional convention in his district renominated him without opposition, which—despite his complaints about the life of a congressman—he found "pleasant." Hayes lingered in Cincinnati for about a week, then joined Lucy and Rud in Ross County, where they had gone to be with Lucy's mother at Aunt Margaret Boggs's farm. Maria Webb's health had deteriorated after little George's death. When her condition became "critical" in mid-August, Hayes and Lucy sent for Birch and Webb. Happy to see them, their grandmother rallied. Her illness kept Hayes from going to Philadelphia on 3 September to the Pro-Congress Convention of Southern Loyalists (designed to offset the earlier pro-Johnson "Arm in Arm" convention), but it did not prevent him from campaigning for reelection. Maria Webb died on 14 September while Lucy sang "Rock of Ages," as she had requested.[36]

Although Hayes had already spoken in five county precincts, the campaign really opened on Saturday, 8 September, with a "great city meeting" at which Hayes's offhand speech "took better" than any speech he had ever delivered. There was a superabundance of laughter and cheers, and after he was done, "a lot of old Kanawha soldiers" jumped onto the stand and "carried on in a style that," he told Lucy, "would have delighted you." Beginning in this "most encouraging" manner, the campaign continued to please Hayes, who predicted that he would be reelected by a large majority.[37]

Hayes regularly delivered a formal speech that was printed and circulated as a campaign document. He declared that there was a Union plan and a rebel plan of Reconstruction before the country. The president and the Democrats embraced the rebel plan and wished to restore the seceded states into the Union with seventy traitors representing them in Congress. The rebel plan would exclude Union men in the South from "every office" and banish many from the states they had tried to save for the Union. It would abandon "the four millions of loyal colored people . . . to such treatment as the ruffian class of the South, educated in the barbarism of slavery and the atrocities of the Rebellion, may choose to give them." In contrast, the Union plan, as embodied in the proposed fourteenth amendment, would remove every relic of slavery from the Constitution and from state institutions and laws, would respect loyalty and make treason odious, and would not repudiate the federal debt incurred in crushing the rebellion.[38]

Hayes predicted that Cincinnati Democrats, who were appealing to "prejudice against negroes," would fail, despite the New York money they were spending. "The negro prejudice is rapidly wearing away," he told Sardis, "but is still very strong among . . . the ignorant and unthinking generally." There was more racial prejudice in Ohio than Hayes perceived, but for the present, it had less appeal than the radical program to strip rebellious southerners of political power by extending equal civil rights to blacks.[39]

Confident that the Republicans would triumph, Hayes urged Guy Bryan to convince Texans to accept the congressional plan of Reconstruction by ratifying the fourteenth amendment. Hayes emphasized that it disfranchised no one and disqualified for officeholding only those who had been Confederate leaders. Hayes warned Bryan that *"this plan contains the best terms you will ever get—and they should be promptly accepted. . . .* Don't let Andy Johnson deceive you. He don't know the Northern people."[40]

As Hayes predicted, the Republicans won a smashing victory in the 9 October 1866 Ohio election. To celebrate, he joined a congressional junket to the end of the Union Pacific Railroad, which had been constructed halfway across Nebraska, and purchased pictures to retain "a very correct notion" of the land and people, "especially of the Pawnees." Hayes was so impressed by the growing towns and cities of the West (especially St. Louis, Kansas City, Leavenworth, Omaha, and Chicago) that he advised William McKinley to settle in one of them.[41]

While Hayes was on his railroad junket, his mother, who was in her seventy-fifth year, died. Although Sophia had appeared to be in good health when he left for the West, she was taken ill at Will Platt's home in Columbus and died there on 30 October, "confident of the future" and surrounded by her grandchildren and Sardis. "Mother," Hayes wrote at the end of her di-

ary, "suffered very little and died in almost perfect possession of her facul-
ties." Hayes arranged for her funeral at Columbus and her burial next to his
father in Delaware. It had been a difficult time for Hayes and Lucy. "We have
lost our Mothers this fall," he told McKinley, and "our little George Crook
died in June."⁴²

With the second session of the Thirty-ninth Congress beginning on 3 December 1866, Hayes and Lucy made plans to return to Washington. They
took the same "rooms again at 100$ for heat fuel & light beginning Dec 1st"
and left Birch and Webb with Sardis in Fremont. The boys did well in school
there and loved to ride Sardis's horse and to watch the pigeons in the pigeon
house. Hayes visited them for a few days in the third week of November, returned to Cincinnati, and on 1 December arrived in Washington with Lucy
and Rud. Initially, Hayes's eight-year-old son did not like going off with his
parents while his older brothers were at Spiegel Grove, but he made friends
with other congressmen's sons and soon enjoyed being in Washington. With
Lucy at his side, Hayes remarked, "The meeting of members after their separation is like old college days."⁴³

Although Hayes had been a "centrist Republican" in the first session of
the Thirty-ninth Congress, the intransigence of a "pig-headed" Johnson and
an unrepentant South and the charismatic leadership of Stevens made him a
radical in the second session. He found the 1 December Republican caucus
of House members "good-tempered and sensible." Its only decision was to
urge the Senate not to confirm "appointments made for political reasons."
Its hope was to prevent Johnson, who had threatened to "kick out" radical
officeholders, from organizing the civil service to support his own Reconstruction policy. To implement its hope, Congress proposed a tenure-of-office bill and a civil-service reform bill. The tenure-of-office bill required the
Senate to approve the removal of any incumbent officeholder whose appointment it had confirmed. On the insistence of radical members of the
House (Hayes among them), the bill included cabinet members, a provision
specifically designed to protect Secretary of War Edwin M. Stanton. Pending
Reconstruction legislation made military rule of the South appear certain,
and radicals wanted a secretary of war who sympathized with their viewpoint. When Johnson vetoed the bill, Congress promptly passed it over his
veto.⁴⁴

The civil-service reform bill, written and sponsored by Thomas A. Jenckes
of Rhode Island, did not fare so well. Going beyond the immediate requirements of the radicals and backed by Republican intellectuals and their allies
in the independent press, it would create a bipartisan commission to curtail
congressional as well as executive patronage. Jenckes's scheme would re-

quire that rank-and-file federal officers be appointed on the basis of their performance on open, competitive examinations. On 6 February 1867, Thaddeus Stevens (who wanted a partisan, radical civil service) successfully moved to kill the Jenckes bill for that Congress by laying it on the table. The close vote of 71 to 67 cut across party lines and split the radicals. In supporting Jenckes, Hayes began a lifelong commitment to civil-service reform.[45]

During the Christmas recess, Hayes and Lucy, who had intended to return to Ohio, became part of a congressional excursion to Memphis and New Orleans. Both cities had suffered race riots in 1866 in which white supremacists had murdered blacks, and the cities' leading citizens wanted to meet with congressmen. These citizens and the managers of southern railroads made the trip possible. A dozen senators and representatives—of whom Sen. Benjamin F. Wade of Ohio was the most prominent—as well as several of their wives went on this social and political trip. The group was predominantly radical Republican and was accompanied by Gen. Oliver Otis Howard, head of the Freedmen's Bureau. While observing southern conditions and meeting southerners in their own bailiwick, the congressional group had a most convivial time. Indeed, Hayes's diary confirms his mother's fear that congressmen were constantly beset by the temptation to drink. On the day of departure, 21 December, the tour had whiskey, crackers, and cheese at Alexandria at 8:30 A.M., had a "good old-fashioned" dinner at Charlottesville, supped at 8 that evening in Lynchburg, and at 11 enjoyed a champagne supper. Subsequent days were filled with sumptuous dining and nights with serious drinking, judging from the arrival of the tour at "Chattanooga, 2 A.M. Drinking." Hayes reported to Sardis that "Lucy is doing her best and enjoying it hugely."[46]

During their Christmas evening in Memphis, Hayes "experienced a new sensation. I went with General Howard to a meeting of colored people and made them a short talk," he reported. "Their eager, earnest faces were very stimulating." Hayes met "the leading Rebels everywhere" and found the former officers "particularly interesting. I get on with them famously," he assured Sardis. "I talk negro suffrage and our extremist radicalism to all of them. They dissent but are polite and cordial." Hayes got the autograph of Gen. Pierre G. T. Beauregard, who had joined them in Mississippi and was "particularly attentive to the ladies of the party," as were the women of his family. On 28 December, the traveling delegates arrived in New Orleans, where they attended the races and visited the mint, the French market, and Jackson Square. But by their second evening in town, there were no speeches at the splendid dinner in their honor, since the radicals and the "*un*reconstructed" had exchanged views all day "with some feeling." After dinner, the congressional party departed for Washington, where it arrived at 6:30 A.M. on 3 January 1867.[47]

When the South, with the exception of Tennessee, took Johnson's advice and rejected the fourteenth amendment, Congress became more radical. "Do you watch the movements here?" Hayes asked his friend Judge William M. Dickson of Cincinnati on 19 January. "What do you think of them? Being myself on the radical side of all of them, I may have lost my sense and would like to hear a cool outsider talk." Conservative Republicans, led by John A. Bingham of Ohio, still wished to reconstruct the South on the basis of the fourteenth amendment, but the radicals, led by Stevens, now wished to go beyond it. They proposed to disqualify rebels from voting, enfranchise blacks, sweep aside the Johnson governments, require new constitutions guaranteeing equal rights to all, and even impeach Johnson. Although a majority of Republicans, Hayes included, agreed with Stevens, on 28 January a combination of Democrats and conservative Republicans recommitted a radical bill proposed by Stevens to the Joint Committee on Reconstruction, which was dominated by moderates. "Nothing will be done," Hayes wrote to Sardis, "on impeachment, or Reconstruction at this session."[48]

Hayes's prediction was wrong. On 6 February, Stevens reported from the committee a military government bill. Going beyond the committee's intent, he interpreted the bill as a radical measure that would regard the unreconstructed states as conquered territories. Some radical and most conservative Republicans raised objections to Stevens's interpretation, but Hayes liked it. "Our new plans suit me exactly," he wrote to Sardis on 7 February. "Grant, Thomas, and Sheridan are now known to be all right." Hayes meant that radicals could trust these previously apolitical generals to look to Congress rather than to Johnson for guidance while administering the South. Stevens tried but failed to push the bill through without amendment on 8 February, and it appeared unlikely that it could pass in time to avert a presidential pocket veto at the end of the lame-duck session on 3 March.[49]

Hayes continued to emphasize the cohesion among Republicans on Reconstruction. On 9 February, he wrote to Warner Bateman that because of personal differences "we *seem* to be much more divided on this subject than we really are." In fact, Hayes emphasized, "We agree to disregard the existing State Governments in the rebellious States, to institute new ones on the basis of loyalty and colored suffrage and to hold these States firmly in the grasp of military power until the process is complete." But there was "no settled purpose" on the impeachment of Johnson. "We are simply 'waiting for the facts.' "[50]

Hayes was correct about essential unity among the Republicans. On 13

February, amid last-ditch efforts to heal the breach between Johnson and conservative Republicans, Stevens saved his military government bill in one of the most dramatic moments in congressional history. James G. Blaine, a moderately conservative Republican, led an effort to amend the bill to require only impartial suffrage (allowing the disfranchisement of most blacks and some whites by literacy or property requirements) by recommitting the bill to the Judiciary Committee. Eight radicals, including Hayes and his ultraradical friend James M. Ashley, joined Blaine, the conservatives, and the Democrats to defeat Stevens. These radicals had been assured by the Judiciary Committee chair that the committee would also disfranchise leading rebels. To achieve a turnaround, Stevens passionately pleaded, in a voice so weak that representatives left their desks to gather around him, that in "this burning crisis . . . we cordially, without guile, without bickering, without small criticisms, lend our aid to promote the great cause of humanity and universal liberty." Touched by Stevens, Hayes and his fellow radicals, as well as some Republican centrists, changed their votes, defeated Blaine's motion, and passed the unamended bill.[51]

Led by John Sherman, the Senate reversed Stevens's victory by amending the military government bill to incorporate features of Blaine's proposal and calling it the Reconstruction bill. Although hinting that he might sign the bill if it included the Blaine "impartial suffrage" amendment, Johnson assured Democrats that he would veto the bill. "Andy *is* or *pretends* to be yielding," Hayes perceived on 15 February. "Many are green enough to believe his professions sincere and are getting ready to meet him *half way*! If we hold firmly to our purposes, I shall not be greatly astonished if he surrenders unconditionally."[52]

Following Stevens, the House refused to concur with the Senate's amendment on 19 February. Only a minority of Republicans, including Hayes, supported Stevens, but he was joined by the Democrats, who hoped that an impasse would kill the bill. "We are in a mixed condition on the reconstruction plans just now," Hayes observed on 20 February, "but will come out all right." That morning, the House's radical caucus decided to accept the Senate bill if it would state that the governments of the rebel states were provisional and under federal government control until their representatives were admitted to Congress, that universal suffrage must be guaranteed under those provisional governments, and that southerners who could not hold office under the proposed fourteenth amendment were still disfranchised and disqualified. Despite objections from Blaine and moderate Republicans, the House adopted these additions and passed the Reconstruction bill. The Senate concurred, but too late for the bill to become a law without Johnson's signature. Johnson, however, was too forthright to use the pocket veto.[53]

Hayes was pleased. "We are getting on just right in politics here," he wrote to Sardis, and reiterated his satisfaction to Murat Halstead, who, in the Cincinnati *Commercial*, had regretted Hayes's radical stand. "The matter is now pretty nearly right," Hayes insisted, "take it coolly . . . and you will, I am confident, come to the same conclusion." As usual, Hayes played down the acrimony among Republicans and explained to Lucy's Uncle Scott Cook, "We did not differ much in principle. . . . I went with the minority of the party in favor of getting as much power away from Rebels as possible." The acrimony, which Hayes minimized, was virtually eliminated by Johnson. He was "in a state of chaos," Hayes heard, over whether to sign or veto the bill. If he vetoed it, he would be "pretty certain to be impeached," and, Hayes noted, "many of the opponents of our party are now advising him to yield." Rejecting their advice, Johnson vetoed the Reconstruction bill on 2 March, effectively uniting disparate Republicans. That same day, both the House and the Senate overrode his veto, and the bill became law.[54]

Although Hayes had "definite and settled views" on Reconstruction, he was "a learner" on "Financial and business questions." In July 1866, Halstead begged him not to "go the whole hog with Morrill and Stevens on the infernal Tariff. It would be an awful business," he warned, "to destroy our gold revenue for the sake of those damned harpies of Pennsylvania and New England." Favoring a modest tariff that would protect "our own labor," Hayes tended to agree with Halstead that the degree of protection advocated by Justin S. Morrill of Vermont and Thaddeus Stevens of Pennsylvania would reduce imports and revenue and fail to reduce the national debt. Suspecting that "the pressure of particular interests" had led representatives to propose duties "too high, either for stability . . . or for Revenue," Hayes in February 1867 tried to cut them "down in all directions." He was also aware that, except for "a few interests," the proposed tariff ignored the West. Despite his opposition, the tariff bill became law on 2 March 1867.[55]

Hayes was faithful in attendance but not a leader in Congress. Inexperienced at legislation and convinced that congressmen talked too much, he became, in Garfield's words, "the most patient listener in the Capitol." Hayes, nevertheless, did important work as chairman of the Joint Committee on the Library. He and Librarian of Congress Ainsworth Rand Spofford had been friends since their days in the Cincinnati Literary Club. In the short period that Hayes chaired the committee, the Library of Congress "vastly" expanded its space and acquired the books and papers of the Smithsonian Institution. Hayes also shepherded through Congress an "unprecedented"

$100,000 appropriation needed to acquire the "rich library of books, pamphlets, manuscripts, and newspaper files" amassed by Peter Force, a Washington printer and journalist and father of Manning F. Force, another literary club member.[56]

Immediately on the expiration of the Thirty-ninth Congress, the Fortieth Congress assembled on 4 March 1867. Its main business was a supplemental Reconstruction bill, which required that federal military commanders register voters, supervise elections, call constitutional conventions, and launch new governments in place of the provisional Johnson governments. To prevent those Johnson regimes from implementing congressional Reconstruction, virtually all Republicans supported this legislation. When Johnson vetoed the supplemental bill, Congress again overrode his veto before recessing from 30 March to 3 July. Hayes, however, remained in Washington for several days on patronage matters to "do a good service" for his city, party, and friends.[57]

With his patronage business completed, Hayes, accompanied by Lucy and Rud, hastened to Fremont. When they arrived on 10 April, Sardis was seriously ill with "lung fever" (pneumonia), but, bolstered by their presence, he was soon out of danger. Leaving Birch and Webb to continue school in Fremont, Hayes, Lucy, and Rud proceeded on 4 May to Cincinnati, where they stayed with Dr. Joe and his bride Annie Matthews, the sister of Stanley Matthews, Hayes's college chum and comrade in arms. While Lucy, who was again pregnant, remained in Cincinnati, Hayes returned to Fremont in early June after looking after political matters—particularly a growing movement to nominate him for governor.[58]

It was still June when Hayes won the Republican gubernatorial nomination. But before the campaign began in August, he moved Lucy into a "new home" in Walnut Hills, ran up to Fremont again, and returned to Washington with Birch and Webb. Despite the added expense of a hundred dollars or so, Hayes wanted his boys to enjoy the Washington experience, especially since he thought that his next few weeks in Congress would "probably [be] my last of public life." Radical Reconstruction was not highly esteemed in Ohio, and Hayes, although a popular war hero, suspected that he would not be elected governor. At first, the boys were subdued on the train to Washington, but before arriving there on 2 July, Webb "was on good terms with the Members of Congress on board; in fact," Hayes told Lucy, "I am afraid that in another day he would have pulled Senator [Zachariah] Chandler's nose and punched Senator [Jacob C.] Howard in the stomach!" In contrast, Birch "took to the guidebook" and was "up on geography, distances, places, etc." The boys enjoyed themselves in Washington. They made trips to Mount

Vernon and Arlington Cemetery, and Hayes took them on the floor of Congress. Birch liked Thaddeus Stevens "the most." Whenever he spoke, both Birch and Webb crowded around him.[59]

Congress remained in session only from 3 to 20 July. Although radicals would have preferred to stay through the summer to impeach Johnson, the Republican caucus decided to consider only amendments to the Reconstruction Act in July and to postpone consideration of impeachment. Congress enacted another supplemental act—clarifying ambiguities in earlier acts but not going beyond them—and postponed the date of reconvening until after the November elections. Hayes leaned toward impeachment. Although on 11 July he sided with the Speaker and a majority of Republicans against the ardent impeachers on a procedural matter, a few moments later he joined that small group (Stevens, Ashley, and others) in their unsuccessful effort to reconvene Congress on 16 October rather than 13 November. With his gubernatorial campaign coming up, Hayes shrewdly made a speech that was suitable for a campaign document and stayed in Washington for a few days after the adjournment while it was being printed. With the boys' Washington days coming to a close, Hayes asked Birch if he wished to go home by way of New York City and Niagara Falls. "No," he replied, "you see I haven't seen Mama for a long time, not since April, and I want to see where she is living." On 24 July, they were "home safely." Although Hayes could have retained his House seat while running for governor, he had already decided to resign, which he did on 7 August, "to take effect from and after 31st day of October 1867."[60]

GOVERNOR

Hayes was first tempted to run for governor when Jacob Dolson Cox decided in early 1867 not to succeed himself after completing his two-year term. Although Hayes had *"no ambition* for Congressional reputation or influence," his sense of duty had not allowed him to resign from Congress and seek the governorship without the support of his Cincinnati constituents. When it appeared, at first, that they wanted him to remain in the House, he told William Henry Smith (Ohio's secretary of state and the first person to seriously suggest that Hayes run for governor) not to put his name forward. Still, his refusal had not been absolute. His ambition for high office was tempered by his desire for a private life with his family. These contradictory drives made Hayes's adeptness at refusing in such a way that allowed his supporters to keep advancing his name less calculating than it might appear.[1]

The Hayes movement continued to flourish, particularly in the Western Reserve, where the Twenty-third had been recruited, and by late May he was wavering. "My *chief personal* objection to being a candidate for governor was removed," he admitted, "when the Legislature squarely stood up to the suffrage issue," extending the vote to blacks in a proposed amendment to the Ohio Constitution, which had to be approved at the next election. By assuring Hayes that "all of the best men" thought that he was "the only one who could carry us . . . triumphantly through the campaign," Smith persuaded him to run. The election of Hayes delegates to the state Republican convention not only settled the gubernatorial nomination but also was a triumph of the radical element, led by Ben Wade, over the moderate followers of Salmon P. Chase. Pleased with the radical platform, Hayes had no regrets about the nomination. He had been an obscure congressman with little influence; now he could become the major political warrior in a pivotal state and strike decisive blows in the ongoing battle for equal rights.[2]

Hayes plunged into the campaign on 5 August. Over the next two months, he spoke once or twice daily while traveling about the state, usually accompanied by a local congressman. Frequent speeches, he confessed to Lucy, made him "quite hoarse but it wears off entirely," he assured her, "as I warm up." Although he was in an uphill fight against the Democrats, who again appealed to racial prejudice, Hayes forthrightly advocated the Negro suffrage amendment and defended radical Reconstruction. Beginning with Lincoln's Gettysburg Address, his set speech affirmed that the Declaration of Independence dedicated the nation to equal rights. Attempts had been made, Hayes noted, "to destroy the great fundamental truth of the Declaration, by limiting the application of the phrase 'all men' to the men of a single race." The South had denied the rights of "over four millions of our countrymen . . . because of their race and color," held them in slavery, and, to perpetuate that slavery, made war to destroy "the great Republic." Hayes linked the leading Ohio Democrats of 1867—George Hunt Pendleton, Clement L. Vallandigham, and Hayes's opponent in the gubernatorial race, Allen G. Thurman—to the attempt to destroy the Union. They had embraced a policy of peace in January 1861 and had "looked smilingly on" while an "armed oligarchy" had tried to establish a nation based on slavery and the denial of human rights.[3]

Having castigated his opponents for abetting slavery and rebellion, Hayes smote them for striving to restore the seceded states and their rebel leaders in a hastily reconstructed Union. Using the same arguments and at times the same words he had used a year earlier, Hayes in 1867 played the emotional chord that had helped bring radicals their 1866 victory. On this occasion, however, the issue was political equality in Ohio, not in the South. The peace Democrats, who had opposed the amendment to the Constitution abolishing slavery, Hayes elaborated, "were bitterly hostile to loyal colored people both North and South." These Democrats, Hayes charged, regarded "treason as no crime and loyalty as no virtue"; they would banish patriots from the states they labored to save, abandon blacks to southern ruffians, and impair the integrity of the public debt. Under the Johnson governments, "civil authorities did not even attempt to prevent" the "atrocious crimes . . . everywhere committed against loyal people." Consequently, Congress passed the Reconstruction acts, which, Hayes argued, completely and exactly "met the evil to be remedied in the South." Democrats opposed this measure "because it commits the people of the nation in favor of manhood suffrage."[4]

If it were wise and just to extend the ballot to blacks in the South, the District of Columbia, and the territories, justice and wisdom demanded that it be extended in Ohio and other northern states. Estimating that there were approximately five million blacks in the United States, Hayes emphasized: "They are not aliens or strangers. . . . They are here by the misfortune of their fathers and the crime of ours. Their labor, privations, and sufferings, unpaid and unrequited, have cleared and redeemed one third of the inhabited territory of the Union. Their toil has added to the resources and wealth of the nation untold millions. Whether we prefer it or not, they are our countrymen, and will remain so forever."[5]

"Our government . . . is not the government of any class, or sect, or nationality, or race," said Hayes. "It is not the government of the native-born, or of the foreign-born, of the rich man, or of the poor man, of the white man, or of the colored man — it is the government of the freeman," it is "the government of the governed." The Ohio Democrats, Hayes charged, were waging "one more campaign on the old and rotten platform of prejudice against colored people." To Hayes, "the plain and monstrous inconsistency and injustice of excluding one seventh of our population from all participation in a Government founded on the consent of the governed in this land of free discussion is simply impossible." Hayes also argued that "impartial suffrage" would secure free public schools for all and would promote popular intelligence, economic progress, and sectional and racial harmony. Hayes was convinced that he and Ohio Republicans deserved victory because they aimed, like Lincoln, to "afford all an unfettered start and a fair chance in the race of life."[6]

Campaigning was taxing, but Hayes "had some good times," especially with men from the Twenty-third. When on Saturday, 31 August, a speech at Hillsboro kept him from catching the last train for Cincinnati, four of his former soldiers took Hayes on a railroad handcar — making "it go very fast"—thirty-seven miles to Loveland. There, Hayes caught a train on the Little Miami Railroad; as it "passed the path in Fulton leading up to Walnut Hills, the conductor slowed up," Hayes jumped off, and he was home about eight or nine o'clock that evening.[7]

Hayes, Lucy, and Rud enjoyed a day of rest before Lucy gave birth to a girl on Monday, 2 September. Although Hayes and Lucy had had difficulty naming their boys, they immediately called their little girl Fanny, for Hayes's beloved sister. The next day, Hayes returned to the campaign trail. When he got to Fremont on 7 September to speak and spend the weekend with his older boys, he heard from Dr. Joe that "Lu & baby are doing first rate." Hayes, in turn, was able to cheer Lucy with news that after their long summer vacation, thirteen-year-old Birch and eleven-year-old Webb were "full of the base ball mania" and "much pleased with their sister."[8]

Birch and Webb remained in Fremont, but by the end of September, the other family members were in their old home in Cincinnati. Hayes closed the campaign there on his forty-fifth birthday, with Oliver P. Morton of Indiana at his side, and regretted that Morton's "noble speech . . . could not be heard by half his audience." Schooled by constant campaigning, Hayes was in excellent voice, reaching all the audience "more easily than ever before" with one of his best speeches.[9]

Hayes fought hard, but it was an uphill battle. The election held on Tuesday, 8 October, was a Republican setback. The suffrage amendment to the Ohio Constitution was defeated; the Republicans lost control of the legislature and, with it, Ben Wade's seat in the Senate; and, although the vote was close, Thurman appeared to be the next governor. Hayes was disappointed but resolved to bear his defeat "cheerfully and with philosophy." He felt "sorry for the boys—especially Birch"—but did not regret the courageous campaign he had waged. The final tally rewarded his courage; to his surprise, he won by a majority of 2,983 votes out of 484,603 cast.[10]

Over the next three months, Hayes organized the move to Columbus, decided on policies and appointments, and wrote his inaugural address. Breaking up housekeeping in Cincinnati, Hayes and Lucy sent a few things to Fremont but, in late December, moved most of their furniture to the house he had rented in Columbus (51 East State Street). Looking forward to a more settled life for the first time in almost seven years, he told Lucy, "I have an impression we shall feel very homelike here."[11]

Hayes consulted with Governor Cox about appointments, but before making any commitments, he wished to speak with Secretary of State William Henry Smith, who had orchestrated his nomination. Hearing rumors and fearing that Hayes had listened too sympathetically to Cox, Smith, who thought that he was Hayes's chief patronage adviser, worked himself into a snit. "Be serene!" Hayes advised him, "I'll talk it all up before jumping in." Although Hayes respected Smith's judgment and wanted his opinions, he also wanted advice from others and was determined to make up his own mind. Remaining offended, Smith complained about rumored appointments and, having resigned his position in order to edit the Cincinnati *Chronicle*, left Columbus in January before Hayes could see him. Unwilling to lose a friend over misunderstandings, Hayes patiently explained, "As to appointments generally I have a preference for meritorious Soldiers *and some* half formed impressions about individuals but the whole matter is open—left so in order to hear what you and others would say."[12]

Composing his inaugural address caused Hayes less trouble than making appointments. He delivered it on 13 January 1868, a snowy, cold Monday, and he boasted that it was the shortest ever delivered in Ohio. In that address, Hayes reaffirmed his commitment to equal voting rights and warned the General Assembly to avoid excessive legislation. Since the divisive debates over the state debt, taxation, banking, currency, and internal improvements had been either settled or transferred to the federal government,

Hayes stressed that only "one important question of principle" remained unsettled: the abolition of "distinctions in political rights based on color." The Democratic legislature, however, continued to work to disfranchise black voters, and, since the governor of Ohio had no veto power, Hayes could do nothing to confound its racist strategy of exploiting Negrophobia to gain white support. The Democrats even voted to rescind Ohio's ratification of the proposed fourteenth amendment, but federal authorities ignored this action, and in 1868 the amendment became part of the Constitution.[13]

Hayes enjoyed his new office. "It strikes me . . . as the pleasantest I have ever had," he wrote to Sardis. "Not too much hard work, plenty of time to read, good society, etc." Lucy, Rud, and Fanny were with him in Columbus, and Birch and Webb were only two hours away with Sardis in Fremont. With "a great snow" that January and its promise of good sleighing, a contented Hayes told his uncle, "My mind is easy now." Life was especially pleasant when Manning F. Force visited in April and Hayes and Lucy invited "about a dozen of the best soldiers hereabouts" and "talked over war stories" until midnight.[14]

Hayes defined his new duties as "putting my autograph at the bottom of papers of various styles." But he also embarked on a quest for the portraits of early Ohio governors, oversaw construction of the Ohio Deaf and Dumb Asylum, urged Otto von Bismarck to appoint Johann B. Stallo (philosopher, scientist, lawyer, teacher, and friend) North German Consul at Cincinnati, responded to queries like the one from Secretary of State William Henry Seward about the status of the temperance movement in Ohio, and, among other routine acts, extradited fugitives from justice.[15]

As the governor of a major state, Hayes was consulted on national issues. He had barely assumed office when Indiana Republicans sounded him out on the currency issue and the payment of the national debt. "The *drift* with us [Ohio Republicans]," Hayes responded, "is toward three (ideas)": to pay the 5/20 bonds in "lawful" but not inflated money, to "withdraw the National Bank currency and substitute lawful money i.e. Greenbacks," and to tax the yield of the bonds like any other property. After the Democratic success in the recent election, thanks in part to George Hunt Pendleton's so-called Ohio Idea of paying the debt with greenbacks, Hayes and Ohio Republicans had positioned themselves rather close to Pendleton's views.[16]

Although willing to drift with his political colleagues on currency matters, Hayes knew his mind on Reconstruction issues. When a member of the Ohio congressional delegation queried by telegraph, "What do Ohio Republicans desire as to impeachment?" Hayes responded, "Conviction." As soon as the Ohio legislature adjourned, he planned to visit Washington during the trial, and he was probably there on Saturday, 16 May 1868, when the crucial Senate vote was taken. Hayes was in Washington to secure from the administration of Benjamin F. Wade (if Johnson were convicted) an appointment for his brother-in-law Dr. Joe as consul at Frankfort, Bremen, Hamburg, or Vienna. Johnson was acquitted by one vote, subsequent attempts to convict him failed, and Dr. Joe did not get his consulate.[17]

Four days after Johnson narrowly escaped conviction, the Republican National Convention met in Chicago. Hayes headed the Ohio delegation and rejoiced at the first-ballot nomination of Ulysses S. Grant. For the vice-presidential nomination, Ben Wade led on the first four ballots, but on the fifth ballot his opponents combined to give the nomination to Schuyler Colfax of Indiana. Except for his friend Wade's failure, Hayes considered the convention "a great success." He was worried, however, that the infamous 17 December 1862 "Jew order" by Grant might cost him Ohio in a close race. Assuming that "Jews, as a class," violated trading regulations, Grant had expelled them from the area under his command. The order had been short-lived—Lincoln quickly rescinded it—but Hayes was still concerned. He asked L. D. Myers, the state printer, how much it would affect "the vote of the Israelites" and how to control its damage.[18]

Hayes's concerns evaporated when on 9 July the Democrats rejected Pendleton and nominated former New York Gov. Horatio Seymour and, as his running mate, the youngest son and namesake of Francis Preston Blair. "Hurrah for Seymour and Blair!" Hayes exclaimed. "The prospect has certainly improved for us." Seymour was vulnerable on three counts: He opposed "the Greenback theory of Mr. Pendleton and the Western Democracy," he was "more completely identified with the peace party than any man except Mr. Pendleton," and he would reconstruct a South that would "be agreeable to the Rebels" and would not give "safety and power to the loyal."[19]

Hayes campaigned arduously throughout Ohio, contrasting Seymour's unenthusiastic support of the war with Grant's contribution to preserving the Union. Confident of victory, Hayes relaxed on election day after voting in Cincinnati. Grant triumphed in Ohio and in the nation with a better than 300,000-vote majority, and Hayes had a "glorious time . . . rejoicing," but two factors made the Republicans uneasy. First, if blacks, who universally voted Republican, had been denied the ballot, the Republicans would have won only a minority of the popular vote, even with Grant. Second, they believed that the Democrats had used fraud to carry New York (with its thirty-three electoral votes) by a 10,000-vote margin out of 850,000 votes cast.[20]

Hayes's optimism led him to believe that the South was progressing toward equal rights for all. A tendency to exaggerate the attitudinal shifts of his college friend Guy Bryan and Bryan's nephew of the same name led to this belief. Talking with young Guy after the Democratic convention, Hayes found his views "cheerful and sensible." Seemingly "free from bigotry," he convinced Hayes that in their county the "Negro business . . . works well— no fuss or trouble." Hayes also appreciated how far his old chum had come and did not expect him to conform to his own radical views. He welcomed Bryan's declarations that he would "strike no more blows"; that he yearned for "peace that springs from *Civil law, justly made,* and *intelligently* executed"; that he would "support the government that protects me"; and that "thinking men of the South" were "willing that the negroe shall have his rights of person and property fully protected." But, Bryan added, "to be equal at the ballot box and in our social relations . . . I am not willing—not willing, because they are not qualified and because *God* has stamped them differently." Emphasizing their widening area of agreement, Hayes ignored their differences. Time was rapidly diminishing their disagreements, he told Bryan in January 1869, and he hoped that hereafter "we shall meet in as complete accord as need be for close friendship."[21]

Immediately after the election, Hayes worked on his annual message to the legislature. On Sunday, 8 November, he was delighted to be interrupted by "screams from [Nurse] Eliza & all," celebrating little Fanny's first steps. The message, delivered 23 November, urged that a proposed revision of Ohio's financial system be adopted; that a fireproof building replace the central Lunatic Asylum (where his sister Fanny had been treated), which had been destroyed by a fire that took six lives; that other state institutions be inspected to prevent similar disasters; that a comprehensive geological survey of Ohio be authorized; and that recent election frauds be prevented by requiring preelection voter registration and minority-party representation on election boards.[22]

After "*several hours*' quiet" and "delightful talk" with Grant in December, Hayes marveled at "how completely and wonderfully he remains unspoiled by his elevation." Other Republican politicians plied Grant with advice and were made uneasy by his failure to respond, but Hayes, thinking " 'pressure' a bad thing" even when applied by good Republicans, had no misgivings about the new president. Grant's inaugural address and cabinet appointments confirmed the fears of many politicians, but Hayes called the address "capital" and the cabinet (which included his friend former Governor Cox) a daring "experiment." It contained "no man of political strength" and "no Presidential aspirants." With "no man being conspicuous," Hayes thought, "Grant's leadership and rule is beyond question. It seems to mean business and not political scheming." He hoped that Grant would "put fitness and qualifications before what is called 'claims' and 'political services.'" Although previously it had been considered impossible, Hayes thought that "if anybody could overthrow the spoils doctrine and practice, Grant is the man."[23]

The Democratic legislature, which Hayes despised, gratified him in one important respect. In April 1869, the geological survey—called by Hayes the "best thing of my administration"—carried "very handsomely in both branches" of the state legislature. "Now comes the important point. Who," Hayes queried, "is to be chief geologist? My prepossessions are for Professor Newberry." John Strong Newberry had been raised in the Western Reserve, studied medicine and geology in Ohio and in Paris, practiced medicine in Cleveland, accompanied numerous western exploring expeditions, served in the Sanitary Commission during the Civil War, and in 1869 was professor of geology and paleontology at the Columbia University School of Mines. When Hayes appointed Newberry, his chief rival—Charles Whittlesey, who had assisted in an 1837–38 partial geological survey of Ohio—worked to remove him. Failing in that, Whittlesey orchestrated "petty criticism and political bickering" throughout Newberry's tenure (1869–82). Legislators criticized Newberry's emphasis on paleontology and his delay in disseminating information that would aid Ohio's mineral industries. Standing by him, Hayes gently nudged Newberry, saying, "the better your showing" in the survey reports, "the more liberal the appropriation" from the legislature. Refusing to be hurried, Newberry continued his in-depth work, which laid the "foundation for most later geologic studies, including studies of mineral resources, stratigraphy, and paleontology." In his frustration, Whittlesey tried unsuccessfully to defeat Hayes's renomination, which occurred by acclamation on 23 June 1869.[24]

In Hayes's acceptance speech to the Republican state convention, he attacked the Democrats for their irresponsibility and their racism. He castigated Democratic legislators for "long sessions, excessive legislation, unnecessary expenditures, and recklessness in authorizing local debts and local taxes." Hayes also hit them for attempting to rescind Ohio's ratification of the Fourteenth Amendment; for rejecting on 4 May 1869 the proposed fifteenth amendment, which would prevent citizens from being denied the vote "on account of race, color, or previous condition of servitude"; for enacting "visible admixture" laws to deprive mixed-race citizens of the vote; and for preventing students and residents of soldiers' homes from voting where they resided. To stop Democrats from designing legislation to prevent Republicans from voting, he pressed for a Republican legislature. Believing "that the

Union Republican party is battling for the right," Hayes remained a warrior and was certain that "the goodness of the cause" would secure its triumph. Once again relying on Lincoln's words, Hayes identified Ohio Republicans with those "whose leading object is to elevate the condition of men, to lift artificial weights from all shoulders, to clear the paths of laudable pursuits for all, and to afford all an unfettered start and a fair chance in the race of life." Lincoln had defined Hayes's mission in politics.[25]

The Democrats offered voters a clear-cut choice. Their convention opposed the fifteenth amendment; wished to tax federal government bonds; and declared that the payment of those bonds in gold, when they had been purchased with greenbacks, was "unjust and extortionate" and would "force upon the people the question of repudiation." It then nominated Hayes's old commander Gen. William S. Rosecrans, who so disliked the platform that he refused to run. After this disastrous beginning, the state committee asked George Hunt Pendleton, their most prominent leader, to oppose Hayes. Pendleton, who had been the Democratic vice-presidential candidate in 1864, ran a strong campaign, mingling a prejudiced appeal to keep blacks from the polls with a popular appeal to pay the war debt with greenbacks.[26]

Finding Pendleton a tougher adversary than Rosecrans would have been, Hayes realized that he was in a "doubtful" race. To confront the Democrats head-on over Negro suffrage (which the voters had rejected in the previous election) and over Pendleton's Ohio Idea would be courting disaster. Even Sardis, who had become an abolitionist during the war, balked at Lucy's bringing Fanny's nurse, Eliza Jane, or any black servant to Spiegel Grove. Hayes, about to launch his campaign for the fifteenth amendment in August 1869, had to assure his uncle that Lucy would bring "a good *white* servant" when she visited. Fortunately for Hayes and Negro suffrage, Pendleton and the Democrats were vulnerable on several issues. To counter the attractiveness of Pendleton's greenback notions concerning the federal debt, Hayes stressed the Democratic legislators' recent irresponsibility concerning state and local debts. He also countered his opponent's appeal to racial prejudice by trumpeting Pendleton's advocacy of peace during the Civil War.[27]

While Hayes contrasted Pendleton's record with that of war Democrats like Rosecrans, Republicans stressed Hayes's heroism. In a speech at Bellefontaine, Gen. George A. Sheridan thundered that when Hayes was leading troops through the quagmire at Opequon, "where was Geo. H. Pendleton? At that very hour, he was the candidate of the 'peace party' for Vice President. At the very instant Hayes was crowning the banners of Ohio with glory, Pendleton was doing all he could to drape the banners all in white in token of surrender. . . . Is there no choice between the man for Governor, the one a soldier tried and true, the other a traitor of the most unquestioned kind?" A Democratic fabrication—that Rosecrans had once collared Hayes and threatened to cut off his shoulder straps—backfired when Rosecrans denied the tale, insisting that Hayes "had both my respect and esteem as an officer and a gentleman, and still retains them."[28]

Hayes's main concern was apathy. "The vote," he feared, "will probably be . . . so light that an adverse result would not surprise me." But with the Democrats equally plagued by apathy, he optimistically figured, "We shall succeed." The election on 12 October was doubtful until the next day. Always preparing himself for defeat with the thought that he would prefer private life, Hayes was "laughing and serene as usual," while those about him wore "anxious faces. . . . It looks as if I was carried through again by a close vote," he wrote to Sardis. "I saw the moon over my right shoulder and I think *that* will win." Hayes's margin of 7,501 votes was larger than his previous win, and this time the Republicans gained the legislature by a narrow margin, making ratification of the fifteenth amendment "almost a certainty." Hayes also thought—prematurely, it turned out—that Pendleton's defeat was the death of "the great Greenback theory."[29]

Reelection pleased Hayes, who liked being governor. He loved Ohio, and he had Lucy and the younger children with him and Birch and Webb accessible in Fremont. Because of the war and politics, Sardis was virtually raising Birch and Webb, and although the governorship had restored some stability to the Hayes household, Hayes preferred the rural environment of Spiegel Grove for his boys rather than the urban experience of Columbus. He corresponded with them about baseball and Sardis's horse Old Ned and kept them posted on Rud and Fanny. Hayes found Rud "queer" because he was lighthearted rather than apprehensive just before an examination, and Fanny could be heard calling "by-by" from the parlor window as Hayes entered the State House.

Hayes attempted to interest Birch and Webb in scholarship rather than hector them in their studies. "I will drop the grammar, and punctuation," he wrote, after he realized that he had played the role of schoolmaster too well, "and write you a few scraps from the early history of the town and region where you now are." He posed problems based on familiar places, such as figuring out the volume of water in a Spiegel Grove spring. Scientific lore fascinated him, and, with his own interest aroused by the geological survey, he piqued their curiosity as well. He sent them fossils that had been found near Columbus and at Delaware and told them of "*septaria*, or large round stones . . . *six* and *eight* feet in diameter," that had been formed near Delaware around the "bones of enormous fishes . . . long since extinct." Hayes de-

Governor Hayes and Fanny

scribed how a local teacher had suspended the Foucault pendulum from the State House dome to demonstrate "that the earth moves from the west to the east." But although "every body saw the result," Hayes noticed that "only a few seemed to fully comprehend it."[30]

Once reelected, Hayes and his family in late 1869 moved to the Seventh

Street home of Supreme Court Justice Noah H. Swayne. It was a larger house with ample grounds, and the $800-a-year rent was cheap. Moving, with its implication of a new beginning, prompted Hayes to take stock of his children in his usual matter-of-fact style. "Fanny is over two years, very handsome, spirited and interesting. Birch [sixteen years of age] came down to help us move. He is a fine looking boy of noble character. A deafness, slight, but noticeable is the greatest drawback which I now see to his future career." (The next month, after he was operated on by Dr. E. Williams of Cincinnati for $25, Hayes thought that he noticed an improvement in Birch's hearing.) Webb at thirteen was "a handsome, cheery, bright boy—with no great fondness or capacity for learning"—and Rud at eleven was "a good scholar and amiable, but [with] a weak constitution."[31]

Hayes was as matter-of-fact about himself and Lucy as he was about their children. At thirty-eight, Lucy was as attractive as ever (eight months earlier she had measured five feet three inches and weighed 127 pounds) and was "in fine health," but she still felt "the remains of her old rheumatism" in her heels if she walked too far. Her humane instincts were as strong as ever. She had been instrumental in the recent establishment of the Soldiers' and Sailors' Orphans' Home at Xenia and had "ransacked" Columbus for money and gifts for the children's Christmas celebration. About himself, at age forty-seven, Hayes observed: "My step is still quick and easy, but both legs have the mark of Rebel missiles, and bad weather brings me certain twinges which indicate that as I get older a cane will be very useful." He was five feet eight and a half inches tall and in April had weighed 171 pounds. When, after the election, he ordered a swallowtail coat, heavy black doeskin pants, and a black silk vest, he requested that "the pants be much fuller in the legs than the fashion, and, as I am getting fatter, fuller in the waist than the last."[32]

With a Republican majority in his second term, Hayes knew that his recommendations would be considered. He planned to discuss "the benevolent and reformatory institutions" in his annual message and to "suggest topics, improvements, or amendments of the Constitution" in his inaugural address. He gathered information for these speeches from the Ohio Board of State Charities, institutions in other states, and the Prison Association of New York.[33]

Trivial matters also occupied Hayes. He responded to congratulatory messages; complained about his unflattering picture in *Harper's Weekly*; wrote letters of recommendation, including one for Jacob A. Camp, his old flame Fanny Perkins's husband; demanded the reinstatement of a federal civil servant in Cincinnati; and tried to discourage petitions for pardons, though he asked Gov. John White Geary of Pennsylvania to have compassion for an Ohio boy who had gone astray in his state. Hayes also thanked Anne C. Mc-Means, Jay Cooke's housekeeper, for a fish caught by Cooke at Gibraltar Island, Put-in-Bay, where Hayes and Lucy had been guests earlier that summer. While they were there, Cooke had interested Hayes in real-estate investments in Duluth, Minnesota, the eastern terminus of the Northern Pacific Railroad. (Hayes subsequently borrowed $8,000 on Sardis's name from John G. Deshler of Columbus to purchase Duluth land.) And Hayes was most aggravated when James Leroy falsely claimed that his son had deposited $800 to $1,000 with Hayes on the morning he was killed at Winchester (19 October 1864), and that Hayes had kept the money. Regarding the accusation as blackmail, Hayes secured government documents to clear his name.[34]

Hayes had his annual message in the hands of the printer by Christmas and "enjoyed the holidays better than ever before. All the boys at home, happy, well-behaved, and promising; little Fan a sunbeam; Lucy improved and appreciated." Fanny's "queer talk" amused Hayes enormously, particularly when she said that she was " '*boosed*' (abused) in a complaining tone whenever she was not in her own opinion well treated." She did not feel "boosed" on Christmas morning. After getting "a carriage, three dolls, candy, a case of peanuts, stockings, &c &c," she said "very prettily 'Kris Kinkle is a mighty *dood* fellow.' "[35]

Hayes's second annual message was delivered in early January 1870. He urged the legislature to ratify the proposed fifteenth amendment and repeal the previous legislature's laws curtailing the voting of Negroes, students, and inmates of soldiers' homes. Concerned with increased taxation and debt on the local level, he advocated legislation limiting municipal taxes and debt. He was thankful that the Board of State Charities (created in 1867, during Cox's administration) had exposed "atrocious" practices in Ohio's care of the mentally ill (one thousand of whom were lodged in county infirmaries and jails) and urged the legislature to provide better facilities for the insane and to establish an asylum for inebriates. On behalf of Lucy's pet project, he asked the state to take over the Soldiers' and Sailors' Orphans' Home at Xenia and to make room for three hundred orphans who were inmates of county infirmaries under conditions "unfit for children." He called for more humane treatment of state prisoners and suggested that the Irish convict system—reformatories for young offenders, graded prisons, paroles, indeterminate sentences—be studied and possibly adopted. And he noted that since

Ohio had accepted the terms of Justin Smith Morrill's Land Grant Act of 1864, the legislature should establish an Ohio "Agricultural and Mechanical College" and stop squabbling over its location. Proclaiming Hayes's agenda for his second term, the message clearly sounded the call for reform.[36]

FOURTEEN

SECOND TERM

At church on 2 January 1870, Hayes mulled over his second inaugural address. He reflected on railroads, temperance, courts, suffrage, minority-party representation on commissions, and "all debts." The inaugural address touched most of these issues, and although it emphasized civil rights, it also positioned Hayes on the new concerns of postwar America. He suggested that the constitutional ban on local aid to railroads be modified to permit "guarded and limited" aid for transportation to undeveloped areas. Hayes also pleaded for administrative and judicial reform and for a heightened awareness of responsibility for society's less fortunate members. Although he believed in the maxim "that government is best which governs least," Hayes did not wish to forget the veteran, "nor his widow, nor his orphan, nor the thousands of other sufferers in our midst."

But if Ohio were to adequately care for "the unfortunate and the erring" and perform its functions effectively, its agencies and its courts needed to be reformed. "For many years," Hayes observed, "political influence and political services have been essential qualifications for employment in the civil service, whether State or National." But civil servants, even "the Warden of the Penitentiary and his subordinates, and the Superintendents of asylums and reformatories and their assistants," were dismissed when their party lost power, no matter how much their experience had enhanced their qualifications. Hayes advised that the "radical reform in the civil service" proposed for the federal government—making "qualifications, and not political services and influence, the chief test in determining appointments" and giving civil servants the "same permanency of place" enjoyed by army and navy officers—be part of the state constitution.

To secure impartial justice from an independent judiciary, Hayes suggested that Ohio follow the federal government's example. He called for judges to be nominated by the governor and confirmed by the state senate; they would serve during good behavior and be paid adequate salaries. "With a dense population crowding into towns and cities, with vast wealth accumulating in the hands of a few persons or corporations," Hayes warned, "it is to be apprehended that the time is coming when judges elected by popular vote, for short official terms, and poorly paid, will not possess the independence required to protect individual rights."[1]

Hayes's first priority was to secure ratification of the fifteenth amendment. Although regular Republicans supported the amendment, a handful of "Republican Reformers" from Hamilton County held the balance of power and threatened to defect on the suffrage issue. Ironically, although these reformers objected to the patronage system, federal patronage conciliated them; in early January, Hayes called for "help" from "the powers that be" in Washington, and by 13 January, he assured Sen. Oliver P. Morton of Indiana that he was *"certain"* of fifty-seven votes.[2]

Hayes's estimate was accurate; Ohio ratified the fifteenth amendment by the slimmest of margins. The final vote was fifty-seven to fifty-five in the house and nineteen to eighteen in the senate. On 30 March 1870, with ratification by three-quarters of the states, it became part of the federal Constitution. Hayes rejoiced in "the final overthrow of the atrocious system which the Republican Party was organized to oppose. By the adoption of the 15th Amendment the principles of the fathers will be fully recognized in the Constitution." The amendment's ratification was "the triumph of justice and humanity," and it gave Hayes "more satisfaction . . . than any act of any General Assembly of the State." When he was in Cincinnati on 4 April 1870 for an election and to have Birch's ears and eyes examined, Hayes recorded: "The colored people vote for the first time under the Fifteenth Amendment. They are very happy and the people generally approve. They vote Republican almost solid." Ratification of the Fifteenth Amendment also achieved a major personal objective for Hayes in his war for equal rights. "I too mean to be out of politics," he wrote to a friend half seriously and half in jest. "The ratification of Fifteenth Amendment gives me the boon of equality before the law, terminates my enlistment, and discharges me cured."[3]

Working with his slim Republican majority, Hayes accomplished much during his second term. He was gratified in early 1870 by legislation that broadened the suffrage, although absenteeism in the house prevented passage of the student voting bill. With the aid of Democratic votes, he achieved what he termed "a noteworthy triumph": the repeal of the visible admixture laws — denying the vote to people of mixed race — even though these laws became unconstitutional after the proclamation of the Fifteenth Amendment. The legislature guaranteed residents of the National Soldiers' Home at Dayton the vote, but the courts (presuming that veterans in the home permanently resided elsewhere) astonished Hayes by overturning that law. To "avoid" that decision, Hayes called for "an Act of Congress."[4]

Hayes was pleased when the state legislature heeded his pleas and established the Agricultural and Mechanical College, which would become Ohio State University. He desired to appoint a strong bipartisan board of trustees (trying unsuccessfully to get George Hunt Pendleton to serve) and corresponded with Dr. John Aston Warder, a distinguished horticulturist and forester, about plans for the college. "I care very little," Hayes said, "as to what Mr. Morrill, or anybody else designed, but I would like to have your views as to what is best." Loving both history and Ohio, Hayes began collecting manuscripts relating to Ohio history for the state library.[5]

The legislature approved the state's takeover of the Soldiers' and Sailors' Orphans' Home at Xenia, which Lucy had helped establish and on which Hayes had spent "much time, money, and labor to make successful." Appointing a board for the Xenia home caused him considerable annoyance and led to a bizarre episode in Ohio legislative history. As befits a civil-service reformer, Hayes initiated the practice of appointing minority-party members to serve on the boards of state institutions. But Hayes's selection of Col. Barnabas Burns of Mansfield for the Orphans' Home board aroused the ire of his Republican neighbors, one of whom assumed that Hayes was too thick-skinned to be disturbed by their complaints. Hurt "deeply" by their "censures," Hayes told his critic that he had consulted "many of our best men" and that if he had made a mistake it was from the best of motives. "One thing is sure," Hayes concluded, "when you come to dispense patronage, you will agree with me that it is no easy job to do satisfactorily."[6]

On the last night of the legislative session, Burns and six other nominees for the Orphans' Home board were almost defeated by the Democrats. By going home early, a Republican senator created a seventeen to seventeen deadlock, making it possible for the Democrats to prevent confirmation of the nominees before adjournment and thus postponing the organization of the Orphans' Home for a year. While Michael Goepper of Cincinnati, a friend of Lucy's, filibustered to prevent adjournment, the absent senator hurried back to Columbus by special locomotive. When he came into the chamber, the Democrats "absquatulated" (fled) to prevent a quorum. Two locked themselves in a privy, and the others tumbled into the street. The assistant sergeant at arms, alert and conscientious even though a Democrat, caught Sen. James Randolph Hubbell of Delaware and brought him back to the chamber. Hubbell's capture achieved a quorum, and the nominees were confirmed. Hayes rejoiced for the Orphans' Home and enjoyed the "very pretty quarrel" that ensued when furious fellow Democrats and Hubbell traded accusations of drunken behavior.[7]

As a defender of murderers while practicing law in Cincinnati, Hayes had accompanied one of his clients to the gallows and found the execution a dreadful experience. During the Civil War, he had approved the execution of a bounty-jumping deserter, but he disliked the death penalty. When in doubt, Governor Hayes commuted the sentence of condemned prisoners and was occasionally criticized for his actions. In slightly more than two years, he commuted "three or four sentences of death . . . on the ground of youth and doubt as to the deliberation and premeditation of the act," but he refused to interfere in four other cases in which the convicts had significant criminal records or had murdered while committing a robbery.[8]

Despite his commitment to humanitarian and political reform, Hayes was not a universal reformer. On 27 April, when Lucy's aunt Margaret Boggs and a Miss Sharpe stopped by in Columbus en route to a women's rights convention at Dayton, Hayes recorded his disapproval of women's suffrage. "The proper discharge of the functions of maternity is inconsistent," he wrote, "with the like discharge of . . . the political duties of . . . citizenship." Hayes, however, made his opposition neither strenuous nor obvious. Phebe McKell, another aunt of Lucy's, believed that "when the proper time (in his estimation) comes for the enfranchisement of my sex I shall count him a staunch and consistent supporter." But for Hayes, the proper time never arrived; nor did it for Lucy. Despite the stand of her aunts and the early influence of Hayes's sister Fanny—with whom she had heard suffragist Lucy Stone lecture—Lucy never backed women's suffrage. It is unlikely that she was overly influenced by her husband, since Lucy always followed her own convictions on reform matters. Indeed, she had been well ahead of Hayes in the movement against slavery and influenced him in the temperance crusade.[9]

Hayes worked for reform within the framework of the Republican party. He was enthusiastic about voting rights for African Americans because, on that issue, human rights and Republican party advantage converged. Hayes's position on alcoholic beverages was calculated to keep both topers and teetotalers in the party. He believed in temperance literally—drinking moderately outside the home—and opposed Prohibition; Lucy, who was a total abstainer and wanted no liquor in the house, did not object to moderate drinking outside her home and opposed Prohibition. When her Lexington relatives sent Kentucky bourbon, she and Hayes promptly expressed it to Sardis, who they knew would enjoy it. Hayes sympathized with those working within the Republican party to stamp out corruption and to rationalize the nation's tax laws, but they disturbed him when they criticized the Grant administration (which, Hayes thought, "does well—reduces the debt, keeps out of difficulty, and lets things float") and began to disrupt the Republican party. Whatever its shortcomings, Hayes preferred it to the Democratic party, which was "led and ruled . . . by New York City plunderers." Fearing that the Liberal Republicans were playing into the hands of the Democrats, Hayes told them that he "wanted no new party and would have nothing to do with organizing . . . one." In fact, the reformers' agenda failed to interest him. Believing that the principle of equal rights had triumphed with the adoption of the Fifteenth Amendment, Hayes was ready to get out of politics.[10]

With the legislature not in session, Hayes traveled about Ohio. Like other elected officials of his time, he had no expense account. Although railroads issued him passes and hotels usually did not charge him (the patronage of a governor was a good advertisement), Hayes could not have made ends meet if Sardis had not subsidized his political career. Hayes's 1870 record of his travels on Decoration (Memorial) Day weekend shows how arduous traveling could be:

Left Columbus Saturday night (28th) 9 or 10 P.M., sleeping car to Steubenville. Got there at 3:30 to 4 A.M. No hackman at depot. Wandered over town hunting United States Hotel. Found it after a long hunt. Nobody awake. Tried to stir out of his bunk a colored servant. After a long delay got him aroused. Said there was no empty bed in the house! Scouted over town until daylight. Went back to hotel; nobody up. Stretched out on chairs in ladies' parlor, got a good nap; disturbed by woman cleaning up. Told her my afflictions. She gave me a poor little room. Slept well.

After awakening, Hayes spent the remainder of that Sunday pleasantly with Anson McCook, one of the "fighting McCooks." On the following day, Hayes gave a "so-so" extemporaneous, thirty-minute speech at a monument in the cemetery, where a great crowd had gathered.[11]

Besides traveling and speaking in Ohio, Hayes made a trip to Washington. "The great statesman" there, he concluded, was his radical friend Sen. Oliver P. Morton of Indiana. "He is a strong, logical debater, who has the faculty of putting an argument in a way that is satisfactory to the best minds, and at the same [time] is understood and appreciated by the most ignorant." The high point of the trip was Hayes's 27 June visit to the great general in the White House. Grant was most cordial on that "sultry night," which followed "a blazing day." Sitting with him on the portico, looking toward the unfinished Washington Monument, Hayes asked him about his health and, in particular, about his headaches. Puffing on a cigar, Grant said that his health was excellent and that for the past year — since he had given up water at meals—he had had no headaches. Although his first three months as president had been hard, he now had "an easy time in his office. . . . San Domingo was his pet topic," Hayes reported, but Grant realized that the treaty to annex that country would not pass the Senate. He was angry about the opposition of Charles Sumner, an impractical, "puffed-up, and unsound" man, and of Carl Schurz, "an infidel and atheist." When Hayes forthrightly told Grant that he "did not know upon what grounds the Administration wanted San Domingo," Grant, "in a rapid, brief, but comprehensive way, set forth its advantages, described the island, its productions, people, etc., etc., in a most capital way."[12]

In September 1870, Hayes took Birch (who was almost seventeen) to Ithaca, New York, to begin his freshman year at Cornell. Admiring the "liberal, progressive, and practical spirit" at that university, Hayes feared that Birch's lack of preparation at Fremont might jeopardize his admission. Too deficient in Greek to enter the classical course, Birch enrolled in the "combined course," which substituted German and French for Greek, and he made up Latin and geometry during his first year. Hayes arranged for tutors in both of these subjects. Birch roomed with two Ohio boys in the Cascadilla, where Cornell President Andrew Dickson White and a dozen professors lived with forty students. Pleased that the teachers knew Birch and would "give him personal attention," Hayes left with a very comfortable feeling.[13]

Lucy feared that Birch might "be led astray . . . at that great College," and Hayes shared her concern with Birch. After suggesting that he eschew liquor and tobacco and play neither cards nor billiards, Hayes realized, "I need not lay down rules"; he assured Birch, "I feel confident you will do what is sensible." Rough sports also concerned Lucy, who winced at the thought of cracked ribs. With Birch playing games "more dangerous to life and limb than a Mexican battle," Hayes, though less concerned than his wife, hoped that skillful surgeons were available to set bones in Ithaca. Lest Birch "forget the main thing," Hayes reminded him, "I am ambitious to see you a scholar. I expect to be gratified." By Christmas vacation, Hayes proudly reported to Sardis that Birch was safely in the class and that his progress in German was "really great."[14]

Hayes delivered the first annual message of his second term on 3 January 1871. "Believing that too frequent changes of the laws and too much legislation are serious evils," he suggested that the legislature defer action, particularly on "the Judiciary, Railroads, Intemperance, and many other important subjects," until after the people decided that year whether to call a constitutional convention (the Ohio constitution required such a vote every twenty years). Hayes was reasonably certain that there would be a convention and that it would reconstitute the legislature "to secure to minorities a fairer representation."

Satisfied that state debt had been reduced, Hayes hoped to curb local taxation and indebtedness. From 1860 to 1870, state taxes had gone up 33 percent, but local taxes had risen almost 170 percent. Hayes feared that these taxes, which were growing faster than the population or wealth of the state, threatened prosperity. Conceding that public works and public debt had been necessary to get Ohio's products to market in the early days, Hayes emphasized that those days were over. "The rule, 'pay as you go,'" he said, "leads to economy in public as well as in private affairs, while the power to contract debts opens the door to wastefulness, extravagance and corruption."

Hayes did not, however, want the state to starve welfare (such as the Orphans' Home) or its employees. Because of inequalities, he advocated putting all state workers on fixed salaries. Under the present system, some city and many county officers, who were compensated by fees, received more money than state supreme court judges. Without mentioning that his own salary failed to cover his expenses, Hayes suggested raising the inadequate salaries of the judges and other officers. He also urged, as an investment, continued legislative support for the geological survey of Ohio. Agriculture could not continue to expand, and future economic growth would depend on mining and manufacturing, based on Ohio's "vast mineral wealth."

Prison reform continued to concern Hayes. He was pleased that, under "prudent and efficient management," the penitentiary earned more than its expenses, that the "condition and treatment" of the prisoners were steadily improving, and that "hateful and degrading" uniforms were disappearing. Hayes suggested that cutting sentences for good behavior be combined with extending sentences for bad behavior, that convicts be classified, that an intermediate prison be erected (using convict labor) for more corrigible inmates, and that the Board of State Charities be asked to collect vice and crime statistics and to help discharged convicts obtain employment. Hayes again attacked the county jails as the most defective part of the state system, complaining that they mixed the innocent and the mentally ill, the young and the old, the novice and the hardened criminal. In contrast, he praised the newly established Girls' Reformatory at White Sulphur Springs as an unqualified success and worthy of liberal support.[15]

"I got off a very successful message," Hayes boasted to Sardis. "Even the *Enquirer*, *Statesman*, and *Crisis* praise it profusely. But it is of small account to say the right thing without firm, strong men to push through the practical

measures. I look to a constitutional convention for the remedy." Former
Governor Cox also praised the message, and Hayes reciprocated by praising
Cox's recent article, "The Civil-Service Reform," in the *North American Review*. Hayes especially liked Cox's suggestion that cabinet officers be able to
participate in congressional debates to explain departmental needs. "I see
here, daily, how much we fail to accomplish for want of it in our State Legislation."[16]

As Hayes expected, he got little from the legislature during his last year as
governor. His time was taken up mainly with administrative and ceremonial
tasks and minor and sometimes irritating chores, such as writing introductions and recommendations. When Col. Stephen W. Dorsey, president of the
Sandusky Tool Company, came armed with a letter from his fellow towns-
man O. Follett and requested a recommendation to the governor of Arkansas, Hayes paraphrased Follett's evaluation. Anything but bashful, Dorsey
had a friend request "an *unqualified endorsement*." After checking with Follett and apparently getting a negative response, Hayes refused to change the
letter. When Dorsey complained of injustice, Hayes responded that he had
followed his "usual habit" and "the usage of businessmen generally when introducing a stranger" and had simply repeated Follett's statements. Dorsey
went to Arkansas, but Hayes had not heard the last of him.[17]

Hayes planned to return to Washington in February, but he delayed his departure because Lucy was again approaching confinement. On the morning
of 8 February 1871, after suffering "intensely," she gave birth to an eleven-
pound boy, whom they called, after their usual delay, Scott Russell. Besides
the attending physician, Aunt Margaret Boggs and Winnie Monroe, "our excellent colored cook, assisted the boy into the world." Three days later,
Hayes left for Washington. When newspapers claimed that his business there
"was to 'fix up' appointments for judges, marshals, etc.," he was miffed, but
he admitted that his main tasks were to get his friend Hastings reappointed
as the U.S. marshal for northern Ohio, to pursue $140,000 in military claims
for Ohio, to hurry along the claim of his uncle Roger Birchard's estate for
federal bonds lost in the fire that had killed him a year earlier, and "to see
things generally."[18]

Hayes arrived in Washington during a heavy snowstorm on Sunday, 12
February. Uncle Roger's bonds, of which there were some fragile remains,
were "*certain* to be restored" and would amount to between $5,000 and
$8,000. He also saw members of the Ohio congressional delegation; talked
about its possible reduction (because of undercounting in Geauga County)
with Census Superintendent Francis A. Walker; and accompanied Columbus
Delano, who had replaced Cox as secretary of the interior, to a cabinet meet-

ing. Grant, who was sitting at the end of the table smoking, rose and greeted Hayes and Delano "pleasantly and cheerfully." As the rest of the cabinet came in, Hayes reported, "we chatted sociably in little groups." Grant discussed bills awaiting his signature with individual cabinet members and signed all but one. He then "turned and talked about San Domingo," specifically about the commissioners he had appointed to consider the annexation of that country, claiming not to know their opinions. "If they reported unfavorably," he insisted, "that would end the matter; if favorably, then he hoped annexation would take place."[19]

The trip to Washington confirmed Hayes's feelings about politics, the Grant administration, and the Republican party. The key issues, he believed, were the South and the debt, and on those two issues as well as the Treaty of Washington (1871), which provided for the arbitration of differences with Great Britain, he found that most Republicans agreed with the administration. In contrast, a "great majority" disagreed with Grant on Santo Domingo but would accept its annexation, and a "vast majority" were vexed with him for appointing the unsavory New York politician Daniel E. Sickles as minister to Spain, for forcing Cox out of the cabinet, and for engineering the removal of Charles Sumner as chairman of the Senate Foreign Relations Committee and replacing him with Simon Cameron, the Pennsylvania corruptionist. But none of these mistakes, Hayes maintained, would "materially affect the public judgment as long as the Administration is *right* on the South and the Democracy *wrong*." He admitted that the Republicans had made "many and mortifying" blunders, but with the rebellion and Reconstruction, "the Democrats have been so big a blunder and crime, that sensible people will still oppose them." Hayes had faith that "the Administration can yet save itself," especially "*if no new causes of dissatisfaction arise.*"[20]

Republican blunders, however, strengthened Hayes's desire to "quit the race for political promotion," even though he could have been nominated for a third term and had as good a chance as anyone to be elected senator from Ohio. Hayes reiterated that the "small questions of today about taxation, appointments, etc." were uninteresting compared with "the glorious struggle against slavery." They were, he decided, not worth "the worry and anxiety" experienced in political life. The excitement, he decided, was not worth the loss of independence. This decision to leave politics was made jointly by Hayes and Lucy. During a visit to Washington in May 1871, again in behalf of Hastings, Hayes—although enjoying the city—saw "no reason here to regret *our* choice and decision." Hayes continued to believe that his mission in politics had been achieved with the passage of the Fourteenth and Fifteenth Amendments.[21]

These amendments had brought African Americans civil equality, and Hayes optimistically believed that they would be free to exercise it throughout the nation. Even after hearing in May what Guy Bryan called the *"truth"* about Texas, "that you, & such as you did not know our condition & treatment, & were deceived," Hayes—ever the conciliator—minimized their differences. Concerning settled issues that Bryan obviously thought were still open, Hayes responded: "There was never a time since 1840 when we were probably nearer together in politics. I am a Republican, and whatever views I have, I shall try to support that party." Hayes believed that the North and the South could be reconciled on the basis of obedience to the new amendments, a universal amnesty policy, and a low protective tariff.[22]

A few weeks later, Bryan visited, and they happily talked "over College days and old times" before disagreeing over Reconstruction. Bryan used a "kind and hearty" thank-you letter to wish that Hayes and his family would "never know ought but peaceful happiness, protected by good laws made by your own race," implying inaccurately that blacks were in control of the Texas legislature and that laws passed by the radical Republicans threatened the safety of white Texans. In late August, after vacationing in Canada, Bryan visited Sardis, whom he called Hayes's *"Father Uncle,"* and observed the beginning of the 1871 Ohio gubernatorial campaign.

Attempting a "new departure" in the campaign, the Democrats accepted the Reconstruction amendments but denounced the way they had been passed. Speaking at Zanesville, Hayes questioned the Democrats' commitment to the amendments. After a relaxed and enjoyable speaking tour throughout the state (enjoyable because he was not a candidate), Hayes felt certain that the Democrats would be beaten "badly." Bryan did not mind Hayes's approach, but he objected to speeches by Edward F. Noyes, nominated to be Hayes's successor, Columbus Delano, and John Sherman. Their speeches attacked the South for murdering and intimidating black Republicans ("Ku Klux" outrages) and, Bryan thought, aimed *"to keep alive the animosities of the war."* Hayes, however, was in agreement with those criticized by Bryan. A few months earlier, Hayes had told Sherman: "You have hit the nail on the head. Nothing unites and harmonizes the Republican party like the conviction that Democratic victories strengthen the reactionary and brutal tendencies of the late rebel states." Hayes's hopes for a Republican victory, vindicating his administration, were rewarded; Noyes triumphed with a 20,000-vote majority.[23]

Although he was ready to denounce reactionary and brutal tendencies in the South (for which the ruffian class was responsible), Hayes wished to encourage the "generous and just" acts of the better elements of both South and North. Despite Bryan's wails about Republican "*despotism*" and his warning that "disgusted" white southerners would "take anything that will rid them of the present encumbrances," Hayes had faith that white southerners of substance would ultimately accept the equal-rights principle. Indeed, Bryan encouraged Hayes in this belief with reassurances that he wished for "good government, under the constitutions and laws of the Federal and State Governments." When Grant advocated a general amnesty in December 1871, Hayes optimistically wrote to Bryan, "There are wrongheaded people on all sides, but the generous and just will in due time win. . . . An era of good feeling prevails here to a degree not seen . . . in fifty years. It will extend and embrace all unless new causes arise."[24]

After voting on 10 October, Hayes hastened to Chicago to help "the sufferers" of that city's terrible fire. Gen. Phil Sheridan gave him "fine quarters at his house" and the use of his army ambulance and mule team "to visit the ruins." Hayes first stopped at the depot for lost children, where he was nearly overcome. Later, while "slowly walking over the debris and contemplating the extent . . . of the destruction," he saw William Henry Smith, his old friend who headed the Western Associated Press. Together, they called on Joseph Medill of the Chicago *Tribune*, and Hayes wrote a short newspaper address to the people of Ohio, asking them to send money, fuel, flour, pork, clothing, and other nonperishable items to Chicago's needy people. He also contributed $100 of his own money to relief work.[25]

The Chicago fire burned out Hayes's hard-luck friend William K. Rogers, and Hayes suffered from the loss. Along with his furniture and books, Rogers lost his family's chief support—rent money from a destroyed block that was partly owned by his wife. As a result of the Chicago fire, Rogers could not pay his share of the Duluth block he was developing with Hayes. What made matters worse was that building the Duluth block had cost double the original $10,000 estimate. "The fire lost friend Rogers his chance of raising five thousand dollars, as he expected, and we are now in need of about eight thousand dollars to complete the building," Hayes wrote. Even though he had already borrowed $6,000 at 7 percent from Austin Birchard, with Sardis as a cosigner, Hayes could handle his remaining $3,000 share for the two lots and the building (he had already paid $9,050), but after the fire he had the added task of helping Rogers raise his $5,000. Although he told Rogers, "It will all come out right," Hayes had difficulty borrowing the money and knew that the situation would make Sardis "anxious and troubled."[26]

Hayes and Lucy were present when his niece Fanny Platt married Dr. Erskine B. Fullerton on 19 October 1871, but a sprained ankle kept him from dancing or attending their "infare" two weeks later. It was his left ankle—

still weak from its injury at Cedar Creek—which he had hurt again while catering to the whims of his grandniece Lily Mitchell. A mute child, she loved to visit Aunt Lu and Uncle Rud and especially to be carried by him. On 2 November, when she objected to the prospect of going home, Hayes gathered her in his arms to carry her home to make the parting easier. He then tripped on the edge of an old mat while running down the steps of his house.[27]

"The tribe is all in, and weighed & measured," Hayes reported to Sardis on Christmas Eve. The family had passed up an invitation from Dr. Joe, the superintendent of the Longview Insane Asylum, to "enjoy a Crazy Christmas" with him and Longview Asylum inmates, but they were gratified to hear that he was caring for Aunt Clara, a former Webb slave who had worked for the Hayes family and was living in Cincinnati. On Christmas morning, the whole family walked "in procession" to breakfast with the Platts, and that evening they "went to the Deaf and Dumb Asylum and saw some of the inmates assisted by ladies of Columbus act some very pretty tragedies." The following day, Hayes, Lucy, and the older boys went to Xenia for Christmas festivities at the Soldier's and Sailors' Orphans' Home. The festivities continued until midnight. It was 2 A.M. when Hayes and his family got home that night.[28]

Hayes sent his final annual message to the Ohio legislature on 1 January 1872. He was pleased to report a reduction in the state's debt but pained to note that local indebtedness had continued to increase. In keeping with his faith in the efficacy of education, he advocated that Ohio establish "institutions for the instruction of teachers in principles and duties" of their calling; urged that the mixed management of schools by township boards and sub-district directors be replaced by a more centralized, purely township system; and demanded that the legislature end the "manifestly unjust" practices that kept black children from attending public schools in several counties.[29]

Hayes applauded the state's penal, reform, and benevolent institutions. Although he did not mention it in this message, he credited the improvement of these institutions to the Board of State Charities, which had been established during Cox's administration. When the board censured Dr. Joseph Webb for mistreating the mentally ill at Longview, Hayes advised him to keep his hot temper in check. After assuring him, "I know you never acted harshly or cruelly, willingly, much less intentionally," Hayes noted, "there are two sides to the question of your grievance." He conceded that the board might be mistaken in Dr. Joe's case but insisted that its work was "important and valuable." He urged the legislature to provide more facilities for the mentally ill (only 1,346 of 3,414 persons judged insane in Ohio were in asylums) and for orphans (only 250 out of 800 were cared for by the state).[30]

Although Hayes was a friend of Jay Cooke and contemplated a career in railroading when he retired from politics, he urged the Ohio legislature to correct railroad abuses. Carrying twelve million passengers in Ohio the previous year and with gross receipts in that state exceeding $30 million, railroads were guilty of "clear and palpable violations of law." Nearly every train that ran in the state carried freight or passengers at illegal, discriminatory rates or fares. The railroads also violated speed limits in towns and cities and at crossings and had been responsible for many deaths in the past year. By investing in express companies and dealing in railroad securities, railroad managers violated Ohio law. Hayes also objected to the "increase or watering of stock" by the railroads, particularly when their objective was to avoid a rate reduction, which was prescribed by Ohio law if net profits reached 10 percent on the capital invested. Hayes urged that five citizens, including the state railroad commissioner, be named to investigate and recommend measures to solve these problems. Railroad abuses, however, would continue, and Hayes would have to deal with their devastating consequences a few years later.[31]

The "extraordinary corruption" in New York City might spread to Ohio, Hayes feared, especially since the causes of corruption already existed there. Those who contracted for public work and supplies, for example, often shared interests with the very officials who gave out contracts or supervised them. Believing that "publicity is a great corrector of official abuses," Hayes asked that the governor be empowered to appoint special investigators to look into the activities of state and local officials suspected of corruption. Hayes also suggested that the state purchase a governor's residence for his successors.[32]

During his last days in office, Hayes fended off those who were urging him to challenge John Sherman for the U.S. Senate. Many Republicans preferred Hayes to Sherman, and all but two or three Democrats were for him. When pushed, Hayes admitted that he would like to be a senator, but not enough, he insisted, to struggle for the honor. Calling himself "a party man," he said, "I must abide by the caucus." Hayes would not campaign either openly or covertly for the job; would not take it unless a majority of the Republicans wanted him to unseat Sherman, which he doubted was the case; and reiterated his wish to get out of politics and to attend to his "private and family affairs." To squelch the movement in his favor, he published a note in Comly's *Ohio State Journal*: "Hayes has not been and will not be a candidate for Senator, either in or out of caucus." Thanks to Hayes's authoritative statement, Sherman received the caucus nomination.[33]

On Monday, 8 January 1872, Hayes retired as governor and told John Herron, "We go out today 'joyfully, joyfully' as little Fan sings." That evening, Hayes and Lucy entertained most of Columbus at a "lively, happy" reception honoring Noyes. They invited the legislature, state and local officials, the press and clergy, New Year's Day callers, and "other gentlemen." Rejoicing in victory and aware of his debt to Hayes, John Sherman also attended. "Oceans of oysters, ice cream, meringues, coffee, etc., etc., left over, were sent next day to the hospital and to friends." Although savoring his newfound freedom, Hayes knew that he had served Ohio well. "True or not," he happily reported to Sardis, "the common remark is that I am the most esteemed of the governors within the memory of people living."[34]

FIFTEEN

INTERLUDE

"I am a free man and jolly as a beggar," Hayes declared on 9 January 1872. But that evening, several members of the Ohio legislature tried to end his freedom. The bell rang just after Hayes had put out the lights in his Columbus home. When he opened the door, state Sen. J. S. Casement and a representative told him, "We want to make you Senator." Insisting that John Sherman was corrupt and "ought to be defeated," they asserted, "His defeat is certain if you consent. Besides, the man now elected Senator over the caucus will be the next President of the United States." The Liberal Republican revolt against Grant was under way, and Casement reasoned that if Hayes could unite dissident Republicans and Democrats and triumph in Ohio, he could do the same on a national level.

Duty, as he conceived it, not friendship or admiration for Sherman, kept Hayes from running against him. Hayes tried to impress the legislators that their caucus votes had committed them to Sherman. Defending their inconsistency, Casement responded "that to beat the trickery and money of Sherman, there must be some concealment of purpose; that if the design had been known, money would have been used to buy Democratic votes." Hayes urged them not to split the Republican party, because Grant's defeat would "give the Government to the enemies of the recent amendments and . . . unsettle all." Insisting that Grant's "defeat by a good Republican would be a good thing," Casement asked Hayes whether he would serve if elected. "In any way, or under any circumstances," Hayes responded, he would not be used to unseat Sherman. As they left, Casement commented that it was "strange to see a man throw away the senatorship," especially "with the Presidency in prospect."

Before going to sleep, Hayes repeated the conversation to Lucy, who laughingly said that she dare not sleep "for fear of some Democrat slipping in." Constant rings of his doorbell soon awakened Hayes. Going down in his nightshirt, he let in his friend John G. Deshler, from whom he had recently borrowed money to invest in Duluth. Deshler told Hayes that a "party" determined to unseat Sherman had been meeting at his house for the past week; they believed that Hayes could be elected, even though Sherman's agents, including two bankers from his hometown, had already bought two

Democrats. When Deshler finally paused, Hayes told him, "I can't honorably do it and there is no use talking." Before leaving, Deshler regretfully admitted, "I must give it up," and added, "I admire your principle, but John Sherman wouldn't do it." After Hayes, upon returning to bed, told Lucy of the conversation, she exclaimed, "Thank fortune we don't want to be elected that way."[1]

Although Hayes and Lucy had decided that their "*permanent residence*" would be the house Sardis had built for them at Spiegel Grove, they moved back to Cincinnati. By the end of January, Hayes had engaged two small rooms and a bath, plus board, "for Lucy, Fanny, Scott R., Winnie (our servant), and self at the Carlisle House, near our old home, at fifty dollars a week." Birch was at Cornell, and Webb and Rud were with Sardis. Lucy preferred boarding in Cincinnati without Webb and Rud to being a guest in Fremont without her black servant and friend Winnie Monroe. Old friends welcomed Hayes and Lucy, and while roaming around town, he saw much growth and had the comforting thought that his house on Sixth Street and the property he had acquired in Millcreek would continue to gain in value.[2]

While pondering his future, Hayes secured temporary office space at Sixth and Walnut Streets. He was clearer about his avocation as a dilettante scholar than about his vocation during what he figured would be at least twenty more years of life. Having just completed a portrait collection of Ohio governors for the state, he decided to collect Ohio books and give them to the "State Library, or other fit place." On his second evening back in Cincinnati, 28 January 1872, he attended the monthly meeting of the literary club he had joined twenty-two years earlier; only four in attendance, including John Herron and Manning Force, matched his length of membership. Hayes was present that spring at Murat Halstead's dinner party honoring William Cullen Bryant, the poet who was editor of the New York *Evening Post*.[3]

To make a living, Hayes contemplated involvement with railroads, which were growing even faster in Ohio than in the nation as a whole. "I want to study up railroad law, and railroad business generally," he decided, "especially as to the construction of railroads." His investments in Duluth real estate heightened his interest in railroad construction. The value of that real estate depended on the westward progress of Jay Cooke's Northern Pacific Railroad. Inspection in March of his Duluth property—of the great docks constructed for the Northern Pacific and of its tracks across the Red River of the North into the Dakota Territory—filled Hayes with enthusiasm.

Chiefly, however, Hayes was interested in railroads closer to home. "Hoping to turn it to the advantage of Fremont," he promoted a railroad from Columbus to Toledo. His suggestion that the upcoming state constitutional convention relax the prohibition on local railroad aid was not entirely a disinterested one. The initial enthusiastic response of M. M. Green of the Hocking Valley Railroad and Benjamin Smith of Cincinnati made Hayes push the project, even though it appeared that the convention would be delayed a year. In the short run, he hoped that a bill authorizing local aid to railroads by popular vote would pass and be proved constitutional. By late April, the Columbus to Toledo railroad appeared likely, but not in the way that Hayes had anticipated. "I can't get it direct to Fremont," he told Sardis, "but I think I succeeded in convincing them that it should go as far as Upper Sandusky and that a branch by Tiffin and Fremont to Put-in-Bay would be a good thing." The slighting of Fremont seemed to dampen Hayes's ardor for railroads. "There is an increasing R.R. mania here," he wrote in a somewhat detached manner to Rogers. "I shall meddle some in it, but probably mainly as a volunteer." By June, Hayes had ceased talking about the Toledo project and thought that he would "take a hand" in "building a new railroad into Cincinnati under the auspices of the Atlantic and Great Western people."[4]

Hayes and his family found living in cramped rooms difficult. Although Lucy was free from the cares of housekeeping, three adults and two children occupying two rooms was trying, and she and Hayes were worried about the health of both Scott Russell and Rud. In February, Rud's "harness to straighten up his shoulders" looked promising and he appeared to be in good health, but by mid-July he had such a bad cough that Hayes suspected tuberculosis. "I fear the change of life is against him. He is now fourteen. A bright, affectionate lad. Tall, slender, & weakly. I must look after his health. Possibly send him South next winter."[5]

Subject to seizures during which he stopped breathing, Scott Russell appeared to be in worse danger. Since he had been "quite healthy" in Columbus, Hayes blamed Scott's "spells" on being "cooped up in the Carlisle House." Because both "little Joey & George . . . [had] died their second Summer," Hayes and Lucy were apprehensive. They decided to spend the summer near Delaware and on 22 May moved to a farmhouse on the Olentangy River, directly opposite the farm that Sophia had owned when Hayes was a boy. Returning to his childhood haunts and hoping that the magical place would restore Scott, Hayes quoted from Shakespeare's *As You Like It*, which he and his sister loved so dearly: "And this our life, exempt from public haunts, finds tongues in trees, books in running brooks, sermons in stones, and good in everything." Rowing on the Olentangy strengthened Rud, and Scott improved for a time. Hayes and Lucy despaired when Scott's spasms got worse in July and August, but then they tapered off; by November, despite an occasional relapse, a relieved Hayes reported that Scott played and romped "more boy-like than ever."[6]

Hayes privately noted that his older boys were not "remarkable for talents, acquirements, or industry" (his mother and sister had often thought the same of him), but he found Fanny a delight. She "is trying to jump the rope & is as persevering as possible," Hayes proudly wrote to Rud. "She says 'now father turn the rope for me I want to *practice*.' She is untiring—If her big brothers," Hayes lectured, "will be half as resolute and constant in their studies, we shall see great progress." Rud was bright and had literary tastes, and Webb studied enough to get into Cornell, with conditions. Sardis, who was paying the college bills, had decided to send him there to be with Birch, who was doing well, but his high jinks occasionally distressed his father, who implored him, after a particularly egregious escapade, "No more such doings . . . *as you love me*."[7]

In retirement from politics, Hayes remained a staunch Republican and worried that Grant, whose administration had been attacked as inept, impolitic, and corrupt, might not be reelected if the Liberal Republicans nominated Charles Francis Adams and the Democrats supported him. The Liberal Republicans met at Cincinnati in early May and nominated Horace Greeley rather than Adams. Hayes "witnessed the intense disappointment" of his friends Stanley Matthews and George Hoadly and was himself astounded by the convention's outcome: Needing wholehearted Democratic support to win, a party of free traders with strength among the beer-loving German element had nominated Greeley, the "bitterest" foe of free trade and a temperance fanatic, whose lifelong motto had been "Anything to beat a Democrat." Adopting the strategy of anyone to beat Grant, the Democrats also nominated Greeley, but Hayes suspected that, rather than vote for him, many of them would "let Grant keep the chair."[8]

Against his will, Hayes was drawn back into politics when the Ohio Republican Committee named him a delegate-at-large to the Republican National Convention in Philadelphia. Rather than resign and "get ranked with the Greeley men," Hayes attended the convention in early June, served on the Committee on Resolutions, which wrote the platform, and supported Grant's renomination. The Philadelphia convention, he reported to Sardis, "was united, harmonious, and the most enthusiastic convention any of us ever saw." He believed that "the unlooked-for enthusiasm" was a strong reaction against the vindictive attacks on Grant.[9]

Despite his prediction that Greeley could not unite disparate elements into a winning coalition, Hayes was worried about Republican prospects. Although he was bombarded with letters urging him to run for Congress in his old district, he did not want to return to Congress, and he told other candidates — including his friend William E. Davis — that he would not run. He realized, however, that if he ran he would improve Grant's chances of carrying Ohio and resolved to do so only if all Republicans — including the other candidates — wanted him to run. Contrary to Hayes's specific instructions, Richard Smith of the Cincinnati *Gazette* told the Second District Nominating Convention that Hayes would accept if nominated. As a result, on 6 August, Hayes got sixty-two votes and Davis fifty-one. Hayes telegraphed both Davis, who felt betrayed, and Smith and declined the nomination. But that evening, Hayes learned from Smith "that the convention had adjourned and that my declination would be disastrous. If I could get out of it creditably I would," he insisted. "But I fear I must stand it." The episode left Hayes chagrined that Davis was hurt, relieved that he had behaved well, flattered to be thought indispensable, and annoyed that his wishes had been ignored.[10]

Hayes's annoyance was heightened a few days later when "responsible parties at Portsmouth," Ohio, asked him "to take charge of the Ohio River Railroad." These promoters had "just voted three hundred thousand dollars" for construction of the road. It seemed to be the opportunity that Hayes had been looking for. "It is a project which I regard with great favor," Hayes wrote to Gen. B. F. Coates, who had contacted him on 10 August, "& one in which it is possible I may desire to engage." His nomination, however, which he had received only because "*the prospect of a defeat was good*," prevented him from accepting the offer. If he were defeated, Hayes could take on the project, but he realized correctly that the promoters would not want to wait sixty days on the chance that he would be beaten.[11]

A week into the campaign in September, Hayes thought that Grant's election was almost sure, but his own was more doubtful than he had supposed. Running in a Greeley stronghold, Hayes knew that his chances would improve if he distanced himself from Grant, but in his effort to ensure Greeley's defeat ("I strike him in every speech"), Hayes drove off the Greeley men. Hayes did not enjoy campaigning away from his family. During the canvass, he learned that Fanny had been "left senseless several hours" after she was thrown by a pony and "hung by one foot in the stirrup, the pony dashing among the trees." Luckily, she had escaped serious injury. He also suffered from an intermittent fever that he found "difficult to throw off" and was forced to "*shirk . . . and sham*." Two weeks before the election, he wrote to Birch that he would soon "be rid of a work which is not at all agreeable." He was spending more money than he had intended, but since it was "positively the last time," he supposed he could stand it. Hayes lost the October election despite his proverbial good luck, and he was glad that he would not have to go back to Washington.[12]

As the news of Grant's victory poured in on the "rainy, raw" presidential election night in November, Hayes was exhilarated by the joyous reaction of the immense crowd standing in the mud outside the Cincinnati *Gazette* office. Grant won by a landslide and did better in Cincinnati than anticipated. Hayes had "no doubt" that his run for Congress had "brought a better vote to the whole ticket than it would have received if I had declined. But what a victory for General Grant! It is simply *'prodigious'*!"[13]

Again out of politics, Hayes faced an uncertain future. After spending the summer at the farm near Delaware and the fall at Chillicothe, Lucy, Fanny, Scott, and Winnie Monroe arrived back in Cincinnati on 18 November. With Hayes, they occupied "two large pleasant rooms" in Brock's Hall at 61 Mound Street, where the company was good but "the boarding unexceptional." Nevertheless, Lucy remained there with the children while Hayes spent Thanksgiving with Sardis, who was disappointed but would not relent on having blacks under his roof. In addition to not wanting to visit Spiegel Grove without Winnie Monroe, Lucy was pregnant again and may have been suffering from morning sickness.

While in Fremont, Hayes took part in celebrating the completion of the Lake Erie and Louisville Railroad to Lima, Ohio. Dr. L. Q. Rawson of Fremont, an old friend of Sardis's, was the president of the road. At Birchard Hall in Fremont, Hayes addressed a meeting favoring a local loan of $134,000 to help extend Rawson's railroad east to Cleveland and to build the new Chicago and New York Air Line Railroad. Taking a shipper's point of view, Hayes argued that where there was no competition, railroad companies took advantage of "produce dealers, manufacturers, and others," and that these proposed roads would lower shipping rates by bringing competition to Sandusky County as well as pay a tenth of its taxes. A two-thirds majority was necessary to approve the loan, and Fremont and Sandusky Township voted for it overwhelmingly.[14]

Already aware that railroad managers exploited monopolistic advantages, Hayes gained insight into their dealings with landowners. Sam Young of Toledo came to Fremont on 3 December hoping to buy 160 acres in East Toledo from Sardis and his partner James Wilson for the Columbus and Toledo Railroad, the same road Hayes had been interested in earlier that year. First offering $700 to $800 an acre, Young finally hinted that he might pay $1,200 an acre. Although Wilson was ready to yield, Hayes "insisted that every acre was worth two thousand dollars." Since he was representing Sardis's interests, which were largely in real estate, Hayes began questioning the wisdom of sweeping legislative grants giving the right of way to railroads. For example, the Toledo and Western had such a grant, but if it decided to build on another route, could it transfer that grant to another company? What were the limits on a railroad's right to condemn for depot and business purposes? Was not a grant to a company that never organized void? Bargaining with Sam Young over part of Sardis's fortune—a fortune that had made it possible for Hayes to pursue a political career uncompromised by questionable payoffs—gave Hayes a new perspective on railroads.[15]

More important to Hayes than railroad promotions or land deals was a proposal Sardis made to him during this visit. Aware that Lucy wished to run her own household, Sardis proposed building a home for his housekeeper, Sarah Jane Grant, and her mother, where he would move the next summer or fall, leaving Spiegel Grove for Hayes and his family. Sardis also asked Hayes to manage his banking and real-estate interests, to which he would soon fall heir. "I think favorably of it," Hayes wrote in his diary, "but must consult Lucy and reflect on it." When he returned to Cincinnati on 5 December, Hayes and Lucy decided that the time was ripe to move to Fremont, and they accepted Sardis's generous offer. With Fanny, they spent Christmas with him in Fremont. For the present, Winnie Monroe was not a problem; she was caring for Scott at Longview, where his Uncle Joe was observing him to suggest treatment for his spasms. After Lucy and Fanny went back to Cincinnati on 10 January, Hayes stayed at Spiegel Grove to plan their move and to keep Sardis company. "When we take possession," Hayes explained to Lucy, "the whole house passes into our hands except Uncle's chamber and sleeping room, which we may use as it stands but not to overhaul and change. . . . I . . . agreed to it all with all my heart." Excited by the prospect, Hayes returned to Cincinnati on 20 January and began reading books on architecture, landscaping, and fruit culture; he made drawings and consulted an architect, but he realized that his plans were for a distant future.[16]

Despite his intention to be in Cincinnati with Lucy, Hayes spent most of the winter with Sardis. Hayes was called back to Spiegel Grove on 6 February when Sardis had convulsions, "severe pains in his head, & . . . blundered strangely in the use of his words." Becoming "wild" from the "grinding" pain, Sardis tried to escape by door or window until calmed by morphine. With Hayes nearby, Sardis improved and, within a couple of days, quipped: "I have one of the worst diseases, consumption, over forty-five years & now the next worse disease, 'apoplex,' has attacked me."[17]

Facing death, Sardis wanted his nephew with him. Hayes stayed and advised Lucy to finish up her calls in Cincinnati, fill one of her big trunks with "as much plunder as you can," and come to Fremont. Lucy, however, was in no hurry to leave Cincinnati. As Sardis became more lucid, he asked Hayes to carry out several bequests. Claiming that Sarah Jane Grant had been like a daughter to him, Sardis wanted to leave her his diamond pin and to pay all the costs of her house above $2,000. Encouraged by his nephew, he gave a valuable tract of land to Fremont for a public library and asked Hayes to serve as a trustee. Having found it "a great comfort to believe & trust in the Saviour," Sardis wanted to give $5,000 to a Home Missionary Society and feared that, although Hayes had "been a good boy," he was "not quite so correct" in his religion as Sardis would have wished.[18]

Whenever Hayes returned to Cincinnati to be with Lucy, Sardis would suffer a relapse, causing Hayes to hasten back to Fremont. Reluctant to leave Cincinnati, yet missing her husband, Lucy became increasingly unhappy, particularly after Hayes spent little more than a week with her before running back to Fremont on 15 March. The deteriorating mental and physical condition of her brother James, whom her brother Joe had admitted to the asylum at Longview, and the convulsions plaguing little Scott further depressed Lucy and tied her to Cincinnati. Vying for Hayes's attention, Lucy and Sardis each had afflictions aplenty. At this inauspicious time, Sardis sent some "word" to Birch and Webb at Cornell, which Lucy perceived as hostile to her. She was possibly oversensitive, since Sardis had been raising Birch and Webb for several years and was in some respects closer to them than she was. Hayes insisted that Lucy was "totally mistaken as to any intended intimation for you" but added that, after sending the offending note, Sardis had "changed his mind as Sarah said he *would* and *ought* at the time." Having confirmed her fears, Hayes then lectured poor Lucy: "Don't *cultivate* suspicion of people. There is enough reality in life that is objectionable without imagining more."

Since Birch and Webb would soon be in Fremont on their spring break from Cornell, Hayes urged Lucy to come up with Fanny for their visit and then either stay or return to Cincinnati "as you please." Hayes reiterated that Winnie, on whom Lucy depended and for whom she had great affection, could not stay at Spiegel Grove as long as it was Sardis's house. Lucy put off facing the future without Winnie and decided to visit Fremont to see her boys and then return to Cincinnati.[19]

On 25 March, when he received a dispatch at Spiegel Grove, Hayes worried that something had happened to the boys en route from Cornell. To his relief and then annoyance, it was word that he—who had been spoken of for the cabinet—had been nominated as assistant U.S. treasurer at Cincinnati. "After what I have been and had and done," Hayes noted, "it would be small

Fanny and Scott with Winnie Monroe

potatoes to grasp this crumb. Thanks be given, I am independent of office for my daily bread!" Yet when Lucy was insulted by the appointment, he assuaged her hurt by calling it "the most important office in the West" and added, "the glory of it is that I have an opportunity to decline a good office!"[20]

Hayes was incredulous when John Sherman temporarily blocked his confirmation by the Senate and postponed the little glory Hayes would derive from refusing the offer. Sherman, who had assured applicants for the position that no appointment would be made until they had all presented their credentials, insisted that he had acted to save his credibility, but Hayes was not mollified. "The action taken was calculated, although not so intended, to injure me and to wound my feelings," Hayes wrote to Sherman, "and frankness requires that I should say that I think you were in error in your views of duty under the circumstances." A month later, Hayes was confirmed, and on 1 May he refused the appointment. Grant's failure to recognize his services, Sherman's bungling, and the "cowardly lies" told to the investigating Poland Committee by congressmen (including Garfield) who had acquired stock in Credit Mobilier (the company constructing the federally subsidized Union Pacific Railroad) under suspiciously favorable circumstances made Hayes glad to be out of politics.[21]

When he refused the treasury post in Cincinnati, Hayes had already become a speculator in Toledo lands. On 22 March 1873, Sardis deeded his half of the valuable 160-acre East Toledo tract to Hayes, and its growing worth inspired his choice of a new profession. "I am now fairly embarked in the business of buying, selling, and improving real estate," Hayes noted a month after getting that tract. "I buy no land except such as I am interested in, and do not intend to take advantage of people's necessities. Paying what is now regarded as a fair price, I believe the growth of Toledo, with judicious improvement, will make purchases sufficiently remunerative." Augustus W. Luckey and his son James B. Luckey of Elmore were Hayes's partners in these real-estate operations, and their talk with him was "of drainage, dock lines, streets, alleys, roads, filling, and excavating." By 30 April, apart from the original 160-acre tract, Hayes had a one-third to one-half interest in tracts in Toledo amounting to 336 acres and costing $145,000. In fifteen to twenty years, he estimated, these lands would be worth at least $1 million.[22]

Lucy at last moved to Spiegel Grove on 3 May 1873. Armed with a letter of recommendation and at least $165, Winnie Monroe went to Chicago. (She would return to the Hayes family fourteen months later.) Hayes chose the date of Lucy's arrival to mark their settlement in Fremont. In an absence of twenty-three years, he had accomplished even more than he had hoped, and he now wished to be useful to his "town, neighbors, and friends," to care for his children, and to contribute to Lucy's "comfort and happiness." After twelve years of "vagabondizing" among several army camps, relatives in four Ohio counties, and the cities of Cincinnati, Columbus, and Washington, Hayes longed for that "fixed home feeling." "We can enjoy life here," he told Lucy, "and bring up the little ones in a quieter and more rational way than was possible with the mode of life we were leading."[23]

When their "plunder" arrived from Columbus on 10 May, it filled a freight car and a half. Although they ate and slept in the main house, Hayes, Lucy, and the children made a newly constructed office and library, where their gear was stored, their headquarters. There, in early July, Lucy read aloud from Harriet Beecher Stowe's *Old Town Folks* while Birch and Rud rearranged the books and Webb pasted clippings into scrapbooks. When they were not popping in and out of the library, Fanny would run "through the grove whooping like any little Shawnee," and accident-prone Scott would occasionally knock his head and trigger a "convulsion" while playing.[24]

On 21 June, there was more than Scott's convulsions to worry about, for on that day Hayes coughed up almost a teaspoon of blood. "I have had a hacking cough, sometimes for several minutes in the night, during the last five or six weeks," he noted; he feared that he might "go like Pease," his cousin and roommate who had died of tuberculosis. To "*prevent*" that fate, but also to "*get ready for the worst*," Hayes thought that he had best "travel to the dry regions" and "get out of debt and settle affairs." His morbid mood was heightened by the death of Lucy's brother James nine days earlier at the Longview Asylum and the precarious state of Sardis's health. But when Hayes coughed up no more blood, his anxiety disappeared. A few months later, on his fifty-first birthday, he admitted to thinner hair, whitening whiskers, several teeth plugged and a few gone. He was also more fleshy, shorter of breath, and had twinges of rheumatism. But his "elastic spirit; fondness for all young people and their employments and amusements"; and his "fresh, ruddy complexion and considerable physical strength" almost persuaded him that he was still a youth.[25]

It was Lucy, not Hayes, whose life was at risk that summer of 1873. She was almost forty-two and was expecting their eighth child. Having gained weight and fearing the hot weather, she "had misgivings about this confinement." Her labor began at 7 P.M. on 31 July with "a pain in her stomach and head," and soon she "began to vomit and retch." Webb, who had no idea that his mother was pregnant, was sent to get her doctor, who gave her an "aromatic and mustard plaster for the pain" and left. When her pain grew worse, a "nurse, engaged for her confinement, . . . was sent for." She and Sarah Jane Grant prepared another plaster, but before it was applied, Lucy told Hayes that "the pains were low down, that she was anxious, believed confinement was near," and, obviously fearing the worst, said, "Oh Ruddy, we have been so happy together for twenty-one years."

Hayes, who "finally went to bed in the office," was soon aroused by Birch with the alarming news, "Mother has had a spasm." The doctor hurried back and called in another physician. Lucy had three seizures before and two seizures after giving birth at 3 A.M. to a nine-pound boy. "The case," Hayes recorded, "was now serious. Morphine was injected into her arm. . . . My anxiety was intense." There were no more convulsions, and Lucy gradually regained her health but could recall nothing from the time her labor began until the next afternoon. The baby, whom they named for their friend Manning Force, survived in a "doubtful" condition.[26]

While Lucy and the baby grew stronger, Hayes served his "town, neighbors, and friends." His main civic interest was the public library and museum, which he had convinced Sardis to endow and on whose board of trustees Hayes was the leading spirit. He sought advice on library buildings and collections; his personal contribution of $3,000, when added to the $15,000 authorized by the town council, secured for the library the highly desirable site of old Fort Stephenson.[27]

This new $3,000 obligation prompted Hayes to analyze his finances on 13 September. He thought that his Toledo and Columbus land holdings were worth about $250,000, and he estimated that their value would probably double in ten years. But he was concerned about "how to carry" his "large" debt of $46,266, and he did not want to be "caught" by falling prices. Five days later, Jay Cooke's banking house failed, precipitating a Wall Street panic that collapsed security prices, started a severe economic depression, and made Hayes's rosy calculations wishful thinking. "The tumbling of the banks" threatened his land speculations, but he and Lucy also felt sorry for "generous and hearty" Jay Cooke. Although the failure of Kraus & Company, an important Toledo bank, caused a "stir" in neighboring towns, including Fremont, Hayes predicted on 28 September, "We are probably now safe, but I must drop various plans I had formed." Among these was a "wood house & hennery." From Duluth, Billy Rogers, who was looking after real estate shared by his wife, Dr. Joe Webb, and Hayes, claimed that the town, which depended on Cooke's railroad, had suffered no direct loss from his failure. With this inane analysis, Rogers could add economic forecasting to his string of failures. By December, he had to report that all the tenants wanted a reduction in their rent, which most of them had not paid for six months.[28]

The panic of 1873 struck a few weeks before an already losing Ohio Republican campaign ended. Hayes, who had not participated, blamed the defeat on the scandals connected with Credit Mobilier and the Salary Grab Act (Congress had voted itself a retroactive pay increase) and a general disillusionment with politics. He also thought that Noyes had erred by running for governor while also a candidate for senator. Somewhat disillusioned himself, Hayes had remained passive and detached.[29]

Hard times in general and the Ohio Democrats' embrace of inflation attracted more voters to their party in 1874. "I regard the inflation acts as wrong in all ways," Hayes wrote to Uncle Austin Birchard. "Personally I am one of the noble army of debtors, and can stand it if others can. But it is a wretched business." When Grant vetoed the inflation bill — a mild measure that would have added at most only $64 million to the national bank and greenback circulation — Hayes rejoiced, saying, "We shall be able to stick to Grant to the end." But Hayes still remained aloof from politics and centered his attention on his family. That August, he did not vote on the proposed new Ohio constitution (it failed at the polls), calling it only slightly better than the old one.[30]

Hayes was more concerned with the fortunes of the Fremont Croghans baseball team, in which his boys were intensely interested, than the fate of the proposed Ohio constitution. His three older boys loved baseball, and Hayes, who called it "a *manly* game," kept them posted. Since Birch excelled in baseball, Hayes was happy "to hear of Webb's improvement in foot ball," remarking, "It is almost as gratifying as fine scholarship." But when he said almost, Hayes meant almost. Reacting to the recent hazing death at Cornell of the son of his friend Gen. Mortimer D. Leggett, Hayes ordered Birch and Webb not to play football with a college team in Cleveland on 25 October. "Cornell can't afford *just now*," he insisted, "to indulge in such nonsense." Since Webb had just joined a fraternity, Hayes "felt greatly troubled" and was disturbed that the verdict of the coroner's jury had not explained the tragedy. Although he knew that no one had tried to kill Leggett, Hayes felt that if the faculty had permitted the "hazardous, and foolish" proceedings that caused his death, it should share in the responsibility. But when he found that his boys had their hearts set on playing in the Ohio game, Hayes telegraphed them, "No objections to the Cleveland affair."[31]

Sarah Jane Grant's house was sufficiently advanced by 26 November, the day before Thanksgiving, for Sardis to move. True to his word, he gave Spiegel Grove to Hayes. "Glad to be housekeeping again," he and Lucy began moving their gear into the main house. They were "in the suds" and did not expect, Hayes wrote to Birch, "to get into full running order until your Christmas vacation. We shall then treat you to some hard work unless we are more lucky in fixing things than I anticipate."[32]

Sardis died on 21 January 1874, less than two months after he moved from Spiegel Grove. Although foggy and dismal, the day began auspiciously for him. His lifelong friend Morrison R. Waite had just been nominated chief justice of the Supreme Court, and Sardis asked Hayes to write a congratulatory letter in which he promised to send Waite an oak cane he had cut in Texas twenty-five years earlier on lands owned by Stephen F. Austin's nephews (Guy Bryan and his brothers). Hayes wrote the note, and Sardis, after seeing how the work was progressing on the house, laid down. At 11 A.M. he "suffered severe pains," and although the pain soon subsided, "his head and face remained as cold as death." He "was cheerful . . . and affectionate" and was glad that Hayes was with him. He "prayed that his sufferings might be short" and "that he might be at rest with Mrs. Valette" (the mistress of the home in which he had lived for years) and Hayes's sister Fanny. Assuming, "with a playful smile," that he would "go to the right place," Sardis joked and was serious by turns as he talked with Hayes, until "a single spasm brought the end."[33]

Sardis's generosity kept Hayes busy. He was the executor of his estate and the most active trustee of the Birchard Library. He cataloged books, listed books to order (Birch and Webb helped select juvenile titles), and prepared temporary quarters for the library in Birchard Hall (an earlier example of Sardis's philanthropy). With the books going on the shelves in May, 1 June was targeted as opening day. Most of Hayes's energies, however, were devoted to improvements at Spiegel Grove. Sardis had managed his affairs so well that, despite the hard times following the panic of 1873, Hayes was able to realize some of his plans. In the spring of 1874, he, Rud, and two handymen cleared two and a half acres for fruit and nut trees, evergreens, berries, and a vegetable garden. By June, workmen had added a kitchen with a new range, effective force pump, and buttery, as well as "bath houses, privies, office, [and] stable"; they also built "closet drawers all over." Lucy was ecstatic in her new home. "You do not know and indeed cannot imagine," she wrote to Birch and Webb, "what comfort and happiness is found in Spiegel Grove."[34]

Upon completing the school year at Cornell, Birch, who was graduating, and Webb had their hearts set on going to the races at Saratoga. Hayes and Lucy decided that it was "all right enough" but wanted them to spend an additional five days visiting the "ancestral Towns" and the kinfolk in Vermont before reaching "Saratoga . . . and the wickedness of the age." "Money is as tight as an Englishman after dinner, but we can raise it," Hayes said. Sending his sons $125, he told them, "Do this trip up in your best style & *conscientiously.*"[35]

All the children were home and under the critical eyes of their parents during the summer of 1874. Hayes did not expect Webb to graduate from Cornell and observed that Birch, who was "ready to begin law," would be helped by "*a little more gab.*" Hayes and Lucy were most anxious about their "invalid," Rud, whom they considered "unfit for hard work or hard study"; they thought it best that he attend "a manual-labor agricultural college." The three younger children presented fewer problems. Fanny was "a boy in climbing, swinging, and playing generally," and Scott, their "handsomest" child, was "too honest to joke." Fond of animals and of each other, he and Fanny spent hours "out in the sand pile." Having just completed his first year, Manning was "a fine, dark-eyed little fellow. Lively and promising."[36]

Almost immediately after his birthday, however, Manning became ill with "a summer complaint" and died. Sarah Jane Grant "was the efficient and untiring nurse of the darling from the time his case became critical," and once he was dead, Hayes wondered if he had been "altogether healthy at any time." Again, Lucy and Hayes grieved for a "dear child." Forgetting his words about Scott and remembering another lost baby, Hayes said that Manning was "probably our handsomest child except Georgey."[37]

Life, which Hayes and Lucy loved too much to remain depressed, soon resumed its normal patterns. By mid-September, Birch had begun to study law in Cincinnati, Webb was back at Cornell, and Winnie Monroe had returned to the household to do the cooking, now that Sardis was gone. "Normal" in the Hayes household could be uproarious. On a hot September Sunday afternoon, Fanny, Lucy, and Winnie were "in a fever—on their ear"—because, just as the quail eggs began hatching, the big black rabbit got out of its cage, and they were trying to round up the dogs and corral them in the breakfast room.[38]

Although seemingly out of politics, Hayes campaigned for his congressman, Charles Foster, in 1874. Foster was popular, but the race was tight. The sick economy and the panacea of inflation prescribed by the Ohio Democrats attracted voters to their party. Observing for himself, Hayes attended a Democratic rally in Fremont where Gov. William Allen bored the crowd, but Pendleton gave a speech that was "as sound and sensible as an argument in favor of an inflation of the currency could be." Hayes found that he enjoyed campaigning again. "Last night at Milan," he wrote to Lucy on 6 October, "I had a fine little hall full of people—women and youngsters with the yeomanry. Was in good trim and without a particle of real preparation, had a good time of it." Even though the 1874 campaign was a disaster for the Republicans, who lost control of the next Congress, Foster was reelected.[39]

Still, Hayes had not returned to politics. Having lost his ardor and the wherewithal to continue his real-estate investments in the economic depression, he devoted himself to cultural pursuits, his community, and his family. He studied the history of the Sandusky Valley and the Wyandot Indian nation. At Governor Allen's behest, he served on the Board of State Managers of the Philadelphia Centennial Exhibition and helped organize committees in each congressional district to encourage the quality of Ohio's representation at the exhibition.[40]

"Be a good boy," Hayes counseled Webb at Cornell. "No drinking or other foolish and ruinous practices." With his mixed feelings about Christianity unchanged, Hayes told him, "I hope you will be benefitted by your church-going. Where the habit does not Christianize, it generally civilizes." On 22 February 1875, Hayes accompanied Rud "to Lansing to deposit him in the freshman class of the Michigan Agricultural College." Hayes would have preferred Ohio State, but Rud feared that Columbus friends and relations would prove too distracting. Hayes objected to the small dormitory rooms with "the two-in-a-bed system" and wished he had taken Rud to Columbus. He left Rud with the admonition to "let your words and conduct be perfectly pure—such as your mother might know without bringing a blush to your cheek." Because of Rud's poor health, Hayes worried that he might not get along, "even in the limited course at Lansing. . . . He is bright and quick, but lacks perseverance."

While in Michigan, Hayes tried to do something "for the world." He spent a few days working to obtain from Republican Governor John J. Bagley a pardon for a young Irish convict whom Hayes and others thought innocent. Since Bagley was "prejudiced against the Irish and Democrats," Hayes was uncertain of success. Bagley also appeared to lack "the independence and manhood to do right at the risk of losing his popularity."[41]

Hayes remained a loyal Republican, but gutless politicians like Bagley annoyed him. Scandals in the War and Treasury Departments of the Grant administration bothered him and confirmed his commitment to civil-service reform. By 1875, many Americans were disturbed by the general malaise they perceived in society. America, they felt, had not lived up to its promise. Quite apart from the economic hard times, which they recognized as temporary, these Americans were convinced that immorality was growing in business and politics and that Reconstruction was not working. Even radicals like Dr. Joe were bothered that "so many bad men, have gotten into place in the Republican Party," and they no longer worried "much about the South." Although Joe still had confidence that the average American would prevent "the Rebels and their friends" from coming into power, he thought that Republicans might benefit from their drubbing in the 1874 elections.[42]

Hayes abhorred corruption, but his abhorrence did not make him abandon his principles and the Republican party. The "danger" of the current age, he thought, was "the snobbish and the sordid." He had contempt for the sordid corruptionists, who were bringing ill repute to Reconstruction, Republicans, and the democratic process; but he had no sympathy for the snobbish elements, who, because of corruption, would abandon the principle of equality and the Republican party. Seeking to avoid both the "sordid" and the "snobbish," he held fast to the equal political rights of the Declaration of Independence and refused to despair of the present or the future.[43]

Hayes managed to be conciliatory and positive even when responding to a Guy Bryan diatribe against the Republican party and racial equality. Reveling in the success of white-supremacy Democrats in 1874 (particularly in their violent southern campaigns stressing the integrated-school requirement in the proposed civil rights bill before Congress), Bryan taunted: "Rud are we done with the Negroe? Are you not satisfied . . . he is not fit to govern himself without the government of the white man? Will the Northern people force the negroe question, & social equality upon us with the view to get the exciting question up again for another canvass? Let us have peace for God sake, & don't ruin the South for party purposes."[44]

Hayes's response indicated his abiding belief in political equality:

It seems to me that the most important thing in Texas, as everywhere else, is *education for all*. I, of course, don't believe in forcing whites and blacks together. But both classes should be fully provided for. I recognize fully the evil of rule by ignorance. . . . You are not so much worse off in this respect than New York, Chicago, and other cities having a large uneducated population. But the remedy is not, I am sure, to be found in the abandonment of the American principle that all must share in government. The whites of the South must do as we do, *forget to drive and learn to lead* the ignorant masses around them.

As usual, Hayes played down their differences and predicted that they would soon vote the same ticket. "But not if you continue to indulge a hope that slavery is in some form to be restored," Hayes warned.[45]

Hayes was content to observe society and politics from Spiegel Grove while keeping track of his family. He noted on 28 March 1875 that Scott Russell was promoted to pants last week, that Fanny did not take to "book larnin," that Rud was homesick in Lansing but wrote cheerful letters, that Webb wrote good letters from Cornell, and that Birch "takes more and more interest in the law." Despite fortnightly migraine headaches, Lucy was healthy, "large but not unwieldy," and Hayes admitted that he also was "getting a little too fat for comfort" but that he was healthy. "The independence of all political and other bother is a happiness."[46]

SIXTEEN

THE CAMPAIGN OF 1876

By the spring of 1875, the Republican party was in disarray in Ohio and in the nation. Led by crusty old William Allen, the Democrats controlled the state, and the deepening economic depression had enabled them to win control of the next House of Representatives, scheduled to meet in December 1875. Desperate to reverse their party's decline, Ohio Republicans turned to their best vote-getter. Their caucus at Columbus on 25 March 1875 unanimously called on Hayes to run a third time for governor. While begging him to join the fray, fellow Republicans suggested that if he were elected governor he would "stand well" for the presidency the next year. "How wild!" Hayes exclaimed. "What a queer lot we are becoming. No body is out of the reach of that mania."

Although flattered, Hayes consistently refused to run. He did not want to oppose Judge Alphonso Taft of Cincinnati, who wanted the nomination, and the inadequate governor's salary would postpone his getting out of debt. Just then, Hayes was enlarging the Spiegel Grove dining room and was so pressed for cash that he asked his Cincinnati friend Dr. John Davis for help. "I find myself at the limit of loans allowed by the Bank I am connected with," he told him, "and am turning in all directions to gather in what I need." Apart from personal considerations, Hayes felt that "the *Butlerism* of the Administration"—the "third term talk, the Civil rights bill, the partisan appointments of the baser sort"—was "all bad & weights on us" and threatened defeat in Ohio.[1]

Hayes's complaints about the "ultra" Civil Rights Act of 1 March 1875 did not mean that he had changed his views on either rebellion or equal rights. In his 1875 Decoration Day address at Toledo, the closest he came to conciliating the South was in a sentence lamely honoring those who had obeyed duty and died for an unworthy cause. As he emphasized to Guy Bryan, Hayes believed in legislating political equality but not social equality. Although Benjamin F. Butler dropped the school-desegregation provision from the bill, the Civil Rights Act barred segregation by railroads and other public carriers, hotels, and places of amusement and affirmed the right of blacks to serve on juries. Like Hayes, most Republicans supported political rights for blacks but were not enthusiastic about this particular measure, which promised a modicum of social equality. Realistic Republicans knew that the act could not be fully enforced by the federal government (which lacked men, money, and stomach for the task) and that, if the act were enforced, it would be strenuously resisted and probably declared unconstitutional by the Supreme Court. Their worst fears were realized. Without producing good results, "the statute had reaped the whirlwind of racist reaction and had served only to weaken the Republican party, to disappoint the blacks, and to further discredit the integrity of the law."[2]

Although reluctant, Hayes decided to heed his party's call if it persisted and if Taft and the other candidates withdrew. Hayes's friends and the party did persist, and although Taft did not withdraw, on 2 June 1875 Hayes was nominated, with 396 votes to Taft's 151. Taft's son Charles graciously moved that the nomination be by acclamation, and William McKinley, who was at the convention, told Hayes, "never did I witness such enthusiasm for a leader as burst forth for you."[3]

"Now that I am in for it I rather like it," Hayes admitted, but he knew that it would be an uphill fight. To get voters to forget the depression and Republican corruption, Hayes planned to identify the Democratic party with slavery, rebellion, and repression as well as repudiation, corruption, and Catholicism. He emphasized that the Republicans were right on the "honest payment" of the national debt in gold rather than in depreciated paper or silver money; were right on equal civil rights for all citizens; were right on destroying slavery, saving the Union, and making "this people one Nation." Republicans were also right, he believed heartily, in resisting Roman Catholic demands that public funds be diverted to parochial schools.[4]

Because of his faith in public schools as the panacea for social ills, Hayes wished to stress the "Catholic Question" and *rebuke the Democracy by a defeat for subserviency to Roman Catholic demands.* Hayes realized that Judge Taft had lost the gubernatorial nomination partly because, in 1870, he had upheld the decision of the Cincinnati school board—in response to Roman Catholic demands—to ban the singing of hymns and the reading of the King James Version of the Bible from the school curriculum. Hayes agreed with this decision and, since it had been upheld by the state supreme court, argued in the campaign that Catholic complaints against the public schools were groundless. "No sectarian flag floats over the school house, & no spirit enters there but that of peace & good will toward all men & creeds." Hayes declared, "We want to bring the children of Protestants, Cath[olics], Jews & Unbelievers together in the common School room."

But in his principled defense of nonsectarian public schools and the separation of church and state, Hayes showed a less admirable willingness to portray the Catholic Church as the enemy of public schools and to identify Catholics with the Democratic party. As a freethinker, he did not share the hostility of ardent Protestants for the Roman Catholic Church, but Hayes knowingly aroused anti-Catholic prejudice to gain votes for the Republican party. In Canton, McKinley thought that the strategy was sound. "The leading topic with us will be the school question. We have here a large catholic population which is thoroughly democratic, a large protestant german element that hitherto have been mainly democratic, they hate the catholics — their votes we must get."[5]

Although the Catholic, or school, question extended beyond the borders of Ohio, the national interest in the Ohio gubernatorial race focused on the currency issue. This focus made little sense, since the governor of Ohio had nothing to do with the nation's money supply. In the Specie Resumption Act of January 1875, Congress had provided for the return to the gold standard on 1 January 1879; greenbacks would be redeemed with gold after that date. To offset the Republican's anti-Catholic campaign in a state with a Protestant majority and to capitalize on the severely depressed condition of industry, the Democrats made currency contraction — resumption — their major issue of the campaign. They demanded that deflation be abandoned and called for a "volume of currency . . . equal to the wants of trade." Governor Allen, whom the Democrats renominated, fought for the inflationary greenback, while Hayes — though up to his "eyes in debt" and able to quip privately that "nothing but *inflation* will relieve me" — regarded the return to the gold standard as both an economic and a moral issue. Hayes argued that inflation benefited wholesale dealers, middlemen, and retailers, who could set prices to "cover the risks of the fickle standard of value" at the expense of farmers and laborers, who were least able to bear the burden. Hayes predicted that inflation would be uncontrolled and would destroy confidence, create crises, spawn bankruptcies, and, by amounting to "*repudiation*," violate the nation's faith, injure the public credit, and be dishonest.[6]

Hayes campaigned without his old zest. After two speeches in one day, he thought his speaking "irregular. . . . Races, baseball, and politics," he concluded, "are for the youngsters." He was ready to do what could be reasonably expected but did not want to speak more than once a day and was sure that "early and earnest discussion by the press" reached more people and was "far more effective" than stump speaking.[7]

Obviously, old concerns were being smothered by new cares engendered by the depression and by nativist fears of Roman Catholic immigrants. "As to Southern affairs," Hayes wrote to Bryan in July, "nothing but good-will now exists towards you," and " 'the let-alone policy' seems now to be the true course." If southerners in the next House of Representatives would be moderate and sensible, like L. Q. C. Lamar of Mississippi, Hayes predicted that "all will be well," but if not, "all will be 'fuss and fury' for a time." But even if that were the case, Hayes wishfully thought, "We are one people at last for all time."[8]

Hayes was overly optimistic about the "moderation and good sense" of southerners. The most violent, disgraceful election in American history was getting under way in Mississippi, where scores of black men soon would be killed, and Lamar, ironically, would be one of the beneficiaries. Perceiving that the public was "tired of these annual autumnal outbreaks in the South," the Grant administration was reluctant to act, and warned by Ohio politicians that intervention in Mississippi might defeat Hayes, did not send troops to compel obedience to the Fourteenth and Fifteenth Amendments. The Democrats took Mississippi by 30,000 votes ("The Revolution of 1875"), confirming that southern politics had become racially polarized. The Republican party was overwhelmingly black in the South, where its small white membership was being depleted by threats of social ostracism. The Democrats in the South now claimed virtually all whites—whether prewar Democrats or Whigs, secessionists or unionists, rabid racists or moderate ones.[9]

The Ohio campaign was extremely close, and Hayes predicted a huge turnout. He anticipated Republican losses in mining and manufacturing districts, exacerbated "by emigration to the west & by immigration on new R.R.s, to the Towns, of Irish"; he expected gains from returning German and Liberal defectors of 1872, from "the waking up of lazy Republicans," and "somewhat" from anti-Catholic Democrats. Late in the campaign, outside speakers—including Carl Schurz, the Liberal Republican and German American leader; and Oliver P. Morton of Indiana, a spoilsman, a soft-money man, and a staunch radical—stumped Ohio for Hayes.[10]

Despite vigorous support from all segments of the Republican party, Hayes feared that he would be beaten by "Hard Times and Plenty of Money to cure it." He anticipated "defeat with very great equanimity." A loss would immediately return him to the quiet life he sought at Spiegel Grove, but a gubernatorial victory would disrupt his life until he either lost the presidential nomination in June 1876 or, if nominated, lost—as was "almost a certainty"—the election in November 1876. When Hayes won by 5,544 votes, the predictions that had initially sounded so wild proved accurate; at least ten Ohio papers backed his candidacy for the presidency. And in *Harper's*

Weekly, the nation's leading illustrated journal, George William Curtis argued that Hayes had demonstrated that reform Republicans could buck the Democratic trend and win. The salient fact, however, was that Hayes had united disparate Republicans.[11]

After the election, Hayes received letters and visitors daily discussing the presidency, but he tried to keep it in perspective. "That 'maggot' I have heard you discourse wisely on these many years," he wrote to his old friend Judge William Johnston of Cincinnati, "you would now put into my head. . . . If other fools, forty in number, rush in, I shall not." Hayes, however, did his candidacy no harm by answering "an urgent appeal" and stumping Pennsylvania for Gov. John F. Hartranft.[12]

Resisting attempts to place the presidential bug in his brain, Hayes turned to the task of governing Ohio. Taking his "seat in the Governor's office once more" was "like getting into old slippers." His brief inaugural address on 10 January 1876 sounded familiar notes. He cautioned against excessive local taxation and indebtedness, urged the legislature to hold short sessions, and called for "just and wise treatment" of those in state institutions. Since the Allen administration had rotated Republicans out of office, Hayes was pressed to replace Democrats with deserving Republicans, but he felt awkward doing so, given his ideas about a nonpartisan civil service. Hayes did his best to strike a political balance among the state's employees, without angering his supporters.[13]

While Hayes decided on appointments, considered pardons, and accomplished other administrative tasks, the fever for his candidacy grew in and out of Ohio. On 21 January, Sen. John Sherman urged Ohio Republicans to send a united Hayes delegation to the national convention. When his old commander, Philip Sheridan, wrote that "his ticket is *Hayes and Wheeler*," Hayes confessed to Lucy, "I am ashamed to say, Who is *Wheeler?*" Hayes did little to organize his supporters. Recognizing that his appeal was "on the score of availability," he decided to "let availability do the work." He realized that corruption in Washington made both parties "more disposed to look for candidates outside of that atmosphere," giving state governors a decided advantage. Yet when Secretary of the Treasury Benjamin H. Bristow, by exposing a corrupt ring of whiskey distillers and federal officials, grew in popularity among reformers, Hayes agreed that he deserved hearty support and might be the best candidate. At the same time, Hayes declared with his usual self-confidence that the "good purposes, and the judgment experience and firmness I possess would enable me to execute the duties of the office well. I do not feel the least fear that I should fail!"[14]

When on 2 April 1876 the "earnest and unanimous" Ohio Republican convention declared for Hayes, he confessed that "the Coronation . . . was really very enjoyable." Although he played the reluctant candidate and pushed neither directly nor indirectly, he wanted the nomination enough to whip Edwin Cowles of the Cleveland *Leader* into line; Cowles, a delegate to the national convention, contemplated voting for James G. Blaine. "If I am to be voted for at all, and as long as I am to be voted for at all," Hayes asked him, "may I not reasonably expect the solid vote of Ohio?" Having intervened sufficiently to achieve unity, Hayes insisted, "*I don't meddle*"; he accepted what was "proposed in or by the Ohio delegation." He trusted it and wanted it to work in harmony. "Be on your guard who you strike," he warned a supporter. "You may unwittingly hit a friend." His "ambition in this business," he declared, was to "behave sensibly, and to do nothing unjust, or uncharitable, even, towards [an] opponent." It was a wise ambition for a favorite son who could get the nomination only if he were acceptable to other candidates whose strength might peak before they had won the prize.[15]

In the first contested Republican convention since 1860, six serious candidates vied for the presidency. Besides Hayes, there were Bristow of Kentucky, the reformers' man; Blaine of Maine, whose strength was among the party faithful; Sen. Roscoe Conkling of New York, the stalwart machine politician, running with the blessing of the Grant administration; Sen. Oliver P. Morton of Indiana, whose radicalism made him the hero of southern Republicans; and John F. Hartranft, the favorite son of Pennsylvania.

Hayes's rivals all had handicaps. Blaine, the front-runner, sustained a severe blow when his enemies leaked the allegation that he had received $64,000 from the Union Pacific Railroad (which, as Speaker of the House, he was in a position to help) for some nearly worthless Little Rock & Fort Smith Railroad bonds. Despite Blaine's denials, delegates supporting other candidates became reluctant to switch to him. Hayes, who was everyone's favorite vice-presidential candidate, secretly instructed the Ohio delegation that he could not run with Blaine. Hayes did not relish defending a man with a questionable record, but at the same time he did not wish to offend the candidate with the most delegates.[16]

The other candidates had drawbacks as well. Morton was in poor health, too radical for moderates on Reconstruction, and too strongly identified with Grant's administration for reformers' tastes. Conkling was even more strongly linked to the administration and was too much of a spoilsman. Bristow was hated by Grant and machine politicians for exposing the whiskey ring. Hartranft, from staunchly Republican Pennsylvania, was not needed to carry his state.

Since the major candidates objected less to Hayes than to one another, his chances as a compromise candidate were good. His public record as a radical Republican was impeccable, though by 1876 he had private doubts about "ultra measures"; he was reform-minded but had loyally supported Grant in 1872; he had fought heroically for the Union during the war; he had stood fearlessly for equal rights and sound money yet was, by nature, a conciliator; and he could carry Ohio, which in 1876 was essential for a Republican victory.[17]

Hayes was a particularly attractive alternative for hard-to-please, reform-minded Bristow supporters like George William Curtis. Hayes's friend Judge William M. Dickson of Cincinnati told Curtis that Hayes "would not consciously nor unconsciously be any man's man." Dickson predicted that, as president, Hayes would try to deal fairly in distributing patronage among the party factions but would select the best men from each division and would raise the qualifications of officeholders. Hayes "would not fully meet the wishes of the advanced reformers, but he would . . . perhaps do as much as the country would bear. I think," Dickson concluded, "his chief excellence is in his intuitive perception of what at the moment is practicably attainable." Upon seeing Dickson's evaluation, Hayes remarked, "you understand me so well."[18]

The convention assembled on 14 June 1876 in Cincinnati. The site, chosen largely at the behest of Bristow and Morton supporters, was teeming with Hayes men. Furthermore, Hayes had in Edward F. Noyes, the leader of the Ohio delegation, a first-rate manager. But, as Hayes remarked, his chances depended more on "the march of events" than "on management."[19]

In his small private office in Columbus, Hayes calmly awaited convention news from his friends. Hayes's family was more caught up in the excitement: Webb was at the convention, Rud was nervously waiting with Hayes, Birch was nervously waiting alone at Harvard Law School, Winnie Monroe was "very anxious," and Fanny was trying to understand what it was all about. On the eve of the convention, "all chance . . . for the great office" seemed gone when Blaine appeared certain of the nomination. But once the convention began, support for Blaine eroded, and before the nominating speeches, it seemed that he would fail.[20]

The convention, however, was driven to near frenzy by Robert G. Ingersoll of Illinois as he nominated Blaine. "Like an armed warrior, like a plumed knight," Ingersoll cried, "James G. Blaine marched down the halls of the American Congress and threw his shining lance full and fair against the brazen foreheads of the defamers of his country and maligners of his honor." The crowd's reaction to Ingersoll's rhetoric, if not logic, led Hayes to conclude that Blaine would be nominated. But Blaine's opponents postponed the balloting until the next day, giving the Hayes men time to project Hayes as the logical compromise candidate. Awakened by "encouraging despatches," Hayes and Lucy "did not readily get to sleep again."

The next morning, 16 June, even while enduring the suspense and coping with the emotions aroused by each telegraphic report, Hayes felt "cheerful and calm" and prepared for victory or defeat. He resolved that, if nominated, "I shall try to do in all things, more than ever before, . . . precisely the thing that is right—to be natural, discreet, wise, moderate, and as firm in the right as it is possible for me to be. And in this Spirit I await the event!"[21]

After the first ballot, Hayes again thought that Blaine would be nominated. With 379 votes needed to win, Blaine had 285, Morton 125, Bristow, 113, Conkling 99, Hayes 61, and Hartranft 58. Blaine's lead was impressive, but allegations of scandal lingered, and supporters of the other candidates hardly budged. After four ballots, Blaine gained only seven votes. On the fifth ballot, a significant break occurred when William A. Howard persuaded the Michigan delegation to give Hayes all twenty-two of its votes rather than merely five, raising his total to 104. On the sixth ballot, he received nine additional votes and Blaine picked up twenty-two, raising his total to 308.[22]

With Blaine gaining momentum as the seventh ballot began, the hearts of Hayes's supporters sank. But when the roll call reached Indiana, its chairman withdrew Morton's name, giving Hayes twenty-five votes and Bristow five. Suddenly "four to five thousand persons," according to the London *Times*, began "jumping, yelling, stamping, waving arms and hats as if . . . stricken with raving madness." Although Iowa and Kansas stayed with Blaine, future Supreme Court Justice John Marshall Harlan, speaking for Kentucky, withdrew Bristow from the race and cast twenty-four votes for Hayes. Tension increased as the roll call continued, with both Hayes and Blaine gaining votes. New York, heeding Conkling, who had never forgiven Blaine for taunting his vain "turkey-gobbler strut," cast sixty-one votes for Hayes and only nine for Blaine. If Blaine could pick up the fifty-eight votes of Pennsylvania, the state of his birth, he still had a chance, but Hartranft supporters divided almost evenly, giving Blaine thirty votes and Hayes twenty-eight. When the roll was completed at 5:30 P.M. on 16 June, Hayes had 384 votes, winning the nomination by five votes, although the twenty-one Bristow votes cast before his withdrawal would probably have gone to Hayes.[23]

"My hand is sore with shaking hands," Hayes wrote to Birch at 6 P.M. Blaine graciously congratulated Hayes, who responded with equal graciousness. Hayes was momentarily overcome with emotion when he thought of

The Republican nominees, 1876

how proud Uncle Sardis and his sister Fanny would have been, but on the whole he remained "calm and self possessed." When the convention selected Congressman William A. Wheeler of New York as its vice-presidential nominee, it fulfilled Sheridan's hopes and achieved a balanced ticket that would run well in the crucial states of New York and Ohio.[24]

"I cannot help thinking," Curtis wrote Hayes, "that your nomination at this juncture is as fortunate for the country as that of Mr. Lincoln in 1860." Curtis believed that Hayes would attract what he and other reformers purported to be the "immense independent vote" in New York. He was sure that the "joyful response" there and elsewhere resulted from "the feeling that while you are a party man and the candidate of the whole party, . . . your sympathies and purposes are for the purification and elevation of the tone of the government."

"I am grateful to you," Hayes told William Henry Smith, who had been promoting his political career since the Civil War. He added, "your sagacity in this matter, take it all in all, is beyond that of any other friend." Hayes also trusted that John Sherman would "never regret" inaugurating and carrying out the movement resulting in his nomination. Responding that Hayes's nomination was "a mathematical deduction," Sherman acknowledged that if anything colored his "reasoning it was your honorable and proper course when during my last canvass for Senator you refused to accept the benefit of a small defection of a few political friends." Hayes was proud that he was "in no way conscious of fault in getting" the nomination, and he determined again, "If elected I shall try to do precisely what is right."[25]

Two weeks later, on 27 June, the Democratic convention met in St. Louis and nominated Gov. Samuel J. Tilden of New York. Tilden had helped smash New York City's corrupt William M. Tweed ring and had then smashed the state's corrupt canal ring. His running mate, Thomas A. Hendricks of Indiana, was from an important, doubtful midwestern state and, in contrast to Tilden's hard-money views, was a soft-money man. Under the circumstances—hard times being endured throughout the country, the corrupt record of the Grant administration, Tilden's reform reputation, the Democrats' straddling of the money issue, and white supremacists in the South intimidating black voters—it seemed likely that Tilden and Hendricks would defeat Hayes and Wheeler. Hayes anticipated "a hot and critical contest"; William Henry Smith warned of "a strong, dangerous enemy"; and Wheeler elaborated that Tilden "is a wonderful organizer and manipulator, has large wealth and is utterly unscrupulous in its use." Confusing prowess with evil, Wheeler and other awed Republicans magnified Tilden into an even more formidable adversary.[26]

As was the custom, neither Hayes nor Tilden participated actively in the campaign, except for writing formal acceptances of their nominations. Tilden's letter approved the Democratic platform, elaborated on his hard-money views, and stressed his commitment to frugality and reform. Hayes's letter approved the Republican platform, stressed the need for civil-service reform, and promised not to seek a second term, lest patronage be used to secure his reelection. The letter also emphasized Hayes's commitment to nonsectarian public schools, to the resumption of specie payments as scheduled in January 1879, and to the promotion of honest and capable local government in the South, when the constitutional rights of all citizens were respected.

"The two parts I took thought about," Hayes wrote, "were the Civil Service, and the South. In the latter, I wanted to plainly talk of the rights of the colored man, and at the same time to say what I could for the interests and feelings of the well disposed white man." Guy Bryan's diatribes against blacks and radical Reconstruction had provoked some of that thought. Hayes realized that coupling home rule in the South with the "sacred" observance of the Constitution—"the parts that are new no less than the parts that are old"—was not what Bryan had in mind, and he advised him "to support any good Democrat ag[ain]st me," since "on one or two topics my notion of the remedy is surely not yours."

Hayes's call for "thorough, radical, and complete" reform of the spoils system arrested the drift of reformers toward Tilden. Initially, Hayes had meant "to say very little" about reform, but by heeding the advice of reformers George William Curtis, Carl Schurz, and Benjamin H. Bristow and shrewd Ohio politicians John Sherman, Charles Foster, and James A. Garfield, he had, as he acknowledged, "hit the nail on the head . . . pretty hard."[27]

Reformers were ecstatic. Hayes attracted back to the Republican party most of the Liberal Republican bolters of 1872, including Carl Schurz, an early practitioner of ethnic politics. Schurz reputedly influenced his fellow German Americans, many of whom were strategically located in closely contested states. Curtis spoke for most reformers when he told Hayes: "The tone and grasp of the letter . . . show unmistakably that it is not the work of a politician. . . . It is this conviction that will carry the letter home to the hearts of Mr. Lincoln's 'plain people,' and assure them that your election will be their triumph."

Hayes's embrace of the one-term principle was not universally applauded. Even some reformers feared that it would be detrimental to their cause; the *Nation* opposed it because the civil service could not be reformed in four years, and Hayes would be as badly needed in 1881 as in 1877. But the most serious objection to the one-term principle came from Grant, who regarded it as a criticism of his own course. Hayes reassured Grant that no such thing was intended; he told Grant that by giving up a second term and clearing the way for rivals for the nomination, he would be guarding against his own misuse of patronage and promoting unity and harmony, which would "surely strengthen my Administration." Hayes gave a political twist to a reform idea in order to retain Grant's friendship and encourage Blaine and Conkling to work for his success, but it is doubtful that anyone outside of reform circles favored the one-term idea.[28]

Having published their letters, Governors Hayes and Tilden acted presidential and pretended to be above the sordid business of electioneering. Hayes, who had determined the strategy and campaigned effectively in three close Ohio gubernatorial elections, observed the campaign from Columbus and Fremont. He wrote encouragingly to friends but shrewdly said nothing beyond his public letter. For a campaign biography, he shipped William Dean Howells half a barrel of what Howells called "glorious material," but despite his moderate views, Hayes warned him to "be careful not to commit me on religion, temperance, or free-trade. Silence is the only safety." Nor would Hayes be smoked out. "On general principles," he told Garfield, "I think explanations and defenses are bad things." Meeting the public on two official visits to the Philadelphia Centennial Exhibition as governor of Ohio was the closest Hayes came to campaigning.[29]

Hayes had little control over his campaign. Party organization was decentralized, with each state committee responsible for its state. The national committee coordinated the overall effort, concentrating its money and attention in doubtful, crucial states. Unfortunately for Hayes, the Republican National Committee in 1876 was ineffective. By placing his minion Alonzo B. Cornell on the committee, Conkling pushed out Chairman Edwin D. Morgan, the former governor of New York and a "tower of strength" as a fund-raiser. Worse yet, the Grant and Blaine people on the committee selected Grant's Secretary of the Interior Zachariah Chandler as the new chairman rather than Hayes's lieutenant, Edward F. Noyes. Although this choice kept him from controlling the coming campaign, Hayes professed to be "entirely content" with Chandler, a former senator from Michigan who was renowned as a spoilsman.[30]

Rarely communicating with Hayes, Chandler failed to give the campaign his undivided attention, which made Hayes loyalists suspicious. Stanley Matthews even warned Hayes that Chandler was part of a plot to throw the election to Tilden. Chandler concentrated on raising campaign funds, but the depression and the bleak prospects for a Republican victory in 1876 made it five times harder to raise money from outside the civil service than it had been in 1872. Having to raise cash to keep his investments afloat, Hayes could make no substantial contribution. When John Sherman urged him to help save the Chicago *Inter Ocean*, a loyal party paper, Hayes confessed that he was "'land-poor,' and in no condition to give the sort of aid required." Finding itself $10,000 in debt, the Republican National Committee briefly ceased operating, but in the end it managed to spend around $200,000— about as much as it had in the two previous campaigns.

Despite Hayes's hope that political assessments would "not be pushed," the national committee raised a hefty proportion of its money by requiring Washington civil servants to give 2 percent of their annual salary. As head of the Interior Department, Chandler was in an ideal position to levy these "voluntary contributions." Schurz was outraged, threatened to quit the campaign, and demanded that Chandler be fired. Hayes, however, realized that money was both necessary and hard to raise. He agreed with his friend Rogers, who told Schurz, "if what [you advise] so earnestly were carried into effect, it would be a surrender of the campaign." Hayes privately exclaimed, "I hate assessments," and he promised Schurz that, if elected, he would see to it that political assessments were abolished "hook, line and sinker." Although Hayes told Richard C. McCormick, the secretary of the national committee, that assessments "ought not to be allowed," McCormick assured him that his letter "was shown to no one and will not be." Chandler continued to assess civil servants in Washington, and Schurz, who was too committed to Hayes to withdraw his support, kept his speaking appointments.[31]

With less than forceful leadership from the national committee, Hayes quietly worked to rally his supporters. In July and early August, he tried to exploit the school issue once again, which he thought would also work in the Protestant South. He backed a constitutional amendment that would prohibit the "application of *any public* money to sectarian schools" but soon found himself vulnerable to charges of nativism. Publication of Hayes's secretary's acknowledgment of a letter of support from the American Alliance caused a panic among his Chicago supporters. Joseph Medill of the Chicago *Tribune* was "downright mad," and William Henry Smith warned Hayes that he had better do something "to aid us with the great foreign population of the Northwest," especially in Chicago and Wisconsin. While maintaining his opposition to Catholic "or any sectarian interference with politics or the schools," Hayes denied any hostility to foreigners, declaring, "I was not a Know-Nothing when my political associates generally ran off after that ephemeral party." Hayes, however, thought that charges of xenophobia could best be "met (*not* by denial or explanation) but by charging Democrats with their Catholic alliance."[32]

As the campaign progressed, it became obvious to Hayes that "*the* issue" was neither civil-service reform nor public support of sectarian schools. "WE MUST CHOOSE OUR OWN TOPICS," he wrote to Garfield. "*The danger of giving the Rebels the Government*, is the topic people are most interested in." Hayes repeatedly urged the Republicans—even reformers like Schurz—to wave the bloody shirt rather than the banner of reform, rejecting the southern-strategy advice of Charles Nordhoff of the New York *Herald*.

Nordhoff had suggested that Hayes confer "*quietly*" with "a few of the prominent old Whig leaders of the Southern states, . . . detach from the Democratic side down there the real Whig vote," and, "without much trouble & with no embarrassing engagements, make sure of carrying Louisiana, North Carolina, Virginia & Arkansas." Nordhoff optimistically argued that "all wise & patriotic" southerners accepted the "later Constitutional Amendments," that federal intervention in local southern affairs would no longer be necessary, and that southern parties were already "re-arranging themselves . . . independent of the color line." In short, he concluded, "The darkies you'll have any how; the white Whigs are what you want to capture."[33]

Reformers, however, refused to "wave the bloody shirt" and were annoyed that it diverted attention from reform. Curtis begged Hayes to show "sympathy with the sincere reform element" of the Republican party in its intraparty struggle with spoilsmen. Hayes assured Curtis that stressing the rebellion issue "does not mean that we are indifferent to Reform" and mentioned as evidence that all six new candidates for Congress from Ohio were his "*intimate* personal friends" and were in agreement with him regarding reform. But, in and around Harvard University, Charles Eliot Norton found that there was "less & less faith that Hayes & Reform are synonymous."[34]

Hayes emphasized the bloody shirt and slighted reform because he realized that the few reformers who would drift to Tilden would be outnumbered by the lethargic rank-and-file Republicans who would be inspired to go to the polls. The situation was so grim that even Maine appeared "horribly doubtful." After the "handsome" Republican gain there in the September election, Hayes congratulated Blaine and urged him to remember, as he campaigned elsewhere, that "our strong ground is the dread of a solid South, rebel rule, etc., etc. I hope you will make these topics prominent in your speeches. It leads people away from 'hard Times,' which is our deadliest foe."[35]

Hayes and the Republicans did not fabricate the bloody shirt issue. In most of the South, Reconstruction had all but ended by 1876 because the Democrats had embraced violence and intimidation to restore white supremacy and destroy the Republican party. Attorney General Alphonso Taft reported to Hayes in August that he was trying to "save" North Carolina, South Carolina, Mississippi, and Louisiana and that with more troops "to sustain the officers of the U.S.," more southern states could be saved for the Republicans. But, he observed, the "Democratic House has crippled us very much" by not appropriating money for the army.

After investigating, Taft told Hayes of the "incredible" wrongs that had been inflicted on southern Republicans. To prevent blacks from voting, the Democratic party used murder as "a common means of intimidation," and its tyranny was so terrible that the Republicans dared not publish the murders or testify to the facts in court. Taft gave up trying to prevent fraud in Mississippi; the Democrats controlled the state government and were frightening off blacks who wished to register. Any Mississippi blacks who did vote "would [be] count[ed] . . . out however great the republican majority should be." In South Carolina, Florida, and Louisiana—the three southern states still controlled by Republicans—Taft resolved that "we shall try to protect the negroes. . . . For it is simply a question whether the 15th Amendment shall be given up."[36]

With Taft's reports in hand, it is no wonder that Hayes sought to rally Republicans around the flag. On 17 September, he noted in his diary thirteen "watchwords" that "might be useful if well circulated." All thirteen rephrased the question, "Are you for the Rebellion, or are you for the Union?" Strong-arm Democratic tactics in the South could help the bloody-shirt-waving Republicans carry the doubtful northern states of Indiana and New York. Republican prospects in Indiana, a hotbed of greenback sentiment, appeared bleak. Gen. Judson Kilpatrick, whose cavalry had made Sherman's march to the sea an especially painful memory for many southerners, wrote to Hayes that a "*bloody shirt campaign, with money*," would save Indiana, but a "*financial* campaign and no money and we are beaten."

Republicans poured $47,000 into Indiana—less than half the $100,000 Oliver P. Morton had requested—and lost the October election by 5,000 votes. As Hayes expected, Ohio went Republican by 9,000 votes, which would likely double for him in November. While urging the Republican National Committee not to give up Indiana, where the party had a "fighting chance," he realized that the Republicans had to either carry New York or salvage enough electoral votes from North and South Carolina, Florida, Mississippi, and Louisiana.[37]

Jolted by losing Indiana, the Grant administration turned to the South.

The 2,800 federal troops stationed in the eleven former Confederate states, although largely symbolic, protected Republican voters and Republican administrations from hostile Democrats. After the October elections, Grant reinforced South Carolina, despite the federal commander's estimate that he had sufficient troops. The additional men made the red-shirted Democratic rifle clubs lie low but not disband. A jubilant South Carolina Republican told Hayes that he would carry the state by 20,000 votes, but the show of federal force lost Hayes the support of some liberals, such as his friend Charles Nordhoff, whose dream of having Republicans capture the southern white Whig vote was destroyed. Ignoring the revolutionary defiance of the Fourteenth and Fifteenth Amendments by southern Democrats, Nordhoff warned Hayes that despite his "good intentions," if he "were elected on a coercion and revolutionary policy," he might "be a mere prisoner" of the high-handed "Chandlers, Mortons, Logans, and Butlers." But even while waving the bloody shirt, Hayes consistently emphasized that if the South obeyed the amendments, it could achieve harmony and home rule. "I stand by the paragraph on the South in my letter," he told Guy Bryan. "The more sinister the reports, the more I am convinced that I have hit the true and only solution. *Time, time*, is the great cure-all in such cases."[38]

Hayes and the Republican strategists believed that New York, the home of Tilden and Conkling, would decide the election. Tilden was a reformer, a popular governor, and a masterful political organizer. His "perfect system" (as Republicans fearfully dubbed it) was to learn each voter's political preference and bombard likely converts—for example, Republican Catholics of French-Canadian origin alienated by Hayes's "school" issue—with appropriate Democratic literature. The Democrats, with their smooth-running system utilizing state and city employees, had "*cowed*" Republicans by mid-October.[39]

Republicans, who controlled the New York customhouse, also knew how to organize the electorate, but their leader was unenthusiastic. Roscoe Conkling would have accepted his defeat by Hayes with better grace if Hayes had ignored civil-service reform in his letter of acceptance. When reformers at the New York Republican convention kept Conkling from nominating his customhouse lieutenant Alonzo B. Cornell for governor and forced his acceptance of compromise nominee Edwin D. Morgan, Conkling realized that he was not in complete control, and his loathing for reformers increased. But Conkling had had enough muscle to keep Cornell as state chairman, and now Cornell's task was to carry New York for Morgan and Hayes, the men who had frustrated his and Conkling's ambitions. With Conkling sulking and Cornell "sour & disappointed," New York Republicans remained uninspired. Hayes tried to flatter Conkling by inviting him to campaign in the West, but Conkling made only one speech during the campaign, and that was in his hometown of Utica. Campaigning among New York Germans, Schurz told Hayes, "If the Republicans do not carry New York, it will be their own fault."[40]

After the Indiana defeat in October, Morgan—who was in touch with Hayes—infused spirit and cash into the Republican campaign in New York. He raised $47,750 in contributions of $1,000 or more from among his friends; he personally wrote to each county chair, had his own agents report on the campaign in each county, and urged Cornell to follow Hayes's advice to send speakers into Republican counties to bring out the vote.[41]

Hayes was assured by Attorney General Alphonso Taft that he could count on "a reasonably honest election in New York." The Republicans had designed the 1871 Federal Elections Act, also called the Enforcement Act, to prevent corrupt Democrats from fraudulently carrying the state. During the campaign of 1876, the Grant administration spent more than $291,000 for 11,501 deputy marshals and 4,863 supervisors; of that sum, more than $80,000 was used to hire 2,300 deputy marshals and 1,144 supervisors in New York City. There, the chief supervisor of federal elections, John I. Davenport, had the residence of each registered voter checked against real-estate maps, mailed notices to registered voters who had given unlikely addresses, and ran newspaper advertisements threatening to arrest anyone attempting to vote whose letter had been marked "addressee unknown." Billy Rogers told Hayes on 2 November that Davenport had boasted that there would not be a hundred fraudulent votes cast in New York City, that businessmen there were stirred up "in our favor," and that Republicans of all hues—including Zach Chandler, Edwin Morgan, Thurlow Weed, and George William Curtis—gave "decided assurance of carrying the State." A few days later, state chairman Alonzo Cornell confidently telegraphed Hayes, "Our electoral vote will be cast for you."[42]

Hayes lacked Cornell's confidence. "The huge registration in New York City looks . . . to our defeat in that State," he wrote in late October. On 26 October, which was Ohio Day at the Philadelphia Centennial Exhibition, Hayes shook some 4,000 hands there and made half a dozen speeches. This encouraged him, and he had some faith in his "*luck*," but he realized that chances were against his election. Despite the Election Law and the work of Taft and Davenport, Hayes predicted that, if he were beaten, it would be "by crime—by bribery, & repeating"—in the North and by "violence and intimidation" in the South.[43]

"I still think," Hayes noted on election day, 7 November 1876, that "Democratic chances [are] the best." Although he believed that the government's effect on business prosperity was exaggerated and that a Tilden victory would not postpone the revival of business, he nevertheless thought that a Democratic victory would be "a calamity," because "we shall have no improvement in Civil Service . . . and the South will drift towards chaos again." With so much crime corrupting the electoral process, especially in the South, Hayes anticipated the danger of a "contested result." In such an event, there was no "means for its decision as ought to be provided by law"; he therefore insisted on 22 October that "this must be attended to hereafter. . . . If a contest comes now it may lead to a conflict of arms. . . . Blood shed and civil war must be averted if possible. If forced to fight I have no fears of failure from lack of courage or firmness."[44]

On the evening of election day, the Hayes family and a few intimate friends became depressed when "Ohio was not doing as well as" they had hoped. Lucy "busied herself about refreshments . . . and soon disappeared . . . abed with a head ache." Although Hayes remained the "most composed, and cheerful of the party," he "never supposed there was a chance for a Republican success" after learning that Tilden would probably carry New York City by 50,000 votes. When Hayes joined Lucy after midnight, they consoled each other with the thought that their lives would be simpler. Hayes wrote: "Both of us felt more anxiety about the South — about the colored people especially than about anything else sinister in the result. . . . There the amendments will be nullified, disorder will continue, prosperity to both whites and colored people, will be pushed off for years." Nevertheless, they "soon fell into a refreshing sleep and the affair seemed over."[45]

THE DISPUTED ELECTION

The affair was not over. While Hayes and Zach Chandler, convinced of defeat and without plans to contest it, slept soundly, Gen. Daniel E. Sickles, on his way home from an after-theater supper, stopped at the nearly deserted Republican National Committee headquarters in New York and made the initial moves that would plunge the nation into a unique crisis. Sickles — whose checkered past mixed politics and diplomacy with seduction and murder — personified for reformers what was wrong with the Grant administration and was an unlikely ally of Rutherford B. Hayes. He scanned the returns, which gave Tilden New York, New Jersey, Connecticut, Indiana, and apparently the entire South, with a plurality of about 250,000 votes and, it seemed, 203 electoral votes (with only 185 needed for victory).

But in these tallies, Sickles found a glimmer of hope. Hayes could win if the Pacific slope, whose returns were not in, went for him and if Republicans retained control of South Carolina, Florida, and Louisiana. Over Chandler's signature, he telegraphed the following audacious message to leading Republicans in South Carolina, Louisiana, Florida, and Oregon: "With your state sure for Hayes, he is elected. Hold your state." By about 6 A.M., he had received encouraging answers from South Carolina and Oregon. Before going home to bed, Sickles again telegraphed "all four states, informing them that the enemy claimed each of them and enjoining vigilance and diligence."[1]

The *New York Times* also refused to believe that Hayes had lost. Encouraging reports from Oregon, South Carolina, Louisiana, and Florida (probably inspired by Sickles's telegrams) and a hint of Democratic uncertainty reinforced the hopes of John C. Reid, the paper's rabid Republican managing editor. In its first edition, the *Times* proclaimed the election "doubtful"; in its second, it claimed victory for Hayes if he carried Florida.[2]

Shortly after 6 A.M., Reid rushed to Republican headquarters to tell Zach Chandler that Associated Press dispatches gave both Florida and Oregon to Hayes and that the *Times* believed he was victorious. There, Reid found only one member of the national committee, William E. Chandler, who had just arrived after voting in New Hampshire. Together, they read the dispatches on Zach Chandler's desk and roused him from a whiskey-induced stupor. He knew nothing of the dispatches and could hardly comprehend their import. "I immediately telegraphed to Florida, Louisiana, South Carolina, Nevada & Oregon," William Chandler reported to Hayes, "that all depended on them and that with them we were safe, to look out for Democratic frauds & to telegraph us when sure." Chandler got off his dispatches at 6:30, "ahead of similar democratic dispatches," he and Reid believed. With responses arriving that morning before other Republicans "came around . . . it seemed as if the dead had been raised."[3]

Unaware that Sickles, Reid, and Chandler had been calculating and telegraphing, Hayes awoke Wednesday morning to find that he was "master" of himself and "contented and cheerful." He went to his office as usual and wrote to Rud, who had transferred to Cornell, to let him know how the folks at home were taking the defeat. "Scott Russell is rejoiced because now we can remain in Columbus where the cousins and friends live, and will not have to go away off to Washington, which he evidently thinks is a very bad place. Fanny shares in this feeling, but has a suspicion that something desirable has been lost. Birch and Webb don't altogether like it, but are cheerful and philosophical about it." Hayes rationalized that he and Lucy had escaped labors and anxieties but regretted that he would not be able "to establish Civil Service reform, and to do a good work for the South."[4]

Soon after writing that letter, however, Hayes learned that his proverbial good luck had not entirely deserted him. During the day, the news indicated that he had carried the Pacific states and, "with a few Republican States in the South," could be victorious. The whole country was "full of excitement and anxiety." Rumors were rife, including a false claim on Wednesday evening that New York was for Hayes, which resulted in "a shouting multitude" rushing to his house. Telling the crowd that he did not believe the rumor, Hayes calmed it by saying that the outcome was still in doubt "owing to the incomplete telegraph communications through some of the Southern and Western States."[5]

Hayes did not claim victory, but on Wednesday evening Zach Chandler claimed it "beyond a doubt." Several days would elapse before unofficial tallies were available in South Carolina, Florida, and Louisiana, and they were subject to review by Republican-controlled returning boards, which were empowered to throw out votes where fraud or intimidation had been practiced. With the sudden power to pick the next president, these boards would be pressed by Democrats to count the actual ballots and by Republicans to throw out votes. Convinced on Wednesday night that the Democrats "were desperate" and that Republicans had to "prepare for any & every possible emergency," William E. Chandler departed posthaste for South Carolina, Florida, and "Louisiana if necessary," he reported to Hayes, "to aid . . . in preventing our being defrauded out of what we have fairly won."[6]

If the decision to contest the election had been left to Hayes, Tilden would have been president. Hayes doubted that the returning boards could or even should overcome the ill-gotten Democratic majorities. He noted that Republican claims to have carried the country by one electoral vote were creating "great uneasiness" and implied that the hasty departure of prominent Republicans and Democrats for points south added to the suspense. After checking the tallies in the Sunday morning papers, he concluded that the Democrats had carried Florida by "fraud and violence" and braced "to accept the inevitable." Hayes believed that by "improper interference with the rights of the colored people," Democrats had deprived him of the presidency. "A fair election in the South," he insisted, "would undoubtedly have given" him a majority of the electoral vote and "a decided preponderance of the popular vote." Hayes never deviated from this belief; his doubts about contesting the election were rooted not in fairness but in questions of practicality and expediency.

Hayes did not make the decision to contest the election; he continued to play a presidential role (as did Tilden). It was able and tenacious Republican leaders who challenged and outclassed Democrats in a sordid struggle for electoral votes. Having decided on Sunday morning that he had lost the presidency, Hayes received a dispatch on Sunday afternoon that opened "it all up again." Former Gov. William Dennison, "a prudent and cautious gentleman" as well as a friend, wired him: "You are undoubtedly elected next President of the U.S. Desperate attempts are being made to defeat you in Louisiana South Carolina & Florida but they will not succeed." Hayes stopped talking about conceding defeat or accepting the inevitable. Believing that a proper canvass of the votes in South Carolina, Louisiana, and Florida would make him the next president, he now wanted that proper canvass.[7]

Although worried about unscrupulous Democrats, Hayes told Schurz that he was also "anxious . . . that in the canvassing of results there should be no taint of dishonesty" among Republicans. Hayes knew that visiting statesmen, including William E. Chandler and Charles B. Farwell (a wealthy Chicago merchant and "the ablest politician and wisest coolest head in Illinois"), were not fastidious in their methods, and he did not want to be—or appear to be—the recipient of stolen goods. He had not participated "in sending leading men South"; to balance the zealous partisans who had been sent, he urged Schurz, whose honesty was above question, to observe the count in Louisiana. But Schurz could not go, and Hayes did little to orchestrate Republican efforts to save the doubtful states. Most of the Republican politicians who observed the count in South Carolina, Florida, and Louisiana were there by invitation from President Grant, who ordered the army to protect the returning boards "in the performance of their duty." But Grant's involvement did not necessarily change the tally. Like Hayes, he was convinced that "the country cannot afford to have the result tainted by the suspicion of illegal or false returns."[8]

Although Hayes's faith that he would have won a fair election was probably justified, Republicans had to prove that he had won an unfair election in three states. Proving that he deserved the electoral votes of South Carolina, which he appeared to carry by 600 to 1,000 votes, was hardly necessary, but winning Florida, which he unofficially lost by ninety-four votes, was a problem; gaining Louisiana, which Tilden unofficially carried by 6,300 votes, was a major difficulty. Unofficial tallies also gave the Democrats the governorship and the legislature in all three states. With Hayes ahead in South Carolina and a Republican returning board determining the outcome there, visiting statesmen concentrated on Florida and Louisiana. In all three states, Republicans had used fraud to counter Democratic fraud, violence, and intimidation. Most of the "bulldozing" had occurred during the campaign, but much of the fraud was practiced on and after a relatively calm election day.

In Florida, it was impossible to determine who would have won a fair election. Repeaters, stuffed ballot boxes, and Democratic ballots printed with the Republican symbol to trick illiterate voters had all been used. In addition, returns from remote areas had been delayed, to be altered as needed. William E. Chandler supervised the struggle to save Florida for Hayes and was aided by agents from the Justice, Treasury, and Post Office Departments, as well as by Hayes's lieutenant Edward F. Noyes. Most visiting statesmen justified their partisans' unlawful acts and zeroed in on those of the opposition. The few who were truly reform-minded were both troubled and ignored. Gen. Lew Wallace—whose *Ben Hur* would be published in 1880—visited Florida at Hayes's behest. Once there, Wallace complained to his wife that both sides were unconscionable. "Nothing is so common as the resort to perjury, unless it is violence—in short, I do not know whom to believe. . . . If we win, our methods are subject to impeachment for possible fraud. If the enemy win, it is the same thing exactly."[9]

To overcome the substantial Democratic lead in Louisiana, Republican visiting statesmen, led by John Sherman, James Garfield, and Charles Farwell, assumed that since blacks constituted a majority of the state's registered voters, the Democrats had intimidated enough of them to carry the state. They ignored the fact that Republican factionalism had alienated some black voters. Telling Hayes of the "atrocious means" used to prevent black Republicans from voting, Sherman assured him that he would have the vote of Louisiana, according to the letter and spirit of its laws. "But," an uneasy Hayes responded, "we are not to allow our friends to defeat one outrage and fraud by another. There must be nothing crooked on our part."[10]

Hayes's unease reflected a realization that his wishes affected neither the returning boards, which quickly got to work, nor the visiting statesmen who hovered over them. Although Tilden also occupied a high moral position, his corrupt nephew Col. William T. Pelton, operating out of Tilden's home, was negotiating to buy off returning board members. Tilden reprimanded his nephew, but he remained in his uncle's household and continued his efforts to buy the election. On 22 November, the all-Republican five-member South Carolina board invalidated the votes in both Edgefield and Laurens Counties and ensured that Republicans would carry the state for Hayes as well as win the legislature and the governorship. When the legislature met on 26 November and Republicans in the lower chamber refused to seat Democrats claiming to be elected from Edgefield and Laurens Counties, the Democrats withdrew and organized a rival state government under Wade Hampton, which the federal troops in the state did not disturb.[11]

Although John Sherman assured Hayes that J. Madison Wells, chair of the all-Republican Louisiana returning board, was "thoroughly honest and conscientious," Wells was auctioning off the presidency. Despite—or perhaps because of—Pelton's interest, the enterprising Wells most likely realized a tidy sum by negotiating with his own party. On 22 November, Farwell assured Hayes's friend William Henry Smith that he was "in constant communication with those who *know*, and they assure me that all will be well." Farwell's confidence most likely resulted from expenditures he made out of his own well-lined pocket. One year later, Smith reminded Hayes that Farwell "in all delicate and important matters last year . . . was our right hand man" and that "his wealth . . . supplied the means when no other could be reached." The result, announced on 5 December, was as Farwell had predicted. Specifically, the board threw out 15,000 votes, 13,000 of which were Democratic. Instead of losing Louisiana, Hayes carried it by more than 3,000 votes, and the Republican state ticket also triumphed. The Democrats, however, set up a rival government, just as they had in South Carolina. Hearing from Sherman, Garfield, and other visiting statesmen that "murder, and hellish cruelties . . . at many polls drove the colored people away, or forced them to vote the Democratic ticket" in Louisiana,

Hayes believed that the board had made a brave as well as a correct decision.[12]

Florida's returning board, which had the novelty of a Democratic member, threw out enough votes to declare, on 6 December, Hayes the victor by 900 votes and the state Republican ticket victorious by a narrower margin. In Columbus, Hayes was "overwhelmed with callers, congratulating" him "on the results declared in Florida and Louisiana. I have no doubt," he told a somewhat dubious Schurz, "that we are justly and legally entitled to the Presidency."[13]

While the Republican returning boards in South Carolina, Louisiana, and Florida were counting their partisans into office, a bizarre development in Oregon played into Democratic hands. Everyone agreed that Hayes had carried that state by more than 1,000 votes, but John W. Watts was both a postmaster and a Republican elector on the ballot, and the Constitution states that a federal officeholder cannot be an elector. Watts assumed that there would be no problem, and upon his election he resigned from the post office, as did a Vermont elector who was also a postmaster. But at the behest of Democratic National Committee Chairman Abram S. Hewitt, Oregon's Democratic governor disqualified Watts and certified a Tilden elector in his place. Hewitt hoped that this maneuver would force the Republicans "to go behind" and reject Oregon's official certified electoral vote. Such a move ought to enable the Democrats to do the same thing with the certificates from the governors of South Carolina, Florida, and Louisiana.[14]

Congress required electors to cast their ballots in the state capitals on 6 December. In thirty-four state capitals, the procedure was routine, but not in Salem, Columbia, Tallahassee, and New Orleans. In those four capitals, both the Republican and the Democratic electors met, voted, and forwarded their conflicting votes to Washington. After the balloting, Tilden had 184 votes and Hayes 165, with both candidates claiming the remaining 20 votes.[15]

On the evening of 6 December, surrounded by family and friends, Hayes and Lucy awaited dispatches confirming the electoral vote. They "had a lively happy little gathering," believing that the decisions of the Republican returning boards were final. But fears about Oregon were confirmed the next day. The governor of Oregon certified one Tilden vote, and Hayes worried that it would be "treated as the true one" and give the election to Tilden. Not anticipating a dispute over the votes of Louisiana, Florida, and South Carolina, Hayes magnified the Oregon problem into a potential crisis, "perhaps fatal to free government," and "would gladly give up all claim to the place, if this would avert the evil." But he soon thought that "the Oregon fraud," as he called it, was "so transparent palpable and disgraceful" that, at worst, it would only complicate matters and at best "be thrown aside without dissent." Convinced that he was "fairly, honestly and lawfully elected," Hayes expected "a general acquiescence in the result among judicious men of all parties."[16]

The Constitution provided that the votes of the electoral college be "directed to the President of the Senate," who "shall, in the presence of the Senate and House of Representatives, open all the Certificates and the votes shall then be counted." The Constitution, however, did not specify whether the presiding officer of the Senate or the combined House and Senate would decide which votes to count when conflicting votes were forwarded to Washington. Since Vice President Henry Wilson had died in 1875, the president of the Senate in 1876 was Thomas W. Ferry, a Michigan Republican who Postmaster General James N. Tyner wished were a "more resolute man." Arguing that Ferry should decide which votes to count, Hayes stated, "My judgment is that neither House of Congress, nor both combined, have any right to interfere in the count. It is for the V.P. to do it all. His action is final. There should be no compromise of our constitutional rights."[17]

Apart from his Ohio circle, few people in Washington agreed with Hayes's hard-line position. Many Republicans and all Democrats objected to such a narrow congressional role. Nor were the Democrats powerless. Although Tilden—who had no stomach for the struggle—provided little leadership, the Democrats controlled the House of Representatives. Citing Republican precedents, they insisted that the combined House and Senate, with its Democratic majority, should decide which votes to count. All but the blindest of partisans realized that concessions and compromise were necessary if the count were to proceed.[18]

Given the decentralized and contentious character of American political parties, disaffected Republicans and Democrats were bound to surface. A few senators and representatives on either side would be ready to sacrifice a national victory for regional, local, or factional advantages. The most conspicuous disaffected Republican was Roscoe Conkling, the boss of New York, who had liked neither Hayes's nomination nor his letter of acceptance and had been virtually silent during the campaign. A Democratic victory would discredit the reform wing of the Republican party and enhance Conkling's power to choose the 1880 Republican nominee. With Hayes tilting toward Conkling's New York enemies, Conkling's chances of patronage might be better with Tilden, especially if Tilden were aware of Conkling's good wishes. On 19 November, Conkling asked a Democrat (who promptly relayed the query to Tilden) whether they were going "to act upon the *good-boy* principle of submission, or whether" they meant "to have it understood that Tilden has been elected and by the Eternal, he shall be inaugurated?" Allied to Conkling were southern Republican senators who were afraid that they would be abandoned if Hayes conciliated the South with home rule in exchange for obedience to the Reconstruction amendments, as promised in his acceptance letter.[19]

Hayes was aware of Conkling's "lack of hearty support" and of his view that Congress, rather than Ferry, should decide which votes to count. From a Conkling emissary, Hayes learned in mid-December that Conkling would support him on how the count should proceed if Hayes would repudiate reformers—such as Carl Schurz and George William Curtis—and not disturb Conkling's New York customhouse lieutenants. Hayes also learned that southern Republican senators would remain loyal if he would continue to back them. Despite these threats and feelers, Hayes made no commitments. He repeated his pledge to "deal fairly and justly by all elements of the party" and reiterated the views he had expressed in his acceptance letter—that to achieve peace and prosperity, "the Southern people must obey the new amendments, and give the colored men all of their rights." His noncommittal attitude did not placate Conkling, whose man tried over the next two weeks to get Hayes to be more specific.[20]

Disaffected Democrats also surfaced. The decisions of the returning boards and Tilden's caution made many members of his party anticipate and accept defeat. Having lost elections for sixteen years, they were habitual losers. Although all Democrats preferred a Tilden victory, some southerners explored what they might gain from capitulation. These southerners wondered whether Hayes would concede the South to the Democrats (home rule) if they acquiesced to his election. In an effort to reach an understanding, Col. William H. Roberts of the New Orleans *Times* met with Hayes on 1 December. Other southern Democratic newspapermen and politicians met counterparts who were close to Hayes. The editor of the Memphis *Avalanche*, Col. Andrew J. Kellar, conferred with both William Henry Smith and Richard Smith of the Cincinnati *Gazette*. Kellar was an independent Democrat who wished to involve "the better class of white southerners" in building a conservative Republican party in the South that would "destroy the color line & save the poor colored people." After meeting with the Smiths, Kellar left for Washington on 14 December to "enter zealously on the great work."

Informed of Kellar's activities by William Henry Smith, Hayes was "hopeful that much good will come from friendly relations with good men" in the South. But he did not move beyond his promise in his letter of acceptance that, if the rights of all were recognized by all, the federal government would promote southern efforts to obtain "honest and capable local government." Confident that Ferry would count him into the presidency, Hayes remained "perfectly free from committals as to *persons* and *policies*."[21]

Even before Kellar arrived in Washington, Garfield told Hayes that Democratic businessmen were "more anxious for quiet than for Tilden" and that "leading southern Democrats in Congress, especially those who were old Whigs," might be separated from their northern associates if they knew that Hayes would treat the South "with kind consideration." For several southern men, kind consideration meant—in addition to home rule and patronage—a federal subsidy for the expansion of the Texas & Pacific Railroad. Although many southern congressmen backed a subsidy bill, which the railroad's president, Thomas A. Scott (also president of the Pennsylvania Railroad), had lobbied for, the Democrats were even more hostile to subsidies than the Republicans were. Estimates of southern Democrats who might be enticed to accept Hayes ran as high as fifty; Garfield was skeptical but thought that the overtures were worth exploring. He told Hayes that if a third of that number would acquiesce in his election, "it would do much to prevent immediate trouble, & to make your future work easier." These southerners wanted Garfield to outline Hayes's southern policy in a speech, but they were "a little vague" about what they wanted, and Garfield was uncertain about Hayes's attitude toward the South, which, apart from his letter of acceptance, had not been friendly.[22]

Republican Congressman John A. Kasson of Iowa, who had been a visiting statesman in Louisiana and Florida, also reported that southerners could be split off from the Democratic majority in the House. Making no mention of the Texas & Pacific Railroad, Kasson said that southerners wished to avoid a "national disorder" and "to recover intelligent white rule in the South," which, he assured Hayes, "need not . . . sacrifice . . . the constitutional rights of the negro, nor should it. Nor will they demand it." Kasson urged Hayes to encourage this group through a Washington spokesman.[23]

Hayes did not elaborate his views beyond his acceptance letter, refused to go to Washington to confer on important points, and did not designate a Washington spokesman. "There are too many cooks at Washington," he told Billy Rogers. "The true thing is, a firm adherence to the Constitution. The V. P. ought to be able to finish the work at one sitting." Hayes continued to rely on Ohio Republicans in Washington—men such as Samuel Shellabarger, Dennison, and John Sherman—to represent him unofficially. "I wish *you* to feel authorized," he told Sherman, "to speak in pretty decided terms for me whenever it seems advisable—to do this, not by reason of specific authority . . . but from your knowledge of my general methods of action." Hayes avoided pledges but left his lieutenants free to give assurances. He feared that an authorized friend might become the focal point of negotiations and fuel charges of "intrigue—bargain and sale. At any rate," he shrewdly concluded, "I see the true position to be 'hands off.'"[24]

With the drift of events in his favor, Hayes was wise to distance himself from Washington intrigues, but William Henry Smith kept him informed. He knew, for example, that Kellar had joined with Henry Van Ness Boynton, the Cincinnati *Gazette*'s correspondent, in exploring Democratic fissures and learned that Kellar, who had left by the morning of 20 December, claimed to have "given a decided impetus" to securing thirty to thirty-six southern Democrats who, in return for home rule, would oppose any "revolutionary" proposition to prevent Ferry from counting the vote. They wanted Hayes to "publicly avow his views," but Boynton explained "that it would be nothing more than a repetition of his letter of acceptance."[25]

Later that same day, Boynton outlined for William Henry Smith a new scheme to attract the thirty to thirty-six votes wanted "for *practical* success"; it involved Tom Scott and the Texas & Pacific Railroad. Elaborating on what Garfield had alluded to earlier, Boynton noted that large areas of the South wanted help for that railroad and that the Republican party no longer favored such subsidies. But if Hayes would support aid for the Texas & Pacific Railroad and if, Boynton continued, "Tom Scott and the prominent representatives of the States I have named could *know* this, Scott with his whole force would come here, and get those votes in spite of all human power, and all the howlings which blusterers North and South could put up." Despite Boynton's exaggeration of the power of Scott's lobby, Smith relayed his letters to Hayes, adding that Joseph Medill of the Chicago *Tribune* and Richard Smith, Boynton's boss at the Cincinnati *Gazette*, were willing to back the scheme. James M. Comly, who was visiting Washington, told Hayes that Garfield as well as Hayes's congressman, Charles Foster, thought that advocating a Texas & Pacific land grant would help their party's cause and might even make Texas a Republican state.[26]

Hayes initially encouraged these negotiations but then pulled back. While maintaining, on 24 December, that he did "not wish to be committed to details," he told Smith that he desired "to restore peace and prosperity to the South" and "would be exceptionally liberal about . . . education and internal improvements of a national character." But, although Boynton desired it, Hayes would not unleash Scott and his lobby by approving, even privately, a land grant to the Texas & Pacific Railroad. With the tide carrying him toward the presidency, he felt uneasy about the Scott lobby and negotiations with southern Democrats, which might cost him the support of "more valuable" southern Republicans. "We are floating still," he wrote to Rogers, " 'sailing the Vesuvian bay'—calmly, quietly. The Dems are afraid of their Southern men in the House, and the Reps are equally doubtful of their Southern men in the Senate. What is gained on one margin is lost on the other." On 3 January, Hayes told Smith, "I am not a believer in the trustworthiness of the forces you hope to rally," but he still planned to support education and internal improvements for the South, hoping to "divide the whites" and help "obliterate the color line." Although taken aback by Hayes's rebuff, Smith continued to pursue "the Southern matter" on his own responsibility. "I look for nothing of value growing out of Southern conservative tendencies in this Congress," Hayes perceptively told Schurz. "Whatever the caucus decides to do will be done, and the influence referred to is too small to control the large House majority."[27]

By January, Hayes's thoughts were more on Republican solidarity than on dissatisfaction among southern Democrats. "We are in some danger . . . from treachery" and "more from mere 'cussedness,' " he wrote to Rogers on 31 December, "but most of all from lack of back bone." To encourage Ferry and to lead congressional Republicans before the count began, Hayes thought of resigning his governorship and boldly claiming the role of president-elect. He consulted Morton, who was enthusiastic, but Sherman convinced him to continue waiting in dignified silence. Bold leadership would not work; too many Republicans rejected the notion that Ferry could decide which electoral votes were valid. Sen. George F. Edmunds of Vermont thought that the Supreme Court should decide; Schurz, despite his friendship with Hayes, agreed. Conkling continued to insist that "the House has an equal voice in the Count." In addition, southern Republican senators— who tended to follow Conkling's lead and owed their seats to Grant's support—feared that if Hayes deferred to reformers such as Benjamin H. Bristow and abandoned them, they would come out ahead by cutting a deal with the Democrats. Even more ominous was Grant's admission to his cabinet, and even to Tilden's lieutenant Hewitt, that he was uncertain who had carried Louisiana and that some Republicans favored a new election in Louisiana.[28]

Realizing that he would not become president if Grant were opposed or even indifferent, Hayes wrote a friendly, well-received letter to Grant just before Christmas. Although Hayes declined Grant's invitation to meet with him, Comly journeyed to Washington and assured Grant that Hayes would not appoint Bristow to a cabinet position. *"At this point in the conversation,"* Comly reported, Grant *"drew the friendly cigars from his pocket,"* and a confidential talk ensued.[29]

Hayes could conciliate Grant, but his lieutenants could not convince Congress to silently observe while Ferry decided the election. George W. McCrary, an Iowa Republican, introduced a resolution calling for a special committee to settle the crisis. The resolution passed the House in mid-December, and a Senate resolution introduced by Edmunds set up a cooperating committee. Ardent Hayes supporters were outraged when Democratic Speaker Samuel J. Randall appointed moderate Republicans to the House committee and were dismayed when Ferry, who did not want to decide the election by himself, appointed Conkling to the Senate committee. Having heard that Conkling believed that the Louisiana returning board had "greatly abused" its discretion, Hayes feared that with his power and hostility, Conkling would inspire a compromise measure that would change the result of the election. His fears were exaggerated. The committees agreed that a commission of five senators, five representatives, and five Supreme Court justices should resolve the dispute. Members of the commission were to be evenly divided between the parties except for the fifth judge—presumably David Davis, a political independent—who would be chosen by the other four justices. In effect, Davis rather than Ferry would decide the election. Both sides agreed that the commission would decide whether to investigate official returns and that its decisions would be final unless they were overturned by both houses, which was highly unlikely.[30]

An expedient measure designed to avoid a conflict, the electoral commission bill was both widely disliked and widely supported. Originating with moderate Republicans, it proved palatable to most Democrats; businessmen, whether Democratic or Republican, were "clamorously in favor of it." Uncompromising Democrats—largely from the South—opposed it, but Tilden accepted it, even though he did not like it; most Democrats thought that it was their best chance for victory. Republican supporters ranged from reformer Carl Schurz to his archenemy President Grant, who lobbied effectively for the measure.[31]

It was in the Hayes camp that support for the measure was lacking. He called it a "surrender, at least in part, of our case" and insisted that Ferry should decide which votes to count. Hayes believed that, by creating the commission, Congress had unconstitutionally usurped the president's power of appointment. But, realizing that the bill was bound to pass and that his opposition might hurt his cause, Hayes complained privately. Garfield called the bill an unconstitutional "surrender of a certainty for an uncertainty." Newspapermen, who had been wooing southern Democratic congressmen, were disappointed by the electoral commission bill, which renewed hopes for a Tilden victory. "The truth is we have had blunder upon blunder at

Washington," William Henry Smith wailed. Spawned by the crisis, their negotiations languished in the more relaxed atmosphere that followed publication of the proposed bill.[32]

Actually, it was absurd for Hayes and his supporters to speak of surrendering a certainty. They had forgotten how up-in-the-air they had been; Hayes had been worried about lack of backbone, and Garfield had feared that some senators might be "treacherous." Charles Foster, however, told Hayes to face up to their untenable position. "Have we a case to surrender?" he asked; reminding Hayes of southern Republicans, he said, "We have a half dozen men in the Senate who I know are disposed to make merchandise" of their power and, "with Conkling, Edmunds and others to hide behind, may play the d[evi]l with us before we get through." Even if Ferry could and would count Hayes in, such a high-handed act would undermine the legitimacy of a Hayes presidency. "The overwhelming reason controlling men," Foster told Hayes, "is that whoever is elected should go in with the best possible title as can be given him." Foster's forcefulness helped Hayes accept the bill gracefully, and when it passed, he declared, "It is a great relief to me." Although he trusted that "the measure will turn out well," he reasoned that "defeat in this way after a full and public hearing before this Commission is not mortifying in any degree, and success will be in all respects more satisfactory." Hayes's equanimity and his capacity to adjust were assets that helped make his luck. George William Curtis found his admiration for Hayes "greatly increased by his tranquil attitude during all the late commotion."[33]

"The Commission," Hayes wrote, "seems to be a good one." Contrary to expectations, the politically independent David Davis was not on the electoral commission. While the bill was being considered, he was the Greenback candidate for senator from Illinois and had no chance of winning until the Democrats—inspired by Tilden's nephew Colonel Pelton—threw their support to him. Pelton and his cohorts believed that by electing Davis they had purchased his support, but they had made a monumental miscalculation. Because he was beholden to the Democrats, Davis refused to serve on the commission. His place was filled by Justice Joseph P. Bradley, a Republican from New Jersey, giving that party an eight-to-seven majority and making the odds in Washington five to one that the next president would be Hayes. Several members of the joint committee creating the commission served on it, but the Hayes camp was thankful that Conkling, who thought its duties "inconvenient if not distasteful," had refused to serve. Morton and Garfield, two of Hayes's staunchest friends, took seats on it. The selection of Garfield, who had helped disqualify Democratic votes in Louisiana, emphasized the political character of the commission.[34]

"The great law suit," Hayes wrote to Birch on 1 February, "begins today. . . . Our chance seems fair." The count proceeded quickly before the joint session of Congress until it referred the disputed returns from Florida to the electoral commission and then recessed. The crucial question was whether the commission should accept or go behind the official returns certified by the governor and the secretary of state. The Democrats argued that testimony taken by both the Senate and the House proved that Tilden had carried Florida and that a partisan returning board and governor had defrauded him of his victory. That view had been upheld by the Florida Supreme Court on 14 December, when it reversed the returning board and allowed the Democrats to take over the state government on 1 January 1877. For the Republicans, William M. Evarts of New York argued against considering evidence that challenged the official returns, since reexamining the vote on the county and local levels would be an endless task and a decision had to be reached by 4 March. As the arguments unfolded, Shellabarger, who also represented the Republicans, wrote to Hayes that "we all *'feel in our bones'* . . . the law and right is with us & we will get through." With each commission member arguing for his own party, it decided by an eight-to-seven vote not to investigate the official returns. On 9 February, by the same vote, it was determined that Hayes had won Florida.[35]

So certain was Hayes of his just title to the presidency that he failed to see how lawyers could differ on the Florida question. Blinded by his own partisanship, he was amazed that the decision was by a strict party vote and mused about the strength of party ties. Confident of success, Hayes had already thought about a cabinet and policies and had noted points to stress in his inaugural address: specie payments; civil-service reform; peace abroad and at home; and a South made prosperous by federal support of education and improvements, by appointments "to aid in good local government," and by its "cheerful acquiescence in the results of the war." In contrast, Tilden, realizing that the strict party vote prophesied his defeat, began planning a European trip.[36]

Angry and stubborn, rudderless Democrats fought on. Possibly they could win Louisiana; if not, they might delay the count and extract concessions from Republicans. Above all, southern Democrats wanted home rule—in effect, white-controlled state governments. If Tilden, who would certainly accede to their wishes, were not elected, they wanted a commitment from Hayes. A minority of southern Democrats were also eager to secure federal support for railroad construction. The threat of a filibuster revived the Kellar and Boynton negotiations for the votes of thirty-five to forty southern Democrats, and when the Democrats were restrained in their delaying tactics, Kellar and Boynton claimed credit for their moderation. After losing Florida, the Democrats remained on the commission, and although they delayed the count by recessing the House until Monday, they did not prevent the count, as some hotheads wished to do. After their overwhelming support for the Electoral Commission Act, most Democrats felt constrained to abide by its results.[37]

On the afternoon of 12 February, Louisiana's conflicting returns were referred to the commission. Because the unofficial returns in Louisiana gave the Democrats a large majority, because the Louisiana returning board was disreputable and lacked a Democratic member, and because Republican frauds were better documented in that state, it presented the Democrats' strongest case—if the commission would go behind the returns and hear evidence. From a technically legal standpoint, however, the Democratic case in Louisiana was identical with the one in Florida. Confident that Bradley and the other Republicans would refuse to go behind the returns, Shellabarger thought "it safe for Mrs. Hayes to begin to get the children ready." Although Lucy's "faith . . . in these 'mixed commissions' " was "weaker than a grain of mustard seed," Shellabarger had once again predicted accurately. A series of eight-to-seven votes on 16 February gave Hayes Louisiana.[38]

After the Louisiana decision, neither Hayes nor the Democrats seriously doubted the ultimate result. On 17 February, he concentrated on his inaugural address and his cabinet. To gain "support from the . . . late rebels," he thought of appointing former Confederate Gen. Joseph E. Johnston to his cabinet. But on the same day, Hayes assured black leaders Frederick Douglass and James Poindexter that he would not sacrifice their rights for the support of white southerners, that he would uphold "the 13*th*, 14*th* and 15*th* amendments."[39]

Frustrated Democrats recessed to delay the count, but in their caucus on 17 February, they again decided not to obstruct the process. With only one southerner voting for a filibuster, Boynton and Kellar were particularly gratified. Boynton could not distinguish between the efforts of the "purely political" negotiations concerning home rule that Kellar conducted and the economic negotiations of the "Scott forces" commanded by Gen. Grenville M. Dodge (the builder of the Union Pacific Railroad) to secure a land grant for the Texas & Pacific Railroad. "Both worked earnestly" and both "contributed much" to the result. But with southern Democrats anxious to commit Hayes to home rule, Kellar begged him "to do or say something" to reassure them.

After the caucus vote, however, Hayes remarked that the "affair now looks extremely well" and remained noncommittal. "I prefer to make no new declarations" beyond my acceptance letter, he had told John Sherman a few days earlier. "But you may say, if you deem it advisable, that you *know* that I will stand by the friendly and encouraging words of that Letter, and by all that they imply. You can not express that too strongly." Aware that his "anxiety to *do* something to promote the pacification of the South" might lead him too far, Hayes kept his lips firmly sealed. But Stanley Matthews (who also argued Hayes's case before the commission) assured Edward A. Burke of Louisiana that Hayes did not like carpetbag rule. Burke was the personal representative of "Governor" Francis T. Nicholls, head of the un-recognized Democratic government, similar to the Wade Hampton govern-ment in South Carolina. At a subsequent meeting on 18 February, Burke also pushed for assurances that strong Republican leaders such as Garfield, Sher-man, Morton, and Blaine would not oppose home rule. When Matthews could not give these assurances, Burke threatened that Louisiana congress-men would ignore the caucus decision and lead a filibuster to prevent Hay-es's inauguration.[40]

If southern Democrats could convince Republicans that their assent was essential to elect Hayes, the Democrats could gain concessions, particularly in Louisiana and South Carolina. Mingled with their threats of filibuster were hints that political and economic concessions not only would cause southern Democrats to acquiesce in Hayes's election but also might win their allegiance to the Republican party. Charles Foster heard from Charles Nordhoff of the New York *Herald*, who again held out the prospect of form-ing "a real and honest Republican party in the South" based on old Whigs, "but only on condition that the carpet-bag leaders are dropped entirely." He suggested that if Hayes appointed two old Whig southerners to his cabinet, he would attract Democrats of that persuasion to the Republicans. But Nordhoff also warned that continued support of Governor Packard would cause an outbreak in Louisiana that would require an army of 100,000 to suppress. "I hardly believe all he says about L[ouisian]a," Foster wrote to Hayes the next day, but he added, "There is no mistaking the general feeling of kindness towards you in the South,—within the past ten days a number of men have assured me of their desire for your success."[41]

Hayes and the Republicans were reluctant to abandon Gov. Stephen B. Packard of Louisiana and Gov. Daniel H. Chamberlain of South Carolina, who were risking their lives to keep their states Republican and to elect Hayes. Their claims to office and Hayes's claim to the presidency were all based on the actions of the returning boards. Even William Henry Smith, while orchestrating the Kellar and Boynton negotiations, exclaimed on 19 February, "You cannot dismiss those gentlemen with a waive of the hand" for "mere party expediency." Foster, who also wished to attract southern Democrats, told Hayes on 16 February that he "did not see how you could throw Packard overboard." John Sherman, whose opinion Hayes valued, wrote on 18 February, "I see no way but the recognition of the Packard government followed by the utmost liberality to the South."[42]

Indeed, Hayes needed the wavering southern Republican support on Monday, 19 February, if the Senate was to ratify the commission's Louisiana decision. Southern Republicans were so upset by negotiations with southern conservatives that they threatened to support Tilden unless Hayes promised them a cabinet position. For leadership, they looked to Conkling, who appeared willing to see Hayes defeated if it would enhance his own power. The Democrats' last hope was that Conkling and his southern allies would object to the commission's decision on Louisiana, but on 19 February he was conspicuously absent. Southern Republican senators were whipped into line; after all, if Tilden won, they would be certain of oblivion. While Democrats despaired of victory after the Senate approved the Louisiana decision, Hayes decided that his cabinet would contain no one from Grant's cabinet and no presidential candidates and that he would make "no appointment to 'take care' of any body."[43]

With defeat certain, delay and the threat of chaos after 4 March were the Democrats' only bargaining chips. But they were dangerous chips to play; the American people, especially those connected with business, did not want chaos. After winning Louisiana with the help of southern Republican senators, Republicans would have to be badly frightened before abandoning those supporters. Having forced recesses on 17 and 19 February, House Democrats caucused anew. At that caucus, Speaker Samuel J. Randall accused southern Democrats of bargaining with Hayes; he predicted that Hayes would continue bayonet rule and ruin them. Randall proposed to delay the count and force the Senate to accept a bill naming Secretary of State Hamilton Fish acting president until a new election could be held. When the caucus did not accept this extreme scheme, its earlier noncooperative yet nonobstructive policy remained in place.

Using Randall's speech for leverage, Kellar and several southern Democrats called on Foster. "The Southern people who had agreed to stand by us in carrying out the Electoral law in good faith," Foster reported to Hayes, "were seized with a fright, if not a panic." They referred to Randall's violent speech and asked for assurances that Hayes would end bayonet rule. After consulting with Matthews, Garfield, and Evarts, Foster planned to make a conciliatory and reassuring speech the next day. Kellar, Smith reported to Hayes, was disheartened and feared that northern Democrats—"Tammany Hall"—would whip into line the southern Whigs and Union Democrats who would give "cheerful support to Gov. Hayes." Kellar urged that Hayes say something and "settle the South" by appointing Kellar's friend Sen. David M. Key of Tennessee to the cabinet.[44]

Apart from commending Foster for his speech—which promised southerners, "The flag shall float over States, not provinces, over freemen, and not subjects"—Hayes kept his peace, and Kellar's fears were not realized. The count reached Oregon on 21 February, and on Friday, 23 February, the commission voted eight to seven to award Oregon's three votes to Hayes. There had been so little suspense over the Oregon vote that by Thursday, Kellar believed that it was no longer necessary for Hayes to say anything. "Gen. Dodge has had the whole of Scott's force at work," Boynton exulted, and "with the purely political part will . . . defeat the desperate men. It is still difficult for me to judge which of these two forces has been the most potent element in the long fight."[45]

Ironically, on the very Thursday that Boynton was so confident of victory over the filibusters, an editorial in the *Ohio State Journal* defended the Packard regime in Louisiana and urged Grant to uphold it with troops. Because Hayes's friend Comly edited the *Journal*, Hayes was thought to have inspired the article, which seemed to confirm Randall's prophecy that he would maintain bayonet rule. Neither Hayes nor Comly, who was ill, had anything to do with the article, but it led southerners to renew demands for assurances that Hayes would not restore bayonet rule. Shellabarger told Hayes of his fear that "they mean to kill us by 'filibustering.'" On Saturday, 24 February, after Oregon was counted for Hayes, the Democrats forced an adjournment until Monday.[46]

Annoyed by the *Ohio State Journal* article, Hayes reiterated, "I stand on my letter," but he did compose a short speech elaborating his plans for the South. He insisted, as he had recently told Frederick Douglass, "that for the protection and welfare of the colored people the 13*th* 14*th*, and 15*th* amendments shall be sacredly observed and faithfully enforced." Since the "tremendous revolution" had left the southern people "impoverished and prostrate," Hayes proposed to do what he could to make them "prosperous and happy. They need economy, honesty, and intelligence in their local governments," he continued. "They need to have such a policy adopted as will cause sectionalism to disappear, and that will tend to wipe out the color line" in politics. "They need to have encouraged immigration, education, and every description of legitimate business and industry." And then, paraphrasing

Foster, Hayes wrote, "We do not want a united North, nor a united South. We want a united country." Hayes did not have to give the speech, but if he had, southerners would have found home rule and internal improvements implied conditionally rather than promised specifically. Refusing to be panicked by the "revolutionary conduct" of House Democrats, Hayes continued to plan for his presidency.[47]

Although Sherman and Garfield thought that the count would be completed on time, other Republicans, including Foster, felt "great anxiety" about the filibuster threat. Grant also took it seriously and moved to resolve the crisis and relieve Hayes of a monumental problem. On Monday morning, 26 February, Grant told Burke that the Nicholls government "should stand in Louisiana" and that public opinion opposed the use of troops to uphold a state government; but, he said, he would not act because he did not want to embarrass Hayes. Later that morning, Burke told Sherman (who was now concerned), Matthews, and Dennison that if they wanted him to call off the filibuster, they should tell Grant that the immediate withdrawal of troops upholding the Republican government in Louisiana would not embarrass Hayes. When Sherman claimed that Grant would not agree, Burke showed them a dispatch to Nicholls that Grant had approved. Sherman, Matthews, and Dennison agreed to see Grant and assured Burke that Hayes would follow Grant's policy. But, knowing Hayes, Sherman wanted assurances that the Nicholls government would protect the rights of blacks and Republicans; knowing the Senate, he wanted assurances that it would not challenge the election of William Pitt Kellogg by the Republican legislature, which would help Republicans retain control of the Senate. That evening, the same men and a few additional colleagues met in Matthews's rooms at Wormley's Hotel and agreed to the bargain outlined that morning.[48]

Had Hayes, who was not the bargaining type, been consulted, he probably would not have authorized the bargain. One did not seem necessary, since Sherman had recently assured him that "*the acquiescents*" among the Democrats were in the ascendancy and that the count would be completed on time. He did not object, however, to assurances being inferred from his letter of acceptance. Actually, the significance of the Wormley's Hotel meeting and the importance of the Kellar and Boynton negotiations and the lobbying of Scott and Dodge have been exaggerated. Had there been no conference at Wormley's and no Texas & Pacific lobby, the count would have been completed on time. Hayes's calm, noncommittal approach in Columbus was the best possible response to the crisis. Democratic support of the filibuster was apparently impervious to negotiators and lobbyists since it had little to do with being southern or northern or being for or against internal improvements. Most Democrats would not delay the count beyond 4 March lest public opinion turn on them and provoke a new wave of Reconstruction legislation, but they were not averse to prolonging the crisis to extract concessions.

Democratic bluffs were moderately successful. Hayes had consistently called for honest and capable local governments in the South, coupled with recognition of the rights of all blacks and whites. Keeping his options open, he had not advocated the abandonment of Republican regimes in Louisiana and South Carolina. Without specific authorization, both Sherman and Foster—who a week earlier would not abandon Packard—joined Matthews and Dennison in committing Hayes to sustaining the Democratic Nicholls government in Louisiana, as long as the civil rights of blacks were respected. Grant regarded this position as inevitable and, with the approval of Hayes's friends, had already taken steps to implement it.[49]

On Tuesday, 27 February, it appeared that the count would proceed smoothly. The electoral commission met at ten that morning and adjourned at seven that night, with the South Carolina case being settled for Hayes by the usual eight-to-seven vote. Congressman Henry Watterson of Kentucky read into the *Congressional Record* Grant's views supporting the Nicholls government in Louisiana and opposing the use of troops to maintain Republican Governor Packard. Burke worked to get the Democratic caucus in New Orleans to agree to respect the constitutional rights of blacks and Republicans and to accept Kellogg's election as senator. Matthews saw Grant, who agreed to rescind his orders to the troops in Louisiana to preserve the status quo—as soon as the count was completed. Matthews also joined with Foster to sign a statement saying that Hayes would allow the people of "South Carolina and Louisiana the right to conduct their own affairs in their own way, subject only to the Constitution of the United States and the laws made in pursuance thereof." Hayes later said that "Foster and Matthews took upon themselves the responsibility of giving assurances without consulting me but always inferentially from their knowledge of my views and temperament," and he acknowledged that they were generally correct. The Wormley's Hotel conference pieces were falling into place, and Boynton, Kellar, and Dodge claimed that their "force" was "strong and solid."[50]

Despite the bargain and the lobby, the count did not go smoothly. On Wednesday, 28 February, according to Garfield, "the Democrats filibustered with all their might" and forced the House to adjourn. The House session that opened at 10 A.M. on Thursday, 1 March, was one of the longest and stormiest in history. Filibusterers made dilatory motions to recess, to reconsider, and to call the roll, but Speaker of the House Randall—in what Hayes understandably considered his finest hour—refused to entertain their motions, adding to the pandemonium. While the uproar was on, Louisiana's Democratic congressmen urged Grant to withdraw the troops immediately, and he approved the draft of a telegram. Signed by his secretary C. C. Sniffen, it alerted Governor Packard that public opinion no longer supported the use of troops to maintain his government. Although he would not send the telegram while the filibuster continued, Grant assured Burke that if the count were finished that evening, Nicholls "would be in peaceful possession tomorrow."

Having extracted all that he could from the filibuster, Burke called it aimless. Congressman William M. Levy returned to the House to announce, "The people of Louisiana have solemn, earnest, and, I believe, truthful assurances from prominent members of the Republican party, high in the confidence of Mr. Hayes, . . . that he will not use the federal authority or the Army to force upon those States governments not of their choice. . . . This, too, is the opinion of President Grant." Perhaps because it was Grant's move or because winning the presidency was so important, erstwhile supporters of radical Reconstruction did not object to abandoning the Republican regimes.

Relying on these commitments to Louisiana and, by extension, to South Carolina, Levy called for the completion of the count, but fifty-seven bitter and disorderly filibusterers paid him no heed and prolonged the struggle until 3:38 A.M. The Senate then assembled in the House chamber, where Wisconsin was counted for Hayes. At 4:10 A.M. on 2 March 1877, Ferry announced that Hayes and Wheeler had 185 votes to 184 for Tilden and Hendricks. "Wherefore, I do declare that Rutherford B. Hayes of Ohio, having received a majority of the whole number of votes is duly elected President of the United States for four years commencing on the 4th day of March, 1877."[51]

EIGHTEEN

TWO NEW POLICIES

Hayes awoke to the good news at Marysville, Pennsylvania. He was traveling with Lucy, Webb, Fanny, Scott, and a small party—including William McKinley, William Henry Smith, and William K. Rogers—in two of Tom Scott's special railroad cars. When they arrived in Washington at about 9:30 A.M. on 2 March, Hayes and his family were escorted to John and Margaret Sherman's home by John and his brother Gen. William T. Sherman.

Following breakfast and a briefing on the recent commitments made by his lieutenants, Hayes, accompanied by John Sherman, called on President Grant. After consulting with Hayes, Grant (through his secretary Sniffen) telegraphed Packard that public opinion opposed the deployment of troops to sustain his government and ordered the withdrawal of federal military support. The troop withdrawal was first delayed in the War Department and then countermanded by General Sherman, in all probability at Hayes's behest and with Grant's tacit approval. Apparently, Hayes did not feel honor bound to immediately fulfill the assurances extracted under duress from his followers by the Louisianans who had claimed, without much foundation, to control the filibusterers. If he were inclined to credit any Democrat with ending the filibuster, it was Speaker of the House Samuel J. Randall of Pennsylvania. Before pulling troops protecting Packard and Chamberlain out of Louisiana and South Carolina, Hayes wanted a stronger commitment to the civil and political rights of black and white Republicans. To avoid an interregnum in the crisis atmosphere of Washington, Grant and Secretary of State Hamilton Fish persuaded Hayes to be privately sworn in at the White House on Saturday evening, 3 March, since the formal inauguration was scheduled for Monday, 5 March. As Hayes moved on to the Capitol with Sherman, he was pleased that the "colored hack drivers and others cheered lustily." There in the vice president's room, he met with a number of senators and representatives of both parties.[1]

Hayes had his inaugural address prepared, but because of his preoccupation with the electoral count, his cabinet was not complete. After winning Louisiana in mid-February, he had resolved to ask John Sherman, who had become a trusted ally and was wise in political and financial matters, to take the Treasury Department and William Maxwell Evarts, a superb lawyer who had experience in foreign affairs, to take the State Department. Hayes had favored Evarts to head that department even prior to his presentation of Hayes's case before the electoral commission. While still in Columbus, Hayes had decided on two daring appointments. To gain the support of reformers, he asked Carl Schurz to serve as secretary of the interior. The Interior Department needed to be reformed, and Schurz was superbly qualified to do that job, but he was despised by Grant and Republican party regulars for his part in the Liberal Republican revolt, which had attempted to deny Grant a second term. To attract respectable, conservative white southerners, Hayes decided to appoint a southern Democrat to the cabinet and toyed briefly with the revolutionary notion of naming Confederate Gen. Joseph E. Johnston secretary of war. Hayes did not offer cabinet positions to his competitors for the nomination or to their satellites or to members of Grant's cabinet. Appointing James G. Blaine, Benjamin H. Bristow, Roscoe Conkling, or Secretary of War James Donald Cameron to the cabinet, Hayes later said, "would have been to invite the intrigues and obstructive acts of personal ambition." But ignoring these powerful party leaders earned Hayes their hostility.[2]

In Washington, senators and representatives besieged Hayes with their cabinet suggestions, and he sought reactions to his ideas. Appointing Johnston proved too impolitic to attempt. Blaine said that it would "harm everybody and help nobody" and then pushed without success his own man, William P. Frye, for the cabinet. "Blaine seemed to claim" the Frye appointment "as a condition of good relations," as did Conkling the appointment of his lieutenant Thomas C. Platt to head the politically sensitive Post Office Department. While pushing Platt, Conkling ingratiatingly praised Hayes's opinions, but having failed in the object of his flattery, he neither called on Hayes nor spoke with him again. Hayes also defied powerful Pennsylvania and Illinois Republicans by refusing to give the War Department to either Cameron or John A. Logan, who had just lost his Senate seat to David Davis; instead he appointed George W. McCrary of Iowa, who had helped originate the Electoral Commission Act and was a friend of railroad lobbyist Grenville M. Dodge. For his southern Democrat, Hayes named Kellar's friend David M. Key of Tennessee as postmaster general. William Henry Smith overoptimistically predicted that Key's appointment would "make . . . conservative men . . . in the State of Tennessee, Arkansas, Miss., & Texas . . . support your administration."[3]

In two ways, Hayes gratified the likes and dislikes of his friend and fellow presidential aspirant Oliver P. Morton of Indiana, who was ill and would die within the year. Hayes appointed Morton's fellow Hoosier Richard W.

Inauguration of President Hayes

Thompson as navy secretary and did not name, as he had planned, John Marshall Harlan as attorney general. For that position, Hayes chose Judge Charles Devens of the Massachusetts Supreme Court, pleasing Devens's law partner, Sen. George F. Hoar, as well as Vice President-Elect Wheeler, who had recommended him. Although Hayes had resolved not to take care of anybody, every cabinet appointment rewarded someone who had helped make him president, and three of his appointments—Evarts, Schurz, and Key—were bound to provoke opposition among Republican Senate leaders.[4]

On Monday, 5 March, in front of the East Portico of the Capitol, before 30,000 spectators, the inaugural ceremony took place. Lucy "wore a black hat, trimmed with white lace, and a scarf of lace about her neck." Under her coat she was "dressed in rich black silk, almost entirely unadorned." After diplomats, Supreme Court justices (except for the two Democrats who had served on the electoral commission and boycotted the ceremony), senators, and representatives were seated, Hayes and Grant appeared arm in arm and proceeded to the front platform, from which Hayes delivered his address. For the most part, he reiterated his letter of acceptance. He discussed five subjects: the South, civil-service reform, the currency question, foreign affairs, and the recent disputed election.[5]

It was clear to Hayes that the South ought to have "wise, honest, and peaceful local self-government." But he insisted that such a government must guard "the interests of both races carefully and equally" and that it must accept and obey the whole Constitution. Hayes also recognized that the federal government was morally obligated "to employ its constitutional power and influence to establish the rights of the people it has emancipated." He reasoned that the political unrest and poverty afflicting the South could "only be removed or remedied by the united and harmonious efforts of both races" and urged that party ties and racial prejudices be surrendered. There was scant comfort in the address for Tom Scott, Grenville Dodge, and other backers of the Texas & Pacific Railroad. Hayes did not mention liberal internal improvements for the South; he merely said that it deserved the considerate care of the federal government, limited by constitutional restraints and economic prudence.

For Hayes, the schoolhouse, not the railroad, was the key to success for the South. The "improvement of the intellectual and moral condition of the people," he maintained, was the basis of prosperity. Insisting that "universal suffrage should rest upon universal education," he emphatically called for "liberal and permanent provision . . . for the support of free schools by the State Governments, and, if need be, supplemented by legitimate aid from national authority."

Hayes's call for a "thorough, radical, and complete" reform of the civil service proved the most memorable part of his address. He wished to "return to the principles and practices of the founders of the Government," who had not allowed members of Congress to dictate civil-service appointments, who had not made appointments merely to reward partisan service, and who had retained public officers as long as their character and work remained satisfactory. Although realizing that he owed his election to the "zealous labors of a political party," he reminded himself "that he serves his party best who serves his country best." Convinced that much of the abuse of the civil service had resulted from presidents' attempts to succeed themselves, he proposed a constitutional amendment that would limit a president to one six-year term.

The third domestic problem that concerned Hayes was the currency question. Noting the depression in commerce and manufacturing, which had prevailed since September 1873, he judged the fluctuating value of greenbacks — fiat paper money (not backed by gold) issued during the Civil War — "one of the greatest obstacles to a return to prosperous times." Accordingly, he called for congressional legislation to implement an early resumption of specie payments (that is, a return to the gold standard by redeeming green-backs in gold coin), a policy that he thought was dictated by wisdom, self-interest, and public opinion.

To preserve good relations with other nations, Hayes wished to maintain "our traditional rule of noninterference in the affairs of foreign nations." He would follow the policy inaugurated by Grant "of submitting to arbitration grave questions in dispute between ourselves and foreign powers." On the home front, arbitration of the disputed election by the two political parties was, Hayes insisted, reason for rejoicing. And he anticipated a conciliatory new southern policy by asking his countrymen to help him secure prosperity, justice, and peace within "a union depending not upon the constraint of force, but upon the loving devotion of a free people."

Reactions to Hayes's address were mixed, but reformers were pleased. "There have been few inaugural addresses superior to that of President Hayes in mingled wisdom, force, and moderation of statement," George William Curtis editorialized in *Harper's Weekly*, adding that Hayes's pro-gram "is unquestionably . . . approved by the intelligence and patriotism of the whole country." Reformers should have been pleased, since Hayes had followed Carl Schurz's advice to stick by his letter of acceptance and "to soften party passions" growing out of the disputed election. So pervasive was Schurz's influence on the inaugural address that Hayes's most quotable line, "he serves his party best who serves his country best," paraphrased Schurz's "You will serve that party best by serving the public interest best."[6]

For partisan Republican leaders in Congress, however, the address's em-phasis on conciliation and reform did not strike a responsive chord. Even the reform-minded Garfield said nothing in his diary about the address, but he did record that, after delivering it, Hayes took the oath of office from Chief Justice Morrison R. Waite and then kissed the Bible "somewhere" in Psalm 118. Perhaps Hayes's kiss landed on the sixth verse: "The Lord is on my side; I will not fear: what can man do unto me?" The charmed life Hayes had led as a soldier and as a politician, surviving battles and winning elections, did little to diminish his quiet self-confidence.[7]

Following the inauguration, the presidential party rode to the White House for a lunch planned by Julia Grant. "There were," Garfield noted, "many indications of relief and joy that no accident had occurred on the route for there were apprehensions of assassination." After lunch, Hayes and Lucy went to the carriage steps to bid the Grants farewell. That after-noon, senators, congressmen, military and naval officers, Supreme Court justices, and members of the diplomatic corps attended a "grand reception"

Taking the oath: Ulysses S. Grant, Morrison R. Waite, and Hayes (*Harper's Weekly*, 24 March 1877)

at the White House. Hayes particularly appreciated his "manly, patriotic, and considerate" old commander Winfield Scott Hancock—a conspicuous Democrat—who advertised his acceptance of Hayes's election by participating in the inauguration ceremony and by being "perhaps, the first officer in uniform" to congratulate Hayes. In the evening, Hayes and Lucy attended a reception at Willard's Hotel, where jubilant Republicans—especially "blue-caped Columbus Cadets"—celebrated into the night. "The city," Mary Clemmer Ames's letter to the Cincinnati *Commercial* observed, "is one blaze of light to-night. For miles on miles the torchlights stream, and the air is all ablaze with red lights and rockets. The mottoes in the windows, the finest flag and streamer flying from housetops, are as clearly visible as at noon-day." Ames noted that "Ohio sails on the top wave, and is a little giddy with triumph."[8]

On Tuesday, the party was over. Smarting over his failure to push Frye into the cabinet, Blaine virtually defied Hayes to abandon the Packard government. Blaine's speech delighted the southern Republican senators but disturbed moderate Republicans, who feared that Blaine and Hayes were on a collision course. When Hayes submitted his cabinet selections to the Senate on Wednesday, a majority of Blaine's colleagues joined him in harassing Hayes. Like Grant, Hayes had not consulted with party leaders about his cabinet appointees, but he lacked Grant's prestige and mandate. Unlike Grant, who had appointed obscure Republicans, Hayes named three highly visible enemies of leading Republican senators to his cabinet. Simon Cameron immediately objected to Evarts, whom he and Conkling disliked, and Blaine successfully moved to refer the nomination to the Committee on Foreign Relations. In an unprecedented action, the Senate then referred all of Hayes's nominations to committee, even that of Sen. John Sherman, and vigorously denounced Evarts, Key, and especially Schurz. Even Schurz's friend Garfield thought that his appointment was "unfortunate and unwise." Rejoicing over the Republican dissension, Democratic senators—led, Hayes gratefully noted, by southerners John B. Gordon, L. Q. C. Lamar, and Benjamin H. Hill—did not oppose Hayes's nominees. Southern Democrats realized that they would aid their worst enemies if they helped defeat Hayes's nominees.[9]

Hayes stood firm, and by Thursday the Senate began to back down. It confirmed Sherman after an hour's debate, apparently because his uncertain fate held up senatorial committee assignments. Sherman immediately lobbied among his former colleagues for his fellow appointees. He was helped by the angry reaction of newspapers and constituents to the senators' obstructive acts. Letters, telegrams, newspaper editorials, and resolutions—approved by meetings of substantial Republicans in New York, Philadelphia, and other cities—urged that the appointees be approved. On Saturday, 10 March, the six remaining nominees were reported favorably from committee and confirmed. The Senate voted unanimously for McCrary, Devens, and Thompson, and only two senators objected to Evarts, Key, and Schurz. Chagrined and unwilling to work with Evarts, Simon Cameron, chairman of the Foreign Relations Committee, resigned from the Senate and had the pliable Pennsylvania legislature name his son James Donald Cameron to succeed him. Hayes had won his first skirmish. A few leading Republicans, relying on the politics of organization, had been outflanked by the new president, relying on the politics of reform and the force of public opinion.[10]

Since the cabinet was largely his creation, Hayes valued its counsel and believed that its members would not subvert the goals of his administration. The cabinet, indeed, proved competent and stable, with its few changes coming late in the administration. In crises, Hayes met with his cabinet daily; in ordinary times, he met with it on Tuesdays and Thursdays from 12 to 2 P.M. Everything from minor appointments to major policies was discussed at these informal and usually harmonious meetings. But it was Hayes who made the decisions and, on occasion, imposed his will on reluctant department heads, including his cabinet's strongest members—Sherman, Evarts, and Schurz. Each week, during a Sunday afternoon drive, Hayes discussed matters of state with Sherman, who proved to be the most valuable member of Hayes's cabinet. He was experienced in financial matters, knowledgeable in politics, and an expert in cajoling senators. Brilliant Evarts and conscientious Schurz were excellent advisers but were mixed blessings, since regular Republicans were suspicious of their political independence.[11]

Hayes needed to rely on his cabinet because he got little guidance from his staff. Unlike presidents a century later, he had few staff members and no offices to study issues and offer counsel and advice, such as the National Security Council or the Office of Management and Budget. Nine staff members, headed by a private secretary, performed prosaic tasks. They received visitors, sorted incoming correspondence, assembled files on potential appointees, answered routine mail, and copied letters and papers that Hayes had written out. He ignored the newly invented typewriter and usually did not dictate to the stenographer on his staff. With few telephones in existence, the Hayes White House got little use from its own phone. The center of communications was the busy White House telegraph office.

Hayes perceived that he needed a strong adviser as his private secretary, but neither William Henry Smith nor Manning F. Force would accept what they regarded as an inferior position. After Gen. Robert P. Kennedy of Bellefontaine, Ohio, also refused, Hayes turned to his loyal but ineffective friend William K. Rogers. He handled Hayes's visitors and correspondence—sometimes badly. For instance, he shielded Hayes from Mark Twain, whom he had confused with the eccentric millionaire faddist George Francis Train. Hayes in time noted that Rogers was "easily duped," trusted all who professed friendship, uncritically admired "almost anything" Hayes did, and lacked "a sense of duty and responsibility." Of great help to Hayes was twenty-one-year-old Webb, who often served successfully as his father's unofficial secretary. With no staff to screen the swarms of applicants or to propose policy alternatives, Hayes, like his predecessors, had to rely on congressmen for advice on appointments and on his cabinet or friends for advice on policy.[12]

Despite his small staff, Hayes strengthened the office of the presidency. His concept of his office differed from that of his immediate predecessors, who had either embraced or enhanced the Whig approach to the presidency. Abraham Lincoln had deferred to Congress in appointments and in other political matters and had given his cabinet members a free hand in running their departments. Andrew Johnson's inept opposition to Congress had brought on the Tenure of Office Act, which had increased congressional power over cabinet members and executive departments. Ulysses S. Grant had been politically astute and often effective, but he had deferred to congressmen and cabinet members for policies and appointments. Hayes, however, refused to let congressmen dictate appointments, did not slavishly follow the opinion of his cabinet, and commanded a unified administration. Although he had been a Whig and was hoping to revive and realign southern Whigs, he moved away from the Whig ideal of a weak president who was subservient to Congress and deferential to his cabinet. In the struggles Hayes had with Congress over his patronage policies and in his desire to use national power to foster education, John Quincy Adams was his role model. But Hayes was a better politician than Adams, and by hard work and tough fighting, he would succeed in reversing the ascendancy of Congress, the independence of cabinet members, and the decline of the presidency.[13]

Unlike his predecessors, Hayes traveled a good deal. Although he enjoyed visiting the various sections of the country, politics was his main objective. By speaking out on these trips—taken in summer and fall when political campaigns were getting under way—he was able to bypass his congressional opponents and take his policies directly to the people in short, informal, issue-stressing speeches. Samuel Ward, the outstanding lobbyist of the day, appreciated what Hayes was doing. "I think," he wrote to Evarts, "these Presidential trips are very salubrious in a social, moral & political point of view. Quidnuncs & grumblers criticize their propriety. But Mr. Hayes is bent upon giving us a Country once more and none but old smooth bores with flintlocks will find any fault." By defining issues for his administration and party rather than merely reacting to Congress, Hayes exercised presi-

Office seekers in the White House waiting for an interview with Hayes

dential leadership and took a step in the direction of the modern presidency.[14]

On taking office, Hayes faced a knotty problem and a huge task. He had to fashion a southern policy, and he had to fill approximately a thousand offices that required senatorial confirmation. With the Senate planning to adjourn in a few weeks, Hayes realized that he could not make good appointments "in such a hurry," so he sensibly decided to fill only the vacant offices while the Senate was in session and to allow the other officials to remain on the job "until he could take his time" deciding whether or not to replace them.[15]

With the exception of a few square miles, Reconstruction had ended before Hayes entered the White House. There were only two Republican governors left in the South, Stephen B. Packard of Louisiana and Daniel H. Chamberlain of South Carolina, and they controlled only the small areas surrounding their statehouses, where they were still protected by federal troops since Grant's order of withdrawal at the close of the electoral vote count had not been carried out. The question confronting Hayes was whether to evacuate or reinforce these Republican "beachheads." That problem had military as well as political, constitutional, and moral dimensions.

There were strong arguments for reinforcement. The canvassing boards of Louisiana and South Carolina had taken into consideration white Democrats' intimidation of black Republican voters in the 1876 election and had declared the Republicans victorious. Since Hayes's claim to the presidency was based on the same canvassing board decisions, his failure to uphold the claims of the remaining Republican governors would undermine his legitimacy. Hayes believed that he had been elected fairly and that Packard and Chamberlain were the legal governors of Louisiana and South Carolina. He knew that the Democrats had violated the recent amendments to the Constitution and that their violence and intimidation had eroded the Republican party in the South.[16]

Hayes wanted the Constitution obeyed and his party to flourish, but restoring the authority of the Republican governors in South Carolina and Louisiana would require more troops. With the nation's meager 25,000-man army scattered in small detachments primarily in the West, few troops were available. The Democrats—who controlled the House of Representatives—refused to appropriate funds for the army beyond 1 July 1877 and were ready to starve it if it continued to prop up Republican regimes in the South. If Hayes sent more troops to the South, he would have to rely on public opinion to force Congress to pass the army appropriation bill.

But northern public opinion appeared unwilling to sustain a renewed military occupation of southern states. The nation continued to suffer from the business depression that had followed the financial panic of 1873, and people were concerned more with economic problems than with the civil rights of blacks or the political fortunes of southern Republicans. Mingling racism with partisanship, northern Democrats cheered southern white supremacists, and by 1876, an increasing number of northern Republicans considered radical Reconstruction, with its emphasis on coercion by the national government, a failed experiment. Waving the bloody shirt had failed to carry the crucial northern states of New York and Indiana for Hayes. The electoral crisis of 1876–77, even though it was resolved in favor of the Republicans, reinforced the doubts of many northern Republicans that the economically dominant whites in the South could be forced to accept racial political equality. Given the state of public opinion, the military option did not exist.

Hayes, however, wanted to use the tenuous military presence in the South as a bargaining chip. Preservation of that bargaining chip had been the primary reason for having Sherman countermand Grant's order withdrawing the military support of Packard. Had Hayes allowed that order to stand, he would have avoided considerable political heat from southern and radical Republicans, but his private thoughts, his public statements, and the commitments made in his name during the electoral count had indicated that he would withdraw the troops and accept home rule only if responsible white southerners promised to allow both black and white Republicans to participate freely in politics.

Hayes's instinct was for a moderate position. In March, when Ohio Republicans filled John Sherman's Senate seat with Stanley Matthews, renowned for his hostility to southern Republican regimes, Hayes considered it "an endorsement of the policy of peace and home rule — of local self government." Such a policy, however, outraged radical Republicans, who wanted to push or shame Hayes into continuing to support the remaining Republican outposts in the South. At the same time, Hayes noted the furor he aroused among conservative Republicans when he nominated Frederick Douglass, "the most distinguished and able colored man in the Nation," as marshal for the District of Columbia — an appointment that Hayes believed "would speak loudest in protest ag[ain]st race prejudice of any place at my disposal." Regarding the reactions to Matthews and Douglass, Hayes observed, "If a liberal policy towards late rebels is adopted, the ultra Republicans are opposed to it; if the colored people are honored, the extremists of the other wing cry out against it. I suspect," he concluded, "I am right in both cases."[17]

Although Hayes wanted "to put aside the bayonet" if southern Democrats guaranteed the civil rights of all, he paused. Prominent Republicans, such as Blaine, were reluctant to abandon Packard and Chamberlain and were skeptical that a liberal southern policy would protect the rights of blacks. Quick action might further inflame the Senate and endanger appointments, but delay would make it possible for Hayes to consider the viability of suggested alternatives (holding new elections, for example) and help dissipate hostility toward his southern policy. Hayes realized that he was "too crowded with business to give thought to these questions." He resolved to seek guidance from his cabinet and from his trusted friend Judge William M. Dickson.[18]

Hayes paused only briefly. The arrest of some black members of Packard's militia by the Democratic Nicholls government led Hayes to bring up the "Louisiana troubles" at the cabinet meeting on 20 March. He found that all but Devens agreed with him that the states themselves should settle contested state elections and that military force should not be used to uphold Packard's government. Even Devens was not decidedly for intervention. Practical and political considerations, rather than constitutional or moral ones, helped Hayes make up his mind. Like Grant, he thought that the people opposed the use of federal forces to uphold one state government against a rival state government. If "the de jure Gov[ernmen]t in a State" has been overthrown, Hayes believed that "the de facto Gov[ernmen]t must be recognized." His amoral, pragmatic approach reflected a realistic appraisal of power; although it sounds more appropriate for foreign than domestic policy, it illustrates the federal nature of the American union, even after the Civil War. Apparently, Hayes felt no hypocrisy in abandoning de jure governments that had put him in the White House, since they had been sustained as long as possible.

Hayes tried to evaluate what radical Reconstruction had accomplished and what was possible at that moment. Having earlier been a radical supporter of the military occupation of the South, he now believed that superior force had failed the blacks by polarizing politics along racial lines. The few troops upholding Republican governments in Louisiana and South Carolina, he reasoned, were counterproductive and would soon be unavailable. With force no longer an option, he decided that only "peaceful methods" could achieve "safety and prosperity for the colored people" and "restore harmony and good feeling between Sections and races." But before he withdrew the troops from Louisiana and South Carolina, Hayes wanted "to make one government out of two in each State" and to secure from those governments certain guarantees. After consulting with his cabinet on 20 March, he decided to send a commission to Louisiana to work toward this goal.[19]

On that same day, Judge Dickson made the same suggestion in a letter to Hayes. A commission, he said, would command the confidence of the old antislavery men and would help Chamberlain, Packard, and their adversaries reach a satisfactory solution. In the same letter, Dickson reassured Hayes that his southern policy was both "right" and "inevitable," since the "bayonet policy . . . *no longer protects*" and could no longer be sustained by the country. Dickson also thought that the blacks might be protected by dividing the white vote through an appeal "to the better sentiment," but if this overture failed and blacks were abused, he inaccurately predicted that "the country will be prepared for repressive measures." Dickson cautioned Hayes, however, not to "drive off the old anti-slavery sentiment" by pushing Chamberlain and Packard "out through the back door" and letting Hampton and Nicholls come in as "*Conquerors*."[20]

From the bleak situation in Louisiana and South Carolina, Hayes was trying to salvage benefits for blacks and the Republican party. Even while urging campaigners to wave the bloody shirt before the election, he had hoped that a policy of conciliation "on the basis of obedience to law and equal rights" would "divide the southern whites, and so protect the colored people." During the count, these views were corroborated by optimistic reports from journalists, such as Nordhoff and Kellar, and reformers, such as Jacob Dolson Cox, that conservative southern Democrats—either Whig or Unionist in background—would acquiesce in his election if he withdrew federal support from the carpetbag-scalawag Packard and Chamberlain governments. These southerners, the reports maintained, might even help Republicans organize the House of Representatives with Garfield as Speaker and come over to the Republican party (carrying five or six former Confederate states with them).

Often detailing hopes as facts, these reports claimed that conservative Democrats were committed to the constitutional rights of blacks and contrasted their "intelligence" and "virtue" with the poverty, ignorance, and corruption of the Packard regime. If Hayes supported this worthy old Whig-Unionist element, the color line could be abolished and a viable two-party system could flourish in the South. If the political color line were not obliterated, the writers of these reports argued, the white Democratic party would triumph, and the "safety, the very existence of political rights" of blacks would be jeopardized. By this line of reasoning, getting rid of the carpetbaggers would benefit southern blacks. Cox, who was preoccupied with corruption, urged Hayes "to choose men for federal office whose reputations shall command the confidence of all classes" and "to moderate the new kindled ambition of the colored people to fill places which neither their experience nor their knowledge of business or of the laws fits them for."

Hayes told Cox that he shared his views "precisely." Believing that the brightest men of any country ought to lead it, Hayes was worried about inefficiency and corruption, but he also wanted white and black Republicans to enjoy their constitutional rights. Although he wished to moderate the role that blacks would play in a revamped Republican party, he did not want to stifle their ambitions. Realizing that African Americans were not responsible for their lack of education, Hayes consistently argued that they deserved support. Both an elitist and a democrat, he believed that all black males should vote and that educated blacks should be officers of the government. Appropriately for a man who favored civil-service reform, Hayes believed that the meritorious should govern and that through public education everyone should have the opportunity to demonstrate merit.[21]

After the inauguration, southern politicians and office seekers angled to affect policy and gain patronage with hints of support. Senators Augustus H. Garland of Arkansas and Ben Hill of Georgia led Kellar to believe that, if rewarded, they would lead a southern administration party, and numerous office seekers insisted that such a movement would be strengthened if they received federal jobs. The spoils system not only provided the civil service with inadequate public officers but also provided political leaders with distorted information from ambitious office seekers. William Henry Smith urged Hayes to forget civil-service reform and to let Postmaster General Key "so organize things in the South as to give you the control of the House" of Representatives. Hayes apparently agreed. "The political outlook," Kellar rejoiced, "is bright and full of hope. I am certain the end will be a complete victory for Hayes over the evil and disreputable elements in both parties."[22]

The Louisiana commission, however, dismayed southerners. To them, it appeared that Hayes had yielded to the radicals and would renege on the conciliatory words in his inaugural address and on the assurances of Sherman, Matthews, Foster, Dennison, and Grant at the close of the count. Fearing that Hayes was about to change his mind, L. Q. C. Lamar of Mississippi urged him to "*do* as you *said* you would do." Randall, the Democratic candidate for Speaker of the House, warned that the Louisiana commission was a ploy to frighten southern Democrats into helping the Republicans organize the House, but Smith and Kellar, who were working toward that end, worried that it would have the opposite effect.[23]

There was no cause for alarm; the Louisiana commission was designed to implement policy, not change it. The crucial step in the hoped-for rapprochement of old southern and northern Whigs was the withdrawal of troops, and Hayes had resolved on 20 March not to use the army to keep Packard and Chamberlain in office. The hope that distributing patronage would blur the color line in southern politics and lure white southerners to the Republican party made the unavoidable abandonment of Chamberlain and Packard more palatable.

Chamberlain was the first to go. South Carolina was less agitated than Louisiana, and Hayes thought that resolving the dispute there might guide the Louisiana commission. A discussion with his cabinet on 22 March confirmed his intention to end the military support of Chamberlain without appointing a South Carolina commission. Later in the month, Hayes conferred with that state's two rival governors. Carrying his carpetbag, Chamberlain traveled anonymously to Washington; Hampton, responding to brass bands and fireworks along his triumphant way, demanded no commission, no compromise, and no troops.

Chamberlain acknowledged that he could not govern without the support of federal troops. He had admitted to others privately that the "North is *tired* of the Southern Question, and wants a settlement, no matter what." Although he knew that Hayes was carrying out the "logic of history," Chamberlain believed that he had won the governorship, and he asked Hayes to appoint a commission to recanvass the votes in South Carolina. Hayes refused that request, and Chamberlain refused to resign. His rival, Hampton, promised to preserve the peace in South Carolina; to recognize the constitutional rights of blacks as well as whites; and to aid in organizing the incoming House of Representatives, with Garfield as Speaker. On the basis of these promises, Hayes ordered the troops withdrawn on 3 April; they left on 10 April, Chamberlain vacated the statehouse, and Hampton moved in on 11 April 1877. Because he remained antagonistic toward Hayes, Chamberlain was offered no position by the administration; he moved to New York, where he practiced law.[24]

It took longer for the Louisiana commission to finesse the abandonment of Packard. William Henry Smith urged Hayes to hurry the commission and warned him that if it should uphold Packard or be slow in recommending his removal, the dream of a southern administration party would not be realized. In a conspiratorial tone, Smith advised the president, "I have confidence in an informal (uninstructed) commission of practical men to pioneer the way for the official com[missio]n. Such men as Rich[ar]d Smith, Medill & Kellar, could drop down at once, quietly get to the bottom & [by] controlling news sources could keep the public in ignorance until the way sh[oul]d be cleared."

Hayes quickly appointed the Louisiana commission and expected it to report promptly. Since no federal funds were available for a commission, Hayes personally borrowed the money to pay its expenses. The commission was chaired by Charles B. Lawrence of Illinois. Its other members were Joseph R. Hawley of Connecticut; John Marshall Harlan of Kentucky; John C. Brown, former governor of Tennessee; and Wayne MacVeagh of Pennsylvania. The commission was a geographical and political mix, but none of its members had conspicuously upheld radical Republican governments in southern states. All the commissioners seemed inclined toward Hayes's hope to conciliate southern whites if they would uphold the equal rights of all citizens, and MacVeagh's views "almost precisely" matched those of the president.[25]

On 2 April, Hayes instructed the commission through Evarts. Since the returning board and both houses of Congress had investigated the recent state election, Hayes did not want the commission to sift through those returns. He wanted it to secure the acknowledgment of one state government in Louisiana or, if that proved impossible, to concentrate on the recognition of a single legislature, since "the legislative power, when undisputed, is quite competent" to resolve "conflicts in the coordinate branches of the Government." Hayes also wanted to be certain that the new Louisiana government would maintain the constitutional rights of all citizens. His instructions emphasized that although he had the right to intervene militarily to protect a state against domestic violence, he did not believe that he had the power to determine disputed elections. Finally, Hayes wanted quick action and hoped that the commission's report would "enable him promptly to execute a purpose he has so much at heart."[26]

Lest the point of the published instructions be missed, Evarts issued "Second Instructions to Louisiana Commission." He bluntly stated that Hayes intended "to remove the troops from the State House" but did not want their removal accompanied by "any outbreak of violence." Through Evarts, Hayes warned of the possibility of future intervention should his constitutional duty demand it, but he hoped that the people of Louisiana would not thwart his desire to end "even an apparent military interference."[27]

The commission arrived in New Orleans in early April. Upset by its instructions, Packard unsuccessfully urged Hayes to have it determine who was legally entitled to govern Louisiana. Hayes's resolve was strengthened by his receipt of a petition signed by hundreds of Louisiana professionals and businessmen, ranging from bishops to bankers, urging that the troops supporting Packard be returned to their barracks. Emphasizing Packard's lack of power beyond the vicinity of the statehouse, the petition concluded: "If local self-government is given us, we pledge ourselves for the loyalty of Louisiana to the Union, for the protection of life and property and civil rights of all her citizens, and for the equal benefit of her laws, without distinction of race, color, or previous condition." Hayes could not have phrased a pledge more pleasing to his ears.[28]

Even though Packard's authority was recognized by the state supreme court, it did not extend much beyond the four New Orleans streets surrounding the St. Louis Hotel, where the statehouse was located. Nevertheless, Packard refused to surrender. Most of the district judges and the parish (county) officers recognized Nicholls. Aware that the nation was watching, the Nicholls regime made the conciliatory gesture of accepting the election of 240 blacks to various positions and appointing twenty-one others to state offices. Running a de facto government from the New Orleans Odd Fellows Hall and encouraged by signs in Washington and South Carolina, the Nicholls forces bided their time. They were further strengthened on 6 April when, at a mass meeting, several thousand supporters pledged "never to submit to the pretended Packard Government; never to pay it a dollar of taxes; never to acknowledge its authority; but to resist it at every point and in every way."

Because neither Nicholls nor Packard would agree to all branches under one government, Hayes's commission worked to create a legislature in which both houses would have a quorum of members whose seats were undisputed. In theory, the Packard and Nicholls legislatures would try to attract each other's undisputed members until one emerged with an uncontested quorum. Although the commission was officially neutral, it tilted toward the Nicholls legislature and counted on the business community to force the politicians into a settlement. Encountering "bad" Republicans and "bulldozing" Democrats, the commissioners quickly became contemptuous of Louisiana politicians. "Of all the states I have ever visited," Harlan wrote to Bristow, "this beats all. Its politics are in utter confusion, and it will puzzle any one to get at the exact truth." Although the Democrats were talking more liberally "as to most matters affecting the colored race" than earlier, Harlan confessed, "I have discovered many things which stir my blood as a Union man & a Republican." He nevertheless wanted an adjustment that would remove "this Southern question from politics."[29]

The commission was above buying politicians, but Kellar was not. Working primarily through Cotton Exchange members, he told William Henry Smith that he was "somewhat confident" on 12 April of securing a legislature, with a quorum conceded by all, that would recognize Nicholls. Kellar most likely bought the six Republican legislators he won over, rationalizing that "the corrupt government in existence, made laws to perpetrate bad government, and a change for reform, must of necessity violate the letter of bad laws enacted for corrupt uses. This is civil revolution, but it is the only remedy of relief."

Kellar was so encouraged that he thought that an administration party fed by federal patronage could be organized in Louisiana. He predicted to Webb Hayes that, under Nicholls, party lines "will not only be obliterated but the party names themselves will be abolished," that intelligent whites and industrious blacks "will unite and support the Administration." Through Webb, Kellar assured Hayes that his southern policy "will accomplish every thing he has at heart. The results of the war, as secured in the Constitutional amendments, will be extended in practical legislation and enforced by public opinion in Louisiana, much beyond my expectation." Although Kellar's prophecies were pleasant to contemplate, Hayes did not take Kellar's political analysis seriously enough to appoint his candidate as collector of customs at New Orleans.[30]

Webb Cook Hayes

The Reconstruction era rapidly ended. From Hayes's perspective, the timing was excellent. On 17 April, the U.S. Senate adjourned, leaving the most vocal critics of Hayes's southern policy without a forum. By 19 April, Kellar and others had induced enough Republicans to join the Nicholls legislature to give it a quorum, and it adopted resolutions that fully accepted the Civil War amendments and pledged "the promotion of kindly relations between the white and colored citizens." Claiming that he had "earnestly sought to obliterate the color line in politics, and consolidate the people on the basis of equal rights and common interests," Nicholls pledged the full and equal protection of the rights of all persons, promised an equal system of tax-supported public education open to all "without regard to race or color," and expressed the wish to foster immigration to hasten Louisiana's economic development. Upon receiving these assurances, the commission wired Hayes that the troops supporting Packard could be withdrawn. That evening, Hayes had reason to celebrate at his first state dinner (honoring two sons of the Russian czar), but the immoderate consumption of wine punch by some less than noble guests left him disturbed. To the joy of temperance advocates, he banned liquor from the White House and, to set a good example, became a total abstainer.

On Friday, 20 April, Hayes directed that the detachment of troops protecting the Packard government "be withdrawn." On Tuesday, 24 April, "at 12 o'clock meridian," the troops left on schedule while crowds cheered, bells rang, and cannons roared. The next day, the Democrats took over the statehouse. Packard, whose legislature had already been dissolved, made no resistance. A brave man who had barely recovered from the effects of an assassin's bullet, he yielded to superior force. "I am," he exclaimed, "wholly discouraged by the fact that, one by one, the Republican State Governments of the South have been forced to succumb to force, fraud, or policy." Packard, however, was compensated for his loss. Hayes appointed him to the lucrative consulate at Liverpool, where the fees he collected rivaled the salary of Hayes himself.[31]

Kellar's vision of the future of southern politics soon proved to be a delusion. Democrats argued that Hayes deserved no credit for having done what they had forced him to do. Despite their promises to accept black participation in the political process (the Civil War amendments), southern Democrats soon set their sights on new goals, such as the repeal of federal election laws, in an ongoing effort to disfranchise black voters. Whiggish whites, having achieved home rule, quickly lost interest in the Republican party. Only a couple of weeks after the troops retired, Comly reported to Hayes from New Orleans that the " 'old Whig' sentiment" had already "petered

out." Southern Republicans, both black and white, feared the further erosion of their strength. Amos T. Akerman of Georgia, who had been Grant's
attorney general, observed that Hayes's course amounted to combating
"lawlessness by letting the lawless have their own way." Kellar's idea that the
"colored voter & laborer will be better protected than under former governments" was contradicted by a South Carolinian who exclaimed to Hayes, "I
am a unprotected freedman. . . . O God Save the Colored People."[32]

Some northern Republicans considered Hayes's course impolitic and
wrong. Among former abolitionists, Wendell Phillips was furious, and William Lloyd Garrison thought that Hayes had made a cowardly compromise
with the "incorrigible enemies of equal rights and legitimate government."
The abandonment of Packard disturbed Charles B. Farwell of Chicago for
personal as well as political reasons. He had been the first visiting statesman
to reach New Orleans, and his "promises . . . made to Kellogg & Packard
immediately upon his arrival determined the course adopted." Benjamin F.
Wade, who had seconded Hayes's nomination, felt "deceived, betrayed, and
humiliated" by Hayes's new departure.[33]

Although most northern Republicans supported Hayes's move, their enthusiasm varied. The reform element was pleased, and so were many practical politicians. Hayes's own representative, Charles Foster, exclaimed, "How
rejoiced I am at the extremely happy undoing of the S.C. & La. muddle.
Here & there a republican may be found who takes the Ben Wade view of
the situation, but, generally speaking, the people of both parties are rejoiced
to know that your policy has been a success, and that a genuine peace is to
again grow up between the north & south." Favoring local self-government,
believing in the supremacy of civil over military authority, and yearning for
peace, northern Republicans were willing to try Hayes's southern policy. If
his strategy could break the color line in politics, win some whites to the Republican party, and protect the rights of blacks, the cause of civil rights
would be advanced throughout the South.

More cautious and self-centered, Garfield thought that Hayes might succeed if southern Democratic supporters of his policy gave "him an administration House," with Garfield as Speaker. "If not," Garfield predicted that
northern Republicans would "not tolerate a continuance of his Southern
Scheme." If the president's strategy failed and white-supremacist governments emerged in South Carolina and Louisiana, as they had in the rest of
the South, the precarious foothold would be lost. And if it were lost, it
would be almost impossible to protect the rights of black voters and to rebuild a strong, southern, black-based Republican party. Hayes realized that
his southern policy was a trial "to staunch antislavery veterans," and he ex-

pected to be condemned for it. "I know they mean well," he wrote. "It is a comfort to know also that I mean well."[34]

Having no practical alternative, Hayes believed that his course was correct and was guardedly optimistic about the future. With northerners tired of Reconstruction, Democrats in control of the House of Representatives and refusing to make military appropriations, and the southern Republican party in disarray, he was, as Chamberlain acknowledged and Bristow expressed it, "carrying out the logic of events" rather than forcing a new policy on the nation. It was, Bristow insisted, "wicked and foolish" for Republicans to attack their president. For Hayes, the choice was not whether to withdraw the troops but when to withdraw them. Using the tenuous federal military presence, he had extracted pledges from the Hampton and Nicholls governments to reject white supremacy, which was more than had been secured from any other so-called redeemer government. Hayes did not share the optimism of Kellar, who proclaimed that a new era of racial justice and political reorganization was at hand. Indeed, Hayes told Dickson, "The Southern men will not yet, if ever, desert their party organization." He had hopes that South Carolina and Louisiana would keep their pledges "that the colored people shall have equal rights to labor, to education, and to the privileges of citizenship." He insisted, "I am confident this is a good work," but he was also realistic, adding, "Time will tell."[35]

To drum up support for his southern policy, Hayes preached reconciliation and civil rights as he toured New England, Ohio, and the South during the summer of 1877. In June, he received an honorary doctor of laws degree while attending Birch's graduation from Harvard Law School. At a banquet in his honor, he was touched by Oliver Wendell Holmes's poem, lauding him as a "Healer of Strife!" To heal strife, Hayes responded, was his "most ardent desire." Approval by New England intellectuals confirmed for Hayes that he was "on the right track."[36]

Hayes's soaring spirits fell when he returned to Washington on 30 June. There he learned from John Sherman that a New Orleans grand jury had indicted J. Madison Wells and Gen. Thomas C. Anderson of the Louisiana returning board. Sherman was irate "at the imprudence and wrong in these indictments," and Hayes was disappointed and embarrassed that these hostile moves were the first fruits of his conciliatory southern policy.[37]

Despite the Louisiana arrests, Hayes retained his faith in the promises of southern politicians. In August, he toured New England with Vice President Wheeler and was delighted with the enthusiastic responses to his "unpremeditated" speeches discouraging "sectionalism and race and class prejudice." After a "rousing evening" in Worcester, Massachusetts, Wheeler told

Hayes that he perceived "a most marked decadence in the feeling of opposition to" the administration's southern policy. In Worcester, Hayes predicted "that equal rights shall be given to all the States; that all citizens, white or black, capitalist or laborer, shall stand equal before the law; that over all the country the United States Government shall be supreme."[38]

On 6 September, scarcely two weeks after completing his New England trip, Hayes, his family, and his cabinet officers set off on a nineteen-day tour of Ohio, Kentucky, Tennessee, Georgia, and Virginia. From Ohio he took a side trip to Richmond, Indiana, to visit Oliver P. Morton, his radical Republican ally who was terminally ill. Deeply moved by the imminent loss of his friend, Hayes kissed Morton on the forehead. Morton, who was also touched, rallied and on 23 October published a vigorous letter supporting Hayes's conciliatory southern policy.

Moving on to the South, Hayes held out the olive branch while stressing that obeying the amendments was a prerequisite of reconciliation. With the South apparently accepting Hayes's terms, the tour was a triumph. Gov. Wade Hampton of South Carolina joined Hayes at Louisville, Kentucky, where the audience applauded its assent when Hayes queried, "My friends, my Confederate friends, do you intend to obey the whole Constitution and Amendments?" At Atlanta, Hayes addressed a crowd of whites and blacks, Democrats and Republicans. He aroused "cheering for several minutes" when he told the blacks that he believed that their "rights and interests would be safer if this great mass of intelligent white men were let alone by the general Government." The crowd also cheered, but less enthusiastically, when Hayes insisted that the Constitution and all its amendments must be "fully and fairly obeyed."[39]

"Received everywhere heartily," Hayes wrote of his southern trip. "The country is again one and united! I am very happy to be able to feel that the course taken has turned out so well." He was similarly encouraged a month later by a trip to Richmond and again that autumn, when he was nominated by the southern members and elected by the unanimous board of the Peabody Education Fund. That fund, intended to combat illiteracy among southern blacks and whites, had been endowed with $3.4 million by George Peabody; Hayes, with his abiding faith in education and his hopes for racial harmony, was a devoted trustee for the remainder of his life. With his hopes becoming his beliefs, Hayes thought that his southern policy was working and that conservative Democrats would ignore color and sectional lines in politics and move into the Republican party.[40]

Hayes was wrong. War wounds were not healed, white southerners neither enforced nor obeyed the amendments, and conservative southern Democrats did not join the Republican party, which shrank in the South to a handful of officeholders. Failing to perceive the pervasiveness and viciousness of racial prejudice, Hayes assumed that the educated, intelligent leaders of the South would deal fairly with the blacks. But even if Hayes had been more astute in assessing southern attitudes, it would have been impossible for him to uphold the rights of blacks. He could neither save the two outposts of radicalism nor mount a counterattack to enforce the amendments. Substituting reason and patriotism for the coercion that had failed in the past and was unfeasible in the present, Hayes tried to persuade white southerners to obey the Reconstruction amendments. For a brief season, he believed that he had succeeded.

"Now for Civil Service Reform," Hayes exclaimed on 22 April 1877. Pleased that his southern problems had apparently receded, he outlined his new program: "Legislation must be prepared & Executive rules and Maxims. We must limit, and narrow the area of patronage—we must diminish the evils of office seeking—we must stop interference of federal officers with elections. We must be relieved of Congressional dictation as to appointments." Recognizing that an administration is transitory, Hayes knew that any lasting civil-service reform would have to be legislated. In counting on Congress to pass the wise reform measure he planned to urge upon it, Hayes underestimated Congress's dependence on the spoils system, its hostility to reform, and its uncooperative attitude toward him.[41]

The next day, Secretary of the Treasury Sherman carried out Hayes's order and appointed John Jay, a reform-minded New York aristocrat, to head a commission to investigate the New York customhouse. He also appointed commissioners to investigate the Philadelphia, New Orleans, and San Francisco customhouses. Sherman was not a civil-service reformer; a month earlier, he had wanted to appoint a friend as New York customhouse auditor, but collector Chester A. Arthur had refused to displace the incumbent, a career officer who had held the post for thirty-five years. It was the warrior Hayes, not Sherman, who fired the first shot in the battle to reform the New York customhouse and to restore the power of appointment to the executive.[42]

When Hayes took office, the federal bureaucracy, especially the field service outside of Washington, was politicized by the spoils system. Nominating candidates, campaigning, keeping track of voters, and getting them out on election day required many devoted party workers. Most of these workers had already secured civil-service positions in return for their labors or hoped to secure one. Although this system worked for the political parties, it was often bad for government service. Politicians—usually members of Congress—dictated appointments, and the civil servants they sponsored, although superb party workers, often did not perform their public tasks adequately. With their tenure insecure and dependent on their patrons' political fortunes, it was difficult for civil servants to develop loyalty to an agency, and their lack of professionalism was matched by a lack of strong national feeling. A civil servant was loyal primarily to his patron—the politician with a local power base who had procured him his job. In addition to providing these politicians with a payroll for their faithful supporters, the civil service was the chief source of campaign funds. Local, state, and federal politicians assessed from 2 to 7 percent of civil servants' yearly salaries; those in lucrative positions paid more.[43]

During his brief congressional career, Hayes had supported the civil-service reform bill proposed by Rhode Island Republican Thomas A. Jenckes. It required that those applicants scoring highest in open, competitive examinations be appointed to government offices. Although it did not pass, an 1871 appropriations bill rider enabled Grant to appoint a commission, headed by George William Curtis, to devise rules for examining applicants for government offices. When Grant ignored its rules in a conspicuous 1873 case, Curtis resigned and Dorman B. Eaton carried on until Congress ceased appropriations in 1875. When Hayes took office, Eaton was still head of this moribund Civil Service Commission.[44]

Among Hayes's cabinet, only Schurz was thoroughly committed to a nonpartisan government service. Other cabinet members were frankly partisan. For example, Key tried to attract old southern Whigs to the Republican party with the bait of postmasterships; and Sherman used Treasury Department patronage to further his presidential ambitions. Indeed, much of the reform program was based on bureaucratic procedures in monarchical Britain and Europe, where there were no mass-based political parties. It appeared to favor an educated elite and did not appeal to democratic Americans. Many citizens believed that the public was best served by rotating employees out of office and bringing in new workers who could easily master the tasks at hand. The fear that American political parties could not function without a partisan civil service bolstered objections to civil-service reform. Even members of America's elite—such as Secretary of State Evarts, whose grandfather had signed both the Declaration of Independence and the Constitution—recognized the connections between the spoils system and the unique American government of the people, by the people, and for the people. On 5 April 1877, Garfield enjoyed a stimulating evening at the Evarts home, where the host asked: "In a Republic

The cabinet (clockwise from Hayes on the left): John Sherman, Richard W. Thompson, Charles Devens, Carl Schurz, David M. Key, George W. McCrary, and William Maxwell Evarts

what political motive is an adequate substitute for patronage?" When guests could not come up with an answer, Garfield concluded, "This is the central difficulty that underlies the Civil Service."[45]

Civil-service reform was difficult, and Hayes moved with characteristic caution. Predictably, his moderation angered the reformers, and even modest reform infuriated the spoilsmen. Hayes's wise decision to avoid wholesale removals and appointments during the first two weeks of his term provoked reformers; believing that the collectors of customs in Boston, New York, and Philadelphia were partisan and corrupt, reformers demanded that they be removed immediately.[46]

At his first cabinet meeting on 12 March, Hayes asked Evarts and Schurz to form a policy on clerical appointments in the Washington departments. Their rules required that appointments be made only at the lowest level and be given to those who had passed a standard, noncompetitive examination. This disappointed reformers, who wanted appointments made on the basis of the British system of open, competitive tests. For more than twenty years, noncompetitive examinations had been required by law and had proved to be no obstacle to spoilsmen. William Grosvenor, of the New York *Tribune*, complained to Schurz on 26 March, "I am afraid the President is making haste *too* slowly: the feeling is not as cordial as it was, & there is now doubt of his steadiness of purpose." Schurz assured Grosvenor that "Hayes makes haste slowly but surely. . . . You need not be anxious."[47]

Hayes and Schurz gave impatient reformers some gratification. When many of his relatives applied for jobs, often through Lucy, Hayes decided that "no person connected with me by blood or marriage will be appointed to office." He angered Dr. Joe Webb and hurt Lucy by refusing to appoint him surgeon general of the modest Marine Hospital Service, which gave medical care to merchant seamen. Joe, who had served with Hayes during the war and had probably saved his life when he was seriously wounded, was well qualified for the job. But Hayes, after the excesses of the Grant administration, eschewed nepotism. Reformers were also encouraged when Schurz, going beyond the rules he and Evarts had formulated, established a three-member board of inquiry to guide his Interior Department appointments, promotions, and removals. Schurz's determination to make no dismissals without cause and to permit no political influence to interfere with removals earned him praise for sounding the keynote of civil-service reform. According to reformer Horace White, writing on 10 April, public opinion in New York was "very favorably disposed to the new Administration & especially towards civil service reform."[48]

Reformers' demands that the New York customhouse "be divorced from the *machinery* of politics" were reinforced in mid-May when Hayes visited New York City and hobnobbed with merchants and reformers. He attended the annual chamber of commerce dinner at Delmonico's restaurant, visited the American Museum of Natural History with Theodore Roosevelt, Sr., before its official opening, breakfasted with John Jacob Astor, and dined with Edwin D. Morgan. Hayes was strengthened in his resolution to reform the civil service by meeting George William Curtis (to whom he offered a foreign mission), John A. Dix, and John Jay, who was investigating the New York customhouse.[49]

Distributing patronage was often fraught with difficulties. Hayes had problems, for example, with the Chicago customhouse and the Louisville post office. Former Sen. John A. Logan of Illinois, a noted spoilsman, was in need, and William Henry Smith proposed that Hayes appoint Logan to a Chicago office. Aware of Logan's financial difficulties and of his outstanding record as a Union general, Hayes was willing to name him collector of customs, but word of his intention "stirred up a hornet's nest" among his reform-minded Chicago supporters. Hayes then abandoned Logan and gave the customhouse to Smith (to whom he owed political debts dating from the Civil War).⁵⁰

In Louisville, Hayes appointed Virginia Campbell Thompson as postmistress, in part to conciliate southerners. She was the widow of a Democratic lawyer and had been recommended by "hosts of good Republicans," including Oliver P. Morton from neighboring Indiana. The appointment, however, outraged John Marshall Harlan, who recalled that the Kentucky delegation had "turned the tide" to Hayes at the Cincinnati nominating convention and protested that the administration distributed its patronage "so as to discourage its friends and delight its enemies." Insisting that "no female can manage so large a Post office," Harlan argued that the appointment could not "be justified by any proper view of civil service reform."

Unlike Harlan, Hayes did not confuse male chauvinism with civil-service reform. He appointed Thompson on 11 June and believed that she would be "a good officer," as would the eighteen other postmistresses he had named by that date. Hayes later wrote to Thompson: "It was particularly pleasing to me to appoint to an important and conspicuous place a woman. It seemed to harmonize with my wish to do what I could to remove the bitterness in the South towards the North and towards the party to which I belonged." Since Hayes aimed to take federal offices *"out of party and personal political management,"* appointing an occasional southern Democrat did not concern him, but "of course," he told Bryan (who wanted him to appoint more southern Democrats), "I shall appoint Republicans generally."⁵¹

Hayes's caution in making changes, coupled with Key's and John Sherman's attitude, made the administration's civil-service reform policy appear weak and vacillating. This was particularly marked after the Jay Commission's first report on the New York customhouse appeared on 24 May. It suggested that 20 percent of the customhouse's 1,262 employees could be immediately dispensed with and that subsequent reductions might be necessary. In the relaxed atmosphere of the customhouse, hours were from nine to four, but work rarely started before ten; since lunch breaks were also taken, employees put in less than a six-hour day. The one rule that was strictly enforced was the paying of political assessments, which some employees recouped by "exacting or accepting from . . . merchants unlawful gratuities." After making these charges, the Jay Commission recommended "the emancipation of the service from partisan control."⁵²

Sherman approved the Jay Commission's minor recommendations but asked Hayes to comment on the recommendations pertaining to political appointments made "without due regard to efficiency," since administration policy was involved. Hayes replied:

It is my wish that the collection of the revenues should be free from partisan control, and organized on a strictly business basis. . . . Party leaders should have no more influence in appointments than other equally respectable citizens. No assessments for political purposes, on officers or subordinates, should be allowed. No useless officer or employee should be retained. No officer should be required or permitted to take part in the management of political organizations, caucuses, conventions, or election campaigns.[53]

Watering down Hayes's forceful commands, Sherman ordered Arthur to trim his force within a month but suggested that "in a government like ours . . . those will be preferred who sympathize with the party in power; but persons in office ought not to be expected to serve their party to the neglect of official duty." Trying not to offend Arthur's patron, Roscoe Conkling, Sherman did not mention political assessments and commended Arthur for approving the Jay Commission's preliminary report. "Mr. Collector, the President wishes the Custom-house to be taken out of politics," George William Curtis paraphrased Sherman's letter. "You will please do it in your own way, only—you will, of course, leave politics in."[54]

Hayes remained cautious, Arthur stayed in office, and the disappointment of reformers increased. Edwin L. Godkin of the *Nation* was "dissatisfied & discouraged, though not ready as yet to make any public declaration to that effect"; Horace White—no longer optimistic—lamented that the collectors at Boston, New York, and Philadelphia had not been summarily replaced by "friends of reform." White feared that the cause of civil-service reform would be "put off for years. For if our enemies can say that, with an Administration of our kind & with a President who didn't want to be reelected, we could still do nothing, will they not convince the country that reform is simply impracticable & that time should not be wasted upon it?"[55]

Hayes moved to mollify reformers. On 22 June 1877, after consulting with Schurz, Jacob Dolson Cox, and Dorman B. Eaton, he prohibited political assessments and forbade "the management of political organizations, caucuses, conventions, or election campaigns" by federal civil servants. Hayes was again popular with reformers; the *Nation* called his order the "best thing he has yet done for politics" after ridding the South of carpetbaggers. But mollifying reformers outraged spoilsmen and also worried several friends. William M. Dickson, who ironically had assured George William Curtis that Hayes would stand up to spoils politicians, told Hayes to "move slowly & tentatively in Civil Service Reform; . . . do not further hazard your influence with your party," he warned, "or you will imperil all." Dickson ar-

gued, like Evarts, that "politics must pay the politician" and urged Hayes to
"give us honest & capable men, but partisans. All else is the cry of Amateur
literary politicians."[56]

In truth, Hayes was not totally committed to the program of the civil-service
reformers. He wanted his order forbidding political activity by officeholders obeyed, but he did not want to destroy Republican party organizations. Influenced more by Sherman than by the cries of "amateur literary
politicians" like Curtis and his friend Charles Eliot Norton, Hayes kept collectors Arthur of New York and W. A. Simmons of Boston in office as long
as they cooperated with reform efforts.[57]

But during the summer of 1877, it appeared to Hayes that Conkling and
his men had no interest in reforming the New York customhouse. William
Grosvenor told Schurz in July that the cutting of its staff, as required by the
Jay Commission report, had been carried out with "outrageous partiality &
knavery. . . . It was, and everybody here knows it, a most impudent avenging of Conkling & his crew, by ousting the men who had become distasteful." Worse, naval officer Alonzo B. Cornell (second in command at the customhouse), encouraged by his political associates, refused to resign from the
Republican National Committee, despite Hayes's order forbidding officeholders from engaging in political activities. Reformers insisted that Cornell
must be removed; if he could defy Hayes with impunity, the administration's
civil-service policy would be broken.[58]

Apart from Cornell's defiance, there were other compelling reasons for
Hayes to attack Conkling's control of the New York customhouse. It collected 70 percent of the nation's customs revenue and was the largest federal
office in the land. Striking a blow for reform there would have a symbolic
impact and, if reform had any merit, would have a practical effect on government service. Apart from reform considerations, Conkling had crossed
Hayes repeatedly. After Hayes had refused to appoint his man Platt to the
cabinet, Conkling had referred to Hayes as "Rutherfraud." Conkling wanted
to destroy the reform wing of the New York Republican party led by Secretary of State Evarts, and Evarts wanted to oust Conkling and rebuild a pro-
administration party from the remains of the old Reuben E. Fenton organization (which Conkling had displaced). Sherman's efforts to avoid a rupture
by retaining Arthur and giving Evarts some appointments failed; neither
Evarts nor the reformers wanted an equilibrium, and Conkling wanted no
reform.[59]

On 6 September 1877, the day he left Washington for Ohio and the South
to preach reconciliation, Hayes attacked Conkling by announcing that Arthur and Cornell would be replaced in a customhouse reorganization. Hayes

moved against them shortly after a supplementary Jay Commission report generously estimated that the undervaluations and excessive damages allowed by New York appraisers had cost the government up to a fourth of its rightful revenues. The necessity of reforming customhouse practices, coupled with Cornell's refusal to obey the president's order, had spurred Hayes to act.[60]

NINETEEN

A TROUBLED SUMMER

Hayes had had little time for civil-service reform in July 1877; unprecedented rioting and bloodshed shattered the nation's peace and demanded his attention. The Great Strike, the closest the United States has ever come to a general strike, had its origin in the depression that followed the panic of 1873. Competition among railroads for the shrinking volume of freight and passengers was particularly fierce among the five trunk lines—the bankrupt Grand Trunk of Canada, the New York Central, the Erie, the Pennsylvania, and the Baltimore & Ohio (B&O)—that linked the Northeast with the Midwest.

To escape bankruptcy, railroads had "to earn more and . . . spend less." To earn more, the four solvent trunk-line roads agreed to pool westbound freight out of New York and to double their rates on it. To spend less, they took turns cutting wages. The giant Pennsylvania Railroad announced that on 1 June it would impose a 10 percent pay cut on its employees earning more than a dollar a day. These men worked twelve-hour shifts, were frequently idle without pay, and performed dangerous tasks (especially brakemen); because of layovers, they often had to spend days away from home at their own expense. In addition, they had already sustained a 20 percent wage cut. On 1 July, the New York Central, the Erie, and a host of other roads cut wages. There were protests but no strikes.[1]

Using the Pennsylvania's formula, the B&O scheduled its pay cut for Monday, 16 July. Its financial condition was weak, but rather than reduce its usual 10 percent stock dividend, as banker Junius S. Morgan had advised, its president John W. Garrett called for a 10 percent wage cut, claiming financial necessity. B&O employees had sustained a wage cut eight months earlier; the number of cars on trains had been increased, but crews had been reduced; and the workers had not been paid since May. They struck on 16 July, but police in Baltimore dispersed the strikers, and Garrett fired them. Strikebreakers kept the trains going.

Outside of Baltimore, Garrett was not as well prepared. Hindered by neither the local police nor a militia company, strikers in Martinsburg, West

Virginia, stopped freight trains. With rail traffic clogged there, the strike spread, and Garrett urged Gov. Henry M. Mathews of West Virginia to ask Hayes to disperse "the rioters" with federal troops. "The loss of an hour," Garrett warned on 17 July, "would most seriously affect us and imperil vast interests." Governor Mathews initially thought that the state militia could protect strikebreakers at Martinsburg, but the militia commander disagreed and called for at least two hundred U.S. Marines. Professing impotence on 18 July, Mathews asked Hayes to send two to three hundred troops to protect "the law abiding people" and to maintain "supremacy of the law." Garrett urged Hayes to act immediately, lest "this difficulty" spread.[2]

Like other political leaders of his time, Hayes thought that strikers had no right to destroy property or prevent others from working. As governor during the 1876 Ohio coal strike, he had ordered the Ohio militia to protect the coal operators' property and the strikebreakers' "right to work." Believing that "rioters" gained strength when authorities hesitated, he had boasted to Garfield that "we shall crush out the law breakers if the courts and juries do not fail." Nevertheless, Hayes did not want to intervene in strikes to break them. He believed that his presidential role was to prevent arson and violence when local and state authorities had exhausted their resources. He sympathized with individual workers, distrusted plutocrats, and did not champion railroad interests. He believed that a day's toil of "eight hours, should never be exceeded," that "colossal fortunes . . . threaten alike good government and our liberties," that railroads should be regulated, and that their stock watering and rate discrimination should be stopped. Cherishing the values of an earlier, simpler age, Hayes disliked the labor agitator and the railroad mogul, but his commitment to maintaining the peace and an individual's right to work benefited management more than labor.[3]

Despite his "prompt, decided policy" as governor in dealing with striking Ohio miners, Hayes was loath to intervene in West Virginia and wired for a full statement of facts. When Mathews responded that available state troops were scarce and that, unless immediate action were taken, "much property may be destroyed and . . . lives lost," the president's skepticism vanished. At 3:50 P.M. on 18 July, he ordered every available man at the Washington Arsenal and at Fort McHenry in Baltimore to Martinsburg via the B&O, which, in keeping with its effort to earn more, charged the federal government for the men's fares.

In 1877, the army was a mere shadow of its wartime self. Its primary tasks were to subdue Native Americans, not strikers, and to maintain order on frontiers, not in railroad centers. That summer, it was at war with the Nez Percé Indians in the Pacific Northwest and, pending the solution of border problems, was facing Mexican army units along the Rio Grande. In addition, with Democrats hostile to the implementation of radical Reconstruction, the army had been without money since 1 July, and its enlisted men had not been paid for months. Even so, the 312 men of the Second U.S. Artillery who were sent from Washington and Baltimore were tough and efficient. When they reached Martinsburg on the morning of 19 July, the city was calm and would remain calm. But in other towns along the B&O Railroad, workers in other industries, the unemployed, tramps, and fourteen- to eighteen-year-old boys joined the strike and quickly outnumbered railroad workers. The strike was not a local problem; its rapid spread illustrated that by 1877 the economy was national in scope and that many of the social problems it engendered could not be solved by state governments.[4]

On Friday, 20 July, rioting erupted in Baltimore. A mob stoned units of the Maryland militia as they marched to the B&O depot to leave for Cumberland, where another mob had paralyzed rail traffic. The militia opened fire, killing ten men and boys and wounding others. An ugly crowd of 15,000 gathered outside the depot, with the militia, local police, railroad officials, the mayor, and Gov. John Lee Carroll all inside. After the mob burned passenger cars and part of the depot, attacked firemen, and exchanged pistol shots with the police, Governor Carroll wired Hayes for federal troops.

Hayes ordered the commandant of Fort McHenry and all his available men to report to Governor Carroll, and he stayed up all night to receive dispatches from Baltimore. On Saturday, Hayes asked Gen. Winfield Scott Hancock, commander of the military division of the Atlantic, to confer with Carroll. In effect, Hayes wanted Hancock, in whom he had great confidence, to take charge of a situation that seemed to be getting out of hand. But shortly after Carroll wired Hayes for help, Baltimore began to calm down. By Sunday, the five hundred U.S. soldiers and marines in that city were not needed.[5]

Baltimore was calm that Sunday morning, but Pittsburgh was burning. The Pennsylvania Railroad had ordered that, starting on the preceding Thursday, all eastbound through freight trains out of Pittsburgh would be doubleheaders (longer trains pulled by two locomotives); the objective was to fire some brakemen and conductors and to work those who remained harder. The timing could not have been worse. Emboldened by news from Martinsburg, workers refused to take the doubleheaders out of the freight yard. After a minor scuffle at a switch, ten policemen got one freight train through that afternoon, but with mill workers, tramps, and boys joining the strikers, it proved to be the last freight train to leave Pittsburgh for several days, even though passenger trains remained on schedule. Since neither the local police nor units of the militia managed to disperse the crowd blocking the track, state authorities—responding to the demands of the Pennsylvania Railroad management—called in the First Division of the Pennsylvania National Guard from Philadelphia. It arrived on Saturday afternoon, 21 July, and dispersed the crowd, but not before killing ten to twenty people. The tracks were cleared, but the slaughter made strikebreakers afraid to man the doubleheaders. When the militia retired to a nearby roundhouse, the angry crowd regrouped and besieged the roundhouse. By morning, the crowd had burned out the Philadelphia guardsmen, killing five of them as they fled Pittsburgh. That Sunday, 22 July, the mob destroyed 104 locomotives, 2,152 railroad cars, and innumerable buildings. By evening, with the rioters tired, drunk, and running out of targets, the Pittsburgh police were able to stop further destruction.[6]

The spreading strike absorbed Hayes's attention. He postponed a visit to Virginia and had a special telegraph line strung to his summer residence at the Soldiers' Home in Washington to keep him informed of the latest developments. While there on Saturday, he learned of the bloodshed in Pittsburgh. That intelligence struck him with particular force, for Rud and Fanny had just passed through Pittsburgh on their way to Columbus to spend the hottest summer weeks with their cousin Laura Platt Mitchell. On Sunday, after attending church, Hayes met with his cabinet and grimly read dispatches from Signal Corps sergeants, who normally observed weather conditions. Stationed throughout the country, they were, in historian Robert V. Bruce's words, "tracking the social storm" that was raging in Pittsburgh and threatening Philadelphia.

The absence of Pennsylvania Gov. John F. Hartranft, who was junketing out West at the expense of Tom Scott, president of the Pennsylvania Railroad, troubled Hayes. Unwilling to send troops to Pennsylvania without a proper request, he took little comfort from Reconstruction legislation empowering presidents to quell civil disorders with federal troops and even less from the fact that there were only 3,000 troops in the military division of the Atlantic. That Sunday afternoon, Scott invoked the spirit of Lincoln and urged Hayes to call for volunteers to put down disturbances along the railroads, arguing that they were highways of interstate commerce. Similar messages from Hartranft and Mayor William S. Stokley of Philadelphia—asking Hayes to suppress the strike rather than keep the peace—indicated that Scott was orchestrating a drive for federal intervention.

Hayes and his cabinet reassembled that Sunday at 10 P.M. at Evarts's house. Although looting and burning had gone on all day in Pittsburgh, they would not intervene without a proper invitation. From Wyoming that evening, Hartranft telegraphed Hayes, asking "for troops to assist in quelling mobs," but since he did not show that he had exhausted all the means at his disposal, Hayes did nothing for Pittsburgh beyond ordering fifty soldiers from Columbus to protect the Allegheny Arsenal. In contrast, he responded immediately to a call from Mayor Stokley of Philadelphia, who detailed why he needed troops to restore order and protect property. (On Monday, the administration also responded to a proper request by Hartranft.) More significantly, Hayes and the cabinet rejected Scott's plea that the federal government intervene on the side of railroad management. Hayes did not feel beholden to Tom Scott for his election, and even if he had, he would not have altered an administration policy to come to his aid. Restricting himself to keeping the peace when states could not do so, Hayes refused to supply soldiers to operate the railroads and break the strike.[7]

By Monday, Hayes had a clear policy. Even prior to a call for help, regulars would be ordered to a trouble spot to protect U.S. property (arsenals and subtreasuries in particular) "and by their presence to promote peace and order," but they would not enforce state law until a formal request had been received and approved. Hayes minimized the federal presence by ordering troops in West Virginia and Maryland to report to state authorities; in Pennsylvania, Governor Hartranft had ordered state militia officers to report to General Hancock, so Hayes was flexible and allowed him to continue to lead "under existing circumstances." The administration was also careful not to intervene and operate railroads on the pretext that the strikers obstructed the mails. Except briefly at Hornellsville, New York, strikers stopped only freight trains, waving through passenger trains and their mail cars. But management, in an attempt to provoke federal intervention, refused to run trains made up only of mail cars. To keep Hayes from drawing the wrong conclusion, strikers in Erie, Pennsylvania, wired him on Tuesday: "The Lake Shore Company has refused to let U.S. mail east of here. We would be pleased if you would . . . direct them to proceed with mails and also passengers." Hayes simply accepted the lack of rail service, and Postmaster General Key sought alternative routes to get the mail through.[8]

The strike spread to other railroads and other states. From Sunday, 22 July, to Tuesday, strikers in Buffalo halted traffic on the New York Central and the Erie, clashing with the New York State militia and the Buffalo police. In Ohio, trains were stopped, but there was no bloodshed. By Tuesday, the strike had spread throughout the Midwest and across the Mississippi River into Missouri and Iowa and had inspired anti-Chinese riots in San Francisco. Hayes coolly noted, however, that violence was diminishing and that U.S. troops were "every where respected."[9]

Although their presence deterred further violence, federal troops arrived too late to confront enraged mobs. The War Department in Washington was the scene of frenzied activity, with troops being ordered to one place only to be intercepted and sent elsewhere. To promote efficiency, Hayes gave General Hancock control over troop movements in the division of the Atlantic on Tuesday, 24 July, but the president continued to monitor the situation closely. When he and Treasury Secretary Sherman worried that Hancock had left $100 million unguarded at the New York subtreasury and customhouse, Hancock quickly returned some men to New York. Although born of confusion, the constant movement of troops through rail centers had a calming effect. "We have not made much noise, it is true," Hancock remarked, "nor did we emblazon our numbers—and that silence led to an exaggeration of the strength of the force at our disposal at whatever point the troops appeared." Had Hayes thrown all the available troops into Pittsburgh, they probably would have fared no better than the Philadelphia militia, and the prestige of U.S. troops—which was crucial—would have been destroyed. Hayes did well to move with caution.[10]

The calm of Hayes contrasted with the hysteria of the press. The memory of the 1871 Paris Commune—which had killed hostages and had been suppressed with much bloodshed—was vivid, and major newspapers blamed the strike on a Communist conspiracy. On the Saturday after the Baltimore riot, the *National Republican* (Washington) called the strike "nothing less than communism in its worst form." But Hayes, when interviewed the next day, saw no evidence that the "spirit of communism" prevailed in the strike, since the strikers did not attack "property in general, but merely . . . that of the railroads with which the strikers had had difficulties." Hayes was essentially correct. The Marxist Workingmen's party, established in 1876, had only a few thousand members in 1877; although it had nothing to do with the commencement of the Great Strike, once it was under way, that party made the most of it.[11]

In Chicago, the Workingmen's party held rallies to build its membership, but it played no part in the three days (24 to 26 July) of violence that followed, except to become a target of the police. That Tuesday, Wednesday, and Thursday, violence shut down the railroad yards, stockyards, packing houses, and factories. On Wednesday, with mobs of strikers and adolescent toughs roving the streets, Mayor Monroe Heath reluctantly called on Hayes for federal troops. Hayes delayed his order until early Thursday morning, perhaps thinking that the two regiments of the Illinois National Guard could keep the peace. That morning, the Chicago police, supported by the militia, repeatedly attacked the rioters as well as innocent bystanders, killing at least eighteen men and boys and wounding many others. By Thursday afternoon, when eight companies of federal troops arrived, they were used to guard property, for the mob had been subdued.[12]

The Workingmen's party played a more important role in St. Louis. A Sunday rally in neighboring East St. Louis, Illinois, was dominated by Workingmen's party speakers and resulted in a decision to strike against six railroads at midnight. Compared with other cities, St. Louis was orderly. The Workingmen's party held well-attended rallies on Monday and Tuesday evenings; at the latter, the leaders warned against violence and called a general strike for an eight-hour workday and against employing children under fourteen. Despite the relative calm, railroad management begged the Hayes administration for federal support. Anticipating trouble, six companies of U.S. infantry arrived in St. Louis under Col. Jefferson C. Davis, who carefully announced that he and his men were there "to protect government and public property," not "to quell the strikers or run the trains." On Wednesday, a crowd of white and black workers shut down factories, but there was no violence and little property damage.

Confronted by an orderly general strike, the St. Louis police did not interfere on Wednesday or on Thursday, when 5,000 men closed down additional factories. The Hayes administration remained aloof, even when a railroad manager wired it: "Stamp out mob now rampant." Clearly enunciating Hayes's policy, Colonel Davis told local authorities that they had to "deal with these difficulties themselves & not call on me for aid until their whole resources are exhausted." On Friday, the St. Louis police and a citizen militia broke up the crowd outside the headquarters of the Workingmen's party. No shots were fired and no stones were thrown, but strike leaders were arrested, ensuring the decline of the strike. The St. Louis experience was unique. Elsewhere, the strike was accompanied by spontaneous, uncontrolled, violent mob action, but there the Marxists organized and controlled a nonviolent strike.[13]

While the strike spread during that hot July week, Hayes and his colleagues refused to panic, despite the widespread cry for volunteers among railroad and business leaders. Actually, many observers commended Hayes's course. "Tell the President," read a blunt telegram to John Sherman from Cincinnati, "a call for volunteers will precipitate a revolution." Charles Nordhoff was "greatly delighted that the President takes so little hand in the riot" and reiterated, "Nothing would be less prudent than any positive action by the Administration, such as calling out volunteers." Speaker of the House Samuel J. Randall, the ranking Democrat in the government, agreed with Nordhoff. When Scott urged Randall to wire Hayes "to call out by proclamation a further force," Randall "abruptly and pointedly" refused.[14]

When Hayes and his cabinet met on Wednesday, 25 July, they did not know that the turning point of the strike had been reached. Railroad managers had insisted that grievances would be discussed only after the men came back to work and the strike had begun to collapse. On that day, the Erie strike ended at Hornellsville, and some New York Central workers at Rochester and Syracuse gave up, although those at Albany and Buffalo held out a bit longer. On the B&O, where it had all started, the freight trains began moving on Friday night, 27 July, and on the Pennsylvania Railroad the first doubleheader out of Pittsburgh left on Sunday, 29 July. Despite pockets of resistance, the strike was over on Monday, 30 July.[15]

Hayes had avoided playing into Tom Scott's hands, but he did not avoid playing into the hands of three antilabor federal judges. U.S. Circuit Court Judge Thomas Drummond of Chicago and U.S. District Court Judges Samuel Hubbel Treat of Springfield, Illinois, and Walter Q. Gresham of Indianapolis held that strikers who had obstructed bankrupt railroads in the custody of federal courts were in contempt of court. Hayes, Evarts, Devens, and the rest of the cabinet accepted the judges' biased reasoning, which identified the courts and the public interest with the labor policies of the receivers or the managers they had appointed. On Thursday, even with abundant signs that the crisis had eased, Hayes decided to send troops to Indiana to help Gresham's marshal keep bankrupt railroads open. Even worse was the administration's decision to urge the policies of Drummond, Treat, and Gresham on federal judges in other strike-bound jurisdictions, including ones in Tennessee, Ohio, and Pennsylvania. Drummond soon became the first federal judge to punish railroad strikers for contempt of court. The federal courts had, in effect, outlawed strikes on bankrupt railroads and set a precedent that had far-reaching effects on organized labor.[16]

Except for embracing the questionable notions of the antilabor judges, Hayes was served well by his legalistic response to the strike. Observing proper procedures meant that federal troops neither provoked nor suppressed rioters. They neither killed nor wounded anyone. By not calling up additional troops and by not operating the railroads under a dubious interpretation of the Commerce Clause, the administration avoided a row over the constitutional powers of the president and avoided a confrontation between strikers and federal forces.

Hayes's moderate course made those who were hostile to labor wish that Grant were back in the White House. Grant was also critical of Hayes, proclaiming that the strike "should have been put down with a strong hand and so summarily as to prevent a like occurrence for a generation." The fashionable preacher, Henry Ward Beecher of Brooklyn, New York, condemned the strikers for "tyrannical opposition to all law and order," jeered at dollar-a-day workers with five children who were not willing to live on bread and water, and proclaimed that God intended "the great to be great and the little to be little" and that the poor must "reap the misfortunes of inferiority."[17]

Beecher may have been fashionable, but on this issue he was in the minority. Believing that the railroads had brought the strike on themselves, most Americans applauded Hayes's moderation. The *Commercial and Financial Chronicle* (New York) criticized Beecher for lacking "either a wise head or a feeling heart," and the New York *World* called his words "suicidal" and "lunatic." *Harper's Monthly* declared that it was the business of the government to prevent future disorders "by removing the discontent which is its cause." In a cabinet discussion on 31 July, Sherman, McCrary, and Evarts favored federal railroad regulation, and Sherman also spoke for it in Ohio.[18]

Since the public tended to blame railroad management for the appalling conditions that had led to the Great Strike, management's victory was illusory. The workers, it appears, gained more than they lost by fighting the wage cuts. Burned by the strike, management improved working conditions; attempted no further wage cuts; and, from October 1877 to early 1880, restored the pay cuts that had precipitated the strike. In addition, railroad managers who were conspicuous during the strike lost prestige. The strike, Nordhoff cheerfully wrote, "finishes Tom Scott, and I shall not be sorry." Indeed, the strike killed Scott's lingering hope for a Texas & Pacific land grant.[19]

After the strike was over, Hayes reacted much as he had a year earlier following the Ohio coal strike: "The strikes have been put down by *force*, but now for the *real* remedy. Cant something [be] done by education of the strikers, by judicious control of the capitalists, by wise general policy to end or diminish the evil? The R.R. strikers, as a rule are good men sober intelligent and industrious."

The administration offered labor sympathy but little of concrete value. Evarts suggested "that an attempt to probe and soothe the labor difficulties by means of a commission . . . would of itself do good and might promise really valuable results." Although Hayes claimed to be willing to do "anything . . . to remove the distress which afflicts laborers" and other members of the administration were aware of "the grievances of the working people," the commission (which Congress would have to fund) did not materialize. When the strike was blamed for the sluggish economy in early August, there was talk of coming to grips with its causes, but when the economy revived, the strike and the plight of labor were all but forgotten. A year later, Hayes met with Labor League president John Pope Hodnett and a hundred of its African American members; with Isaac Cohen, an organizer of black workers in the Workingmen's Relief Association; and with workers from the Washington and Boston navy yards. He promised to look into their grievances, but his inquiries achieved few if any results. Despite his generous impulses, Hayes did not come up with ways to educate strikers or control capitalists and found no wise general policy to diminish the grievances of working people.[20]

During the summer of 1877, Hayes faced serious but more conventional problems along the Mexican border and with the Nez Percé Indian nation. For years, relations with Mexico had been strained by marauders crossing into Texas and rustling the cattle of U.S. ranchers. Political instability made it difficult for Mexico to control its border. Benito Juárez, leader of the liberal anticlerical forces in Mexico, had dominated that country before and after Archduke Maximilian's 1864–67 reign as emperor. When Juárez died in 1872, his successor, Sebastián Lerdo de Tejada, continued his liberal policies. On 20 November 1876, however, two weeks after the Hayes-Tilden election, Porfirio Díaz overthrew Lerdo de Tejada and assumed the office of president on 2 May 1877, two months after Hayes's inauguration. Consolidating his position, Díaz wielded absolute power until he was overthrown in 1911. In 1877, however, Hayes had no idea whether Díaz could prevent border incursions any better than his predecessors had. On 1 June 1877, Hayes ordered Gen. Edward O. C. Ord to keep "lawless bands" from invading the United States, even if his troops had to cross into Mexico to punish offending outlaws. Protesting Hayes's order, the Díaz regime sent troops and a cabinet minister to the border to protect Mexico's sovereignty.

Critics in the United States echoed Díaz's protests. Some speculated that the administration wanted to provoke a war with Mexico so that it could annex several Mexican states and drive from public memory the recent abandonment of Republican regimes in South Carolina and Louisiana. Aggression against Mexico, they maintained, would be another blandishment by the administration for white southern Democrats, who had coveted that territory since the days of James K. Polk. Still smarting because Hayes had ignored his suggestion for the cabinet and unhappy with the administration's southern policy, James G. Blaine attacked its Mexican policy. After noting in a Fourth of July speech the "kindly" assurance "that in no event shall any Mexican territory be acquired or annexed to the United States," Blaine sug-

President Hayes

gested, "as in many cases of similar design and movement, the most important feature may be that which is specially disavowed." The implication that he had lied angered Hayes, who declared, "There is nothing secret or underhand in the Mexican policy." Evarts characteristically quipped that, being habitually truthful, he was able to conceal his diplomatic objectives from those who expected him to be deceptive.[21]

Although Hayes and Evarts were telling the truth, there was some basis for Blaine's speculations. William S. Rosecrans wanted the Hayes administration to play a larger role in Mexican affairs and to "secure for our commercial and manufacturing interests, the lion share of the commerce of ten millions of people." Rosecrans was not only the original colonel of Hayes's Twenty-third Ohio Volunteers; he was also Andrew Johnson's minister to Mexico in 1868 and 1869 and a promoter of mining and railroad interests there. The fact that Rosecrans was a Democrat neither discouraged him nor diminished Hayes's admiration for his old commander. Rosecrans advocated the building of railroads through Mexico's populous and productive "tablelands" and tying these roads into a North American system. He suggested that the best way for Mexico to subsidize the construction "would be to sell to the U.S. the sparsely settled states of Sonora, Chihuahua, Coahuila, Nuevo Leon and Tamaulipas and the Territory of Lower California." Rosecrans recognized that the Mexican constitution's prohibition against the sale or alienation of Mexican soil would have to be amended and that opposition by the Mexican "political class" to "Northern annexation" was "practically a monomania capable of overturning any government not backed by money, power and popularity." Still, he believed that it was the manifest destiny of the United States to consolidate "the family of Western Republics under our leadership."[22]

Rosecrans's ideas combined old territorial ambitions with new economic ones, but they did not determine Hayes's Mexican policy. Although Hayes believed that the annexation of adjacent territory both north and south "seems to be, according to the phrase of 1844, our 'manifest destiny,'" he was "not in favor of artificial stimulants to this tendency." Neither Hayes nor Díaz wished to buy or sell northern Mexico; neither were they willing to go to war over vexing border problems. Hayes told Ord that if Mexican forces opposed his pursuit of cattle thieves, "our troops must retire across the river and report such opposition to the War Department." Despite Díaz's bombastic talk, he agreed to pursue outlaws jointly with Ord, and Ord tried to prevent Mexican revolutionaries from using the United States as a base for raids into Mexico. On 22 July 1877, he arrested Gen. Mariano Escobeda, who was recruiting troops in Texas to overthrow Díaz. After several months, these desultory revolutionary activities ceased to challenge Díaz, whose regime was recognized by the Hayes administration on 23 March 1878. By 24 February 1880, Mexico sufficiently controlled the border for Hayes to revoke the 1 June 1877 order permitting Ord to follow outlaws into Mexico. Many years later, Woodrow Wilson's administration would confront a similar problem with less satisfactory results.[23]

The Nez Percé war, which broke out in June 1877, originated in a classic fashion. The ancient home of the bands that constituted the Nez Percé Indian nation was in the mountainous region surrounding the point where Oregon, Washington, and Idaho meet. The Nez Percés deified their ancestral land ("the Earth is my mother"), and to exchange it for other land was tantamount to renouncing their religion. In 1855, the federal government had guaranteed this area to them, but white intruders discovered gold in the heart of the region in 1860. Those who rushed to mine the gold and stayed to raise cattle and crops paid no heed to the fact that they were trespassers. Abetting covetous settlers were federal Indian agents, who bribed and coerced the chiefs of some Nez Percé bands to agree to an 1863 treaty removing their people to a reservation at Lapwai, Idaho. Other Nez Percé bands refused to agree to the treaty and remained on their land. One of these bands, which was led by Chief Joseph, stayed in the Wallowa Valley of northeastern Oregon and tried to live peaceably with its white neighbors. Many white settlers were fond of Joseph—a feeling that he reciprocated—but others were contemptuous of Indian rights and wanted to force the nontreaty Nez Percés onto the Lapwai Reservation.[24]

By vacillating, the Grant administration exacerbated matters. On 16 June 1873, Grant ordered that Joseph's band be given part of the Wallowa Valley for a reservation, but a vigorous protest by white settlers, the governor, and the Oregon congressional delegation made Grant waver. In June 1875, after the Indian Bureau reexamined the case, he rescinded his earlier order; on 6 January 1877, Grant decided that the 1863 treaty obligated all Nez Percés to move to the Lapwai Reservation. Joseph was frustrated because the whites failed to understand that "the country they claim belonged to my father, and when he died it was given to me and my people." He was determined not to leave it "until I am compelled to."

When Hayes took office in March, he was apparently unaware of the Indian Bureau's policy toward the nontreaty Nez Percés. Schurz, while learning the ropes of his new job, did not interfere with the implementation of decisions made by the previous administration. Joseph and his fellow nontreaty Nez Percé chiefs, Looking Glass and White Bird, still hoped to reason with the Indian Bureau and the U.S. Army, but at a council on 14 May, Gen. Oliver Otis Howard insisted that if the Nez Percés did not move within thirty days, they would be forced off their land. Faced with the option of moving or fighting, Joseph and other nontreaty Nez Percé chiefs agreed to move.[25]

Physically and psychologically, the move was difficult. With not enough time to round up its thousands of cattle and horses, which were scattered throughout the Wallowa Valley, Joseph's band abandoned some of their livestock to the settlers and lost some of it while crossing the swollen Snake River into Idaho. Pushing on to the Salmon River, Joseph's band camped a few miles from the reservation with the other nontreaty Nez Percés on 2 June. Hoping to enjoy their last two weeks of freedom, Joseph and his younger brother Ollokot went hunting.

But the camp smoldered with resentment. A young brave from White Bird's band decided to avenge the murder of his father, which had occurred two years earlier. He and two friends murdered four whites who were known for their hostility to Nez Percés. In the wake of these killings, seventeen warriors (all but one from White Bird's band) joined the avenging braves on a two-day rampage, killing fourteen or fifteen settlers along the Salmon River. When Joseph and Ollokot returned from their hunting trip, they tried to persuade everyone to wait for the army and explain what had happened, hoping to save all but the guilty from punishment.

Joseph's counsel was not heeded. He and Ollokot, along with their people, joined White Bird's band, which was already on the move. The addition of the Wallowa band strengthened those in flight, but Joseph still hoped that Howard would send emissaries and that a war could be averted. Joseph and White Bird moved their bands to a defensible position on White Bird Creek and waited. Unfortunately, Capt. David Perry—in command of the pursuing cavalry and a band of trigger-happy civilian volunteers—sent no emissaries before he attacked at dawn on 17 June 1877 and suffered a disastrous defeat. The outmanned and outgunned Nez Percés killed thirty-four of Perry's command and captured sixty-three rifles and numerous pistols; only three of their own warriors were wounded.

While Howard called for reinforcements and advanced to White Bird Canyon, Joseph withdrew to a new position across the Salmon River. "No general," Howard remarked, "could have chosen a safer position, or one that would be more likely to puzzle and obstruct a pursuing foe." Despite his professional admiration for his adversary, Howard relentlessly pursued the Nez Percés, who were encumbered by their old and infirm, by women and children, and by their possessions and livestock, including 2,500 to 3,500 horses.[26]

By early July, the Nez Percés were outfighting and, despite encumbrances, outmaneuvering the U.S. Army. According to the Associated Press, Hayes and his cabinet considered removing Howard but ultimately left him in command. The elusive Nez Percés had begun their 1,700-mile retreat, seeking safety among the Crows in Montana and, when that failed, with Sitting Bull in the Old Woman's Country—Queen Victoria's Canada. After the annihilation of George A. Custer and his command a year earlier, Sitting Bull and his Sioux had fled to Canada, where they were not welcome but remained for several years. As the Nez Percés retreated, they alarmed Hayes's friend and old political ally Gov. Benjamin F. Potts of Montana, who wanted to raise five hundred volunteers. Having had enough of troublemaking civilian volunteers, the Hayes administration assured him that the army did not need his help.[27]

But Potts's worries and the Nez Percés' plight were not the primary concerns of the administration, which was in the midst of the Great Strike and Mexican border problems. Although he wanted to be just, Hayes seems not to have understood the crux of the problem: that the government was illegally forcing the nontreaty Nez Percés off their land. He noted to Schurz that the Indians should lay down their arms, leave their lands, go to the reservation, "take *separate* titles" to land, and "give up the Murderers." Hayes thought that a commission should determine their guilt or innocence and that those who were found guilty should "be dealt with according to the law applicable to white men." Before the Battle of White Bird, Captain Perry could have secured all these objectives, if he had only asked.[28]

In October, Col. Nelson A. Miles and four hundred men finally cornered the Nez Percés at Bear Paw Mountain in Montana. After a five-day battle in which both sides suffered heavy losses, Howard reinforced Miles. Joseph surrendered with the understanding, agreed to by Miles and Howard, that the prisoners could return to the Northwest. The prisoners included 87 men, 184 women, and 147 children, but more than 200 Nez Percés had escaped to join Sitting Bull in Canada. Joseph, whose clothes were riddled with bullet holes, proudly but not defiantly gave his rifle to Miles and, through an interpreter, addressed his old adversary Howard: "I am tired of fighting. Our chiefs are killed. . . . It is cold, and we have no blankets. The little children are freezing to death. . . . Hear me, my chiefs! I am tired. My heart is sick and sad. From where the sun now stands I will fight no more forever."[29]

The cost of this unjust and needless war was high. The retreating Nez Percés lost sixty-five men and fifty-five women and children; the U.S. Army lost 180 men. The federal government spent $1,873,410 to make dependent, albeit proud, paupers of the once-prosperous Nez Percés. To the dismay of Miles, who to his death remained an advocate of the Nez Percés, Gens. Philip Sheridan and William T. Sherman refused to honor Miles's promise to Joseph; instead, they ordered the Nez Percés to the Indian Territory (present-day Oklahoma). Indeed, Sherman wanted to execute Joseph and the other Nez Percé leaders. In November 1877, Miles appealed to Sheridan to permit him to take a Nez Percé delegation to Washington; Sheridan refused, and General Sherman, Commissioner of Indian Affairs Ezra A. Hayt, Secretary of War McCrary, and Secretary of Interior Schurz backed Sheridan's decision. Accustomed to the cool mountains of the Northwest, the Nez Percés suffered sixty-eight more deaths in the hot southern plains during the first year of their captivity. Although Hayt permitted them to move to a better location on the Ponca Indian Reserve, almost every child born there died.

Eloquent, wise, and humane, Joseph continued to struggle for the rights of the Nez Percés. Although he won the admiration of white Americans, he failed to win justice for his people. In January 1879, he was permitted to travel to Washington, D.C., to plead for permission to return to the Northwest. Although Joseph spoke to a large gathering of distinguished officials, saw Hayes and Schurz, and published a stirring interview in the influential *North American Review*, Miles's pledge to him at Bear Paw Mountain was not honored. Indictments were still out in Idaho for those who had murdered along the Salmon River, and both the War Department and the Interior Department feared trouble if the Nez Percé exiles returned. Two years later, when Miles asked Hayes to let the Nez Percés go back to Idaho, the president turned to Schurz, who advised against it. He feared that "private vengeance," as well as public indictments, would destroy "a large portion of that tribe." In the 1880s, after Hayes had left office, the Nez Percés were finally allowed to return to the Northwest, but most of them, including Joseph, were kept at Colville, Washington. In 1899 and again in 1900, Joseph visited his beloved Wallowa Valley, but the white settlers there refused to sell him even a small piece of the land that had belonged to him and his forebears. Joseph died at Colville in 1904.[30]

The Nez Percé war underscored an Indian policy that was at best inadequate and at worst unconscionable. It also illustrated the need for civil-service reform by exposing the Indian Bureau's failure to implement policy. Had a just, consistent policy been administered by knowledgeable agents, the Nez Percé war would not have happened. John B. Wolff, an ardent advocate for Native Americans, advised Schurz and Hayes that reconstruction of the Indian Bureau on business principles would save ten to fifteen million dol-

lars annually, avert Indian wars, and make most Native Americans self-supporting within five years. Self-sufficiency would eliminate the contractors,
who defrauded both Native Americans and the government. "If the Indians
are dealt by *justly*," Wolff insisted, "they will give us little trouble." But if
treated unjustly, they will "obey the instinct of life and like Joseph . . . refuse
to die like dogs, and so sell their lives for the highest price in other lives."[31]

The Nez Percé war and the arguments of advocates like Wolff led Hayes to
rethink his Indian policy. In his first annual message, he admitted that
"many, if not most, of our Indian wars have had their origin in broken promises and acts of injustice upon our part." He urged Congress to approve
prompt and liberal appropriations to keep the government's promises to aid
Indians on reservations with "cattle and agricultural implements," so that
they could support themselves, and to establish and maintain "schools to
bring them under the control of civilized influences." He requested legislation allowing self-sufficient Indians "who are willing to detach themselves
from their tribal relations" to be "admitted to the benefit of the homestead
act and the privileges of citizenship."

Hayes also supported Schurz's efforts to "purify the Indian service, so that
every dollar appropriated by Congress shall redound to the benefit of the Indians, as intended." Investigations begun while the Nez Percé war was under
way revealed that a ring within the bureau had received gifts from Indian
contractors, who were defrauding both the Native Americans and the government. Bureau head John Q. Smith, an honest man with neither judgment
nor business capacity, had already resigned to take the Montreal consulate,
so when Schurz fired members of the ring, the way was clear to reorganize
the Indian service. Since Ezra A. Hayt, the new head, had consulted with Indian-rights activists and was known as an opponent of frauds in the Indian
Bureau, Hayes felt confident that relations with Native Americans would
improve.[32]

Despite unfair dealings with the Nez Percés, relations with Native Americans had begun to improve under President Grant. Rather than allow western politicians to nominate Indian agents (as part of their spoils of office),
Grant had relied on Protestant clergymen for advice in making these appointments. This practice may have been unconstitutional and certainly discriminated against Roman Catholics, but it did secure better agents. Hayes
followed Grant's example but did not relinquish his appointing power.
When the Red Cloud Agency suddenly became vacant, Hayes wrote to Rev.
Robert C. Rogers of the New York Bible House that, since the agency was in
a critical condition, "It is my desire to appoint Dr McGillicuddy, lately connected with the army as a surgeon, who has Indian experience and is well ac-

quainted with the Red Cloud Sioux. No delay being admissible I should be glad to appoint him with your assent."[33]

Having learned from the Nez Percé war, Hayes took pains to avoid further conflicts with Native Americans. "Always," he noted, "the Numbers and prowess of the Indians have been underrated." He avoided high-handed acts. When Jay Gould and the Union Pacific Railroad lobbied extensively to build the Oregon and Utah Railroad through the Fort Hall Reservation, the administration refused to permit the railroad's construction unless the Indians approved. Hayes also restrained white settlers to preserve peace. In December 1878, the army prevented civilian volunteers from attacking Chief Moses and his band for refusing to move to a reservation in the Washington Territory. With some of his people, Moses journeyed to Washington, D.C., and negotiated with Schurz. On 18 April, Hayes "by Executive Order set aside a very large reservation in the Northern parts of Washington Territory" for Moses and his band. "We are friendly toward you," Hayes said, "and want to deal with you with exact justice." The administration also frustrated the governor and citizens of Colorado when it prevented the 1879 "White River massacre" by Utes from escalating into a war.

Hayes restrained the army as well. In January 1879, some Sioux followers of Sitting Bull began to straggle back to the United States from Canada, where they had fled after annihilating Custer and his men. Hayes neither sought to punish them nor regarded them as hostile as long as they remained peaceful. Although Miles reported in July that they were "very demonstrative, and were being reinforced by other straggling bands," Hayes insisted that he "be very careful in his movements, and do everything to avoid a conflict."[34]

Determined to make the administration's policy flexible and perceptive, Hayes recognized that the realities of reservation life demanded local police officers. That important innovation occurred in 1878, when, following recommendations by Hayt and Schurz, Congress appropriated funds to appoint Native American police. Before that date, agents had relied on the army to combat serious crime. In 1883, after Hayes left office, the policy was expanded to include the appointment of Native American judges. By mixing Anglo-Saxon jurisprudence with Indian customs, policemen and judges were able to keep order on the reservations and proved to be effective agents of acculturation. E. M. Marble, who succeeded Hayt as commissioner of Indian affairs, declared that the appointment of Indian police, "at first undertaken as an experiment, is now looked upon as a necessity."[35]

Matters pertaining to Native Americans (who tended to live in remote areas) were among the most difficult tasks confronting Hayes. Friction abounded — between whites and Indians; between easterners, who championed Indian rights, and westerners, who ignored them; and between the Interior and the War Departments. Although the Indian Bureau was lodged in the Interior Department, the army often had to enforce decisions affecting Native Americans (despite the presence of Indian police).

A persistent problem was the encroachment of settlers into the Indian Territory (present-day Oklahoma). In late April 1879, Hayes proclaimed that anyone who attempted to settle in the Indian Territory would be expelled. Those holding "genuine permits from the Cherokee Nation for *grazing purposes* only" could stay, but the army was to clear from Cherokee lands the illegal, "evil-disposed" settlers (who often claimed to be either half-breed Cherokees or citizens of the Cherokee nation). Despite this proclamation, intruders persisted, and there were false reports that Hayes had changed his mind. This led him to reissue his proclamation on 12 February 1880, reiterating his determination to prevent incursions. When "Capt." David L. Payne, the most persistent intruder, again led settlers into the Indian Territory, Hayes insisted on prosecuting him. In the long run, however, the trespassers were victorious. When Congress opened the Indian Territory to settlement in 1889, these intruders were already occupying choice land.[36]

The presidency was hard and, at times, disheartening work. Shaping southern and civil-service policies, responding to labor and Indian troubles, absorbing hostile criticism, and coping with "official annoyances" could be debilitating and demoralizing. Hayes was buoyed by his loving family, interesting visitors, diverting entertainment, and refreshing travels. Reflecting Lucy's spirit, the Hayes White House was lively and informal, and Hayes was proud of its atmosphere.

Music was especially stressed. A superb contralto, Lucy enjoyed singing folk and gospel songs and loved to hear talented musicians. She often invited vocalists and instrumentalists to perform popular and classical music at the White House for friends and political associates and also gave informal receptions for these artists. When the Hutchinson family entertained the Hayeses with songs, including "Grandfather's Clock," in the Red Parlor, little Fanny amused those present by singing "There Was a Little Kitten." Marie Selika, "the celebrated colored prima donna," sang a varied program of arias and songs with "remarkable power, sweetness, and versatility" in the Green Room. On Sunday evenings, Lucy led a "sing" in the upstairs library, with Schurz or the children's governess at the piano. Friends from Ohio and members of the administration and Congress — including Vice President

A hymn sing at the White House: Carl Schurz at the piano, Lucy and Scott Hayes in the foreground, and in the background Vice President William A. Wheeler with his hand on Hayes's chair and John Sherman sharing a hymnal with Fanny Hayes. The young woman leaning on the piano is probably Emily Platt. (*Frank Leslie's Illustrated Newspaper*, 3 April 1880)

Wheeler with his "sweet, clear voice" and even General Sherman—gathered to sing gospel songs. Responding to Lucy's love of music, a quartet sang on 26 October 1877 to inaugurate service on the new telephone line connecting the White House and the Treasury Department. But when Lucy requested that they sing louder, the concert abruptly ended: With his powerful bass voice, W. A. Widney struck high C in the final bar of "The Grave Digger," smashing "to atoms" the "sounding board of the telephone."[37]

Arriving in a steady stream, visitors encouraged, informed, amused, and pestered Hayes. Clara Barton told him of her plans to mitigate the cruelties of war, and he urged Evarts to "give her a hearing and such encouragement and aid as may be deemed by you fit." But Evarts opposed ratification of the 1864 Geneva Convention, postponing the establishment of the American Red Cross until 1881, during the next administration. Another visitor brought to Hayes's attention a new "ink for cancelling stamps, and also a process for making stamps intended to prevent the frauds now practiced," which prompted Hayes to ask Key to investigate. Many crackpot inventors called, but on the evening that the Hutchinson family sang, Hayes managed to get the genuine article. At 11 P.M., after Lucy, her guests, and the children had retired, Hayes contacted Thomas A. Edison, who was in town demonstrating his phonograph, and asked him to bring his new invention to the White House. When he arrived, Edison found "Hayes and several others waiting, among them . . . Carl Schurz who was playing the piano. . . . The exhibition continued till about 12:30 A.M., when Mrs. Hayes and several other ladies who had been induced to get up and dress, appeared." It was 3:30 that morning before Edison left the White House.[38]

There were also annoyances. When Marian Neil—the daughter of an old Cincinnati friend and the wife of Col. John B. Neil, Hayes's private secretary during his second term as governor—called, a delighted Hayes greeted her with a kiss. She was in town with her husband, the assistant postmaster in Salt Lake City, who sought a consulship in France. His quest was aided by Lycurgus Edgerton, who wanted Neil to sell Utah mining stock abroad. When Neil did not get a consulate, Edgerton was enraged and threatened to expose Hayes for his broken promises to Neil and for his gross insult to Marian. Insisting that "there was no offense," Hayes would not be blackmailed, and John and Marian Neil apologized profusely for Edgerton's behavior. No one took the publicity seriously, but John Herron could not resist teasing Hayes about "the various naughty things that you have been doing." Neil was especially disturbed, since Hayes had told him that he would favorably consider him for any suitable vacant position in Utah, and he had already applied for appointment as receiver in the Salt Lake City land office. Although the appointment was delayed, Neil received it, and in July 1880, Hayes appointed him governor of the Territory of Idaho.[39]

Hayes traveled to renew his spirits as well as to attract support for his policies. When his friend Murat Halstead of the Cincinnati *Commercial* criticized his trips, Hayes responded: "You have no idea how much they are needed. Eight months of wearying worry over details is enough to kill a strong man. Every month a man in this place ought to shake off its oppression. Nothing does it better than a 'popular bath,' a 'junketing,' or a journey." Hayes frequently got out of town for ceremonial purposes. From 21 to 24 December 1877, he and Lucy enjoyed "a most happy" visit to New York, where he helped open the American Museum of Natural History (which he had previewed in May), attended a Union League reception, and dined with the New England Society, where he and George William Curtis conversed briefly on civil-service reform. In April 1878, the president was in Chester, Pennsylvania, for the launching of a steamship and enjoyed the colorful scene and the cheering crowd. After the launch, he was "crowded into the loft of one of the shipyard buildings to dine," and while "holding a piece of cake in his left hand," he shook hands "with the crowd who surged around him, eager for a grasp." Two months later, in June 1878, Hayes and Lucy sailed up the Hudson for a lovely visit to West Point. A week later, they were delighted to go down the Potomac to Mount Vernon, sleep in Lafayette's room, and, as did George and Martha Washington, go to Pohick Church.[40]

After their New York trip — opening the Museum of Natural History and hobnobbing with supporters — Hayes and Lucy returned to Washington to celebrate Christmas in the White House. There, they found that the "presents to the children made them and their parents equally happy." But the high point of the holiday season — indeed, the social event of Hayes and Lucy's four years in the White House — occurred on 30 December 1877. Surrounded by close relatives and friends — including the Platts, Herrons, Forces, and Davises — and White House staff members, Hayes and Lucy celebrated their twenty-fifth anniversary by repeating their wedding vows in the Blue Room. Dr. L. D. McCabe again conducted the ceremony. Lucy was "as merry as a girl" in her "quaint," twenty-five-year-old wedding dress, and Laura Platt Mitchell once again held Lucy's hand during the ceremony. Fanny and Scott were also christened, along with Lucy's new namesake Lucy Hayes Herron. Manning Force read letters and poems from friends, and presents were received. The celebration was marred only by the absence of Lucy's brother Joe, who remained angry because Hayes would not relax his ban on nepotism and give him an appointment.[41]

With the New Year's reception at the White House, the Washington social season was in full swing. Lucy, who was primarily responsible for social events in the White House, asked Harriet Herron, Eliza Davis, Frances Force, and Laura Mitchell to assist her. The reception started at 11 A.M. with the arrival of the cabinet and foreign ministers and continued at 11:30 with the arrival of judges, senators, and congressmen. Army and navy officers arrived at noon, heads of bureaus at 12:30, and veterans' groups at 12:45. From 1 to 2 P.M., the gates were thrown open for all citizens to attend.

On Tuesday evening, 15 January, the Hayeses gave their first formal levee, which the friendly press characterized as "a grand success." It was not quite as large as those in the early days of the Grant administration, and — perhaps reflecting Lucy's preference for modesty — low-cut and short-sleeved gowns "were the exception rather than the rule." In her own dress, Lucy combined simplicity with elegance. At the Hayes's second levee on 5 February, she wore "a rich garnet velvet dress, trimmed with silk of the same color. At her throat a bunch of pink roses nestled among the folds of the white *crepe lisse*." Although Lucy preferred more informal gatherings, presidential levees were among the most fascinating scenes available in America and, as one woman remarked, "as good as a trip abroad, for among the gay throng were to be seen representatives of every nationality."[42]

The Hayes White House was western in its friendliness, good humor, openness, and unpretentiousness. It could hardly be pretentious with Stanley Matthews's wife Mary Ann regaling Washington society with tales of White House rats so numerous as to scamper over the presidential bed and so bold as to nibble on the presidential toes. Unfazed by rats, Hayes and Lucy remained unflappable. Clover Adams (who was as snobbish and cultivated as her historian husband Henry) was pleased in November 1877 to be "very simply and graciously" received by Lucy. "She is quite nice looking," Clover reported, "dark with smooth black hair combed low over her ears and a high comb behind—her dress a plain untrimmed black silk, a broad white Smyrna lace tie round her neck—no jewelry." But Clover described Hayes as "the same Ohio type as Garfield and Stanley Matthews—stout, sandy hair, ordinary and very complacent. Mr. Hayes looks amiable and respectable—not a ray of force or intellect in forehead, eye or mouth."[43]

Lucy inaugurated "informal" Saturday afternoon (3 to 5 P.M.) receptions on 5 January 1878, with all in attendance "on an equal footing, the ladies generally appearing in street costume and always retaining their bonnets." To lift her spirits, help her entertain, and put guests at ease, she invited young relatives and friends from Ohio to the White House. Hayes's comrade in arms Russell Hastings was so charmed by one of these helpers—Hayes's niece Emily Platt—that he married her, lending credence to the accusation by the "old cats" of Washington society that Lucy was "marrying off her young lady guests during this administration." To her friend Wheeler, Lucy protested, "I am getting too much credit in the Match making business which don't suit me," but Hastings fondly recalled that "all through the winter" Lucy "kept the house filled with young people and fun and frolic reigned all day and well into the night." During winter evenings, Lucy "was always at home to her near friends who were living in Washington or were visiting the city for a few days." Hastings came often with the McKinleys and remembered that "the family usually went from the dinner table directly to the Red Parlor"; Lucy, "with her young lady guests grouped about her, seemed as queenly as any woman who ever wore a crown."

Lucy may have looked like a queen to Hastings, but she was neither haughty nor remote, and her warmth made the Red Parlor appealing. The New York *Graphic*'s correspondent observed: "She is so vivacious and so re-

Lucy Hayes in the stunning cream and gold dress she wore at the state dinner for the grand dukes of Russia

sponsive that everybody leaves her presence with a vague idea that he is the one person whom she was longing to see. . . . She is one of the most sympathetic of conversationalists; . . . is rather serious and reserved and an eloquent listener, but she manages to speak the right word at the right moment, and make everybody else do the same."

Hayes sometimes "graced" the Red Parlor, "but his official duties more frequently called him to the Cabinet room." In any event, Lucy's warmth and sympathetic ear were always available to him, and Hayes, who early in his administration was constantly attacked in and out of his party, was strengthened.[44]

TWENTY

CONGRESS TRIUMPHANT

After enjoying adulation while touring the South in September 1877, Hayes returned to Washington to confront the hostility of New York politicians. On 26 September, with naval officer Alonzo Cornell of the customhouse and other officeholders in attendance, Roscoe Conkling launched a counterattack at the state Republican convention in Rochester. Congressman Thomas C. Platt, whom Hayes had refused to appoint postmaster general, made a "violent and abusive attack" on the administration; the convention platform, which Conkling wrote, ignored the Hayes administration while piously calling for an ideal civil service. George William Curtis tried to amend the platform with a resolution commending Hayes for his efforts to pacify the South and to correct "evils and abuses in the Civil Service."[1]

Conkling responded vehemently. He insisted that New York Republicans had the right to criticize Hayes, and he vilified reformers in general and Curtis in particular as "man-milliners, the dilettanti and carpet knights of politics," who "forget that parties are not built up by deportment, or by ladies' magazines, or gush." In conclusion, Conkling sneered: "When Dr. Johnson defined patriotism as the last refuge of a scoundrel, he was unconscious of the then undeveloped capabilities and uses of the word reform."[2]

Conkling's speech made a profound impression on all present. "Had all the Gall & bitterness of Tophet been breathed into Conkling," a delegate remarked, "he could not have shown more than he did, toward Curtis & Hayes." Although Conkling's followers loved his performance, his enemies knew that he had "put himself frankly at the head of the malcontents" and would lose in the long run. William Henry Smith believed that Conkling's vituperative hostility had played into Hayes's hands and wondered, "Was there ever as lucky a fellow as Hayes?"[3]

Although Conkling's bombast stiffened Hayes's resolve to defeat him and to improve the civil service, it was a portent of what Hayes could expect from Congress. By gratifying the reformers, he had offended the organization men in his party (they blamed losses in the October election in Ohio on his civil-service order); by conciliating southern Democrats but not converting them, he had alienated many Republicans.[4]

Because Congress had adjourned in March without appropriating funds for the army, Hayes called the Forty-fifth Congress for a special session beginning 15 October 1877. Hoping to give Republicans who were opposed to his southern policy time to calm down and southern Democrats time to align themselves with his administration, he had postponed the special session as long as possible. But the Republicans proved to be more divided than the Democrats, who reelected Samuel J. Randall Speaker of the House. Although Garfield had received every Republican vote cast, five protectionist and inflationist Republican congressmen from Pennsylvania had abstained from voting. Furthermore, although the much-needed army appropriation passed, congressional Democrats united to oppose political equality for African Americans. Aiming to cripple the Reconstruction amendments, the Democrats tried to prevent the president's use of the army as a "*posse comitatus*," but the Republicans salvaged its use when "expressly authorized by the Constitution."[5]

Hayes's main struggle in the fall of 1877, however, was with Conkling over the New York customhouse. In place of Arthur, Cornell, and surveyor George H. Sharpe, Hayes named politicians favored by Evarts rather than nonpartisan civil-service reformers. For collector, he nominated Theodore Roosevelt, Sr.; for naval officer, L. Bradford Prince; and for surveyor, Edwin A. Merritt. Although Roosevelt was acceptable to reformers, Merritt had been a political lieutenant of Reuben E. Fenton, whom Conkling in 1870 had displaced as the head of New York Republicans, and Prince had allegedly received financial help from New York City's notorious Tweed ring. Nevertheless, reformers acquiesced in their nominations. Curtis realized that Hayes's position was "very difficult," that he could not "do all that he would," and that there "must be many inconsistencies and many mistakes." But, he told Silas W. Burt, a civil-service reformer employed in the customhouse, "I think that we should not despair so long as the general tendencies of the administration are right."[6]

The nominations were in immediate trouble. Conkling chaired the Senate Committee on Commerce to which they were referred, and Hayes's relations with Congress were at a low point. Although Garfield thought that "the atmosphere of praise" in which a president lives had "partially blinded" Hayes "to the dangers and criticisms of his course," John Sherman, his liaison with Congress, told Hayes the sober truth. There was, Sherman detailed, "a very decided opposition to the Administration in both Houses of Congress, among the Republican members." Specifically, they objected to Evarts,

Schurz, and Key in the cabinet, to making the civil service nonpartisan, to the pacification of the South, and, most bitterly, to any attempt to "deprive Congressmen of all control and share of the patronage of the Government." Although his equanimity was disturbed, Hayes believed that "a large majority of the best people are in full accord with me." He resolved "to keep cool—to treat all adversaries considerately respectfully and kindly but . . . to satisfy them of my sincerity and firmness."[7]

On 15 November, Conkling, as chairman of the Commerce Committee, asked Sherman to explain why customhouse changes were necessary. Sherman's reply stressed that collector Arthur's opposition to the program contemplated by the administration following its receipt of the Jay Commission reports necessitated his removal. On 23 November, Arthur (who, although a spoilsman, was a reasonably effective collector and was popular with New York businessmen) attacked the Jay Commission as "partial and one-sided." He claimed that its charges were based on hearsay, "misstatements," and "misrepresentation" and that he had practiced civil-service reform by removing workers only for cause and by promoting efficient workers. Jay answered him by illustrating "the character & extent of the abuses & the corruption" in the customhouse with quotations not only from him but also from Cornell and Sharpe.[8]

On 30 November 1877, Conkling won his first victory; the Commerce Committee unanimously voted, with three Democratic abstentions, to reject Hayes's nominations. "The political situation seems extremely confused," Schurz observed. "The struggle for mastery in the Senate has re-inflamed party feeling to such an extent that men, who some time ago talked and acted very sensibly, are entirely off their balance." Although Schurz claimed that the administration took "things with great coolness," Hayes and his colleagues appeared to be in disarray. Tilden's observation on 4 November— that "this administration will be the greatest failure the Country ever saw"— was extreme, but reformers were disheartened. In late October, Attorney General Devens had explained to officeholders that although Hayes's order forbade them to take "part in the management of political organizations, caucuses, conventions, or election campaigns," they were allowed "to express their views on public questions either orally or through the press." In short, they could campaign if it did not interfere with the performance of their duties. This explanation had been provoked by collector Simmons of Boston, whose strict obedience to Hayes's order was keeping his customhouse personnel out of the 1877 Massachusetts campaign. The administration was eager for the reelection of Gov. Alexander H. Rice, who had been nominated by a convention that "cordially endorsed" Hayes. To win, Rice needed help from the customhouse. With it, Rice triumphed and Hayes rejoiced, but reformers were unhappy with his administration's drift away from reform.[9]

Hayes's struggle to regain control of the nominating power appeared ludicrous when Secretary of State Evarts (who could not "hold his tongue") asked the Pennsylvania and Illinois congressional delegations to nominate ministers to Great Britain and Germany. Pennsylvania named Simon Cameron, its venerable spoilsman boss, and Illinois suggested Robert G. Ingersoll, who had heralded James G. Blaine as a plumed knight. Since both suggestions were unacceptable to Hayes, Evarts's poor judgment disappointed spoilsmen and peeved reformers. Offering Arthur the Paris consulate to seduce him out of the customhouse further eroded the administration's reform position.[10]

Hayes's first annual message, forwarded to Congress on 3 December 1877—the first day of its regular session—issued a low-key call for civil-service reform. Hayes stressed that the executive should control appointments, pledged that he would cooperate with Congress in systematizing subordinate appointments, and requested an appropriation for the Civil Service Commission, which had been languishing since 1875 without funds. Hayes's friend Dickson, however, again warned him that "we must . . . have rotation in office & appointments on political considerations." Sensing that "the party don't want to be troubled about personal matters," Dickson had no sympathy for either Conkling or Evarts and told Hayes that he should make them "settle their strife or go out like Burr & Hamilton & settle one of them."[11]

For Hayes, it was not a personal matter between rival politicians but a constitutional issue—the "Senatorial usurpation" of the president's power to appoint—and he resubmitted his New York nominations. He believed that "the claim of a single Senator to control all nominations in his State" was "preposterous" and would "fall of its own weight," and that its fall would be "the first and most important step" in reforming the civil service. Hayes wondered whether he "should not insist that all who receive important places . . . be on the right side of this vital question." Admitting that achieving a nonpartisan civil service by using partisan methods was "rather radical," he decided not to do so unless "the war goes on."[12]

Initially, Conkling defended Arthur and Cornell before the Senate on the plausible grounds that their four-year terms had not expired and that they did not merit dismissal. But on 12 December 1877, when the crucial vote was taken in executive session, Conkling called the nominations an attack on "the courtesy of the Senate" and "an attempt to degrade him personally." Because Sharpe's term had expired, the Senate approved Merritt as surveyor, but it rejected both Roosevelt and Prince. Only six Republicans—two of them from Massachusetts—joined with nineteen Democrats to support the president; twenty-eight Republicans and three Democrats sided with Conkling. "The Senate," lamented Evarts's friend Richard Henry Dana, Jr., "is the citadel of the Spoils System."[13]

Discouraged reformers blamed Hayes for Conkling's victory. If Hayes's "hands were clean," said Horace White, Conkling would have been defeated. From Massachusetts, Hayes's friend Edward L. Pierce wrote: "The *natural* friends of the administration are lukewarm, and the defeat of Roosevelt has added discouragement to discontent. Some things have gone wrong in Civil Service." Despite his closeness to Hayes, Curtis claimed in *Harper's Weekly* that Conkling had defeated the administration "with weapons which its own inconsistency had furnished." "We are somewhat adrift," Henry Cabot Lodge complained, "as to what civil service reform means in the Presidential mind & the reform element is sadly dispirited."[14]

This defeat hammered home to Hayes how hard it was to wrest control of appointments from Congress. He became more aware of how dependent he was on others for guidance, how undependable and self-serving political allies could be, and how quickly reformers could lose confidence in him after losing a battle. "No one can know the difficulties and obstacles in the way who has not been in this place," Hayes told Pierce. "Mere lack of time to give due consideration to the duty in hand—the variety of things claiming attention—the thoughtlessness of friends—the falsehoods I hear from men apparently trustworthy &c &c &c."

Like subsequent historians and many of his contemporaries, Hayes used the metaphor of war in conceptualizing his struggle with Conkling and his fellow spoilsmen. For Hayes, that imagery was a source of strength. A seasoned, determined campaigner who was not given to quick decisions but was unshakable once his mind was made up, Hayes was confident that he would prevail. Recognizing that Conkling "was talented and able," Hayes was also aware that his judgment was warped by "inordinate egotism and self-will" and knew that "if he could not rule, he would not 'play.'" Conkling, Hayes perceived, based his power not on measures or issues but on "his manipulation of men and patronage" and on his "impressive presence and manner." For the present, Hayes realized that a fresh assault would fail because "the friends of a real reform are a minority," but he would bide his time. In his diary entry of 13 December 1877, he observed: "In the language of the press 'Senator Conkling has won a great victory over the Administration.' . . . But the end is not yet. I am right, and shall not give up the contest."[15]

Congress also disagreed with Hayes on the currency question. After taking office, he and Sherman, who had written the Resumption Act, began to build a gold reserve to meet the demands of 1 January 1879, when greenbacks would be redeemed in gold, and to reduce the interest payments on the federal debt. In July 1877, Sherman arranged for a $77 million bond sale at 4 percent interest, using some of the funds to retire 6 percent bonds and the rest as a gold reserve for the resumption of specie payments. After July, the Great Strike and silver agitation undermined fiscal confidence, and few government bonds were sold during the remainder of the year. Suffering from depression and deflation, the West and the South pressed for the repeal of the Resumption Act and for the unlimited coinage of silver at a sixteen-to-one ratio with gold. By the summer of 1877, Ohio and Pennsylvania Republicans joined with southern Democrats and western Republicans to demand free silver. There was even a rumor in Washington that Hayes would sign a silver-coinage bill.[16]

During the special session of the Forty-fifth Congress, the House considered the questions of silver and resumption. On 5 November, it overwhelmingly passed (164 to 34) a silver bill presented by Democrat Richard P. ("Silver Dick") Bland of Missouri. Bland's bill, which the free-silver plank of the 1896 Democratic platform later reiterated, called for the unlimited coinage of the old standard silver dollar of 412.5 troy grains. Given the temper of the times, it was not surprising that the silver bill passed the House; that it passed by such a wide margin and without debate was noteworthy, as were the bill's adherents. Among them were Ohio Republicans Charles Foster, who was Hayes's own congressman; Jacob Dolson Cox, a hero of civil-service reformers, most of whom supported hard money; and William McKinley, who in 1896 would be the champion of the gold standard.[17]

Because of delays in the Senate, Hayes did not have to veto an inflationary bill during the special session. On 21 November, Iowa Republican William B. Allison, from the Senate Committee on Finance, reported an amended silver bill requiring that from two to four million silver dollars must be coined monthly, leaving the precise number to the discretion of the treasury secretary. The Senate failed to act on this limited silver-coinage bill before the close of the special session. The House had also voted (133 to 120) to repeal the Resumption Act of 1875, but the Republican-controlled Senate ignored that inflationary measure.[18]

Hayes's first annual message expressed his hostility to inflation, whether it was achieved by printing greenbacks or by coining silver. Although he was a wealthy debtor who would have been enriched by inflation, the currency question was one of honesty, not one of expediency for him or the government (with its Civil War debt). He perceived that "the rich, the speculative, the operating, the money-dealing classes" profited from "a variable currency," while wage earners suffered. Indeed, inflation involved both moral imperatives and economic verities. The speedy resumption of specie payments for greenbacks—the return to the gold standard—Hayes argued, was a fiscal necessity, demanded by fundamental economic law. Even though resumption might bring difficulty and distress to some citizens, it would facilitate commerce, provide fiscal stability, promote public confidence, and revive the economy. If the nation retained an irredeemable paper currency, he insisted, the current depression would end in "disorder, dishonor, and disaster."

Hayes did not object to coining silver, as long as its ratio to gold reflected its commercial value and it did not cause inflation. He further emphasized that because market fluctuations made an absolute equality of the intrinsic value of gold and silver coins unattainable, silver coinage should be limited. The $2 billion public debt, Hayes asserted, should be paid not in inflated paper or silver dollars but in gold or its equivalent. To place this debt in perspective, the nation's income for the year ending 30 June 1877 was $269 million, and its expenditures were $239 million, leaving a $30 million surplus for the sinking fund to retire the debt. "You have staid the onward march of repudiation," his friend W. M. Dickson exclaimed, and "steadied the exchanges round the world." But Hayes's unyielding stands on specie resumption and silver coinage pleased only New York and New England and had little effect on Congress.[19]

The question of remonetizing silver troubled Hayes. Soon after Congress received his annual message, his friend Sen. Stanley Matthews spread "uneasiness" in financial circles and among bondholders as far away as London by proposing that the federal debt be repaid in silver. Members of Congress were determined to respond to their constituents' demands rather than to the falling prices of U.S. bonds. By February, it was clear that although the "unlimited silver people" could not muster up a two-thirds majority to override a veto, a bill with Allison's amendment providing for the limited coinage of silver would pass, despite a veto. To "avoid injury to the public credit," many opponents of inflation were prepared to compromise and minimize the amount of silver coined.[20]

Hayes, however, remained firm on the silver question. "It is now almost a certainty that the Silver bill will pass in such shape that I must withhold my signature," he wrote on 3 February. Insisting that he would veto any "measure which stains our credit," he added, "We must keep that untainted. We are a debtor nation. Low rates of interest on the vast indebtedness we must carry for many years is the important end to be kept in view. Expediency and justice both demand honest coinage." Hard-money men argued that in the United States, with its large public debt, the interest rates yielded by government bonds were bound to regulate other interest rates. The 1875 Specie Resumption Act had caused interest rates to fall because it had given investors confidence that the nation was rebuilding its depressed economy on the "bed-rock" of gold. Consequently, hard-money men argued that even the limited coinage of silver would undermine the public credit, raise interest rates, and hurt debtors.[21]

On 15 February, the Senate passed the Bland bill with Allison's amendments, limiting the coinage of silver to between $2 and $4 million a month. The Senate also called for an international bimetal convention. As expected, on 21 February, the House accepted the bill as amended by the Senate. Hardcore opposition in both houses centered on the northeastern seaboard. Most senators representing the remainder of the country accepted a limited quantity of silver dollars.

Despite the Bland-Allison bill's limit on silver dollars, Hayes resolved to veto it. Murat Halstead warned him that a successful veto would protract "dissension about dollars" and lead to economic and political disaster. "Business will perish," Halstead prophesied, and "the second Congress of your administration will be worse than the first." Halstead's views were backed by Cincinnati's leading bankers and businessmen, but Hayes was unmoved. On 26 February, he sought his cabinet's reaction to his veto message. Schurz, Devens, and Key wanted the bill vetoed; Sherman and McCrary supported a veto but equivocated. Sherman was fearful of its consequences and quoted August Belmont, a prominent New York banker and Democratic politician, who considered the bill "*bad*" but wanted it approved. McCrary hoped that the bill would pass over a veto, since he feared, like Halstead, that a successful veto would bring the Democrats into power. In contrast, Navy Secretary Thompson opposed the veto on both policy and constitutional grounds. He believed that the bill was wise and noted that it was supported almost unanimously by the people and had been passed by more than two-thirds of both houses of Congress. Acknowledging that he was an old Whig and testifying that the old Whig doctrine was sound, Thompson emphasized that the veto was to be used not for policy or for expediency but for "a violation of the Constitution, or haste or mistake."

Hayes countered Thompson by insisting that his veto was based on principle not policy. "The faith of the nation was to be violated—the obligation of contracts was impaired by the law." Thompson lectured Hayes that the Constitution denied states, but not Congress, the right to impair contracts; he further insisted "that no obligation was in fact impaired—that contracts were made in view of the right of Congress to alter legal tender." Evarts rescued Hayes by repudiating the old Whig doctrine, arguing that the president did more than merely execute the laws; the Constitution made the president "part of the Law making power," and it was within his rights to veto constitutional measures that he did not approve of.[22]

Hayes vetoed the Bland-Allison bill on 28 February. He emphasized that it impaired both public and private contract obligations and would injure the public credit. He argued that the intrinsic worth of a 412.5-grain silver dollar was only ninety to ninety-two cents in gold, yet the Bland-Allison bill made it legal tender for existing debts. Hayes doubted that the silver dollars authorized by the bill would be as valuable as gold dollars and concluded: "A currency worth less than it purports to be worth will in the end defraud not only creditors, but all who are engaged in legitimate business, and none more surely than those who are dependent on their daily labor for their daily bread."[23]

Not sharing Hayes's moral perceptions and more sensitive to political realities, Congress quickly overrode his veto, making the Bland-Allison bill law. The backbone of the president's support came from the Northeast (Blaine and Conkling both agreed with him), where creditors had political clout and numerous national banks provided adequate currency and moderate interest rates. Further west, Garfield opposed the bill, but other Ohioans deserted Hayes. In the Senate, Stanley Matthews conspicuously supported the bill, and Jacob Dolson Cox, Charles Foster, J. Warren Keifer, and William McKinley joined the overwhelming majority in the House to override the veto.

But Hayes did not let a political setback—even on an issue he defined in moral terms—undermine his personal relations. That evening, the Fosters, along with Albert Bierstadt (whose scenic western paintings Hayes had long admired), attended a congenial state dinner, with Speaker Randall as guest of honor and key southern Democrats in attendance. Still believing that the Bland-Allison Act authorized "what . . . is dishonest," Hayes resolved to minimize its effect by coining only the $2 million monthly minimum and by keeping those silver dollars equal in value to gold dollars. Trusting "that in fact no actual dishonesty will be permitted under it," Hayes concluded that there were political advantages in the way things had worked out and optimistically looked to the future. "The veto and the passage of the silver bill over it will I hope leave us more united," he wrote to Gov. Benjamin F. Prescott of New Hampshire. "The money questions of the future—and I look for enough of them speedily, will find Republicans more united—far more—than they were on the silver bill."[24]

The main money question Hayes referred to was specie resumption—the return to the gold standard by redeeming greenbacks at face value in gold, even though they had been issued during the Civil War as fiat money. In the spring of 1878, he and Sherman prepared for resumption and attempted to conciliate the moderate soft-money men. In fact, many moderates, including Jacob Dolson Cox and Murat Halstead, had supported the Bland-Allison Act to prevent the repeal of the Resumption Act of 1875. A move to repeal it had gathered impressive support in late 1877, but the Bland bill had shouldered repeal aside in January and February of 1878. After the passage of the Bland-Allison Act and intense lobbying by Sherman, who brought home what Hayes called the "*truth*," several inflation-minded senators and representatives who had wished to repeal the Resumption Act were willing to wait until they had monitored the effects of the Bland-Allison Act.

With his plans to secure an adequate supply of gold, Sherman managed to reassure dubious congressmen that the return to specie payments was feasible. In April, he negotiated a loan at 4.5 percent with an international syndicate of bankers for $50 million in European gold to augment the $70 million in gold already in the U.S. Treasury. News of this contract virtually wiped out the premium on gold, and Hayes rejoiced that resumption of payments in specie seemed secure. To make it certain, the president, displaying his pragmatic streak, agreed to a bargain; this may have been his method of conveying the "*truth*" to the moderate soft-money men. He would approve a bill to retain the $346 million in greenbacks in circulation—repealing the part of the 1875 Resumption Act that would reduce them to $300 million by January 1879—if the inflationists would stop agitating for the repeal of resumption.[25]

Shortly after Hayes went down to self-righteous defeat over the Bland-Allison Act, he reflected on his first year in office. He admitted that misrepresentations had led him to make "serious mistakes, mainly in appointments," but he believed that his policies were "right" and that he had "been firm and self possessed on the most difficult and trying occasions." He realized that as "a non partisan President" he would "be feebly supported, if at all, in Congress or by the Press," but he was "content to abide the judgment—the sober second thought of the people," and he was certain that his administration had already strengthened the Republican party. "We are in a period when old questions are settled, and the new are not yet brought forward. Extreme party action if continued in such a time would ruin the Party. Moderation is its only chance."[26]

Hayes believed that his policies were successful. He was proud that the South enjoyed "peace, safety, order"; that during the Great Strike, federal troops had upheld order while shooting no one; that his Mexican policy was eliminating border problems; that he had "adhered to the policy of a sound currency"; and that reforms had been introduced to make the civil service less partisan. He boasted with justification that his major appointments—cabinet members, ministers abroad, judges, and bureau chiefs—were excellent. His finest appointment was that of John Marshall Harlan of Kentucky to the Supreme Court seat vacated by David Davis of Illinois. Harlan sustained Hayes's judgment by interpreting the Constitution over the next thirty-four years (1877–1911) to extend the power of the federal government, to uphold the civil rights of individuals, and to curtail the monopolistic power of giant corporations. Although Hayes turned to congressmen for advice, he resisted their dictation of appointments, and his administration made no removals except for cause. For his first year in office, Hayes believed that his record on appointments and removals was the best since that of John Quincy Adams.[27]

Hayes sensed, from his excursions, that the people applauded his moderation, but he was aware that politicians, reformers, and even friends called his presidency a failure. To his critics, it was clear that his southern policy had alienated radical Republicans without attracting old southern Whigs or even making them intolerant of the vicious behavior of many southern Democrats; he had embraced too much reform for the politicians and not enough for the reformers. Garfield thought that Hayes's "vague notions" and "wretched practice" of civil-service reform were "the chief mischief with his administration." He noted, "The impression is deepening that he is not large enough for the place he holds," and he believed that Hayes's election "has been an almost fatal blow to his party."[28]

Whitelaw Reid of the New York *Tribune* thought that Hayes had surrendered his leadership to Schurz, with disastrous results. "I don't think we differ very much about the Administration," Reid wrote to William Henry Smith, Hayes's trusted lieutenant and the recently confirmed collector at Chicago. He believed that the Hayes administration combined "the boasting of Schurz & Co." (which led to impossible expectations) with "hopelessly impracticable and inconsistent" methods. As a result, Reid concluded, "no human being of either party . . . pretends that the Administration thus far has been a success." He was losing hope that Hayes would either line up with his party or persuade it to line up with him.[29]

The most virulent attacks on Hayes came from spoilsmen within his own party. Sen. Timothy O. Howe of Wisconsin thought that he, rather than Harlan, should have been appointed to the Supreme Court. Encouraged to speak out by Blaine, Conkling, and Don Cameron, Howe exploded on 25 March with a vituperative attack on Hayes for abandoning southern Republicans and on Schurz for supporting civil-service reform. Blaine chimed in, and a few days later the usually friendly *National Republican* claimed that Hayes had created "discontent with the Administration in Republican circles." He had listened courteously when the Pennsylvania congressional delegation had asserted that "Western Pennsylvania" had "a proscriptive right to the Registership of the Treasury" and then rejected its candidate for the post.[30]

The results of these attacks were disappointing to spoilsmen. The very day of Howe's speech, Schurz apparently suffered a heart attack at his office. After medical treatment, he rallied; two days later, Hayes predicted his speedy return to the Interior Department. Flooded by complimentary letters, Schurz commented, "If such men as Howe and Blaine would only go on a little while longer, they would succeed in making the administration positively popular." Having learned their lesson, spoilsmen began to show more restraint. A Republican congressional caucus in early April voted down a resolution to condemn Hayes's order forbidding "federal office holders from managing the party politics of the Country." That this hostile resolution was even proposed illustrates the estrangement between many Republicans and the administration. Hayes, however, kept his sense of humor. On the day after Howe's attack, he told Vice President Wheeler, who presided over the Senate, "I too have a grievance." For over four months, an irresponsible clerk had not sent Hayes the record of the executive proceedings of the Senate. "Can you make the waters move?" the president asked, and added, "I still live."[31]

Reformers were almost as angry with Hayes as spoilsmen were. Jacob Dolson Cox insisted that Hayes "had utterly failed to accomplish anything in the way of Civil Service reform, and that he had pursued no system that could be defended by any class of politicians." Shortly after seeing Hayes, Wayne MacVeagh—a Philadelphia reformer and a member of the 1877 Louisiana commission—told fellow reformer Charles Eliot Norton: "The Pres*t*. is genuinely noble and true-hearted,—only slow and patient and half-blind. But why should we complain of him when Mr. Evarts saddens everybody but his enemies day by day. It is enough to make one's heart break when he reflects what possibility of great glory was before us and to what distant future it seems to have receded."[32]

Glory for reformers receded even further in the spring of 1878 when Hayes reinterpreted his civil-service order to permit political contributions by federal officers (campaigning had already been allowed by a previous clarification). Hayes stated that he intended to contribute but added that any employee refusing to contribute would not be removed. Trying to distinguish between contributions and assessments, he insisted to Curtis that "the order issued last June stands without alteration," but Curtis agreed with Cox that Hayes "has broken up one system without establishing another."[33]

It was obvious to reformers that Hayes had retreated. By the end of May, the Republican Congressional Campaign Committee issued its usual circular to federal officeholders, stipulating the amount they were to contribute and assuring "those who happen to be in Federal employ that there will be no objection in any official quarter to such voluntary contribution." Although Schurz composed a notice emphasizing that noncontributing clerks would retain their positions, and Hayes adopted it as a guide for all executive departments, it was feared that only Interior Department employees would take the Schurz notice seriously.[34]

Even temperance advocates turned on Hayes and Lucy. They were pleased with the ban on liquor in the White House and were honored when, on Washington's Birthday, Hayes reviewed the "Cold Water Army" of total abstainers. At that time, he testified that the consumption of "Ardent Spirits" was needless and hurtful and that he was convinced that its "entire disuse" would promote health, virtue, and happiness. But in April, Hayes and Lucy offended the more ardent spirits among the temperance advocates when they did not object to a claret punch being served at a dinner for them in Philadelphia. These advocates were angered when Lucy assured her hosts: "It is a great mistake to suppose that I desire to dictate my views to others in this matter of the use of wine and such drinks. I do not use them myself nor in my family, but I have no thought of shunning those who think and act differently. . . . I want people to enjoy themselves in the manner that is most pleasing to them." The Lucy Hayes Temperance Society of Washington changed its name. "As you have been read out of your 'Temperance Society,' " her friend Wheeler teased, "I trust you will now have no objection to accepting that bottle of old Kentucky Whiskey from Judge Harlan. *Serve it at once.* It is good for *damp feet!*"[35]

With radical, reform, and spoils-minded Republicans all attacking Hayes in the spring of 1878, the Democrats moved in for the kill and challenged his title to the presidency. That threat had been building over a long period. The June 1877 indictment of J. Madison Wells and Gen. Thomas C. Anderson of the Louisiana returning board for altering election returns was not an isolated attempt to attribute the Hayes victory to fraud. Upon his return from Europe in October 1877, Tilden blamed his loss on "a great fraud which the American people have not condoned and never will condone – never, never, never." The Democratic press harped on "the great fraud" and was aided in December 1877 when William E. Chandler, the Republican national committeeman who had played a key role in the election dispute, accused Hayes of reneging on one bargain to keep another.

Angered that Hayes had abandoned Packard in Louisiana and Chamberlain in South Carolina, Chandler charged that Hayes had done so to fulfill "a bargain" made during the count. But, Chandler added, in so doing, Hayes had failed to carry out the earlier "assurances" given by "Senator Sherman and his associates" to the Louisiana returning board that its members would be protected "from evil consequences" if they did the "extraordinary even if justifiable work" of correcting the returns. When Chandler made this attack in an unsuccessful attempt to swing the New Hampshire Republican convention against the administration, the Democratic press pounced on his admission that Hayes's lieutenants had made promises to the returning board. Chandler's talk of bargains and the fact that so many returning board members had received patronage plums from a reform administration added credence to Democratic charges of Republican fraud.

Montgomery Blair, who had been Lincoln's postmaster general and an ardent Tilden supporter in 1876, followed Chandler's lead. Blair argued that when Hayes disregarded the returns that had elected Packard and Chamberlain, he admitted that the identical returns that had seated him were "false and fraudulent." In January 1878, as a member of the Maryland state legislature, Blair demanded that Congress ask the courts to determine who had been elected president in 1876. The legislature modified Blair's proposal to instruct the Maryland attorney general to institute a suit in the Supreme Court if Congress passed such legislation. The suit would charge that fraudulent returns from other states had denied Maryland the full effect of its electoral vote and would ask the Court to revise the count and declare Tilden the victor.[36]

In the meantime, Anderson, the acting collector of the port of New Orleans, was convicted of tampering with election returns and jailed, but Hayes secured his release by exerting pressure on the Louisiana Supreme Court "especially" through his friend General Hancock. Ignoring the fact that the Nicholls administration had prosecuted Anderson, Hayes was encouraged that "for the first time the better classes have overruled the violent."[37]

After being slowed by the release of Anderson in March, Democratic momentum for an investigation increased. Two Republican election officials in Florida and Louisiana, disappointed in not having received offices from the Hayes administration, admitted that they had committed frauds in the recent election. S. B. McLin of the Florida returning board claimed that its vote should have gone to Tilden. Although McLin had been nominated by Hayes as chief justice of the New Mexico Territory, his appointment was not confirmed by the Senate because of opposition by Simon B. Conover, a Republican senator from his own state. McLin declared that "excitement . . . partisan zeal," and "promises made by Governor Noyes, that if Mr. Hayes became President I should be rewarded . . . had a strong control over my judgment and action." Allegations by James E. Anderson (not to be confused with acting collector Thomas C. Anderson) enabled Democrats to claim that Louisiana Republicans in East and West Feliciana Parishes planned not to vote so that they could blame their low turnout on Democratic violence and make it plausible for the returning board to throw out the votes of these parishes, depriving Tilden of his huge majorities.[38]

On 17 May 1878, the House of Representatives, dominated by Democrats, adopted the resolution of Clarkson N. Potter of New York to investigate the "alleged false and fraudulent" elections in Louisiana and Florida. Believing that Tilden Democrats such as Blair, aided by Republicans of the "Chandler sort," were responsible for the Potter resolution, Hayes denounced it as a revolutionary partisan proceeding that would disturb business, revive sectional strife, deepen the color line, increase the power of Tammany Hall, and harm the South as well as the rest of the country. If the Republicans, he added prophetically, "manage well their side of the controversy I suspect it will damage its authors."[39]

Hayes had no qualms about the role he had played in the period between the election and his entering the White House. Even before rereading the letters he had received from Noyes, Matthews, and Chandler during that period, Hayes stated, "I neither knew nor suspected fraud on our side. The danger was fraud by our adversaries." Although Hayes had nothing to hide personally, he had by late 1877 become aware, through William Henry Smith, that men such as Henry Van Ness Boynton and Charles B. Farwell possessed information that could be embarrassing. Smith was particularly anxious that Hayes humor Boynton—who was unhappy with the president—and welcome Farwell warmly when he visited the White House. Hayes was cordial to both men, and since neither of them was slated to testify before the Potter committee, he was confident that the witnesses the Democrats had lined up would merely "raise a dust" and would hurt neither Noyes nor Sherman.[40]

Hayes considered any effort to unseat him through the courts "another rebellion." After taking part in an 1878 Memorial Day service at Gettysburg, he uttered the day's most memorable words. In a conversation at a reception there, he vowed to go to war rather than submit to removal by any means other than the constitutional process of impeachment. An enterprising newspaperman, George Alfred Townsend, overheard Hayes's remarks and published them as "an interview." After discussing the Townsend interview with numerous Republicans and Democrats, William Henry Smith told Hayes that his emphatic determination was of "great importance" and left "the situation good." William M. Dickson also applauded Hayes and warned that if the Democrats controlled the next Congress "they will attempt to seat Tilden & will do it unless you *in time arrest* him & if necessary *shoot* him." The investigation spawned by Potter's resolution was, as Hayes said, the "event now on the scene."[41]

The Potter resolution unified squabbling Republicans, produced division among Democrats, and thoroughly aroused the public. Although some Democrats agreed with Blair and wished to unseat Hayes, others merely wanted to identify the Republicans with fraud. A few, such as Alexander H. Stephens, the former vice president of the Confederacy, denounced the Potter resolution as "most unwise, most unfortunate, and most mischievous." A somewhat relieved Hayes wrote to Lucy, who, with Fanny in tow, was fishing in the Adirondacks with Vice President Wheeler, "Politically we are getting into a more lovely frame of mind. Hampton and other Southern men talk out, and the dissentient Republicans are in better temper."[42]

The eleven-member Potter committee, which Speaker Randall stacked with Hayes's enemies, speedily got under way. Its hearings, however, did the Republicans little harm. On 1 June, it heard the testimony of James E. Anderson, the supervisor of registration of East Feliciana Parish, Louisiana. He claimed that Sherman had written a letter promising him and D. A. Weber, supervisor of registration at West Feliciana, that if they stood firm—in other words, maintained that the election was not fair and free in their parishes— they would "be provided for as soon after the 4th of March as may be practicable." When Weber was "mysteriously" murdered in March, Sherman's original letter disappeared, leaving only a copy.

According to Anderson's story, he had called on Hayes after the inauguration, told him that the election in both Felicianas was "a cheat," and secured a recommendation to Evarts to give him a consulship in a warm climate.

When the consulship did not materialize, Anderson again called at the White House on 13 June 1877, this time with Gen. T. C. H. Smith, who was then the appointments clerk of the Treasury Department and Hayes's personal friend. Anderson did not see Hayes, but Smith did; according to Anderson, Smith told him that "the President for political considerations wanted something satisfactory done for him." Hayes, as requested, furnished the committee with copies of his correspondence that concerned Anderson but denied receiving a letter from Matthews urging an appointment for Anderson, although Matthews had given Anderson a testimonial.

Accusations by "the scamp Anderson" annoyed Hayes, who attempted to set the record straight in his diary. Anderson, Hayes wrote, "came to me, one of the throng of office seekers early in my term," with a strong recommendation from a trustworthy citizen of Steubenville, Ohio, and testimonials from Senators Matthews and Kellogg and several Louisiana representatives, claiming that he had risked his life for the Republican party and could not safely return to his home and business. "Nothing was said," Hayes emphasized, "which led me to suspect that he had been guilty of any crookedness, or that any promises had been made to him." Anderson, who appeared to be intelligent and capable, claimed that his wife's delicate health required a mild climate and secured an endorsement from Hayes. Evarts found a small consulship for Anderson, but subsequent derogatory information, including facts from Matthews suggesting that Anderson was "trying to levy blackmail," led Hayes to order his character investigated. The result was that Anderson received no office.

Hayes denied hearing from Anderson that the election in the Felicianas was fraudulent. If, Hayes elaborated, "he told me that the Feliciana business was 'a cheat' . . . it was on one of the occasions when he was under the influence of liquor, and excited. . . . I certainly never promised him office, and never intended to give him office after I had been informed of his true character and conduct." But, Hayes admitted, he would have appointed Anderson if he had been a proper candidate and not "a great scoundrel." On 2 June, at a White House dinner featuring a fifteen-pound salmon trout that Lucy had caught on Lake Saranac, Sherman, Schurz, Thompson, and Key of the cabinet and Garfield, McKinley, and Keifer of the House mulled over Anderson's story and decided that it was "too thin to do serious harm."[43]

The diners were right. In testimony before the Potter committee, Sherman denied that there was a Republican conspiracy in the Felicianas. He also denied writing to Anderson or Weber or encouraging them to commit offenses. Sherman aggressively told the committee that he could prove that the election in those parishes was "governed and controlled by force, violence, and intimidation." Later that month, the committee discovered that the letter Anderson had attributed to Sherman was a fabrication. Anderson's unimpressive testimony, coupled with Hayes's openness, determination, and public support, undermined rabid Democrats like Montgomery Blair who wished to unseat Hayes through a judicial process. On 14 June, Republicans and moderate Democrats passed two resolutions denying that Congress, the courts, or any tribunal could reverse the declaration by the Forty-fourth Congress that Hayes and Wheeler had been elected. "As to the Potter investigation," Sherman wrote to a London correspondent in late June, "the general impression here is that it is fizzling out."[44]

Congress was also fizzling out. After much confusion and drunkenness during an all-night session, it adjourned on 20 June at 7 A.M. To be available for last-minute adjustments, Hayes had arrived at the Capitol at 8 P.M. the preceding night, following the "quiet, beautiful" White House wedding of his niece Emily Platt and Russell Hastings. With many members of the enrollment committee and clerks of the House too drunk to dispatch business, Hayes and his cabinet had to remain all night in the president's room in the Capitol. His only pleasure that night was derived from the proficiency of the "colored member [Joseph H.] Rainey of South Carolina [who] kept sober and alone secured attention to the Sundry Civil Service bill appropriating many millions, perhaps 18,000,000!" Hayes's disgust and anger with the irresponsible Congress were heightened when someone lost or stole "one or two important pages relating to the Hot Springs" Reservation in Arkansas, resulting in the loss of the $27,000 to compensate the commission that was settling conflicting claims to that reservation. Hayes had to request the commissioners to proceed on faith that the next Congress would remember them in a new appropriations bill.[45]

The chaotic scene was a fitting close to a long, troublesome session. Congress had passed the Bland-Allison Act, and though resumption appeared to be safe, Hayes feared that the inflationists had won too much. Congress had also opposed Hayes's modest attempts to reform the civil service. With the Senate rejecting his nominees for the New York customhouse, federal legislators still claimed the power to appoint federal administrators in their states. The Potter committee, while attempting to prove that Hayes had gained the presidency through fraud, had revealed that his administration's distribution of patronage was not a "thorough, radical, and complete" reform of the civil service. During his cross-examination of witnesses before the Potter committee, Ben Butler had exposed "the bastard character of Mr. Hayes' pretended reform" when he forced Gen. T. C. H. Smith to admit that "he had never made, or observed, or even heard of, an appointment for other than political reasons." When Congress adjourned, the Senate was so hostile to Hayes that only "half a dozen of the seventy-six Senators followed the time-honored custom and dropped in to pay their respects" during the long night he spent in the Senate wing of the Capitol.[46]

TWENTY-ONE

HAYES TAKES CHARGE

Despite attacks by reformers and congressmen, Hayes's confidence remained unshaken. He was a moderate who would not abandon his principles, but he was also a realist who would attempt only that which was possible. He was willing to experiment with civil-service reform in a few offices—Schurz's Interior Department, for example—but he did not insist that appointments in the Treasury Department under Sherman, a responsible spoilsman, be any less political than Gen. T. C. H. Smith had admitted they were to the Potter committee. "The progress is no doubt slow," Hayes wrote to Curtis, "but there is progress." Not insisting on immediate results, Hayes was willing to let the final goal wait for generations, as long as gradual improvement was shown. Having faith that the formal and informal education of children and adults was the key to instituting reforms and achieving equality, Hayes conspicuously supported schools for disadvantaged groups and seized every opportunity to instruct the public. In February 1878, he spoke at Howard University; in May and June, he attended exercises at the National Deaf Mute (Gallaudet) College, Hampton Normal and Industrial Institute, and the Washington "High School for colored children." The adjournment of Congress and the scattering of its members enabled the president to counterattack by drumming up public support for civil-service reform and sound money.[1]

On 11 July 1878, Hayes revived the spirit of reformers by suspending collector Arthur and naval officer Cornell from the New York customhouse. Celebrating reformers could not foresee the long-term results of this move—Arthur becoming president of the United States and Cornell governor of New York—but Thurlow Weed, an astute New York politician, warned Evarts that by removing these men, he "was preparing crowns for his victims." Hayes replaced Arthur with surveyor Edwin A. Merritt and Cornell with deputy naval officer Silas W. Burt, who would assume their posts immediately, since Congress was not in session. "This action," Charles Eliot Norton rejoiced, "puts a new face on affairs."[2]

Many people thought that the New York changes were a blow against

Conkling rather than one for reform, but Hayes insisted, "My course is not based on personal grounds." The New York daily press disapproved of the action, and Curtis hoped that Hayes would be neither "amazed nor disheartened by the outcry." Merritt's appointment lent credence to the cynical charge that the administration was planning to destroy Conkling by reorganizing the New York Republican party around the spoils-minded followers of his predecessor, Reuben E. Fenton. Evarts frankly avowed "that these changes are both useful to the public service and to the unity of the party." Accusing "the political management now displeasured" with bringing the party "to its low estate in New York," he recognized that the new collector would be the political manager of the New York Republican party.[3]

Although Curtis urged the promotion of deputy surveyor James I. Benedict to surveyor, Hayes appointed Gen. Charles K. Graham, a Union veteran, a civil engineer, and a Fenton Republican who was connected with neither the customs service nor reform. That move seemed to confirm that the president had removed Arthur and Cornell in order to build an administration machine. Continuing to suggest that worthy subordinates be promoted in the customhouse, Curtis warned Hayes "that certain appointments, such as I have seen mentioned as probable, would be so apparently conclusive proof that the change is merely of one faction for another, that the result could only be disastrous. . . . The selection of gentlemen, for instance, known only as 'Fenton politicians' would be fatal to all possibility of explanation and defense."[4]

The complaints of reformers that followed each of his appointments rankled Hayes. "We have only a per cent on our side—not enough to quarrel, or sulk about things. Let us get together," he wrote to Curtis. "The harshest blows many crotchety reformers strike are against each other." Insisting that he was not using Fenton politicians to construct an administration machine, Hayes parried that he did not wish to "proscribe people who have been active in politics." For example, he did not fire Thomas L. James, New York City's Conklingite postmaster, who was "a capital officer" and was appreciated by reformers and businessmen for rewarding "merit" in the post office. In October 1878, Hayes visited James in New York and observed the operation of civil-service reform in a huge field office. James removed officers only for cause; usually hired Republicans, but insisted on their fitness and integrity; promoted on the basis of competitive examinations; protected employees who did not pay political assessments; and believed that he and his workers did more for their party by providing "good and efficient postal service than by controlling primaries and dictating nominations."[5]

But the currency, not civil-service reform, was Hayes's major concern in

In the Dakota Territory: Hayes, with his arms folded, and Lucy, holding a plaid shawl, are standing in front of their traveling companions.

1878. In September, he toured as far west as the Dakota Territory, stopping in Pennsylvania, Ohio, Illinois, Wisconsin, and Minnesota. With the fall campaign in full swing, his primary objective was to convince inflation-minded midwesterners—among whom the "spread of the Greenback heresy" was "appalling"—that the resumption of specie payments in January 1879 would strengthen the economy. Deferring to the prevailing idea that political campaigning was beneath the dignity of the president, Hayes spoke briefly about issues rather than candidates; he managed to appear above politics while campaigning for his policies. "The great question before the Country," he insisted, "is whether we shall have a sound Currency or not. All other questions are either of the past, or of subordinate importance."

Hayes loved the cities and the countryside and was received warmly from Pittsburgh to Fargo. When he, Lucy, Birch, Webb, and Rud arrived in Chicago, "an immense concourse of citizens cheered lustily," threw their hats in the air, and called for the president. A five-mile-long parade commenced at noon, with Hayes standing in his carriage followed by 150 visiting fire companies; in the evening, a reception was held at the Grand Pacific Hotel. Further west, the vastness and grandeur of the country thrilled Hayes and Lucy. The wheat farms were so immense that one "could walk in a straight line five miles across the field." In "a wild prairie wind on Red River," when numerous "ladies were losing hats and locks of artificial hair," Lucy assured Hayes that even "if my hair does fly so as to make a Potawatomie of me, there is no danger of my losing it!"[6]

At the tristate fair in Toledo, Hayes gave his most elaborate speech of the trip before 75,000 people. The depression of the past five years, he claimed, was the natural aftermath of the war—with its "fast living" and high interest rates—and retrenchment during the hard times had brought strong signs of a healthy economy and a prosperous future. The $2.4 billion debt had been cut by a third, the 7.3 percent interest rate once paid by the government had declined more than a third, and the 12 to 15 percent paid by private borrowers had declined similarly. The "fickle" greenback currency, which had fluctuated at around sixty cents on the dollar (with the businessman charging "enough to make himself safe, and the consumer" paying "the loss"), was at "ninety-nine and one-half" and "as unchangeable as Lake Erie." The trade balance, which had been unfavorable by $100 million before the panic of 1873, was favorable by over $200 million in 1878. Not only was the country exporting more wheat and corn, but watches made in Elgin, Illinois, and in New England were being sold at "the foot of the Alps." Boasting that the United States "is getting rich," Hayes assured his audience that "we are all getting out of the panic, and nothing but our unwisdom will get us into it again. . . . Too much legislation on financial subjects is the bane of our times," he warned.[7]

Hayes believed that his extensive western trip was the happiest and most useful trip he had made. "It certainly strengthened my administration," he remarked, "and our greetings showed that we were already strong." Hard-money men heartily agreed, and Hayes hoped that Congress would take note and "be in better temper next winter."[8]

Although support for his civil-service and currency policies was growing among Republicans, southern Democrats defied federal law and rejected Hayes's conciliatory southern policy. Southern mountaineers who distilled illicit whiskey routinely refused to pay the federal excise tax unless compelled to do so by superior force. Although they did not question the federal government's right to tax whiskey, state officers and judges winked at violations. In the summer of 1878, state judges in the northwest corner of South Carolina did more than wink: State authorities arrested and indicted for murder Internal Revenue officers who had accidentally killed an escaped prisoner charged with illicit distilling. When the Hayes administration attempted to get the case tried in the U.S. Circuit Court, the South Carolina courts refused to transfer it, held the federal officers without bail, declared the jailing of the three illicit distillers unlawful and oppressive, and instructed the Pickens County grand jury to investigate local "outrages" by Internal Revenue officers. Hayes was particularly disturbed when a state circuit judge declared that U.S. laws were unconstitutional. Aware that a recent proviso attached to an appropriations bill prevented federal officers from using the army as a *posse comitatus* to enforce the laws, Hayes was determined to enforce revenue laws even if it meant "the calling out of volunteers . . . like the Whiskey rebellion in the time of Washington."[9]

Hayes's optimism for the future of the South was undermined by a realistic appraisal of the present. Joseph H. Rainey, a black congressman who was highly regarded by Hayes, and Stephen A. Swailes, a black state senator, told Hayes that in South Carolina, with the complicity of the Hampton government, "the Whites are resorting to intimidation and violence to prevent the colored people from organising for the elections." Swailes reported that both the Columbia *Register* and the Charleston *News and Courier* had urged the whites to defy federal authorities. When Swailes asked what he should tell his people at home, Hayes replied, "Tell them that they shall have all the protection the law will give."

Hayes asked the Justice Department to investigate and prosecute these and other outrages, but he and his cabinet soon realized that with a hostile Congress, an apathetic public, and a South divided on the color line, the law gave little protection. "The whites," Hayes noted, "have the intelligence, the property and the courage which make power. The negroes are for the most part ignorant, poor and timid. My view is that the whites must be divided there before a better state of things will prevail." But Hayes's efforts to break the color line and to attract white southerners to the Republican party had failed.[10]

Yale president Theodore Dwight Woolsey suggested a different tactic to breach the solid South. He urged Hayes to vindicate the principle of free speech by speaking in South Carolina before election day. Although concurring with this "important" suggestion, Hayes did not break his engagements (fairs in Maryland on 24 and 31 October) to carry it out. "I trust we shall never have another election for Congressmen in the South without meetings of the sort you desire," he told Woolsey, but the idea of pitting the prestige of the presidency against repressive white supremacists was not pursued. Perhaps he decided that the move would be too partisan and demean the presidency. After the election, Hayes noted angrily that despite pledges by the Hampton and Nicholls governments to uphold the constitutional rights of all citizens, South Carolina and Louisiana had prevented blacks from voting by legislation, fraud, intimidation, and "violence of the most atrocious character."[11]

The political rights of blacks were violated throughout the South. Reports of outrages in Alabama led Attorney General Devens to order the U.S. attorney in Montgomery to prosecute those who prevented or tried to prevent citizens from voting, but Devens's move had little effect. The Galveston *News* reported that Democrats at Marshall, Texas, had "bulldozed the usual Republican majority of the county" from 1,500 votes to 150. Finding themselves still defeated, they seized the ballot boxes and appointed a "committee of citizens" to count the votes. Declaring all the Democratic candidates elected, this committee, supported by "an armed mob," installed the fraudulent candidates.

The election of 1878 was a setback for Hayes. The Democrats were victorious, and widespread violence in the South went unpunished. In November, federal marshals arrested twenty-two South Carolinians for intimidating black voters, but legal maneuvering and all-white juries prevented convictions. Hayes's conciliatory policy had not split white southerners; the Democrats whom Key had rewarded with post offices had not attracted whites to the Republican party; and rather than fading, the color line had become more pronounced in southern politics. Still convinced that the color line had to be broken before any "good results" could be had in the South, Hayes clung to one shred of hope. Since "a host of people of both colors took no part" in the election, he blamed the outcome on the "unorganized" condition of "the better elements of the South," which Hayes still thought of as "our side."[12]

As Hayes prepared his second annual message to Congress, "Southern outrages" committed during the recent campaign continued to anger him. He resolved to "reiterate the sound opinions" he had long held on the subject. "What good people demand is exact justice," he wrote, "equality before the law, perfect freedom of political speech and action and no denial of rights to any citizen on account of color or race." The denial of black citizens' rights throughout Louisiana and South Carolina and in some congressional districts elsewhere was so much on his mind that it was the only subject he elaborated on in his 2 December annual message. He suggested that Congress should not seat the victors in these dubious elections, vowed to bring offenders to justice, and asked Congress for money to implement the 1870 and 1871 acts to enforce the Fourteenth and Fifteenth Amendments. Hayes was convinced that peace and prosperity required "the maintenance in full vigor of . . . free speech, free press, and free suffrage."

Still, Hayes professed that his southern policy was widely accepted and "safely vindicated." He wrote to Guy Bryan that "people are weary of sectional controversy" and predicted that "it will gradually drop out of sight." When Bryan countered that his annual message would prolong sectional animosity, Hayes told him:

My theory of the Southern situation is this. Let the rights of the colored people be secured and the laws enforced . . . by the action of the civil tribunals and wait for the healing influences of time and reflection to solve and remove the remaining difficulties. This will be a slow process, but the world moves faster than formerly, and it is plain that the politicians on both sides who seek to thrive by agitation and bitterness are losing rapidly their hold.

Hayes's southern policy depended on the Pauline trinity of faith, hope, and charity. His theory rested on a faith that the rights of blacks could be secured by civil tribunals, on a hope that a better sort of white southern politician would emerge to obliterate the color line in southern politics, and on a spirit of community and fraternity in the South. His thinking was wishful and unrealistic, but it was born of his realistic belief that civil processes — not military force — and a two-party system in the South were the only feasible methods to protect the civil rights of blacks. Law enforcement, however, was starved by a hostile Democratic House, and the so-called better sort of politician had no desire to protect the rights of blacks or to leave the party that had committed the outrages. Nor did southern outrages keep Democrats from winning elections in the rest of the nation. Already controlling the House of Representatives, they would gain control of the new Senate and ignore Hayes's plea for money to enforce the election laws.[13]

Despite Democratic gains, Hayes found some gratification in the election. Benjamin F. Butler, the Democratic gubernatorial candidate in Massachusetts, suffered a crushing defeat, which Hayes termed one of the best events since the war. Butler, who was a spoilsman and an inflationist and had just abandoned the Republican party, was the personification of political evil to Hayes. After a more sober look at the election a few days later, Hayes concluded that Butlerism, with its inflationary schemes, still lived. The president worried that the discontented might unite in one party, "with cheap money and plenty of it as its watchwords," and might even rule the country.[14]

The recent election made it clear that Hayes's modest reform initiatives prevented civil servants from managing but not from fighting political wars. Even the New York customhouse remained in politics, with Hayes's complicity. During that campaign, New York Congressman Anson G. McCook requested the temporary suspension of an order cutting down customhouse personnel, and it was granted. After the election, he asked Sherman to make the suspension permanent, complaining that it would "seriously affect several of my best friends, who stood by me in the late campaign." Wishing to apprise but not "embarrass" Hayes, Sherman forwarded McCook's plea with the comment that it "presents fairly the claim of our Friend McCook that we must govern the N.Y. Customs House so as to keep in those who help him whether their services are needed or not." Collector Merritt, Sherman added, "recommends the restorations proposed."[15]

William Henry Smith, the Chicago collector, was also in politics, but not to the extent he wished. He complained to Hayes that his celebrated civil-service order kept "a good many agents of the Executive," including himself, from the June 1878 Illinois state Republican convention. As a result, resolutions endorsing Hayes "in handsome and strong language" were not adopted because, without Smith, "there was no one sufficiently aggressive to carry them through."[16]

Although Hayes condemned conspicuous political activities by office-holders, he accepted less overt politicking. Naval officer Cornell's position on the Republican National Committee had been unacceptable, but Postmaster James's support for Arthur, Cornell, and Conkling, though regrettable, was acceptable. Hayes warned Sen. Stephen W. Dorsey, who had encouraged federal officers in Arkansas to manage political conventions, that he wanted the practice stopped. Hayes appointed his own supporters to office, but he told them not to remove subordinates except for "undoubted reasons," and he wished neither to tap their pay nor to dragoon them into electioneering.

Hayes was both a reformer and a practical politician. His letters to George William Curtis during the 1878 campaign emphasized his commitment to reform and his toleration of political dissent among efficient civil servants; his correspondence with Evarts, Key, and William Henry Smith revealed a willingness to use appointments to secure support for his administration. Hayes's support of reform and his recognition of the demands of practical politics were reflected in his appointments to the New York customhouse. Burt, whose appointment gratified reformers, would make the naval office politically neutral, while collector Merritt and surveyor Graham would strive to strengthen Hayes supporters in the New York Republican party. Out in Chicago, collector Smith identified local politicians who supported the administration and advised Hayes on post office appointments. In the South, Hayes appointed postmasters to attract Democrats to the Republican party. But when Key had to urge Col. D. G. Potts, postmaster of Petersburg, Virginia, to support the Republican incumbent for Congress, two things were obvious: Hayes's southern strategy was not working, and his administration expected the postmasters it had appointed to support its candidates.[17]

Republicans in the lame-duck Congress that assembled in December 1878 were friendlier to Hayes than they had been in their last session. Apparently they were chastened by his successful tour and by their unsuccessful campaign. The anger Hayes expressed in his second annual message over southern attacks on Republicans also struck a responsive chord, and they could not quarrel with the administration's careful preparation for specie resumption. Urging Congress to eschew financial legislation, Hayes predicted that the resumption of specie payments "will take place at the appointed time, will be successfully and easily maintained, and . . . will be followed by a healthful and enduring revival of business prosperity."

A month later, the appointed time arrived. More gold was exchanged for convenient paper greenbacks than greenbacks for gold, indicating a trust in the nation's capacity to remain on the gold standard. As Hayes had predicted, interest rates fell; resumption gave confidence to businessmen and stimulated additional economic activity. Later that year, thanks to a favorable trade balance, Sherman decided to "pay out gold on called bonds, as a mode of getting rid of the gold, and . . . distributing it in large amounts throughout the country."[18]

The Pension Arrears Act, which Hayes signed on 25 January 1879 after much cabinet discussion, soon dug into the gold surplus. Despite estimates that it would cost from $50 to $150 million in back pensions for disabled Union veterans, this act passed with bipartisan support because some inflation-minded lawmakers hoped to create fiscal problems for Hayes; other legislators posed as friends of the veteran but expected Hayes to veto the measure. William M. Dickson urged Hayes to veto it, arguing, "The Union may be bought too dearly if all is to be given the soldiers." But Hayes, refusing to "haggle . . . with those who gave health and blood and life" to their country, cheerfully signed the bill. It supplanted special congressional legislation for pension seekers with the more evenhanded bureaucratic procedures of the Pension Office. Under the new act, pensions began on the day of honorable discharge rather than on the date of the application (a difference of thousands of dollars for some), reminding many veterans of previously ignored service-related injuries.[19]

With his annual message out of the way, on 8 December 1878, Hayes turned his attention to "the Civil Service in case the N.Y. appointments are confirmed. The first step in any adequate and permanent reform is the divorce of the Legislative from the nominating power. With this, *reform* can and will successfully proceed. Without it reform is impossible." A few days later, however, as he tried to pick a postmaster for Lebanon, Ohio, from among eight candidates, Hayes recognized how difficult it was to make certain appointments without consulting Congress.[20]

As expected, Conkling opposed the confirmation of Merritt, Burt, and

Conkling riding high before his fall (*Puck*, 29 January 1879)

Graham. Hayes believed that although most senators would prefer to confirm, many would oppose it because of "Senatorial courtesy, the Senatorial prerogative, and the fear of C[onkling]'s vengeance." Conkling "is like Butler," Hayes observed, "more powerful because he is vindictive and not restrained by conscience. The most noticeable weakness of Congressmen, is their timidity. . . . They do not vote according to their convictions [but] from fear of consequences."[21]

Conkling appeared to be as powerful as ever. In January 1879, the Republican majority in the New York legislature reelected him for a third senatorial term, and the Speaker of the assembly lauded him as the peer of Webster, Clay, and Calhoun. On principle, Hayes had made no attempt to defeat Conkling or any other hostile senator, but he must have realized that interference would have been fruitless. In the Senate, Conkling seemed to be on his way to another victory. On 15 January 1879, Sherman made charges of inefficiency and corruption against Arthur and Cornell in an executive session; at Conkling's shrewd behest, these charges were kept secret. On 24 January, Conkling's Commerce Committee advised the Senate to reject the Merritt, Burt, and Graham nominations.

Not regarding Conkling as invincible, Hayes took the offensive and publicized what Conkling had stifled. Hayes told the Senate that the New York customhouse, which collected two-thirds of the nation's customs revenue, was of national significance and "should be conducted on business principles." Arthur and Cornell had made it "a center of partisan political management," and Hayes had no hope that they would manage it as James administered the New York Post Office. Taking the New York customhouse out of politics, they had insisted, would force them "to surrender their personal and political rights."[22]

The administration defeated Conkling when, on 3 February 1879, the Senate confirmed the appointments of Merritt and Burt; a few days later, Graham was confirmed. Most Republicans sided with Conkling, but thanks to Sherman's "extraordinary personal efforts," which included pursuing senators to their lodgings, a minority of them supported the administration, as did most Democrats, who were happy to keep the Republicans divided. Hayes exulted in Conkling's defeat, ending "the Senatorial courtesy pretension," and in the triumph of the principle "that public offices ought not to be party machines."

Although most reformers thought that the "defeat of Conkling *is glorious,*" his clever defense of Arthur and Cornell "created a profound sensation." Adopting the reform "principle that efficiency and fidelity . . . constitute the sole title to retention in the public service," Conkling asserted that since Arthur and Cornell had been efficient and faithful, the Hayes administration itself had violated the principles of civil-service reform and was acting out of "petty, perverse spite." Conkling quoted from Sherman's private political letters to Arthur. Responding to Sherman's requests, Arthur—for "manifest reasons"—had provided a place in the customhouse for a son of Supreme Court Justice Joseph P. Bradley, who had cast the deciding vote for Hayes on the electoral commission. He had also accepted as a deputy collector J. Q. Howard, the author of a Hayes campaign biography. Having had the bad form to reveal personal correspondence, Conkling then denounced the "undignified, unprincipled, and in every way unworthy" behavior of Sherman, who had secured the votes of senators with personal appeals and by distributing seventeen customhouse appointments among them. Although the *New York Times* commented that "the public service will hardly be elevated by the removal of one officer for being too much a politician to make way for another who has never been anything but a politician," most reformers regarded Conkling's defeat as so great a "gain for the country . . . that we can well afford to disregard the motives of the disputants."[23]

The self-righteous indignation of Conkling, a spoilsman, was absurd; Hayes would recommend his political supporters for offices they were qualified to fill, but he was no spoilsman. Upon receiving reports that made him anxious about New Orleans customs officers, for example, Hayes asked Sherman to investigate quietly. "If a change seems best let us get the best men possible without regard to past 'services.'" Even though Hayes did recommend his friends, his reluctance to fire able civil servants to make way for them marks him as the least partisan president between John Quincy Adams and Theodore Roosevelt. "I want him to know," Hayes said of the new St. Louis postmaster, "that I wish him to be cautious and deliberate as to removals of subordinates—remove none but for undoubted reasons—prefer to retain in case of doubt—no sweeping removals." Hayes applied this no-removal-without-cause principle to himself as well. He wished to find a place for a Mr. Hayden in the Post Office Department, but Key told him "that Mr. Hayden cannot be given employment in this Department without removing some member of our force, and I know of no just cause for removal of any one."[24]

Despite the requests of Sherman and the designs of Evarts, Hayes had decided to make the New York customhouse a showcase for reform. He ordered Merritt to conduct his office "on strictly business principles" and urged that neither the recommendation of congressmen nor that of "other influential persons should be specially regarded. . . . Let no man be put out merely because he is Mr. Arthur's friend, and no man put in merely because he is our friend." Hayes directed naval officer Burt, collector Merritt, and surveyor Graham to devise regulations based on the Grant Civil Service Commission rules, with which Burt had experience. Curtis conferred with the new leadership and reported to Hayes his satisfaction that "the babe" of civil-service reform was "not given to its deadly enemies to nurse."[25]

Publication of Hayes's letter to Merritt brought praise from reformers, and this praise grew louder when the new rules were published. They applied to all New York customhouse and subtreasury appointees, with the exception of those in a few offices of special trust. Appointments were made from the three candidates who had scored highest on a competitive examination administered by one of three boards of examiners. New appointees could enter only at the lowest grade; higher vacancies were to be filled by promotions within the customhouse. Naval officer Silas W. Burt, an early and ardent civil-service reformer, was the dynamic force behind the New York customhouse rules. With little faith in open, competitive examinations, collector Merritt believed that the experiment would fail and assured Burt, "If you can revive this corpse you are entitled to all the glory." Burt's success was striking. The highly critical *New York Times* admitted in July that "after four months' experience, it is simple justice to say that the reform has been applied there in good faith, and with a degree of pertinacity, a patient attempt to make it successful, and an enlightened appreciation of its nature and its scope, which have been an agreeable disappointment to the doubters."[26]

At the time that Merritt and Burt were confirmed, the Potter investigation—designed to undermine Hayes's title to the presidency—was confounding its Democratic authors. In the spring of 1878, the investigation had failed to prove allegations of Republican fraud; in the fall and winter, it had to confront Democratic corruption. The New York *Tribune* published dispatches it had deciphered, revealing that Tilden's nephew, Col. William T. Pelton, had tried to bribe the Florida and South Carolina canvassing boards. As a result, the Democrats had to include the dispatches in the Potter investigation. Pelton's testimony that he had tried to buy the presidency for his uncle, and Tilden's admission that after squelching those bribery attempts he had allowed his nephew to remain in his household—where Pelton had continued his negotiations—destroyed Democratic hopes of nominating Tilden in 1880 and capitalizing on "the great fraud." For Hayes, the first week in

February 1878 brought relief: He defeated Conkling, and the Potter investigation degenerated into a self-destructive farce.[27]

After his triumph over Conkling and the Potter committee, Hayes was roundly criticized in early 1879 for pardoning a free-love advocate. As governor, Hayes had been pilloried in the press for "his unprecedented use of the pardoning power." As president, he issued 284 pardons between 4 March 1877 and 20 May 1878. Pardons were unpopular, but Hayes was not afraid to give them if he believed that there had been a miscarriage of justice. He also continued to support the less-than-fashionable movement to reform prisons.[28]

Hayes's most unpopular pardon angered the Protestant clergy, who were among his strongest supporters. The benefactor of this pardon was Ezra Hervey Heywood, an ardent abolitionist, pacifist, and women's rights advocate. He had become notorious after 1873 when he and his wife, Angela Fiducia Tilton, founded the New England Free Love League. Coincidentally, that same year, Anthony Comstock secured passage of a federal law closing the mail to obscene materials and was appointed both an unpaid agent of the Post Office Department and the secretary of the Society for the Suppression of Vice. Making no attempt to distinguish radical ideas from pornography, Comstock pursued panderers and avant-gardists with equal fervor. In 1877, using an alias, he received publications from Heywood, including his pamphlet *Cupid's Yokes: or, The Binding Forces of Conjugal Life*, and later arrested him in Boston at a Free Love League meeting. In June 1878, Comstock secured Heywood's conviction for mailing obscene matter. When Heywood was fined $100 and sentenced to two years in jail, 4,000 to 6,000 people protested at Faneuil Hall.

Although Hayes's first cousin John Humphrey Noyes was more notorious for his bizarre view of marriage than was Heywood, Hayes's own views on marriage were unshakably conventional. Nor did he brook pornographers. "A man guilty of circulating writing or publishing obscene books — books intended or calculated to corrupt the young," he insisted, "would find no favor with me." Hayes, however, agreed with the recommendation of the Department of Justice and pardoned Heywood after he had served six months in jail. Heywood was ill and had not intended to violate the law, and in Hayes's judgment, the pamphlet was not obscene, so the law had not been violated. Hayes perceived that Heywood's offense was "not that he discussed a question in an objectionable manner, but that he was on the wrong side of the question." Hayes was as convinced as those who assailed him for the pardon that Heywood was wrong, but the president felt that it was not a crime under U.S. laws to advocate the abolition of marriage. "In this case," he concluded, "the writings were objectionable but were not obscene, lascivious, lewd, or corrupting in the criminal sense." Although certain that he was correct in granting the pardon, the president did not defend himself in public, preferring not to give Heywood further publicity. Hayes also advised clergymen and journalists to stop advertising Heywood and his beliefs by attacking the pardon.[29]

Even though he had offended them, Protestant clergymen continued to support Hayes. Tending to be Republicans, these ministers perceived the Democratic party much as their peer Samuel Dickinson Burchard would a few years later: as the party whose antecedents were "rum, romanism, and rebellion." Protestant ministers particularly liked Hayes for his temperance and antislavery views. In addition, his opposition to public aid for parochial schools had frustrated Roman Catholics in Ohio, and his upright character helped the country forget the corruption of the Grant regime.

Upon becoming president, Hayes did not change his religious attitudes to curry favor with the clergy. He remained, in his own words, a "non-church member, a non-professor of religion," and a "worshipper" of Ralph Waldo Emerson. Although urged to do so by clergymen, he would not change his views. He generously supported the church of Lucy's choice and contributed to other churches, including the Roman Catholic church in Fremont, for building programs and special projects. He always attended church regularly, first to please his mother, then to please Lucy, and finally to please himself. Never a confirmed Christian, he once acknowledged that he was close to Methodism, since every night he slept with one of that persuasion.[30]

Clergymen were pleased when Hayes stopped serving alcoholic beverages at White House functions. Dissipation bothered Hayes. He noted that young men were made reckless by too much wine and did disgraceful things during receptions held by both the British and Mexican ministers. But his move produced grumbling and ridicule even among his close associates. Evarts quipped that at White House dinners, the water flowed like wine. Convinced that Americans were not able to hold their liquor, Hayes had resolved to set an example as well as gratify Lucy and other temperance advocates. After "the venerable historian" George Bancroft (with whom Lucy promenaded) called Hayes and Lucy's "official entertainment to the Diplomatic Corps" on 25 February 1879 "the finest affair ever had in the White House," Hayes thought: "The exclusion of wine from the list of refreshments has turned out exceedingly well." He was pleased and surprised that "many of

Rutherford and Lucy Hayes at the Foundry Methodist Church (*Harper's Bazaar*, 19 April 1879)

the Foreign gentlemen speak of it with approval" and resolved: "We shall stick to it." Publicity of this dry reception, on the heels of the Heywood pardon, helped assuage the wrath of the religious press.[31]

Vicious critics of Hayes blamed his abstinence on stinginess, while those of a gentler nature believed that he was being duped by White House stewards in collusion with capital tipplers. Ben: Perley Poore, a Washington correspondent with a colon fixation, reported that concealed within the oranges at what became known as the "Life-Saving Station" was a delicious frozen Roman punch liberally laced with "strong old Santa Croix rum." Hayes, however, claimed: "The joke of the Roman punch oranges was not on us but on the drinking people. My orders were to flavor them *rather strongly* with the same flavor that is found in Jamaica rum. . . . This took! There was not a drop of spirits in them!"

Hayes and Lucy saved money on wine and liquor, but economy was not their aim: They entertained lavishly. The menu at that 25 February reception for the diplomatic corps, which hundreds attended, was: "Salmon a la Vatelle, sauce a la Ravegotte, boned turkey and truffles, game pates and truffles, ham glace, filet de valaille a la Carlette, chicken salads, lobster salads, oyster pates, scalloped oysters, chicken croquet on truffles, terrapin (diamond back), sandwiches, tea, coffee, and chocolate." On the dessert tables were "Meringues baskets, Newgate pyramids, Charlotte russe jellies, water ices," and candied fruit, plus the notorious oranges.[32]

Hayes's support among Protestant ministers was further strengthened when he did not pardon the offender in the next celebrated obscenity case. On 5 June 1879, Comstock obtained the conviction of De Robigne Mortimer Bennett for sending obscene matter through the mails. Earlier the purveyor of "Dr. Bennett's Quick Cure, Golden Liniment, Worm Lozenges, and Root and Plant Pills," Bennett had become during the 1870s the freethinking editor of the *Truthseeker*. His specific offense was to mail Ezra Heywood's pamphlet *Cupid's Yokes*. After Hayes pardoned Heywood, Judge Samuel Blatchford found *Cupid's Yokes* obscene in a landmark decision and sentenced Bennett to thirteen months in the penitentiary and fined him $300. Bennett applied for a pardon, but the president refused to grant it. The opinion of Blatchford, whom Hayes admired, and the large number of copies that Bennett had sold led the president to reverse his earlier decision and to conclude that *Cupid's Yokes* contained many indecent passages "not required for the argument" and was "obscenity to make money."

Hayes, however, was uneasy about his inconsistency. Robert G. Ingersoll urged him to pardon Bennett, arguing that *Cupid's Yokes* was opposed to religion but "was not, in any fair sense, obscene." Apparently, Attorney General Devens was of the same opinion. Hayes realized that an atheistic, immoral work was not necessarily obscene and that the "true rule as to obscene matter is does it tend to excite the passions or to inflame the sensual appetite, or desires of the Young." Nevertheless, he thought that the "pardoning power must not be used to nullify or repeal Statutes, nor to overrule the judgments of the Courts." The pardoning power, he decided, should be saved for "palpable mistakes, hasty decisions, newly discovered facts."

Hayes feared that a pardon for Bennett would "nullify the law as expounded by the judicial department" and would be an abuse of the pardoning power. But the president's doubts lingered. "I was never satisfied, as I would wish," Hayes confessed in 1892, "with the correctness of the result to which I came chiefly in deference to the courts. 'Cupid's Yokes' was a free-love pamphlet of bad principles, and in bad taste, but Colonel Ingersoll had abundant reason for his argument that it was not, in the legal sense, 'an obscene publication.' "[33]

In February 1879, Congress passed a bill restricting Chinese immigration to the United States. White workers were hostile to Chinese workers, who, in the 1870s, constituted a quarter of California wage earners and a much higher percentage of San Francisco workers. The depression following the panic of 1873 made cheap Chinese labor appealing to factory owners and offensive to white workers. "Anticoolie" clubs attracted white laborers and small manufacturers who had difficulty competing with shops that used Chinese labor.[34]

As early as the late 1860s, anti-Chinese statements were a successful political ploy in the West, and by 1876, the national conventions of both parties adopted anti-Chinese planks. The Democratic plank was explicitly racist; the Republican one—which called for a congressional investigation of the moral and material effects of the "immigration and importation of Mongolians"—was implicitly racist. In October and November 1876, a joint congressional committee chaired by Oliver P. Morton, a champion of human rights, held public hearings in San Francisco on Chinese immigration. The majority report called for the renegotiation of the 1868 Burlingame Treaty to eliminate unrestricted Chinese immigration. Morton's minority report, appearing after his death, claimed that Chinese laborers benefited the West. It noted that the hostility toward them was racially motivated and argued against restricting their immigration. Emphatically a minority view, Morton's report was a dying gasp of abolitionist commitment to racial equality.[35]

The Great Strike of 1877 inspired anti-Chinese riots in San Francisco. That fall, the Workingmen's party—led by Denis Kearney, a demagogue who wished to "stop the leprous Chinamen from landing," and not to be confused with the Marxist Workingmen's party in St. Louis—expanded and became a major force in state politics by early 1878. At the California constitutional convention that year, the Workingmen's party secured articles preventing Chinese from voting and prohibiting their employment on state or local public works or by corporations operating under California law. Although everyone realized that these racist articles were unconstitutional and would be struck down, Congress received the message from California. After an hour's debate, the House passed a bill allowing each incoming vessel to land no more than fifteen Chinese passengers. Despite the hostility of a remnant of antislavery Republicans and of a bipartisan group sensitive to the international obligations of the United States, the measure also passed the Senate. The upper house specifically amended the bill to abrogate articles five and six of the Burlingame Treaty, which permitted voluntary immigration to China and the United States by citizens of both countries and protected them during their stays in the other nation.[36]

Outside of Congress, eastern reformers and the Protestant clergy opposed Chinese exclusion. In New York, on 21 February, Curtis reported to Hayes that there was "so general and strong a protest against the Chinese bill as an act of bad faith, and so universal a hope of a veto, that I venture to add my most earnest wish that you may see the bill, as I do, as a most flagrant breach of the National faith. If Asiatic immigration be undesirable, this is certainly not the way to apply the remedy; and that the Republican party should be the first to shut the gates of America on mankind is amazing."[37]

All Californians did not agree with those pressing for anti-Chinese legislation. The poet Joaquin Miller was disgusted because members of Congress "from the Pacific called *personally* to urge an unjust cause. I have *lived* with and *labored* with the Chinese for nearly a quarter of a century," he told Hayes, "and know more about them than all that Delegation put together. . . . The Chinese is . . . far better than those now crying out against him." But few agreed with Miller. The California constitutional convention thanked Congress for passing the fifteen-passenger bill, and a bipartisan Republican and Democratic rally in San Francisco urged Hayes to sign the bill into law. "Our Countrymen on the Pacific Coast," Hayes noted, "with great unanimity, and with the utmost earnestness desire a change in our relations with China."[38]

Despite this pressure, Hayes resolved to "stand for the sacred observance of treaties." He noted that the vital articles of the Burlingame Treaty, which Congress wished to "abrogate without notice, without negotiation," were "of our own making." He also believed that West Coast exclusionists could secure "relief . . . long before there is any material increase of their present difficulties without any violation of national faith, and without any real or substantial departure from our traditional policy on the subject of immigration." Why Hayes thought that exclusion would not constitute a departure from American immigration policy is difficult to understand, unless he saw a parallel—which he did not express—between prohibiting the importation of slaves from Africa after 1808 and of workers from China after 1879.

On 1 March, Hayes vetoed the Chinese exclusion bill. Since the Forty-fifth Congress was about to expire, he could have killed the bill by not signing it, but he was too forthright to use the pocket veto. West of the Rocky Mountains, his veto was bitterly denounced, and he was even burned in effigy. Although Hayes wrote virtually every state paper he signed, he was not satisfied with his own veto message and adopted Evarts's more detailed but less explicit exposition of how this restrictive bill would affect relations with China and the standing of the United States among the nations of the world. Rather than stress the racial-equality argument embraced by Oliver P. Morton, the veto message argued that the fifteen-passenger bill amounted to a "denunciation" of the Burlingame Treaty, which was advantageous to the United States. Although Chinese immigrants would lose the advantages they had enjoyed under the treaty, so would American merchants and missionaries working in China. "Fortunately," Hayes accurately noted, Chinese migration to the West Coast was slowing down, and its "instant suppression" was not required, despite the urgency with which it had been demanded. The problem could be handled by diplomatic negotiations.[39]

The exclusion bill forced Hayes to examine his own and his countrymen's attitudes on race relations. "If we could put ourselves in" the places of white Californians, he recognized, "it is absolutely certain that we should think and feel as they do." He realized, however, that the problem was not the Chinese laborer but the tendency of the powerful white race to bully other races. He believed that the equal-rights principle in the Declaration of Independence applied to all Americans, not just to whites, but he observed: "Our experience in dealing with the weaker races—the negroes and indians for example is not encouraging. We shall oppress the Chinamen, and their presence will make hoodlums or vagabonds of their oppressors."

During Hayes's presidency—to say nothing of his lifetime—southern "bulldozers" intimidated blacks, settlers violated the original inhabitants' rights to their ancestral lands, and rioters murdered Chinese workers. Indians and blacks had long been part of the American scene, but the Chinese were recent arrivals. They were a "labor invasion" without wives, mothers, and children, and Hayes feared that they could be neither assimilated nor admitted into the bosom of American society. "I therefore," Hayes concluded, "would consider with favor measures to discourage the Chinese from coming to our shores."[40]

The veto, which Congress could not override, neither answered nor closed the Chinese question. For an expert opinion, the administration turned to

George Frederick Seward, the nephew of William H. Seward, Lincoln's secretary of state. Having served as a consul in China from 1861 to 1876 and as
the minister to China since 1876, George Seward was by March 1879 an old
China hand. He was also in trouble. Two days after Hayes vetoed the Chinese immigration bill, the Democrats in the House of Representatives tried
to impeach him for "high crimes and misdemeanors while in office." He was
an arbitrary administrator, they alleged, who had defrauded the Chinese
government by embezzlement, bribery, and extortion while helping to build
China's first railroad. Although Seward, a "contumacious witness," angered
Democrats by not producing his accounts, they failed to impeach him because Republicans prevented a quorum by refusing to vote.[41]

After narrowly escaping impeachment, Seward prepared a confidential
memorandum dated 25 March 1879, for Evarts and Hayes on the Chinese
question. To preserve good relations with China and "allay the anxiety felt
in this country regarding Chinese immigration," Seward suggested that both
countries take steps to prevent contract immigration. He assumed that a
strengthened consular service, which would issue a certificate to each immi-
grant who attested to his voluntary status, would largely take care of the
problem. Stating "that the Chinese are not an emigrating people," Seward
had no fear that the United States was about to witness a larger immigration
from China, but the Burlingame Treaty could be revised if it should prove
desirable.

Seward's main concern was trade with China. Although it was unimportant in 1879, he did not want the migration issue to jeopardize the future of
that trade. Emphasizing the vast potential market, he predicted, "our people
will avail of it if we do not cut off their opportunities." Having implemented
U.S. Far Eastern policy (which was essentially the open-door policy in all
but name) since 1861, Seward knew that it "recognized the identity of all legitimate foreign interests in China and in Japan, and the wisdom of cooperation with other governments to advance those interests and to stand in the
way of irregular procedure and selfish purposes on the part of any of them."
American policy endeavored "to sustain and support both Empires alike in
the name of one common humanity and of alliances which should be productive of continuously increasing advantages." Eight months after Seward
wrote his memorandum, John Hay joined the Hayes administration as assistant secretary of state and became intimately acquainted with America's desire to sustain and trade freely with the Chinese and Japanese empires. When
Hay became secretary of state twenty years later, that understanding made it
quite natural for him to adopt, without fuss, the open-door notes, which

forcefully restated what Seward had regarded in 1879 as a well-defined U.S. policy. [42]

Despite Seward's questionable ethics in China and evasive tactics on Capitol Hill, Hayes and Evarts sent him back to China to negotiate changes in the Burlingame Treaty, with instructions based largely on his 25 March memorandum. His problems, however, undermined his usefulness, and he was recalled on 27 December 1879. In his place as minister and chief negotiator, Hayes appointed James B. Angell, president of the University of Michigan. He had been recommended by Sen. George F. Edmunds, whom Hayes had praised for not badgering the administration with suggestions for collectorships and postmasterships. John F. Swift, a California Republican renowned for his antimonopoly and anti-Chinese views, and William H. Trescott of South Carolina, a diplomatic historian with diplomatic experience, were appointed as commissioners to work with Angell.

With Angell chairing the American mission, negotiations proceeded smoothly and quickly. Swift wished to exclude the Chinese, but Angell and Trescott—reflecting the view of the Hayes administration—wanted to curb the influx of Chinese without jeopardizing the advantages of American merchants and missionaries in China. Working harmoniously, the Angell mission and the Chinese plenipotentiaries had agreed on both an immigration treaty and a commerce treaty by 17 November 1880. The immigration treaty enabled the United States to regulate, limit, and suspend—but not prohibit—the immigration of Chinese laborers. The commerce treaty secured new commercial advantages for Americans but prohibited either country from shipping opium into the other. When these treaties were ratified in 1881, Hayes had left office. The next year, after attempting to pass a twenty-year suspension of Chinese immigration, Congress settled for a ten-year suspension. [43]

RIDERS, POLITICS, AND REFORM

On 3 March 1879, two days after Hayes vetoed the Chinese immigration bill, the Forty-fifth Congress adjourned without appropriating funds to keep the army and civil service functioning during the fiscal year beginning 1 July 1879. The Republican Senate had refused to pass appropriations bills to which the Democratic House had attached provisions (called riders) that would alter the election laws and other legislation, and the Democrats had refused to pass the appropriations bills without the riders. These votes, taken in the waning days of the Forty-fifth Congress, followed strict party lines and unified the divisive elements in both parties. Blaine, Conkling, and Hayes supporters joined to rally around their party's standard, just as all Democrats, with or without Whig antecedents or hard- or soft-money proclivities, united. As a result, Hayes was forced to call the Forty-sixth Congress to meet in special session on 18 March, to prevent government functions from grinding to a halt on 1 July. Hayes was angered by "Democratic attempts to revolutionize the Gov[ernmen]t of our fathers" and annoyed that the extra session compelled him to give up a projected trip to California. Members of Congress were surprised and dissatisfied that the president had called the special session so soon after the expiration of the previous Congress.

With control of both houses of the incoming Congress, the Democrats seemed to have repeal of the election laws within their grasp. The targeted laws dated from the Civil War and Reconstruction years and were designed to protect black and white Republicans in both the North and the South from fraud, intimidation, and violence at the polls. The election laws—also known as the Force or Enforcement Acts—made hindering voters a federal offense and authorized the federal courts to appoint and pay supervisors of congressional elections and their deputy marshals "in any city or town having upward of twenty thousand inhabitants . . . or . . . in any county or parish, in any congressional district." The election laws were effective and important to all Republicans. Additional legislation prevented former Confederates from serving as jurors in federal courts and permitted federal troops to keep the peace at the polls. Many Republicans were ready to retreat on the test oaths for jurors, and Hayes did not think that troops should be stationed at the polls, but he believed that civil authorities should be able to call in troops if they were necessary to keep the peace. All Republicans were united in backing the election laws, which relied on federal civil authority to ensure honest elections.[1]

The Democrats believed that repeal of the election laws would bring them the presidency in 1880. "The practical object of the 'so-called' Democrats is very plain," Hayes heard from his friend Judge William Johnston of Cincinnati. "They want to kill with impunity so many negroes as may be necessary to frighten the survivors from the polls in the South; and . . . to stuff the ballot-boxes of New York after the manner of 1868." Hayes had managed to win in 1876 without New York, but with Florida, Louisiana, South Carolina, and the rest of the South now firmly in Democratic hands, Republicans knew that they would have to carry New York to win any presidential election in the foreseeable future. And to carry New York without the election laws in force would be most difficult.[2]

Hayes was determined to veto any attempt to halt federal supervision of national elections. He predicted that the Democrats "will stop the wheels . . . of government if I do not yield my convictions in favor of the election laws. It will be a severe, perhaps a long contest. I do not fear it—I do not even dread it. The people will not allow this Revolutionary course to triumph." Wishing neither to increase the prevailing excitement nor to provoke the Democrats, Hayes calmly requested in his 19 March message to the special session of Congress that it appropriate funds for the executive, legislative, and judicial branches of the government and for the army.[3]

Democrats were uncertain about their tactics. Many of them favored passing separate bills repealing the election laws (rather than relying on riders to appropriations bills) and holding back the appropriations bills until Hayes approved the repeal bills. For over a week, Washington was awash with rumors about the Democrats' program and speculation about the president's response. In his diary, Hayes acknowledged that he would approve separate bills repealing the "laws authorizing soldiers to be sent to the polls at elections to keep the peace" and prescribing test oaths for federal jurors. He would not allow the elimination of legislation designed to protect elections, but he was willing to let Congress tinker with election laws if the changes promoted free and fair elections, which Hayes firmly believed would produce Republican majorities in Congress.[4]

Hayes was determined to retain federal civil control of congressional elections and insisted that federal civil authorities be able to call on the military to suppress violence. "Experience," he emphatically stated, "has shown that the protection and conduct of National elections can not safely be left to the States." Despite their talk of separate legislation, the Democrats of the new Congress, like those of the previous one, decided to attach riders to appropriations bills. William O. Stoddard, who had been one of Lincoln's secretaries, noted that the "future *status* of the presidency" depended on Hayes's "wisdom and firmness" in meeting this "proposed Congressional coercion of the Executive." He urged Hayes to show "what the Yankees call 'clean grit' " and "not yield an inch," enabling the American people to "point to the White House with the proud assurance that *there* is *our* 'majority.' "[5]

Hayes, who was outraged by the rider tactic, agreed with Stoddard. "It is," he exclaimed, "an unconstitutional and revolutionary attempt" by the Democrats, with their bare congressional majority, "to deprive the Executive of one of his most important prerogatives. To coerce him to approve a measure which he in fact does not approve." Having earlier defended his appointing power from an attack by Republican senators, Hayes now defended his veto power from an onslaught by both houses of the Democratic Congress. "I stand," he affirmed, "for 'the equal' and Constitutional 'independence of the Executive.' " Hayes feared that if he did not stand firm, the House of Representatives would "become a despotism with unlimited power."[6]

On 27 March, the Democrats introduced the army appropriations bill with a rider that would prevent federal military and civil authorities from keeping the peace at the polls. Hayes did not think that the army should be routinely stationed at the polls, and on that very day, he told William Henry Smith that he did "not care to use the military." But if a military presence were deemed necessary by federal civil authorities, he wanted to be able to use it. Recalling the intimidation of black voters by rifle clubs, Hayes asked, "If the red shirts can be present at the polls in S[outh] C[arolina] why can not the blue coats be called in also?"[7]

While Congress debated the army appropriations bill and its rider, Hayes consulted fellow Republicans and refined his position. Naturally, he emphasized the nobler constitutional issues at stake rather than the practical political effect of the rider on the Republican and Democratic parties. Evarts thought that the Democrats were simply making issues for the next presidential election, but Hayes considered the controversy "a new form of the old conflict between ultra state rights, and the National doctrines." On another level, he believed that it was an attempt to destroy the balance of power in the federal government and, as such, a revolutionary attack on the Constitution. Specifically, he thought that the House Democrats were trying to use their control over appropriations to gain control over "the judicial and executive authority." Although riders had been in the legislative bag of tricks since the days of Andrew Jackson, they had seldom affected major issues. Hayes despised all riders, but those proposed by the Democrats in 1879—designed to coerce an unwilling president into repealing major legislation that enforced the Constitution—were, he believed, unprecedented in the country's legislative history. Relishing the coming battle with Congress, Hayes confidently predicted, "This *particular* thing will, I suspect, never grow into a practice after the fate which this attempt will meet."[8]

Although Hayes was determined to use his veto power, there were rumors that he might sign a modified bill repealing the election laws. Republicans responded with alarm. "There must be *no compromise* in this matter!" one passionate Chicagoan warned. "Even the slightest yielding—now—on the part of the President to the demands of the Bull-dozing Brigadiers—would not only ruin *him*—but would *ruin the Republican Party* and *endanger the Nation*." Even Murat Halstead, who knew Hayes well, was uncertain. Hayes responded:

It almost angers me to see in the *Commercial* that you are shaky on the question of my probable action. Now let me assure you that everybody here ought to know my soundness on two questions.

  1. The right, duty and necessity of National protection at National elections.

  2. The duty of the President not to allow Congress to usurp his power to share in legislation.

It does not require half the nerve to maintain the right side of the latter question that it did to stand against the Congressional claim to the appointing power.[9]

The struggle over the election laws, which pitted Republicans against Democrats, revived the passions of the Civil War just as the Fitz John Porter case resurfaced. From the beginning, this case had been mired by politics, and now the timing was especially bad. A Democrat and a loyal lieutenant of Gen. George B. McClellan, Porter had been court-martialed, found guilty, and dismissed from the army for failing to obey Gen. John Pope's order to attack the enemy during the Second Battle of Bull Run. Although Porter had long sought exoneration, Grant—first as commanding general of the army and then as president—had kept the case closed.

Politics and friendship had led Hayes to assume that Porter was guilty. Hayes had been a radical during the early Reconstruction years; he was an associate of Garfield, who had served on Porter's court-martial, and was a friend of Manning F. Force, whose wife's sister was married to Pope. Aware, however, that the passions of war could distort justice, Hayes dismayed close friends by appointing a board of army officers to reexamine the case. New evidence revealing the precise strength of the Confederates opposite Porter and an able presentation by his distinguished counsel, Joseph H. Choate, helped convince the board that if Porter had obeyed the order (which Pope had based on an erroneous view of the situation), the attack would have invited disaster.[10]

The board's report shook Hayes's confidence in Porter's conviction. Had he not been struggling with the Democrats and rallying the old radical Republicans to his side in the battle of the riders, he might have taken a stand in Porter's favor. As it was, the report nudged him into a noncommittal position. Claiming that his opportunity to examine the evidence was "too limited to express a decided opinion," he sent the board's report and evidence to Congress, stating that the case deserved its attention. Had the board simply exonerated Porter and recommended his restoration to the army, its views might have been accepted. But its praise of Porter's conduct made ardent Republicans bristle, as did its somewhat dubious conclusion that it was Porter's grasp of the Confederates' actual strength—rather than his innate caution and contempt for Pope—that had kept him from obeying the order to attack.[11]

A year later, in March 1880, Hayes admitted that he had felt inclined to accept the board's conclusion about Porter. But the hostile opinions of Force, Jacob Dolson Cox, and Garfield, as well as debate in Congress, caused the president to revert toward his earlier view. No bill for Porter's relief passed until 1886, when Grover Cleveland, a Democratic president, signed the measure into law. A minor interruption during the ongoing battle of the riders, the Porter case augmented the wartime feelings that the riders had revived.[12]

On 25 April, after a lengthy debate, Congress passed the army appropriations bill with the rider by a strict party vote. The president, who already had most of his veto message written, added the last paragraphs to it that night. Since the public was uncertain of his response, there was considerable "betting and selling of pools" in Washington and New York.[13]

Hayes's veto message of 29 April objected to both the substance and the method of the rider. It was a "radical, dangerous, and unconstitutional" attempt by the House to force legislation on the Senate and the president; if enacted, it would prevent federal officers, whether civil or military, from keeping the peace at the polls. If the intent of the rider was to prevent the U.S. Army from intimidating voters at the polls, it was unnecessary, because under existing laws, "there can be no military interference with the elections." But, he continued, the rider also prohibited civil authorities from keeping the peace at congressional elections, which are of national as well as local significance. "It is the right of every citizen," Hayes emphasized, "to cast one unintimidated ballot and to have his ballot honestly counted." In a strictly party vote on 1 May, the Democrats could not override Hayes's veto.[14]

The Republican reaction to Hayes's veto was ecstatic. "Never before in my political experience have I known greater satisfaction among members of our party on any political event," John Sherman wrote from New York. In Chicago, according to William Henry Smith, the message produced "nothing but words of commendation." Smith himself considered the message good politics and broad statesmanship; it solidified and strengthened the Republican party by bringing back some of its members who had voted with the Democrats. Hayes also caused further merriment among Republicans when he mentioned to the correspondent from the Cincinnati *Commercial* that the Confederate constitution, to which a majority of the Democratic House and Senate caucus had sworn allegiance, prohibited riders by allowing the president an item veto in appropriations bills. Sherman also reported that the deadlock between Hayes and Congress had not slowed the economic recovery following the resumption of specie payments four months earlier.[15]

In early May, the Democrats changed their tactics and pushed a bill—not a rider—through Congress that would prohibit federal troops from keeping the peace at the polls unless they were requested to do so by state authorities. The Democrats, Hayes remarked, had passed a measure repealing many valuable laws: "They call them war measures, and seem to think that as the War is ended these laws should now be mustered out. We are ready to muster out the soldiers, but we dont muster out the flag nor the powers of the law and of the Constitution, which enabled us to gain the victory. We dont muster in again the evils that caused the War. Besides it is for the victors to say what shall remain—not for the vanquished."[16]

Hayes was up to the challenge. "The use of troops at the polls," he realized, "is a favorite battle cry of our opponents, utterly without foundation in recent facts, and yet if not fully understood capable of mischief." Hayes vetoed the bill on 12 May. Military interference at elections had already been prohibited, but, he observed, the national government should be able to use its military force wherever it is necessary to enforce the Constitution and laws of the United States. The proposed bill, Hayes pointed out, would allow state authorities to call on federal troops "to maintain the conduct of a State election" but would forbid federal authorities to call on the army or navy "to maintain the conduct of a national election against the same local violence that would overthrow it."[17]

Republicans of all shades backed Hayes's judgment that the vetoed bill would have granted state supremacy over national authority. Sitting at his desk in the House of Representatives, Garfield wrote to Hayes: "The message has just been read; and I know the House so well as an index of the public mind that I cannot be mistaken when I tell you, that no speech or paper ever emanated from your hand that will strike so deep into the heart and minds of the American people, and live so long in their gratitude as this noble and masterly paper of today."

On 13 May, the House failed to muster the two-thirds majority needed to override the veto, as Republicans rallied behind Hayes. Whitelaw Reid, whose New York *Tribune* had been hostile to the president, wrote: "I want in a word to tell you how glad I am for the matter as well as the manner of the last veto, and to say how proud I am of the fact—now visible to everybody—that the Republican party stands united and solid behind its chief."[18]

"What will the Democrats now do?" Dickson wondered. "Can they frame an innocent bill, one that does not subordinate the Nation to the State?" What they did was to persist in retaining the rider, repealing the election laws, which they had added to an $18 million legislative, executive, and judicial appropriations bill. By a strictly party vote, the House had adopted the bill on 26 April. Hayes planned his veto while the Senate debated its version of the bill in May. Normally an affable, placid man, Hayes became the steely adversary he had been on the battlefield: "I am glad . . . to do something for the true principles of the Constitution. My first veto maintained the prerogatives of the Executive . . . against the grasping ambition of the House of Representatives. The second maintained the right of the Executive branch . . . to enforce the laws, and now I am likely . . . to do something for purity and fairness in elections."[19]

As anticipated, the Senate passed the $18 million appropriations bill with its rider, and Hayes returned it to the House with his veto on 29 May. "I have not in such work been careful as to style," the president commented on his vetoes, "except to have my papers state principles in a way to satisfy men of ability and culture that the statement is sound, and to so phrase and put my propositions that the plain people can readily understand them." Apart from opposing riders on appropriations bills in principle, Hayes attacked this particular rider because it would destroy the federal government's control over congressional elections. The bill would allow federal marshals and supervisors merely to observe elections; it would provide neither protection for those voting nor punishment for those violating the law. In addition, Hayes argued that the election laws were both constitutional and necessary. The people, he asserted, "do not think that a free election means freedom from the wholesome restraints of law." Neither do they think that the place of election "should be a sanctuary for lawlessness and crime." The House again failed to override the president's veto.[20]

The Democrats were in a quandary. It was clear that Hayes gained strength with each veto. He had unified Republicans for the 1880 presidential campaign. Even George William Curtis, who in April had deplored the Republican emphasis on rebels and revolution, in May editorialized in *Harper's Weekly*: "The extra session . . . has revealed the Democratic party as the champion of state sovereignty as against the Union, and as toying with revolution upon an utterly false cry. It has united the Republican party enthusiastically in defense of the principle which was established by the war. It has given the Republicans a patriotic, constitutional, and conservative platform, upon which all intelligent citizens will gladly stand."[21]

The Democrats had woefully miscalculated. Their desire to pose as the defenders of liberty by eliminating federal interference with elections had been frustrated by Hayes's vetoes, which hammered home the message that the federal government had the right and the duty to prevent the voter intimidation and election frauds that the Democrats apparently had in mind. The plight of the Democrats concerned Garfield. "For them," he told Hayes, "there would seem to be no way out except perseverance in the direction of revolution, or an ignominious backing down." When Hayes responded playfully that he saw no reason for Republicans to worry over the Democrats' predicament, Garfield insisted: "But, Mr. President, the situation to them is very serious. If they go ahead in the way of revolution they are ruined and the country is embarrassed, and if they back squarely down and vote appropriations, they will surrender so completely that their political future is one of disaster." Hayes did not worry about a Democratic disaster. "A square backing down is their best way out," he insisted, "and for my part I will await that result with complacency."

William Henry Smith and Ohio Representatives William McKinley and Amos Townsend were present when Garfield unburdened himself. Smith noted:

The firm and cheerful tone of the President had an inspiring effect on General Garfield, whose principal weakness is a lack of moral courage. A man of great ability, with good impulses and an honorable ambition, he too often surprises his friends and mars his own prospects by yielding in the very midst of a contest. In this respect Mr. Hayes is his opposite; slow to accept the gage of battle, never himself provoking opposition, when once he has seen the necessity and has entered the lists he is vigorous and unfaltering: his faith and courage are sufficient to carry with him a host.[22]

Smith was too hard on Garfield, who had moral courage but often questioned the wisdom of the course he was taking. His introspective nature, confirmed by his Christian experience, caused him to examine and reexamine his actions. In contrast, Hayes was not introspective and had not experienced conversion; he adhered firmly to his course of action once he made up his mind. His self-confidence, which had served him well during Civil War battles, was useful in the White House.

While Hayes confidently awaited the future, the Democrats caucused in early June to find a way out of their predicament. Having unwittingly united and strengthened the Republicans in and out of Congress, the Democrats wished to retreat without further damaging their own party. They decided to pass the major appropriations bills but maneuvered to salvage something from the battle of the riders. By mid-June, Congress had passed an army appropriations bill and a legislative, executive, and judicial appropriations bill without political restrictions, both of which Hayes signed. It did not bother him that the Democrats had added to the army bill a face-saving, meaningless clause preventing the army from being used as a police force at the polls. The civil authorities, including marshals and their deputies, were the ones who policed the polls. Only if they could not enforce the election laws, Hayes noted, would the army be called in, and then not as a police force "but as part of the military power," which "may be used whenever it is necessary to enforce the laws."[23]

Still, the battle of the riders was not over yet. Congress had excluded provisions for the payment of deputy marshals and supervisors of elections as well as other judicial expenses from the legislative, executive, and judicial bill and placed them in a supplemental judicial appropriations bill, which included riders. On 23 June 1879, Hayes vetoed this supplemental bill, which forbade the "payment of general or special deputy marshals for service in connection with elections or on election day." The measure left the powers and duties of the supervisors of elections untouched but deprived them of the protection of the deputy marshals, who were "clothed with authority to enforce the election laws." Hayes stated the case baldly: "The object is to prevent any adequate control by the United States over the national

Hayes at bat for the Union (*Daily Graphic*, 3 June 1879)

elections." As usual, the Republican minority in Congress sustained Hayes's veto.[24]

This fourth veto threw the Democrats into confusion. Hard-line Democrats could not force an adjournment without further appropriations, because seventeen of their party had joined with Greenbackers and Republicans to keep Congress in session. After several caucuses, the Democrats were still in a quandary, but Hayes reported that "the probability seems to be that the Democrats will pass a judicial Expenses [bill] without the objectionable section . . . and also without any provision for Marshals or their deputies. Another bill for the Marshals, with the objectionable rider attached will also be sent to me."[25]

Hayes was right. The Democratic Congress passed a judicial expenses bill that excluded marshals and included riders repealing the test oath for jurors and providing for nonpartisan juries. Not objecting to these provisions, Hayes approved the bill but resolved to veto a companion appropriations bill for federal marshals with an "objectionable rider." Adopted by Congress on 28 June, this bill once again attempted to prevent the compensation of marshals and their deputies while they were enforcing the election laws. Reiterating the position he had taken a week earlier, Hayes vetoed the federal marshal bill on 30 June. The House sustained his veto, and on the following day, as the new fiscal year began, Congress adjourned. Hayes had saved the election laws, but the Democrats had prevented the appropriation of the $600,000 needed for marshals.[26]

The fight was over, and Hayes experienced "one of the 'ups' of political life." His earlier stand against the usurpation of the appointing power by Conkling and other Republican senators was now balanced by his stand against the "pretensions" to power of a "bare" Democratic majority of Congress. The president enjoyed enormous popularity among Republicans and cautioned himself: "When the [New York] Tribune can say 'The President has the Courtesy of a Chesterfield and the firmness of a Jackson,'(!) I must be prepared for the reactionary counterblast." But for the present, he basked in the praise. Murat Halstead told him that he had restored the Republican party, which had been "broken down and degraded under Grant," and the Philadelphia *Public Ledger* urged Hayes to run for a second term.[27]

Hayes would not renounce his pledge to seek only one term. During the battle of the riders, he told William Henry Smith to count him out in 1880. If Smith persisted in organizing a movement for his renomination, Hayes insisted, "I will put my foot on it at once. I have had enough of it, and firmly adhere to my original determination." Hayes thought that he could accomplish more as a lame duck than as a candidate for reelection. If he were a candidate, he believed, he "would be annoyed and hindered in the work" he had set his heart on "to accomplish as the distinguishing features" of his administration. "The first half of my term was so full of trouble and embarrassments as to be a continual struggle," he said, "but our difficulties are over, we are moving harmoniously along and I do not propose to invite a new season of embarrassment" by considering a second term. Smith realized that the president was not playing games. "Mr. Hayes's 'no' once expressed," he knew, "was always a very decisive syllable."[28]

At four o'clock on Sunday afternoon, 25 May 1879, Hayes went on his weekly ride with Secretary of the Treasury John Sherman, whose own presidential ambitions were unbounded. Ironically, Hayes's one-term principle, adopted to prevent the president from prostituting the civil service to secure his reelection, led his treasury secretary to use patronage in an attempt to secure the nomination. The next day, having visited Blaine of Maine and Logan of Illinois, Smith spoke with Sherman about his prospects for 1880. "It is evident," Smith reported, that Sherman "thinks Heaven is smiling upon him, and so it is, but will it continue to do so?" While Sherman and Blaine were anxious to take up residence in the White House, Hayes and Lucy agreed on 6 June that the pledge to vacate it after four years was one of their "greatest comforts."[29]

During his spectacular battle with Congress, Hayes also continued his routine administrative work and pushed for further civil-service reform. In April 1879, he ordered that the regulations governing appointments and promotions in the New York customhouse and New York post office be examined and adopted by other postmasters and collectors heading large federal offices. Wishing to be flexible, he had his private secretary, William K. Rogers, add: "Any alteration or addition that you may deem advisable will be favorably considered." A follow-up letter on 1 November queried "whether specific rules have been adopted . . . and, if so, with what result."[30]

Throughout the remainder of 1879, Sherman, Key, and Hayes received the reactions of postmasters and collectors to the New York rules. Virtually all these field civil servants had been in politics and resisted changing the habits of a lifetime. Nor were they ready to exchange, at the behest of a lame-duck administration, a half-century-old spoils tradition for the reformers' panacea of open, competitive examinations.

D. V. Bell, collector of customs at Detroit, insisted on 5 May that the New York rules, designed for a huge operation, would be cumbersome, inconvenient, and disadvantageous in his small office. Since only a few vacancies occurred in his force of approximately sixty, he believed that he could ascertain "the ability, integrity, habits, education, industry and history of any applicant far more fully" than could an examining board. Advancing the plausible argument that competitive examinations would favor inexperienced young men fresh out of high school or college, Bell recommended that no rules be adopted for his district. After he was told that the Treasury Department wanted the rules implemented, he sent in the names of his examiners and his modified regulations, but, given his attitude toward the competitive system, his assurances that the rules would "be observed as closely as is practicable in this District" did not augur well for reform in Detroit. In Chicago, after promising that the New York rules would be examined and applied if "practicable," collector William Henry Smith conveniently lost his copy of them and took no action until after the fall elections. When Smith finally introduced the new system, his qualms about open, competitive examinations led him to suggest that the responsible official should have "wide latitude in choosing between competitors."[31]

Hayes made some progress toward instituting civil-service reform in the major field offices. In Boston, where there was strong local support for reform, postmaster E. S. Tobey approved the New York rules; in Buffalo, collector John Tyler nominated as inspector of customs the highest-scoring individual among twenty who took a competitive examination. Tyler may have been especially cooperative because an extramarital affair had nearly cost him his job. In response to Hayes's query, Curtis (after consulting with Buffalo reformers) replied that the charge was "unfortunately true" but that "the girl was common," and removal for that reason "would necessarily ruin Mr. Tyler and his most worthy wife and family" and would not benefit the public service. After weighing Tyler's questionable private life against his proper public life, Hayes left him in office.[32]

Whether they embraced or rejected civil-service reform, administrators tried to eliminate theft. James N. Tyner, the first assistant postmaster general, related how his department apprehended Hilan H. Husted, who accounted for the payment of "short postage" on registered mail nationwide. Husted had been reporting very few stamps received, so his mail was interrupted and a record made of the stamps sent to him. Tyner reported: "At the end of fifteen days . . . the special agents in charge of the matter pounced upon him. The amount . . . found in his drawer, ready to be reported, was only about one-half what it should have been, and in his pocket was found the sum of one hundred dollars in postage stamps. . . . It was, also, discovered that he had arranged . . . with a druggist in this city, for the sale of stamps, and there were other circumstances that fastened his guilt upon him." But while Husted was pilfering stamps, Second Assistant Postmaster General Thomas J. Brady was defrauding the government of thousands of dollars by overpaying star-route mail contractors. If legal requirements were met and political needs served, some officials tolerated graft.[33]

Hayes wanted competent and honest officers, but evaluating them was difficult, especially if they were remote from Washington. Officials making field trips often reported on personnel problems in departments other than their own. In May 1879, for example, Tyner, while in San Francisco on post office business, reported to Hayes through Key that the internal revenue collector was unfit for office. Even with the railroad and the telegraph, the president had a complex task in administering the vast United States.[34]

Despite his good intentions, Hayes occasionally caused problems for his department heads. For example, he and other politicians made the manning of ships Navy Secretary Thompson's most vexing problem. Many naval officers marshaled every political connection they had to resist going to sea unless a good climate or sightseeing opportunity was in the offing. "I find myself especially embarrassed," Thompson told Hayes in September 1879, "by the detachment of several officers made by your order from Ships about to sail to the South Atlantic." One of them was angling for a Mediterranean cruise, "where *they all* desire to go," and a second wished "to avoid going to sea at all." Thompson asked Hayes not to allow himself "to be importuned and persuaded by the friends of officers" who were "*shirking* duty" and "demoralizing" the service. Thompson stressed that assignments were made from the roster without favoritism, and that interference undermined "all department orders and we shall never know what officers are on board any ship until she gets out of port."[35]

On 5 July 1879, Hayes and his family took up their usual summer residence at the Soldiers' Home on the outskirts of Washington. "Somewhat affected by the Washington malaria," he was anxious to get away and eager to have the local marshes drained. His malarial symptoms included "slight headache at night—bad dreams, a tendency of blood to the head—flushed face at times." But Hayes remained in the District of Columbia during July and August looking after affairs of state, mediating between the conflicting demands of politicians and reformers, attending church regularly (he had not missed a Sunday morning service since the beginning of his presidency), and thinking of his "talks to the people" during his projected midwestern tour. Avoiding "mere electioneering topics," he planned to stress the success of resumption, to exhort northern industrialists and southern landowners and merchants not to "oppress" white and black labor, and to preach that "the less public officers have to do with the management of party politics the better it will be for the public service, and for their party."[36]

While Hayes prepared to hit the campaign trail in his low-key manner, other politicians tried to enlist the civil service in their campaigns. For those

Hayes with his family

whose political lives were at stake, any commitment to a nonpartisan civil service evaporated as elections drew near. With his earlier order that civil servants refrain from political management and his introduction of the New York rules into the field service, Hayes had taken the first steps to convert a partisan civil service into a nonpolitical bureaucracy. But without congressional legislation, permanent reform was impossible. Hayes's administration would be gone in less than two years, and none of the three leading candidates to succeed him—Grant, Blaine, and Sherman—was an advocate of civil-service reform.

Even in the New York customhouse, the administration's showcase, reform could not be taken for granted. On one occasion, when George William Curtis insisted that collector Merritt appoint a candidate from among those placing highest on a competitive examination, Merritt, who had "no original interest or convictions" on reform, was visibly "chafed" by the interference of "one who is not in any official position." Having used reform methods to fill one position, he ignored the results of an examination and nominated as inspector W. H. Grace, who had been "convicted . . . of a flagrant assault upon Surveyor Sharpe." Although Sherman approved the nomination, the acting collector (Merritt was out of town) refused to administer the oath of office to Grace, since his appointment violated the rules. A distraught Curtis protested that the appointment of Grace would be a "breach of good faith" and that if it were made, the reform scheme should be abandoned as "impracticable. The Collector certainly ought to be able to see that such a system as he has pledged himself to cannot be, at the same time observed and disregarded." Hayes immediately told Sherman, "You know my earnest desire to keep the New York office above all criticism. Please deal judiciously and kindly, but with the utmost firmness in this and all such matters."[37]

Although federal employees in Baltimore and Cincinnati also were defying the president's civil-service reform policy, attention focused on New York, where a governor would be elected in the fall of 1879. New York was the seat of Roscoe Conkling, the most conspicuous spoilsman; it was the site of the most serious reform efforts; and it was the home of George William Curtis, the most indefatigable civil-service reformer. But with a Republican gubernatorial nominee to select in early September, neither the supporters of Conkling nor those of the administration (except for die-hard reformers like Curtis) were against using the civil service to achieve victory. As the convention approached, the president's June 1877 order was increasingly disobeyed.[38]

The best candidate from the administration's standpoint was Sherman S. Rogers of Buffalo; Conkling's man was Alonzo Cornell, whom Hayes had dismissed from the New York customhouse. Scandal increased the administration's chances of defeating Conkling, who was enamored with Chief Justice Salmon P. Chase's daughter, Kate Chase Sprague. Their affair came to an abrupt and public end in the summer of 1879 when her husband, former Sen. William Sprague of Rhode Island (an alcoholic who had neglected her), used a shotgun to chase Conkling from their summer home at Narragansett Pier. Conkling's attire, or lack of it, depended on the scurrility and hostility of the newspaper printing the story. "This exposure of C[onkling]'s rottenness will do good in one direction," Hayes commented. "It will weaken his political power, which is bad and only bad."[39]

To defeat Conkling, collector Merritt begged Hayes to let him attend the state convention, and administration Republicans pressed the president to replace John Tyler at Buffalo with William H. Daniels, who would work for Rogers's nomination. Curtis warned Hayes: "It would be rather singular that Mr. Tyler, whose conduct conforms precisely to the wishes of the administration, should make way for a gentleman, the sole reason of whose appointment is that he would do with zeal and success, precisely what the administration desires should not be done. . . . I should infinitely prefer that the Convention should nominate Cornell than that you should appoint Daniels."[40]

Resisting pressure, Hayes did nothing. He refused to unleash Merritt or replace Tyler. "Consistency" demanded that he keep the New York customhouse out of the convention, and Tyler did not merit dismissal. Hayes wished to set a "correct line of action" for "the political conduct of Office holders." He told Curtis: "We have simply let New York politics alone. Of course we are deeply interested in the result, but we have not interfered to control it."[41]

Dominated by officeholders who defied Hayes and remained loyal to Conkling in spite of his personal and political problems, the 1879 New York State Republican convention at Saratoga nominated Cornell for governor. Practical politicians in the administration blamed the outcome on civil-service reform; reformers drew the opposite conclusion. Angered and frustrated, Curtis told Hayes: "The Convention was carried against us by deliberate disregard of your order. . . . Should this conduct be disregarded by the Executive, the same means will secure the State Presidential Convention next year. The position of the Administration and its character require the summary removal of such offenders. No 'cause' can be more stringent than 'packing' caucuses and conventions."

Reform at the New York customhouse and post office and a reform-minded collector at the Buffalo customhouse had not kept government officers at these locations out of politics. Curtis emphasized that, besides obeying the civil-service order themselves, heads of offices must be convinced of its wisdom and must insist that their subordinates obey it. "If Mr. Burt was the head of the whole Custom House," Curtis declared, "every subordinate would know that he erred at his peril. . . . I mean no reflection upon General Merritt. But as you know, he acquiesces where Mr. Burt believes." And at the post office, Curtis believed that James should compel officers who had been appointed under the spoils system to conform to the new system. Having insisted before the convention that Tyler not be replaced by Daniels at Buffalo, Curtis told Hayes after the convention: "If Mr. Tyler is content to sit in his office and be ignorant of what is done by his subordinates . . . I should replace him with a collector who would take care that they all did as he did."[42]

On 8 September, a few days after Curtis had pleaded for the blood of New York spoilsmen, Hayes left Washington for the Midwest. With him were Lucy, Birch, Fanny, and Scott. Their first stop was the Cincinnati Industrial Exposition, where Hayes gave a speech, met former associates (including recently retired Rep. Jacob Dolson Cox and Gen. Philip Sheridan), attended a reception at William S. Groesbeck's mansion ("the largest and finest west of the Mountains"), saw old friends, and held a political powwow with collector William Henry Smith. Hayes was disturbed by newspaper reports that Smith was reorganizing the Republican party in Chicago, contrary to Hayes's order prohibiting political activity by officeholders. "Your relations to me," Hayes told him, "make it more embarrassing. . . . Other government officials ask to be permitted to do the same as you." Claiming that he had been "grossly misrepresented," Smith said that he had "merely" called a meeting at the request of "the most prominent and respectable business men of Chicago," who wished to drive "the disreputable element" from the leadership of the party. Seeing through Smith's alibi, Hayes responded: "If the business men of Chicago have not sufficient ability to organize for themselves and to purify the party . . . let it go. But they will find out how to do it, and find the men to lead them. But our duty is to . . . attend to the public business. We must refrain from political management in the interest of a decent civil service — to vindicate the principles we have already avowed."

To the annoyance of Smith, a committee insisting on an audience with the president ended the confidential chat. Smith wanted to tell Hayes that the people clamoring for civil-service reform and objecting to low-flung politics would not respect an administration that failed to protect itself and its friends. "With hands tied and the enemy free," Smith concluded, "defeat is inevitable." The nomination of Cornell at Saratoga seemed to confirm

Smith's point, but Hayes felt that if he had ignored his civil-service order to avoid defeat at Saratoga, he would, in his hypocrisy, have suffered a greater defeat.[43]

Frustration over the perpetual parade of patronage problems helped make civil-service reform attractive to Hayes. The strain of being president was "hard to bear" and grew harder as time passed. Time-consuming and emotionally taxing major policy decisions were inevitable, but petty patronage matters were also wearing and could be avoided if reform were adopted. While in Cincinnati, for example, Hayes obliged John Sherman by discussing with Assistant Treasurer Alexander M. Stem allegations that he had discriminated against veterans in his appointments at the U.S. subtreasury in that city. While in Fremont on his way west, Hayes had to decide if the Cheyenne postmaster could serve in the Wyoming territorial legislature and had to resolve a factional dispute over the Erie, Pennsylvania, post office.[44]

After a brief rest at Fremont, Hayes left for the West on 22 September, determined to conserve his strength. "I shall make no more full speeches," he told John Sherman, "and shall get off with as little talking as may be!" In this "swing around the circle," Hayes visited Indiana, Illinois, Missouri, and Kansas; he gave many short speeches and shook hands by the hour. As always, he discussed issues that he had embraced, fully realizing the value of advertising his views among the people. "It is public opinion that rules in this Republic," he told his audience in St. Joseph, Missouri. He stressed that his currency policy had brought prosperity, bolstered exports, and was responsible for the favorable balance of trade. Emphasizing the supremacy of the nation over the states, he insisted that all citizens had "equal civil and political rights" and reiterated that the federal government was concerned that these rights be enjoyed "on every inch of American soil." Everywhere, Hayes extolled the "popular system of free school education." It was his recipe for building prosperous communities fit for self-government. Hayes's trip was a triumph; wherever he went, the president received a warm welcome.[45]

Hayes got back to Fremont the day before his fifty-seventh birthday and remained at Spiegel Grove to vote in the Ohio election and to relax for two and a half weeks. From Washington, John Sherman assured him that the Supreme Court's traditional formal call on the president at the beginning of its October term could easily be postponed a week, as could the filling of a few vacancies among internal revenue collectors.[46]

While celebrating his birthday, Hayes walked around Spiegel Grove with William Henry Smith, discussing "public affairs . . . with great freedom and . . . good sense." Buoyed by his trip, Hayes spoke of business prosperity and full employment and of a "once more cheerful and contented" people. Turn-

Meeting the people (*Frank Leslie's Illustrated Newspaper*, 14 July 1877)

ing to politics, he blamed Grant's shortcomings as president on his lack of confidence in civil matters and his consequent dependence on Conkling for guidance. After Hayes spoke of the danger of a third Grant term (with Conkling in control), Smith again tried to persuade Hayes to consider a second term, but he emphatically said, "*That cannot and ought not to be.*" Predicting that public life was a habit he would leave with regret, Smith persisted, but Hayes maintained that he would go back to his books and private life "with a feeling of keen satisfaction."[47]

The return of prosperity helped the Republicans in the 1879 campaign. The election in Ohio, Hayes reported, "has gone strongly with us. . . . This is a valuable victory. Two questions were debated mainly. The Currency and the Supremacy of the General Gov[ernmen]t. Inflation and States rights are badly beaten." It gratified Hayes to have his uncompromising support of the gold standard and his conviction that Congress should appropriate funds "to execute all laws" vindicated by Ohio.[48]

After the October elections, interest focused on the New York campaign. Cornell was running for governor, and Arthur, who was now the Republican state chairman, was managing the campaign. Republican reformers were becoming genuine independents. They planned to scratch Cornell's name from the Republican ballot and either leave the space blank or write in the name of the Democratic nominee and incumbent, Gov. Lucius Robinson. Their defection, however, was offset by Tammany Hall Democrats, who refused to support Robinson, a Tilden protégé, and ran their own leader, "Honest" John Kelly. Cornell's nomination and campaign placed the Hayes administration in a ludicrous position. As head of his party, Hayes could not support a Democrat, but neither could he support Cornell as governor after he had declared him unfit to serve in the New York customhouse.

Hayes was annoyed by his predicament, but party loyalty triumphed. Although he thought Conkling a "corrupt and thoroughly rotten man," Hayes and his administration, particularly Evarts and Sherman, supported Conkling's nominee. In early October, Sherman posted Hayes on the vexing campaign: "The outlook in New York is a little more mixed than formerly. . . . The Cornell Committee are calling for help and will need all they can get. You have probably noticed my letter in response to a very urgent one from Arthur." Sherman, as a potential presidential candidate, was anxious to place others in his debt and campaigned for Cornell. Hayes even asked Schurz to permit Interior Department clerks to return to New York to vote.[49]

On the whole, the November elections pleased Hayes. "The Republican victory yesterday," he wrote in his diary, "was complete everywhere in the North except in New York." There, Republicans carried the legislature and elected Cornell governor—thanks to bolting Tammany Democrats—but lost three of the seven state officers to the Democrats. "I did all I could to save the cause," Hayes wrote, "by urging friends to lay aside their opposition. But there was too much Conkling in the ticket."[50]

The administration's course exasperated reformers, who, in turn, exasperated Hayes. Hayes wrote to reformer Wayne MacVeagh: "The great embarrassment in dealing with my 'friends' (not you) is they are without experience in practical affairs—have never been responsible for results—are without training in actual government, or law making—are soon hot and soon cold. You cant fight but one battle at a time—*two* at the most. This they don't know." MacVeagh agreed that many reformers lacked "political sense" but told Hayes that Sherman and Evarts exhibited "a grievous lack of the same article." Their behavior in the recent New York election had given the administration's commitment to civil-service reform the "air of humbug." Edward Cary, the editor of the *New York Times*, wrote: "I have little or no patience with Mr. Hayes. He is the victim of 'goody' rather than good intentions & his contributions to the pavement of the road to the infernal regions are vast & various."[51]

TWENTY-THREE

THE SUCCESSION

Triumphs in the 1879 elections augured well for the Republican party. The maneuvering of presidential candidates has always produced excitement and speculation, but in 1880 the fight for the Republican nomination was spectacular. Because Hayes kept his pledge to serve only one term, the struggle was among Grant, Blaine, and Sherman. The first two were popular but seriously flawed, and Sherman's inside track gave him a chance.

After the fall elections, Hayes turned from politics to affairs of state. The second session of the Forty-sixth Congress would meet on 1 December 1879, and his third annual message was due at that time. Hayes decided to address the currency question once again and reiterate his hard-money position. Although William Henry Smith warned him that another currency battle would incite attacks from "crazy speculating theorists," and cabinet members Thompson and Evarts told him to "do nothing to change the issues now before the Country," Hayes rejected their counsel. "The sooner we take the true position, the easier it will be to convince the people of its wisdom," he insisted.[1]

Hayes's message stressed the economic success of his monetary policy. Confidence in the government's capacity to make specie payments continued, and the excess of precious metals deposited and exchanged for greenbacks was about $40 million for the first eleven months of 1879. The strong business revival that year had resulted from the resumption of specie payments, Hayes proudly explained, which particularly benefited foreign trade, interest rates, and public credit. Beginning in 1873 and continuing throughout the Hayes administration, the United States had enjoyed a favorable balance of trade and consistently imported gold. This influx of gold, primarily in payment for enormous exports of wheat, moderated interest rates and enabled John Sherman to sell at par value (or above) 4 percent bonds, refinancing as much of the national debt as the law permitted. Since March 1877, this policy of funding the debt at lower interest rates had saved $14.3 million.

Hayes wished to pay off the debt rapidly but would not tamper with duties protecting American industry. Since receipts during the fiscal year ending 30 June 1879 ($273.8 million) barely covered the government's expenditures ($266.9 million), Hayes suggested that a duty on tea and coffee would bring several million dollars into the treasury for debt reduction. Although he had tilted toward free trade as a congressman and had avoided the tariff issue as a presidential candidate, President Hayes embraced protection, since, under it, American prosperity had surpassed that of other nations.

Prosperity, however, had failed to reconcile Hayes to a limited coinage of silver dollars or to a fixed amount of greenbacks in circulation ($346 million). Even when greenbacks could be readily redeemed in gold, Hayes believed that they threatened the gold standard. He urged Congress to allow the treasury secretary to suspend silver coinage, since the market value of silver dollars was uniformly less than that of gold dollars, and to retire all greenbacks, because he thought that paper money based wholly on the authority and credit of the government was unconstitutional (except in extreme emergencies) and a violation of sound financial principles.[2]

Despite the mutual exasperation between reformers and Hayes, he devoted the largest section of his message to civil-service reform. At his request, Dorman B. Eaton, the chairman of the Civil Service Commission (established in 1871 and without funds since 1875), studied the British civil service and found that open, competitive examinations supervised by a commission were used with success for the appointment of almost every subordinate British and Indian public officer. When submitting the study (which Eaton had made at his own expense) to Congress, Hayes asked it to decide whether British reform measures were adaptable "to our institutions and social life."

Hayes obviously thought that the British measures were adaptable. The power to appoint and remove subordinate civil servants, he maintained, should not "be used to aid a friend or reward a partisan, but is a trust, to be exercised in the public interest." Although acknowledging that the civil service was largely the president's responsibility, he insisted "that nothing adequate can be accomplished without cooperation on the part of Congress and considerate and intelligent support among the people." Stressing that appointments based on competitive examinations in Schurz's Department of the Interior and in a number of post offices and customhouses—most notably in New York City—were "salutary in a marked degree," Hayes wished to extend their use and requested funds for the Civil Service Commission. An active commission backed by Congress could also perpetuate his ban on political assessments and on political activities by officeholders.[3]

With his message out of the way, Hayes and his colleagues turned to presidential politics. Blaine, who had been hostile to Hayes, made overtures of friendship to which Hayes (who was almost never vindictive) responded positively. Despite his preference for Sherman, Hayes officially remained neutral. Knowing that a Republican defeat in 1880 was a "possibility, and that the question of availability must be considered" by the nominating convention, he let events take their course, just as he had with his own nomination.[4]

Hayes did not think that Sherman could be nominated. He expected Grant to be named and preferred him to Blaine, whose "railroad transactions," Hayes believed, "would defeat him before the people." Fearing, however, that another term would further diminish Grant's reputation, Hayes met with him privately on the day after Christmas at the residence of John Welsh in Philadelphia. For two hours, the president tried to dissuade his predecessor from seeking the nomination. While Hayes faced Grant in Philadelphia, Sherman urged his own followers to stress the nation's hostility to a third term. "The real contest," Sherman thought, "will be between Blaine and me. If Ohio is solid for me I have every reasonable assurance of success."[5]

As 1880 began, foreign affairs vied with politics for Hayes's attention. Except for the problems along the Mexican border and over Chinese immigrants, the administration had experienced no difficulties in conducting foreign affairs. In 1878, Hayes contributed to peace in South America by arbitrating a dispute between Argentina and Paraguay over the Chaco territory. When he awarded the territory to Paraguay, it gratefully renamed Villa Occidental in that region Villa Hayes, and the department of which it was the capital was later named Presidente Hayes. While Hayes was being honored in this way, a proposal to build a Panama canal was posing a new problem.[6]

Schemes to connect Atlantic and Pacific shipping lanes through Mexico, Nicaragua, or Panama experienced a dramatic revival in May 1879, when the Congres International d'Etudes du Canal Interoceanique met in Paris. Although 136 delegates from twenty-two countries (including naval officers Daniel Ammen and Aniceto Garcia Menocal from the United States) attended the meeting, Ferdinand de Lesseps, the builder of the Suez Canal, dominated the proceedings. With little forethought, he proposed that a sea-level, $240 million Panama canal be built by 1892. Having surveyed the route, Menocal knew that a sea-level Panama canal was impossible; he favored a canal with locks through Nicaragua. Ignoring the opinions of Menocal and of other expert engineers, the gathering caught the vision of de Lesseps and enthusiastically endorsed his proposal. De Lesseps immediately organized a private syndicate to build the canal and, although he had little success in raising money, journeyed to Panama in December 1879 and assured everyone, "The canal will be made."[7]

De Lesseps's ill-conceived, grandiose dream provoked Hayes's concern. He would have been uneasy about any non-American attempt to join the oceans across Central America, but because little more than a decade had elapsed since Napoleon III had made Maximilian the short-lived emperor of Mexico, a French project made him doubly suspicious. Hayes was determined that the United States should control any interocean canal. In taking this stand, he ignored the 1850 Clayton-Bulwer Treaty with Great Britain, which stipulated that neither country would seek "exclusive control" over such a venture. Hayes had not mentioned the de Lesseps project in his annual message, but he had anticipated a Nicaraguan canal "under the protective auspices of the United States." On 9 January 1880, he ordered two naval vessels to Caribbean and Pacific ports in the Chiriqui grant to establish naval stations strategically located between the proposed Panama and Nicaragua canals. Hayes thought that these bases would "give us a foothold which will be of vast service in controlling the passage from Ocean to Ocean either at Panama or at Nicaragua Lake." Congress, however, ignored Hayes's later request that it appropriate $200,000 for the Chiriqui bases.[8]

As was his custom when confronted with an important issue, Hayes sorted out his ideas before discussing them with his cabinet. On 7 February 1880, he concluded that the United States deemed the unobstructed use of an interoceanic canal in peace and in war, for commerce or for defense, as "essential to their safety and prosperity." Consequently, "the United States will not consent that any European power shall control the Railroad or Canal across the Isthmus of Central America"; indeed, "the United States will insist that this passage way shall always remain under American control."

Although adamant that Europe must not control the canal, Hayes was unsure of the role of "our sister republics. . . . The control must be exclusively either in the Country through which it passes," he wrote, "or in the United States, or under the joint control of American Republics." Then, apparently unaware of a contradiction, he added, "The United States should control this great highway between that part of our Country" on the Atlantic and that on the Pacific. "It must be held and controlled by America — by the American Republics." Hayes apparently thought that the Central American republics would neither wish nor dare to differ with the United States, which he sometimes referred to in the singular and sometimes in the plural. His grammatical inconsistency reflects the ongoing transformation of his country from a collection of states into a unified nation.[9]

Hayes remained preoccupied with the canal, despite family and social dis-

Guests arriving and departing for a White House reception (*Harper's Weekly*, 17 March 1877)

tractions. On Saturday evening, 7 February 1880, he and Lucy gave their largest, gayest, and last reception of the season. Although attendance at the event rivaled that of the Andrew Jackson inauguration-reception fiasco, the crowd was good-natured and well-behaved rather than uncouth and unruly. (But then, Jackson's punch differed from that which the Hayeses served.) On both occasions, some guests could not get into the White House, others could not get into the Blue Room, and some of those who got in had to exit "through windows because they could not get out at the door." The following day, Scott's ninth birthday, was bright and beautiful, but that did not keep Hayes from further ruminations in his diary about the canal. After arguing, "The interest of the U.S. in the . . . interoceanic canal or Railroad does not rest on the Monroe doctrine alone," he emphasized national security over prosperity, declaring that U.S. control "is essential for National defense."[10]

On 10 February, Hayes laid his "matured distinct and decisive" opinion before his cabinet. To warn de Lesseps and his associates "of the principles of the United States," Hayes planned to send a special message to Congress.

Evarts, who was collecting treaties, correspondence, and other relevant material, did not favor prompt action, but the rest of the cabinet enthusiastically supported the president. Schurz, who later would be an ardent anti-imperialist, said, "No European nation under similar circumstances would hesitate an instant to assert its rights in such a case, and to give decided expression of its purpose to maintain them." With a smile, Thompson (who would later change his mind when the price was right) said, "You know these have been my views all along." After further consultation, Hayes emphatically concluded, "The true policy of the United States as to a canal across any part of the Isthmus is either a canal under American control, or no canal."[11]

Some Americans did not consider the proposed canal a threat to the prosperity or security of the United States. De Lesseps's company was not connected with the French government, and Americans were free to purchase its stock. George William Curtis editorialized in *Harper's Weekly* that the de Lesseps enterprise did not jeopardize American interests, violate the Monroe Doctrine (which opposed new European colonies, but not investments in the Western Hemisphere), or even concern the American people. "If a private company of Frenchmen can raise the means to open a canal through the Isthmus of Panama," he asked, "why should the government of the United States take action?"[12]

Curtis, however, reversed himself two weeks later after hearing from Hayes's secretary William K. Rogers. No longer backing a policy of inaction, Curtis suggested that perhaps de Lesseps was taking the first step in establishing a European foothold and that the Monroe Doctrine would certainly apply to commercial enterprises projected "upon this continent under the authority, patronage, control, or protection of European governments." He concluded that although the de Lesseps enterprise was not "an infraction of our traditional policy," it did involve "very serious possibilities" that required the United States to define its attitude "authoritatively." Although Evarts's quip that the administration had "not been well edited" accurately reflected hostile Democratic publications, the cool Republican press, and lukewarm reform newspapers, the Hayes administration was certainly well served by *Harper's Weekly.*[13]

From Panama, de Lesseps arrived in New York for a U.S. tour, which would be both a triumph and a defeat. Hailed in New York, he was feted by 250 notables at Delmonico's. He took pains to disarm hostile Americans by insisting that his venture was a private enterprise, in no way contradicting the Monroe Doctrine. He welcomed American investors and was willing to locate his company's headquarters in New York or Washington, but American capitalists, fearing that his project would not succeed, held back their support. Although honors and praise were showered upon de Lesseps by the American people, these accolades were for his Suez achievement rather than for his Panama dream.

Yet because there was a chance that de Lesseps might succeed, Congress and the public shared Hayes's apprehensions concerning an interocean canal constructed by foreigners. Hayes had courteously received de Lesseps, but as he outlined his vision for Panama before the House Interoceanic Canal Committee, Hayes released the text of his special message to the Senate on 8 March 1880. This message unequivocally stated: "The policy of this country is a canal under American control." It condemned all foreign schemes to connect the Atlantic and Pacific Oceans. Hayes anticipated the Theodore Roosevelt Corollary to the Monroe Doctrine by warning foreign investors that "the United States would deem wholly inadmissible" any intervention on this continent by a European power to protect such investors. If the investors relied on the United States for protection, it must exercise enough control over projects "to protect its national interests and maintain the rights of those whose private capital is embarked in the work."

Hayes then spelled out the vital American interests at stake in the proposed canal: "It would be the great ocean thoroughfare between our Atlantic and our Pacific shores, and virtually a part of the coast line of the United States. Our merely commercial interest in it is greater than that of all other countries, while its relations to our power and prosperity as a nation, to our means of defense, our unity, peace, and safety, are matters of paramount concern to the people of the United States." This message to the Senate was accompanied by documents and a report from Evarts, which, although stressing the nation's special interest in the canal, rested its case on the 1846 treaty with New Grenada rather than on Hayes's broad principles. Realizing that his attack on a private venture went beyond any earlier American position, Hayes did not mention the Monroe Doctrine.

The Third French Republic quickly assured Hayes that it had no political ambitions in the New World, and de Lesseps refused to be devastated by the administration's hostility toward his project. Twisting Hayes's meaning, he audaciously welcomed the protection of the United States and cabled his son Charles in Paris: "The message of President Hayes guarantees the political security of the canal." A born promoter, de Lesseps took off on a whirlwind transcontinental rail tour, during which he created headlines all the way to San Francisco and back.[14]

Although de Lesseps had publicized his scheme and had lined up American bankers to market canal company stock, he left New York on 1 April

1880 without having persuaded American capitalists to invest in his project. The French people, however, supported him as he plunged ahead, and Hayes was plagued by the canal issue for the rest of his term. To attract American investors, de Lesseps formed an American committee and offered its presidency to Grant, who rejected it; then, in a maneuver calculated to suggest governmental support, he offered the job to Secretary of the Navy Thompson. When Hayes heard of the offer in late August 1880, he warned Thompson that "of course, you would not think of accepting an employment, or connection with the American Syndicate . . . while you continue in the administration." But the $25,000-a-year salary tempted Thompson, whose taste for high living could not be satiated by his $8,000-a-year cabinet salary. By early December, Thompson had accepted the syndicate presidency and, despite Hayes's admonition, planned to remain in the cabinet. Hayes, who had just reiterated his position on the canal in his fourth annual message, was infuriated by Thompson's action and immediately told him that he accepted his resignation.[15]

Within days, Thompson ably defended his new employers before the House Foreign Affairs Committee. He claimed that the proposed canal was a private enterprise that posed no threat to "the absolute sovereignty and independence of the South American states," which the Monroe Doctrine protected. Indeed, he insisted that the United States would threaten that sovereignty if the committee were to adopt the militant resolution it was considering, which invoked the Monroe Doctrine against a foreign-built canal. After Thompson's testimony, the committee recommended a milder resolution that, without condemning de Lesseps's scheme, declared that any attempt by a European government to build a canal would violate the Monroe Doctrine. Ignoring the committee's recommendations, the House passed no resolution. Although Hayes was unable to stop the canal before he left office, his aggressive stand had produced a quick denial of interest by France. Hayes also laid down a line of thought that, in his view, was quite distinct from the Monroe Doctrine. Theodore Roosevelt would later claim that line of thought as a corollary of the Monroe Doctrine.[16]

In January 1880, Hayes considered the Mormon Church in Utah to be as great a threat to American institutions as the French presence in Panama would be to American security. Mormon leaders demanded and received obedience from their followers, who made up more than 95 percent of those living in the Utah Territory. Defying the social customs and religious practices of mainstream America, as well as violating an 1862 federal law, the

Mormon Church sanctioned polygamy, and its members practiced it. This defiance of federal law, as well as the Mormon Church's secular activities, alarmed Hayes. The problem he faced with the Mormons was analogous to the problem of the South during Reconstruction, and his reaction to it echoed his earlier radicalism. In a federal system that emphasizes local authority, how should the federal government treat a tyrannical local majority that sometimes uses violence to achieve its ends? As president, Hayes appointed the governor of the Utah Territory, but the Mormon Church controlled both the legislature and, through juries, the courts. In Utah, the oppressed were women, although many of them believed the Mormon prophets Joseph Smith and Brigham Young, who taught that marrying a man with at least three wives secured a woman an exalted place in heaven.[17]

Hayes fervently believed in the separation of church and state and was determined to wrench control of Utah from the Mormon Church. In January 1880, when he had to either reappoint or replace the incumbent governor of the Utah Territory (who was reputedly "*too thick*" with the Mormons), his cabinet was divided between those who would reappoint and those who, like Hayes, wanted a new governor to establish a more vigorous policy. Division in Washington and the complicated situation in Utah made the appointment a difficult one, but Hayes resolved to regain for the government the temporal power that the Mormon Church had assumed. "Mormonism as a sectarian idea is nothing, but as a system of government it is our duty to deal with it as an enemy to our institutions, and its supporters and leaders as criminals." In mid-January 1880, Hayes appointed E. H. Murray, a friend of Justice John Marshall Harlan, as governor of Utah.[18]

A month earlier, in his annual message, Hayes had promised Congress that the 1862 law against polygamy—recently declared by the Supreme Court not to be in conflict with the First Amendment—would "be firmly and effectively executed." To help the new governor of the Utah Territory eradicate "the infamies of a law breaking and law defying institution," he called for more federal legislation. Since Congress did not legislate that year, Hayes urged in his next annual message that the government of Utah be reorganized to break Mormon political power. Taking an idea from the Northwest Ordinance of 1787, he recommended that Utah be governed by a governor and judges or commissioners appointed by the president and confirmed by the Senate. If Congress should balk at depriving Utah of its local government, Hayes suggested that "the right to vote, hold office, and sit on juries in the Territory of Utah be confined to those who neither practice nor uphold polygamy."

Congress followed neither prescription. It took a less extreme course and, in time, achieved some success. Even though the Edmunds Act of 1882 greatly increased arrests for polygamy, Mormons did not give up its practice until 1890. That year, the Supreme Court upheld the Edmunds-Tucker Act of 1887, which threatened Mormon institutions by dissolving the church as a corporate entity. With the Mormon Church no longer sanctioning polygamy, Utah became a state in 1896.[19]

"I am now in the last year of the Presidency," Hayes wrote in March 1880, "and look forward to its close as a school boy longs for the coming vacation." When Guy Bryan complained that Hayes had not written, he responded, "I dont write many letters except on compulsion. My writing is enormous in an office way. I neglect my friends from sheer weariness." Also, the spectacular receptions the Hayeses gave during the social season in January and February were tiring and occasionally trying affairs. Although called "a gay succession of brilliant scenes," the New Year's reception was marred by Col. Henry C. De Ahna, whose renomination as collector of Alaska had been rejected by the Senate. Upon reaching Hayes in the receiving line, he denounced the president (rather than the Senate) for "bringing on him and his family disgrace, hardships, suffering and sickness" and persisted so long that it was necessary for the police to eject him from the White House. Even the more successful receptions were exhausting, since Hayes and Lucy would stand for hours shaking the hands of an endless procession of guests.[20]

On the upside, informal musical evenings at the White House were relaxing, some ceremonial duties were rewarding, and many of the guests were entertaining. On 30 March, Hayes formally opened the Metropolitan Museum of Art in New York, after which he and Lucy dined most elegantly with John Jacob Astor. Among the White House guests that Hayes particularly enjoyed were Elinor Mead, his first cousin once removed, and her novelist husband William Dean Howells, who visited in May. Hayes not only took Howells on a walk every evening at half past nine but, as Elinor reported, rapped on their door each morning for "him to go with him for a turn before breakfast." The turn on 11 May was "two miles or more between 6 & 7 A.M." to the new buildings of the Bureau of Printing and Engraving and the Smithsonian Institution.[21]

Elinor Mead also mentioned that "it is very quiet here" because "Cousin Lucy has just lost her brother Joseph" and only wishes to see old friends. Dr. Joe, who was only fifty-three, had died suddenly on 27 April after suffering "an apoplectic stroke." He had never forgiven Hayes for not appointing him head of the Marine Hospital Service. Hayes had realized that Joe was a sick man and, noting that he suffered from "chills and fevers . . . had severe headaches . . . [and] was of a bilious temperament," Hayes had even feared that Joe might "become insane." Saddened but not regretting his course, Hayes preferred to remember Joe "as he was" during the Civil War—"an affectionate, warm hearted, honest and brave man, possessed of uncommon talents of observation, good judgment, and the faculty of making those around him happy."[22]

Hayes was wearying of the affairs of state. He was tired of chatting with a constant stream of visitors and of reading endless documents. He and his cabinet spent hours considering who to appoint as postmaster here or internal revenue collector there, as well as considering minor technical matters that should have been decided at a lower level. On two occasions in March, for example, they discussed whether the duty imposed on "iron imported for cotton-ties, barrel-hoops, etc." should be classed as hoop iron and charged a specific duty, as domestic manufacturers argued, or be classed simply as manufactured iron and subjected to a lower duty, as importers and a New York court maintained. Failing to resolve the problem, the cabinet left the final decision to Treasury Secretary John Sherman.[23]

More important and more troubling to Hayes and his cabinet was the case of Cadet Johnson Chesnut Whittaker, the only African American attending the U.S. Military Academy at West Point. Born a slave, Whittaker had entered the academy in 1876, after attending the University of South Carolina for two years. Although he was hazed and ostracized by white cadets, the superintendent of West Point, Gen. John M. Schofield, did not intervene. Believing that these student actions were useful tools in shaping nonconformists into an acceptable mold, he failed to see that, when applied relentlessly to Whittaker, their aim and result were discrimination, which was officially banned at the academy. Intense loneliness hampered Whittaker academically. After being held back one year, in the spring of 1880 he was at the top of the lowest sixth of his class. On the night of 5 April, three masked assailants beat him, cut his hair, slashed his ear, bound his hands and feet, and left him on the floor, where he was found the next morning.[24]

With neither Schofield nor the cadets willing to believe Whittaker's story, a speedy investigation by Lt. Col. Henry M. Lazelle, the commandant of cadets, concluded on 8 April that Whittaker had faked the assault. Denying any motive to attack himself, Whittaker asked for a further investigation by a court of inquiry. Schofield granted the request, appointed four West Point officers to the board and another officer to serve as Whittaker's counsel, and ordered the inquiry to begin the next day. Although Schofield admitted to Gen. William T. Sherman on 11 April that the affair was "a perplexing mystery," he told the New York press that Whittaker had mutilated himself to avoid an upcoming examination.

Within days, the "outrage committed on Cadet Whittaker" and "the attitude of the officers and cadets at the academy" were widely debated in the press. Conservatives sided with Schofield, his faculty, and the cadets; the old antislavery element championed Whittaker. Whittaker was particularly gratified by the support and advice of his former teacher, Richard T. Greener, who was dean of Howard University Law School and the first African American to graduate from Harvard College. By 14 April, Hayes and his cabinet decided that Whittaker needed additional legal counsel and asked District Attorney Martin I. Townsend of New York to appear in his behalf. Townsend's aggressive manner and repeated challenges to the West Point code of conduct offended the court and infuriated Schofield, who commended "the Corps of Cadets for their bearing under the injurious suspicions cast upon them" and expressed "confidence in their honor and integrity."

Townsend's defense made good newspaper copy but failed to help Whittaker. On 29 May 1880, the court of inquiry concluded that he had slashed himself in perpetrating a hoax. Schofield wanted to dismiss him on disciplinary grounds, but Hayes insisted that he could be dismissed only for academic reasons. In the June examinations immediately following the inquiry, Whittaker's grades plummeted, but adverse publicity had put West Point on the defensive, and Schofield did not dismiss him.

The Whittaker case alerted Hayes to the racism that prevailed at the military academy and to its inadequate educational standards. Yet, although Hayes wished to improve the quality of education at West Point, he tried to save from dismissal John C. Kilbreth (the nephew of a friend), who had failed both French and mathematics. On 18 July, Hayes thought it best to "pardon the West Point boys, all of them—Whittaker included," and Schofield reluctantly reinstated Kilbreth.[25]

Forgiving by nature, the president felt that the military academy was more responsible for the Whittaker case than the cadets involved. The academy, he judged, was "not on a satisfactory footing in several important respects." He believed that a West Point education failed to develop the moral perceptions and philosophical resources of American army officers. He discussed "the condition and want of West Point" with his friend Gen. Thomas L. Casey and concluded that the chaplain there should be replaced with "a young and vigorous preacher of real character" and that the curriculum should include "larger attention . . . to General literature. Our officers should have higher resources for happiness than are now resorted to in the Western

Posts." In the year preceding 10 February 1881, Hayes pardoned or reduced the sentences of thirty-one army officers found guilty of "drunkenness and much resulting scandalous conduct," and later that month he stopped the sale of "intoxicating liquors" at army posts.[26]

In July 1880, with little time remaining in his administration, Hayes turned to Manning F. Force for advice "*whether* to, and *how* to reorganize West Point." Force agreed that West Point should be "radically" reorganized and that Hayes should do the reorganizing that summer. Reflecting "a very general feeling through the country," Force condemned the cliquish tone of the military academy, as it was administered by Schofield, as "unAmerican" and "unrepublican" and recommended that a new superintendent be appointed with a "large discretion in the matter of . . . reorganization." Although Force thought that his wife's brother-in-law, Gen. John Pope, would be ideal for the task, he conceded that Pope was more valuable in his present command of the Department of the Missouri. In mentioning Pope, who blamed his failure at the 1862 battle of Second Bull Run on Fitz John Porter's inactivity, Force reminded Hayes of another dimension to the Whittaker case. As president of the board of general officers that had reviewed Porter's conduct at Bull Run and reported in his favor, Schofield had offended Pope and Force in 1879. The role of Schofield on that board magnified Force's hostility to his administration of West Point.[27]

"You," Hayes told Force, "have hit the nail on the head in every point you make," but Hayes realized that if Pope were at West Point, Porter's champions would oppose any reform he might propose. Hayes suggested several candidates, but Force disparaged them all. "You see," Hayes commented, "how little progress I am making. This is nothing new. In all affairs of government the same difficulty is met. Who?"[28]

Despite doubts about a replacement, Hayes informed Schofield on 17 August that he would be removed to ensure fair treatment of black cadets. Although he had anticipated the change, Schofield was outraged. Recalling his own excellent war record, he insisted to a sympathetic General Sherman that "very few men now living" had furthered the "freedom and equal rights" of blacks as much as he had. Now, Schofield believed, he was being ousted "for the purpose . . . of alluring the colored vote." Defending his own course and the behavior of the cadets, Schofield insisted to Hayes that the presence of blacks at West Point increased racial prejudice, that cadets had a right to avoid contact with blacks, and that it was unreasonable to force social intimacy between the races at West Point when this intimacy was rejected by the rest of the country.[29]

Carefully considering the conflicting interests involved, Hayes took months to decide on Schofield's successor. Evaluating the arguments of West Pointers against non–West Pointers, Porter's champions against Pope's champions, and racists against civil libertarians, Hayes appointed Gen. Oliver Otis Howard in December. This action angered General Sherman, who had not been consulted and who did not wish Schofield disturbed. But Hayes knew that Howard, the former head of the Freedmen's Bureau and of Howard University, would insist that black cadets be treated fairly. Furthermore, the arguments of law professor Greener buttressed Hayes's view and convinced Howard that Whittaker deserved a fair trial. On 29 December, on Howard's recommendation, Hayes ordered a court-martial and made certain that a majority of the ten officers involved were not West Pointers.[30]

The trial got under way in early 1881 and lasted more than four months—long after Hayes had left the presidency. Although Whittaker was ably defended by former South Carolina Gov. Daniel H. Chamberlain and was unshaken by vigorous cross-examination, he was found guilty of faking the attack and of lying to the court of inquiry and was dismissed from West Point. Whittaker appealed, and on 22 March 1882, President Chester A. Arthur, following the recommendation of Judge Advocate General David G. Swaim, disapproved of the findings and the sentence. The day before, however, Secretary of War Robert Todd Lincoln, son of the emancipator, had ordered Whittaker discharged from West Point for failing a philosophy examination back in 1880, immediately after his ordeal before the court of inquiry.[31]

Since 1880 was a presidential election year, politics got more attention than did polygamy, the proposed Panama canal, and West Point. No one was more involved in politics than John Sherman. Despite his chief's commitment to civil-service reform, Sherman used the enormous patronage of the Treasury Department to line up delegates to support his presidential candidacy. For example, by sending collector William Henry Smith of Chicago to New Orleans to ascertain "the reliable Sherman men in the Gov[ernmen]t service," Sherman and Smith violated Hayes's celebrated 22 June 1877 order prohibiting the management of political campaigns by officeholders.[32]

While Sherman and Smith behaved like spoilsmen, Hayes and Schurz continued to strive for a politically neutral civil service. As Hayes emphasized in his third annual message, legislation was needed to make reform stick. The problem was, he acknowledged to Curtis, that in Congress there were "no *champions* of Civil Service reform." Those who "would *float* or *lean* that way" needed "some earnest man to propose the bills, to make the argument, and champion the cause as a hobby." Hayes still believed that the first step should be "to regulate by law the conduct of members of Congress with respect to what is called, and, unhappily, properly called, patronage." Curtis agreed that "patronage and Congressional interference" should be restricted and cheered Hayes with word that Eaton's book on the British civil service, which Harper & Brothers had just published, was arousing great interest.[33]

With no champion in Congress and no reform legislation in the offing, civil-service reform depended largely on Hayes. The capacity of minor appointees and the degree and direction of their politicization depended on the quality and attitude of their supervisors, whom Hayes and his immediate subordinates appointed. They were constantly badgered by reformers as well as spoilsmen to appoint their candidates to these major positions. The difference was that while spoilsmen scrambled for offices to strengthen their machines, reformers scrambled for appointments to improve the public service and to make spoilsmen less powerful. For example, in January 1880, Curtis was particularly interested in a New York patronage matter. Although he knew little about the qualifications of either candidate for postmaster at Geneseo, he urged Hayes to appoint John F. Bishop, the anti-Conkling candidate. Bishop was backed by the state comptroller, James W. Wadsworth, "who stands against the ruthless despotism of the machine" and is "one of the props of better politics in this state." Ever willing to damage the Conkling machine, Hayes appointed Bishop.[34]

Just as Sherman's attempt to recruit delegates was part of the 1880 presidential campaign, so was the renewed Democratic effort to cripple the election laws. House Democrats attached a rider to an $8 million deficiency-appropriations bill, which passed both houses on 29 April. Hayes had urged Congress to appropriate funds to protect voting rights, but the rider took the power to appoint special deputy marshals away from the district marshal and gave it to the federal circuit court or, if it were not in session, to the district court. Since its object was to divide and undermine the authority, responsibility, and effectiveness of federal officers who supervised elections, Hayes vetoed the bill on 4 May. Because the appropriations were needed for government operations, the rider was, Hayes noted in his diary, a thinly disguised "measure of coercion." Again beaten back, the Democratic Congress passed a deficiency-appropriations bill containing neither the rider nor compensation for the services of deputy marshals at elections. Although deputy marshals would not receive five dollars a day from the federal government, Hayes approved the bill. It kept the government operating and left election laws intact.[35]

Rallying once more, the Democrats pushed through a bill that was almost identical to the recent rider: The courts would appoint deputy marshals, over whom district marshals would have no control. Making clear their aim to undermine the federal supervision of elections, the Democrats rejected a Republican amendment that would allow the courts to appoint deputy marshals but give the deputies the powers named in the existing election laws and place them, "like other deputy marshals, under the orders and control of the marshal of the district." Hayes again thwarted the Democrats. His veto message on 15 June did not object to court-appointed deputies supervising elections, but it did object to divorcing them from existing election laws that had been enacted to prevent fraud and bloodshed.

To buttress his position, Hayes quoted from the recent Maryland election case—*Ex Parte Siebold*, 1879—in which the Supreme Court had held that the election laws were constitutional. The majority opinion of Justice Bradley emphasized that "violence, fraud, corruption, and irregularity . . . have frequently prevailed" at recent elections for members of the House of Representatives. Asserting the supremacy of federal laws, he maintained that the national government "must necessarily have power to command obedience, preserve order, and keep the peace," or "it is no government." Bradley further stated that "no person or power in this land has the right to resist or question its authority so long as it keeps within the bounds of its jurisdiction."

Under this new bill, Hayes argued, the marshal could not appoint, remove, or control deputy marshals at elections. With no powers under the election laws, the proposed deputy marshals could not ensure "peaceable, orderly, and lawful elections." By discriminating against the authority of the United States, specifically "the powers of the United States officers at national elections," the proposed bill "violates the true principles of the Constitution."[36]

This last veto by Hayes in defense of the election laws was obscured by the struggle for the Republican presidential nomination. Although officially neutral, Hayes was not a disinterested spectator. If Grant or Blaine were nominated, Hayes, and particularly his southern and civil-service policies, would be repudiated by the convention. If Sherman were named, however, the administration and its policies (no matter how much Sherman might have deviated from them) would be endorsed.

In May, before the Chicago convention opened, Grant led the field. Although his backers exuded confidence publicly, Hayes learned that some of them feared that their man could not be nominated. In Illinois, for example, "the energy of John A. Logan and the devotion of the machine at his back" appeared, "through sharp practice," to make that state's delegation practically solid for Grant. But Logan confessed to William Henry Smith that he had little hope for Grant and thought that John Sherman "might be nominated"; Logan was, Smith perceived, "really fighting for his own political existence." Appalled by Logan's desperate, "high handed proceedings" in Illinois, Sherman exclaimed that the tactics of Grant's followers, suppressing "the wishes of the minority, and in some cases, the majority . . . will make it suicidal to press his nomination." Indeed, Sherman began to fear that Grant's reckless handlers "would prefer defeat with Grant to success with anyone else."[37]

Sherman's prediction that the high-handed methods of Grant's supporters would backfire was correct. They failed to secure a majority of delegates. Weakened by Hayes's civil-service policies and challenged by reformers and by Blaine's people, Grant supporters resorted to a desperate ploy to force his nomination. James Donald Cameron, chairman of the Republican National Committee, planned to apply the unit rule to all votes from the moment he called the convention to order on 2 June 1880. Under this rule, all the votes of a state delegation were awarded to the candidate backed by the majority of its delegates. This would enable Conkling, Cameron, and Logan to ignore the opposition within their New York, Pennsylvania, and Illinois delegations and give Grant the unanimous support of these states.

Their plan failed even before the convention met. Grant's opponents on the national committee forced Cameron to nominate George Frisbie Hoar, an enemy of the unit rule and a strong supporter of the Hayes administration, as the convention's temporary chairman. With Hoar in the chair, the convention ousted some Grant delegates from Illinois who had been the beneficiaries of Logan's high-handedness. "Logan was completely vanquished," Birch wrote to Lucy, and "Conkling sneered at every thing and every-body, but seemed to get the worse in every encounter."

Before the balloting began, Hayes concluded that Grant would not be nominated because of "the unpopularity of the managers of his canvass, and of their methods. . . . The immediately valuable result is the condemnation of the machine as organized & managed by Conkling and Cameron." Hayes regretted that "our first soldier and a man of many sterling qualities should be so humiliated and degraded as he has been by his unprincipled supporters." Even though Blaine's chances were good, Hayes thought that Sherman or a fourth candidate might win.

Grant's supporters could not muster the 378 votes needed to win his nomination, but they remained loyal to him. On the first ballot, he received 304 votes; on the thirty-sixth and last ballot, he had 306 votes. The supporters of the other candidates were also disciplined. Blaine had 284 votes on the first ballot and 275 on the thirty-fourth; Sherman started with 93, advanced to 120 on the thirtieth, and still had 99 on the thirty-fifth ballot.

The break came on 8 June with the thirty-fourth ballot. James A. Garfield, who was managing the Sherman forces at the convention, was embarrassed and flattered to receive one or two votes between the second and the thirty-third ballots. When on the next ballot his total jumped to seventeen, the anti-Grant forces had found their candidate. On the thirty-fifth ballot, most of Blaine's supporters went over to Garfield, and on the thirty-sixth ballot, virtually all of Sherman's men shifted to give Garfield the nomination. To win New York's crucial electoral vote in the ensuing campaign, Garfield's friends wanted to give it the vice-presidential candidate, but Conkling ordered his minions to reject the nomination. The New York delegation caucused without Conkling and named Chester A. Arthur, who defied Conkling and accepted the honor.[38]

Although Hayes was close to Sherman, he called Garfield's nomination "the best that was possible." The convention gave Hayes "much personal gratification" with the defeat of his bitter enemies, the success of a friend ("Ohio to the front also and again!"), and the endorsement of his own administration and civil-service reform. Hayes regarded the nomination of Arthur, whom he had fired from the New York customhouse, as a "sop thrown to Conkling" that emphasized "the completeness of his defeat" (which was precisely the way Conkling felt). Garfield, Hayes thought, was "the ideal candidate"; he had risen from poverty and obscurity—from the boy on the canal towpath—to scholar, major general, statesman, and presidential candidate. Carried away by his enthusiasm, Hayes exclaimed, "The truth is no man ever started so low that accomplished so much in all our history. Not Franklin or Lincoln even."[39]

Sherman was not enthusiastic, but, considering his disappointment, he behaved well. He became "satisfied that while Garfield had the hope that he would be the dark horse that he faithfully and loyally" supported Sherman's candidacy until the convention turned to him. In addition to the pain of his defeat, Sherman had financial problems. His forces had spent $2,800 in Chicago at the very time he had committed himself to building a home in Washington. But his nervy Chicago manager came to his aid by insisting that since Garfield had been nominated, his friends must assume Sherman's bills. Fearing Sherman's wrath, Garfield's friends complied. Personally, Garfield wanted neither to be thought guilty of duplicity nor to have his campaign sabotaged by the Treasury Department. Although Hayes later came to believe that Garfield could have been more faithful to Sherman by forcefully quashing his own candidacy, at the time, Hayes assured Garfield that Sherman did not feel betrayed.[40]

A "little hoarse from much talking but . . . natural and sensible," Garfield discussed campaign plans with Hayes, who suggested three topics. With the battle of the riders still in his mind, Hayes stressed the Democrats' attempt "to reestablish the States Rights doctrine of Calhoun and the Rebellion, and the resistance to these reactionary movements by the Republican party." Hayes also wanted to advertise the "prosperous condition of the Gov[ernmen]t and the People by reason of Republican measures & administration," and, finally, he wanted the campaign to exploit "the character, life, and Services of Gen. Garfield."[41]

TWENTY-FOUR

THE GARFIELD CAMPAIGN

Garfield's nomination marked the beginning of the wind-down of the Hayes administration. Although he would be president for nine more months, Hayes became more reflective about the accomplishments of his administration and less concerned with its present and future. No longer at the center of politics, he became an observer at its edge. After meeting Hayes immediately following the convention, Garfield did not seek his advice on strategy, principles, or issues but did request appointments to help heal party strife and ensure a Republican triumph.

On 16 June, Garfield relayed to Hayes a telegram he had received from Portland, Oregon, claiming that John Kelly "should be reappointed Collector at this port," since "any change now would endanger the success of the republican party here in November." Two weeks later, after claiming to be unwilling to annoy the president "with letters in reference to removals or appointments," Garfield repeated warnings from Oregon and elsewhere that Kelly's removal would "seriously affect our prospects." Since Navy Secretary Thompson (who had not yet been dismissed) planned to visit the West Coast, Hayes accepted his offer to investigate but told him to "hear fully *both* sides."[1]

In addition, Garfield wished to use the Philadelphia postmastership "to heal the dissensions which the contest in Chicago has produced." Since Hayes planned to move former Gov. John F. Hartranft from the post office to the customhouse, Garfield consulted with "several prominent Pennsylvania gentlemen" and then asked Hayes to appoint as postmaster Peter A. B. Widener. A traction magnate and former city treasurer, Widener was "a man of wealth and influence and not politically obnoxious to either wing of the party." That move, Garfield believed, would "greatly aid in the Campaign."

After receiving a second anxious letter, Hayes told Garfield, "The Philadelphia Post Office is still in the hands of Gen. Hartranft. When he leaves it, if he does leave it, I will look carefully into the case. I am doing nothing to hurt the cause if I can avoid it. You will of course be appealed to by all sorts of people and will be perfectly free to make known to me whatever you wish me to know. My purpose is to allow no danger to come through me." Garfield got the point. "I want you to give me credit," he responded, "for many requests I do not make—or rather—for not making very many of those which I am asked to do."[2]

Although Hayes wished to cooperate with Garfield, he followed his own counsel, as always, and nominated Gen. Henry Shippen Huidekoper for postmaster of Philadelphia. Appointing any of the strongly backed candidates, Hayes explained, "would have offended some powerful faction." Huidekoper, a man of education and social standing who had lost an arm at Gettysburg, would offend no one and would be an excellent officer, which was, Hayes said, "the consideration which does and should win." Meanwhile, out on the West Coast, Thompson discovered that the factional struggle over Kelly's reappointment or nonreappointment as collector of Portland would not jeopardize Republican control of Oregon.[3]

Hayes was disappointed in Garfield as a candidate. His letter of acceptance, which would be his only public opportunity to address campaign issues, abandoned what Hayes had won in his struggle with Conkling over senatorial courtesy. The letter also ignored the successful application of an appointments policy based on open, competitive examinations in the New York customhouse. Reform legislation, Garfield said, should regulate the tenure of civil servants rather than the way they were appointed. "To select wisely," he would "seek and receive" guidance from Congress.

Believing just the opposite, Hayes exclaimed: "The first great step in the reform is to abolish Congressional patronage—to restore to the Executive the appointing power which has been usurped by Congress, and especially by the Senate." Hayes had taken that step and was "filling the important places of Collector of the Ports, and Post Master at Philadelphia almost without a suggestion even from Senators or Representatives!" Garfield's attempt "to be politic—to trim—to talk so equivocally as to have the benefit of opposing no body," made Hayes fear that what he had gained for reform might be lost. Disgusted reformers called the letter cowardly and unworthy, and Curtis feared that Garfield, whose "fiber" was not "steel," would follow no firm civil-service policy. Nevertheless, reformers supported him, for they realized that the Democrats and their nominee, Gen. Winfield Scott Hancock, would not reform the civil service.[4]

From the viewpoint of Hayes and members of his cabinet—Schurz and Sherman in particular—Garfield made further mistakes. Still, he retained their support and received their encouragement and advice. After he impetuously responded to a hostile letter, Hayes warned him, as he had been warned earlier, that the first rule for a candidate should be "absolute and complete divorce from your inkstand." He should write *"no letters to strangers*, or to anybody else *on politics*." To Hayes, Garfield's most questionable move, however, was his New York trip to conciliate Conkling. Because Hayes had won the 1876 election with nineteen electoral votes from southern states that the Republicans could no longer win, Garfield obviously had to win some states that Tilden had carried. New York (thirty-five votes), Indiana (fifteen), and Connecticut (six) were possibilities. To win, Garfield needed organization, money, and hard work, but Hayes's civil-service policies threatened to wither political organizations and to shrink party revenues from assessments on officeholders. In contrast, the spoilsmen were adept at extracting cash from civil servants, and if the members of the Conkling machine worked at it, they would most likely be able to wrest New York from the Democrats.[5]

With the reform vote still safe, Garfield wrote to Hayes that he was going to New York to promote party peace. Garfield insisted that "leading men of all shades of republicanism" be invited to the meeting and reassured Hayes that "if . . . the purpose of this meeting is to secure any concessions to the N.Y. men who are sulking—they will find no help in me beyond what I would give to any Republican." The 5 August meeting of Republican politicians at the Fifth Avenue Hotel included Sherman, who thought that Garfield should not have attended "a mere political meeting," and Blaine. Conkling, who was nearby enjoying the sea breezes on Coney Island, sent his lieutenants. To the amusement of Hayes, Lucy—in New York to shop for their approaching western trip—was also at the Fifth Avenue Hotel. Conkling's lieutenants later claimed that a conciliatory Garfield had promised them the spoils of New York. Accepting their version, Conkling ceased his sulking, took to the stump, and worked effectively for the Republican party but refrained from mentioning Garfield in a generous way.[6]

Although the New York meeting activated Conkling, it left Garfield troubled. Ever introspective, he realized that he had led the Conkling men to expect more than he planned to give them and that his ambiguity—born of the twin desires to win the election and to please everybody—would later plague him. "If I finished the N.Y. trip without mistakes, I shall be glad," he confided to Hayes.[7]

Hayes remained presidential and did not campaign overtly, but he followed his advice to Garfield and dropped "a good seed at every available point." He noted that an "effective" partisan speech would contrast the Democratic platform, which insisted that a free ballot must "be maintained in every part of the United States," with what the Democrats had done "in South Carolina, Mississippi, Louisiana and other States" to disfranchise blacks and to deprive Republicans of a majority in both houses of Congress. It would also stress that the Democratic party had failed to achieve "complete pacification" by refusing "to faithfully observe the 15*th* amendment" and would insist that this unrest injured the South by causing immigrants to avoid it; this would explain why in 1880 "only one city out of the *twenty*" with a population over 100,000 was southern. Hayes restrained himself and did not make a genuine campaign speech until the final day of the campaign, but these ideas influenced the frequent talks he gave while traveling.[8]

Avoiding blatant politics in his speeches at college commencements and soldier gatherings, Hayes preached equal rights. He spoke at his alma mater Kenyon and at Yale, where he received an honorary doctor of laws degree; he addressed Ohio veterans at Columbus on 11 August, where he shared the platform with General Sherman (who made his "war . . . is all hell" speech); and at Canton on 1 September, he spoke at the reunion of his Twenty-third Ohio Regiment. To veterans, Hayes emphasized that although the war had destroyed slavery, "its evils live after it." Many parts of the South still lacked "that intelligent self-government without which, in America at least, great and permanent prosperity is impossible." Hayes argued that self-government rested on universal suffrage and had to be based on universal education. "My hobby," he wrote while preparing for his speech at Columbus, "more and more is likely to be Common School Education, or universal education."

Hayes knew that universal education could not be accomplished without federal aid, because southern states and western territories were too impoverished to educate all their children. Federal subsidies—either land grants, for which there were ample precedents, or direct appropriations—had to supplement inadequate local systems. Wherever the work of the schoolmaster "shall be well done, in all our borders," Hayes predicted at Columbus, "it will be found that there, also, the principles of the Declaration of Independence will be cherished, the sentiment of nationality will prevail, the equal rights amendments will be cheerfully obeyed, and there will be 'the home of freedom and the refuge of the oppressed of every race.'"[9]

Hayes's letter to Frank Hatton, editor of the Burlington, Iowa, *Hawkeye*, stressing the necessity of an educated electorate was widely circulated as a campaign document. Although the "perpetuity of the Union" had been established and the Supreme Court had sustained the "supremacy of the National Government" by upholding the "validity of the federal election laws," there was still, Hayes wrote, "a dangerous practical denial of the equal rights with respect to voting secured to colored citizens by the Fifteenth Amendment to the Constitution."[10]

Hayes's point—that it was difficult for a demagogue to manipulate an educated electorate—was well taken. Demagogues routinely exploited poor southern whites by playing the race card when there were issues in which poor blacks and poor whites shared common interests. Unquestionably, education would improve the economic status of impoverished citizens, and educated blacks would be better able to protest their disfranchisement than would ignorant blacks. The most pressing problem for southern blacks, however, was not deceptive demagogues but brutalizing bullies. During Hayes's administration, Democratic strength in Congress and growing apathy among Republicans made enforcing the Fourteenth and Fifteenth Amendments impossible. Although Hayes managed to keep the Force Acts (i.e., election laws) on the books, they were not enforced in the South. Realizing that there was little immediate chance that the election laws would give blacks the vote, Hayes pinned his hopes on education. But Congress also failed to enact the Blair bill, which embodied Hayes's ideas on federal aid to education.[11]

The presidential campaign focused attention on the electoral college and on the census, which determined the strength of states in that college and in Congress. Hayes consulted with Francis Amasa Walker, superintendent of the tenth census (1880), about Republican allegations that southern enumerators had exaggerated the population of their region in general and of South Carolina in particular. A professor of political economy and history at Yale University's Sheffield Scientific School, Walker had reorganized the Bureau of Statistics and had directed the ninth census (1870). He was chagrined, however, when that census proved unreliable, particularly in the South. He had been handicapped by inadequate authority in the 1850 law governing the census; by Congress, which cut off his compensation in 1870; and by the spoils system, which failed to provide capable personnel.

When Hayes took office, Walker was still the unpaid superintendent of the census. Hayes urged making the Census Office permanent and maintaining its machinery continuously. In 1879, Congress responded with a law enabling Walker—who was at last paid $5,000—to set up a Washington Census Office with a staff of twenty and to select his own enumerators for the tenth census. With the full support of the Hayes administration and with a stellar group of assistants, Walker presented to the nation an outstanding census in twenty-two volumes. Hayes, who had faith that Walker and his staff would correct frauds, advised Garfield to "go slow on the complaints about the Census," since the two fastest-growing districts (one in Kentucky and the other in South Carolina) had "staunch Republican Supervisors."[12]

The presidential campaign was of paramount importance, but Hayes also kept posted on two construction projects. An addition to his Fremont home was progressing nicely under the supervision of his son Webb, and stonemasons had resumed their work on the Washington Monument. To Hayes, the unfinished monument was "a reproach to the nation"; to Lucy, the stunted structure looked more like a classical ruin than a tribute to the country's first president. The gigantic obelisk, designed by Robert Mills, was started in 1848 by the Washington National Monument Association and halted in 1855 when Mills died with only 152 feet of its projected 600-foot shaft completed. Over the next twenty years, while critics disparaged the monument's design and engineers doubted that its foundation could bear its massive weight, the association had difficulty raising money until Congress provided funds on 2 August 1876.

Not about to throw money away, Congress attached conditions to its appropriation. Before the project could proceed, the foundation had to be strengthened. Meanwhile, other designs were suggested, including a proposal by Hayes's cousin Larkin Goldsmith Mead that an eighty-five-foot hammered bronze statue of Washington be placed on the existing column. Coordinating the efforts of those who wanted the monument completed, Hayes worked closely with the commissioner of public buildings, Gen. Thomas L. Casey (who became a family friend and often introduced guests at large White House receptions). After careful study, Casey made a towering obelisk again feasible with a plan to strengthen the foundation by means of "a hoop skirt." In June 1878, Congress authorized $36,000 for this work.

Hayes and his associates "decided that the monument should overtop all other tall structures." Initially, they fixed its height at 550 feet, reflecting research on the heights of tall structures by Librarian of Congress Ainsworth Rand Spofford (Hayes's old Cincinnati Literary Club associate). It was, however, George Perkins Marsh, American minister to Italy, who determined the height of the monument. Personifying the cultivated nineteenth-century diplomat with unbounded scholarly interests, Marsh had served in Italy since 1861. Although interested primarily in linguistics, he also collected reptiles and engravings for the Smithsonian Institution and, in 1864, published one of the earliest works on the environment. With a reputation as a universal genius, he was consulted by Hayes and his associates on the Washington Monument project. Marsh did not disappoint them. "Singularly and fortunately," Hayes recorded, Marsh "discovered that there was a rule which determined the height of an obelisk by reference to the dimension of its base; and that by the rule our monument should be 555 feet high."[13]

Although Edward Clark, the architect of the Capitol, gave constant and indispensable aid to the work, Hayes put Casey in charge of constructing the remainder of the monument. When it was completed in 1885, the Washington Monument was the tallest structure in the world. Although it was subsequently dwarfed by steel towers, it will probably remain the world's tallest masonry structure. To put the monument in a proper setting, Hayes wished to realize the plans of Pierre L'Enfant and Andrew Jackson Downing for "laying out *as one park* all of the public ground from the Capitol to the Potomac." To achieve part of that dream and to improve both health and navigation, Hayes urged Congress to appropriate funds to reclaim "the marshes in the harbors of the cities of Washington and Georgetown." The mall, however, was not created until the railroad station, the train tracks, and the surrounding "jumbled mass of shacks (temporary Civil War barracks), assorted gardens and plots" were finally removed in the twentieth century.[14]

When the first stone in the renewed construction of the monument was laid on 7 August 1880 (with Hayes looking on), the Garfield campaign was just beginning to raise money from civil servants. Hayes had prohibited political assessments in June 1877, but by early 1878 he had explained that he did not object to officeholders making voluntary contributions. Although Hayes insisted that no one would be dismissed for refusing to contribute, civil servants were apprehensive in 1880 when they received circulars stipulating the amount they were expected to give. As a congressman, Garfield had condemned these assessments, but as a presidential candidate, he wrote to the chief assessor in Washington: "Please say to Brady that I hope he will give us all the assistance he can. I think he can help effectually. Please tell me how the Departments generally are doing." Thomas J. Brady, Hayes's second assistant postmaster general, was busily engaged not only in assessing officeholders but also, unknown to Hayes and Garfield, in defrauding the Post Office Department of money that was earmarked for its star routes in sparsely populated areas.[15]

The star-route frauds, for which Brady was primarily responsible, also helped finance Garfield's campaign. These special postal routes—which were designated on lists by three stars for "certainty, celerity, and security"—were mostly in the West and depended on "stagecoach, buckboard and saddle horse" for transportation. Marauders, topography, and climate made them difficult and dangerous. There were 9,225 star routes (some of them handling only three letters a week) for which $5.9 million was appropriated in 1878. Between 1878 and 1880, Brady and his accomplices furnished sham petitions requesting that service be expedited on ninety-three of these routes. Improved service jumped annual operating costs from $762,858 to $2,723,464, which required a deficiency appropriation that made Hayes and some congressmen suspicious. The House Committee on Appropriations, which was dominated by Democrats, investigated; but after "active and angry controversy," Congress sustained Brady and appropriated the money.

Whether star-route mail service in remote areas should be restricted or liberally furnished had always been controversial. Since he identified with the West, Hayes agreed in principle with Postmaster General David M. Key and First Assistant Postmaster General James N. Tyner's liberal policy. They both thought that increased star-route appropriations reflected expanded service and were not an indication of possible corruption. But, despite their opinions, Hayes feared skulduggery and insisted that no new star-route liabilities be incurred without a review by Key, the cabinet, and himself. Hayes believed that this drastic solution—requiring a presidential decision on mail routes handling only a few letters a week—would stop what he later described as "crooked or even inconsiderate action."[16]

Despite Key's failure to divine what Brady was up to, Hayes's cabinet served him well. His chief advisers—Sherman, Evarts, Schurz, and Devens—remained with him throughout his presidency and helped make his administration extremely stable. Hayes made only three cabinet changes, and they occurred late in his administration. In December 1879, when George W. McCrary resigned as secretary of war to become a federal circuit judge, Alexander Ramsey of Minnesota took over the War Department. A second change occurred in late August 1880 when Key, whom Hayes had made a U.S. district judge for eastern and middle Tennessee, began his judicial duties. Although "every republican state Senator & state officer" in New York urged that New York's reforming postmaster, Thomas L. James, fill Key's place, Hayes did not appoint him, probably because of his loyalty to Roscoe Conkling. Hayes asked Horace Maynard—a Tennessean like Key, but a radical Republican rather than a moderate Democrat—to head the politically sensitive Post Office Department. Hayes made his final cabinet change when he replaced Navy Secretary Thompson with Nathan Goff, Jr., of West Virginia, who served only two months.[17]

During the summer of 1880, Hayes and Lucy prepared for a visit to the West Coast in September. Hayes, who was five feet eight inches tall, discovered in July that his weight had crept up to 190 pounds and resolved to lose five to eight pounds with "warm morning walks." He also had to trim the size of the party accompanying them. Hayes explained that, with "several hundred miles of staging & ambulancing," it would be a difficult trip, and the "ladies have been cut down of necessity." Though it looked "mean and under other circumstances would be mean," Hayes invited William Dean Howells and Maj. W. D. Bickham without their wives, but neither of them accepted.[18]

Leaving "dull" Washington on the evening of 26 August, Hayes was absent during the height of the campaign, when civil servants were pressed to pay political assessments. Coming just before the election of his successor, this pleasant trip enabled Hayes to take a bow for a job well done. People everywhere thronged to applaud him. The first leg of the journey was a ride to Fremont in the beautiful new car belonging to Charles Edmund Pugh, superintendent of inspection of the Pennsylvania Railroad. Hayes and his family rested almost a week at Spiegel Grove, where they celebrated Lucy's forty-ninth birthday, and Hayes acknowledged, "I never loved her so much as now."

On 1 September, Hayes left by train for California. He was accompanied by Lucy, sons Birch and Rud, favorite niece Laura Platt Mitchell, and old friends John and Harriet Herron. Fanny and Scott were left at Spiegel Grove under the supervision of Webb, who had accompanied Schurz on a western tour the previous summer. The party (whose number fluctuated around nineteen) also included General Sherman (who planned the trip), his daughter Rachel, and Secretary of War Ramsey. After an overnight stop in Chicago, the travelers proceeded to Salt Lake City, Utah. They made frequent stops along the way, during which Hayes, Sherman, and Ramsey would say a few words and Lucy would make an appearance. Although informal and nonpartisan in these talks, Hayes realized that by appearing with the popular, though apolitical, General Sherman and discussing broad principles and transcendent issues, he was helping Garfield and the Republican party. As Hayes and Lucy moved west, they were increasingly captivated by the scenery. In Utah, for example, as their train passed through Echo Canyon, with its 800- to 1,200-foot walls, Birch, Rud, and three friends rode on the locomotive's cowcatcher while Hayes and Lucy were with the engineer in the cab.[19]

Upon reaching Salt Lake City, Hayes and his friends were entertained by "governor Murray and the gentiles." Consistent with his abhorrence of theocracy, Hayes refused the hospitality of the city but did meet "John Taylor, George O. Cannon and several other leading Mormons, including some ladies." When the presidential party "mingled fraternally" with these Mormons, "nothing disagreeable occurred." The first president to visit the West Coast while in office, Hayes arrived in San Francisco on 9 September, the thirtieth anniversary of California's admission to the union. The people back east expect "you to build the empire here that shall dominate the commerce of the Pacific," Hayes told the gathered throng. "I doubt not that you will meet their expectations."

During rounds of California "parades, receptions, balls, banquets, and sight-seeing expeditions," Hayes and Sherman pleased crowds by speaking often. Hayes stressed the nation's prosperity and the virtues of sound money and called for eradicating illiteracy and sectional and racial prejudice. Captivated by the climate, the mountain scenery, the enormous resources, the enterprising people of the Pacific slope, and their hospitality, Hayes pronounced the home of Darius Ogden Mills (president of the Bank of California) and his wife Jane "the finest place I have ever seen." Hayes met with settlers from Fresno and Tulare Counties who were struggling against the Southern Pacific Railroad, as well as with former Gov. Leland Stanford of that railroad.[20]

On 22 September, at the state capitol in Sacramento, Hayes predicted that California, Oregon, and the territories of Washington and Alaska, with their population of 1 to 1.5 million, would someday support 50 million people. He reminded Californians that "three great principles, set forth in three great charters" made the United States the earth's most desirable place to live. The Declaration of Independence gave us "equal rights of all men before the law . . . the very foundation-stone of our institutions. . . . Whatever difficulties you have here," he assured his hearers (referring to Californians' hostility toward Asian laborers), "will all work out right if the Anglo-Saxon race will stand on that great principle of equal rights of all men." The second great charter, the Northwest Ordinance of 1787, promoted free public schools. "If you are to have one race, equal suffrage, universal suffrage," Hayes reasoned, "you can only do it by having universal education. . . . With the motto of equal rights and universal education, every community is safe." The essence of the third charter, the Constitution, he stated, is the perpetual union of separate states balancing "one supreme" nation with "local self-government." Equal rights, universal education, and perpetual union made the United States unique, and Californians were in "the vanguard of progress" at the end of civilization's westward march. "You have reached the margin," Hayes declared, "and now it is for you . . . to see that in the future, as in the past, American institutions and the American name shall lose nothing at your hands."[21]

From Sacramento, the president's party journeyed north to the end of the railroad at Redding and then by stagecoach into Oregon, with General Sherman riding "shotgun" beside the coachman. Although the Democratic town of Jacksonville refused to welcome Hayes officially, the Hayeses, the Herrons, and Sherman were greeted by the local Republicans at Madame de Robaum Holt's new hotel, where they stayed. When they were about to leave the next morning, Madame Holt, apparently rejecting the almost universal notion that the prestige of entertaining the president was sufficient compensation, presented a bill of $100 for five guests. Taken aback, John Herron handed her $25, with the flippant remark that they did not intend to buy the hotel. Rather than bring Madame Holt business, the episode gave her hotel a reputation for exorbitant prices, for which she blamed the president.

The encounter with Madame Holt did not lessen Hayes and Lucy's enthusiasm for Oregon. Following their 275-mile stagecoach ride from Redding to the railhead at Roseburg, Lucy exclaimed to her "little darling" Fanny, "What a beautiful country we have passed through — what magnificent scenery grand majestic trees and of fruits the most luscious I ever tasted." While in Portland, Hayes and Lucy took a fifty-mile side trip to Forest Grove to visit a federally financed "Indian school with about twenty or thirty scholars." Speaking there, Hayes emphasized his pleasure that Indian boys and girls were being prepared "to become part of the great American family. . . . This country was once theirs," Hayes reminded those of his listeners who were not Indians. "They owned it as much as you own your farms. We have displaced them and are now completing that work."[22]

The Hayes party stopped at the Vancouver barracks, Washington Territory, before ascending the Columbia River. There they were entertained by the commander of the Department of the Columbia, Gen. Oliver Otis Howard (who would succeed Schofield as superintendent at West Point). On Sunday, 3 October, Hayes and Lucy drove out to the Piute camp and once again saw Sarah Winnemucca, the chief's daughter who was an effective champion of her people. Earlier at the White House, she had pleaded with Hayes and Schurz to let the Piutes move from the Yakima Reservation, Washington Territory, to the Malheur Agency in Oregon, where they had been happy. Schurz was agreeable to the move, but the Yakima Indian agent opposed it. Once again, Winnemucca petitioned Hayes to gather her people at "one place where they could live permanently and be cared for and instructed," and her eloquence moved Lucy to tears. Although Hayes remembered the petition, the agent prevailed, and the Piutes remained on the Yakima Reservation.

Hayes and his party left Vancouver on his fifty-eighth birthday, 4 October 1880. They traveled by steamboat and railroad up the Columbia River, and upon reaching Walla Walla, Washington, Hayes exclaimed: "The grandeur of the views has not been exaggerated." While there, Hayes shook hands with "fifty Umatilla Indians, of both sexes, in paint and feathers," and he and his party watched "a war-dance which lasted an hour." Next, they lis-

In Yosemite Valley: On the far right Hayes, with a dark hat, is seated by the driver; Lucy, in a light hat, is the fourth person from the right.

tened to a concert by the First U.S. Cavalry Band, which featured selections from Richard Wagner's *Lohengrin* and Franz Schubert's *Unfinished Symphony.* Although Hayes and Lucy enjoyed the concert, they found the war dance "wild and fantastic beyond comprehension, and all the party said it was the most novel and interesting scene of the entire trip." Returning down-river to Portland, Hayes declared that in America only the valleys of the St. Lawrence and the Hudson compared with the beauty of the Columbia.

Moving north to the Washington Territory, Hayes cruised Puget Sound for a week and discovered that, with "Mt Rainier and the Cascade Mts and the Olympic Mts in sight," it rivaled the beauty of the Sierra Nevadas of California and Mount Hood and the Dalles of Oregon. The presidential party returned to San Francisco by sea, enjoying "wonderfully fine weather." No one seemed to enjoy that three-day trip more than Lucy, who, Laura Mitchell reported to Fanny and Scott, "sings, and talks, and laughs like the jolliest Jack Tar of them all."[23]

When they arrived back in San Francisco on 18 October, Hayes and his party left immediately for the Yosemite Valley. Arriving at Modesto, their train interrupted a Democratic rally. "Rows ensued, and the uproar continued some time" when the Republican band welcoming Hayes drowned out the Democratic speeches. But the raucousness subsided, and the "train moved off amid cheers." From Madera, they took the Yosemite stage line into the valley and were "delighted" with its spectacular scenery. They then headed south to Los Angeles, arriving on Saturday, 23 October. They spent a busy day viewing orange groves and vineyards, attending an agricultural fair, and visiting the University of Southern California. Aware of fleeting time, they departed Saturday evening, reaching Tucson at noon the next day. There, Hayes attended a reception, talked with three hundred schoolchildren, and met with a hundred Papagos and their chief before departing at 5:30 P.M. On Monday morning, 25 October, Hayes and his party arrived at the end of the Southern Pacific Railroad, twenty miles east of Shakespeare, New Mexico.

Eager to get home to vote for Garfield, Hayes began the most arduous and dangerous lap of his journey. He and his party were forced to abandon their luxurious railroad accommodations for horse-drawn army ambulances. With cavalry escorting them through rugged territory frequented by hostile Apaches, they left immediately, changed horses at Cow Springs and at the Memembres River, and reached Fort Cummings, New Mexico, at 8:00 P.M. (having endured an eleven-hour, sixty-four-mile trip). No longer needing their escort, they pushed on at daybreak and covered sixty additional miles before spending Tuesday night in a comfortable camp at Palomas on the Rio Grande. On Wednesday, they went twenty-eight miles up the Rio Grande, fording it at Fest's Crossing near Fort McRae, and traveled an additional twenty miles before reaching the end of the Atchison, Topeka & Santa Fe Railroad track near Round Mountain, San Marcial, New Mexico. Two hundred miles down that track was Santa Fe, where Hayes and his companions arrived at 10:00 A.M. on Thursday, 28 October, and enjoyed a grand fiesta. The next morning, the Hayeses departed for home by way of Kansas City, sacrificing their projected visit to Denver. At 1:30 A.M. on Monday, 1 November, they arrived at Fremont. "You seem to have come by telegraph in company with the dispatches announcing your intention to leave," Manning Force marveled.

Hayes and his party had traveled by rail, steamship, stagecoach, and ambulance; they had enjoyed sumptuous accommodations and endured primitive ones. An American, republican version of an English royal progress, the journey cost Hayes $575.40 (the expenses of his immediate party of nine). "Our trip," he summed up, "was most fortunate in all of its circumstances.

Superb weather, good health and no accidents. A most gratifying reception greeted us everywhere from the people and from noted and interesting individuals." The grand sights they had seen, Hayes confessed, left him and Lucy "with a certain incapacity to tell the exact truth."[24]

Since there had been grumbling in October that Hayes preferred vacationing in the West to voting in Ohio, his friends were relieved at his arrival. On election eve, seven hundred torch-bearing Republicans marched through Fremont and out to Spiegel Grove, where Hayes—rationalizing that it was "too late" to affect the campaign—made a political speech. He declared that those who "stood by the banner of the union," who wish to protect "home industries against foreign competition," who favor a "sound financial policy," and who "think that every child in the country should be educated at the expense of the country" are those who "are all throwing up their hats and shouting that Garfield will be elected to-morrow."

Hayes was confident that Garfield would win the presidency. Before leaving for California, Hayes had told him: "We are on safe and strong ground and if you were now to sit cross-legged and look wise . . . no sagacious politician would find fault." Garfield's victory, Hayes rejoiced, was too decisive to be disputed. Despite a few qualms, Hayes had faith that Garfield would uphold "the supremacy of the general Government," would foster prosperity through sound money, would not turn the civil service over to the spoilsmen, and would generally continue Hayes's policies. The president knew that Garfield's victory was his victory. John Sherman agreed. "Our strength in this campaign," he wrote to Hayes, "has been in the success of your admin. This is universally conceded by all intelligent men. No one has ignored it but Conkling and he has done it in the most offensive way possible."[25]

Three days after the election, the Cleveland Republican Business Men's Club also maintained that Hayes's record had made Garfield's victory possible. Grateful for what he termed a rather extravagant compliment, but one that he thought he deserved, Hayes responded: "It has been my firm purpose to do that which appeared to me for the good of the whole country and that of each and all of its inhabitants," and in so doing "I have to some extent promoted the success of the Republican party." Garfield's election proved the truth of the most memorable words in Hayes's inaugural address—indeed, the most enduring words Hayes ever spoke: "He serves his party best who serves his country best."[26]

TWENTY-FIVE

LAME DUCK

Buoyed by his "delightful & instructive" West Coast trip and by the election results, Hayes returned to Washington on 6 November. After an absence of seventy-one days, he was ready to enjoy his four months as a lame duck. His most pressing task was preparing his fourth annual message, which he sent to Congress on 6 December 1880. Informed by almost four years of experience, Hayes wished to make the most of this last opportunity to communicate with the country as president. Since he was proud of his administration's accomplishments but aware of his unfinished tasks, his message both summed up the past and challenged the future.[1]

For special discussion and congressional action, Hayes singled out civil rights for blacks, civil-service reform, and polygamy in Utah. Meeting Mormons had reconciled him to neither their polygamy nor their political power; to compel their obedience to federal law, Hayes advocated that Congress drastically curtail local self-government in the Utah Territory. Since in "several of the late slaveholding States" blacks were recently deprived of their voting rights, he urged the House and Senate to investigate violations of the Fifteenth Amendment and to appropriate funds for the executive to prosecute those who deprived citizens of their constitutional rights. Again stressing education as the guarantor of suffrage rights, Hayes asked Congress to supplement local educational funds in states that had inadequate public school systems. With the successful application of the merit system during the past two years to more than two thousand positions in the New York customhouse and post office, Hayes asked Congress for $25,000 to enable a commission to devise and supervise a system of competitive examinations for use throughout the civil service. Hayes also asked for legislation to protect government workers from political assessments, to stop the encroachment upon the president's appointing power by members of Congress, and to repeal the Tenure of Office Act of 2 March 1867, which required that the Senate approve the removal of those appointees it had confirmed.[2]

De Lesseps's proposed canal through Panama both perturbed Hayes and widened his outlook to global proportions. To improve communication and to stimulate shipping and trade, he suggested that Congress subsidize mail steamship lines to Latin America, the Far East, and Australia and the laying

of a telegraph cable from San Francisco to Hawaii, and from there to the Far
East and Australia. He also suggested that an expanded navy, whose ships
would circulate in all quarters of the globe, was necessary for both commerce and defense. Since Congress did not feel threatened by other powers,
any rationale for replacing rotten and rusted vessels had to stress commerce.
The sudden urge to promote commerce and enlarge the navy was prompted
by the de Lesseps project; Hayes's primary concern in Panama remained control of any sea link between the East and West Coasts of the United States.[3]

The federal government's receipts for the fiscal year ending 30 June 1880
reflected the nation's booming economy. A 22 percent increase in income to
$333.5 million had exceeded expenditures by $65.9 million. This surplus,
Hayes proudly stated, had enabled his administration to reduce the federal
debt (about $2 billion when he took office) to $1.886 million; if Hayes's estimate were realized, it would be reduced by another $90 million during the
current year. Hayes continued his attack on the silver dollars minted under
the Bland-Allison Act, noting that with their inconvenient weight and their
intrinsic market value at seven-eighths of gold dollars, nearly two-thirds of
them were almost immediately returned to the treasury. If silver dollars were
to be minted, Hayes preferred that they be larger and as valuable as the gold
dollar. "Our own recent financial history shows how surely money becomes
abundant whenever confidence in the exact performance of moneyed obligations is established," Hayes concluded.[4]

Hayes also made numerous practical suggestions. He thought that Congress should appropriate enough money for the 30,000-man army it had authorized (rather than allowing the army only enough money for 25,000 men)
and should let the War Department sell its obsolete small army posts along
old wagon routes and build larger, more efficient quarters at points with
good rail connections. Newly aware of the needs of the Pacific Northwest,
Hayes called for a twenty-foot channel extending a hundred miles up the Columbia River and for an adequate local territorial government for Alaska,
where only the presence of the navy ship *Jamestown* prevented anarchy. Anticipating the 1892 demands of the Populist party, he backed the suggestion
of Postmaster General Horace Maynard that a system of postal savings be
adopted.[5]

Hayes emphasized several constructive suggestions by Schurz. Favoring
the orderly utilization, but not waste, of the nation's natural resources,
Hayes asked Congress to codify the land laws, as prepared by the Public
Lands Commission, and to pass special legislation to prevent the "wasteful
depredations committed on our public timber lands." He commended the
consolidation of the various geological and geographical surveys of the West

into the Geological Survey, with Clarence King as its director, and urged that its work include the entire country.[6]

With the past year "unusually free from disturbances," Hayes was pleased that Indian affairs were "in a more hopeful condition." The Indian police had helped maintain law and order on the reservations; rather than making war, the Native Americans had "made gratifying progress in agriculture, herding, and mechanical pursuits," as well as in the wagon freighting business. As Hayes desired, the Interior Department had increased educational possibilities for Native American children. Besides building new boarding schools at Indian agencies, it had sent eastern Cherokee children to boarding schools in North Carolina, increased Indian pupils at Hampton Institute in Virginia, and established Indian schools at Carlisle, Pennsylvania, in 1879 and at Forest Grove, Oregon, in 1880 (the school Hayes had recently inspected). The pupils at these schools received an elementary English education as well as instruction in housework, agriculture, and mechanical pursuits. The Interior Department's "permanent civilization fund" paid for the education of these children, but the fund was so reduced that Hayes—who wanted the program to expand—requested a specific appropriation. Neither Hayes nor most of his contemporaries realized that acculturation had devastating effects and that the cultural identity of Native American children at boarding schools was especially at risk.

Along with Schurz, Hayes proposed that Congress allot reservation lands to individual Indian owners. The proposed bill would not allow Indians to sell their private land but would permit the sale of other reservation land to white settlers if the Native Americans consented and the money from the land sale were used to benefit them. Hayes felt that this measure, buttressed by vigorous educational efforts, would promote the merging of Native Americans with "the great body of American citizenship."[7]

Two days after he had assured Congress of the hopeful state of Indian affairs, a troubled Hayes wrote in his diary: "A great . . . wrong has been done to the Poncas." Too late for Hayes to investigate before delivering his upbeat message, Massachusetts Sens. George F. Hoar and Henry L. Dawes had protested the removal of the Ponca Indians from their lands in northeastern Nebraska and southeastern Dakota Territory, for which they blamed Schurz. Hoar urged the president to redress the wrong so that his administration could "take its place in history as the purest and freest from stain since the inauguration of Washington." Loyal to his lieutenant, Hayes replied, "*I suppose General Schurz has been most shamefully treated in this affair*, but," Hayes admitted, "I may be mistaken." Dawes was so hostile to Schurz that he feared for the safety of the Poncas should they visit the Interior Department to ask for redress. Hayes assured Dawes that "nothing unfair or inconsiderate" would be done to them and reminded him pointedly, "This is the first time that you have called my attention to the subject" of the Poncas.

Thanks to Hoar, Dawes, and protest meetings, the Poncas remained on Hayes's mind. Everyone the president spoke with agreed that the Poncas had been wronged, but with Dawes blaming Schurz and Schurz claiming that Congress and Dawes—a member of the Senate Committee on Indian Affairs—were at fault, Hayes decided to study congressional debates and reports by the commissioner of Indian affairs for the previous four years.[8]

The Ponca problem was rooted in the 1868 treaty between the United States and the Sioux, traditional enemies of the Poncas. This treaty gave the Sioux the 96,000-acre Ponca Reserve along the Missouri River, even though it had been guaranteed to the Poncas by 1858 and 1867 treaties. The Poncas remained there, but the Sioux harassed them until the Poncas asked to be moved to the reservation of the Omahas, a kindred tribe in Nebraska. In 1874 and 1875, the commissioner of Indian affairs urged that the Poncas be granted their wish, but Congress failed to act. In September 1875, their chiefs petitioned to be removed to the Indian Territory but later insisted that they had asked to live with the Omahas.

In 1876, Congress appropriated $25,000 to remove the Poncas to the Indian Territory if they agreed to relinquish their claims to their old reserve. Upon receiving assurances from the Indian Bureau that the Poncas agreed to do so, Congress appropriated an additional $15,000 on 3 March 1877 to move them and to provide for the Sioux to take over Ponca lands. But a majority of the Poncas were opposed to leaving. With Schurz still learning his job, the change of administration did not change the decision to move the Poncas. The Hayes administration was six weeks old when 175 Poncas willingly departed for the Indian Territory on 17 April. A month later, the approach of four cavalry companies forced most of the 550 remaining Poncas to begin a similar trek. They made the journey from the Dakota Territory to present-day Oklahoma "under great difficulties and hardships, occasioned by unprecedented storms and floods." After arriving, they were ravaged by disease and harassed by white adventurers, who rustled their cattle and ponies and smuggled whiskey into their camps. Most of the Poncas did not like their new location, so, as a last resort, their chiefs pleaded their case in Washington.

Four Ponca chiefs—White Eagle, Standing Buffalo, Standing Bear, and Big Chief—visited the White House and asked Hayes to intercede. One chief told the president: "I was living on the old reservation, but all at once I was taken up as by a whirlwind and disturbed in my place just as I had learned to

An Indian conference at the White House (*Harper's Weekly*, 22 January 1881)

plow, and was made to take another road which is new to me. We are all perishing where we are now. In less than three months' time over thirty people have died, and so have many cattle." Touched by this appeal, Hayes responded, "I will do the best I can for you." To his later regret, he followed the advice of Schurz (who had consulted with William Welsh, a prominent

Indian-rights advocate) and did not let the Poncas return home, lest they be destroyed by the Sioux nation.[9]

Schurz, however, asked the Poncas to search the Indian Territory for a suitable tract as large as the 96,000 acres they had left. He also assured them that they would be compensated for the log houses, furnishings, and implements they had been forced to leave in Dakota. In his 1877 annual report to Congress, Schurz listed the hardships the Poncas had suffered, emphasized that they were a friendly, well-behaved people who were "entitled to more than ordinary care at the hands of the Government," and recommended a liberal provision to aid their resettlement.

The Poncas found lands more to their liking at the Salt Fork of the Arkansas River, but Congress ignored Schurz's repeated requests to indemnify them for their losses and to help them gain title to their new reservation. The new Ponca lands in the Indian Territory proved to be better than their land in Dakota. As they became acclimated to their new surroundings, most Poncas were content with their location, but a minority wished to return to their revered ancestral land, especially to bury their dead. Schurz insisted, however, that none of them return, even though the Sioux had abandoned the Ponca lands and become peaceful.[10]

Probably no one would have noticed the Poncas' difficulties if the death of Standing Bear's grandchild had not made this Ponca chief's desire to return to the home of his people more urgent. Setting off in early 1879 with the remains of the child, Standing Bear and thirty-four followers endured terrible hardships on a 600-mile winter journey before they were arrested by the army in Nebraska, where they had stopped to rest among the Omahas. Their dramatic story attracted support, and they were soon freed on a writ of habeas corpus. On 30 April 1879, Judge Elmer S. Dundy of the federal district court ruled that the constitutional guarantee that no person shall be deprived of life, liberty, or property without due process of law applied to the Poncas.

Rather than risk his control over Indian nations by appealing to the Supreme Court, Schurz ignored the ruling except as it applied to Standing Bear and his followers. Standing Bear embarked on an eastern speaking tour accompanied by Bright Eyes, a gifted young Omaha whose education in the government school on the Omaha Reservation and in Elizabeth, New Jersey, had not impaired her cultural identity. Bright Eyes captivated audiences with her forceful eloquence and graceful dignity. She and Standing Bear aroused many Americans to the injustice that had been done to uprooted Native Americans, particularly the Poncas, and stirred Congress from its torpor. Senator Dawes introduced a bill, and the Senate Committee on Indian Affairs recommended on 31 May 1880 that the Poncas be allowed to return home, but Schurz stubbornly insisted that they stay put in the Indian Territory.[11]

Hayes decided that the situation required an investigation by a special commission. He consulted with Senator Hoar about its composition and agreed to allow the Ponca Relief Committee of Boston to appoint up to half the commissioners if the committee would pay the expenses of those it named. Hayes lamented that he was restricted to the army or the Interior Department for his own appointments, since he had no contingency fund to compensate commission members. On 18 December 1880, he appointed Brig. Gens. George Crook and Nelson A. Miles; William Stickney, the secretary of the Board of Indian Commissioners; and Walter Allen of Newton, Massachusetts, the Boston committee's man. After conferring with the Poncas in the Indian Territory and in Dakota, where some of them remained, the commission suggested that they be allowed to live where they desired. The commission found that the 521 Poncas in the Indian Territory wished to stay there, and the 150 Poncas in Dakota and Nebraska wanted to remain close to their ancestors.[12]

Hayes and Schurz agreed with the commission. "I have found good reason . . . to regret," Schurz confessed, the removal of the Pawnees, the northern Cheyennes, and the Poncas to the Indian Territory. Schurz drafted and Hayes revised the message of 1 February 1881 to accompany the commission's report to Congress. Hayes requested that Congress compensate the Poncas, allow them to choose where they would live, and let them gain title to their land as individuals, with the proviso that it be nontransferable ("inalienable") for a period of years to protect them from scheming whites. "In short," Hayes declared, "nothing should be left undone to show to the Indians that the Government of the United States regards their rights as equally sacred with those of its citizens."[13]

The determination of Standing Bear and the eloquence of Bright Eyes enabled Hayes to reiterate his four main ideas for Indian policy: First, young Indians of both sexes should receive an industrial and general education that would "enable them to be self-supporting and capable of self-protection in a civilized community." Second, Indians should be allotted land "in severalty, inalienable for a certain period." Third, Indians should receive "fair compensation for their lands not required for individual allotments, the amount to be invested, with suitable safeguards, for their benefit." Fourth, after meeting these prerequisites, Indians who were citizens of their own nations should become citizens of the United States.

Having considered the Native American problem in general, Hayes returned to the injustice done to the Poncas. He was "deeply sensible" that, as president, "when the wrong was consummated . . . enough of the responsibility for that wrong justly attaches to me to make it my particular duty . . . to give to these injured people that measure of redress which is required alike by justice and by humanity." Unaware that Schurz had a hand in its composition, Dawes expressed his "great gratification" to Hayes for his Ponca message: "Every word of it meets my hearty commendation, and is worthy of your high office and high character. In my opinion it will pass into history as a great state paper, marking an epoch in our dealings with the weak and defenseless more conspicuous and grand than any other public expression from the head of the nation for many years." As Schurz and Hayes suggested, Congress appropriated $165,000 for the Poncas. Although Dawes continued to attack Schurz, he incorporated his and Hayes's ideas on land and citizenship for Native Americans into the Dawes Severalty Act of 1887.[14]

In addition to the problems of the Poncas, other matters vied for Hayes's attention during his last months in office. "A perpetual stream, growing too, of matters that must be attended to is pouring in upon me," he complained, "and I haven't time to eat or sleep." When William Strong resigned from the Supreme Court in December 1880, Hayes responded to the universal feeling that the South should be represented on the Court by appointing William Burnham Woods, a Republican carpetbagger who had migrated from Ohio to Alabama. Despite assurances from Justice Bradley that Woods, a federal circuit court judge, viewed the Constitution as did Hayes, Woods proved to be a mediocre justice remembered for protecting the rights of states but not those of blacks. On the civil-rights question, he thought like Bradley, but neither of them viewed the Constitution as did Hayes and his friend Justice Harlan.[15]

Having instituted civil-service reform in a few offices, Hayes was shrewd to publicize its value. On 3 December 1880, he asked Dorman B. Eaton, who had already documented the successful application of the merit system in Great Britain, to report on open, competitive examinations for appointments and promotions in the New York customhouse and post office. Eaton reported in February 1881 that these examinations were highly successful in both places. Never before, he insisted, had so much time been given to proper work and so little to partisan politics. Economy, efficiency, promptness, and high morale characterized the service. Even though political activity had not been eliminated entirely, Eaton was encouraged by its decline. He and his fellow reformers justifiably believed that their colleague, naval officer Silas W. Burt, was responsible for the success of the experiment in the customhouse and that Thomas L. James, a Conkling Republican, was responsible for its success in the post office. In 1880, the volume of mail had increased a third over that in 1875, yet it was delivered for $20,000 less, even though collections and deliveries had been increased. James achieved efficiency by working his men ten and eleven hours a day and kept them on their toes by adjusting their salaries according to their performance on periodic examinations. Aware that vast increases in mail volume made new workers necessary, James hoped to cut labor costs further by hiring boys. Ideal working conditions were not synonymous with civil-service reform.[16]

During his last weeks in office, Hayes concentrated on easing Garfield's transition into the presidency. To shield him from adverse reaction, he offered to make certain personnel moves before leaving office. Thinking that his ideas on Garfield's cabinet might prove useful, Hayes suggested that Horace Davis, a businessman and congressman from California and a nephew of historian George Bancroft, would "represent well the Pacific Coast" and that former Gov. Elisha M. Pease of Texas, collector of customs at Galveston, "would be a wise, safe and popular Southern member" in the cabinet.[17]

Hayes also passed on plugs for Sherman and Blaine. In Vice President Wheeler's view, it would "be regarded as ungenerous in you and a disregard of the public interests if Sherman is not retained" in the Treasury Department. "Blaine is favorably spoken of for Secy of State in all quarters," Hayes added, "but probably he wouldn't accept. Why not offer it?" A month later, when it appeared that Hayes had miscalculated and Blaine would accept the State Department, Hayes disingenuously wrote, "It is deemed fortunate and wise." He then warned, "The saving clause in the whole business is, *the faith that you will be President.*" After it became apparent that Garfield did not want Sherman (who personified specie resumption) in his cabinet, Hayes mentioned that Sen. William Windom of Minnesota was a favorite for the Treasury Department. Among those Hayes had recommended, only Blaine (whom Hayes distrusted and really did not want appointed) and Windom made Garfield's cabinet. Unlike Hayes, Garfield was willing to sacrifice executive independence in cabinet selections to secure good relations with Congress. "I like Horace Davis," Garfield explained to Hayes, "and I wish he had the support of his delegation, but fear he has not."[18]

Military retirements and promotions were particularly prickly, and Garfield hoped that Hayes would settle these problems. Hayes spared him the heat by appointing Garfield's Civil War army aide and crony Maj. David G. Swaim as judge advocate general, so that he would be at Garfield's side in

Washington. Garfield enjoyed playing cards and billiards with Swaim, had borrowed $6,500 for his Washington home — about half its cost — from him, and had employed him in the recent campaign. Swaim, Hayes also realized, would be useful in making a smooth transition to the new administration. In addition, Hayes promoted to brigadier general Garfield's friend William B. Hazen and made him chief signal officer of the army.[19]

Forcing army officers to retire at three-quarters pay was painful. "I shall look with interest," Garfield wrote to Hayes, "upon the retirement of Army officers & hope you may be well through it before I go in." When Hayes retired Gen. Edward O. C. Ord, who was stationed in Texas, it was in spite of the support he had mustered from Collis P. Huntington of the Central Pacific Railroad; Thomas A. Scott of the Texas & Pacific and Pennsylvania Railroads; William T. Sherman, the commanding general of the army; and even civil-service reformer Wayne MacVeagh.[20]

Doing the dirty work to make Garfield's beginning easier created problems for Hayes. Even though Sherman had traveled with him to the West Coast, Hayes noted in January: "I have for the present lost the friendship of Gen Sherman. Several things have occurred to which this may be attributed. 1. I recommended the promotion of Gen Grant to a Captain Generalcy. 2. I retired certain officers, notably Gen Ord, against his advice and wish. 3. I promoted Gens Hazen and Miles against his wish." Sherman was also angry that Hayes had not consulted him before replacing Schofield at West Point over the Whittaker case.

Hayes, who had been a nonprofessional officer, was imposing his authority as commander-in-chief of the army, and Sherman resented it. The old soldier wanted his professional advice followed by the president and felt that Hayes — who was gratifying Grant, Garfield, and Sherman's brother John in personnel moves — was promoting the interests of the Republican party rather than those of the army. Although unyielding in his respect for Grant, Sherman had opposed special legislation to create a new title for Grant and felt that his own position had been "misunderstood in high circles." Maintaining that "all should be treated alike," Sherman feared that Grant's special treatment might "prejudice the interest and harmony of the Service" and insisted that, like other officers, Grant should be retired at three-quarters pay rather than be given a salary increase and a new rank. Sherman thought correctly that the promotion of Miles, who had married his niece and was too willing to use this connection to advance his career, would lead to charges of nepotism. And Hazen, through his Garfield connection, was an early and effective "whistle blower" who had not endeared himself to his colleagues by helping to expose the corrupt post-trader system in Grant's War Department.[21]

Hayes wished to collaborate with Garfield on a last-minute cabinet appointment. After firing Secretary of the Navy Thompson for his involvement with de Lesseps, Hayes asked Garfield to select Thompson's replacement, but Garfield could not decide quickly enough. Hayes had to act fast because the Tenure of Office Act, he explained to Garfield, "prevented all expenditures in the Dept after ten days of a vacant secretaryship." Hayes asked Nathan Goff, a district attorney in West Virginia, to complete Thompson's term, with the understanding that when Garfield took office, he would reappoint Goff to his old post.[22]

Garfield reciprocated by agreeing to remember Hayes's few requests for friends and by helping him with a Supreme Court appointment. When his old Columbus landlord, Justice Noah H. Swayne, retired from the Supreme Court, Hayes nominated Stanley Matthews, his college friend and Garfield's 1877 rival for the Senate. But to Hayes's surprise, Matthews was not confirmed. Hostile senators claimed he was close to railroad and corporate interests and insisted that since he had been a negotiator during the crisis of 1877, Hayes was rewarding him for past services. Hayes obviously wanted Matthews confirmed, but he did not appoint Sen. Don Cameron's candidate for the surveyorship in the Philadelphia customhouse (Nathan C. Elsbree of Towanda, Pennsylvania) when Cameron approached him through Matthews and implied that the Elsbree appointment was the price of his vote. Garfield later renewed the nomination, and Matthews was confirmed by a margin of one vote, with Cameron voting in his favor. Matthews proved to be a hardworking judge who enhanced federal control of interstate commerce and, notably in *Yick Wo v. Hopkins* (1886), defended minority rights, but he did not uphold the constitutionality of the 1875 Civil Rights Act.[23]

Hayes and Garfield wanted the nominations on which they had collaborated confirmed quickly, to avoid their overlap into Garfield's administration. The problem, Hayes noted, was that "so many are interested in particular cases, in rejections, that by combining all such opposers into a general opposition it is possible that postponement will result." Undaunted, he continued to appoint Garfield's choices. But the Senate, inspired, some observers believed, "by the spite and hatred of Senator Conkling," had not confirmed about a hundred of his nominees when Hayes left office.[24]

Although some of Garfield's decisions made Hayes apprehensive, their correspondence remained cordial. Aware that Garfield would not be able to afford equipage appropriate for his new office, Hayes left his horses and carriage for Garfield's use. Hayes also suggested that the Garfields stay in the

White House when they came to Washington before the inauguration, and Garfield accepted that gracious invitation for his mother and his boys. Yet despite his friendship for Garfield, Hayes shared the fear of many of their contemporaries that he lacked backbone. Vice President Wheeler, while chatting with Hayes about Garfield, remarked, "I have said forty times, if he had one tenth of your amiable obstinacy and independence he would be a great success." Garfield's plan to "restore wine and liquor to the White House" was evidence, Hayes believed, that he "lacks the grit to face fashionable ridicule."[25]

Despite his placid nature, Hayes was agitated enough to write Garfield a memorandum on temperance in the White House. Whatever may be true of Europeans, Hayes declared, "the American who drinks wine is in danger of becoming the victim of drunkenness, licentiousness, and gambling." He believed that Garfield would "grievously disappoint thousands of the best people who supported" him if he were to bring wine and liquor back to the White House. Bringing alcohol back, Hayes warned, would "revive the Temperance party, which has now dropped almost out of sight, and give it votes enough to put in jeopardy the Republican ascendancy in Maine, New Hampshire, Connecticut, New York, Ohio, Indiana, and in perhaps thirty northern congressional districts"; in addition, it would "seriously damage your personal reputation and your political prospects" for reelection. Hayes's analysis of the temperance vote was prophetic. In 1880, the Prohibitionists won only 1,517 votes in New York State, but in 1884, they piled up 25,016 votes, causing the Republicans to lose New York by 1,149 votes and thereby lose the national election. Perhaps recalling his own reaction in January 1880 to "a state dinner at the President's . . . wet down with coffee and cold water," Garfield was unimpressed by Hayes's arguments.[26]

Temperance advocates, however, often annoyed Hayes and embarrassed Lucy. Against their better judgment, the president and Lucy agreed to let the Women's Christian Temperance Union (WCTU) sponsor a White House portrait of Lucy. Both self-effacing and proud, Lucy preferred to be "enshrined" in the "hearts of the people" rather than on canvas and was insulted that the WCTU begged ten-cent contributions for the picture. When it became apparent in January 1881 that the WCTU, without consulting Lucy, was using the portrait as a gimmick to raise money for temperance publications, Hayes ordered that the fund-raising be stopped, with "as little publicity and friction as possible," as soon as funds sufficient for the portrait were raised. Noting the diversity of opinion among temperance advocates—there were those who wanted "a political temperance party," those who worked for prohibition "through the old political organizations," and those who,

Daniel Huntington's portrait of Lucy W. Hayes for the WCTU

like Hayes and Lucy, wished to advance temperance by example, explanation, and exhortation—Hayes emphasized that there could be no agreement
on what literature to publish. Despite this unpleasantness, Fanny expressed
the whole family's feeling about Daniel Huntington's flattering portrait
when she exclaimed, "Mama's picture is perfectly splendid."[27]

Temperance did not dampen the genial social temperaments of Hayes and
Lucy. Departing from their custom, they often dined out during their last
winter in Washington. Their dinner with George Bancroft was memorable,
not only for his "conversation and vigor" while telling stories of John C.
Calhoun and Henry Clay but also for the "agreeable and intelligent" guests
who were present. These included Caroline Edgar (Mrs. Jerome Napoleon)
Bonaparte, the granddaughter of Daniel Webster, who told of his midnight-
to-dawn preparation for his reply to Robert Y. Hayne; and Henry Adams,
who characteristically and undiplomatically declared, "Our system of Govt
has failed utterly in many respects." At a dinner honoring Grant, who "was
interesting and talkative," Sen. George F. Edmunds, Hayes noted, told
"good anecdotes, and is *both* witty and humorous—a rare combination."
But the best storyteller in Washington was apparently John Hay, who was
"timely and apt in using" his "prodigious" fund of stories.[28]

When not stepping out, Hayes and Lucy continued to make the White
House sparkle with their dinners and receptions. As usual, "Lucy had gathered a fine bevy of young ladies" to help with the large receptions, including
Lizzie Mills, whose parents Hayes and Lucy had recently visited in California. On New Year's Day 1881, the "severe cold" reduced the number of
callers but enabled John Philip Sousa's Marine Band to play from a more
central and warmer location. Frigid temperatures cut into the attendance at
Lucy's Saturday afternoon reception a week later, but the weather was no
longer a factor for her 29 January reception, when she was assisted by Mary
Logan and Edith Davis, the wives of Sen. John A. Logan and Rep. Horace
Davis. The "royal help-meet" trio that these women formed with Lucy provoked the *National Republican* to reflect that "there is no place where a
really bright, sweet woman, with proper tact, can make of herself a more
charming personality and power or do more to advance a husband's career"
than in Washington. At Lucy's last Saturday afternoon reception, "dames of
high degree" attended in a multitude, making it "dangerous to life and limb
to be wedged in that struggling crowd." Despite "prolonged handshaking,"
Lucy showed no weariness and acted pleased to greet "each individual of the
thousands who passed in review."[29]

Paralleling Lucy's Saturday afternoon affairs were the fortnightly levees on Tuesday evenings, with Sousa and the Marine Band providing entertainment. The last of these, held on Washington's Birthday, "was a literal crush," but what Hayes called "our great social event" was his and Lucy's diplomatic reception two days later. For two hours, they shook hands with 2,000 to 3,000 guests, including the cabinet, members of the diplomatic corps, most of the Supreme Court, army and navy officers, many senators, and fifteen representatives who skipped a night session until they were forced to return to the House for a vote. The White House was festooned with flags and flowers, the band played, and "the glittering uniforms and court suits, reflected in the great mirrors by the light of many chandeliers," created a brilliant effect.[30]

Although Hayes was comfortable at formal affairs, he and Lucy both preferred informality. "Lucy," he remarked, "is well enough in all respects in the duties of a State dinner, but she feels unequal to them, and therefore *hates* State dinners." The dinner for Grant that provoked these remarks was, like the others, extremely formal and "passed off in good style." At these affairs, a balance between men and women was maintained. Each "gentleman," upon arrival, received an envelope containing the name of his dinner partner. Ushers conducted the guests to the Blue Parlor, where—after paying their respects to the president and Lucy—the men would seek out their partners, making each "lady" aware of her "fate." At seven o'clock, a double procession, led by Hayes and Lucy, would form in the Red Parlor and enter the dining room, where individuals were seated by name cards. Only the men were furnished with a diagram of the table that gave the names of the other guests. In 1881, the Hayeses introduced their "beautiful" but derisively criticized set of porcelain dishes designed by Theodore R. Davis and made by Haviland of Limoges. These dishes spectacularly—and, for many guests, far too realistically—reproduced the fauna and flora about to be consumed as well as "fearful" wilderness scenes. After dinner, the guests promenaded for an hour or more, often in Lucy's spectacular, gas-lit greenhouses (which grew to twelve during the Hayes years). Before ten, the guests went home or party-hopped to less formal and more intoxicating gatherings.

Despite the somewhat oppressive formality, which the presence of Hayes and Lucy helped mitigate, an invitation to a state dinner was prized. White-law Reid of the New York *Tribune* journeyed to Washington to attend the first state dinner of 1881 and, as Lucy planned, basked in the company of Lizzie Mills, whom he would marry in a few months. Reid not only wooed Lizzie at that dinner but also patched up his quarrel with Sen. Matthew Carpenter of Wisconsin (who died a month later). Bitter antagonists accepted invitations from Hayes and Lucy, who did their best to maintain friendly social relations with political friends and foes, but many guests were invited simply because the president and his wife enjoyed their company. Indeed, the Hayeses had such a good time at the Bancroft dinner that, a few nights later, they reciprocated with a state dinner for Bancroft, the Bonapartes, Henry and Clover Adams, John and Clara Hay, Daniel C. Gilman (president of Johns Hopkins University), and his wife Elisabeth Dwight Woolsey Gilman, among others. Clover Adams was pleased that Gilman escorted her to the table but found that "to eat one's soup calmly" from a plate "with a coyote springing at you . . . is intimidating."[31]

Lucy may have been an uneasy hostess at formal events, but she put her guests at ease. People liked her, and Hayes was gratified by "the heartiness and warmth of friendship for Lucy." He was pleased in particular when newspapers that were unfriendly to him paid compliments to her graciousness. He was proud that she remained beautiful as she grew older and was pleased that her happy spirit permeated the White House. Among relatives and friends, Lucy's name was synonymous with "happy, hilarious times," and she filled her children's Washington days with fun. She also provided fun for Washington's children. After Congress forbade the rolling of Easter eggs on the Capitol grounds, Lucy hosted the first Easter egg roll on the White House lawn on 22 April 1878.[32]

Holidays were given over to Fanny and Scott, who in 1881 were thirteen and ten years old. At the sounding of a bell on Christmas, they raced to bring presents from the Red Room to the library, where family, servants, and friends waited expectantly. Whether sledding after a winter's snow, taking "lessons at the swimming school," or attending their dancing master's costume ball as Martha Washington and an orderly sergeant of their father's Twenty-third Regiment, Fanny and Scott were fond of each other's company. And Hayes loved watching them and their friends—"a merry crowd of little folks"—at play. While a "noisy happy party of thirty" played "blindman's buff and other sports in the East room and halls" during Scott's seventh birthday celebration, the president had stood nearby talking "country and religion" with a governor, a general, and a bishop.[33]

Hayes understood and enjoyed his children. He noted how his "Little Fanny in the presence of strangers spoke lightly" of the death of Old Whitey, the beloved warhorse who had been put to pasture at Spiegel Grove, and then went off for "a good cry." Webb, who served as his father's standby and unofficial secretary, was "full of social and friendly qualities" that made up for his lack of scholarship. He was the only one of the three older boys to live with his parents in the White House. His older brother Birchard, "conscien-

Hayes with his sons Rud and Birchard

tious, scholarly, but not so practical," was practicing law in Toledo; Rud, the family's third son, was at Cornell studying natural sciences, an area in which he was "quick," though he was "slow in others." On the few occasions when the president's family circle was complete, these young men and their friends made White House dinners "unusually chatty and lively." Besides their three older sons and their nephew Ruddy Platt, those joining Hayes and Lucy for their last White House family dinner were Ohio friends John and Harriet Herron and Eliza and John Davis.[34]

Hayes and Lucy entertained lavishly, but his annual salary of $50,000 apparently covered their expenditures. Yearly White House expenses, he estimated, were a bit under $25,000; in addition, Hayes spent from $6,000 to $7,000 annually "for the advantage of the Republican cause." He told Garfield that he could probably save $20,000 a year while president, although Hayes had "not quite" saved that much. Considerably in debt when he became president, Hayes noted that, despite what he had saved during his White House years, "I shall leave here in debt from twenty thousand to twenty-five thousand dollars, but with a good credit, plenty of property, and in no sense needing pecuniary aid or sympathy. If the times continue good a few years longer, I am sure of a competency—a happy independence." Five months later, Hayes sought to refinance his debts with a low-interest loan for between $25,000 and $30,000. "It *will be my only debt*," he confided, and "I am always punctual in interest &c." He estimated that, at current prices, his property was worth between $200,000 and $300,000.[35]

On 3 March, just before leaving office, Hayes struck a last blow for a sound monetary system. He vetoed a bill to refund the national debt with 3 percent bonds (which he favored) because it also stipulated that only these 3 percent bonds could be received as "security for national-bank circulation." This requirement, Hayes warned, would destroy the "efficient and admirable" national banking system, and the withdrawal of national bank notes from circulation would "bring serious embarrassment and disaster to the business of the country." Hayes returned the bill—which reflected rural hostility to the national banking system—to the House of Representatives, where the Republicans, with the help of three Democrats, sustained his veto.[36]

On the evening of 3 March, Hayes and Lucy entertained his cabinet and the Garfield family at a state dinner. At the inauguration the next day, George W. Julian, an old abolitionist who had supported Tilden, noted that Hayes "looked as sweet & lamblike as possible, but Garfield's face looked worn." After the inauguration, Hayes and Lucy served the Garfields lunch at the White House, enjoyed the inaugural parade with them, and left to spend the night in the new home of John and Margaret Sherman before departing the next morning for Fremont. When the Garfields walked back to the White House after the parade, young Rud Hayes was just leaving to join his parents in their carriage. Seizing Lucretia Garfield by the hand, he said, "Permit me to hope that you will spend four as happy years in this mansion as we have done."[37]

TWENTY-SIX

SPIEGEL GROVE

Eleven miles out of Washington at Severn, Maryland, Hayes's train crashed into two locomotives returning to the capital from Baltimore. Although no one in Hayes's party was seriously hurt, two people aboard the train were killed (Lucy comforted the ten-year-old son of one of the victims), and the three wrecked engines "could scarcely be told apart." Somewhat shaken, Hayes and his family reached Baltimore that evening. After dining with their friends Samuel M. and Augusta Shoemaker, they boarded a Pullman car and arrived at 8:00 A.M. Sunday in Altoona, where Hayes wrote letters while they rested. He assured Garfield that with his cabinet and his "sound and admirable" inaugural address, his troubles were "*all over.*" He complimented John Sherman for his "extremely felicitous" remarks on leaving the Treasury Department (which would help dispel the notion that he was "cold in temperament") and acknowledged that "to no one am I so much indebted for the Career in public life which is now closed as I am to you." After stopping in Cleveland with their "kinfolk" Linus and Louise Austin, the Hayeses reached Fremont at nightfall on Tuesday.[1]

A "throng of men, women, and children" with "bands, torches and banners" met the train and triumphantly escorted Hayes and Lucy home. From the veranda of their recently enlarged house, Hayes spoke of what a former president should do to occupy himself. "Let him . . . promote the welfare and the happiness of his family, his town, his State, and his country." That work, he prophesied, would yield "more individual contentment and gratification" than public life. As he and Lucy "shook hands with a large part of the meeting," Hayes began a new career.[2]

During his first days at Spiegel Grove, however, Hayes's old career kept him busy. On 9 March alone, he received forty-two letters. Many of these praised the success of his administration, and others congratulated him on escaping injury when the trains collided at Severn. Civil-service reformers were particularly grateful for Hayes's support. Schurz spoke movingly of Hayes's "friendship and confidence" and of his own affection for him and his family; Curtis declared, "No President has been more malignantly assailed than you have been, but few will be more gratefully remembered"; and Burt acknowledged prophetically, "To your almost unaided action the country is indebted for the initiation of reform and such progress as ensures its successful accomplishment."[3]

Hayes, however, was annoyed with those civil-service reformers who thought that their reform was the only one, who thought that men to accomplish it "were as plenty as blackberries," and who failed to appreciate Evarts and Sherman. Even if these cabinet members "cared nothing for a formal reform of the civil service," Hayes rhetorically queried, "were they not the only men for their places?" Indeed, Sherman was confident that neither he nor Hayes "need regret our part in your administration" but was critical of Evarts. "I have always felt," he wrote, "that Mr. Evarts unkindly involved you in the N.Y. quarrel which might have been avoided or postponed, and that when we were in it he displayed great weakness." Evarts admitted to Hayes that he feared "that the New York hostilities . . . were aggravated by jealousies or repugnances which I drew," but later, when Garfield too had trouble with Conkling, Evarts was relieved of his guilt feelings. Whether Evarts was responsible for the New York fight or irresponsible in it, Hayes realized his virtues. "I do not attempt to tell how much the good fortune of my administration is due to you," he wrote to him, "and how much my own personal happiness in the course of it has been promoted by you." Lucy could have added that of all the Washington wives, Helen Evarts "attracted her the most."

In addition, Hayes thanked William Henry Smith, who was not enamored with civil-service reform, for supporting his political career. "You were at the cradle and you have followed the hearse 'of this ambitious life.' . . . No man ever had a more sincere, a more judicious, and a more unselfish friend than, in this matter, I have found in you. You have been generous, considerate, and forgiving."[4]

Those whose interests Hayes had promoted were lavish in their praise. Lyman Abbott of the *Christian Union* could have alluded to the high moral tone and temperance of the Hayes White House but chose to emphasize that "the quiet courage" of the administration, "which has provoked no conflicts & evaded none, will be more & more esteemed." Specifically, under the leadership of Hayes, "the country passed the financial crisis, & came to the *wise & honest* determination to pay its debts in the worlds currency, & the crisis of administrative reform, in crystallizing a national purpose to make the offices serve the people." In addition, the officers and teachers of the Hampton Normal and Agricultural Institute for Negroes and Indians thanked Hayes and Lucy for their "constant kindness" and "greatest encouragement." They had visited the institute often, and Lucy had sponsored a scholarship student there. One of Hayes's last acts was to save for the school's continued use the chapel in the National Cemetery on the school's campus.[5]

After an absence of over five years, Hayes and Lucy returned to a different Spiegel Grove. The large and as yet uncompleted addition doubled the veranda (which Hayes loved), provided "a large pleasant parlor . . . and a cozy Library room back of it . . . with sliding doors between," as well as "nice" bedrooms upstairs. In mid-April, Lucy wrote to former Vice President Wheeler that "the workmen are still with us — this week the plasterers will finish and the carpenters follow next."[6]

Hayes quickly moved back into the civic life of Fremont and its neighboring towns. He functioned once again as a trustee of the Birchard Library and was appointed to the boards of trustees of Western Reserve University, Green Springs Academy, and Oakwood Cemetery; subsequently he also served on those of Ohio Wesleyan University and Ohio State University. He was on the board of the Fremont Methodist Episcopal church, which he attended with Lucy but still would not join, and was named a director of the First National Bank of Fremont. Refusing to regard any of these posts as honorific, Hayes declared, "I mean to give due attention to all these matters." He joined the New York Civil Service Reform Association, rejoined the International Order of Odd Fellows, joined fellow veterans in the Grand Army of the Republic (GAR), and helped establish the Loyal Legion of Ohio, becoming its first commander. Hayes was tireless in attending army reunions — even of outfits in which he had not served — dedications of monuments to war heroes, and Decoration Day exercises.[7]

As he watched from Fremont, Hayes quickly perceived that many of Garfield's problems stemmed from his repudiation of Hayes's civil-service policy. He agreed with public printer John D. Defrees that Garfield's "unfortunate" promise to consult with congressmen on appointments led them to demand that fellow Republicans be fired to make way for "their special favorites." By resisting many of these requests, Garfield fulfilled the prediction of Defrees that within thirty days of the inauguration "Conkling and his toadies would denounce Gen. Garfield."[8]

Garfield particularly dismayed Hayes by replacing the New York collector of customs, Edwin A. Merritt (before his four-year term was over) with William Henry Robertson, a Blaine lieutenant. "What a muss Garfield has already made of it," Wheeler wrote to Lucy. "Or rather what a muss Blaine has made of it. So far *he* is 'running' G." And John Sherman wrote to Hayes, "I do not like the removal of Merritt . . . and I feel chagrined that the attack came from Garfield or rather from Blaine." But if Merritt's removal dismayed Hayes, Robertson's appointment enraged Conkling. Like Hayes,

Garfield had flouted "senatorial courtesy," and Conkling demanded that his colleagues reject the Robertson nomination. When Conkling was defeated and he and his colleague Thomas C. Platt resigned from the Senate, Hayes hoped that they had destroyed themselves and senatorial courtesy. This prospect, Hayes concluded, "almost reconciles me to the removal of Merritt."

When Lucretia Garfield became seriously ill, Hayes again sympathized with Garfield. But when her illness was blamed on the "notoriously unhealthy" White House, Hayes and particularly Lucy, who loved "the old house," emphatically disagreed. Writing to John Hay, who was editing the New York *Tribune* while Whitelaw and Lizzie Reid were on their honeymoon, Hayes stressed that "no family—including servants, children, guests, and Mrs. Hayes and myself were ever healthier in any house than we were in the White House. During four years there was no serious case of sickness." Hayes admitted that at night and "after the beginning of dog days," residents were exposed "to the malaria of the Potomac marshes," which is why the Hayeses retreated to the Soldiers' Home from early July until after the first October frost. When Lucretia Garfield's fever broke and she began to recover—shortly after Conkling's resignation—the personal and political stresses on Garfield eased.[9]

Despite Hayes's warm personal feelings for Garfield and his delight at Conkling's apparent political demise, the "wretched business" of the customhouse had shaken Hayes's confidence in his successor. It galled him to agree with Conkling and Platt's "strong point" that removing Merritt violated "all sound principles" of administration. Distinguishing between his and Garfield's administrations, Hayes believed: "The capital mistake is to attempt to build up an Administration or a party by the use of the offices as patronage. The offices should be filled for the good of the service. Country first and party afterwards." Trying to discover the root of Garfield's problems, Hayes concluded that "his long and brilliant career in Congress," where "traditions and courtesies . . . stand in the way of the Executive," was at fault. Yet Hayes still banked on Garfield's good intentions and had "hope for the future."[10]

As Garfield's troubles receded, Hayes was forced to confront a problem of his own. He had been out of office less than two months when Postmaster General Thomas L. James exposed the star-route frauds perpetrated during Hayes's administration. As the scandal broke, the connection between the frauds and the 1880 election, in which Garfield had triumphed, became apparent. Stephen W. Dorsey, a former carpetbag senator from Arkansas, was secretary of the Republican National Committee. Along with Marshall Jewell, Dorsey had run Garfield's campaign and had worked his greatest miracle in Indiana with star-route money. Among star-route contractors were Dorsey's brother, his brother-in-law, and a former partner. These three men controlled twenty-four contracts that had originally been worth $55,246 but had increased to $501,072. A small part of the increase went for additional service; the rest was put to private and political use. Dorsey later made the preposterous claim that he had spent $400,000 on the Indiana campaign.[11]

Hayes was disturbed and defensive. The fear that someone he was compelled to trust would prove false had been realized. He had been suspicious of increased star-route costs but had been reassured by Key and Tyner, who had faith in the "good reputation" of the chief culprit, Thomas J. Brady. Knowing that he had done "the right thing as it then appeared," Hayes characteristically resolved, "I do not and shall not deny or explain until the case requires it. Haste to deny or explain is always a sign of weakness. *I feel strong.*"[12]

The star-route frauds were suddenly overshadowed when word came on 2 July that Garfield had been seriously wounded by an assassin. Hayes and Lucy could think of nothing else that Saturday, but by 7:00 A.M. the next day, they received an encouraging dispatch that, after a "refreshing sleep," Garfield was "cheerful and hopeful" and that "his courage and fortitude" were "great." Although somewhat relieved, Hayes continued to be apprehensive, since Garfield's death "would be a national calamity," placing the anti-civil-service reform, stalwart wing of the Republican party in power. "Arthur for President! Conkling the power behind the throne, superior to the throne!"

Hayes arrested his pessimism with the thought that "the people are at last the government. If they are wise and firm and virtuous, all will yet be well." Hayes also realized that Arthur's past as a stalwart spoilsman did not predetermine his behavior should he become president. "If Arthur comes in, he should have a fair trial. He should be encouraged to do well by a warm and sympathetic support as far as he is right." Hayes buoyed himself further by remembering that Arthur wrote a "creditable" letter accepting the vice-presidential nomination. "But," Hayes emphasized, "our hopes and prayers are for Garfield."

When it appeared in early July that Garfield would recover, Hayes predicted that the attempt on his life by Charles Guiteau, a deranged stalwart office seeker, "will vastly increase the President's power and popularity. Stalwartism, which is synonymous with extreme, not to say, bitter and savage partisanship, will lose power." If Garfield would seize "his great opportunity," a "true and genuine reform of the civil service" would be possible.[13]

Garfield lingered during that summer "of universal anxiety and gloom."

Because of personal ties and political fears, Hayes's concern for Garfield's suffering was constant. On receiving an optimistic dispatch, Hayes and Lucy experienced the "greatest relief and joy" and were depressed whenever Garfield's condition weakened. When the mockingbird that had sung for them in the White House died, Hayes felt "a foolish presentiment that the death of the bird presages that of President Garfield." On 19 September, at 11:00 P.M., when the telegraph operator in Fremont telephoned that Garfield had died at 10:30, Hayes was overcome with fear before he reassured himself: "'Assassination does not change history.' The march of events will go on." But his deep "personal grief" remained.[14]

Hayes recognized, however, that the nation's grief could be channeled to change history. Journeying to Washington and later to Cleveland for Garfield's funeral services, Hayes was convinced that "nothing could exceed the universality and depth of feeling shown by all sorts of people." Even before Garfield died, Hayes wrote to his fellow civil-service reformer Silas W. Burt that "recent events have given the cause great advantages. We now have a clear field. Now is the time to push." In a public letter, Hayes instructed the grieving nation that the "lesson" of Garfield's assassination "is the folly, the wickedness, and the danger of the extreme and bitter partisanship," which "is greatly aggravated" by the spoils system. "The required reform" of the civil service "will be accomplished whenever the people imperatively demand it, not only of their Executive, but also of their legislative officers. With it, the class to which the assassin belongs will lose . . . the temptation to try 'to administer government by assassination.'" Along with other prominent men of both parties, Hayes signed an "address" by the New York Civil Service Reform Association linking the spoils system with murder.[15]

While president, Hayes had resolved to make education, particularly the education of disadvantaged Americans, his "hobby." In retirement, pushing wider educational advantages for all citizens became his most important activity. He remained a diligent trustee of the Peabody Educational Fund, whose mission was to improve schools in the South. A week after returning to Spiegel Grove following Garfield's burial, Hayes and Lucy left for a Peabody meeting in New York and remained for two weeks. Because of a railroad rate war, the normal thirteen-dollar ticket to New York was reduced to four dollars.

Hayes loved New York, particularly when viewed from the Sixth Avenue elevated railroad, but Lucy found it "bewildering" and was pained by "the contrasts of condition between the prosperous and the unfortunate." He enjoyed seeing his colleagues on the Peabody board, including General Grant (who "looked well and turned down his glasses at our trustee dinner") and Hamilton Fish (who gave the trustees lunch at his home, which was beautifully situated opposite West Point). Hayes also saw Schurz and Silas W. Burt of the customhouse and viewed the pictures and statuary of the Metropolitan Museum of Art. He was most impressed by the size and age of the recently arrived obelisk called Cleopatra's Needle. For an hour in the morning and another in the early afternoon, Hayes posed for William Merritt Chase, who was making good progress on Hayes's portrait for the Harvard Law School. But Hayes, who preferred the flattering style of Huntington, was not pleased by what he suspected was "a very truthful likeness. I would like it better if [it] was not so gray, not so cramped about the eyes, and not quite so corpulent. But," he wondered, "is not this quarreling with nature?" Seven months later, when Hayes arrived for some final sittings, he found the "portrait improved."[16]

While Hayes was in New York, Leonard W. Bacon, a Congregational minister from Norwich, Connecticut, interested him in a new educational project. Bacon's parishioner John Fox Slater, a wealthy textile manufacturer, wished to create a $1 million fund to "teach the colored people of the South" in nondenominational but Protestant schools. The new fund would be modeled on the $2 million Peabody Fund, which promoted the education of both black and white southerners. After conferring with Bacon and Slater, Hayes agreed to become president of the Slater Fund.

During the fall and winter of 1881–82, Hayes helped work out plans and select leaders for the Slater Fund. At his suggestion, a New York State charter was secured, and at the suggestion of Robert C. Winthrop, the words "*Protestant*" and "*colored*" were dropped, but Slater's objective remained "the uplifting of the lately emancipated population of the Southern States, and their posterity, by conferring upon them the blessings of Christian education." The trustees controlled the investment of the fund (which Slater increased by $200,000), whose earnings were to be used for neither land nor buildings. If, after thirty-three years, three-quarters of the trustees agreed, they could dissolve the trust and use its capital to provide scholarships for "poor students of the colored race."[17]

By the spring of 1882, Bacon, Slater, and Hayes had selected ten trustees, who met for the first time on 18 May in New York City. After engaging in some "conversational debate, brief and to the purpose," the Slater board elected members to a finance, a bylaws, and an executive committee. Hayes had wanted Bacon on the board but he had disqualified himself, fearing that his polemical style (he was currently attacking Sunday laws in Connecticut) would provoke opposition to the fund and its purpose. Because white supremacists perceived that education would improve the economic, political, and social position of blacks, the Slater Fund and its purpose were controversial from the start.[18]

Bacon urged the Slater board to select Atticus Green Haygood as its agent. A former Confederate chaplain, a Methodist minister, and the president of Emory College in Atlanta, Haygood had just published *Our Brother in Black*, an "audacious" book for a southerner to write. In it, he argued that God had willed the death of slavery, that Negroes were in the South to stay, that they were citizens with the right to vote, and that, as voters, they *"must be educated"* to utilize the "tremendous engine of political power" that was the ballot. Certain that, "right or wrong, wise or foolish," the South would not accept racial integration, Haygood favored segregated schools. So convinced was he of the necessity of "this educational work" that he proclaimed it *"God's work."* Like Bacon, Hayes was impressed by *Our Brother in Black*, and queries about its author produced favorable reactions. At the 5 October meeting of the Slater Fund, the board agreed to ask Haygood to become its general agent, and on 13 November he accepted the offer.[19]

While remaining an active trustee of the Peabody Fund, Hayes became the major force in the Slater Fund. Adjustments and understandings were made to his satisfaction. For example, he was reassured that the fund was not intended "for young *men* only," but "for all young persons of both sexes, white as well as black," willing to "engage in the education of the colored pupils." Bacon "fully re-assured" Hayes that Slater's intent was that *"man & he* are of the 'common gender,' except where the restricted use is apparent." Hayes was also concerned that Slater's words "Christian education" in his letter defining the trust might prevent aid to public schools. Again Bacon assured Hayes that Slater used "Christian education" in "the largest & most general sense," defining public-school education in Massachusetts and Connecticut as Christian, since it was "leavened with a predominant & salutary Christian influence."[20]

By the 5 October meeting of the Slater Fund, Hayes (who had celebrated his sixtieth birthday the day before) was clear on two ideas. He felt that the limited fund should be used to help those "who help themselves" and to support schools providing some form of industrial education. Hayes believed in manual training for his own children as well as the children of former slaves. "We must not divorce the mind from the hand," he reiterated. "Let the normal instruction be that men must earn their own living, and that by the labor of their hands as far as may be. This is the gospel of salvation for the colored man. Let the labor not be servile, but in manly occupations like those of the carpenter, the farmer, and the blacksmith."[21]

Hayes also urged that the Slater Fund be invested prudently. Slater had invested half the fund's capital—over half a million dollars—at 6 percent in the bonds of a railroad from Louisville to Chicago, and the finance committee had invested the remainder of it in railroad securities. Hayes "vastly" preferred investing in government bonds or mortgages and feared that "Slater's anxiety to get a good income from his fund . . . will lead to unsafe investments. I shall insist," he resolved, "on better security even with the loss of interest." Although the fund's treasurer Morris K. Jesup assured him of the "favorable condition" of the New Albany, Louisville, and Chicago Railroad, Hayes remained unenthusiastic about the purchase of railroad bonds. "Individuals invest their surplus," Hayes argued, but a trust fund "has no surplus" and must anticipate frequent hard times during its lifetime, "when at least three-fourths of all the RRs of the country will fail to pay their interest."[22]

The deeper Hayes became involved in education, the more he realized that, in a democratic republic, wise laws and efficient administration depended on the educational level of the population. There was, he believed, too much emphasis on passing laws, too much "time . . . wasted . . . in trying to force the stream to flow higher than its source," and too little emphasis on general education. The "character" of the people, which in a democracy "is sovereign," is formed by the "press, pulpit, railroad, schools and colleges and universities." These "great educators," by raising standards and developing the capacity for "intelligent and general discussion," are responsible for the simultaneously progressive and conservative "force of our institutions."[23]

When Hayes contemplated legislation prohibiting the sale of alcoholic beverages, he observed that enforceable laws are those that "embody the settled public opinion of the people who enacted them and whom they are to govern. . . . But if they embody only the sentiments of a bare majority . . . they will, if strenuously opposed," fail and even "injure the cause they are framed to advance." These reflections were probably informed in part by his experience with the Enforcement Acts. As president, Hayes had insisted that the Fourteenth and Fifteenth Amendments be obeyed, but efforts to enforce the election laws were frustrated by hostile local courts, an uncooperative Congress, and an indifferent public. As president, Hayes had found it impossible to overcome actively racist southerners and passively racist northerners, but in retirement, with education as his chief weapon, he hoped to prevail.[24]

Ignoring the growing intransigence of white southerners, Hayes continued to believe that their hostility to blacks had been engendered by the army's presence in the South. He remained convinced that his southern policy (local self-government coupled with political rights for all, enforced by civil authorities) "would bring ultimate safety and prosperity to the colored people and restore good feeling between the hostile sections." Hayes had not expected a quick transformation of the racist attitudes of southern whites, but by 1883, he believed optimistic reports that African Americans were as well treated in the South as in the North. Hayes assured Benjamin Tucker Tanner (a black minister and educator) that the policy he had instituted was doing "its work . . . slowly and surely." In large measure, Hayes's devotion to education, particularly the education of black southerners, was to ensure the "ultimate" success of his southern policy. But despite his optimism about progress, he knew and admitted to Tanner that racism was an enormous nationwide problem. "Certain it is, the people of the North have not in the last six years made greater progress in getting away from barbarism in the treatment of the colored man than the people of the South have made in the same period. . . . How few can say sincerely with Dr. Haygood, 'our *brother* in black.' "[25]

Although Hayes rightly declared in March 1883 that his "chief interest in pending public questions is on the subject of education in the South," he remained intrigued by politics. In September 1882, he and Lucy were delighted to catch up on capital gossip while entertaining the reporter Austine Snead. "Nothing," Hayes declared, "could be further from our desire than to return to Washington and enter again its whirl . . . but we are interested in seeing Washington with the *roof off*." When William K. Rogers stopped by, it was "exceedingly pleasant to talk over the years at Washington," and when William Henry Smith visited, they reviewed Hayes's political career. In retirement, Hayes defended his own course while observing his successors.[26]

Hayes was particularly irked in October 1881 by an anonymous leak to the press concerning the star-route frauds. Claims were made that, in 1879, First Assistant Postmaster General James N. Tyner had reported these frauds to Key, who did nothing because "it would hurt the party"; that Hayes was aware of Tyner's discovery but did nothing; and finally that Tyner's report to Postmaster General James broke the scandal. Hayes, as usual, took no public notice, nor did he let William Henry Smith dispute the anonymous insinuations. After telling Key that Tyner had always expressed confidence in "both the honesty and efficiency of Brady," Hayes queried him, "How is your recollection on this point?" At the time, Key still believed Thomas J.

Brady—his second assistant postmaster general—to be an honest man despite his implication in the frauds. Key responded that Tyner, having starved the star routes in the past, had criticized the Brady-backed policy of expediting some of the star routes but had repeatedly endorsed Brady's "honesty, ability and efficient service." Key believed that James was "playing . . . the demagogue" and that he had reduced star-route expenses not by eliminating corruption but by eliminating star routes in areas where railroads had expanded.

Hayes appreciated Key's "straightforward" reply but disagreed about Brady, thinking him corrupt. Tyner had not informed Hayes earlier of his doubts about star-route contracts, nor had Key relayed Tyner's doubts to the president. Indeed, Hayes had been led to believe that Tyner favored increasing star-route expenditures. Hayes's first intimation of a possible problem with the star-route contracts came not from the Post Office Department but from Rep. Joseph R. Hawley when Congress investigated and subsequently approved appropriations for extended service. Believing that "Brady and his set of Stalwarts were always my enemies," Hayes fervently reassured William Henry Smith, "One thing you may be sure of, I was not a party to covering up anything." The Arthur administration eventually brought Dorsey and Brady to trial, but after protracted litigation they were acquitted.[27]

Although sensitive to Arthur's awkward position as the beneficiary of an assassination by a deranged political ally, Hayes was critical of his first annual message. Because of its "non-committalism," Hayes labeled it "almost VanBurenish." Instead of backing civil-service reform legislation, Arthur merely declared that he would carry out reform if it were legislated. Instead of attacking the union of church and state in Utah, Arthur dealt with polygamy as if it—rather than government by "an irresponsible priesthood"—were at the heart of the Mormon question. Instead of recognizing the national government's "duty" to improve southern schools so that they would make former slaves informed voters, Arthur, although sympathetic, doubted the constitutionality of federal aid to education. Hayes, however, considered Arthur's failure to comment on "the Southern situation" a tacit endorsement of Hayes's southern policy. In thinking over Arthur's message, Hayes charitably concluded: "Perhaps in the present prosperous condition of the country this caution is politically wise. We want to be let alone. King Log is not a bad king sometimes."[28]

Hayes's charitable feelings toward Arthur disappeared in 1882. In July, Sherman told Hayes that Arthur wanted not only to "undo all you did, but to remove from office all your appointees," including Hayes's friend Clark Waggoner, the Toledo collector of internal revenue. Hayes, who had sus-

On the veranda at Spiegel Grove: Lucy, Hayes, and dogs with William Henry Smith

pected for some time that Arthur wanted "to get even," agreed with Sherman. "No merit will save any officer" of my administration, the former president acknowledged. "Only fear of public opinion spares those who are left." From Tennessee, Key confirmed that, whenever it dared, the Arthur administration was "quietly remov[ing] from office those who were opposed to Stalwartism." In Congress, stalwart John A. Logan, reverting to his earlier hostility, teamed up with Democrat James B. Beck to block Hayes's reimbursement for the expenses of the 1877 Louisiana commission, which he had paid. Hayes refused to let this parsimony bother him. In July 1882, he was no longer "in need. Land sells at fair prices," he explained to Sherman, "and I am independent again. My income is not large, but it is sufficient, and my debts are now in manageable shape. A year or two more of these good times and I am as easy as an old shoe."[29]

On 4 January 1883, Hayes agreed with Key that Arthur's course had brought the resounding Republican defeat in the 1882 congressional elections. Yet, despite Arthur's errors, Hayes was optimistic. The nation was prosperous, the southern question was "no longer threatening," and a chastened Congress was enacting civil-service reform legislation written by Dorman B. Eaton and introduced by the Ohio Democrat George H. Pendleton. When the Pendleton Act passed, Silas W. Burt once again credited the "rapid progress of the reform" to Hayes, who, by establishing the merit system in New York, had created "a practical basis for the arguments of the reformers." Hayes was also far enough removed from the assassination to place some of the blame for the Republican malaise on Garfield. Although Garfield was "the best popular debater of his time" in Congress, Hayes considered him weak and vacillating and "not executive in his talents."[30]

Politics and education were important to Hayes, but in his retirement he also devoted himself to his family and to Spiegel Grove. Although he and Lucy employed a staff of four, Hayes supervised the planting of trees and bushes, often pitched in with the outdoor work, and occasionally suffered for his enthusiasm. He stepped "carelessly on a chunk," was sharply reminded of Cedar Creek, and walked with a crutch for a few days. His most persistent problem, however, was poison ivy. In July 1882, while removing branches and brush, he "was badly poisoned" and suffered a "week of worry and pain" while treating his swollen hands, eyes, and face with "sugar of lead" and salt water. Still, the beauty of the grove more than compensated for the pain it occasionally caused. In the spring, Hayes rejoiced in the blooming dogwood, apple, and crabapple trees; in the fall, he found the brilliant foliage most satisfying.[31]

Interesting visitors heightened the joy of living at Spiegel Grove for Hayes and Lucy. Besides talking politics with visiting former associates, Hayes got acquainted with his new Slater Fund associate Atticus G. Haygood. In May 1882, he enjoyed meeting the talented African American Fisk Jubilee Singers, who stayed at Spiegel Grove while staging a "successful" concert in Fremont. When all the children were home, Hayes found "happiness enough!" In 1882, Birch, who continued to practice law in Toledo, and Webb, who was secretary and treasurer of the Whipple Lock Manufacturing Company in Cleveland, came home nearly every weekend. But Rud, who studied civil engineering at the Massachusetts Institute of Technology for a time, made it home only for major holidays. In September 1882, fifteen-year-old Fanny joined Mollie Garfield at Miss Mittleberger's School in Cleveland. Sorely missing his daughter's animated presence, Hayes feared that Fanny might be overworked and worried more about her deportment than her scholarship. Scott Russell remained at home until May 1883, when he started attending Green Springs Academy, eight miles away. When he returned home for the summer vacation and camped out in the grove with friends, Hayes was up before dawn "to see how the young soldiers got through the night."[32]

Hayes and Lucy welcomed his sister Fanny's grandchildren as though they were their own. When Laura Platt Mitchell's daughter Fanny came down with scarlet fever in March 1882, Laura shipped her other children—Lily, Jeannie, and John—to Spiegel Grove. "They are lovely and interesting children and think Aunt Lu is Divine Providence!" Hayes reported. When Lucy ran off to visit friends in Toledo, he and the children hunted eggs, shot at a target, built a huge fire, and read poetry before bedtime. Hayes was delighted to find that each "of these little folks" had a favorite Longfellow poem.[33]

Christmas 1882, "with the *whole family* at home," was the high point of the year. Webb, even "more uproarious" than usual, found an ally in Rud, and together they teased Adda Cook—Lucy's cousin and a member of the household—about a beau, "telling her 'don't deny—don't explain. Live it down.'" Among his presents, Hayes especially prized mittens and scarves that would be useful for sleighing. Five days later, after he and Lucy celebrated their thirtieth wedding anniversary, Hayes declared, "No holiday season was ever happier with us than this." Lucy, however, had recently suffered severe spasmodic pains, and these "symptoms of ill health" gave them "anxiety. But on the whole," Hayes concluded, "she is so strong, our children are so promising and good, that as a family we may deem ourselves peculiarly blessed."[34]

TWENTY-SEVEN

POPULAR EDUCATION

Lucy was more ill than Hayes had supposed. For about six months, she would be plagued by frequent intense "pain in the region of the liver," possibly caused by gallbladder disease. Dr. Thomas Stilwell prescribed "hot applications," quinine, and fifteen drops of opium. Later, "chlo____," possibly chloroform, seemed more effective in staving off attacks, and Hayes had a bathroom put in next to their bedroom for Lucy's convenience. After a few weeks' relief, the attacks returned in March 1883 but were relieved "at once" by hypodermic injections, apparently of opium, administered by Dr. John B. Rice, whom Stilwell had called in. In late April, when Hayes was in New York for a Slater trustee meeting, Lucy suffered another attack, and he rushed home to be with her.[1]

Between her debilitating attacks, Lucy functioned quite normally at home and continued her good works in the community. In January, Hayes invited a band, a glee club, and two hundred members of the GAR to Spiegel Grove. He proudly noted that "Lucy with her usual tact and magnetic cheerfulness looked after the happiness of all," until an attack forced her to withdraw unobtrusively. For a couple of weeks after the great flood of the Sandusky River on 4 February 1883, Lucy and Adda Cook went daily "to the City Hall to aid in the work for the sufferers"; Hayes played a leading role in organizing the relief effort and contributed a hundred of the thousand dollars raised. When Fanny came home from school and accompanied her mother on the piano, Lucy's singing, Hayes reported, "was as charming as ever. Not artistic, I suppose, but I never heard finer." By July, with "her rheumatic troubles" on the wane, Lucy was again in full stride. Along with Hayes, she was a guest of Henry and Ellen Bowen of Roseland Park, Woodstock, Connecticut, who had a "large and delightful" family of seven "stalwart" sons and three daughters. At Roseland Park, the main diversions were polo, swimming, and driving, and Hayes proudly told Fanny, "Your mother's best thing was her bath with 'all the boys' in the little lake."[2]

Hayes and Lucy were in Woodstock for his Fourth of July address urging the support of national aid to education, as embodied in the Blair bill. Its chief beneficiaries would be black children in the South, and racist southerners and parsimonious northerners opposed it. In December 1883, Hayes thought of another way to secure national aid for education. Amid talk of repealing the excise tax on whiskey or dividing its proceeds among the states, Hayes urged Whitelaw Reid of the influential New York *Tribune* to advocate distributing this revenue to the states for education. Exhibiting the prejudices of the age, Reid refused, maintaining, "The negroes do not have the intelligence and the whites do not have the inclination to secure for the blacks the full benefit of any Educational provisions that may be made for them." Had either the Blair bill or Hayes's whiskey-tax distribution scheme passed, millions of dollars would have gone into educating the poor of both races.[3]

With only thousands to distribute, Hayes continued his work for the Peabody and Slater Funds. In April 1883, Slater trustees agreed that students should be trained to use their hands as well as their heads and voted to use the available $20,000 to support "the very best Schools" that teach handicrafts. When Haygood rejected a plea from Howard University, saying that other points in the South needed aid more than Washington, D. C., Hayes got him to change his mind, since Howard was "beginning an Industrial Department."[4]

Hayes also spent much time and energy on church and community affairs. In 1883, he contributed over three hundred books, a card catalog, and $1,000 to the Birchard Library, and he agreed to pay a quarter of the $18,000 to $20,000 estimated cost of the new Methodist church building. When its minister Rev. D. D. Mather lost his pulpit for what Hayes described as "imprudent but not in the least licentious conduct with women," Hayes, Lucy, and other church leaders journeyed to Cleveland and successfully urged Bishop Randolph Foster to restore Mather. Harmony in the divided church, however, was not restored. Finding his position too awkward, Mather left the following year.[5]

Although living fully in the present, Hayes reveled in the history of the nation, including the recent events in which he had participated. Anxious to separate myths from "exact facts," he researched the landing of the Pilgrims, studied the Founding Fathers in George Bancroft's *History of the Constitution*, and rejoiced that "the work of Washington in the crisis of 1783–87" really was great. Though Hayes demythologized his childhood heroes, he infused the Civil War with spiritual values; it had become for him a crusade that transformed America. Inspired by Ralph Waldo Emerson's descripton of the war as a "battle for humanity," opening new "vistas" that "overpaid" its "cost of life," Hayes declared that the victory of the Union was also "the triumph of religion, of virtue, of knowledge. . . . During those four years, whatever our motives, whatever our lives, we were fighting on God's side. We were doing His work."[6]

Hayes championed and loved to associate with his fellow crusaders. He and Lucy attended annual reunions of the Twenty-third and of the Army of West Virginia, which gave her the distinction of being "the first woman ever chosen an honorary member of an army society." As commander of the Ohio Loyal Legion, Hayes frequently went to its monthly meetings in Cincinnati. "The legion," he admitted, "has taken the place of the . . . Literary Club. . . . The military circles are interested in the same things with myself, and so we *endure*, if not enjoy, each other." Hayes and Lucy also participated wholeheartedly in the activities of the Fremont GAR.[7]

Republican blunders following his retirement continued to disturb Hayes. Arthur, he perceived, had "stood in the way of every reform" until heavy congressional losses in 1882 forced him to approve the Pendleton Act. The Republican-dominated Court, including Hayes's appointee William B. Woods and his friend Stanley Matthews, also disappointed him by declaring the 1875 Civil Rights Act unconstitutional. Hayes had doubted the political wisdom of passing that act, but he shared the constitutional views of his friend and appointee John Marshall Harlan, the lone dissenter in the civil rights cases, who was "gratified" by Hayes's approval and added, "I am particularly delighted that Mrs. Hayes approves not only the *sentiment* of the dissent, but my views on the merely legal question involved in the cases."[8]

Preparing himself for a possible Democratic victory in the next election, Hayes wrote to Guy Bryan in October 1883: "When one party has had six Presidential terms, a change, merely for the sake of change, has something in its favor. But your leaders have a talent for blundering. Out of power a quarter of a century has lost to them the faculty of statesmanship under responsibility. They will probably throw away their chance."[9]

Within a few months, Ohio Democrats did blunder. Having carried the legislature, they refused to reelect Pendleton, a Democrat, to the Senate "solely because he was for civil service reform." In his place, they put Henry B. Payne, whose son Oliver, the treasurer of Standard Oil Company, reputedly invested $100,000 in making his father senator. This act disgusted the growing body of independent, reform-minded voters and offended the workingmen, whose votes, Hayes noted, "largely belong to the Democratic party. Their loss will destroy the power of the Democracy."[10]

To Hayes's regret, the "blunder and misfortune" of James G. Blaine's Republican nomination in 1884 offset Democratic mistakes. Observing that members of the reform element "doubt his personal integrity" and those of the "Stalwart element, the Grant men of 1880, do not like him," Hayes concluded that Blaine was "not the most *available* man and not the *best* man" that could have been named. He thought that Blaine was "a scheming demagogue, selfish and reckless," who would "gladly be wrong to be President," but Hayes supported him because he was a Republican, was able, and would "be a better President than he has been politician."[11]

Hayes feared that the Democratic nominee, Gov. Grover Cleveland of New York, would attract independent Republicans and Germans while retaining the loyalty of the Irish and Tammany Hall. With the campaign exploiting scandals rather than exploring issues, Hayes thought that greater care should be taken in naming candidates. He deplored the fathering of an illegitimate child by Cleveland as a "dark blot on his personal life," although he knew that it did "not imply entire unfitness for his public life." A careful rereading of Blaine's June 1876 speech on the Mulligan letters convinced Hayes that Blaine had covered up corrupt railroad transactions. Saying that the "steady warm" election day rain would not hurt the Republicans, Hayes voted and went off to Cincinnati for a Loyal Legion meeting. That evening, he and John Herron joined Murat Halstead at the *Commercial-Gazette* to monitor election returns. New York would determine the victor, and there the vote was incredibly close. When the Republicans lost that state and the election, Hayes, writing to Lucy, blamed it on the "record of our candidate and factional griefs," adding, "I dread the turning back of the hands of the clock in the Southern business and in the reform of the civil service."[12]

Hayes, however, quickly put the election and politics into perspective. Since Cleveland was "pledged to the right side" of the civil-service reform issue, Hayes became less fearful of wholesale changes and requested Schurz to ask Cleveland not to fire faithful White House servants. Hayes realized that Cleveland faced a "practical difficulty" in making cabinet appointments: There were simply not enough "men of good standing" in the Democratic party who were sympathetic to civil-service reform. More cheering to Hayes was the strength of the Republican party in defeat. He was certain that it would have triumphed if it had been led by John or William T. Sherman, Joseph R. Hawley, Walter Q. Gresham, or Benjamin Harrison. Even with Blaine, it carried the Senate, came close to winning the House, and, as Hayes told an unsympathetic Guy Bryan, would have carried four to six southern states and the presidency if the Reconstruction amendments had been obeyed. But Hayes did not wish to exaggerate the impact of political campaigns on "the march of events. . . . The people are the government. Their character does not change with the results of elections," but only with "generations" of education.[13]

As for politics, Hayes declared, "I am a looker-on except as to education.

On that, *I am persistent*, in and out of season, before all sorts of audiences." Hayes did not exaggerate. On Decoration Day at Springfield, Ohio, he spoke on national aid to education, which he insisted was "needed to secure the fruits of the Union victory." The entire system of education, he stressed, was impractical and did not fit young men and women for the duties of life. Believing that the Slater Fund was on the cutting edge of the movement for industrial education, he told his audience what it was doing in the South. At the end of 1884, Hayes was "daily writing to Members of Congress in behalf of the bill in aid of education by the general Government."[14]

With its mix of the practical, the humanitarian, and the social, Hayes found his work on the Slater and Peabody Funds satisfying. At the October 1884 Peabody Fund trustee meeting, Grant was "genial, talkative, and interesting" and in "better health and spirits" than expected, considering the recent loss of his fortune; Hamilton Fish regaled him even more than usual with Albert Gallatin stories. Evarts and Hayes opposed the majority decision to cut off aid to Mississippi because the state had refused to pay its debt on bonds held by the Peabody Fund. Insisting that Mississippi children should not suffer because their legislature lacked principle, Hayes said, "Educate the children and the State will pay its debts."[15]

As president of the Slater Fund, Hayes had more influence. Atticus G. Haygood, the Slater Fund agent, implemented Hayes's ideas on industrial education. "I am simply astonished," he wrote to Hayes, "at the influence of this Fund in making College work for Colored people *practical*." Having dealt with Haygood more than the other trustees had, Hayes found Haygood's first year's work "most encouraging and satisfactory." The other trustees, however, insisted that Haygood should spend "more time with the board and especially more time examining industrial schools at the North and attending the schools aided by us in term time." As a result, Hayes persuaded Haygood to resign the presidency of Emory College.[16]

Beginning in 1885, Haygood devoted his full time to the Slater Fund. When board members remained at odds with him, Hayes did his best to harmonize the dissonant voices. Daniel Coit Gilman and other board members demanded more information on the postwar education of southern blacks and the integration of manual labor and intellectual training in northern schools. Because of these demands, Haygood found the "undertones" of the January 1885 meeting "utterly unsatisfactory. There seemed to be a notion that the chief end of the Slater Board was to *study* the Negro Question," he complained. He thought the idea of further studies "preposterous" and a waste of time and money. Hayes agreed and told Gilman that he felt "no special need" for further investigation "beyond the conference we can have with each other." Gilman conceded that Haygood's recent pamphlet on Negro education in the southern states covered the field, and if Haygood analyzed in depth the education of blacks in Georgia, he would be content. At the May meeting, Haygood staved off his critics by reading "excellent" excerpts from his printed report and from his report on Georgia.[17]

A further compromise was necessary after the May meeting. Treasurer Morris K. Jesup, backed by letters from Samuel Chapman Armstrong of the Hampton Institute and President Edmund Asa Ware of Atlanta University, urged putting the "Slater force into three or four schools for teaching trades." Haygood countered that it was "unthinkable" for him to "make the superintending of three or four machine shops my life work" and, through Hayes, reminded Jesup that Slater's chief idea "was to help . . . prepare young men & women to teach." Like Haygood, Hayes thought of industrial education in conjunction with book learning. His "educational hobbies" included the teaching of more "American history and biography, . . . English language and literature and modern languages," and industrial education. Not totally rejecting Jesup's idea, the board earmarked $3,000 of its available $30,000 for the Hampton Institute, making it necessary for Haygood "to pinch at many other places."

Despite limited funds, Haygood saw "*buds* of promise" and Hayes saw "encouraging progress" in their work as they looked south. In 1885, Haygood sensed that blacks were doing more to help themselves and southern whites were exhibiting a "helping spirit"; Hayes fueled his optimism by rationalizing that "elections and politics in this country correspond with battles and war in other times and countries. Whatever of departing evils remains is sure to show itself last in the excitements of political contests." Hayes was "fully persuaded" that the evil of inequality was coming to its end.[18]

In Ohio, Hayes struck a blow for education when he helped reorganize Western Reserve University. It had been renamed Adelbert College of Western Reserve University after receiving a generous gift from Amasa J. Stone in memory of his son, but the medical department had been promised $250,000 by another donor if it could disassociate itself from the name Adelbert. University trustees asked Hayes to work out a plan that would be satisfying to the new donor and to the family of Amasa Stone. Hayes called on his former assistant secretary of state John Hay, who was Stone's son-in-law. They agreed to call the institution Western Reserve University (with Adelbert College as one of its schools). Hayes chaired the reorganization meeting on 15 April 1884, and perhaps out of gratitude, Western Reserve rescued another of Hayes's educational responsibilities by adopting the ailing Green Springs Academy as a preparatory school for Adelbert College.[19]

Hayes also reinvolved himself in prison reform. Given his desire to rehabilitate criminals, he considered this another educational endeavor. The National Prison Reform Association was reorganized on 7 September 1883 at Saratoga and chose Hayes (who was at Spiegel Grove) as president, William M. F. Round as secretary, and Theodore Roosevelt (who was on his way to the Badlands in the Dakota Territory) as treasurer. When Hayes was in New York a month later for a Peabody Fund meeting, he called on Round, and their discussion made him glad to be officially associated with prison reform again. Hayes realized the dimensions of his new task when he noted the statement of his fellow reformer Franklin B. Sanborn in *Harper's Weekly* that there were 45,000 convicts in 130 prisons in the United States.[20]

Meetings of the National Prison Reform Association were instructive. At Saratoga in September 1884, Hayes (who was still criticized for his generous use of the pardoning power) heard papers on pardons, extradition, punishment, and the causes of crime. He believed that prisons themselves caused crime. In Samuel Taylor Coleridge's words, imprisoned convicts became "hopelessly deformed / By sights of ever more deformity." Echoing Coleridge, reformer Eugene Smith would show at the association's next annual meeting that county "jails were training-schools for crime — compulsory under law, and at public expense." To separate hardened criminals from novices, Smith advocated "complete isolation," as required by the Ohio Jail Plan. Hayes — who with Lucy was on the inspection committee of the Sandusky County Jail — noted that such isolation was "unfortunately rarely found even in Ohio."[21]

For "a non-church member, a non-professor of religion," Hayes spent an inordinate amount of time in church and on church business. He continued to serve as a key member of the Methodist building committee and, with the congregation no longer divided, rarely missed a Sunday service; he even attended revivals. Unmoved during these emotional meetings, he calmly noted that converts — usually belonging to "the middle and poorer classes" — were evenly divided between young and old, male and female. On St. Patrick's Day 1884, Hayes joined Father J. D. Bowles and his Roman Catholic parishioners of St. Ann's for "good feelings" and "good music" at the Opera Hall and was among those making "the usual speeches." Considering Christianity "the best religion the world has ever had," Hayes thought that "a man or a community adopting it is virtuous, prosperous, and happy." But for him, supporting Christianity did not mean subscribing to a dogma or encouraging attempts by missionaries to convert a "cultured people" like the Chinese.[22]

Books nourished Hayes spiritually and intellectually. Ralph Waldo Emerson continued to exert the strongest influence on his thought, but he disliked Emerson's friend Henry David Thoreau, who Hayes believed was "not a patriot" and deserved to go to jail for his civil disobedience. In early 1885, Hayes read John Fiske, Charles Darwin, and Herbert Spencer on evolution. He also read novels and poetry, but history and biography remained his favorites, and he found Thomas Carlyle especially provocative. Never the docile follower of Congress, Hayes applied Carlyle's observation that William Pitt was "a despotic sovereign, though a temporary one," to the American presidency.[23]

Initially, Hayes thought that the current temporary despot, Grover Cleveland, was "doing extremely well." He was "sound on the currency, the tariff, and the reform of the civil service," and his appointments abroad—particularly that of George Pendleton to Germany—were good. But in late August 1885, Hayes—still an ardent Republican—believed that, despite "the sincere repugnance of a reform President," the "spoils system is . . . in power at Washington." In its "desire to sustain the President," the National Civil Service Reform League tended "to wink at the violations of principle which are of daily occurrence. . . . The sweep is not rapid, but it will no doubt be 'clean.'" Hayes warned that failure to condemn Democratic spoils practices would strengthen the growing apprehension that the Reform League might be annexed by "*the* Spoils Party of the Country."[24]

Since most civil-service reformers had supported Cleveland, Hayes's relationship with these mugwumps was strained. In January 1885, he complained that "some friends of the cause" belittled his work in attacking "Senatorial prerogative" and "Congressional patronage," in preventing party management by officeholders, and in establishing reform in the New York customhouse. Although Curtis "spoke kindly" of Hayes's reform efforts when they met in New York in October 1884, by the end of 1885, Hayes had "noticed with regret during the last three years a disposition in Mr. Curtis to disparage my ability." Hayes was particularly incensed that Curtis had erroneously credited Sherman with writing Hayes's veto of the 1878 Bland-Allison Silver Coinage Act.[25]

Despite the defection of mugwumps and prohibitionists, the Republican party was healthy in 1885. When the Republican majority in the New York legislature elected Evarts to Conkling's old Senate seat, Hayes called it "our victory" and labeled it a "vindication of my Administration." In the fall,

Hayes was further pleased, despite the divisive "bloody-shirt course of the canvass," that the Republicans carried Ohio, ensuring John Sherman's return to the Senate. Lunching with Governor-elect Joseph B. Foraker, Hayes suggested that if he would identify the Republican party with regulating but not prohibiting the sale of alcoholic beverages, he would arrest defections to the Prohibition party. In New York, those defections had cost Blaine the recent presidential election.[26]

The divisive and derisive nature of prohibition and temperance (which even divided the Fremont GAR) aggravated Hayes. Frequent accusations that parsimony had moved him and Lucy to banish wine from the White House incensed him, since he had spent more on entertaining than any previous president. He was also bothered by the press's delight when a piece of Omaha real estate that he owned with Ralph Buckland was leased for the sale of liquor without their knowledge. "The exclusion of wine from the White House," Hayes insisted, was "at the bottom of three-fourths of all the lies" told about him. "The man who does that which avails in reforms or other good works always has clubs thrown at him," he philosophized. "The nobodies are passed over in Silence, or with good natured unmeaning compliments after they leave high places."[27]

Hayes and Lucy opposed prohibition but remained on good terms with temperance advocates. He attempted to steer Frances Willard of the WCTU gently away from a dependence on "courts, ballot-boxes, and legislatures" and toward awakening the consciousness and consciences of individuals. To advance moral reforms, he did not believe in resorting "to force—not even to the force of law." When Lucy was in Chicago, he reminded her that if "Miss *Willard* . . . calls you need *promise* nothing but smother her with politeness." Hayes was angered by the exaggerations of "a temperance krank" who asked him for data on the "three thousand pardons of whiskey convicts in 1877–1881" (when all of his pardons did not even approach that number). He demanded the authority for the statement and warned that "a good cause often suffers by the reckless and baseless statements of its injudicious and excitable friends."[28]

As former presidents, Hayes and Arthur were together at the funeral of Ulysses S. Grant on Saturday, 8 August 1885. Earlier that year, Hayes had twice visited his former commander and was comforted to find him happy and secure in the hold he had "on the hearts of his countrymen." Despite the fact that Hayes had once fired Arthur, they conversed "without any reserve or embarrassment on either side." After waiting for two to three hours, they joined the huge procession near the catafalque and spent the next five hours moving slowly past a decorous multitude of spectators to the grave site.

"President Arthur," Hayes noted gratefully, "proved an excellent companion for such a drive." Hayes found "the ships in the Hudson, and the whole scene . . . unspeakably impressive and affecting." Back at their hotel, Arthur spoke "kind words" to him and, after "a hearty good-bye," they parted. In little more than a year, Hayes and Cleveland would attend Arthur's funeral.[29]

"Our life at Washington," Hayes noted, "led us to know rather aged people. They are going — going." When Cleveland's vice president, Thomas A. Hendricks, died in late November, Hayes attended his funeral in Indianapolis. Even though Hendricks had been Tilden's running mate and a soft-money advocate, he and Hayes had always been cordial. When he was in the House and Hendricks in the Senate, Hayes recalled that they "had long and agreeable talks on public affairs and personages" on the train returning home to the West. After Hendricks's funeral, Hayes proceeded to Cincinnati, where extreme partisans criticized him. "I see you were at the funeral of that _____ old Copperhead," former Governor Noyes needled him at the Loyal Legion meeting.[30]

In February 1885, Hayes's financial problems eclipsed his other concerns. The Fremont Harvester Company, in which Sardis and Hayes had invested "for the benefit of the community" and for which Hayes had signed notes, went bankrupt. In addition, a challenge to the constitutionality of the Ohio savings bank law threatened Hayes's investment in the Fremont Savings Bank. "Urgent private business" connected with these problems prevented him from attending the 21 February dedication of the Washington Monument, whose completion had long been his favorite project. Hayes's financial picture was further complicated by his pledge to pay a quarter of what the Methodist church raised toward its debt for its new building.[31]

Hayes's financial difficulties worsened. His bank investments were imperiled by imprudent management, the affairs of the Harvester Company were even worse than early reports had indicated, and the church's pledge drive succeeded beyond expectations. Although Hayes was relieved to hear on 24 February that the Ohio Supreme Court upheld the savings bank law, he had been "vexed" to discover on 23 February that the First National Bank of Fremont, in which he had invested $41,000, had not reduced its dangerously high loans to the Malt Works, as he had supposed. The bank had carried them for years on the strength of its partners' notes. After "some sharp words," the bank's president stopped trying to "bluff" Hayes and admitted neglecting "his duty." By early March, Hayes anticipated that the Harvester Company's failure would cost him $12,000 to $15,000; with his other debts, his "load [would be] too heavy for comfort. But with economy and careful management," he hoped to pull through "without large sacrifices of property."[32]

Amid these financial difficulties, Hayes was surprised and delighted when Senator Sherman secured from Congress $3,950 to reimburse him for the expenses of the 1877 commission that had finessed the end of Reconstruction in Louisiana. Hayes maintained that the money was "the smallest part" of his gratification. He chose to view the payment as "an all-sufficient reply to the foolish 'fraud' cry of the [New York] *Sun* and a few other implacables in both parties."[33]

Realizing that their assets in land more than covered their 1885 losses, Hayes and Lucy refused to let their financial upset get them down. They were more pained on 4 March by the loss of Grymme, their greyhound, than by their financial troubles. Grymme was killed at a Lake Shore railroad crossing, where he stood his ground, expecting the train, like the teams of horses, to turn out for him. "I miss him everywhere," Lucy wrote almost a week later, "his joyous loving greeting . . . his dignified trot when going with the Carriage—the greeting from the children 'Oh there is Mrs. Hayes and Grymme.'" Hayes and Lucy decided to bury Grymme in Spiegel Grove, next to the warhorse Old Whitey. By April, with his financial crisis abating, Hayes was traveling again and presided over the fifth congress of the Loyal Legion in Chicago, where he particularly relished the "enthusiastic and stirring" banquet, during which those present stamped around the tables singing "Tramp, Tramp, Tramp, the Boys Are Marching."[34]

Hayes read Civil War memoirs avidly and rejoiced in 1886 that rivalries and "harsh and cruel criticisms among officers . . . under the same flag" were abating. No book on the war thrilled him more than the "intensely interesting and very valuable" *Personal Memoirs* of Grant, which appeared shortly after Grant's death. On reading the first volume, Hayes declared, "It is graphic and simple and as truthful as truth itself." Hayes exulted that "our matchless comrade and companion, our illustrious commander . . . speaks today to more minds, with a higher authority, and gets back a readier and heartier reply than ever before." Grant's appraisal—in his second volume—of Hayes "brought tears" to his eyes. "His conduct on the field," Grant wrote, "was marked by conspicuous gallantry as well as the display of qualities of a higher order than that of mere personal daring. This might well have been expected of one who could write . . . : 'Any officer fit for duty who at this crisis would abandon his post to electioneer for a seat in Congress ought to be scalped.'" Hayes never received a compliment that meant more to him than those words. But he was nearly as pleased to learn a few years later that George Crook had called him "as brave a man as ever wore a shoulder-strap."[35]

Praise was sweet, but criticism, particularly unwarranted criticism, rankled Hayes. If he thought that others had misrepresented the past, he was quick to set the record straight. When an anonymous writer blamed him for Gen. David Hunter's failure to destroy Jubal Early's army, Hayes—through his friend James M. Comly—ably defended himself but tried not to disparage Hunter, who had been unreasonably criticized for the Lynchburg raid. Hayes's legal training and his love of history demanded that sound evidence be used in reconstructing the past. He considered the publication of private conversations, for example, an invasion of privacy and, because no one remembers them correctly, of little historical value. "Leave it to the '*thin-brained*' to quote from memory conversations of long ago," he warned Comly. Hayes came to expect, but never accepted, a less than scrupulous use of sources by partisans of military heroes, political leaders, and reform causes.[36]

The use of sources by a scholar in an article published by the American Historical Association also disappointed Hayes. When Lucy M. Salmon, in a "carefully prepared" article on the president's appointing power, adopted "the accusations of a hostile and partisan paper," Edwin L. Godkin's *Nation*, Hayes complained. Rightfully proud of his appointments, he was particularly irked by Salmon's accusation that "honors were conferred upon unknown men and personal friends as well as upon some who had been foremost in the questionable events connected with the action of the returning boards." That action, Hayes insisted, was justified because the Fifteenth Amendment had been ignored (the ignoring of which Godkin and the *Nation* viewed "with complacency if not approval"); an examination of his appointments and the policies on which they were based would reveal a high degree of creditability and a low level of political partisanship. Salmon's repetition of Godkin's accusation, Hayes concluded, was "utterly unworthy of a place in a historical article." In contrast, Albert Bushnell Hart's book on the veto power, "in which ample justice" was done to him, pleased Hayes.[37]

As if to punctuate his objection to Salmon's article, a month after reading it, Hayes helped save the job of Louisville's postmistress, whom local Democrats were trying to replace. Hayes emphasized that he had appointed Virginia Campbell Thompson not because she was a Republican (he had thought her a Democrat, and his assumption had been confirmed by the opposition to her among Kentucky Republicans) but because he was convinced that she "would be a good officer" and that her appointment would gratify "good people," would reduce southern bitterness against the North and the Republican party, and would put a woman in "an important and conspicuous place."[38]

TWENTY-EIGHT

SOCIAL JUSTICE

Feeling increasingly alienated from civil-service reformers—who were tilting toward the Democrats and showing little concern for social issues—Hayes shifted his emphasis from political reform to social justice. Multiplying strikes and boycotts and the spectacular growth of the Knights of Labor in 1885 and early 1886 bothered Hayes. Believing that "strikes and boycotting are akin to war, and can be justified only on grounds [of] . . . intolerable injustice and oppression," he feared that a situation of that magnitude was in the offing and declared: "The question for the country now is how to secure a more equal distribution of property. . . . There can be no republican institutions with vast masses of property . . . in a few hands, and large masses of voters without property. . . . Let no man get by inheritance . . . more than . . . an income of fifteen thousand per year, or an estate of five hundred thousand dollars."[1]

Hayes returned to this "capital and labor question" again and again. When on St. Patrick's Day he addressed Father Edward Hannin's St. Patrick's Institute in Toledo, he advocated "such measures and laws as will give to every workingman a reasonable hope that by industry, temperance, and frugality he can secure a home for himself and his family, education for his children, and a comfortable support for old age." Two days later, he elaborated in his diary: "No man . . . can use a large fortune so that it will do half as much good in the world as it would if it were . . . in the hands of workmen who had earned it by industry and frugality." The next day, when he met Cornelius Vanderbilt ("one of our railroad kings"), who had inherited the bulk of his father's $100 million estate, Hayes thought "of the inconsistency of allowing such vast and irresponsible power . . . to be vested by law in the hands of one man." To Hayes, men like Vanderbilt provoked labor violence and threatened democracy. Americans, Hayes suspected, would have to choose either "to limit and control great wealth, corporations, and the like, or [to] resort to a strong military government" to keep peace. He asked, "Shall the interest of railroad kings be chiefly regarded, or shall the interest of the people be paramount?"[2]

In the unusually beautiful spring of 1886, strikes, especially on railroads, mounted toward a May Day climax. To better understand strikes, Hayes read James F. Hudson's *The Railways and the Republic* (1886) and found that its argument, favoring railroad reform, was grounded on facts. At the end of April, while attending the encampment of the Ohio GAR, Hayes spoke on the labor and railroad problems. So eager was he for railroad regulation that he thanked both Sen. Shelby M. Cullom and Rep. John H. Reagan for their strikingly different interstate commerce bills designed to make railroads more accountable to the public. A general strike had been called for in Chicago in early May, and Hayes castigated railroads for causing the violence he anticipated: "It may be truly said," he wrote in his diary, "that for twenty-five years, at least, railroad workingmen have had too little, and railroad capitalists and managers . . . have had too much. . . . The railroads should be under a wise, watchful, and powerful supervision by the Government. No violence, no lawlessness, destructive of life and property, should be allowed. It should be suppressed instantly and with a strong hand."[3]

As Hayes feared, violence erupted in Chicago. It culminated at the Haymarket when a bomb exploded among policemen who were breaking up a small anarchist rally. Although he advocated "extensive reforms" by the federal government to ensure labor a "fair share of the wealth it creates," Hayes believed above all else in "*the supremacy of law.*" Far more wrought up than he had been during the Great Strike of 1877, Hayes called "all of the lawless agitators and their followers anarchists. They train under the red flag. . . . It is the enemy . . . of honest industry in America. Rally under the old flag—the Stars and Stripes—the emblem of liberty regulated by law."[4]

Hayes perceived that America had changed since the 1877 Great Strike. "In Congress, in state legislatures, in city councils, in the courts, in the political conventions, in the press, in the pulpit, in the circles of the educated and the talented," Hayes saw the influence of money "growing greater and greater. Excessive wealth in the hands of the few means extreme poverty, ignorance, vice, and wretchedness as the lot of the many," he counseled. In Ohio, "the Standard Oil Monopoly . . . is offensive; it destroys individual enterprise; . . . it is a menace to the people." By electing a governor and a senator with its money, it has "attempted to seize political power and usurp the functions of the State." The "government of the people, by the people, and for the people" had become "a government of corporations, by corporations, and for corporations." Before the Civil War, the great problem was how to rid the country of slavery without destroying society. "Now the great problem," Hayes perceived, "is to rid our country of the conflict between wealth and poverty without destroying either society or civilization, or liberty & free government."[5]

Hayes believed that the people must first be convinced that the excessive power of excessive wealth was "the evil" to be eradicated, the problem to be solved. Once convinced, the people could "earnestly seek" and find remedies based on an exhaustive exploration of the treatments available. Hayes appreciated Henry George's exposure, in *Progress and Poverty*, of "the rottenness of the present system," but although he was "not yet ready" for George's confiscatory single tax on growing land values, Hayes advocated legislation (just short of confiscation) "regulating corporations, descents of property, wills, trusts, taxation, and a host of other important interests, not omitting lands and other property." Hayes stressed that, in proportion to their estates, millionaires *"pay less than half as much as ordinary citizens, whereas they ought to pay more"* taxes. "The Interstate Commerce law, one of the crudest ever passed, is yet one of the most beneficent in its results. The government should say to dangerous combinations, 'Thus far, and no further.' " After lifelong acceptance of John Marshall's Dartmouth College decision, protecting corporations from state regulation, Hayes decided that "it was a mistake . . . that . . . gave to capital a power that should rest only with the people."[6]

Hayes also believed that universal industrial education would eliminate class strife at home and enhance America's image abroad. Since he equated education with high wages and ignorance with low wages, Hayes thought that schools—especially schools with a new curriculum—could help mitigate the maldistribution of wealth, prevent the "division of society into castes, which prevails in the old world," and promote democratic principles. "Every American boy and girl should have that training of the hand and eye which industrial schools furnish"; that, Hayes believed, would give them "an equal chance and a fair start."

Egalitarianism and education were inextricably linked in Hayes's mind. When he congratulated Leland Stanford on his establishment of Stanford University, Hayes particularly praised him for making it nonsectarian and providing for manual training. Exposing business and political leaders to industrial education would foster their understanding of, and respect for, labor and would reduce class conflict. "No man," Hayes emphasized, "is fit to make or administer laws in this country who holds in contempt labor or the laborer."[7]

Hayes shared many of the concerns of his cousin Elinor's husband, William Dean Howells, whom he found "more and more a man of wisdom and heart." Believing that Howells's latest book, *Annie Kilburn*, which he had finished reading in January 1889, "opens the democratic side of the coming questions," Hayes searched for but could not find "a ready word for the doctrine of true equality of rights. Its foes call it nihilism, communism, socialism, and the like," he noted. "Howells would perhaps call it justice. It is the doctrine of the Declaration of Independence, and of the Sermon on the Mount. But what is a proper and *favorable* word or phrase to designate it?"[8]

While complaining about the maldistribution of wealth in America, Hayes continued to work for better schools and prisons. In March 1886, he pressed once again for congressional support for the Blair bill. When Comly implied opposition in his Toledo newspaper, Hayes told him, "The South cannot get an efficient school system without this aid. It is the only hope." Although three-fourths of the Senate passed the Blair bill that month, it encountered opposition in the House. To Hayes's dismay, Slater Fund trustees—influenced by Morris K. Jesup—refused to petition Congress in the bill's favor. Laissez-faire, states' rights, and racism eventually defeated the Blair bill, which would have prevented racial discrimination in the distribution of funds while permitting segregated schools. Led by Samuel J. Randall, the Democratic House of Representatives smothered it.[9]

In 1886, Hayes stepped up his activities for prison reform. He spoke in July to the thirteenth National Conference of Charities and Corrections at Saint Paul; in November, he journeyed to Mansfield for "the laying of the corner stone of Ohio's great reformatory, the intermediate penitentiary," and continued to Atlanta for the National Prison Association Congress. The main reason for meeting in Atlanta was to attack Georgia's leasing of convicts. Chained together, gangs of prisoners worked under conditions worse than those of slavery. In what he proudly told Lucy was his "best" performance ever, Hayes spoke of the deplorable conditions that made the National Prison Association necessary; but, he admitted, it was the "*brave* and eloquent" Slater Fund agent Atticus G. Haygood who "cut the Georgia lease system to the quick." The congress provoked Georgians to contemplate a separate prison for women and a reformatory for juveniles, and Haygood believed that the "best thought & sentiment" of Georgia was against the contract labor system. While together in Atlanta, Hayes and Haygood visited Clark University for the Slater Fund and found the school's progress "encouraging in every way."[10]

In his prison-reform work, Hayes added a twist reflecting his social concerns. Connecting crime with crowded dwellings and poverty in his 1888 address to the Prison Congress in Boston, he found crime's cause rooted in "the crimes of the wealthy," specifically in their greed and "extravagance," which deprived an underclass of a decent income. Apart from redistributing wealth to prevent crime, Hayes backed manual training of the young and a restructuring of "our Prison systems" to mitigate their "evils." He wished to reform the corrigibles in enlightened institutions and permanently jail the incorrigible offenders at other facilities, where they would "earn by labor their own support." Expecting that the "privileged class" would label his speech "a little 'communistic' in its tendency," he was delighted to tell Lucy that he had "never *read* a speech so well" and that "it was received most flatteringly." When the assembly passed a "resolution on the absolute need in all prisons of *skilled and remunerative labor*," Hayes felt repaid for his efforts.[11]

At the 1888 Ohio centennial celebration in Columbus, Hayes left off hobnobbing with governors to go with Elijah G. Coffin, the warden of the Ohio penitentiary, to see the gallows "where murderers are now executed." Hayes thought the new system, which permitted only about thirty or forty witnesses rather than the general public, "the best mode" of execution. Nevertheless, he emphatically declared, "I think the time for capital punishment has passed."[12]

"Educational and benevolent" work and his lively family kept Hayes active, "cheerful and contented." He was not discouraged by the loss of $12,000 in February 1886 when the Whipple Manufacturing Company, of which Webb was secretary and treasurer, burned to the ground. Nor did he let his feeling that Webb spent too much time playing polo and participating in the "Cleveland Cavalry troop" intrude on his heartfelt sympathy for him and the 175 men who had lost their jobs. Insisting "we are greatly blessed," Hayes soon signed $6,000 in notes to start Webb in the National Carbon Company of Cleveland, which specialized in "making carbon for electric lights."[13]

By the end of 1886, the blessings had taken a nuptial turn with a delightful "marrying mania." On 30 December, on Hayes and Lucy's thirty-fourth anniversary, Birch married Mary Sherman of Norwalk (no relation of John or William T. Sherman); on 4 January 1887, Lucy's niece Adda Cook married R. W. Huntington and left Spiegel Grove for Mississippi; and a few days later, Hayes's nephew and namesake Ruddy Platt married Maryette Smith, the granddaughter of Joseph R. Swan, a distinguished Ohio jurist. In April, when Ruddy and Maryette visited Spiegel Grove, a pleased Hayes wrote, "With Birch and his lovely wife, and Webb to stir up a riot, the house was in a very lively and enjoyable state while the dear young people were with us."[14]

Enjoying both books and companionship, Hayes often joined the two by reading aloud with Lucy and guests. Mary and Birch were excellent readers, and in 1887, while their new home—a wedding present from Hayes and Lucy—was being built in Toledo, they were often at Spiegel Grove. When Mary began reading a new William Dean Howells story, Hayes admired his skill but wanted to tell him, "Don't let this story, so happily begun, leave a bad taste in our mouths." After Howells called in May and "warmly commended Tolstoy's writings," Hayes began *Anna Karenina*, marking passages that especially appealed to him. He too believed, "To sleep, you must work; and to be happy, you must also work" and search for truth and never find it.[15]

Actually, Hayes overdid work. On 9 April 1887, he became overheated after five hours of yard work and then rested on his porch with Theodore Roosevelt's "vigorous, dogmatic, and a little scattering" biography of Thomas Hart Benton, Andrew Jackson's lieutenant and the father-in-law of John Charles Frémont. Although Hayes found time for reading—and even wiled away a few hours with French detective novels—he was "loaded down to the guards with educational, benevolent, and other miscellaneous public work." Since he "made it a rule through life to attend well to the humblest duties," he realized, "I *must* not attempt to do more." Determined to trim his tasks, Hayes gave up the time-consuming leadership of the Croghan Lodge of the Odd Fellows and felt that since "temperance has become popular and has powerful friends in almost every circle, Mrs. Hayes and I can leave the laboring oar to others." In fact, Hayes did not sympathize with many temperance advocates, who were either cranks—"against theatre-going, card-playing, and dancing"—or relied "too much on the constable" and not enough on "education, morality, and religion" to make drinking "disreputable in public opinion."[16]

As he dropped other activities, Hayes increased his work for education. In 1887, Governor Foraker named him a trustee of Ohio State University. Considering the university next in importance to the state's legislature, governor, and judiciary, Hayes immediately began preparing for his new duties. Proud of his role in founding the university, Hayes also noted that he, perhaps more than anyone else, was responsible for acquiring its land in Columbus, which was "already worth twice as much as the land-grant fund."

Hayes found that, as a former president, he was "not suspected of wanting any personal promotion or advancement" and could wield great influence. He emphasized that by accepting the federal land grant for the university, Ohio was legally obligated "to build up and support the institution" it had been neglecting. Hayes worked to improve industrial training at the university and advanced for Ohio students the same ideas he pushed for southern black students through the Slater Fund. He believed: "The study of rhetoric will not make an orator or a writer. Declamation, debate, the habit of composition must be formed by practice. Work must go with study. Geology and other sciences are to be learned well only by practical work. Thoroughly to understand a theory, we must be able to put it into practice."

In May, Hayes made a "hasty" tour of Ohio State University. He found the geological collection "very valuable," the equipment in general "creditable," the military drill "good"; but he identified the library, "mechanical industrial education," and "agricultural manual training" as "weak points." The main problem facing the board was the willingness of the "Grange element" to starve the university because it "neglected" farming interests. To "restore harmony," Hayes suggested in November that the university board grant to the agricultural "experiment station all the land and other privileges in our power," with the understanding that "the friends of the experiment station will aid the university in all proper ways." At a critical meeting on 10 December 1887, the boards of the university and the experiment station adjusted their differences "in a friendly spirit," giving Hayes "hope that the farmers of the State will be content with the university as an institution for practical education, and give it a support heretofore denied." Aware that the new peace was largely his work, Hayes was "very solicitous that all may turn out well." He wanted Ohio State University to succeed not only because he was a passionate Buckeye but also because he was the school's chief founder.[17]

Hayes's commitment to training the hands as well as the minds of students made the farmers of Ohio appreciate his presence on the board of Ohio State University. *Farm and Fireside* quoted him approvingly: "No education for a boy or girl, rich or poor, black or white, is what it should be that does not prepare the young to make a living by manual labor on the farm, in the shop, or in the domestic employments of women. This, not merely because to make a living is the essential thing, but because such training builds up the intellect and character in a way and to an extent that no mere study of books can do." While Hayes was in New York on Slater Fund business, he visited the Industrial Training Normal School run by Nicholas Murray Butler, the president of the Industrial Education Association, in order to learn more about industrial education from its practitioners.[18]

The Slater and Peabody Funds continued to make substantial demands on Hayes. On the Slater board, he still mediated between Haygood and the trustees. They complained that Haygood was partial to Methodists, reported irregularly, failed to make the twice-yearly visits to each institution receiving Slater money, and neglected to keep a diary of his activities. For his part, Haygood felt rebuked for "independence of method & action." Appreciating Haygood's effective work, Hayes did not mind his idiosyncratic behavior. He was pleased with Haygood's December 1888 address at Columbus to the Freedmen's Aid Society. His "wonderful talk . . . was humorous, pithy, pathetic, and convincing," and to top it off, Haygood had praised

Hayes's "course as President." The Slater board, particularly treasurer Morris K. Jesup, was often exasperating in its narrowness. Not only had Jesup convinced the board not to back the Blair bill; he had—to Hayes's amazement—questioned the board's "power" to accept gifts when Smith Hirst, a "studious" Quaker farmer from Colerain, Ohio, donated $2,000 to the Slater Fund.

Although annoyed by the Slater board and occasionally discouraged in his efforts to prick "Southern white consciences," Haygood felt that progress was being made. School attendance was increasing, the quality of both students and their education was improving, black parents were making greater sacrifices to educate their children, and industrial education was aiding "other educational processes" and winning white support for black education. "Notwithstanding occasional outbreaks of prejudice and ignorance," Haygood discerned a "growing sentiment among Southern white people in favor of the education of the Negro Race." Haygood's optimism concerning the attitudes of the white race and improvements in black education confirmed Hayes's faith that the southern policy he had instituted as president was working for blacks as well as whites.[19]

Hayes's commitment to industrial education extended to his own family. Scott attended the Manual Training School of Toledo (and, in December 1887, brought home "nine specimens of his work as a blacksmith"). After Fanny finished Miss Porter's School and enjoyed a long vacation with her cousin Emily Hastings in Bermuda, Hayes tried unsuccessfully to make her a "burning and shining" example of manual training.[20]

Hayes used every opportunity to "preach" on industrial education and to broaden school curricula. By unanimous invitation, he addressed the Ohio House of Representatives on Washington's Birthday 1888 and "was received with enthusiasm." A few days later, he went "to Cleveland to stir up the Methodist alumni" of Ohio Wesleyan University and got a commitment to begin a manual training experiment with printing. At the 7 March board meeting of Western Reserve University, he was pleased to report, "We added a musical department," but he regretted that "the gymnasium does not walk off as it should."[21]

Although insisting on high moral standards for his own children and students in general, Hayes had a high tolerance for high spirits. Webb at thirty-two was still so "full of fun and life" that Hayes and Lucy dubbed him "Anarchy"; they thought it "lively and pleasant" when, after a Republican election victory, a party of fourteen broom-carrying young people arrived at Spiegel Grove "singing and hurrahing" at 11:00 P.M. Hayes thought that W. H. Scott, the tactless president of Ohio State University, was "rather severe, and somewhat hasty" in dismissing two boys for skipping prayers. Hayes believed that students should be attracted, not driven, to religious services and urged Scott to restore the boys. After he adamantly refused, Hayes concluded that Scott had demonstrated his "insufficiency" for the presidency of Ohio State University. With his own children, Hayes wanted the germ, not the husk, of morality. He advised his son Scott, who had completed his manual training and was heading for Cornell University: "Be a good scholar if you can, but in any event be a gentleman in the best sense of the word—truthful, honorable, polite, and kind, with the Golden Rule as your guide. Do nothing that would give pain to your mother if she knew it."[22]

Hayes treasured his family even more when, on 2 October 1887, Birch and Mary had a son, whom they named for Hayes. Every bit the proud grandfather, he found little Rutherford "uncommonly fine looking for one so young," and Lucy seized every opportunity to go to Toledo to be with her grandson while his parents settled into their new home. Before a month had passed, Hayes read aloud "to Mary & the boy . . . from Dr. O. W. Holmes's 'Hundred Days in Europe,' his comparison between now and fifty years ago," and he wondered what changes the boy, "if he lives," would see over the next fifty years.[23]

Hayes and Lucy were as hospitable at Spiegel Grove as they had been in the White House. In keeping with their egalitarian ideas about democracy and community, on 1 December 1887, they entertained about three hundred workers of the "newly-established manufactures" that had been attracted to Fremont by cheap natural gas, including a railroad spike factory, carbon works, drop-forge works, shear works, and fifth-wheel works. The grateful board of trade suggested "no refreshments," but Hayes and Lucy "insisted on 'breaking bread' and 'eating salt'" with their guests and served oysters, eggs, hams, hot biscuits, bread, and coffee. Entertaining in this manner was natural for Lucy and Hayes, who affectionately referred to their section of Ohio as "this level country,—level society as well as scenery."[24]

Although less partisan in his politics as he grew older, Hayes was not quite the "calm outsider" he claimed to be. He did not like Cleveland's niggardly attitude toward veterans' pensions, but he refused to be outraged when, in 1887, the president ordered captured rebel flags returned to their states of origin. Hayes also thought that Cleveland erred—and "brightened Republican prospects"—when he made the tariff the major issue in 1888. "For more than twenty years," Hayes recalled, "existing legislation has enticed capital and labor into manufactures. . . . To strike them down now . . . looks like cruelty and bad faith." Both parties ignored Hayes's list of imperative reforms: the single six-year presidential term; universal education supplemented, when necessary, by national aid; industrial training for all young people; and the reduction of "existing capital and labor troubles" by controlling "the irresponsible power" of both wealth and numbers.[25]

The political campaign of 1888 intensified Hayes's commitment to a single six-year term. From experience, he knew that presidents were surrounded by flatterers and had more difficulty keeping in touch with reality as their years in office mounted. Furthermore, presidents let their desire to get reelected influence their policies and appointments more than was good for the country. Although he generally thought well of Cleveland and was pleased that the "independent and honorable" Allen G. Thurman had been nominated as his 1888 running mate, Hayes sensed that "Cleveland was so swallowed up in his own egotism" that he could not see "the whole world around him." As for the Republicans, Hayes felt bad that they had named their most "available" man, Benjamin Harrison of Indiana, rather than their fittest candidate, John Sherman. Having himself been the available man in 1876, Hayes realized that the choice of Harrison was politically sound and tried to console his friend Sherman with "the reflection that . . . the man of great and valuable service . . . must be content to leave the Presidency to the less conspicuous and deserving." Hayes assured his protégé McKinley, who had had an outside chance for the nomination, that he had "gained gloriously" by "manfully" remaining loyal to Sherman. "Men in political life must be ambitious. But the surest path to the White House is his who never allows his ambition to get there to stand in the way of any duty, large or small." Proud of the way McKinley had handled himself, Hayes concluded, "I could not help telling you how my young hero looked to his old friend."[26]

Harrison and his running mate, Levi P. Morton of New York, were excellent candidates. Harrison flattered Hayes by requesting a copy of his acceptance letter, saying that Blaine had called it "the best ever written." Despite the rain on election day (which Hayes consistently maintained did not matter but which political pundits insisted kept rural Republicans from the polls), Harrison triumphed. Although he respected Cleveland and his young wife, Frances, Hayes rejoiced "that such good people as General and Mrs. Harrison are to carry their clean ways and pure lives into the White House. Besides," he added, "I do hate Cleveland's course towards the veterans." When in Indianapolis on Loyal Legion business in December, Hayes called on the Harrisons and was "*very*" cordially received; he returned the next day for "a full talk." Since Harrison was particularly interested in "the details of household affairs at Washington," Hayes suggested that he consult Webb.

Lucy, too, tried to help. "I hope you will enjoy and love the old House as I did," she wrote to Caroline Harrison. "No new house will ever have its charms."[27]

Hayes gave Harrison both solicited and unsolicited advice on promotions and appointments. When Harrison requested "the name of a Southern-born man in the Union army for Secretary of War," Hayes suggested either Nathan Goff of West Virginia (his secretary of the navy) or William Cassius Goodloe of Kentucky (his minister to Belgium). Hayes worked with vigor to secure a promotion for his beloved commander George Crook. From among those "anxious to serve their country" in soft, lucrative federal positions, Hayes was committed to his neighbor Gen. William H. Gibson ("one of God's noblemen") for commissioner of pensions; resolved to "do the friendliest things I can" for Jacob A. Camp, who had failed to succeed in other areas after beating Hayes out for the hand of Fanny Perkins; requested the Ohio pension office at Columbus for his niece Laura's husband, Gen. John G. Mitchell, who had suffered business reverses; wanted Clark Waggoner restored as collector of internal revenue at Toledo; asked for the reappointment of Capt. Thomas B. Reed as postmaster of Fairmount, West Virginia (it was Reed who had notified Lucy that Hayes had not been killed at Cedar Creek); and wanted George C. Tanner retained as consul in Nova Scotia.[28]

Despite his objection to congressional pressure on the executive, Hayes went beyond merely suggesting appointments. He asked Justice John Marshall Harlan to see Harrison about the appointments for Mitchell, Reed, and Tanner. After visiting Harrison, Harlan called on Postmaster General John Wanamaker for Reed, who was reappointed, and on Secretary of State James G. Blaine for Tanner. Greatly touched that Hayes had not joined the mugwumps in 1884, Blaine promised to retain and possibly promote Tanner. Mitchell's appointment took longer and required more pressure, but in April 1890, Harrison wrote to Hayes, "It gave me great pleasure to oblige you in the matter of the appointment of General Mitchell. There was a good deal of opposition from friends of other candidates." Although gratified that his influence had secured these appointments of friends and relations, Hayes—unaware of any contradiction—was disturbed that Harrison, like Garfield, had turned "appointments over to the Senators and Representatives. They will use it to pay debts," Hayes sadly noted. "It is a return to the spoils system."[29]

Since reliving the Civil War was perhaps his most congenial activity, Hayes continued to spend much time on veterans' affairs. He believed that the nation owed an incalculable debt to the veterans of "the best war ever fought." Appreciating, in turn, his companionship and support, fellow veterans delighted in acknowledging his presence with "three cheers and a tiger." Following the death of Philip Sheridan (who was only fifty-seven), Hayes was named commander in chief of the Military Order of the Loyal Legion in October 1888. Hayes, the senior vice commander in chief, was the logical successor, but he had suggested that Sherman or Schofield, with their military reputations, would be more appropriate. When the honor came to him, however, he was delighted. "Nothing," he wrote to Lucy, "could have been done more handsomely. . . . This is on the whole the pleasantest of the honors that have come to me since Washington."[30]

Although Hayes emphasized that the national government was obliged to aid Union veterans, he felt that private citizens should help the "disabled and destitute" who had fought against the nation. Reminding other northerners that these former enemies "share with us . . . the destiny of America," Hayes insisted, "Whatever, therefore, we . . . can do to remove burdens from their shoulders and to brighten their lives is surely in the pathway of humanity and patriotism."[31]

The death of friends, his daughter Fanny's partial hearing loss, and his own "first symptoms" of old age bothered Hayes. The surgical removal of polyps in Fanny's nose—supposedly the cause of her deafness—especially concerned Hayes in the spring of 1888. Thinking of his own approaching death, he took pains to make his will "satisfactory to all." In June, he learned that he had a mild case of diabetes, having "used sugar to excess" all his days. A month later, a meat diet, "aided" by arsenic prescribed for his drinks, had caused the complaint to disappear. Hayes was also mildly concerned when "limestone, as big as a fair-sized tooth, . . . worked out of a little tumor" under his tongue. In April, he nursed a severe cold with the sedative aconite, which brought "some ugly dreams" along with relief. Hayes dealt with the problems of aging by trying to keep busy and by recalling men like John Quincy Adams and Thaddeus Stevens, who had accomplished "their best work long after middle life."[32]

Hayes's own health problems were overshadowed by his friends' deaths. "They have been the blessing and comfort of my life," he attested. "Their loss has been the cause of my greatest suffering and sadness." Linus Austin, his cousin and warm friend, died in April 1887; in June, Hayes traveled to Malone, New York, to attend the funeral of his vice president, William A. Wheeler. "He was one of the few Vice-Presidents," Hayes wrote, "who was on cordial terms—intimately and sincerely friendly—with the President. Our family all were heartily fond of him. He came often to the White House and often expressed in strong language the pleasure his visits gave him. In character he was sterling gold." Less than two months later, Hayes's war comrade James M. Comly died, after much suffering. Perhaps even worse, Manning F. Force suffered from "insane delusions" that even his best friends suspected him of dishonesty and were treating him with contempt. Facing these losses, Hayes despondently wrote, "As friends go it is less important to live."[33]

In 1888, Hayes mourned the death of his old family friend, "dear, dear . . . beloved" Morrison R. Waite, chief justice of the Supreme Court, with whom he had been associated on the Peabody and Slater Funds. Hayes was even more affected a year later when Stanley Matthews died. As students, lawyers, warriors, and politicians, Hayes and Matthews had been intimate friends for fifty years. Since their friendship had inspired him to insist on Matthews's appointment to the Supreme Court, Hayes was gratified when Justice Harlan characterized him as "a rapid worker; accurate and skilful; wise and able." Before leaving Spiegel Grove to attend Matthews's funeral, Hayes wrote to Guy Bryan, "You are the last!"[34]

The most difficult death for Hayes and Lucy was that of their grandson Rutherford, who was not yet fourteen months old. Lucy was devastated, and Hayes grieved deeply for the "beautiful boy—gone forever." Besides his own grief, Hayes felt the anguish of Birch and particularly of Mary; he considered Mary "the perfection of womanhood," and she reminded him of his "sister Fanny—the dear, dear memory of early life." On a "mournful" Thanksgiving, they brought little Rutherford to Spiegel Grove and buried him on the following day in the cemetery, under a beautiful white pine, by the side of little Manning Force. In her agony, Lucy found comfort in Birch and Mary's second son, six-week-old Sherman Otis, and in the thought that her own little Manning was "no longer *alone!*"[35]

Hayes and Lucy took comfort from each other. Above all, Hayes enjoyed her company and threw himself wholeheartedly into projects that were dear to her heart. When on 6 February 1888 the new Methodist church burned completely, he worked to rebuild her *"elegant little church."* In the spring of 1889, Hayes also commenced work on the addition of a kitchen and dining room at Spiegel Grove, built to Lucy's specifications. The addition would make it easier to entertain. Although Lucy occasionally had "little *down* spells," Hayes proudly noted that "all sorts of people stimulate her to a fine flow of spirits." When entertaining three hundred veterans and their families, Hayes observed, "Lucy was in her best estate. Making all happy." Her health was good on her fifty-seventh birthday (28 August 1888), and he appreciated that "her constitution preserves her beauty." When she attended a funeral or a meeting of the Woman's Home Missionary Society (of which she was the head), he missed her dreadfully, no matter how many young folks surrounded him. "Lucy gone," he wrote in his diary, "the home is gone."

Hayes particularly liked to have Lucy accompany him on his travels. In early April 1888, they visited Columbus for dinner with Laura, Chillicothe for a wedding, Marietta for its centennial, and Cleveland for a Loyal Legion banquet. Hayes pronounced it "a most delightful tour . . . with Lucy, who was everywhere the life of all circles, especially at Cleveland with the Loyal Legion." While attending further celebrations of the Ohio centennial in September with Lucy and Fanny, Hayes declared that it was perhaps their finest visit to Columbus.[36]

Hayes used his greatest superlatives, however, to describe the visit he and Lucy made to New York in April and May 1889, when Fanny accompanied them to the centennial of Washington's inauguration. Hayes made short speeches in response to toasts to the presidency and to the United States, enjoyed seeing Grover and Frances Cleveland, and was proud of Harrison's "handsome speaking." Hayes attended "a semi-political symposium" on the South at Col. Elliott F. Shepard's home, where Gov. John B. Gordon of Georgia praised him for his noble and equitable treatment of all sections of the country. In thanking Gordon, Hayes reminded the southerners present that "we must accept as settled" the right of Negro suffrage and recognize education as one of the "remedies for evils." New York City itself again enthralled Hayes. "Nothing could be more inspiring in the way of city growth and material prosperity," he insisted, after traversing Central, Morningside, and Riverside Parks "and the boulevard and great streets, Seventh Avenue, St. Nicholas, etc. . . . A few years will see the part of New York north of Central Park the finest city the world ever had."[37]

Six weeks later, on 21 June 1889, Hayes, accompanied by his niece Laura, was returning from an Ohio State University board meeting when Rud met them at the station with "very bad news." Looking "as if something awful was on his mind," he sobbed out that Lucy had been felled by paralysis that afternoon. Lucy had been sewing by the window in the bedroom when her servant Ella Graves noticed that she was having difficulty threading a needle. When Ella went to her, Lucy sank back in her chair, unable to speak and in tears. Fanny and her friends, who were playing tennis just outside the window, ran in, and cousin Lucy Keeler called Rud at the bank where he worked and rushed out for Dr. John B. Rice, who came immediately and helped Lucy into bed. When Hayes arrived by her side, Lucy pressed his hand and tried to smile."[38]

Lucy's stroke did not surprise Hayes. "In church some days before," she had lost her balance when she rose to sing. Sitting down immediately, she had tried twice to stand before she was able to rise. Left with "a decided numbness on the left side," Lucy considered the attack "a notification" that the end was near. With Hayes, she discussed her desire for a simple funeral with singing but no sermon. She did not want her virtues exaggerated beyond recognition, she insisted. She feared not death but "paralysis that would deprive her of locomotion" or "loss of mind as was the case with her brother James." If either of these calamities occurred, she told Hayes "not to let friends see her. She wanted to be remembered as she had been in active life." When a friend had noticed that "she did not move about among people as formerly," Lucy had merely smiled and said, "We old folks must conceal our infirmities."[39]

No longer able to conceal her infirmities, Lucy, who appeared to be unconscious most of the time, occasionally comforted members of her family by indicating an awareness of their presence. By Saturday, they had all gathered around her. Fearful that he had seen her "glorious eyes" for the last time, Hayes took comfort from the fact that she continued to grasp his hand "with the old affection." Lucy also responded positively to his query, "Do you hear me darling?" By Monday morning, her rapid pulse, high temperature, and labored breathing told Hayes that her "end is now inevitable."

Continuing to watch by her side that day and into the night, Hayes was grateful that Lucy was not suffering and thankful to have been her husband. "Few men," he noted after midnight, "in this most important relation in life have been so blessed as I have been. From early mature manhood to the threshold of old age I have enjoyed her society in the most intimate of all relations. How all of my friends love her! My comrades of the war almost worship her." Thinking back over the past months, he decided, "our last days together have been our best days." Putting aside his diary, in which he had recorded his innermost thoughts, Hayes lay down beside Lucy, "holding her hand & once . . . kissing her brow." Toward morning, the doctors indicated that her end was very near, and the whole family gathered in the bedroom. When she was dead, Hayes kissed Lucy good-bye, gazed again "upon her fine face," and sobbed once before walking on the porch with Fanny and his other children in the "bracing" morning air.[40]

TWENTY-NINE

WITHOUT LUCY

Although Spiegel Grove was still lovely, Hayes found that without Lucy "*the soul*" had left it. "Doing things that seem to be useful in the present emergency, or in contriving what will perpetuate and do honor" to Lucy got Hayes through the first days without her. He was thankful that she had died without suffering the long-term mind or body damage she had dreaded; that she had partaken fully of life's offerings "from first love to the grandmother's joy"; and that the "letters of friends and the words of the press show how well she and her work are understood and valued. This *does* console and strengthen. I enjoy while I weep the kind things said."[1]

The funeral on Friday, 28 June, was "gratifying and consoling." Old and dear friends attending included John and Harriet Herron, John and Eliza Davis, and Carrie Little. Eliza Jane Burrell, a former Webb family slave whom Lucy had taught to read and had employed in her household, came from Canada. Dr. L. D. McCabe of Ohio Wesleyan University, who had married Lucy and Hayes, "led in the services and made a heart-warm talk at the end." As Hayes left Lucy's grave, he saw "one of our humblest citizens . . . an acquaintance since boyhood, known as 'Indian King.' His sad, tear-covered face told how Lucy was loved and admired by the lowly of the earth."

When the carpenters returned on the Monday after Lucy's funeral to continue work on the addition, Hayes "shook hands with each one of them" and found sympathy in each "warm grasp." That evening, he returned to "the old room and bed" and slept better than he had since Lucy's stroke. He decided to "gather there a few of her favorite things—not enough to prevent it from being as nearly as she left it as may be—and so live with her and near her . . . the rest of my days."

To keep the memory of Lucy fresh for himself and his children, Hayes noted her appearance and virtues. "She was very beautiful in her prime and changed with years less than most persons do. Her eyes were simply perfect—large, hazel, dark, flashing, tender. . . . Her hair [was] always a beautiful raven black, with a single red hair or dark auburn here and there. The few gray hairs" added by the time of her death had "not changed its general appearance." Her speaking and singing voice "was of extraordinary excellence, of great compass, penetration, and distinctiveness, and as sweet and tender as can be imagined." Although Lucy was a church-going Methodist, she cared "little for the formalities of religion" and refused to force her opinions on others. Recalling her many acts of kindness, Hayes remembered Lucy as "the Golden Rule incarnate."[2]

Even though "a new sad world had . . . taken possession of all things," Hayes did not mope. He acknowledged over seven hundred dispatches and letters of sympathy, and, knowing that Lucy "was fond of fame, wanted to be remembered," he began organizing her papers for a memorial volume. His niece Laura remained with him for six weeks, and others visited, including Charles L. Mead and his family and William Henry Smith. Hayes's morale got its biggest boost in August when Harriet Herron and her daughters Lucy Webb and Elinor arrived.[3]

This visit carried Hayes "forward a long way." "Next after Lucy, no woman, not of my blood, was ever so near and dear!" he acknowledged. He loved to read with Harriet, and they began with Tennyson's "noble poem" *In Memoriam*, which appropriately moved from "doubt to rest and peace." With Harriet for company, Hayes began to take note of the beauties and the problems of the world about him, despite a "frequent *pang*" as they "walked around the grove," viewing "scenes in which Lucy was such a figure."[4]

By the end of August, when the new addition was completed, Hayes resumed his old activities. In early September, he attended the annual reunion of the Twenty-third at Lakeside, where good words about Lucy comforted him; two weeks later, when the Tenth Ohio Cavalry held its reunion in Fremont, Fanny—who had taken over the Spiegel Grove household—held a reception that made Hayes proud. In what was becoming a familiar theme, he suggested to his fellow veterans that, rather than boast about themselves or criticize others, they should work to "secure a sweeping, radical, and beneficent change in our pension laws" to aid the veterans who were no longer able to provide for themselves. A year later, in Ottawa, Kansas, Hayes likened the nation's obligation to pay its defenders' pensions to its obligation to pay its creditors the interest on Civil War bonds in gold.[5]

In the autumn, Hayes and Fanny traveled east. On 28 September, they arrived at the Mohonk Lake House—where they were the guests of Albert K. and Eliza P. C. Smiley—for the annual conference on improving the condition of Native Americans. When president, Hayes had appointed Smiley to the Board of Indian Commissioners, and Smiley had helped Schurz root corruption out of the Indian Bureau. Meeting with the conference participants and enjoying the "wild mountain scenery in juxtaposition with cultivated farms" gave Hayes a lift. Before leaving, he proposed that a conference to

Spiegel Grove after it was enlarged in 1889

help six million Negroes "rise to the full stature of American citizenship" be held the next year, and Smiley agreed. By 3 October, Hayes and Fanny were in New York for his Peabody trustee meeting, where he agreed to chair a committee to explore the feasibility of establishing a Peabody Normal School at Nashville. On the next day, his sixty-seventh birthday, his mood changed. He sorely missed Lucy, particularly as he recalled their last New York visit. "How easily," Hayes thought, "I could now let go of life!"[6]

But Hayes held on. That afternoon, he began a restorative ten-day New England pilgrimage, primarily to his ancestral homes in Vermont and Connecticut. Arriving late one evening in West Brattleboro, he awoke the next day charmed by his surroundings:

> I am writing before breakfast in the little room over the hall in the old Hayes home, where my grandfather lived as a young man with his young wife more than one hundred years ago, and where my father was born and to which he brought my mother as his bride seventy-six years ago! . . . I slept in what was once part of the *ballroom* in the Hayes Inn, where balls, card parties, and flip drinking were enjoyed—dispensed by my grandfather and grandmother . . . for more than twenty years at the close of the last century and the beginning of this.[7]

Back in New York, Hayes rendezvoused with Fanny and visited Harriet Herron and her sister-in-law (and his old girlfriend) Helen Kelley Collins. Although he also met with Schurz and other friends, he was in town for an important Slater trustee meeting. The finance committee had challenged Atticus Haygood's judgment in recommending the funding of an industrial education program at Clark University (Atlanta) rather than one at Atlanta University, but after "a practical mechanical engineer" investigated and agreed with Haygood, his views prevailed. This controversy helped Daniel Coit Gilman recognize Haygood's "unusual excellence" and made him realize that Hayes and Haygood were "the most important factors in the Exec. Comm." of the Slater Fund. Traveling to Philadelphia, Hayes presided at the Loyal Legion banquet on 17 October and then, still accompanied by Fanny, returned to Spiegel Grove. As he approached home after his "delightful trip of three weeks," he "thought of Lucy gone" and felt "the sinking of the heart," for she would not be there to greet him "in her lovely way."[8]

But Hayes was comforted by the beauty of his grove and occupied by thoughts of Scott and little Sherman. "I never saw anything finer than old Spiegel is now in her fall dress and colors," he declared. "The dark red or maroon of the great white oaks, in contrast with the lighter colors of maples and hickories, make a picture of wonderful beauty." On 19 October, the twenty-fifth anniversary of Cedar Creek, Hayes savored again that victorious afternoon, but he interrupted his memories to worry about the future of his youngest child, who was neither studious nor industrious. Fearing that "public life is not favorable to the best training of our young people," Hayes resolved to be considerate of Scott's feelings while trying to "lead him into better paths." Scott had decided to quit Cornell and pursue a business career, and by January 1890, his work in the First National Bank of Fremont encouraged Hayes. The youngest generation created less trouble and more joy. "Little Sherman plays with life and sport to the delight of all of us," Hayes reported. "Just begins to show signs of standing & walking. Creeps in a queer way. No words yet, but he calls back when I repeat sounds 'a-e-i-o-' almost an imitation."[9]

Books led Hayes out of "sorrowful paths." He responded enthusiastically to Harriet's suggestion that they have a "little Chautauqua" reading and studying circle. Hayes proposed beginning with "my ancient favorite Emerson," whose "writings have done for me far more than all other reading." After reading Emerson's "Immortality," Hayes confessed to Harriet that, despite his "longing after immortality," he realized that "we believe, or disbelieve, or are in doubt according to our own make-up — to accidents, to education, to environment." Unlike his daughter-in-law Mary and his niece

Laura, who took comfort from the thought that Lucy and little Ruddy were "*now happy together*," Hayes did not believe that "the conscious person . . . will meet you in the world beyond." But Emerson prepared him "to meet the disappointments and griefs of this mortal life" and left him "far more content with whatever may come."[10]

In November 1889, Hayes and Fanny attended the National Prison Association Congress and a Peabody committee meeting in Nashville. The congress, with its "good papers, liberal sentiments, harmony, and good social relations," encouraged Hayes. He was particularly impressed by Dr. R. M. Cunningham of Alabama, "who showed up in a lively way the horror" of his state's convict lease system, and he was proud that Fanny behaved "in a most winning and lively way." Despite diarrhea "caused by imprudent eating of oysters & fresh fruit," Hayes also managed his Peabody business. His committee unanimously adopted the normal school (established in 1875) at "Nashville as the site of the final Peabody memorial." There were 330 students already in attendance, two-thirds of them young women. "I anticipate the growth of a great institution—the best of its sort anywhere," Hayes enthusiastically reported. The Peabody Trust accepted his recommendation and "appropriated about seventeen thousand dollars as the beginning" of its transformation into the vastly influential George Peabody College for Teachers. A few Peabody trustees opposed the policy of "concentration" and wished to set up a normal school in each state, but Hayes and the majority argued that they should concentrate on "an ideal, a model—the great Normal College at Nashville."[11]

The holiday season was difficult, but, with the help of "little Sherman & all of the rest of the family," Christmas 1889 "happily passed." Even though loyalty to Lucy seemed "to compel" him "to indulge mournful thoughts," Hayes was becoming "more hopeful" as his life resumed its normal rhythm. Apart from pressing for educational and prison reform, he was consumed by "the great question of 'nihilism,'" as he called the "opposition to plutocracy," and appreciated novels such as Charles Dudley Warner's *A Little Journey in the World* (1889) and Mark Twain's *A Connecticut Yankee in King Arthur's Court* (1889). Hayes agreed with the "purpose" of Howells's latest book, *A Hazard of New Fortunes* (1890), which showed that crime, vice, and wretchedness resulted from "our present social system—a system that fosters the giant evils of great riches and hopeless poverty." Cyrenus Osborne Ward's study of the conditions of laborers in Greece and Rome, *The Ancient Lowly* (1889), inspired Hayes to define the progress of society as "the improvement in the condition of the workingmen." Impediments to progress were obvious to Hayes. "We have got rid of the fetish of the divine right of kings, and that slavery is of divine origin and authority. But the divine right of property has taken its place. The tendency is towards . . . 'a government of the rich, by the rich, and for the rich.' "[12]

Doing what he conceived to be his duty was good therapy for Hayes. As a dutiful father, he occasionally gave advice to his children. "Be good — conscientiously good," Hayes urged Webb on his thirty-fourth birthday. "Do not let your bachelor ways crystallize so that you can't soften them away when you come to have a wife and family of your own." Hayes responded to all correspondents, including schoolchildren. He encouraged one child, who was his namesake and who was berated by classmates for his opposition to local-option prohibition, to "always try to have the courage of your convictions, and vote *as your judgment and conscience dictate*," but warned that the only absolutely safe rule on drinking *"is total abstinence."* Despite his eminent status in veterans' affairs, Hayes continued to participate in the ranks. On 19 March 1890, he attended the funeral of a railroad-crossing watchman. "I marched in the snow with the comrades from the hall to his dwelling and back to the church by the side of a tall negro — the comrade who bears the colors." Hayes became better acquainted with Robert Keys, the tall black comrade, and reported that he was an excellent speaker.[13]

Without Lucy, Hayes traveled even more and refused to let personal discomfort slacken his pace. While in Cleveland for a Western Reserve University board meeting on a cold and icy March day in 1890, Hayes "fell heavily" when attempting "to jump" on a trolley car. Despite injuring his wrist, hip, and knee, he went on to Cincinnati for the funeral of his old opponent George Hunt Pendleton and doubled back to Columbus to help Laura's husband campaign for the local pension agency. Hayes was scarcely back in Spiegel Grove before he was off to Chicago for the funeral of his "dear friend and best beloved commander, General George Crook." Despite diarrhea, he was in Cleveland on 5 April to plan the dedication of the Garfield monument on Decoration Day. Ten days later, he was in Philadelphia attending Loyal Legion meetings.[14]

On 17 April, Webb and Rud saw Hayes and Fanny off on what Hayes would term "the finest visit I ever made." With Rud taking snapshots with his Kodak, they departed from New York for Bermuda on the *Trinidad*. Sailing away, they enjoyed a "noble view of New York harbor, 'Liberty,' etc." Although most passengers were seasick, Hayes went to meals, read newspapers (finding, with pleasure, that the Philadelphia *Inquirer* had commended what he termed the "nihilistic paragraphs" in his Loyal Legion speech), and

Hayes and Fanny leaving for Bermuda

bragged to Fanny that he "did not suffer." Managing to be adorable even while seasick, she kissed him before hissing, "You scorpion!"

As they entered the rocky, crooked passage into the harbor of Hamilton, Bermuda, at 5:30 A.M. on 20 April, Hayes and Fanny were on the bridge. Hayes recorded, "we took in scenery and coffee with great satisfaction. . . . We soon got into the intricate channel. The colored pilots pointed out the frequent shoals, easily seen by the color of the water and the buoys constantly in view and near to each other." As they passed Soncy, the home of Hayes's niece Emily, Fanny (who had visited two years earlier) waved her handkerchief. Russell Hastings, Emily's husband and Hayes's Civil War comrade, took them ashore in his own boat as the *Trinidad* approached its landing. "What a paradise of a home we found Soncy to be," Hayes exclaimed. "I wept to think that Lucy never saw it. Nothing finer or lovelier was ever seen in a dream."

Over the next eleven days, Hayes reveled in the scenery and climate and enjoyed a series of parties in his honor. Marked in their attentions, British officials placed at his disposal a steam launch and the governor's carriage. Reminding him of "Kentucky gentlemen and ladies," the islanders, Hayes decided, had retained "the virtues and manners of the slave period," which made conditions "very pleasant for strangers." He was intrigued by the old capital of St. George, with its "narrow crooked streets," and especially by its police magistrate, W. C. J. Hyland, with his Civil War tales of rebels and their "blockade running, drinking, and rioting." Charmed by Bermuda's natural beauty, Hayes found the rocks, caves, trees, and flowers fascinating and the water perfect for bathing. Clad "in undershirt, drawers, & slippers," he went ten steps from his room to the beach, where, in the company of Fanny, Emily, and Hastings, he had "the best swim in the world."[15]

Back in New York in early May for a Slater Fund trustees' meeting, Hayes visited friends and relations, including Isabella Mead (Charley Mead was out of town), Carl Schurz, and Gen. William T. Sherman. At first speaking cheerfully of his son Thomas Ewing, who had become a Catholic priest, Sherman soon "complained that after he had spent thousands of dollars for his education they [the church] now took it all,—made him a teacher with almost no salary and so practically confiscated him." While Hayes had his picture made at the Sarony Gallery (where his favorite picture of Lucy had been taken), Fanny saw her physician, who assured her that her still-impaired hearing would not get worse and suggested that it might improve. Hayes also attended a splendid Loyal Legion banquet at Delmonico's. "I made a 'rattling speech,' offhand and scattering," he reported, "but it took the audience. Hardly ever have I been applauded with such enthusiasm. . . . Our outing is fortunately crowned and ended. Philadelphia, Bermuda, New York! I cannot expect to see many—perhaps no other—such enjoyments."[16]

Arriving back at Spiegel Grove, Hayes plunged into preparations for the upcoming Lake Mohonk conference on the Negro question, over which he had agreed to preside. Asked about his goals for this gathering, Hayes called it "a tentative effort . . . to reach the truth on the negro question and to assist in the formation of sound opinions among the people as to their duty on the whole subject." When John C. Covert of the Cleveland *Leader* sent Hayes a paper he had prepared, Hayes found it "too exclusively political and partisan to be useful in that body . . . of educators, philanthropists, and religious leaders." Hoping to attract members of "all sects and parties" to work for change, Hayes was determined to avoid anything that would needlessly "breed ill-will between the Negro and his white neighbor." For him, three questions were appropriate:

1. What is the actual condition of the negro with respect to intelligence, morality, and religion?
2. How can public attention be attracted to the deplorable situation?
3. What additional aid can be given and what new agencies and methods can be employed to uplift the negro?[17]

Among the 1890 Mohonk conferees, there were fewer representatives from the South than Hayes had "hoped for, but enough to leaven the lump." After being elected president of the conference, Hayes suggested that the participants discuss "the best methods for uplifting the colored people" and for "forming and enlightening that public opinion which [is] in fact, the Government." For three days (4 to 6 June), papers—primarily on education, housing, and crime—were read and discussed. Commissioner of Education William T. Harris, for example, discussed the link between illiteracy and crime. The most challenging speech, "pungent, dramatic, original, and daring," was by Albion W. Tourgee, a North Carolina carpetbagger and author, who—standing up for blacks—"rebuked the churches, the North, the South." Hayes was impressed, but he also noted that President Andrew D. White of Cornell University (who was pessimistic about improving the condition of blacks in the near future) "replied to him in an effective speech."

By nature a harmonizer and an optimist, Hayes closed the conference with words of hope. "Whether what we have said or done shall live or die, our impressions, our convictions are stronger than before, that the much injured race in whose behalf we have met has large possibilities—an important future—a part to play, in the history of our American society." Responding to the assertion that blacks "had no history," Hayes argued:

> The gifts required to take a place in history . . . belong to them. We were told of their success in weighty tables of figures by Mr. Harris. President White told of the great men he met in Santo Domingo, in Hayti, and other West Indian islands. Let me add a small item to that shining list of prophetic facts. . . . I was a few days ago in Bermuda.

The entrance to its principal port is a long, intricate, difficult, and dangerous passage. The [black] man who has charge of the ship, taking it in and out, can be no weakling.[18]

In early June, Hayes attended the funeral in Delaware of Lucy's girlhood friend Carrie Williams Little, in whose wedding cake Hayes had found the ring that he had given to Lucy and she, in turn, had given back to him. Aware that "the dear links" that held him "to the paradise" of his life were "parting one by one," he reveled in his memories. Each morning before six, he visited the Sulphur Spring, where he had first met Lucy. Being in Delaware also brought early recollections of "Mother, Uncle, Fanny." Hayes stopped at his family's cemetery plot, where he noted that all was "well enough," except that his brother was identified on the monument as "Lorenzo Berchard."[19]

In August 1890, William Henry Smith visited Hayes at Spiegel Grove, where, Smith reported, they gossiped about the past, analyzed the present, and speculated about the future. They spoke of Kate Chase Sprague's affair with Conkling and his "brutality" in "compelling his wife to attend the dinner at Washington at which Mrs. Sprague appeared"; they talked of Garfield and concluded that as leader of the Sherman forces at the 1880 convention, he should have squelched any talk of himself as a nominee. Hayes was also "full of the questions of the day." Familiar with Edward Bellamy's utopian novel *Looking Backward, 2000–1887* (1888) and the literature of the Nationalist party, which advocated Bellamy's views, Hayes agreed with it that wealth was badly distributed and welcomed "agitation of the subject." But he preferred Henry George's scheme of a single land tax to Bellamy's remedy of a collectivized society operated by a disciplined industrial army. Hayes looked to the federal government to preserve domestic peace not with an army (which, in the long run, would not work) but with regulatory legislation that would narrow the gap between the rich and the poor.[20]

In the summer of 1890, while visiting Webb and the First Cleveland Cavalry Troop in camp, Hayes suffered an "attack of *dizziness, vertigo.*" Although he at first thought that it had been "cured by a *laxative*," the dizziness returned. Even when he was "lying down the bed" seemed "to swim or almost run over." Pronouncing his heart "strong and sound," Dr. Frederick S. Hilbish called the sickness "stomach dizziness" and prescribed "purgatives" and a spare diet. Aware that death might be near, Hayes was not afraid. He felt assured that his adult children no longer needed him and that they would lead productive lives. "Well, let the end come," he wrote in his diary. "The charm of life left me when Lucy died."[21]

Still, duty kept Hayes going. As he met college and fund trustees, visited reformatories and relatives, attended army reunions, and gave speeches, the vertigo seemed to disappear. And then, while at church on 19 October 1890, at the close of a "noble sermon" during which he had planned a Loyal Legion speech, Hayes wondered, "Did I feel or only imagine a numbness of head, of the right leg, and a difficulty in controlling the tongue?" Hayes again thought of following Lucy, but when nothing further occurred, he dismissed the attack as the effects of "an unusually bad cold." Lucy was even more on his mind on 27 October when he received a copy of Eliza Davis's *In Memoriam*, prepared especially for the Woman's Home Missionary Society, of which Lucy had been president. "With swimming eyes I read it," he wrote Auntie Davis, "and look and look at the portraits!"[22]

The October Slater Fund meeting in New York was particularly important. A successor to Atticus G. Haygood, who had been appointed a Methodist bishop, had to be selected. With virtually the entire board present, Hayes successfully recommended J. L. M. Curry, the agent of the Peabody Fund, for the position. Hayes then caught the Congressional Limited to Baltimore to meet with Curry and arrange for his taking over of Haygood's duties. While there, he also visited Johns Hopkins University, where he addressed the history class of Herbert Baxter Adams on "The Condition of Negroes in the Virginia Military Land District of Ohio." Hayes found that blacks born and educated between the Scioto, Little Miami, and Ohio Rivers "show a considerable advance in the good qualities of civilization, and proper appreciation of citizenship," in contrast to the "not encouraging" situation of blacks in the South. Arguing that education had made the difference, he was "rather hopeful" that southern blacks would do better in the future. To encourage them, Hayes made a promise: "If there is any young colored man in the South whom we find to have a talent for art or literature, or any especial aptitude for study, we are willing to give him money from the education funds to send him to Europe or to give him an advanced education, but hitherto their chief and almost only gift has been that of oratory." Nationally reported, Hayes's lecture alerted talented blacks to write to the Slater Fund for support. Among them was a young Harvard graduate student in political science named William Edward Burghardt Du Bois.[23]

Hayes was back in Fremont for the 1890 election, which did not bode well for the Republicans. When they had lost the Ohio governorship and legislature in 1889, Hayes had blamed Governor Foraker—who, although "very popular with the hurrah boys," was too partisan and too much a spoilsman—and President Harrison—who had jeopardized the soldier vote by dismissing his commissioner of pensions, James Tanner. Always a loyal Republican, Hayes took scant comfort from his son Rud's remark that Foraker's loss left Hayes the only Ohio governor elected to a third term. By 1890, Republicans also had the burden of the McKinley tariff of that year, which the Democrats had "misrepresented," Hayes said, "as increasing the cost of all goods." The Republicans were set back, and even McKinley lost his seat in Congress. "The sober second thought," Hayes accurately predicted, "will perhaps elect him governor. The seesaw of political life is to be counted on."[24]

Despite his concern for McKinley's career, Hayes was more interested in reform than in politics. Two days after the election, he spoke on prison reform in Fremont while laying the cornerstone of the new county jail, which, on his recommendation, had been modeled on the jail in Pickaway County. Hayes probably used the same speech eleven days later, when he addressed the Congregational Club of Chicago on the spirit of the Golden Rule. "When reformers, religious teachers, and statesmen, and the general public" embrace "the spirit of true fraternity" or "absolute justice," he prophesied, "there will no longer be a negro problem, nor a problem of capital and labor, nor any question as to the treatment of the criminal."[25]

Hayes rejected the laissez-faire attitudes of the social Darwinists. "The unrestricted competition so commonly advocated does not leave us the survival of the fittest," he wrote. "The unscrupulous succeed best in accumulating wealth." Finding monopoly always hateful, he thought that the natural gas company in northwest Ohio (controlled by the Standard Oil monopoly) was despicable to induce factories to locate in Fremont and then cut off their gas supply when it became more profitable to sell gas for domestic purposes. To bring about a more equitable society, Hayes would rely on "state action, state regulation, state control," as well as the Golden Rule, but he was against state socialism, communism, and anarchism.[26]

As 1890 drew to a close, Hayes read everything he could find "on the negro." He was more than ever convinced "that education will help him wherever he needs help, will strengthen where he is weak, and will aid him to overcome all evil tendencies. The question then is how best to educate him." Hayes wanted the second Mohonk conference on the Negro, planned for the summer, to help answer that question. In Cleveland, he discussed the conference with John C. Covert of the *Leader*, who suggested that Hayes involve John D. Rockefeller, the Standard Oil monopolist. Hayes, who would have enlisted the devil himself in the cause of good education, asked Smiley to invite Rockefeller. With "enough ill nature" in Congress and the press, Hayes wanted a constructive meeting that would deal with present problems, chart a course for the future, and not dwell on past offenses.[27]

The bittersweet end of the year brought a fresh reminder of Hayes's generation's tenuous hold on life. Even though his thoughts never left Lucy, Hayes spent a happy Christmas with all his children at Birch and Mary's home, where they enjoyed little Sherman and his new brother Webb. The next morning, Hayes was "plunged into sorrow" by news that Dr. John Davis, the husband of Lucy's friend Eliza Davis, had died on Christmas Day. With Fanny, Hayes went to Cincinnati for Davis's funeral. Two days later, Hayes was back at Spiegel Grove grieving on his and Lucy's wedding anniversary until Horton Force, Manning Force's son, came over from Sandusky with his ice skates. "He is a bright fine specimen in all respects of a 12 year old," Hayes enthused, "cheerful, happy, fond of books, of sports, and all good things."[28]

JOINING LUCY

On New Year's Day 1891, Hayes lamented the passing of two customs. When he was young, "the old year was 'watched out' and the New Year was 'watched in' with prayers, hymns, and solemn exhortations." But when he stopped at the Methodist church before 9 P.M., he found the lights out and the prayer meeting ended, enabling those attending to welcome the new year more festively. The "happy old custom of New Year's calling," Hayes also noted, "has nearly disappeared." But he visited his old law partner Ralph Buckland and "talked over the usual topics" before they "naturally drifted into the war."[1]

"In many ways," Hayes declared in April 1891, "the War for the Union is the grandest event in all the secular annals of our Race. . . . It was a victory that blessed the victors and blessed at least equally the vanquished, and still more the innocent cause of it, the Negro." Although he thought that the southerners had been "*mistaken*," Hayes had no rancor for them. His heartfelt desire was, "Let us become one people." With most blacks living in the South, he believed that keeping hostile attitudes alive would delay progress toward political equality and educational and economic opportunity. Realizing that "the Negro Question" would have to be answered primarily by southerners, Hayes felt that the sooner the North and South were "one people," the sooner the problem would be solved.[2]

For Hayes, the ultimate solution remained education. In June 1891, he presided over the second Mohonk conference on the Negro question and found discussions "useful and inspiring." But by 1892, Hayes was aware of the political setbacks blacks had suffered in the South and was disturbed that "no question is raised as to the systematic and organized suppression of the negro vote."[3]

Despite setbacks, Hayes hoped for a better future as he worked to advance the educational opportunities for southern blacks. Reversing the policy of Haygood, J. L. M. Curry, the new Slater Fund agent, wished to achieve striking advances in a few schools and to spend Slater funds accordingly. In November 1891, Hayes and Curry inspected schools in six southern states and confirmed that the diffusion of funds was "wasteful," that more selectivity was "imperative," and that industrial training as an "auxiliary" to mental training was "indispensable." They were disappointed in the quality of manual training, which was often badly taught and seldom integrated into overall instruction. But programs at Tougaloo, Fisk, and Clark Universities encouraged Hayes. Influenced by the report of Hayes and Curry, the Slater board divided its funds among fewer schools.[4]

Hayes also played a supporting role in the early career of W. E. B. Du Bois, scholar and militant agitator for equality. Following Hayes's talk at Johns Hopkins University, Du Bois applied for a Slater Fund grant to continue his studies abroad. Although impressed by his credentials, the Slater board, whose funds were limited, did not grant aid to Du Bois or any other applicants at its May 1891 meeting. Hurt by his rejection and insisting that he had neither believed Hayes's offer nor expected help, Du Bois castigated the former president:

> You went before a number of keenly observant men who looked upon you as an authority in the matter, and told them in substance that the Negroes of the United States either couldn't or wouldn't embrace a most liberal opportunity for advancement. That statement went all over the country. When now finally you receive three or four applications for the fulfillment of that offer, the offer is suddenly withdrawn. . . . I think you owe an apology to the Negro people. We are ready to furnish competent men for every European scholarship furnished us. . . . But we can't educate ourselves on nothing and we can't have the moral courage to try if in the midst of our work, our friends turn public sentiment against us by making statements which injure us and which they cannot stand by. . . . I find men willing to help me thro' cheap theological schools, I find men willing to help me use my hands before I have got my brains in working order, . . . but I never found a man willing to help me get a Harvard Ph.D.[5]

Understanding Du Bois's disappointment, Hayes did not take umbrage at his criticism but encouraged him to renew his application the following year. Du Bois did so, requesting a grant or a loan to obtain "training in a European University for at least a year." With Hayes and Gilman supporting his application, Slater Fund trustees voted Du Bois a $375 grant plus a loan for the same amount in April 1892. On hearing the good news, Du Bois immediately thanked Hayes for his support. Reacting to Du Bois's short autobiography, Hayes noted gladly that he was "sensible, sufficiently religious, able, and a fair speaker," and hoped he would "turn out well."[6]

Although he continued to serve on the boards of Western Reserve and

Ohio Wesleyan Universities, Hayes worked especially hard for Ohio State University. He fought for an annual "one-twentieth mill" tax for it by writing to legislators and addressing the state senate finance committee; then, when that tax was forthcoming, he fought to avoid sharing the fund with Wilberforce University, a Methodist institution for black students. Since Ohio State University was the only state "institution for the higher education in science, in art, in mechanics, in agriculture, in practical knowledge," he did not want to share funds from the new tax with other colleges. But Hayes did urge the state to use other funds to equip and support an industrial department at Wilberforce.

With adequate funding in sight, Hayes believed that Ohio State was "at the forks of the road" and wanted to build a "credible institution" with a "generous regard for the plain people. The mechanics and farmers must see in our actions that their interests, wishes, and feelings are first in our thoughts." At the 5 May 1891 board meeting, Hayes wrote the unanimously adopted resolution for the construction of a manual training building, costing $45,000 with equipment; a geological museum and library; and a combined armory, assembly room, and gymnasium.[7]

Hayes helped select locations and arrange for the planning of the three new buildings, and the board placed him "in charge of the manual training department." Recognizing Hayes's contribution to Ohio State University, its trustees made him board president on 23 November 1892. Earlier, while he was absent inspecting southern schools for the Slater Fund, they had named the new industrial arts building Hayes Hall. The honor was compounded for Hayes, since the motion had been proposed by a Democrat and unanimously carried by a board with a Democratic majority.[8]

Hayes was convinced that failing to provide universal education and economic opportunity caused crime by spreading ignorance, poverty, and discontent. Although he believed that criminals were responsible for their acts, he refused to excuse the repressive elements in society whose actions, he believed, spawned crime. "Whoever interferes with equal rights and equal opportunities," he concluded, "is in some sense, in some . . . real degree, responsible for the crimes committed in the community." Hayes also agreed with Francis Wayland, dean of Yale Law School, who declared that the state had a duty and a responsibility with respect to the treatment of children. But state responsibility did not absolve the people of their responsibility. Hayes reminded the Ohio State Conference of Charities and Correction in 1892 that citizens must aid and inform "public officers in their duties with respect to the dependent, defective, and criminal members of society."[9]

As a result of his reading and his "almost seventy years of experience," Hayes believed in "the capacity of men and women for self-improvement." He appreciated Shakespeare's statement, "By use (habit) we can almost change the stamp of nature." He believed that "the young can train themselves to good dispositions, to good minds, *to steady nerves*, to courage, to self-control," just as he had overcome his youthful nervousness. Hayes claimed to have mastered relaxation so well that he could fall "into a sweet sleep" during a painful dental procedure involving "pounding, grinding, and filing."[10]

Hayes expected the United States, a mature democracy, to exercise the same self-control when dealing with other nations that mature individuals were expected to exhibit. He was disappointed by Harrison's warlike reaction to the mob attack in Valparaiso, which killed two American sailors and injured several others. "Chile consents to do all we can reasonably demand," he commented. "My regret is that our Government blustered and bullied. President Harrison in his message argued like a prosecutor—made the most of the case against our weak sister. Forbearance, charity, friendship, arbitration should have been in our words and thoughts." Hayes also thought that Italy overreacted when a New Orleans mob lynched eleven Italian immigrants who had been acquitted of assassinating its chief of police. The immigrants, Hayes reasoned, had opted to live in America, making their lynching "a question for America alone to deal with."[11]

William McKinley—Hayes's main political interest—ran for governor in 1891. As a former president, Hayes avoided partisanship, but he rooted for McKinley. While presiding at a meeting of the Ohio Farmers' Alliance, Hayes introduced McKinley with words about his early life and their service in the Twenty-third. Besides making McKinley governor, the election secured a Republican legislature, which, to Hayes's delight, reelected John Sherman to the Senate over the opposition of Joseph B. Foraker. The election also made McKinley a possible presidential nominee in 1892. When Harrison was renominated, McKinley "won new laurels" by his conduct and was well positioned for 1896. Carried away by his affection, Hayes extravagantly hailed him as "the man with the purest fame and the most brilliant record of any statesman in our political history."[12]

With Harrison again pitted against Cleveland, Hayes predicted Cleveland's triumph, but it was more decisive than Hayes had foreseen. Cleveland won, Hayes believed, because the "labor vote, holding the balance of power and better organized than ever before, joined the Democrats." Workingmen did not believe that they got "their share of the profits" or were "in an equal degree benefitted by protection" when they "saw the capitalists going to Europe to spend the fortunes acquired in America." Hayes wondered whether the Democrats would enact a "free-trade or revenue tariff" and, if they did, whether workers would get better wages. If reducing the tariff did not improve wages, perhaps McKinley would win the presidency in 1896 by asking, "What laborer gets better wages by reason of the new law?"[13]

Hayes's regard for McKinley owed more to their shared wartime experiences than to their shared political views. As the years of his presidency receded, the lure of politics diminished for Hayes, but he remained a warrior to the end, keeping bright memories of the Civil War and the luster of its soldiers. When Gen. William T. Sherman died in February 1891, Hayes, who had found him "the most interesting and original character . . . in the world," went to New York for his funeral and accompanied his body to St. Louis for burial. Although Hayes already belonged to the GAR and to the Loyal Legion and believed that there were "too many army societies," he joined the Union Veterans' Union. "If I can't have unity by inducing others to join the older societies, I will try to have it by uniting with them," he said.[14]

Usually accompanied by one of his children, Hayes addressed meetings of veterans and other groups on topics such as education and equal rights. But as he grew older, his health problems multiplied, and travel used him up "more than ever before." Nevertheless, Hayes insisted on "duties first" and kept to a grueling schedule. Between his ailments, he paced back and forth on the Spiegel Grove porch before breakfast and continued to clear brush and prune trees. When his *stomach vertigo* flared up in January 1891 and his diabetes in April, he attempted to control both by diet. "Hot lemonade with a little whiskey" threw off the severe cold he caught in March on a trip to Boston to participate in a memorial service for his attorney general, Charles Devens; bathing his eyes in hot water helped relieve them from the redness caused by another cold. In April and May, Hayes suffered from the "prevailing" grippe and influenza; then came diarrhea, cured by "a bottle of blackberry brandy with Bermuda ginger"; followed by a toothache that resisted "quinine, hot foot baths, & a plaster for the gums" and ended only when a dentist killed the nerve.[15]

In early April 1892, Hayes had his worst bout with poison ivy. He applied a solution of sulphate and soda water to his "swollen face and blood-shot eyes" and, despite the pain and the look of "just coming out of a spree," met his appointments. After speaking on education and manual training at the University of Wooster in Ohio, he attended the Slater Fund meetings in New

York. While there, the poison ivy reached the "last place" on Hayes's person. Subsequent swelling "substantially closed" Hayes's rectum for almost a week. Despite his discomfort, he noted the "great growth and beauty" of Harlem, admired the "grand view" while walking across the Brooklyn Bridge, and stopped for a chat at the City Club. The talk at the club of "divorcing city affairs from national politics" was congenial, since Hayes already believed that state concerns—education, social services, agriculture, forestry, and geology—"ought to be managed independent of party." Back in Ohio and "after a good deal of pain," Hayes's poison-ivy-induced constipation was finally relieved by a Cleveland physician. Weak but game, Hayes sampled grapefruit for the first time and found it "refreshing." Upon returning to Spiegel Grove, he declared meaningfully, "Home is the place for the old."[16]

As Hayes regained his strength, memories of his ordeal faded, and in the summer of 1892 he resumed traveling. His trip to Kenyon College, on the fiftieth anniversary of his graduation, was pure pleasure. There, comfortable in his old surroundings, he "was most heartily greeted and made a scattering talk of fifteen minutes." In early July, his trip to Cleveland to arrange with Myron T. Herrick for a loan of $50,000 to improve his Duluth property was pure business.[17]

Although Hayes was wealthy, his finances were not tidy. In September 1891, after meeting with Birch, Webb, and Rud "on *our* business affairs," he noted, "debts large and increasing. I have said yes to appeals too often during the last ten years. *The interest on my debts now exceeds my income.* But the real estate is worth three hundred thousand dollars and in the long run it probably increases in value faster than the debts. But the situation is embarrassing and needs attention." Continuing his generous ways, Hayes reminded himself on 31 December 1891, "My recent gifts to needy relatives and friends are far beyond my means."[18]

Despite his frequent trips, Hayes was apprehensive about attending the September 1892 GAR National Encampment in Washington. Since leaving the White House at the end of his presidency, he had returned to Washington only once, for Garfield's funeral. Now the critical condition of Harrison's wife Caroline brought memories of Lucy's death and made Hayes reluctant to make the trip. "But the good and much loved comrades of the Army of West Virginia, of the 'Old Kanawha Division,'" expected him, and Mary F. and Robert Stead, Manning Force's niece and her husband, made the trip more appealing by inviting Hayes to stay in their home, where he found "no fuss, no fidgets, but a careful regard for all my needs."

Informing his diary that "I go not for pleasure," Hayes, accompanied by

Scott, had the time of his life. On their arrival, a policeman recognized Hayes, took them to a hack, and helped arrange for the delivery of their luggage. With Scott, he attended the Foundry Methodist Church on Sunday, sitting in the pew he had occupied with Lucy during their White House years. Hayes also called on William T. Crump, his "old orderly of the war and steward in the White House, . . . at his plain but clean and orderly" Crump's Hotel and Cafe. Hayes spent his mornings at Ohio headquarters at Riggs House and attended meetings in a tent (where, one evening when the electric lights failed, the men carried on in the dark) and "in the noble hall of the Pension Department."

Appropriately for a battle-scarred warrior, a champion of pensions for veterans, and a former president, Hayes was enthusiastically cheered, especially while marching in the ranks on the "day of the great parade."

> I had tramped afoot [Hayes explained] with my comrades in post duties at home, at State Encampments, and at the National Encampment in Detroit. It struck me as the thing to do to follow these precedents at Washington. The people looking on and the comrades approved by applause in a very gratifying way. Nothing of the sort could have been better than the demonstration on Fifteenth Street—Treasury on one side, Riggs House on the other—and as I approached the stand, Senator Hawley led in the cheering. It was enough to stir the blood of the coldest and oldest.[19]

On 4 October, Hayes celebrated his seventieth birthday with Fanny, Birch, Mary, and his grandsons. Two days later, he left with Fanny for another Mohonk conference on American Indians, Peabody and Slater meetings, and New York's quadricentennial celebration of Columbus's first voyage to America. On 11 October, they viewed the "august" naval procession and, on the anniversary of the landfall, watched the "stupendous" parade for an hour before Hayes left for a Peabody trustees' meeting. There he carried the point he had lost in 1884: that schools in states that had repudiated their debts (Mississippi and Florida in 1892) should not be excluded from grants.

At Mohonk House, Hayes and Fanny "found a large attendance at the Indian Conference." Among those present were Sen. Henry L. Dawes, author of the Dawes Severalty Act (1887), which to a large extent codified the Indian policy of Schurz and Hayes; Commissioner of Indian Affairs Thomas J. Morgan; the Boston publisher H. O. Houghton; Hayes's friends Edward L. and Moses Pierce; and Civil Service Commissioner Theodore Roosevelt, who was writing and publishing his four-volume *Winning of the West*

(1889–96). The conference wound up with resolutions approving Dawes and his act, which—with little understanding of cultural values or realities—attempted to mold Native Americans into individualistic farmers. With the presidential campaign nearing its end, Hayes especially enjoyed political discussions with conference participants.[20]

As Hayes and Fanny left Mohonk with Houghton and his daughter Alberta on a "clear, crisp" 17 October, they exchanged the cheer "M-O-H-O-N-K, Mohonk, Rah! Rah!" with those remaining. Changing trains at Albany, Hayes and Fanny arrived in Chicago after an "agreeable all-night swift ride." There they were joined by Rud for ceremonies dedicating the World's Columbian Exposition. They took the Illinois Central out to the Chicago World's Fair grounds and inspected George B. Post's Manufactures and Liberal Arts Building (the largest in the world), which seated 45,000. Hayes found it "astounding in size and beauty"; the overall effect of the White City, planned for the fair by Frederick Law Olmsted and Daniel H. Burnham, was "stupendous, amazing, unequalled." Hayes was also delighted by Chicago itself, with its lake shore and park, its statues of Lincoln and Grant, and its private dwellings.

Hayes was flattered by the accolades he received from the crowds. He also appreciated the attentions of his old friends William Henry Smith and Justice John Marshall Harlan. For Hayes, the highlight of the Civic Parade on 20 October was the Carlisle Indian School "marching with hoes, rakes, spades, and other instruments of husbandry." On the following "great day of dedication," as a participant in the procession, he heard more cries of " 'Hayes,' 'Hayes,' 'Hayes' " than he had heard since leaving the presidency. However, the speeches that followed were, with one exception, inaudible, "too long," or "of no importance."[21]

As the year ended, Hayes was doing remarkably well. Thanksgiving at Spiegel Grove was heartwarming, largely because his grandsons Sherman and Webb "gave great delight to all with their drums, marching, both in jackets & breeches." Thinking of Lucy, Hayes recalled that "Thanksgiving with her to guide and direct was a perpetual joy!" But his longing for her did not rob that day of its cheer. On the next night, Hayes's "darling Fanny" and three other young women—Fanny Pease, Lucy Keeler, and Mary Miller—threw a "swell" affair. Called a musicale, it featured a Cleveland vocalist, Julia Severance Millikin, and a German pianist, Anna Bern. "All but about twenty-five or thirty" of the more than 250 invited friends accepted, Hayes recorded. With this throng—all "in their best array"—seated for refreshments, it was no wonder that their "number strained the capacity of old Spiegel." Present were at least eight of the single and married women who

Hayes and Sherman Otis Hayes

Sleigh ride: Hayes with the reins, Scott by the sleigh, and a bevy of women passengers

accompanied Hayes on his frequent carriage or sleigh rides—often to the cemetery or along the Sandusky River. One of these "intimate lady friends" had received "an anonymous letter" complaining that she was "too loving" with Hayes. Although the letter hurt her, Hayes dismissed it as "a mixture of envy and malice" and insisted that their friendly relationship was "not open to criticism."[22]

Hayes entered into the spirit of the holiday season. Having not heard for "some months" from Guy Bryan, his increasingly "morbid" college friend, and fearful that his feelings were "hurt over something," Hayes took time to write to him. Snow and the season's first sleighing on Sunday, 25 December, brought Hayes the Christmas he loved. After a "glorious" family time, he called that evening on Dr. Thomas and Annie Stilwell and on the Keelers, where he was delighted to find Lucy Keeler at home, since her "active, culti-vated mind" was "one of the few in my home range."[23]

The day after Christmas, Hayes left his family at Spiegel Grove to travel in behalf of education. In Cleveland that evening, he addressed the second annual banquet of the Kenyon Association in a "rambling" speech "on old times at Kenyon and . . . lasting college friendships," which he illustrated by reading, just after midnight, Bryan's response to his recent letter. On the train to Columbus the next day, Hayes "had a full, good talk" with McKinley, whose plans to reorganize Ohio State University troubled Hayes. Believing that Ohio State "stands well, is growing in favor, *needs* no change," Hayes suggested to his protégé that it "would be hurt by a seeming partisan measure" and warned him that he had indulged in "too much reorganization of State institutions already" for his "personal interests. *All* appointments *hurt*. Five friends are made cold or hostile for every appointment; no *new* friends are made. All *patronage* is perilous to men of real ability or merit. It aids only those who lack other claims to public support."

While in Columbus, Hayes addressed the Ohio College Association on manual training. Having "got it off well," he met with Wilbur H. Siebert, an instructor in history at the university, who was preparing a paper on the Underground Railroad. For his benefit, Hayes reminisced about "the winters when the Ohio was frozen over, 1851–2, 1855–6, . . . and the exodus of fugitive slaves." He also remembered the other underground railroad—the brutal one "running *South* to *slavery* with *free* colored men from this region" as kidnapped passengers.[24]

As the old year ended and the new year began, Hayes's thoughts danced between death and life. He thought of Lucy on 30 December, their fortieth wedding anniversary, and noted that among their wedding guests only the Herrons, Professor McCabe, and Eliza Davis—who was "near death's door"—still lived. But life reasserted itself when he took Lucy Keeler and Julia Haynes for a drive and then watched little Sherman and Webb enjoying Fanny's party for the forty children who attended the catechism class she helped teach. On New Year's Eve, Hayes briefly appeared at a party where Rud, Fanny, and her naval officer friend Harry E. Smith—whom she would later marry and divorce—were celebrating, and he called New Year's Day, which he always enjoyed, "one of the best." But on the morrow, he noted that for some time he had had "a trouble of the bladder." To cope with it, he resolved to reduce his liquids to a cup of coffee or mineral water at each meal. But he did not let his "trouble" interfere with the "great sleighing!" he enjoyed with "the young ladies" in the first week of January. After hearing "a fair sermon" on 8 January, Hayes declared, "I am a Christian according to my conscience . . . not of course by the orthodox standard. But I am content, and have a feeling of trust and safety." Accompanied by Rud, Hayes then drove "around the grave of Lucy in the sleigh. My feeling," he noted, "was one of longing to be quietly resting . . . by her side!"[25]

Hayes was up by 6:00 A.M. Monday morning to catch a train for Columbus to prepare for an Ohio State University board meeting on Tuesday. "How long is this going to last?" he asked Rud, who took him to the station. "These trips are wearisome, although the duty is very pleasant, and the objects those in which I am greatly interested." The board meeting, over which he presided, was fairly routine. Despite the bitterly cold weather, Hayes found time to visit relatives, dine with his faithful friend William K. Rogers, and call on McKinley. From Columbus, Hayes went to Cleveland; on Friday, he braved the deep snow and bitter cold to consult, as he had in the past, with Newton M. Anderson of the University School about the Manual Training Department at Ohio State. Later, Hayes had his usual good time with Webb at the home of Auntie Austin.[26]

En route to Spiegel Grove with Webb on Saturday, 14 January 1893, Hayes felt abnormally cold as they entered their train at the Cleveland railroad station. Calling for a stimulant, he returned to the station's platform while Webb procured him brandy and urged that they return to Auntie Austin's home. But Hayes insisted, "I would rather die in Spiegel Grove than live anywhere else." While getting back on the train, he suffered an attack of angina pectoris with violent chest pains, reminiscent of his wounded arm and broken ribs at South Mountain. "It is in the same old place," he said, while stoically bearing the pain. Webb telegraphed ahead, and Dr. Hilbish met the train at Fremont with opiates, which brought Hayes relief.

Confined in bed for the first time since his South Mountain wound, Hayes was restless. He had always wanted to "die well & at the right time," and he felt that his time had come. "And yet," he said, "I am not unhappy; my life is an exceptionally happy one." Sunday was the coldest day of the year, with the mercury below zero, and Dr. Hilbish feared that Hayes might get pneumonia. Laughing at Lucy Keeler, who brought a hot brick to warm his bed and tried "to keep the bedclothes round him," Hayes kidded her about roasting him. His condition worsened on Monday afternoon but seemed to stabilize on Tuesday. Often he mentioned his recent visit with Rud to Lucy's grave and his desire to be by her side. "I know that I am going where Lucy is," he told Dr. Hilbish. That evening, 17 January 1893, at 11 P.M., with only a nurse present, Hayes suddenly died.[27]

The funeral services on Friday, 20 January, were short and simple. A stream of people had viewed his remains on Thursday evening in his flag-bedecked room and on Friday morning as he lay in state in the dining room, with "the ribbon of the Loyal Legion around his neck; medals of the Army of

West Virginia & the Cumberland on one side, & the 23d badge on the other." At noon, the family was honored by the arrival of President-elect Cleveland, who said that he was following Hayes's example and "was very glad to come." Governor McKinley was on hand, as were members of President Harrison's cabinet. Among Hayes's old friends, Manning Force, William Henry Smith, and John Herron were present. Harriet Herron could not come; her daughter (who was Lucy Hayes's namesake) was ill with what was feared to be typhoid fever. Dr. McCabe arrived from Delaware just before the two o'clock service began. The house was packed with friends and officials, while thousands of people waited outside in the snow. The service, consisting of the Twenty-third Psalm, the hymn "It Is Well With My Soul," a touching and simple prayer, and another hymn, "God Be With You Till We Meet Again," concluded with all repeating the Lord's Prayer. Then the doors were opened and a long procession, organized by Col. Henry C. Corbin and led by military units, moved to the cemetery for the grave-side service. Although a number of dignitaries were honorary pallbearers, the body of Hayes was borne by his comrades of the Twenty-third. At the grave, the military ritual of the GAR, "a prayer, the salute from the guns, the 'taps' sounded upon bugle and horn, and the benediction," was a "solemn and impressive" farewell.[28]

Written tributes were also impressive. Most came from expected sources—president and Congress, governor and legislature, university boards and educational funds, reform organizations and military societies—but those that emanated from less obvious quarters—Democrats and priests, for example—would have given Hayes special pleasure. Almost all these statements celebrated his character and accomplishments, but one promised the ultimate fulfillment of his work and dreams. From Berlin, W. E. B. Du Bois wrote to the trustees of the Slater Fund: "I am especially grateful to the memory of him, your late head, through whose initiative my case was brought before you, and whose tireless energy and singleheartedness for the interests of my Race, God has at last crowned. I shall, believe me, ever strive that these efforts shall not be wholly without results."[29]

AFTERWORD

"I have no fears as to the standing of" my administration, Hayes declared, if "impartial writers . . . have the facts before them." But Hayes has suffered more than most presidents at the hands of writers who have judged him in a context divorced from his times. His southern policy has been singled out for particular criticism. Although W. E. B. Du Bois appreciated Hayes's personal support, when he published *Black Reconstruction in America: . . . 1860–1880* (1935), he criticized the promises made to white southerners by Hayes's lieutenants and their apparent fulfillment by the Hayes's administration. Subsequent revisionists, most recently and notably William Gillette in *Retreat from Reconstruction: 1869–1879* (1979) and Eric Foner in *Reconstruction: America's Unfinished Revolution, 1863–1877* (1988), have been even more negative in their views of Hayes as president.[1]

But few contemporaries would have quarreled with Hayes's own evaluation of his accomplishments. He was proud that, after finding "the country divided and distracted and every interest depressed," his administration had "left it united, harmonious, and prosperous." When his administration began, Hayes also found the Republican party "discordant, disheartened, and weak," and he left it "strong, confident, and victorious." Fearless on the battlefields of politics as well as of war, Hayes believed that he had successfully confronted many issues: "The Southern question; the money question; the hard times and riots; the Indian question; the Chinese question; the reform of the civil service; the partisan bitterness growing out of a disputed election; a hostile Congress; and a party long in power on the verge of defeat." Boasting of his own presidency, Hayes remarked that, apart from Lincoln's administration, "it would be difficult to find one which began with so rough a situation, and few which closed with so smooth a sea." In 1876, Henry Adams had dismissed Hayes as "a third-rate nonentity" and voted for Tilden, but by 1880, Adams—a caustic critic of politicians—acknowledged that Hayes had conducted "a most successful administration."[2]

Shortly after Hayes left the White House, the luster of his presidency began to dim. Mark Twain's prediction that the Hayes administration "would steadily rise into higher & higher prominence, as time & distance give it a right perspective," has not come to pass. Time and distance have resulted in changed values and different perspectives from those of the Gilded Age. Subsequent generations have tended to view its laissez-faire ideas of government, its paternalistic notions of reform, and its major political and economic players with disdain. That attitude has led late-twentieth-century historians to either reject or fail to understand the solutions Hayes embraced for many problems. He has been criticized for withdrawing military support for Republican governments in Louisiana and South Carolina, for championing the gold standard, for breaking the Great Strike of 1877, for espousing an Indian policy that aimed at acculturation, for negotiating a treaty that led to Chinese exclusion, for being inconsistent in his support for civil-service reform, and for not effectively leading Congress. He has also been subjected to considerable derision for banning liquor from the White House and dismissed as unimportant and uninteresting.[3]

It is, however, unfair to dismiss Hayes so summarily. Too often, he has been measured against the ideals of a later era, and his limited options have not been appreciated. Other actions of his have been misrepresented, and when his views and moves were prophetic, they have been ignored. Take, for example, the criticism that he abandoned Reconstruction governments. Hayes entered the White House with the poorest mandate of any president ever. With the public preoccupied with a depressed economy and unwilling to continue military intervention in southern politics, and with a hostile House of Representatives refusing to appropriate money for the army, Hayes was boxed in. He had no choice but to withdraw the troops in the two southern states where Republicans had a precarious foothold and try to bargain a few concessions in return. Before carrying out that inevitable withdrawal, Hayes demonstrated his commitment to voting rights for blacks by securing a pledge from the South Carolina and Louisiana governments to respect those rights. But, because of the pervasive racism that prevailed in the South and because northerners had lost interest in Reconstruction aims and the will to back them up, that commitment could not be enforced.

Historians have also failed to acknowledge the success of Hayes's monetary orthodoxy, and they have misrepresented his role in the Great Strike. He set his face against the inflationary schemes of greenbackers and silverites and sought the monetary stability provided by the gold standard for international trade, domestic business, and American labor. The evidence suggests that it was the proper course at the time. The United States' return to the gold standard during his administration was accompanied by a stunning economic revival. And Hayes, neither friendly to railroads nor hostile to labor, did not break the Great Strike of 1877. In fact, he refused to respond to the call of railroad moguls for troops to operate the railroads. He used the army to keep the peace only when help was properly requested by state and local authorities who were no longer able to cope with riots. When railroad management claimed to be unable to transport the mail, Hayes refused to intervene to get it through.

Hayes's paternalistic Indian policy—which aimed at integrating Native Americans into the economy of the West as agriculturalists, herders, and wagoners—has been judged by the ideals of a later era. He failed to appreciate the diverse cultures of the first Americans. Still, Hayes's course was fundamentally decent; in stopping the cruel removal of Native Americans to the Indian Territory, it built on the Grant administration's policy of peace, which was light years ahead of previous policies.

Although Hayes was burned in effigy for vetoing a Chinese exclusion bill, he was cognizant of the temper of both California and Congress and negotiated a new treaty restricting but not prohibiting Chinese immigration. Hayes's civil-service policy infuriated spoils politicians, who feared that it would destroy the Republican party; it frustrated reformers, who were unwilling to advance toward their goal in stages. Pleasing no one, Hayes kept the party sufficiently united and its machinery sufficiently intact to win the election of 1880. At the same time, he was conducting a successful civil-service reform experiment in the New York customhouse and post office—the largest and most complex offices in the country. Silas W. Burt, the soul of reform in the customhouse, credited Hayes with proving the feasibility of reform and making possible the passage of the 1883 Pendleton Civil Service Reform Act.

Hayes is also significant for his strikingly modern actions to enhance the power of the presidency. He engaged in a titanic struggle with Republican senators (particularly Roscoe Conkling) over the power of appointment. Senators had magnified their power to confirm appointments by the executive into the right to nominate federal officers in their states (senatorial courtesy). In a battle over the head of the New York customhouse, Hayes defeated Conkling and senatorial courtesy. By the end of the Hayes administration, senators and congressmen could suggest nominees but could not control appointments. Even more important, during the second half of his term, Hayes fought the Democratic congressional majority over the president's legislative role. The Democrats refused to vote funds for the civil and military operations of the government without "riders" attached to appropriations bills. The riders were obnoxious to Hayes because, if accepted, they would repeal the election laws—designed to protect the civil and voting rights of southern blacks under the Fourteenth and Fifteenth Amendments—and would promote ballot-box stuffing in northern cities. Hayes also recognized the rider device as an effort by congressional Democrats to destroy the president's veto power. In a battle royal, Hayes, ever the warrior, successfully vetoed appropriations bill after appropriations bill. He gained political ground with each veto by spelling out in detail to the public his constitutional and political objections to the riders. His actions forced the Democrats to surrender.

Hayes's vetoes in the battle of the riders illustrate his appreciation for public opinion, which he termed "the government." Unlike congressmen who depended on their organizations, Hayes depended on the public. Long before Theodore Roosevelt entered the national stage, Hayes made the presidency into a "bully pulpit," exploiting issues that would arouse public opinion and traveling more than any previous president. Although he eschewed electioneering on his trips, Hayes seized every available opportunity to address topics close to his heart, and his detailed ideas received good press coverage.

Anything but an inept politician, Hayes shrewdly played presidential politics. He was far more clever than the Conklings and the Blaines, who criticized him when he refused to let them dominate his administration. Uncannily aware of what was possible, Hayes avoided the impossible, lest he split the Republican party. His middle-of-the-road positions on issues such as civil-service reform and temperance kept the party together, but few historians single out middle-of-the-road positions for praise. His attitude toward temperance is a case in point. Hayes banned liquor from the White House as much to gain political advantage as to curb boorish behavior. He realized that temperance advocates in the Republican party would applaud his move and not desert to the Prohibitionists—a third-party movement he abhorred—and he knew that the wets would stay in the party, since his symbolic act did not harm them. Hayes's view that, rather than coerce society not to drink, public opinion should be persuaded that drinking is disreputable is strikingly close to the 1990s crusade of Mothers against Drunk Driving (MADD).[4]

Hayes did make a serious mistake, however, in refusing to run for reelection. Presidents who serve only one term are usually written off as mediocrities, while those acclaimed as great have invariably been reelected. A second term enables presidents to implement more fully their policy initiatives. Four more years would have allowed Hayes to widen the executive application of civil-service reform principles, and if he had secured a Republican Congress, he could have enforced the election laws and protected black voters in the South. He was the last nineteenth-century president with a genuine interest in securing voting rights for blacks, and had he succeeded in obtaining these rights, subsequent history might have been quite different.

Before and after his presidency, Hayes fought wholeheartedly for equality. He viewed the Civil War as a war against slavery, and no president has received as many wounds fighting for his country as he did. With the exception of Jimmy Carter, no retired president has been more involved in social causes than Hayes. Recognizing that the American government and its laws could be no better than its people, Hayes labored constantly to broaden educational opportunities for ordinary as well as gifted students of all races, from grade school through graduate training. He was a major dispenser of two educational funds dedicated to improving the education of southern blacks and whites, and he fought for federal subsidies to educate the children of all races in poor school districts. Hayes believed that education would improve the economic status of the disadvantaged, enlighten the intolerant, and achieve the fair start in life envisioned by Lincoln—and the political equality declared by Jefferson—as part of everyone's birthright. In addition, Hayes hoped that education would prove, in the long run, that his southern policy—substituting persuasion for the bayonet—was not merely the only possible policy but also the only real solution to southern problems.

Closely related to Hayes's faith in the schoolhouse was his interest in prison reform and in reducing crime. In his early years as a defense attorney, Hayes worked to keep his clients from the gallows; as an executive, he was generous with pardons; and in retirement, he opposed the death penalty. Hayes was convinced that criminals could be reformed and that crime was the product of poverty and desperation and could be reduced by a more equitable distribution of wealth.

In the last decade of his life, Hayes believed that the disparity in wealth between industrial "kings" and laboring men was the greatest problem facing his country. A century later, the excessive compensation of executives and their resulting remoteness from labor have been cited as a cause of the United States' declining industrial performance. Hayes favored confiscatory inheritance taxes, federal regulation of industry, and universal industrial education so that everyone—from financial moguls and political leaders to humble citizens—would experience and appreciate what manual labor involved. A common knowledge of manual labor and what it entailed, Hayes believed, would improve laws and policies and reduce class tensions.

Hayes was a precursor of the Progressive movement. Profoundly believing in equal rights and deeply concerned over the threat of plutocracy, he had faith that federal regulation would restore a balance in society and save American democracy. Hayes saw social Darwinism for what it was. Unregulated competition, he believed, resulted not in the survival of the fittest but in the triumph of the most predatory corporations. His reaction to the problems of the 1890s, like his earlier response to slavery, combined a sensitive nature, a judicious temperament, and a pragmatic attitude. Near the end of his life, Hayes perhaps most accurately assessed his own position, concluding, "I am 'a radical in thought (and principle) and a conservative in method' (and conduct)."[5]

A NOTE ON SOURCES

This biography is based on the incomparable resources of the Rutherford B. Hayes Presidential Center in Fremont, Ohio. Besides the voluminous papers and diaries of Hayes and members of his family, the library holdings include copies of Hayes materials housed at other collections throughout the country. These numerous collections are cited in pertinent endnotes. The diaries and a portion of the correspondence have been edited by Charles Richard Williams in *The Diary and Letters of Rutherford Birchard Hayes: Nineteenth President of the United States*, 5 vols. (Columbus: Ohio State Archaeological and Historical Society, 1922–1926). Williams eliminated abbreviations and made the punctuation more consistent but preserved the meaning of what he edited. The diary of the presidential years has been meticulously reproduced by T. Harry Williams in *Hayes: The Diary of a President, 1875–1881, Covering the Disputed Election, the End of Reconstruction, and the Beginning of Civil Service* (New York: David McKay, 1964). Wherever possible I have quoted from these readily available sources. I have also used the Carl Schurz and John Sherman papers in the Library of Congress and the George William Curtis and Charles Eliot Norton papers at Harvard University.

Charles Richard Williams also wrote an appreciative *Life of Rutherford Birchard Hayes: Nineteenth President of the United States*, 2 vols. (Columbus: Ohio State Archaeological and Historical Society, 1914), which is factually accurate and includes many speeches and pertinent newspaper accounts. I am indebted to Harry Barnard, *Rutherford B. Hayes and His America* (Indianapolis: Bobbs-Merrill, 1954), for his work on Hayes's early years, to Kenneth E. Davison, *The Presidency of Rutherford B. Hayes* (Westport, Conn.: Greenwood Press, 1972), and to Emily Apt Geer for her insights in *First Lady: The Life of Lucy Webb Hayes* (Kent and Fremont, Ohio: Kent State University Press and Rutherford B. Hayes Presidential Center, 1984).

T. Harry Williams, *Hayes of the Twenty-third: The Civil War Volunteer Officer* (New York: Alfred A. Knopf, 1965), has been helpful in tracing Hayes's Civil War career, as has E. B. Long and Barbara Long's *Civil War Day by Day: An Almanac, 1861–1865* (New York: Da Capo Press, 1971). On Reconstruction issues, I benefited from David Donald, *The Politics of Reconstruction, 1863–1867* (Baton Rouge: Louisiana State University Press, 1965), Michael Les

Benedict, *A Compromise of Principle: Congressional Republicans and Reconstruction* (New York: W. W. Norton, 1974), Hans L. Trefousse, *Andrew Johnson: A Biography* (New York: W. W. Norton, 1989), and Eric L. McKitrick, *Andrew Johnson and Reconstruction* (Chicago: University of Chicago Press, 1960).

Keith Ian Polakoff, *The Politics of Inertia: The Election of 1876 and the End of Reconstruction* (Baton Rouge: Louisiana State University Press, 1973), and C. Vann Woodward, *Reunion and Reaction: The Compromise of 1877 and the End of Reconstruction* (Garden City, N.Y.: Doubleday, 1956), have been most useful, but also of help on the end of Reconstruction were William Gillette, *Retreat from Reconstruction: 1869–1879* (Baton Rouge: Louisiana State University Press, 1979), and Stanley P. Hirshson, *Farewell to the Bloody Shirt: Northern Republicans & the Southern Negro, 1877–1893* (Bloomington: Indiana University Press, 1962). As collections of convenient source materials, Edward McPherson's *Hand-Book of Politics*, coming out every two years for use in elections from 1872 to 1894 (reprint, New York: Da Capo Press, 1972), is unmatched.

I have relied on several biographies of political leaders including Allan Peskin, *Garfield: A Biography* (Kent, Ohio: Kent State University Press, 1978), Thomas C. Reeves, *Gentleman Boss: The Life of Chester Alan Arthur* (New York: Alfred A. Knopf, 1975), David M. Jordan, *Roscoe Conkling of New York: Voice in the Senate* (Ithaca, N.Y.: Cornell University Press, 1971), Hans L. Trefousse, *Carl Schurz: A Biography* (Knoxville: University of Tennessee Press, 1982), and Chester L. Barrows, *Williams M. Evarts: Lawyer, Diplomat, Statesman* (Chapel Hill: University of North Carolina Press, 1941).

On other issues during Hayes's presidency, I have depended on Irwin Unger, *The Greenback Era: A Social and Political History of American Finance, 1865–1879* (Princeton, N.J.: Princeton University Press, 1964), Robert V. Bruce, *1877: Year of Violence* (Indianapolis: Bobbs-Merrill, 1959), Alvin M. Josephy, Jr., *The Nez Perce Indians and the Opening of the Northwest* (New Haven, Conn.: Yale University Press, 1965), Alexander Saxon, *The Indispensable Enemy: Labor and the Anti-Chinese Movement in California* (Berkeley: University of California Press, 1971), and David McCullough, *The Path between the Seas: The Creation of the Panama Canal* (New York: Simon and Schuster, 1977). On Hayes's significant postpresidential career, I was helped by Louis D. Rubin, Jr., *Teach the Freeman: The Correspondence of Rutherford B. Hayes and the Slater Fund for Negro Education, 1881–1893*, 2 vols. (Baton Rouge: Louisiana State University Press, 1959). For other sources used in writing this biography, refer to its endnotes.

NOTES

Introduction

1. Thomas Wolfe, "The Four Lost Men," in *From Death to Morning* (New York: Charles Scribner's Sons, 1935), pp. 114–33, quote on p. 121.

2. William Gillette, *Retreat from Reconstruction, 1869–1879* (Baton Rouge: Louisiana State University Press, 1979), pp. 347–48.

3. Eric Foner, *Reconstruction: America's Unfinished Revolution, 1863–1877* (New

York: Harper & Row, 1988), pp. 582–85; Robert V. Bruce, *1877: Year of Violence* (Indianapolis: Bobbs-Merrill, 1959), pp. 259–60.

4. Charles Richard Williams, *The Life of Rutherford Birchard Hayes: Nineteenth President of the United States*, 2 vols. (Columbus: Ohio State Archaeological and Historical Society, 1914), 2: 295–96.

5. T. Harry Williams, ed., *Hayes: The Diary of a President, 1875–1881* (New York: David McKay, 1964), 6 June 1879, p. 227; hereafter cited as RBH, *Diary.* Chicago *Times*, 6 Sept. 1878, quoted in Richard Kenin and Justin Wintle, eds., *The Dictionary of Biographical Quotation of British and American Subjects* (New York: Alfred A. Knopf, 1978), p. 368; RBH to Murat Halstead, 13 July 1878, Halstead Papers, Cincinnati Historical Society, copy HPC; Henry Adams to Henry Cabot Lodge, 13 May 1880, in J. C. Levenson et al., eds., *The Letters of Henry Adams, 1858–1918*, 6 vols. (Cambridge, Mass.: Harvard University Press, 1982–88), 2: 400.

6. RBH, Diary, 17 Feb. 1882, in Charles Richard Williams, ed., *The Diary and Letters of Rutherford Birchard Hayes: Nineteenth President of the United States*, 5 vols. (Columbus: Ohio State Archaeological and Historical Society, 1922–26), 4: 68. Hereafter cited as *D&L*.

7. Ulysses S. Grant, *Personal Memoirs*, 2 vols. (New York: Charles L. Webster & Company, 1885–86), 2: 340.

8. W. E. B. DuBois to DCG, no date, in Louis D. Rubin, Jr., *Teach the Freeman: The Correspondence of Rutherford B. Hayes and the Slater Fund for Negro Education, 1881–1893*, 2 vols. (Baton Rouge: Louisiana State University Press, 1959), 2: 281.

9. RBH, MS Diary, 15 Apr. 1892, HPC.

10. Samuel Langhorne Clemens to RBH, 10 Apr. 1882, HPC.

Chapter 1. Ohio and New England

1. Genealogical charts and tables, HPC; *Delaware Patron and Franklin Chronicle*, 24 July 1822; Harry Barnard, *Rutherford B. Hayes and His America* (Indianapolis: Bobbs-Merrill, 1954), pp. 48–49, 56–61, 70. Drusilla caught the fatal "spotted fever" from a dying soldier she took into her home and nursed after he was abandoned on the roadside by a recruiting officer. RBH to BAH, 18 Jan. 1871, HPC.

2. Genealogical charts and tables, HPC; RBH, Diary, 14 Dec. 1860, in *D&L*, 1: 568; Barnard, *Hayes*, pp. 50–55, 59–68. The wedding date of 19 September, usually given as 13 September, is from notes in RBH's writing, "Extracts from Town Records Wilmington Vt.," HPC. "Roseate cheeks" and "rubicund hair" were Rutherford Hayes, Jr.'s, own words.

3. RBH, Diary, 29 Dec. 1891, in *D&L*, 5: 43; genealogical charts and tables, HPC; Barnard, *Hayes*, pp. 20, 68–70.

4. RBH, Diary, 31 Aug. 1872, in *D&L*, 3: 212, Barnard, *Hayes*, p. 73.

5. SBH to RBH, 20 July 1839, SBH to Dyer Bancroft, 26 Sept. 1824, HPC.

6. RBH to SBH, 8 Jan. 1844, HPC; Barnard, *Hayes*, pp. 73–74, 79–80.

7. RBH, "Recollections of My Sister Fanny, 1856," in *D&L*, 1: 5–7, additions from MS, HPC; FAHP to RBH, 20 July 1852, HPC; Barnard, *Hayes*, p. 21.

8. Barnard, *Hayes*, p. 85; FAHP to RBH, 3 Oct. 1847, HPC; RBH to Clark Waggoner, 7 Jan. 1881, in *D&L*, 3: 636.

9. RBH, "My Sister Fanny," in *D&L*, 1: 11.

10. RBH, Genealogical Notes, appended to vol. 4 of MS Diary, HPC; RBH, "My Sister Fanny," in *D&L*, 1: 4; Anna C. Smith Pabst, *Berlin Township & Delaware County, Ohio History: Told by Contemporaries* (Delaware, 1958), 2: 9.

11. SBH to Austin and Roger Birchard, 3 Sept. 1825, HPC; RBH, "My Sister Fanny," corrected from MS, HPC, RBH to FAHP, 8 Aug. 1847, in *D&L*, 1: 4–5, 212.

12. RBH, "My Sister Fanny," in *D&L*, 1: 5, corrected from MS, HPC; FAHP to RBH, 3 Oct. 1847, HPC.

13. RBH, Diary, 10 Sept., 3 Oct. 1871, in *D&L*, 3: 161–63, 165–66; Barnard, *Hayes*, pp. 29–30; RBH, Genealogical Notes.

14. SBH to Austin and Roger Birchard, 3 Sept. 1825, 21 July 1827, and SBH to Roger Birchard, 14 May 1826, HPC; RBH, Genealogical Notes.

15. RBH, Genealogical Notes; RBH, "My Sister Fanny," in *D&L*, 1: 4, 8; Barnard, *Hayes*, pp. 94–98.

16. SBH to Austin and Roger Birchard, 4 Nov. 1830, HPC.

17. RBH, "My Sister Fanny," in *D&L*, 1: 8–9, corrected from MS, HPC; RBH, Diary, 11 Feb. 1876, in *D&L*, 3: 304.

18. Barnard, *Hayes*, pp. 74, 83–84, 90–91.

19. Ibid., pp. 90–91; RBH, Diary, 7 Nov. 1841, in *D&L*, 1: 73–74.

20. Barnard, *Hayes*, pp. 81–83, 86–87, 90–91, 97–98.

21. RBH, "Visit to New England," RBH, Diary, 4 June 1887, in *D&L* 1: 1, 4: 328; RBH to FAHP, 4 June 1854, RBH to Austin Birchard, 14 May 1874, HPC.

22. RBH, Genealogical Notes; RBH, "Visit to New England," RBH, Diary, 4 June 1887, in *D&L* 1: 1, 4: 328; Barnard, *Hayes*, pp. 58–60.

23. RBH, Genealogical Notes; Belinda Elliot McLellan, 8 Dec. 1870, in Genealogical materials, HPC; RBH, "My Sister Fanny," RBH, Diary, 18 Feb. 1844, in *D&L* 1: 10, 143.

24. RBH, "Visit to New England," RBH, "My Sister Fanny," RBH, Diary, 12 July 1841, 18 Feb. 1844, in *D&L* 1: 1, 10, 64, 143–44.

25. RBH, "Visit to New England," in *D&L* 1: 1; *Dictionary of American Biography*, s.v. "Noyes, John Humphrey"; hereafter cited as *DAB*.

26. RBH, "Visit to New England," in *D&L* 1: 2, corrected from MS, HPC; *DAB*, s.vv. "Mead, Larkin Goldsmith," "Mead, William Rutherford."

27. "The Hayes Family," Rutland (Vt.) *Herald*, Aug. 1877?, in Hayes Scrapbook, 91: 74, HPC; RBH, "Visit to New England," in *D&L*, 1: 2, corrected from MS.

28. RBH, "Visit to New England," RBH, "My Sister Fanny," in *D&L*, 1: 2–3, 10, corrected from MS, HPC.

29. RBH, "Visit to New England," in *D&L*, 1: 3; SBH to SB, 6 Oct. 1834, HPC. Cousin John Pease was Linda Hayes Elliot's son by a previous marriage.

30. RBH, "My Sister Fanny," RBH, Diary, 12 Mar. 1888, in *D&L*, 1: 10–11, 4:374–75; SBH to SB, 23 Apr., 9 May 1835, HPC.

31. RBH, Diary, 11 Feb. 1876, in *D&L*, 3: 304; Barnard, *Hayes*, p. 98.

32. SBH to SB, 26 Mar., May 1836, HPC.

33. RBH to SB, 21 June 1836, in *D&L*, 1: 13, SBH to SB, 8 July 1836, HPC.

34. RBH to SB, 21 June, 20 Sept. 1836, in *D&L*, 1: 13–14; SBH to SB, 11 Sept., 16, 27 Oct., 28 Nov. 1836, 1 May 1837, HPC.

35. RBH to SBH 13 [23?] Oct. 1836, in *D&L*, 1: 14.

36. SBH to SB, 28 Nov. 1836, 11 Jan., 8 Mar. 1837, HPC.

37. RBH to FAHP, 4 Apr. 1837, in SBH to FAHP, 1 Apr. 1837, HPC.

38. SBH to SB, 28 Nov. 1836; FAHP to RBH, [Apr. 1837], HPC.

39. RBH, "My Sister Fanny," RBH to SB, 13 Aug. 1870, in *D&L*, 1: 7, 3: 116–17; SBH to SB, 1 May 1837, SBH to FAHP, June 1837, HPC. Fanny, but apparently not Rud, made a deep impression on Finch.

40. FAHP to SB, 7 July 1837, 4 Jan. 1838, HPC; SBH to SB, 17 May, 27 June 1837, in Barnard, *Hayes*, pp. 98–99; RBH, "My Sister Fanny," in *D&L*, 1: 11. For evidence of Rud's awakened interest in the opposite sex, see RBH to Manly Covell, 6 Jan. 1838, RBH to Harriet Moody, 24 Feb. 1838, RBH, Diary, 12 Mar. 1892, in *D&L*, 1: 16–19, 5: 63–64.

41. SBH to SB, Aug. 1837, 14 June 1866, HPC.
42. SBH to SB, [Oct. 1837], HPC. On Webb's school, see *D&L*, 1: 15.
43. SBH to SB, 1 Dec. 1837, HPC.
44. RBH to SB, 9 Dec. 1837, RBH to Manly D. Covell, 6 Jan. 1838, in *D&L*, 1: 15–18; Isaac Webb to SB, 31 Jan. 1838, HPC.
45. RBH, Diary, 27 Feb. 1892, in *D&L*, 5: 61; Barnard, *Hayes*, pp. 100–101; Isaac Webb to SB, 29 Sept. 1838, HPC.
46. RBH to Manly D. Covell, 6 Jan. 1838, RBH to SB, 5, 28 Apr., 6 June 1838, RBH to SBH, 7 July 1838, in *D&L*, 1: 17, 19–23; FAHP to SB, 29 Apr. 1838, HPC.
47. RBH to SB, 9 Dec. 1837, RBH to Harriet Moody, 24 Feb. 1838, RBH to SBH, 30 Aug. 1838, in *D&L*, 1: 16, 19, 24; RBH to SBH, 7 July 1838, HPC.
48. Isaac Webb to SB, 30 Apr. 1838, RBH to SB, 6 June, 18 Sept. 1838, RBH to SBH, 30 Aug. 1838, in *D&L*, 1: 21–22, 25; SBH to SB, 6, 18 Aug. 1838, Isaac Webb to SB, 29 Sept. 1838, HPC. Sam Weller in Dickens's *Pickwick Papers* (1836–37) said "wery" for "very."
49. RBH to SB, 18 Sept. 1838, RBH, Diary, 4–9 Oct. 1838, RBH, "My Sister Fanny," in *D&L*, 1: 12, 26; RBH to William G. Lane, 20 Nov. 1838, Yale University, copy HPC.
50. RBH, "My Sister Fanny," in *D&L*, 1: 12; RBH to FAHP, [5] Aug. 1839; SBH to SB, 29 Apr. 1838, 8 July 1839, HPC. The Union was probably modeled on the Oxford University debating society of that name.
51. SBH to SB, 6 Oct. 1838, HPC; RBH, 1839 Account Book, in Barnard, *Hayes*, p. 103.
52. Isaac Webb to SB, 29 Sept. 1838, HPC.

Chapter 2. Kenyon and Harvard

1. SBH to SB, 6 Oct. 1838, 2 Mar. 1839, SBH to RBH, 11 Nov., 12 Dec. 1838, HPC; RBH, Diary, 31 Oct.–3 Nov. 1838, in *D&L*, 1: 27.
2. RBH to William G. Lane, 20 Nov. 1838, Yale University, copy HPC; RBH, Diary, 27 Nov. 1838, 4 Oct. 1892, in *D&L*, 1: 27, 5: 111. Later in life, Hayes preferred that his children skate on shallow ponds, since thin ice was "the only form of danger" he was "uneasy about." RBH to SB, 12 Dec. 1868, HPC.
3. RBH, Diary, 21 Dec. 1838–1 Jan. 1839, in *D&L*, 1: 27; FAHP to SB, 6 Jan. 1839, and SBH to RBH, 11 Jan. 1839, HPC.
4. RBH, Diary, 18 Jan. 1839, RBH to FAHP, 5 Feb. 1839, in *D&L*, 1: 27–29.
5. SBH to RBH, 12 Dec. 1838, HPC; RBH to FAHP, 5 Feb. 1839, in *D&L*, 1: 29–30.
6. FAHP to RBH, 20 Jan., 25 Feb. 1839, FAHP to SB, 3 Mar. 1839, HPC; RBH to SBH, 10 Mar. 1839, in *D&L*, 1: 30–32.
7. RBH to SBH, 10 Mar. 1839, RBH, Diary, 23 Mar. 1889, in *D&L*, 1: 30–32, 4: 458; Barnard, *Hayes*, p. 108; William B. Bodine, *The Kenyon Book* (Columbus, 1890), p. 364. Sparrow was, in effect, the president of Kenyon, since the nominal president was the Episcopal bishop of Ohio, who was not directly involved in the college's administration. On nagging Rud, see FAHP to RBH, 26 May 1839, and SBH to RBH, no date [1839 or 1840] and 12 June 1840, HPC.
8. RBH to FAHP, 13 May 1839, RBH to SBH, 13 May, 5 Aug. 1839, in *D&L*, 1: 33–34, 36.
9. RBH to FAHP, 9 July 1839, RBH, Diary, 3 July 1841, in *D&L*, 1: 34–35, 61–62. Hayes was friendly with the Kentuckian, Thomas M. Kane; in New Orleans, seven years after the altercation on the Fourth at Kenyon, Kane was killed in a duel growing out of a "dispute in a ballroom about positions." RBH, Diary, 9 Oct. 1846, in *D&L*, 1: 187.
10. RBH to SBH, 5 Aug. 1839, in *D&L*, 1: 36–37.
11. SBH to SB, 8 July 1839, SBH to RBH, 20 July 1839, HPC. In April 1838, Fanny de-

feated Will Platt in two out of three games of chess and beat him "fairly" at marksmanship by putting her last shot "exactly in the centre of the mark." FAHP to SB, 29 Apr. 1838, HPC.

12. FAHP to RBH, 22 July 1839, HPC.

13. RBH to FAHP, 5 Aug. 1839, HPC.

14. SBH to RBH, 5 Nov. 1839, RBH to FAHP, 1 Dec. 1839, SB to Austin Birchard, 16 Sept. 1839, FAHP to RBH, 5 Nov. 1839, FAHP to SB, 24 Oct., 7 Nov. 1839, HPC; RBH to SBH, 4 May 1840, in *D&L*, 1: 37. In his effort to build a case for incestuous feelings between Rud and Fanny, Barnard claims without documentation that Rud avoided Fanny's wedding by remaining at Kenyon. Barnard, *Hayes*, p. 111. In all probability, Rud did attend the wedding. Sophia expected both Rud and Sardis to be in Delaware in late August; Rud was home on 16 September when Sardis and Sophia first wrote to Vermont relatives following the wedding, and no mention was made of his absence. SBH to RBH, 20 July 1839, SB and SBH to Austin Birchard, 16 Sept. 1839, HPC.

15. "Excerpts from Philomathesian Society Minute Book, 1832–1848," Kenyon College, copy HPC; RBH, "Discussions — Forensics — &c.," "Selections from Poets," 1 Nov. 1838, "Russian Proverbs — Pinkerton," "Extracts — Figures," Notes on Debates, HPC; Robert Pinkerton, *Russia: Or, Miscellaneous Observations on the Past and Present State of That Country and Its Inhabitants* (London, 1833), pp. 349–56; SB to Austin Birchard, 1 Apr. 1839, in Barnard, *Hayes*, p. 114. For Hayes's training in speech and debate at Kenyon, particularly his extracurricular work in the Philomathesian Society, see Wyman W. Parker, "Rutherford B. Hayes as a Student of Speech at Kenyon College," *The Quarterly Journal of Speech* 39 (1953): 291–95.

16. RBH to FAHP, 22 June 1840, FAHP to RBH, 19 Jan., 3 July 1840, HPC. Columbus Delano, who was later an inadequate secretary of the interior under President Ulysses S. Grant, defended Sawyer, who apparently was acquitted.

17. RBH to R. T. Russel, 24 Apr. 1840, HPC; RBH, "A History of the Presidential Campaign of 1840, Begun June 25, 1840," in *D&L*, 1: 40–44.

18. RBH to SBH, 11 Oct. 1840, in *D&L*, 1: 45; GMB to RBH, 3 Apr. 1892, SBH to RBH, 16 Oct. 1840, SBH to SB, 17 Dec. 1840, HPC; Bodine, *Kenyon Book*, p. 363.

19. RBH, Diary, 10 Feb. 1841, RBH to SBH, 10 Feb. 1841, in *D&L*, 1: 45–50; SBH to RBH, 16 Feb. 1841, HPC.

20. RBH, Diary, 11 June 1841, in *D&L*, 1: 54–55.

21. RBH, Diary, 17 June 1841, in *D&L*, 1: 55–56.

22. RBH, Diary, 19 June 1841, in *D&L*, 1: 56–57.

23. Ibid., 1: 57.

24. FAHP to RBH, 18 June 1841, RBH to FAHP, 22 June 1841, HPC; RBH to FAHP, 13 May 1839, RBH, Diary, 21 June 1841, in *D&L*, 1: 33, 57–58.

25. RBH, Diary, 25, 29 June 1841, in *D&L*, 1: 58–60.

26. "Philomathesian Society Minute Book," Kenyon College, copy HPC.

27. RBH, Diary, 3 July, 7 Oct. 1841, in *D&L*, 1: 61–62, 70; "Philomathesian Society Minute Book," Kenyon College, copy HPC; Bodine, *Kenyon Book*, p. 364; Barnard, *Hayes*, pp. 119–20.

28. WHS, Private Memoranda, 14 Dec. 1887, HPC.

29. RBH, Diary, 7 Nov. 1841, 6 Jan. 1842, in *D&L*, 1: 73, 82–83.

30. RBH to SBH, 25 Oct. 1841, HPC; RBH, Diary, 17, 29 Oct., 1, 7 Nov. 1841, in *D&L*, 1: 70–74. For examples of Fanny urging Hayes to diligently study in order to lay "*the piers which are to support the future bridge of his fame*" and to "sound the family trumpet far & wide," see FAHP to RBH, 2 Mar. 1840, 4 Mar. 1841, HPC.

31. RBH to FAHP, 4 Dec. 1841, RBH, Diary, 10 Dec. 1841, 25 Jan. 1842, in *D&L*, 1: 80–82, 90–91; Wyman W. Parker, "The College Reading of a President," *Library Quar-*

terly 21 (1951): 107–12; "Books Withdrawn from the Philomathesian Library by R. B. Hayes," Kenyon College.

32. RBH, Diary, 1 Aug., 28 Nov. 1841, 1 Aug. 1855, in *D&L*, 1: 65–66, 74–77, 489; RBH to WAP, June 1841, RBH to FAHP, 19 July 1841, HPC.

33. RBH to FAHP, 4 Oct. 1841, HPC; RBH to FAHP, 31 Jan., 7 Feb. 1842, in *D&L*, 1: 91, 93.

34. RBH to SBH, 10 Jan. 1842, in *D&L*, 1: 84–86. Sophia need not have worried about Rud's morals. A college friend recalled him "as one of the purest boys I ever knew." Bodine, *Kenyon Book*, p. 364.

35. FAHP to RBH, 29 Nov. 1841, HPC; RBH to FAHP, 7 Feb., 14, 15 Apr. 1842, in *D&L*, 1: 94, 100; Barnard, *Hayes*, p. 109. Case realized his ambition after study at the University of Pennsylvania.

36. RBH to FAHP, 7 Feb. 1842, in *D&L*, 1: 93–94; SBH to RBH, 14 Mar. 1842, HPC.

37. RBH to FAHP, 7 Feb. 1842, S. J. Johnson to SBH, 15 Mar. 1842, in *D&L*, 1: 94, 97.

38. "Philomathesian Society Minute Book," Kenyon College, copy HPC; SBH to SB, 4 July 1842, HPC.

39. WAP to RBH, 17, 22 Apr. 1842, WAP to SB, 24 Apr. 1842, SBH to Austin Birchard, 17 July 1842, HPC. Postpartum psychosis is the rarest and most dangerous form of postpartum depression. Terra Ziporyn, "True Blue? Postpartum Depression," *Harvard Health Letter* 17 (Feb. 1992): 1–3.

40. WAP to RBH, 22, 24 Apr. 1842, WAP to SB, 24 Apr. 1842, HPC.

41. RBH to WAP, 25 Apr. 1842, in *D&L*, 1: 100; WAP to RBH, 24 Apr. 1842, HPC; Norman Dain, *Concepts of Insanity in the United States, 1789–1865* (New Brunswick, N.J.: Rutgers University Press, 1964).

42. RBH to WAP, 25 Apr. 1842, SBH to RBH, 30 Apr. 1842, HPC; RBH, Diary, 4 Oct. 1892, in *D&L*, 5: 111.

43. RBH to WAP, 31 May 1842, RBH to SBH, 13 June 1842, in *D&L*, 1: 100–102; SBH to SB, 4 July 1842, HPC.

44. SBH to Austin Birchard, 17 July 1842, WAP to RBH, 18 July 1842, WAP to SB, 1 Aug. 1842, HPC; Barnard, *Hayes*, p. 127.

45. RBH, Diary, 6 Jan. 1842, RBH to SBH, 18 July 1842, in *D&L*, 1: 82, 104; SBH to SB, 19 Sept. 1841, RBH to S. S. Perry [c. 14 Sept. 1842], HPC; Bodine, *Kenyon Book*, p. 363.

46. Wyman W. Parker, "President Hayes's Graduation Speeches," *Ohio State Archaeological and Historical Quarterly* 63 (1954): 135–46; for an effusive contemporary reaction, see *Democratic Banner* (Mount Vernon, Ohio), 9 Aug. 1842.

47. RBH to S. S. Perry [c. 14 Sept. 1842], HPC.

48. RBH to SBH, 18 July 1842, in *D&L*, 1: 105; WAP to RBH, 24 Aug. 1842, SBH to SB, 25 Aug. 1842, RBH to SB, 14 Sept. 1842, RBH to S. S. Perry [c. 14 Sept. 1842], SB to Austin Birchard, 14 Nov. 1842, HPC.

49. SBH to SB, 25 Aug., 14 Sept. 1842, RBH to SB, 29 Oct. 1842, FAHP to SB, 25 Aug. 1843, HPC. Sardis had, at Sophia's request, given Fanny $200 to buy clothes in New York. "You know," Sophia explained, "how independent she likes to be."

50. RBH to FAHP, 7 Feb. 1842, in *D&L*, 1: 94; RBH to SB, 14 Sept., 29 Oct. 1842, RBH to S. S. Perry [c. 14 Sept. 1842], HPC.

51. RBH, Diary, 12, 19, 26 Nov. 1842, in *D&L*, 1: 107–10. Hayes was reading William Chillingworth's *Works* (1836), including *The Religion of Protestants: A Safe Way to Salvation*, and Richard Whately's *Logic* (1826) "to discipline the reasoning faculty."

52. RBH, Diary, 28 Aug. 1843, RBH to SBH, 12 Oct. 1845, RBH to FAH, 6 Mar. 1887, in *D&L*, 1: 112, 173, 4: 313; RBH to SB, 17 June 1843, SBH to SB, 17 June 1843, FAHP to RBH, 24 Sept. 1843, SB to Austin Birchard, 21 Aug. 1843, HPC. Barnard mistakenly as-

sumes that Hayes spent "one of his happiest, most carefree periods" of his life reading law at Columbus. Barnard, *Hayes*, p. 128.

53. RBH, Diary, 28 Aug. 1843, RBH to SBH, 27 Aug. 1843, in *D&L*, 1: 112; Thomas Sparrow to _____, 5 Aug. 1843, HPC.

54. RBH, Diary, 1 Sept. 1843, in *D&L*, 1: 113.

55. RBH, Diary, 29, 31 Aug., 21 Dec. 1843, 4 Jan., 18 Feb. 1844, in *D&L*, 1: 112–13, 131, 136, 144. Story had written the opinion of the Supreme Court in *Prigg* v. *Pennsylvania* (1842), which declared unconstitutional the Pennsylvania personal liberty law of 1826 (and similar statutes in other northern states), because legislation on fugitive slaves was "exclusive in the national government."

56. RBH to SB, 24 Sept. 1843, RBH to FAHP, 8 Dec. 1844, HPC; RBH, Diary, 27 Oct., 15 Nov. 1843, in *D&L*, 1: 122, 127.

57. RBH, Diary, 27 Oct., 27 Nov., 3, 21, 25 Dec. 1843, 13, 22, 31 Jan. 1844, in *D&L*, 1: 121, 127, 129–30, 132–33, 137, 139, 143; Russel Blaine Nye, *The Cultural Life of the New Nation: 1776–1830* (New York: Harper & Brothers, 1960), pp. 33–36.

58. RBH, Diary, 25 Oct, 27 Nov. 1843, 15, 22 Jan., 3, 11, 18 Mar., 1 Oct. 1844, in *D&L*, 1: 120, 127, 139, 147–48, 160; RBH to SB, 15 Apr. 1844, RBH to SBH, 1 Oct. 1844, HPC.

59. RBH to FAHP, 30 Oct. 1843, in *D&L*, 1: 122–25.

60. RBH, Diary, 27 Nov. 1843, in *D&L*, 1: 128; FAHP to RBH, 25 Feb. 1844, RBH to FAHP, 8 Dec. 1844, HPC.

61. RBH, Diary, 20 Sept., 15, 30 Nov. 1843, in *D&L*, 1: 115, 126–29; RBH to SB, 24 Sept. 1843, HPC.

62. RBH, Diary, 31 Dec. 1843, 12, 26 May 1844, in *D&L*, 1: 134–36, 150–52; *DAB*, s.v. "Walker, James."

63. RBH, Diary, 14 Nov. 1843, 12 May 1844, in *D&L*, 1: 126, 150.

64. RBH, Diary, 25 Oct. 1843, in *D&L*, 1: 120–21.

65. RBH, Diary, 18 Feb. 1844, in *D&L*, 1: 143–44; RBH to SB, 25 Feb. 1844, HPC. Mary Birchard would die in the Ashtabula, Ohio, railroad disaster of 29 December 1876. By then, Hayes thought her "a kind-hearted, lovable woman." RBH, Diary, 2 Jan. 1877, in *D&L*, 3: 398–99.

66. RBH, Diary, 8 Apr., 18 May 1844, RBH to FAHP, 2 June 1844, in *D&L*, 1: 149, 151, 153–54; RBH to SB, 15 Apr. 1844, HPC.

67. RBH, Diary, 18 May 1844, in *D&L*, 1: 151; RBH to SB, 15 Jan. 1844, SB to RBH, 30 Jan. 1844, SBH to SB, 10 Apr. 1844, FAHP to RBH, 17 Apr. 1844, HPC.

68. RBH, Diary, 26 Feb., 12 May 1844, in *D&L*, 1: 145, 150; RBH to SB, 15 Apr. 1844, RBH to SBH, 8 Jan. 1844, HPC.

69. RBH, Diary, 21 Sept. 1844, in *D&L*, 1: 159; RBH to SB, 8 Aug. 1844, RBH to SBH, 1 Sept. 1844, HPC.

70. RBH, Diary, 21 Sept. 1844, in *D&L*, 1: 159–60; RBH to SBH, 1 Oct. 1844, HPC; newspaper clipping, Scrapbook, HPC.

71. RBH, Diary, 26 Sept. 1843, 9 Nov. 1844, in *D&L*, 1: 116–17, 161–62; RBH endorsement on Electoral Tickets, Massachusetts, 1844, dated 11 Nov. 1844; RBH to WAP, 10 Nov. 1844, RBH to FAHP, 8 Dec. 1844, HPC.

72. RBH, Diary, 31 Jan. 1844, in *D&L*, 1: 143; GMB to RBH, 1 July 1844, RBH to SB, 8 Dec. 1844, HPC.

73. RBH, Diary, 5 Oct. 1844, in *D&L*, 1: 161; RBH to SB, 8 Dec. 1844, HPC.

74. RBH, Diary, 1 Jan. 1845, in *D&L*, 1: 162. Hayes's bachelor of laws degree from Harvard Law School is dated 27 August 1845. Kenneth E. Davison, *The Presidency of Rutherford B. Hayes* (Westport, Conn.: Greenwood Press, 1972), p. 5.

Chapter 3. Lower Sandusky

1. RBH to SBH, 8 Jan. 1844, RBH to SB, 15 Jan, 28 July, 8 Aug. 1844, RBH to FAHP, 8 Dec. 1844, HPC. At the close of the Civil War, Hayes advised a young man to "go to a large City or to a Town that is rapidly growing to importance" to set up a practice. "A large City like St. Louis, Memphis &c &c is more discouraging than a smaller town at first, but success is just as certain, and far more remunerative." Hayes gave William McKinley similar advice a year later. RBH to R. L. Nye, 9 Aug. 1865, HPC; RBH to William McKinley, 6 Nov. 1866, in *D&L*, 5: 149–50.

2. RBH to FAHP, 8 Dec. 1844, RBH to Austin Birchard, 2 Feb. 1845, HPC. In 1862, during the Civil War, Olds was arrested for disloyalty and imprisoned in Fort Lafayette, but while there, he was elected to the Ohio state legislature. *Biographical Directory of the American Congress*, s.v. "Olds, Edson Baldwin"; hereafter cited as *Biog. Dir. of Cong.*

3. RBH to William G. Lane, 16 Mar. 1845, Yale University Library, copy HPC. "Dead" was slang for a complete failure in a recitation. *Oxford English Dictionary*, s.v. "Dead"; hereafter cited as *OED*.

4. RBH to William G. Lane, 16 Mar, 12 Apr. 1845, Yale University, copy HPC. Hayes granted Douglass permission to quote from his valedictory tribute. D. B. Douglass to RBH, 28 Jan. 1845, SBH to SB, 31 Mar. 1845, HPC; Parker, "Graduation Speeches," p. 137.

5. RBH to FAHP, 20 Apr. 1845, RBH, Diary, 12 Apr., 7 May 1845, in *D&L*, 1: 163–65; RBH to William G. Lane, 12 Apr. 1845, Yale University, copy HPC.

6. RBH to FAHP, 20 Apr. 1845, RBH to Janette Elliot, 20 Aug. 1846, in *D&L*, 1: 165–66, 181; RBH to William G. Lane, 11 Aug. 1845, Yale University, copy HPC.

7. RBH to William G. Lane, 12 Apr., 1 June, 11 Aug. 1845, Yale University, copy HPC; RBH, Diary, 15 Apr. 1845, RBH to FAHP, 1 June 1845, in *D&L*, 1: 163–64, 166.

8. RBH to FAHP, 20 Apr., 27 Aug. 1845, in *D&L*, 1: 165, 172; FAHP to RBH, 11 Sept. 1845, HPC.

9. RBH to SBH, 9 June, 27 Aug. 1845, in *D&L*, 1: 168, 170–71.

10. RBH to FAHP, 1 June 1845, RBH to SBH, 20 Aug. 1845, in *D&L*, 1: 167–68; RBH to William G. Lane, 11 Aug. 1845, Yale University, copy HPC.

11. RBH to William G. Lane, 1 June, 13, 22 Sept., 21 Oct. 1845, RBH to Ebenezer Lane, 22 Sept. 1845, Yale University, copies HPC; RBH to SBH, 12 Oct. 1845, in *D&L*, 1: 173–74.

12. RBH to SBH, 2 Nov. 1845, HPC; RBH to FAHP, 28 Feb. 1846, RBH, Diary, 4 Oct. 1846, in *D&L* 1: 176, 184.

13. Account by Clark Waggoner, Toledo, 4 Mar. 1885, RBH, Scrapbook, 12: 72, HPC. On hearing from Hayes about "wading in the mud, and upsetting in the stage," Sophia was grateful "to our merciful Preserver that you were kept safe from all *danger*." Fanny lovingly mocked Hayes: "Your hairbreadth escapes,—your unprecedented sufferings from hunger & fatigue awoke sympathy in many a feeling breast & with a sigh parted many a rosy lip." SBH to RBH, Feb. 1846, FAHP to RBH, 22 Feb. 1846, HPC.

14. RBH to FAHP, 28 Feb. 1846, in *D&L*, 1: 175.

15. FAHP to RBH, 22 Feb., 14 Mar. 1846, HPC; RBH to FAHP, 28 Feb. 1846, in *D&L*, 1: 175–76.

16. RBH to Ebenezer Lane, 28 Mar. 1846, Historical Society of Pennsylvania, copy HPC; RBH to William G. Lane, 11 July 1846, Yale University, copy HPC; "Buckland & Hayes," 1 Apr. 1846, WHS Papers, Ohio Historical Society, copy HPC; SBH to RBH, 13 May 1846, HPC; RBH, Diary, 4 Oct. 1846, in *D&L*, 1: 184.

17. RBH to William G. Lane, 11 July, 10 Oct. 1846, Yale University, copies HPC; RBH, Diary, 4 Oct. 1846, in *D&L*, 1: 185.

18. RBH to William G. Lane, 11 July, 10, 15 Oct. 1846, Yale University, copies HPC.

19. RBH to FAHP, 7 July 1846, in *D&L*, 1: 176–77; RBH to William G. Lane, 11 July, 10 Oct. 1846, Yale University, copies HPC; SBH to SB, 4 Aug. 1846, HPC.

20. RBH to SB, 11 Nov. 1846, HPC; RBH, Diary, 4 Oct. 1846, in *D&L*, 1: 184–85.

21. RBH, Diary, 23 Dec. 1846, in *D&L*, 1: 192–93.

22. RBH to FAHP, 27 Dec. 1846, 6 Jan. 1847, RBH, MS Diary, 1 Feb. 1847, HPC.

23. RBH to SBH, 16 Feb. 1847, RBH to FAHP, 22 Mar. 1847, in *D&L*, 1: 194–99.

24. RBH to FAHP, 13 Apr. 1847, in *D&L*, 1: 199–202.

25. Ibid., RBH to SBH, 31 May 1847, in *D&L*, 1: 199–203; RBH to Ebenezer Lane, 1, 8 June 1847, Chicago Historical Society, copies HPC; RBH to William G. Lane, 26 June 1847, Yale University, copy HPC. Pease died of tuberculosis on 2 January 1860. RBH, Diary, 5 Jan. 1860, in *D&L*, 1: 547–48.

26. RBH to SBH, 31 May 1847, RBH, Diary, 1 June, July 1847, in *D&L*, 1: 203–5, 208; RBH to Ebenezer Lane, 1, 8 June 1847, Chicago Historical Society, copies HPC.

27. RBH, Diary, 1 June 1847, in *D&L*, 1: 204–5. The wild oats he contemplated did not include sexual exploits: "Whatever other evils may befall me, I shall now remain as pure as need be." Ibid.

28. RBH to SB, 13 June 1847, RBH to FAHP, 8 Aug. 1847, in *D&L*, 1: 206–7, 213; RBH to SB, 19 June 1847, RBH to Dear Friend, 18 June 1847, SBH to SB, 19 June 1847, HPC; RBH to William G. Lane, 26 June 1847, Yale University, copy HPC.

29. SBH to SB, 18, 19 June 1847, FAHP to RBH, 15 June 1847, HPC. Barnard thinks that Hayes's illness was psychosomatic and stemmed from his "bad emotional state." He also claims that "Sardis, abetted by Fanny and Sophia, and aided by Will Platt, had reached both physicians and convinced them that it was to Hayes's benefit, regardless of his physical condition, that they advise him to abandon the war plan." Barnard offers no evidence to support this assertion that Hayes's family and physicians behaved slyly at best or unethically at worst. The evidence, on the contrary, shows that the family believed that Hayes was seriously ill and that competent physicians would not send him off to war. If Sardis had "reached" anyone, it would have been Dr. Daniel Drake, whom he urged Hayes to see, but since Sardis was unaware that Drake resided in Louisville, Kentucky (from 1840 to 1849), Sardis obviously had not contacted him. See RBH to SB, 8 June 1847, SB to RBH, 13 June 1847, HPC; *DAB*, s.v. "Drake, Daniel." For Barnard's version, see his *Hayes*, pp. 156–58, 160.

30. RBH to SB, 1 July 1847, RBH, Diary, July 1847, in *D&L*, 1: 208; RBH to Dear Friend, 18 June 1847, HPC; *DAB*, s.v. "Mussey, Reuben Dimond."

31. RBH to FAHP, 19 July 1847, RBH, Diary, July 1847, RBH to LWH, 4 Aug. 1851, in *D&L*, 1: 208–9, 379; RBH to SB, 27 June 1847, SBH to SB, 17 July 1847, HPC; Emily Apt Geer, *First Lady: The Life of Lucy Webb Hayes* (Kent and Fremont, Ohio: Kent State University Press and Rutherford B. Hayes Presidential Center, 1984), p. 7.

32. RBH to FAHP, 19 July 1847, RBH to SBH, 29 July 1847, in *D&L*, 1: 208–10; RBH, MS Diary, 4 Oct. 1847, HPC.

33. Hayes liked Martha Billings Hayes (Uncle Russell's wife), Larkin Goldsmith Mead, Dyer Bancroft ("a curious old philosopher" with whom Hayes was "amazingly pleased"), and Belinda Elliot's husband R. W. B. McLelland. In sharp contrast to these impressive in-laws was his "queer hair-brained" Uncle Roger Birchard. RBH to SBH, 29 July 1847, RBH to FAHP, 8 Aug., 23 Oct. 1847, in *D&L* 1: 210–12, 222; RBH, MS Diary, 4 Oct. 1847, HPC.

34. RBH to SBH, 29 July 1847, in *D&L* 1: 210; RBH, MS Diary, 4 Oct. 1847, HPC; *DAB*, s.v. "Noyes, John Humphrey." On the sexual practices of Noyes and his followers, see John D'Emilio and Estelle B. Freedman, *Intimate Matters: A History of Sexuality in America* (New York: Harper & Row, 1988), pp. 118–20.

35. RBH to FAHP, 8 Aug. 1847, RBH, MS Diary, 4 Oct. 1847, HPC.

36. RBH to FAHP, 8 Aug., Oct. 1847, HPC.

37. RBH to FAHP, 8, 30 Aug., 19 Sept. 1847, in *D&L*, 1:213–18; RBH to FAHP, Oct. 1847, RBH, MS Diary, 4 Oct. 1847, HPC. Camp ultimately married Fanny Perkins and brought her home to Sandusky City, Ohio, but Hayes apparently never called on them.

38. FAHP to RBH, 24 Oct. 1847, HPC.

39. RBH to SBH, 30 May 1847, in *D&L* 1: 202; RBH, MS Diary, 4 Oct. 1847, FAHP to RBH, 15 June 1847, RBH to FAHP, Oct. 1847, HPC.

40. RBH to SBH, 16 Oct. 1847, RBH to FAHP, 23 Oct. 1847, in *D&L*, 1: 220–21; FAHP to RBH, Sept. 1847, SBH to RBH, 17 Nov. 1847, HPC.

41. RBH to FAHP, 22 Nov. 1847, in *D&L* 1: 224; FAHP to Harriet Platt, 12 Jan. 1848, FAHP to RBH, 6, 17 Feb. 1848, HPC.

42. FAHP to RBH, 10 June, Oct. 1848, HPC; RBH to SBH, 18 June 1848, RBH to FAHP, 9 July 1848, RBH, Diary, 26 Sept. 1847–21 Nov. 1848, in *D&L* 1: 229–31, 234.

43. RBH to SBH, 27 Sept. 1847, RBH to FAHP, 28 Jan., 16 Apr., 9 July, 18 Sept. 1848, RBH, Diary, 26 Sept. 1847–21 Nov. 1848, in *D&L* 1: 219, 227, 229–30, 232, 234; FAHP to RBH, 4 Mar. 1848, HPC.

44. RBH to Austin Birchard, 12 Nov. 1848, HPC.

45. RBH, Diary, 21 Nov.–13 Dec. 1848, RBH to FAHP, 16 Dec. 1848, in *D&L* 1: 235–37, 240.

46. RBH, Diary, 13, 15, 18, 19 Dec. 1848, in *D&L* 1: 237–39. If Moses were not the "young Jew," the making sport of a fellow Jew would probably have made him all the more anxious to demonstrate that he would not be victimized by a cheat.

47. RBH, Diary, 16, 20 Dec. 1848, RBH to FAHP, 16 Dec. 1848, in *D&L* 1: 238–39, 241, 243–44.

48. RBH, Diary, 21–23 Dec. 1848, RBH to FAHP, 16 Dec. 1848, in *D&L* 1: 239–40, 243–44.

49. RBH, Diary, 24–25 Dec. 1848, RBH to WAP, 26 Dec. 1848, in *D&L* 1: 244–45; *DAB*, s.v. "Worth, William Jenkins."

50. RBH, Diary, 26–27 Dec. 1848, RBH to WAP, 26 Dec. 1848, in *D&L* 1: 245–46.

51. RBH, Diary, 29–30 Dec. 1848, in *D&L* 1: 246–47.

52. RBH, Diary, 25 Jan. 1849, RBH to FAHP, 1 Jan. 1849, in *D&L* 1: 248, 253.

53. RBH, Diary, 28 Dec. 1848, 2, 17, 19–24 Jan., 5 Feb. 1849, RBH to FAHP, 1 Jan. 1849, in *D&L* 1: 246–8, 251, 253, 257.

54. RBH, Diary, 18, 30 Jan. 1849, RBH to SBH, 27 Jan. 1849, in *D&L*, 1: 252, 254–55. Bryan's mother died in 1851, after having been an invalid for years. GMB to RBH, 13 Oct. 1851, HPC.

55. RBH, Diary, 7 Feb.–9 Mar. 1849, RBH to FAHP, 10 Mar. 1849, in *D&L* 1: 257–66; RBH to John R. Pease, 10 Mar. 1849, HPC.

56. RBH, Diary, 11–22 Mar. 1849, RBH to FAHP, 10 Mar. 1849, in *D&L* 1: 264–67; GMB to RBH, 13 May 1849, HPC.

57. RBH, MS Diary, 25 Mar.–6 Apr. 1849, FAHP to Anne Platt (Mrs. William C.) Hickok, Apr. 1849, RBH to George W. Jones, 26 June 1849, HPC.

58. RBH, Diary, Apr.–Dec. 1849; RBH to FAHP, 4 May 1849, RBH to SBH, 27 June, 27 Aug. 1849, in *D&L* 1: 268–70; RBH to George W. Jones, 26 June 1849, HPC.

59. RBH, Diary, Apr.–Dec. 1849, in *D&L* 1: 268; RBH to Henry Howe, 22 Jan. 1889, HPC. Croghan had successfully defended Fort Stephenson (located on the site of Fremont) on 1 August 1813 against an attack by a superior force of British and Indians and had recently (8 January 1849) died of cholera in New Orleans. *DAB*, s.v. "Croghan, George."

60. RBH, Diary, Apr.–Dec. 1849, RBH to FAHP, 9 Sept. 1849, in *D&L* 1: 268, 271.

61. RBH, Diary, Apr.–Dec. 1849, RBH to SB, 4, 6, 16 Dec. 1849, in *D&L* 1: 268, 273–74; RBH to SB, 23, 27 Dec. 1849, HPC.

Chapter 4. Cincinnati

1. RBH, Diary, 1 Jan., 12 Apr. 1850, 24 Dec. 1859, in *D&L* 1: 275, 291, 547; RBH, MS Diary, 1 Jan. 1850, HPC.

2. SBH to RBH, 31 Dec. 1850, HPC.

3. RBH, Diary, 1, 31 Jan. 1850, RBH to SB, 5 Mar. 1850, in *D&L*, 1: 275, 280–81, 288; RBH to SB, 13 Feb. 1850, HPC.

4. RBH, Diary, 8 Jan. 1850, RBH to SB, 19 Feb. 1850, in *D&L*, 1: 277, 283–84.

5. RBH to WAP, 14 Jan. 1850, RBH to SB, 19 Feb. 1850, in *D&L*, 1: 277, 285.

6. RBH, Diary, 19 Feb. 1850, 9 Jan. 1890, RBH to SB, 4 Jan., 19 Feb. 1850, RBH to WAP, 14 Jan. 1850, in *D&L*, 1: 276–78, 283–85, 4: 536–37; RBH, MS Diary, 8 Jan. 1850, RBH to SB, 16 Jan. 1850, RBH to R. C. Phillips, 3 Feb. 1871, HPC. Along with eleven friends, Ainsworth Rand Spofford (who, in 1861, would become Librarian of Congress) established the literary club in October 1849. Robert C. Vitz, *The Queen and the Arts: Cultural Life in Nineteenth-Century Cincinnati* (Kent, Ohio: Kent State University Press, 1989), pp. 54–55.

7. RBH, MS Diary, 5 Jan. 1850, HPC; RBH, Diary, 1 Jan. 1850, RBH to WAP, 14 Jan. 1850, RBH to John A. Little, 20 Jan. 1850, in *D&L*, 1: 275, 278–79.

8. RBH to FAHP, 13 Feb. 1850, RBH to SB, 5 Mar. 1850, HPC; RBH, Diary, 1, 3, 6, 11 Mar. 1850, in *D&L*, 1: 286–89.

9. RBH, Diary, 11, 17 Mar. 1850, in *D&L*, 1: 288–90.

10. RBH, Diary, 12, 17, 26 Apr., 18, 27 July 1850, in *D&L*, 1: 290–95, 318–19.

11. RBH, Diary, 8 Jan. 1851, in *D&L*, 1: 342.

12. RBH, Diary, 11 Mar., 11 May 1850, RBH to SB, 18 Apr. 1850, in *D&L*, 1: 289, 293–94, 296; FAHP to RBH, 5 May 1850, SBH to RBH, 5 May 1850, HPC.

13. RBH to SB, 18 Apr., 13, 22 May, 9 July 1850, in *D&L*, 1: 294, 297, 300, 318; RBH to SB, 11 July 1850, SBH to SB, 19 July 1850, HPC.

14. RBH to SB, 16, 30 Oct. 1850, 22, 24 May 1851, RBH, Diary, 17 June 1851, RBH to SBH, 26 July 1851, in *D&L*, 1: 325–28, 361–62, 367, 374.

15. RBH, Diary, 11 May 1850, RBH to GMB, 6 June 1850, in *D&L*, 1: 296, 310. Whittier's lines are from "Ichabod," which Hayes copied in its entirety. When in law school, Hayes applauded Joseph Story's attack on abolitionists for opposing the return of fugitive slaves to the South. RBH, Diary, 21 Dec. 1843, in *D&L*, 1: 131.

16. RBH, Diary, 3, 17 Mar., 17 Apr., 18, 20 Sept., 22 Nov., 1, 14 Dec. 1850, RBH to SB, 17 Dec. 1850, in *D&L*, 1: 286, 289, 292, 322–23, 338–41.

17. RBH, Diary, 24, 26 May 1850, RBH to FAHP, 12 June 1850, in *D&L*, 1: 301–5, 313–16; FAHP to RBH, 9 June 1850, HPC; Ralph L. Rusk, *The Life of Ralph Waldo Emerson* (New York: Charles Scribner's Sons, 1949), pp. 380–81. Emerson spoke on "Natural Aristocracy," on "Eloquence," on "The Spirit of the Age," on "England," and on "Books" and gave three additional metaphysical lectures on the identity of "Intellect and Nature."

18. RBH, Diary, 24 Oct. 1850, in *D&L*, 1: 326–27.

19. RBH, Diary, 4 May 1850, in *D&L*, 1: 295.

20. RBH, Diary, 27 July, 31 Oct. 1850, 10 June 1890, in *D&L*, 1: 319, 329, 4: 580; *Fremont Democratic Messenger*, 7 Jan. 1886.

21. RBH, Diary, 16 Nov. 1850, 8 Jan. 1851, RBH to FAHP, 20 Nov. 1850, in *D&L*, 1: 334, 337, 342–43.

22. RBH to FAHP, 7, 20 Nov. 1850, RBH to SB, 25 Nov., 5, 22 Dec. 1850, 14 Jan. 1851, RBH, Diary, 22 Nov., 9 Dec. 1850, 26 Jan., 23 April, 9, 21 May 1851, in *D&L*, 1: 331, 336, 338–341, 343–44, 356, 360.

23. RBH, Diary, 21 Nov. 1850, 26, 30 Jan., 29 Mar., 4 Apr., 15 May 1851, in *D&L*, 1: 337, 343–48, 352, 354, 357–58; FAHP to RBH, 22 Apr. 1851, HPC.

24. RBH, Diary, 4 Nov. 1850, 9, 17 Apr. 1851, RBH to FAHP, 8 June 1851, in *D&L*, 1: 330, 354–55, 363. Ik Marvel was the pseudonym of Donald Grant Mitchell. Hayes was particularly amused by Ik Marvel's tale in *Fresh Gleanings* (made popular by a Broadway musical) "of the barber and pastry cook—the barber cut the throats of his customers and the cook made their carcasses into mince pies—and the two gained great wealth thereby—and were esteemed of the aristocracy, for in those days as in ours people looked at the tax duplicate as the substitute for the herald's registry of olden times—as the registry of merit!" RBH, MS Diary, 16 July 1851, HPC.

25. RBH, Diary, 18 May 1851, in *D&L*, 1: 358; RBH, MS Diary, 18 May 1851, HPC.

26. RBH, MS Diary, 18 May 1851, HPC; RBH, Diary, 23 May 1851, in *D&L*, 1: 361–62.

27. RBH, Diary, 14 June 1851, in *D&L*, 1: 364–66.

28. RBH, Diary, 14 June 1851, RBH to LWH, 22 June 1851, in *D&L*, 1: 364–66, 368; *Fremont Daily Messenger*, 7 Jan. 1886.

29. RBH to LWH, 22 June, 19 Sept. 1851, in *D&L*, 1: 370, 397.

30. RBH to LWH, 22 June 1851, HPC; RBH to LWH, 22 June 1851, RBH, Diary, 28 July 1851, in *D&L*, 1: 367–69, 375–76. Hayes slightly misquoted the line from John Milton's "Comus." The line is: "It were a journey like the path to heaven."

31. RBH, Diary, 23, 28 July, 16, 21 Aug., 13 Oct. 1851, RBH to LWH, 21 Aug., 9, 19 Sept. 1851, RBH to SBH, 16 Oct. 1847, in *D&L*, 1: 220, 373, 375, 384–85, 387, 390–91, 393–98.

32. RBH to LWH, 21 Aug. 1851, RBH, Diary, 24 July, 13 Aug. 1851, in *D&L*, 1: 374, 383, 388–89; RBH, MS Diary, 1 Aug. 1851, HPC.

33. RBH to LWH, 21 Aug. 1851, RBH, Diary, 16, 18, 20 Aug. 1851, in *D&L*, 1: 384–87, 389.

34. RBH to FAHP, 8 Nov. 1852, in *D&L*, 1: 430–31.

35. RBH, Diary, 5 Jan., 1 Apr., 24 Sept., 14 Oct., 3 Nov. 1852, RBH to SBH, 13 Sept. 1852, RBH to SB, 4 July, 14 Sept., 2, 17, 31 Oct. 1852, RBH to FAHP, 8 Nov. 1852, in *D&L*, 1: 404, 408, 410, 420–23, 425–30; SBH to RBH, 11, 12 Feb. 1852, HPC.

36. RBH to LWH, 17 July, 22 Aug. 1852, in *D&L*, 1: 411–12, 417–18; FAHP to LWH, c. 22 Aug. 1852, HPC.

37. RBH to LWH, 10 Aug. 1851, 22 Aug. 1852, RBH to SB, 7 Sept., 22, 31 Oct., 20 Nov. 1852, in *D&L*, 1: 382, 418–19, 427–28, 434–35; FAHP to LWH, c. 22 Aug. 1852, RBH to Samuel Galloway, 19 Nov. 1852, HPC.

38. RBH to SB, 3, 19, 22 Dec. 1852, RBH to FAHP, 15 Dec. 1852, in *D&L*, 1: 435, 437–38; SBH to RBH, Dec. 1852, FAHP to RBH, 18 Dec. 1852, FAHP to Anne Platt Hickok, 7 Mar. 1853, HPC.

39. RBH, Diary, 30 Dec. 1852, in *D&L*, 1: 438; FAHP to Charlotte Birchard DeWitt, 14 Mar. 1853, HPC.

Chapter 5. Law and Family

1. RBH, Diary, 7 Jan. 1853, 31 Oct. 1871, RBH to SB, 13 Jan. 1853, in *D&L*, 1: 438–39, 3: 170. Ewing had been on the opposite side of Hayes in the Boswell case.

2. RBH, Diary, 17 Jan. 1852, in *D&L*, 1: 407.

3. RBH, Diary, 1 Apr. 1852, RBH to SB, 5 Apr. 1852, in *D&L*, 1: 408; RBH to ?, 18 Feb. 1852, RBH, MS Diary, 28 Sept. 1853, HPC; C. R. Williams, *Hayes*, 1: 89; J. J. Quinn, "Homicidal Insanity—The Case of Nancy Farrer," *Western Lancet* 16 (Nov. 1855): 654. Years later, Hayes blamed his youthful nervousness on the number of insane near relatives on both sides of his family, and he singled out his conduct in the Nancy Farrer case as

proof that he could control himself under the worst of circumstances. RBH, Diary, 4 Oct. 1892, in *D&L*, 5: 111.

4. SBH to RBH, 3 Apr. 1852, HPC.

5. RBH to SB, 5 Apr. 1852, in *D&L*, 1: 408; Cincinnati *Times*, 22? Apr. 1852 (dateline 21 Apr.), Nancy Farrer File, HPC; Quinn, "Homicidal Insanity," p. 654.

6. RBH, Diary, 20 May 1851, RBH to SB, 1 May 1852, in *D&L*, 1: 360, 409; SBH to SB, 15 May 1852, "The Governor's Decision in the Case of James Summons," 10 Mar. 1857, RBH, Scrapbook, 2: 57, HPC.

7. Pass for execution, 26 Nov. 1852, with notation by RBH, HPC; Cincinnati *Enquirer*, 27, 28 Nov. 1852. A dray is a low cart without sides; a dray pin is a stake on the sides or ends to hold a load on board.

8. RBH to SB, 15, 30 May 1852, in *D&L*, 1: 409; RBH to SB, 11 Nov. 1852, HPC.

9. RBH to SB, 22 Jan. 1853, in *D&L*, 1: 439–40; FAHP to SB, 31 Jan. 1853, HPC; C. R. Williams, *Hayes*, 1: 91.

10. RBH to SB, 22 Jan. 1853, RBH to GMB, 22 Jan. 1855, in *D&L*, 1: 439, 476; RBH to SB, 28 Jan. 1855, 30 Nov. 1856, 22 Feb. 1857, "The Governors Decision in the Case of James Summons," 10 Mar. 1857, RBH, Scrapbook, 2: 57, HPC.

11. FAHP to SB, 31 Jan. 1853, FAHP to Charlotte Birchard DeWitt, 14 Mar. 1853, HPC; RBH, Diary, 5 Aug. 1889, in *D&L*, 4: 497.

12. RBH, Diary, 14 Oct. 1852, in *D&L*, 1: 425; *Nancy Farrer v. The State of Ohio*, 2 Ohio State Reports, 54–82.

13. RBH, Diary, Dec. 1854, in *D&L*, 1: 475; Quinn, "Homicidal Insanity," pp. 654–69.

14. RBH, Diary, Feb. 1853, 11 July 1889, RBH to SB, 4 Feb. 1853, in *D&L*, 1: 440–41, 4: 486.

15. RBH, Diary, 27 Feb., 4, 11 Mar. 1853, in *D&L*, 1: 444, 446.

16. RBH, Diary, 24 Apr. 1853, in *D&L*, 1: 449.

17. RBH to SB, 25 Sept., 10, 18 Nov. 1852, 4, 9 Feb., 1 Apr. 1853, in *D&L*, 1: 422–23, 432–34, 441–42, 447–48.

18. RBH, Diary, 11 Apr. 1853, RBH to SB, 14 Apr., 18 May, 6 June 1853, RBH to Ralph Buckland, 8 June 1853, in *D&L*, 1: 448–52; RBH to SB, 4 May 1853, RBH, Memorandum, 14 June 1853, HPC. Hayes, however, felt free in 1869 "to camp on" Will Lane and his wife in Sandusky. RBH to William G. Lane, 19 July 1869, Yale University, copy HPC.

19. RBH to SB, 24 May 1853, HPC; RBH to Ralph Buckland, 8 June 1853, RBH to SB, 22 June 1853, in *D&L*, 1: 451–52.

20. RBH to SBH, 23 Oct. 1853, RBH to FAHP, 25 Dec. 1853, in *D&L*, 1: 455–56, 458; RBH to SB, 25 Dec. 1853, RBH to GMB, 9 Feb. 1854, HPC.

21. RBH, Diary, 28 June, Sept., 6 Nov. 1853, 2 July 1889, in *D&L*, 1: 453, 456, 4: 479–80; RBH to SBH, 9 Aug. 1853, RBH to SB, 8 Jan. 1854, RBH to FAHP, 4 June 1854, HPC.

22. RBH, Diary, 6 Nov. 1853, 18 Nov. 1883, RBH to GMB, 20 Nov. 1853, in *D&L*, 1: 456, 458, 4: 129; James Webb to ?, 14 June 1833, RBH to FAHP, 9 Nov. 1853, RBH to LWH, 4 Dec. 1853, RBH, MS Diary, 15, 25 Nov. 1853, HPC; C. R. Williams, *Hayes*, 1: 77–78.

23. RBH, Diary, 4 Sept. 1854, RBH to SB, 7 Apr., 1 Aug., 3, 29 Sept. 1854, in *D&L*, 1: 460, 466, 468–69; RBH to SB, 9 Sept. 1854, HPC.

24. RBH, Diary, 4 Sept. 1854, in *D&L*, 1: 468.

25. RBH, Diary, 25 Dec. 1854, in *D&L*, 1: 475; SBH to SB, 4 Jan. 1855, HPC.

26. RBH to SB, 13 Oct. 1854, in *D&L*, 1: 470.

27. RBH to LWH, 4 Sept. 1853, HPC; C. R. Williams, *Hayes*, 1: 95 n. 2; Barnard, *Hayes*, pp. 189–91.

28. Newspaper clipping, 1855, RBH, Scrapbook, 6: 70, HPC; C. R. Williams, *Hayes*, 1: 94.

29. C. R. Williams, *Hayes*, 1: 94.

30. FAHP to SB, 6 Apr. 1855, newspaper clipping, 1855, RBH, Scrapbook, 6: 70, HPC; C. R. Williams, *Hayes*, 1: 95. The Rosetta case antedated by five years the Lemmon case, which resulted in the same conclusion in New York and in which William M. Evarts played a leading role.

31. SBH to RBH and LWH, 4 Apr. 1855, FAHP to LWH, 15 Apr. 1855, RBH to LWH, 24 Mar. 1873, HPC.

32. FAHP to LPM, 6 May 1855, HPC; RBH to FAHP, 1 July 1855, in *D&L*, 1: 485–86.

33. RBH to SB, 23 Mar. 1855, HPC; RBH to W. H. Gibson, 6 May, 18, 23, 25 June 1855, Seneca County Museum, Tiffin, Ohio, copies HPC; RBH to LWH, 24 June 1855, RBH to SB, 15 July 1855, in *D&L*, 1: 483, 489. Sams (Uncle Sams) were probably nativists, Sambos were probably Free-Soilers, and Locos were former Democrats.

34. RBH, Memoranda, undated [1868–72, 1876–77], HPC; RBH, Diary, 7 Oct. 1855, RBH to SB, 14 Oct. 1855, RBH to GMB, 16 Apr. 1856, in *D&L*, 1: 491, 496–97.

35. RBH, Diary, 23 Mar. 1856, RBH to SBH, 10 June 1856, in *D&L*, 1: 496–97; RBH to SB, 20 Mar. 1856, RBH to SBH, 13 Apr. 1856, HPC.

36. RBH, Diary, July 1856, in *D&L*, 1: 498; RBH to LWH, 3 July 1856, RBH to JTW, 4, 5 July 1856, JTW to RBH, 6 July 1856, RBH to Russell Hayes, 19 July 1856, HPC.

37. RBH, Diary, July 1856, RBH to GMB, 23 July 1856, in *D&L*, 1: 498–500.

Chapter 6. Politics

1. RBH, Diary, 29 July 1856, in *D&L*, 1: 500–501; RBH to SB, 26 July, 24 Sept. 1856, HPC; RBH to WKR, 28 Sept. 1856, RBH Papers, LC, copy HPC.

2. RBH to SB, 20, 31 Aug., 8 Sept. 1856, John W. Herron to RBH, 20 Aug. 1856, R. H. Stephenson to WKR, 7 Sept. 1856, HPC; RBH to WKR, 24, 31 Aug., 28 Sept., 21 Oct. 1856, RBH Papers, LC, copies HPC.

3. RBH, Diary, 30 Oct., 2 Nov. 1856, in *D&L*, 1: 502–3; RBH to WKR, 10, 25 Nov. 1856, RBH Papers, LC, copies HPC.

4. RBH, Diary, 30 Oct., 28 Dec. 1856, in *D&L*, 1: 502, 506; RBH to WKR, 24 Aug., 28 Sept., 1856, RBH Papers, LC, copies HPC.

5. RBH, Diary, 4, 8, 25 Jan., 26 Apr. 1857, in *D&L*, 1: 508–9, 511–12; RBH to WKR, 4 Jan. 1857, RBH Papers, LC, copy HPC.

6. GMB to RBH, 1 Jan. 1857, HPC.

7. RBH to GMB, 24 Jan., 31 May, 10 July 1857, in *D&L*, 1: 510–11, 516–17, 519.

8. RBH to SBH, 21 Jan. 1857, RBH to LWH, 4 or 5 July 1857, in *D&L*, 1: 509, 518; RBH, MS Diary, 26 Apr. 1857, RBH to SB, 1 Feb. 1857, HPC.

9. RBH to SBH, 4 Oct. 1857, RBH to WAP, 8 Oct. 1857, in *D&L*, 1: 520–21; RBH to SB, 28 Sept., 2, 6, 7, 14, 16, 21, 25 Oct., 12, 22, 24, 29 Nov., 6, 17, 25 Dec. 1857, HPC.

10. RBH to LWH, 29 Nov., 4 Dec. 1857, RBH to SB, 17, 25 Dec. 1857, WAP to SB, 22 Dec. 1857, HPC; RBH to LWH, 11 Dec. 1857, RBH, Diary, 24 Nov., 25 Dec. 1857, 10 Jan. 1858, in *D&L*, 1: 521–22.

11. RBH to SB, 14 Oct., 12 Nov. 1857, HPC; RBH to LWH, 11 Dec. 1857, RBH to GMB, 5 Apr. 1858, in *D&L*, 1: 522–24; RBH to Stephen A. Douglas, 1 Jan. 1858, Stephen A. Douglas Papers, University of Chicago, copy HPC. Hayes was glad that Guy Bryan avoided the Kansas issue in his "maiden effort in the House," but Hayes might not have been so pleased if he had agreed with Bryan's views on Kansas.

12. RBH to GMB, 5 Apr. 1858, RBH, Diary, 13 June 1858, in *D&L*, 1: 524–25; RBH to SB, 31 Jan., 21 Mar. 1858, HPC.

13. RBH to SB, 21 Mar., 21 Apr. 1858, RBH to SBH, 22 June 1858, HPC.

14. RBH, Diary, 24 June, 23 July 1858, in *D&L*, 1: 525–26; RBH to SB, 6, 15, 19 July, 5 Aug. 1858, RBH to SBH, 21 July 1858, HPC.

15. RBH to LWH, 15 Sept. 1858 (misdated 1857), 2 Oct. 1858, RBH to GMB, 11 Oct. 1858, in *D&L*, 1: 520, 533–35.

16. RBH to LWH, 30 Sept., 4 Oct. 1858, in *D&L*, 1: 533–34; RBH to SB, 21 Oct. 1858, HPC.

17. RBH to WKR, 28 Sept. 1856, RBH Papers, LC, copy HPC; RBH to SB, 27 Oct. 1858, HPC; RBH to SB, 30 Nov. 1858, 17 Mar. 1861, in *D&L*, 1: 536, 2: 6; Barnard, *Hayes*, p. 201.

18. RBH, Diary, 3 Dec. 1890, in *D&L*, 4: 619; C. R. Williams, *Hayes*, 1: 108; Barnard, *Hayes*, pp. 202–3. There are discrepancies among these accounts. I have followed Williams for the most part.

19. William Disney, Cincinnati *Commercial Gazette*, 31 Jan. 1893, in C. R. Williams, *Hayes*, 1: 108; RBH to SB, 31 Dec. 1858, in *D&L*, 1: 540; RBH to Finance Committee, City Council, 13 Dec. 1858, City Solicitor, Office Records, Outgoing, 7 Jan. 1858–20 Feb. 1868, Letterpress Copies, City of Cincinnati, copy HPC.

20. RBH to SB, 9, 17 Dec. 1858, RBH, Diary, 3 Dec. 1890, in *D&L*, 1: 536–37, 4: 619.

21. RBH to N. W. Thomas, Mayor, 9 Dec. 1858, RBH to Jas. A. Blundell, 14 Mar. 1859, City Solicitor, Office Records, Outgoing, 7 Jan. 1858–20 Feb. 1868, Letterpress Copies, City of Cincinnati, copies HPC; RBH to SB, 24 June 1859, HPC.

22. RBH to Board of City Improvements, 13, 20 Dec. 1858, RBH to City Council, 12 Jan. 1859, City Solicitor, Office Records, Outgoing, 7 Jan. 1858 to 20 Feb. 1868, Letterpress Copies, City of Cincinnati, copies HPC.

23. RBH to SB, 24 June, 12, 23 Aug. 1859, HPC; RBH to SBH, 5 Apr. 1859, in *D&L*, 1: 540–41; Barnard, *Hayes*, pp. 63, 203.

24. RBH to LWH, 17 July 1852, RBH to M. F. Round, 30 Aug. 1889, in *D&L*, 1: 412, 4: 505–6.

25. RBH to SB, 27 Apr., 5 May, 23, 31 July, 30 Oct. 1859, SB to RBH, 7, 12 July 1859, RBH to SBH, 17 July 1859, HPC; RBH to SBH, 2 Dec. 1859, in *D&L*, 1: 545.

26. RBH to SB, 26 Sept. 1859, HPC; RBH, Diary, 23 Oct. 1859, in *D&L*, 1: 544.

27. RBH, MS Diary, 26 Dec. 1859, 5 Jan. 4, 20 Feb. 1860, RBH to SB, 26 Feb. 1860, HPC; RBH to SB, 4 Feb. 1860, RBH, Diary, 15 Apr. 1860, in *D&L*, 1: 551, 554.

28. RBH to A. P. Russell, 14 Sept. 1859, Whelpley Collection, Cincinnati Historical Society, copy HPC. Hayes knew that Russell would convey this information to Lincoln.

29. "Our Two Greatest Presidents," interview, c. 1892, HPC. At the McCormick reaper trial, Edwin M. Stanton and his associates snubbed Lincoln, but Hayes could "not recall anything" about Lincoln "being snubbed."

30. Ibid., RBH to LPM, 17 Oct. 1859, HPC; C. R. Williams, *Hayes*, 1: 111. Barnard, *Hayes*, pp. 108–9, mistakenly places Lincoln's visit in his presidential campaign of 1860.

31. RBH to LPM, 20 Apr. 1860, 1 Apr. 1875, HPC.

32. RBH to LWH, 5 July 1860, in *D&L*, 1: 559–60. Hayes had recently purchased Robert Burton's *The Anatomy of Melancholy* "to muse over." RBH, MS Diary, 22 Jan. 1860, HPC.

33. RBH to SB, 6 June 1860, RBH to JTW, 26 Aug. 1860, RBH, MS Diary, 9 Sept. 1860, HPC; RBH to SBH, 2, 8 Sept. 1860, in *D&L*, 1: 562–63.

34. RBH to SB, 11, 23 May, 20, 30 Sept. 1860, RBH, Diary, 24 June, 29 Sept. 1860, in *D&L*, 1: 555, 557–58, 563–64.

35. RBH to SB, 7, 15 Oct. 1860, in *D&L*, 1: 564–65; RBH to LPM, 9 Oct. 1860, RBH to SB, 30 Oct. 1860, HPC.

36. RBH, Diary, 6 Nov. 1860, in *D&L*, 1: 566.

Chapter 7. War

1. RBH to SB, 9 Dec. 1860, in *D&L*, 1: 567; RBH to SB, 21 Dec. 1860, HPC.

2. RBH, Diary, 4 Jan. 1861, in *D&L*, 2: 2.

3. RBH to SB, 12 Jan. 1861, in *D&L*, 2: 3–4.

4. RBH, Diary, 27 Jan. 1861, in *D&L*, 2: 4.

5. RBH to SB, 13, 15 Feb. 1861, in *D&L*, 2: 4–5; SBH to SB, 26 Feb. 1861, RBH to LPM, 13 Feb. 1861, HPC. Hayes especially wanted his cousin Elinor Mead, who was a newspaper correspondent in Columbus that winter, to observe Lincoln's bow. (She later married William Dean Howells.)

6. RBH to SB, 15 Feb. 1861, in *D&L*, 2: 5–6.

7. RBH to SB, 17, 24, 29 Mar. 1861, in *D&L*, 2: 6–7; RBH to LPM, 1 Apr. 1861, HPC.

8. RBH to SB, 2, 10 Apr. 1861, in *D&L*, 2: 8.

9. RBH to SB, 15 Apr. 1861, RBH, Diary, 10 May 1861, in *D&L*, 2: 9, 16; C. R. Williams, *Hayes*, 1: 120.

10. RBH to SB, 15, 20 Apr. 1861, in *D&L*, 2: 9–10. Joseph Rockwell Swan was a distinguished jurist, and John W. Andrews was an outstanding lawyer.

11. RBH to SB, 19, 20, 23, 25 [28], 30 Apr. 1861, RBH, Memorandum, Apr. 1861, RBH, Diary, 9 Jan. 1890, in *D&L*, 2: 9–12, 4: 536–37.

12. RBH to GMB, 8 May 1861, RBH to SB, 12 May 1861, in *D&L*, 2: 13, 17.

13. RBH to GMB, 8 May 1861, in *D&L*, 2: 13–15.

14. RBH to GMB, 8 May 1861, RBH, Diary, 15 May 1861, in *D&L*, 2: 14–15, 17.

15. RBH to SB, 16, 23, 26, 31 May, 5, 9, 10 June 1861, RBH, Diary, 19 May 1861, in *D&L*, 2: 17–21.

16. RBH to SB, 9, 10, 12 June 1861, RBH to LWH, 10 June 1861, in *D&L*, 2: 21, 23–24.

17. RBH, Diary, 10, 13 June 1861, RBH to LWH, 10 June 1861, RBH to JTW, 10 June 1861, RBH to MFF, 10, 12 June 1861, in *D&L*, 2: 22–28.

18. RBH to JTW, 10 June 1861, RBH to MFF, 12 June 1861, RBH to SB, 14 June 1861, RBH, Diary, 13 June 1861, in *D&L*, 2: 22, 24–25, 27.

19. RBH, Diary, 13 June 1861, RBH to LWH, 16 June 1861, in *D&L*, 2: 27–28, 30.

20. RBH, Diary, 16 June 1861, RBH to LWH, 16 June 1861, in *D&L*, 2: 28–30; RBH to SBH, 15 June 1861, HPC.

21. RBH to LWH, 16 June 1861, RBH to SB, 20 June 1861, in *D&L*, 2: 29–30, 32.

22. RBH to SB, 20, 28 June 1861, RBH to LWH, 30 June 1861, in *D&L*, 2: 32, 34–35.

23. RBH to LWH, 27, 30 June, 2, 6 July 1861, RBH to SB, 5 July 1861, RBH, Diary, 23 July 1861, in *D&L*, 2: 33–37, 41.

24. RBH to Salmon P. Chase, 29 June 1861, Chase Papers, LC, copy HPC; RBH to SB, 18 July 1861, in *D&L*, 2: 38–39; T. Harry Williams, *Hayes of the Twenty-third: The Civil War Volunteer Officer* (New York: Alfred A. Knopf, 1965), pp. 45–46.

25. RBH to LWH, 6 July 1861, RBH to SB, 11, 21 July 1861, in *D&L*, 2: 37–39; RBH to SB, 14 July 1861, HPC. Jacob Ammen's brother Daniel, a renowned naval officer, also became Hayes's friend.

26. RBH, Diary, 22, 23 July 1861, in *D&L*, 2: 40–41.

27. RBH, Diary, 24, 25 July 1861, RBH to SB, 23, 24 July 1861, in *D&L*, 2: 42–44; SBH to SB, 25 July 1861, HPC.

28. RBH, Diary, 27 July 1861, RBH to LWH, 27 July 1861, in *D&L*, 2: 45–46.

29. RBH, Diary, 28, 29 July 1861, in *D&L*, 2: 47.

30. RBH to SB, 30 July 1861, RBH to LWH, 30 July 1861, in *D&L*, 2: 48–50.

31. RBH, Diary, 1–7 Aug. 1861, RBH to LWH, 1, 15 Aug. 1861, RBH to LPM, 4 Aug. 1861, RBH to SBH, 6 Aug. 1861, in *D&L*, 2: 52–58, 66–67.

32. RBH, Diary, 12, 13, 15, 17 Aug. 1861, RBH to SB, 17 Aug. 1861, RBH to LWH, 17 Aug. 1861, in *D&L*, 2: 63–65, 67–68, 70.

33. RBH, Diary, 18–20, 22–24, 26–28 Aug. 1861, RBH to LWH, 17, 22, 24, 25, 26, 30 Aug. 1861, RBH to SBH, 21 Aug. 1861, RBH to SB, 26 Aug. 1861, in *D&L*, 2: 71–82.

34. RBH to LWH, 5 Sept. 1861, in *D&L*, 2: 85–87.

35. RBH, Diary, 1, 4 Sept., 1 Oct. 1861, in *D&L*, 2: 83, 104.

36. RBH, Diary, 6–10 Sept. 1861, RBH to LWH, 11 Sept. 1861, RBH to SB, 14 Sept. 1861, in *D&L*, 2: 87–92; RBH, "Sept. 10th 1861 — Carnifex Ferry," HPC.

37. RBH to SB, 14 Sept. 1861, RBH to LWH, 15, 19 Sept. 1861, in *D&L*, 2: 92–94, 96.

38. RBH to LWH, 11, 15 Sept. 1861, RBH to SB, 14 Sept. 1861, in *D&L*, 2: 90, 92–94.

39. RBH, Diary, 5, 19, 20 Sept. 1861, RBH to LWH, 19 A.M., 19 P.M., 22, 27 Sept., 3, 9 Oct. 1861, RBH to SB, 3 Oct. 1861, in *D&L*, 2: 87, 95–97, 99–100, 103, 106–7, 111; General Orders — No. 22, Army of Western Virginia, 19 Sept. 1861, HPC.

40. RBH to LWH, 7 Oct. 1861, RBH to WAP, 9 Oct. 1861, in *D&L*, 2: 108–9, 112–14.

41. RBH to LWH, 7, 18 Oct. 1861, RBH to SB, 27 Oct. 1861, in *D&L*, 2: 108–9, 118, 123.

42. RBH to LWH, 19, 21, 27 Oct. 1861, RBH to SB, 27 Oct. 1861, in *D&L*, 2: 119–26; SB to RBH, 21 Oct. 1861, HPC.

43. RBH to SB, 19, 27 Oct., 4 Nov. 1861, RBH, Diary, 29 Oct., 3, 12 Nov. 1861, in *D&L*, 2: 121, 123, 127, 136–37, 145.

44. RBH, Diary, 29 Oct., 3 Nov. 1861, in *D&L*, 2: 126–27, 136.

45. RBH, Diary, 13–18 Nov. 1861, RBH to LWH, 19 Nov. 1861, RBH to SBH, 25 Nov. 1861, in *D&L*, 2: 145–49.

46. RBH, MS Diary, 24–27, 29 Nov. 1861, HPC; RBH, Diary, 31 Oct., 8, 22 Nov. 1861, RBH to SBH, 9 Nov. 1861, in *D&L*, 2: 133, 139–40, 142, 150.

47. RBH, Diary, 29 Oct. 1861, in *D&L*, 2: 127–28.

Chapter 8. War in Earnest

1. RBH, Diary, 28 Nov. 1861, RBH to LPM, 29 Nov. 1861, in *D&L*, 2: 151–53.

2. RBH, Diary, 1, 2, 5, 7 Dec. 1861, RBH to LWH, 2 Dec. 1861, in *D&L*, 2: 155–56.

3. RBH, Diary, 6, 16 Dec. 1861, in *D&L*, 2: 156, 159–60.

4. RBH, Diary, 31 Oct., 30 Nov., 5, 17, 25 Dec. 1861, in *D&L*, 2: 133, 154, 156, 160–61, 168. Moore did resign in March 1862. RBH, Diary, 10 Mar. 1862, in *D&L*, 2: 205.

5. RBH, Diary, 15, 23, 26, 31 Dec. 1861, RBH to LWH, 29 Dec. 1861, 12–13, 16 Jan. 1862, in *D&L*, 2: 158, 165, 169, 171–72, 185–86, 189.

6. RBH, Diary, 21 Dec. 1861, in *D&L*, 2: 164–65. Bullock had a three-year-old nephew in New York named Theodore Roosevelt.

7. RBH, Diary, 22 Dec. 1861, 2 Jan. 1862, in *D&L*, 2: 165, 173–74.

8. RBH, Diary, 2, 15 Jan. 1862, RBH to LWH, 27 Nov. 1861, RBH to SB, 19 Dec. 1861, 16 Jan. 1862, in *D&L*, 2: 151, 163, 173, 188–89.

9. RBH, Diary, 28 Jan., 1–4 Feb. 1862, in *D&L*, 2: 195, 197–98.

10. RBH, Diary, 13 Dec. 1861, in *D&L*, 2: 158. A photograph dated 22 February 1860 shows Hayes with a neatly trimmed beard. *D&L*, 1: 552 facing.

11. RBH, Diary, 4, 11, 17 Feb. 1862, RBH to LWH, 14 Feb. 1862, RBH to SB, 18 Feb. 1862, RBH to SBH, 22 Feb. 1862, in *D&L*, 2: 198–200.

12. RBH, Diary, 28 Feb., 8, 12 Mar. 1862, RBH to LWH, 1, 9, 13 Mar. 1862, in *D&L*, 2: 201, 204–7.

13. RBH, Diary, 17 Jan., 13, 21 Mar. 1862, RBH to LWH, 22 Mar. 1862, in *D&L*, 2: 190, 206, 213–15.

14. RBH, Diary, 27 Mar. 1862, in *D&L*, 2: 218–19.

15. RBH, Diary, 22, 24 Jan., 17 Mar., 4 Apr. 1862, in *D&L*, 2: 193, 210–11, 223; T. H. Williams, *Hayes of the Twenty-third*, p. 103.

16. RBH, Diary, 12 Mar., 8, 20 Apr. 1862, RBH to LWH, 20 Apr. 1862, in *D&L*, 2: 205, 225, 231–33.

17. RBH, Diary, 1, 5 May 1862, RBH to LWH, 2 May 1862, RBH to Scammon, 4, 5 May 1862, in *D&L*, 2: 238–40, 245–49, 251.

18. RBH, Diary, 29 Apr., 6, 7 May 1862, RBH to Scammon, 8 A.M. 5, 5, 4:30 A.M. 8 May 1862, in *D&L*, 2: 237, 251–55, 258.

19. RBH, Diary, 8–11 May 1862, RBH to Scammon, 7, 4:30 A.M. 8, 7 P.M. 8, 9, 11 May 1862, RBH to LWH, 11, 26 May 1862, RBH to FAH, 10 May 1887, in *D&L*, 2: 255–67, 280, 4: 324.

20. RBH to LWH, 11–12 May 1862, RBH, Diary, 17 May 1862, in *D&L*, 2: 267–68, 271.

21. RBH to SB, 20 May 1862, RBH to LWH, 20 May 1862, RBH, Diary, 18, 20 May 1862, in *D&L*, 2: 271–74.

22. RBH to LWH, 20 May, 3 June 1862, RBH, Diary, 24 May 1862, in *D&L*, 2: 274, 277, 285.

23. RBH to LWH, 26 May, 12 June 1862, RBH, Diary, 31 May, 2, 16 June 1862, in *D&L*, 2: 280, 283–84, 288–89, 291.

24. RBH, Diary, 31 May, 2, 5 June 1862, in *D&L*, 2: 283–84, 286; Allan Peskin, *Garfield: A Biography* (Kent, Ohio: Kent State University Press, 1978), pp. 137–40.

25. RBH, Diary, 1 June 1862, RBH to LWH, 12 June 1862, in *D&L*, 2: 284, 288.

26. RBH to SBH, 10 July 1862, RBH, Diary, 7, 10 July 1862, in *D&L*, 2: 298–300.

27. RBH, Diary, 1, 3, 7, 8 July 1862, RBH to LWH, 6, 14 July 1862, in *D&L*, 2: 295–96, 298–99, 303.

28. RBH, Diary, 11, 13 July 1862, RBH to LWH, 14 July 1862, in *D&L*, 2: 301–2.

29. RBH, Diary, 23, 29 July 1862, RBH to LWH, 23–24 July, 6 Aug. 1862, in *D&L*, 2: 307–9, 312, 317.

30. RBH, Diary, 24, 26 July, 6, 7 Aug. 1862, RBH to LWH, 7 Aug. 1862, RBH to SB, 8 Aug. 1862, in *D&L*, 2: 309–12, 315–20. The diary says that eight men nearly died, but Hayes's letter to Lucy says that five appeared to be dead before being doused.

31. RBH, Diary, 9–12 Aug. 1862, RBH to LWH, 10 Aug. 1862, RBH to SB, 12 Aug. 1862, in *D&L*, 2: 321–27.

32. RBH to LWH, 18–19 Aug. 1862, in *D&L*, 2: 328–29

33. RBH, Diary, 25–30 Aug. 1862, RBH to LWH, 25, 30 Aug. 1862, RBH to SB, 25 Aug. 1862, in *D&L*, 2: 330–33.

34. RBH, Diary, 2 Sept. 1862, RBH to LWH, 1, 4 Sept. 1862, RBH to SBH, 1 Sept. 1862, in *D&L*, 2: 336–39, 343.

35. RBH, Diary, 27 June, 1–3 Sept. 1862, RBH to SB, 3 Sept. 1862, RBH to LWH, 4 Sept. 1862, in *D&L*, 2: 294, 335, 339–41, 344.

36. RBH to SB, 3 Sept. 1862, RBH to LWH, 4 Sept. 1862, in *D&L*, 2: 340–41, 343–44.

37. RBH, Diary, 5, 6, 7 Sept. 1862, RBH to SB, 6 Sept. 1862, RBH to LWH, 6 Sept. 1862, in *D&L*, 2: 345–46.

38. RBH, Diary, 7, 8 Sept. 1862, in *D&L*, 2: 346–47; RBH to Jacob D. Cox, 8 Sept. 1882, in C. R. Williams, *Hayes*, 1: 195.

39. RBH, Diary, 7, 8 Sept. 1862, RBH to SB, 8 Sept. 1862, in *D&L*, 2: 347–49.

40. RBH to LWH, 10 Sept. 1862, in *D&L*, 2: 350–51.

41. RBH to LWH, 13 Sept. 1862, RBH to SB, 13 Sept. 1862, in *D&L*, 2: 352–53.

42. Kenneth P. Williams, *Lincoln Finds a General: A Military Study of the Civil War*, 5 vols. (New York: Macmillan, 1949–59), 1: 376–82. Cox's division was used to "bad roads and rugged, wooded mountains."

43. RBH, Diary, 18 Sept., 8 Dec. 1862, in *D&L*, 2: 355–57, 372; RBH, "South Mountain," JTW to SB, 15 Sept. 1862, JTW to Maria Cook Webb, 15 Sept. 1862, HPC; Geer, *First Lady*, p. 56.

Chapter 9. Western Virginia Interlude

1. T. H. Williams, *Hayes of the Twenty-third*, pp. 139–40; C. R. Williams, *Hayes*, 1: 200–201; K. P. Williams, *Lincoln Finds a General*, 1: 381–83; JTW to Maria Cook Webb, 15 Sept. 1862, HPC.

2. RBH to WAP, 15 Sept. 1862, RBH to Maria Cook Webb, 15 Sept. 1862, RBH to SBH, 16 Sept. 1862, RBH, Diary, 18 Sept. 1862, in *D&L*, 2: 353–54, 357; JTW to SB, 15 Sept. 1862, HPC. Ella was probably a Rudy daughter.

3. RBH to SBH, 16, 18 Sept. 1862, RBH, Diary, 18 Sept. 1862, in *D&L*, 2: 354, 357–58; RBH, "South Mountain," HPC.

4. RBH, Diary, 19–20 Sept. 1862, in *D&L*, 2: 358; JTW to SB, 19–20 Sept. 1862, HPC.

5. LWH, "Lucy's Search for Her Husband," HPC; Geer, *First Lady*, pp. 56–58; RBH to LWH, 14 Dec. 1862, RBH, Diary, 12 Dec. 1862, in *D&L*, 2: 373–75.

6. RBH to SB, 26 Sept., 1 Oct. 1862, RBH to SBH, 26 Sept., 1 Oct. 1862, RBH, Diary, 4 Oct. 1862, in *D&L*, 2: 359–61; RBH to SBH, 4 Oct. 1862, in C. R. Williams, *Hayes*, 1: 203.

7. J. D. Cox to RBH, 2 Oct. 1862, in C. R. Williams, *Hayes*, 1: 202; RBH, "South Mountain," J. M. Comly to RBH, 5 Oct. 1862, HPC.

8. RBH to SB, 23 Oct. 1862, in *D&L*, 2: 362; John W. Herron to RBH, 25 Sept. 1862, RBH, "South Mountain," HPC; C. R. Williams, *Hayes*, 1: 203.

9. RBH to SB, 17, 23, 31 Oct., 8, 12, Nov. 1862, in *D&L*, 2: 362–64.

10. RBH to SBH, 24 Nov. 1862, RBH to LWH, 1 Dec. 1862, RBH, Diary, 2 Dec. 1862, in *D&L*, 2: 364, 366–68.

11. RBH to LWH, 14 Dec. 1862, RBH, Diary, 4 Dec. 1862, in *D&L*, 2: 370, 375; RBH, MS Diary, 14 Dec. 1862, HPC.

12. RBH to LWH, 8, 14, 28 Dec. 1862, RBH to SB, 5 Dec. 1862, RBH, Diary, 3–5, 8, 12, 15, 17 Dec. 1862, in *D&L*, 2: 370–75, 381.

13. RBH to LWH, 8, 28, 31 Dec. 1862, RBH to SBH, 22 Dec. 1862, RBH, Diary, 19 Dec. 1862, in *D&L*, 2: 372, 376, 379, 381–82.

14. RBH to SB, 20 Dec. 1862, 12 Jan. 1863, RBH, Diary, 18, 20 Dec. 1862, 24 Mar. 1863, in *D&L*, 2: 376–78, 388, 397. On Hayes's reading, see RBH to LWH, 14 Dec. 1862, 4 Jan. 1863, RBH, Diary, 22–23 Dec. 1862, 17 Jan. 1863, in *D&L*, 2: 374–75, 379–80, 384, 390.

15. RBH to SBH, 25 Jan. 1863, RBH to SB, 8, 24 Feb., 4, 9 Mar. 1863, RBH, Diary, 11, 17–18 Jan., 18–19 Feb., 15, 22 Mar. 1863, in *D&L*, 2: 387, 390–95.

16. RBH to LWH, 21 Mar., 1 Apr., 2, 7 May 1863, RBH to SB, 22 Mar. 1863, RBH to SBH, 22 Mar. 1863, RBH, Diary, 7 Jan., 15 Mar., 22 Apr. 1863, in *D&L*, 2: 387, 394–96, 401, 406–9.

17. RBH, Diary, 24, 27 Mar. 1863, RBH to SB, [4?] May 1863 (misdated 20 May), 17 May 1863, in *D&L*, 2: 397–98, 410.

18. RBH to LWH, 17 May 1863, RBH to SB, 25 May, 14–15, 25 June 1863, RBH to SBH, 19 June 1863, RBH, Diary, 25 June, 1 July 1863, in *D&L*, 2: 409, 411–15; Geer, *First Lady*, p. 64.

19. RBH to LWH, 6 July 1863, RBH to SB, [4?] May, 1, 6 July 1863, RBH to SBH, 8 July 1863, RBH, Diary, 7 July 1863, in *D&L*, 2: 410, 415–17. Lincoln also thought that Meade, a Pennsylvanian, would fight well on his "dunghill," but he disliked references to "our soil" and "their soil," since the soil controlled by the Confederacy was "our soil."

20. RBH to LWH, 16 July 1863, RBH to SBH, 16 July 1863, RBH, Diary, 9–12, 16 July 1863, in *D&L*, 2: 417–19.

21. RBH to LWH, 22 July 1863, RBH to SB, 22 July 1863, RBH, Diary, 22 July 1863, in *D&L*, 2: 420–21; C. R. Williams, *Hayes*, 1: 210–12.

22. RBH to LWH, 26 July, 15, 23 Aug., 4 Sept. 1863, RBH to SB, 6 Aug. 1863, RBH, Diary, 19 Aug. 1863, in *D&L*, 2: 424, 427–29, 432; Geer, *First Lady*, p. 66.

23. RBH to SB, 12 Jan., 25 Aug. 1863, RBH, Diary, 11 Jan., 21, 30 Sept. 1863, in *D&L*, 2: 387–88, 430, 436–37.

24. RBH to LWH, 11 Sept. 1863, RBH to SB, 24 Sept., 7, 19, 21 Oct. 1863, RBH to SBH, 28 Sept., 10 Oct. 1863, RBH to BAH, 2 Oct. 1863, in *D&L*, 2: 434–41; Geer, *First Lady*, p. 69. The poem "Casabianca" by Felicia Dorothea Hemans immortalized the boy who "stood [with his dying father] on the burning deck, / Whence all but he had fled."

25. RBH, Diary, 15 Oct. 1863, in *D&L*, 2: 440.

26. RBH to SBH, 25 Oct. 1863, RBH to SB, 8 Nov. 1863, RBH, Diary, 18 Dec. 1863, in *D&L*, 2: 442, 445, 447; C. R. Williams, *Hayes*, 1: 214–15.

27. RBH, Diary, 31 Oct., 7 Nov. 1863, 18 Jan. 1864, RBH to SBH, 1 Nov. 1863, RBH to SB, 1 Jan. 1864, in *D&L*, 2: 443–44, 449–50; Cincinnati *Gazette*, 14 Feb. 1864.

28. RBH, Diary, 21 Nov. 1863, RBH to SBH, 17 Jan., 29 Feb., 26 Mar. 1864, RBH to SB, 7 Oct. 1863, 24 Jan., 7 Feb., 11 Mar. 1864, in *D&L*, 2: 439, 445, 449–52; Geer, *First Lady*, p. 69.

29. RBH to SB, 3, 20 Apr. 1864, RBH to SBH, 9, 24 Apr., 1 May 1864, RBH, Diary, 26 Apr. 1864, in *D&L*, 2: 453–55.

30. RBH to LWH, 1 May 1864, RBH, Diary, 1 Jan. 1890, in *D&L*, 2: 455, 4: 535, D. B. Ainger to William T. Crump, 20 Mar. 1890, HPC; Geer, *First Lady*, p. 70.

Chapter 10. The Valleys of Virginia

1. RBH, Diary, 2–5 May 1864, in *D&L*, 2: 455–56; RBH, "Cloyd Mountain," HPC; T. H. Williams, *Hayes of the Twenty-third*, pp. 170–71.

2. RBH, Diary, 6–8 May 1864, in *D&L*, 2: 456; RBH, "Cloyd Mountain," HPC.

3. RBH, Diary, 9 May 1864, RBH to LWH, 13, 19 May 1864, RBH to SB, 19 May 1864, in *D&L*, 2: 456–58, 461–64; RBH, "Cloyd Mountain," HPC; T. H. Williams, *Hayes of the Twenty-third*, pp. 174–80.

4. RBH, Diary, 10 May 1864, RBH to LWH, 19 May 1864, in *D&L*, 2: 457, 462–63; RBH, "Cloyd Mountain," HPC; T. H. Williams, *Hayes of the Twenty-third*, pp. 180–81.

5. T. H. Williams, *Hayes of the Twenty-third*, pp. 181–83. Williams is mildly critical of Crook for not pushing up the railroad to Staunton.

6. RBH, Diary, 10–12, 20 May 1864, in *D&L*, 2: 457–58, 464; RBH, MS Diary, 12 May 1864, HPC; T. H. Williams, *Hayes of the Twenty-third*, pp. 184–85.

7. RBH, Diary, 13–18 May 1864, in *D&L*, 2: 458–61; T. H. Williams, *Hayes of the Twenty-third*, pp. 185–86.

8. RBH, Diary, 19, 21 May 1864, RBH to LWH, 19, 25 May 1864, RBH to SB, 19 May 1864, in *D&L*, 2: 461–66.

9. RBH, Diary, 31 May 1864, RBH to LWH, 25, 29 May, 8 June 1864, RBH to SB, 26, 29 May 1864, in *D&L*, 2: 465–69, 472. When little Webb sent Crook his love via a letter from Lucy, Crook told Hayes, "Webb is a fine boy." He prophesied (with uncanny accuracy, considering Webb would win the Congressional Medal of Honor), "He will make a soldier."

10. RBH, Diary, 1–8 June 1864, RBH to LWH, 8, 9 June 1864, in *D&L*, 2: 469–73.

11. RBH, Diary, 12 June 1864, RBH to LWH, 12 June, 2 July 1864, in *D&L*, 2: 473–74, 478–79; T. H. Williams, *Hayes of the Twenty-third*, pp. 193–94.

12. RBH, Diary, 30 June 1864, in *D&L*, 2: 474–75; T. H. Williams, *Hayes of the Twenty-third*, pp. 195–97.

13. RBH, Diary, 30 June 1864, in *D&L*, 2: 474–75; T. H. Williams, *Hayes of the Twenty-third*, pp. 198–201.

14. RBH to LWH, 30 June, 2, 5 July 1864, RBH to SB, 30 June, 2 July 1864, RBH to SBH, 30 June 1864, in *D&L*, 2: 475–81.

15. RBH to LWH, 2 July 1864, in *D&L*, 2: 478–79; William Ernest Smith, *The Francis Preston Blair Family in Politics*, 2 vols. (New York: Macmillan, 1933), 2: 271–76. To Montgomery Blair's dismay, Gen. Benjamin F. Butler burned Confederate Secretary of War James A. Seddon's house near Fredericksburg in retaliation.

16. RBH to SBH, 2, 12 July 1864, RBH, Diary, 7 July 1864, in *D&L*, 2: 480, 482; RBH, MS Diary, 8–17 July 1864, HPC.

17. RBH to LWH, 20 July 1864, RBH, Diary, 17–24 July 1864, in *D&L*, 2: 484–85.

18. RBH, Diary, 24 July 1864, RBH to LWH, 26 July 1864, in *D&L*, 2: 485–86; RBH to C. B. Hayslip, 8 Aug. 1864, RBH, "Winchester," HPC; T. H. Williams, *Hayes of the Twenty-third*, pp. 218–20.

19. RBH, Diary, 24–26 July 1864, RBH to LWH, 26 July 1864, in *D&L*, 2: 485–87; RBH, "Winchester," JTW to Maria Cook Webb, 28 July 1864, HPC; T. H. Williams, *Hayes of the Twenty-third*, pp. 220–23.

20. RBH, Diary, 27–29 July 1864, RBH to LWH, 29 July 1864, RBH to SB, 30 July 1864, in *D&L*, 2: 487–88.

21. RBH, MS Diary, 30–31 July 1864, HPC; RBH to LWH, 2 Aug. 1864, RBH to SB, 30–31 July 1864, in *D&L*, 2: 487–89.

22. RBH, Diary, 5 Aug. 1864, RBH to LWH, 2, 8 Aug. 1864, in *D&L*, 2: 489–90, 492; RBH to BAH, 4 Aug. 1864, JTW to WCH and RPH, 4 Aug. 1864, HPC. The law permitted draftees who did not wish to serve to hire someone to take their place.

23. RBH to LWH, 8 Aug. 1864, in *D&L*, 2: 492; RBH, MS Diary, 6–8 Aug. 1864, HPC; T. H. Williams, *Hayes of the Twenty-third*, p. 233.

24. RBH, MS Diary, 8–27 Aug. 1864, HPC; T. H. Williams, *Hayes of the Twenty-third*, pp. 234–39; RBH to LWH, 23 Aug. 1864, RBH to SB, 27 Aug. 1864, in *D&L*, 2: 495–96, 498.

25. RBH, MS Diary, 28 Aug.–2 Sept. 1864, HPC; RBH to Scott Cook, 22 Aug. 1864, Scott Cook Collection, Western Reserve Historical Society, copy HPC; RBH to LWH, 8, 23 Aug., 1 Sept. 1864, RBH to WHS, 24 Aug. 1864, RBH to SB, 30 July, 30 Aug. 1864, in *D&L*, 2: 488, 493, 496–97, 500–502. Hayes's presence in Ohio was not crucial for the Union (Republican) party there, but capable officers in Sherman's army, such as John A. Logan of Illinois and Frank Blair of Missouri, were also major political players and better served the Union at the hustings than at the front.

26. RBH to P. G. Bier, 12 Sept. 1864, RBH, MS Diary, 3–4 Sept. 1864, RBH, "Berryville," HPC; RBH to LWH, 4 Sept. 1864, in *D&L*, 2: 503; T. H. Williams, *Hayes of the Twenty-third*, pp. 240–42.

27. RBH to LWH, 4 Sept. 1864, in *D&L*, 2: 502–3.

28. RBH to SB, 6 Sept. 1864, in *D&L*, 2: 503–4.

29. RBH, MS Diary, 4–19 Sept. 1864, HPC; RBH to LWH, 9, 13, 17 Sept. 1864, RBH to SB, 12 Sept. 1864, in *D&L*, 2: 504–7.

30. RBH to P. G. Bier, 13 Oct. 1864, RBH to ?, 20 May 1865, HPC; RBH to LWH, 17, 21 Sept. 1864, RBH to SB, 26 Sept., 20 Dec. 1864, in *D&L*, 2: 507–11, 513–14, 551; T. H. Williams, *Hayes of the Twenty-third*, pp. 245–64.

31. RBH, MS Diary, 20–22 Sept. 1864, 7 Sept. 1883, RBH to P. G. Bier, 14 Oct. 1864, RBH, "Fisher's Hill," Russell Hastings, "The Battle of Fisher Hill: Fought 22d Sept.

1864," HPC; RBH to LWH, 26 Sept. 1864, RBH to SB, 26 Sept. 1864, in *D&L*, 2: 513–14; T. H. Williams, *Hayes of the Twenty-third*, pp. 265–75. Sheridan relieved Averell of his command. Although Williams uncritically worships Sheridan, he criticizes Hayes for uncritically worshiping Crook.

32. RBH, MS Diary, 23–29 Sept. 1864, HPC; RBH to LWH, 27–29 Sept., 1–2 Oct. 1864, RBH to SB, 27 Sept. 1864, RBH to SBH, 27 Sept. 1864, in *D&L*, 2: 515–16, 518–21.

33. RBH, MS Diary, 1–10 Oct. 1864, HPC; RBH to LWH, 1, 2, 10 Oct. 1864, RBH to SBH, 2 Oct. 1864, RBH to Matthew Scott Cook, 12 Oct. 1864, in *D&L*, 2: 519–24.

34. RBH, MS Diary, 11 Oct. 1864, HPC; RBH, Diary, 13–15, 17–18, Oct. 1864, 1 Sept. 1889, RBH to LWH, 15 Oct. 1864, RBH to SBH, 15 Oct. 1864, RBH to SB, 15 Oct. 1864, in *D&L*, 2: 524–27, 4: 506.

35. RBH, Diary, 19 Oct. 1864, RBH to LWH, 21 Oct. 1864, RBH to SB, 21 Oct. 1864, RBH to John M. Gould, 10 Jan. 1884, in *D&L*, 2: 527–29, 4: 136–37; T. H. Williams, *Hayes of the Twenty-third*, pp. 287–312; Thomas A. Lewis, *The Guns of Cedar Creek* (New York: Harper & Row, 1988). His injured ankle would bother Hayes in the future. RBH to BAH, 22 Nov. 1871, HPC. Thomas Buchanan Read immortalized "Sheridan's Ride" in verse. Although he exaggerated the eleven and a half miles covered to twenty and the speed of Sheridan's steed, he captured Sheridan's effect on his men.

Chapter 11. The End of the War

1. RBH to LWH, 21 Oct., 13 Nov. 1864, RBH, Diary, 1 Jan. 1890, in *D&L*, 2: 528, 536, 4: 535; LWH to RBH, 3 Jan. 1865, Geer, *First Lady*, pp. 76–77.

2. JTW to Maria Cook Webb, 19–20 Oct. 1864, RBH, MS Diary, 26 Oct. 1864, HPC; RBH to LWH, 25, 27 Oct. 1864, in *D&L*, 2: 529–31; T. H. Williams, *Hayes of the Twenty-third*, pp. 311–12.

3. RBH, MS Diary, 26–27 Oct. 1864, RBH to SB, 27 Oct. 1864, HPC; T. H. Williams, *Hayes of the Twenty-third*, pp. 312, 315; C. R. Williams, *Hayes*, 1: 259–60, n. 1. In trying to parry unjust criticism, Hayes unfairly blamed General Wright, the commander of the whole army, for the surprise; he was not forthright in admitting the shortcomings of Crook's corps, including his own division, that fateful foggy morning. RBH, Diary, 28 Oct. 1864, in *D&L*, 2: 531; RBH to B. R. Cowan, 25 Oct. 1864, Cowan to RBH, 2 Nov. 1864, HPC.

4. RBH, Diary, 8–10 Nov. 1864, in *D&L*, 2: 535; C. R. Williams, *Hayes*, 1: 263–64.

5. RBH, Diary, 9 Nov. 1864, RBH to LWH, 20, 23 Nov. 1864, in *D&L*, 2: 535, 540.

6. RBH, Diary, 9–10, 17, 23, 26 Nov., 12 Dec. 1864, RBH to SB, 2 Nov. 1864, RBH to LWH, 17 Nov., 6 Dec. 1864, RBH to SBH, 6 Dec. 1864, in *D&L*, 2: 532, 535, 537–39, 541, 543–44, 546.

7. RBH, Diary, 9–10 Dec. 1864, 3 Jan. 1865, RBH to LWH, 9 Dec. 1864, RBH to SB, 6 Jan. 1865, in *D&L*, 2: 545–46, 553, 555. Hayes did not put on Crook's shoulder straps until 3 January 1865, when he received official notification that he had been promoted (dating from 19 October 1864) "for gallantry and meritorious services in the Battles of Opequon, Fisher's Hill, and Cedar Creek."

8. RBH, Diary, 17 Dec. 1864, RBH to SB, 12 Dec. 1865, RBH to LWH, 17 Dec. 1864, in *D&L*, 2: 546–49.

9. RBH, MS Diary, 18–21 Dec. 1864, RBH to BAH, 23 Dec. 1864, HPC; RBH, Diary, 22–28, 30–31 Dec. 1864, RBH to SB, 20 Dec. 1864, in *D&L*, 2: 550–53.

10. RBH, Diary, 2–3, 5, 9 Jan. 1865, RBH to LWH, 1, 5 Jan. 1865, RBH to SB, 6, 8 Jan. 1865, in *D&L*, 2: 553–55; RBH, MS Diary, 8, 10–12 Jan. 1865, RBH to SBH, 1 Jan. 1865,

HPC; RBH, "Oath of Office," 3 Jan. 1865, Adjutant General Oaths, no. 55, Army of West Virginia, National Archives, copy HPC.

11. RBH, MS Diary, 12–21 Jan. 1865, RBH to LWH, 16 (misdated 15) Jan. 1865, HPC; RBH to SBH, 22 Jan. 1865, in *D&L*, 2: 556.

12. RBH, MS Diary, 22–31 Jan., 1–9 Feb. 1865, HPC; RBH to Warner M. Bateman, 10 Feb. 1865, Bateman-Hayes Correspondence, Western Reserve Historical Society, Cleveland, Ohio, copy HPC; RBH to SB, 1 Feb. 1865, RBH to SBH, 6 Feb. 1865, RBH to LWH, 12 Feb. 1865, HPC.

13. RBH, MS Diary, 10, 16–17 Feb. 1865, RBH to SB, 17 Feb. 1865, HPC; RBH to LWH, 12 Feb. 1865, in *D&L*, 2: 557. Unless John Quincy Adams engaged his father in similar sport, Hayes and McKinley were the only future U.S. presidents to participate together in a snowball fight.

14. RBH to SB, 10 Feb. 1865, HPC; RBH, Diary, 21 Feb. 1865, RBH to LWH, 23 Feb. 1865, in *D&L*, 2: 559, 562. Carrying his desire to emulate Crook to an extreme, Hayes mused to Lucy, "If it could be without stain I would rather like now to be captured. It would be a good experience." RBH to LWH, 23 Feb. 1865, in *D&L*, 2: 562. Although contradicted by his diary and his private correspondence, Hayes's official report of the incident says, "no inquiry was made for me or Gen. Duval." RBH to U. S. Grant?, 21 Feb. 1865, Harvard University, copy HPC.

15. RBH, MS Diary, 24 Feb. 1865, HPC; RBH to LWH, 21, 23 Feb. 1865, RBH to SBH, 22 Feb. 1865, in *D&L*, 2: 560–62.

16. RBH to SB, 12 Dec. 1864, RBH to LWH, 12 Feb. 1865, in *D&L*, 2: 548, 557; RBH to SBH, 25 Feb. 1865, HPC; RBH to MFF, 15 Feb. 1865, MFF Papers, University of Washington, Seattle, copy HPC.

17. RBH to LWH, 23 Feb. 1865, RBH to SBH, 11 Mar. 1865, RBH to SB, 18, 24 Mar. 1865, in *D&L*, 2: 562, 566, 568–69. Over the next twenty years, Hayes would be friendly with Hancock even though he was a Democrat in politics; Hayes found him to be "through and through pure gold." RBH, Diary, 5 Apr. 1886, in *D&L*, 4: 279–80.

18. RBH to SBH, 5 Mar. 1865, HPC; RBH to LWH, 15, 23 Feb., 5, 12 Mar. 1865, RBH to SB, 2 Mar. 1865, RBH to WHS, 4 Mar. 1865, in *D&L*, 2: 558, 561–64, 566.

19. RBH to LWH, 12 Mar. 1865, in *D&L*, 2: 566.

20. RBH to LWH, 21 Mar., 8 Apr. 1865, RBH to SB, 24 Mar. 1865, RBH to Russell Hastings, 3 Apr. 1865, in *D&L*, 2: 568–69, 571–72; T. H. Williams, *Hayes of the Twenty-third*, p. 320; C. R. Williams, *Hayes*, 1: 268.

21. RBH to SB, 21 Mar. 1865, RBH to LWH, 5, 8 Apr. 1865, in *D&L*, 2: 568, 571–73; RBH to The Officers and Men of the First Brigade, First Division, Department of West Virginia, 6 Apr. 1865, in C. R. Williams, *Hayes*, 1: 269–70 n.

22. RBH to LWH, 8, 12 Apr. 1865, RBH to SBH, 9 Apr. 1865, RBH to William Johnston, 10 Apr. 1865, RBH to SB, 12 Apr. 1865, in *D&L*, 2: 572–75.

23. RBH, Diary, 15 Apr. 1865, RBH to LWH, 16 Apr. 1865, in *D&L*, 2: 575–77.

24. RBH to SB, 21 Apr. 1865, RBH to LWH, 28 Apr., 9 May 1865, in *D&L*, 2: 580, 582.

25. RBH, Diary, 29 Apr. 1865, RBH to LWH, 5, 9 May 1865, RBH to SBH, 7 May 1865, RBH to LPM, 9 May 1865, RBH to SB, 7 May 1865, in *D&L*, 2: 580–83; RBH to SBH, 7 May 1865, HPC; RBH to R. L. Nye, 5 May 1865, Campus Martius Museum, Marietta, Ohio, copy HPC.

26. RBH to SBH, 12, 14, 20 May 1865, RBH to Russell Hastings, 20 May 1865, RBH to SB, 20 May 1865, in *D&L*, 2: 583–84; RBH to SBH, 16 May 1865, HPC; RBH to Thomas Meline, 20 May 1865, Record Group 94, National Archives, copy HPC.

27. RBH to Maria Cook Webb, 22 May 1865, RBH to SB, 27 May 1865, HPC; E. B. Long and Barbara Long, *The Civil War Day by Day: An Almanac, 1861–1865* (New York: Da Capo Press, 1971), pp. 689–90. The description of the reviews is from the Longs' *Almanac*, which is enormously useful in pinpointing events of the Civil War.

28. Geer, *First Lady*, p. 78.

29. RBH to SBH, 28 May, 11 June 1865, RBH, Diary, 6 Jan. 1891, in *D&L*, 2: 584–85, 4: 630.

30. RBH, Diary, 13 May, 1886, 15 July 1892, in *D&L*, 4: 286–88, 5: 96; C. R. Williams, *Hayes*, 1: 273–75; Barnard, *Hayes*, p. 219; T. H. Williams, *Hayes of the Twenty-third*, pp. 19–30, 324. Hayes was sent his commission of major general by brevet over a year later, in July 1866. RBH to J. C. Kelton, 4 Aug. 1866, National Archives, copy HPC.

31. RBH to SBH, 20 May, 11 June 1865, in *D&L*, 2: 583, 585.

Chapter 12. Congressman

1. RBH, Diary, 8 Mar. 1865, 27 Dec. 1892, in *D&L*, 2: 565, 5: 131. For Thomas Jefferson's reference to a similar observation by Louis XIV, see Dumas Malone, *Jefferson and His Time*, 6 vols. (Boston: Little, Brown, 1948–81), 5: 169.

2. RBH to WHS, 4 Mar. 1865, in *D&L*, 2: 564.

3. RBH to LWH, 5 May, 22 June, 9 July 1865, RBH to SB, 6 July 1865, in *D&L*, 2: 581, 3: 1–2.

4. RBH to SB, 24 Mar., 6 July 1865, RBH to LWH, 25 Aug. 1865, in *D&L*, 2: 569–70, 3: 2–3; RBH to SB, 24 Aug. 1865, RBH to SBH, 24 Aug. 1865, SBH to SB, 17 Aug. 1865, SBH to Charlotte Birchard DeWitt, 13 Sept. 1865, HPC.

5. RBH to GMB, 30 Aug. 1865, GMB Papers, University of Texas, copy HPC; W. J. Bryan to RBH, 21 Sept. 1865, HPC.

6. RBH to SBH, 13, 24 Sept. 1865, RBH to SB, 11 Oct., 1 Nov. 1865, HPC; RBH to James Williams, 18 Sept. 1865, Western Reserve Historical Society, copy HPC; RBH to LWH, 1 Oct. 1865, RBH to SBH, 22 Oct. 1865, in *D&L*, 3: 4.

7. RBH to GMB, 9 Nov. 1865 (misdated 1868), in *D&L*, 3: 55–56.

8. RBH to SB, 5, 8 Nov. 1865, SBH to BAH, 19 Nov. 1865, SBH, MS Diary, 20 Nov. 1865, HPC.

9. RBH, Diary, 30 Nov., 1 Dec. 1865, in *D&L*, 3: 5–6.

10. RBH, Diary, 1 Dec. 1865, in *D&L*, 3: 6–7.

11. RBH, Diary, 2, 4 Dec. 1865, in *D&L*, 3: 7–8; RBH to Warner M. Bateman, 4 Dec. 1865, Western Reserve Historical Society, copy HPC.

12. RBH, Diary, 1, 3 Dec. 1865, RBH to LWH, 7 Dec. 1865, in *D&L*, 3: 7–9.

13. RBH, Diary, 16 Dec. 1865, RBH to LWH, 17 Dec. 1865, in *D&L*, 3: 11–12.

14. RBH to SBH, 8 Dec. 1865, RBH to BAH, 12 Dec. 1865, HPC; RBH to LWH, 7 Dec. 1865, in *D&L*, 3: 10.

15. RBH, Diary, 2 Dec. 1865, 8 Jan. 1866, RBH to LWH, 7 Dec. 1865, in *D&L*, 3: 8–10, 12.

16. RBH to SB, 11 Dec. 1865, in *D&L*, 3: 10–11.

17. RBH, MS Diary, 8, 9 Jan. 1866, RBH to BAH, 6 Jan. 1866, RBH to SBH, 7 Jan. 1866, SBH, MS Diary, 29 Dec. 1865, HPC; RBH to LWH, 10 Jan. 1866, in *D&L*, 3: 13.

18. RBH, Diary, 12 Dec. 1865, 10 Jan. 1866, in *D&L*, 3: 11–13. Hayes thought that Rep. Glenni W. Scofield made "a shrewd and pithy speech," which Hayes might have recalled when he appointed him register of the Treasury in 1878.

19. RBH to SBH, 21, 28 Jan., 4 Feb. 1866, RBH to SB, 28 Feb. 1866, in *D&L*, 3: 14–15, 17–18; RBH to LWH, 8 Mar. 1866, RBH to BAH, 12 Apr. 1866, HPC.

20. RBH to SBH, 4 Feb. 1866, in *D&L*, 3: 17.

21. RBH to LWH, 28 Feb., 29 Mar. 1866, in *D&L*, 3: 19, 21; RBH to LWH, 4 Mar. 1866, HPC.

22. RBH to SB, 2 Mar., 15 Apr. 1866, RBH to LWH, 15 Apr. 1866, in *D&L*, 3: 19, 23–24.

23. RBH to Warner M. Bateman, 31 Jan., 1 Feb. 1866, HPC; RBH to Murat Halstead, 2 Feb. 1866, RBH to SB, 28 Feb. 1866, RBH to LWH, 4 Apr. 1866, in *D&L*, 3: 16–18, 22; Eric L. McKitrick, *Andrew Johnson and Reconstruction* (Chicago: University of Chicago Press, 1960), pp. 336–39.

24. RBH to SB, 2, 4 Mar. 1866, RBH to LWH, 22, 29 Mar. 1866, in *D&L*, 3: 19–21.

25. RBH to Friedrich Hassaurek, 8 Apr. 1866, Kenyon College, copy HPC.

26. RBH to MFF, 17 Mar. 1866, in *D&L*, 3: 20.

27. RBH to SBH, 12 Apr. 1866, RBH to LWH, 8, 19 Apr. 1866, RBH to SB, 15 Apr. 1866, in *D&L*, 3: 22–24.

28. McKitrick, *Andrew Johnson and Reconstruction*, pp. 349–52; Hans L. Trefousse, *Andrew Johnson: A Biography* (New York: W. W. Norton, 1989), pp. 250–52.

29. RBH to SBH, 29 Apr., 16 May 1866, RBH to SB, 2 May 1866, HPC; RBH to Warner M. Bateman, 15 May 1866, Western Reserve Historical Society, copy HPC; RBH to LWH, 10, 13 May 1866, in *D&L*, 3: 24–25.

30. RBH, Diary, 15 May 1866, in *D&L*, 3: 25; Edward McPherson, *The Political History of the United States of America During the Period of Reconstruction: April 15, 1865–July 15, 1870* (New York: Da Capo Press, 1972), pp. 114–17.

31. RBH to LWH, 16 May 1866, in *D&L*, 3: 25. Fullerton, who was in charge of the Freedmen's Bureau in Louisiana, seemed bent on its destruction. On corruption and its use as an issue in post–Civil War America, see Mark Wahlgren Summers, *The Era of Good Stealings* (New York: Oxford University Press, 1993).

32. RBH to SBH, 16, 25 May 1866, RBH to SB, 22 May 1866, HPC; RBH, Diary, 24 May 1866, RBH to LWH, 6 June 1866, in *D&L*, 3: 25–26.

33. RBH to LWH, 3 June 1866, HPC; RBH to LWH, 14, 16 June 1866, in *D&L*, 3: 27.

34. RBH, Diary, 14 June 1866, RBH to LWH, 6, 14 June 1866, in *D&L*, 3: 26–27; RBH to LWH, 6 June 1866, RBH to BAH, 8 June 1866, HPC; McKitrick, *Andrew Johnson and Reconstruction*, pp. 353–56; Trefousse, *Andrew Johnson*, p. 252.

35. RBH to LWH, 12 July 1866, in *D&L*, 3: 29; *Congressional Globe*, 39th Cong., 1st sess., 3851 (16 July 1866); McKitrick, *Andrew Johnson and Reconstruction*, p. 357; Trefousse, *Andrew Johnson*, pp. 252–54; McPherson, *Reconstruction*, pp. 74, 151.

36. RBH to SB, 7 July, 6, 15, 27 Aug., 16 Sept. 1866, RBH to LWH, 27 Aug. 1866, in *D&L*, 3: 28–31; RBH to LWH, 12–13 July 1866, RBH to SBH, 31 July, 4 Aug. 1866, RBH to SB, 18 Aug. 1866, RBH to JTW, 16 Sept. 1866, HPC.

37. RBH to LWH, 9 Sept. 1866, RBH to SB, 23 Sept. 1866, RBH to GMB, 1 Oct. 1866, in *D&L*, 3: 30–32.

38. C. R. Williams, *Hayes*, 1: 283–88.

39. RBH to SB, 6 Oct. 1866, in *D&L*, 3: 33–34.

40. RBH to GMB, 1 Oct. 1866, in *D&L*, 3: 32–33.

41. RBH to LWH, 15, 22 Oct. 1866, RBH to William McKinley, 6 Nov. 1866, RBH to SB, 13 Dec. 1866, in *D&L*, 3: 34, 36, 5: 149–50; RBH to Thomas C. Durant, 3 Oct. 1866, University of Iowa, copy HPC. The promoters of the Union Pacific depended on federal government loans and private investors for funds to build the road and were careful to cultivate congressmen. Robert William Fogel, *The Union Pacific Railroad: A Case in Premature Enterprise* (Baltimore: Johns Hopkins University Press, 1960), pp. 57–60. Hayes was not involved in the premier scandal of the day. Upright and unimportant, he was not offered stock in Credit Mobilier (which was building the Union Pacific) by Congressman Oakes Ames.

42. RBH to GMB, 5 Nov. 1866, in *D&L*, 3: 35, RBH to William McKinley, 6 Nov. 1866, RBH entry in SBH, Diary, 4 Nov. 1866, HPC. George had actually died in May.

43. RBH to LWH, 20 Nov. 1866, RBH to SB, 1, 13 Dec. 1866, in *D&L*, 3: 35–36; RBH to Col. ?, 31 Oct. 1866, HPC.

44. RBH to SB, 1–2 Dec. 1866, in *D&L*, 3: 36; Ari Hoogenboom, *Outlawing the Spoils: A History of the Civil Service Reform Movement, 1865–1883* (Urbana: University of Illinois Press, 1961), pp. 31–32.

45. *Congressional Globe*, 39th Cong., 2d sess., 1036 (6 Feb. 1867); Hoogenboom, *Outlawing the Spoils*, pp. 30–31.

46. RBH, MS Diary, 21–24 Dec. 1866, HPC; RBH to SB, 19, 24 Dec. 1866, in *D&L*, 3: 36–37; Cincinnati *Gazette*, 25, 27–28, 31 Dec. 1866; C. R. Williams, *Hayes*, 1: 288–89; Hans L. Trefousse, *The Radical Republicans: Lincoln's Vanguard for Racial Justice* (New York: Alfred A. Knopf, 1969), pp. 351–52. While his parents went south, Rud—accompanied by either James M. Ashley or Rowland Trowbridge—joined his brothers at Fremont.

47. RBH to SB, 26, 28 Dec. 1866, in *D&L*, 3: 37–38; RBH, MS Diary, 25–31 Dec. 1866, 1–3 Jan. 1867, HPC; Cincinnati *Gazette*, 31 Dec. 1866; Trefousse, *Radical Republicans*, p. 351.

48. RBH to William M. Dickson, 19 Jan. 1967, RBH to SB, 30 Jan. 1867, in *D&L*, 3: 38–39; RBH to BAH, 22 Jan. 1867, HPC; Michael Les Benedict, *A Compromise of Principle: Congressional Republicans and Reconstruction, 1863–1869* (New York: W. W. Norton, 1974), pp. 216–20.

49. RBH to SB, 7 Feb. 1867, in *D&L*, 3: 41; Benedict, *Compromise of Principle*, pp. 223–27. The political awareness of these West Pointers represented a sharp break with the past.

50. RBH to Warner Bateman, 9 Feb. 1867, HPC.

51. Benedict, *Compromise of Principle*, pp. 231–33.

52. RBH to Timothy C. Day, 15 Feb. 1867, Charles Roberts Autograph Collection, Haverford College Library, copy HPC; Benedict, *Compromise of Principle*, pp. 233–36; David Donald, *The Politics of Reconstruction, 1863–1867* (Baton Rouge: Louisiana State University Press, 1965), pp. 77–78.

53. RBH to SB, 20 Feb. 1867, HPC; Benedict, *Compromise of Principle*, pp. 236–39; Donald, *Politics of Reconstruction*, pp. 80–81.

54. RBH to Murat Halstead, 22 Feb. 1867, Halstead Papers, Cincinnati Historical Society, copy HPC; RBH to SB, 22 Feb. 1867, in *D&L*, 3: 41; RBH to Scott Cook, 24 Feb. 1867, Scott Cook Collection, Western Reserve Historical Society, copy HPC; Benedict, *Compromise of Principle*, pp. 239–40.

55. Murat Halstead to RBH, 6 July 1866, HPC; RBH to Timothy C. Day, 15 Feb. 1867, Charles Roberts Autograph Collection, copy HPC; RBH to Frank R. Jones?, 10 Mar. 1867, Jones Collection, Cincinnati Historical Society, copy HPC; RBH to Scott Cook, 24 Feb. 1867, Scott Cook Collection, Western Reserve Historical Society, copy HPC; RBH to James M. Comly, 9 June 1867, James M. Comly Papers, Ohio Historical Society, copy HPC. Hayes illustrated his moderation by voting to reduce the one–dollar tariff on one hundred pounds of railroad bar iron to seventy cents but refusing to cut it to fifty cents. *Congressional Globe*, 39th Cong., 1st sess., 3722–25 (10 July 1866). On several votes during the tariff debate, Hayes opposed the high protectionists. *Congressional Globe*, 39th Cong., 2d sess., 1592, 1658–59 (26, 28 Feb. 1867).

56. RBH to MFF, 23 Feb. 1867, in *D&L*, 3: 42; C. R. Williams, *Hayes*, 1: 281–82; John Y. Cole, "The Library of Congress and American Scholarship, 1865–1939," in Phyllis Dain and John Y. Cole, eds., *Libraries and Scholarly Communication in the United States: The Historical Dimension* (Westport, Conn.: Greenwood Press, 1990), p. 47.

57. RBH to SB, 6 Apr. 1867, in *D&L*, 3: 42; Benedict, *Compromise of Principle*, pp. 240–43.

58. RBH to JTW, 14 Apr. 1867, RBH to SB, 6 May 1867, HPC; RBH to LWH, 2 June 1867, in *D&L*, 3: 44; Fremont *Journal*, 12 Apr. 1867.

59. RBH to SB, 20 June 1867, RBH to LWH, 2, 11 July 1867, in *D&L*, 3: 45; RBH to LWH, 29 June, 5, 18, 20, 21 July 1867, HPC.

60. Benedict, *Compromise of Principle*, pp. 253–55, 359; RBH to LWH, 21 July 1867, RBH to Jacob Dolson Cox, 7 Aug. 1867, HPC; RBH to LWH, 14 July 1867, RBH to SB, 25 July 1867, in *D&L*, 3: 46; *Congressional Globe*, 40th Cong., 1st sess., 590 (11 July 1867).

Chapter 13. Governor

1. RBH to WHS, 29 Jan., Feb. 1867, RBH to SB, 2 Feb. 1867, in *D&L*, 3: 39–40; C. R. Williams, *Hayes*, 1: 290.

2. RBH to WHS, 23, 25 May 1867, WHS to RBH, 24? May 1867, RBH to SB, 21 May, 12, 20 June 1867, in *D&L*, 3: 42–45; Benedict, *Compromise of Principle*, p. 267.

3. RBH to General [Benjamin R. Cowan], 24 Aug. 1867, Gates W. McGarrah Papers, LC, copy HPC; RBH to LWH, 25 Aug. 1867, in *D&L*, 3: 47; C. R. Williams, *Hayes*, 1: 293–306. Hayes's set speech supports Gary Wills's thesis in *Lincoln at Gettysburg: The Words That Remade America* (New York: Simon & Schuster, 1992) that the Gettysburg Address fundamentally changed the country with its emphasis on the Declaration of Independence rather than the Constitution.

4. C. R. Williams, *Hayes*, 1: 306–15.

5. Ibid., 1: 315–16.

6. Ibid., 1: 316–20. Hayes was quoting from Lincoln's "Message to Congress in Special Session, July 4, 1861." See Roy P. Basler et al., eds., *The Collected Works of Abraham Lincoln*, 8 vols. (New Brunswick, N.J.: Rutgers University Press, 1953), 4: 438. Hereafter cited as Lincoln, *Collected Works*.

7. RBH to BAH and WCH, 1 Sept. 1867, RBH, MS Diary, 2 Sept. 1883, 2 Sept. 1890, HPC; RBH, Diary, 2 Sept. 1888, in *D&L*, 4: 404.

8. JTW to RBH, c. 4 Sept. 1867, RBH to LWH, 8 Sept. 1867, HPC.

9. RBH to SB, 6 Oct. 1867, in *D&L*, 3: 48.

10. RBH to SB, 9 Oct. 1867, in *D&L*, 3: 49; C. R. Williams, *Hayes*, 1: 328.

11. RBH to BAH and WCH, 28 Oct. 1867, HPC; RBH to LWH, 27 Dec. 1867, in *D&L*, 3: 50; *Ohio State Journal*, 30 Dec. 1867.

12. RBH to WHS, 17 Nov. 1867, in *D&L*, 3: 49; RBH to WHS, 19 Dec. 1867, 7 Jan. 1868, HPC.

13. RBH to SB, 11, 13 Jan. 1868, in *D&L*, 3: 50; RBH, *Inaugural Address of Rutherford B. Hayes, Governor of Ohio, to the Fifty-eighth General Assembly, Monday, January 13, 1868* (Columbus, 1868); RBH, MS Diary, 9 Jan. 1888, HPC; C. R. Williams, *Hayes*, 1: 331.

14. RBH to SB, 17 Jan. 1868, in *D&L*, 3: 51; RBH to SB, 21 Jan. 1868, RBH to BAH and WCH, 15, 20 Apr. 1868, HPC.

15. RBH to WHS, 17 Feb. 1868, RBH to Otto von Bismarck, 15 Apr. 1868, in *D&L*, 3: 51–52; RBH to WHS, 16 Jan. 1868, RBH to C. G. Hawley, 4 Apr. 1868, RBH to William Henry Seward, 17 Jan. 1868, RBH to Chairman Finance Committee, 3 Feb. 1868, Ohio Governors' Letter Press Copy Book, Ohio Historical Society, copy HPC.

16. RBH to Conrad Baker, 24 Jan. 1868, Indiana Historical Society, copy HPC; Irwin Unger, *The Greenback Era: A Social and Political History of American Finance, 1865–1879* (Princeton, N.J.: Princeton University Press, 1964), pp. 82–89.

17. J. C. Lee to RBH, 5 May 1868, RBH to J. C. Lee, 6 May 1868, in *D&L*, 3: 52; JTW to LWH, 2 Apr. 1868, RBH to Dr. [James Webb], 28 Apr. 1868, RBH to BAH, 8 May 1868, HPC.

18. RBH to LWH, 23 May 1868, in *D&L*, 3: 52–53; RBH to L. Myers, 28 May 1868,

HPC; McPherson, *Reconstruction*, pp. 364–66; Long and Long, *Civil War Day by Day*, p. 297.

19. RBH, Diary, 9 July 1868, RBH to SB, 14 July 1868, in *D&L*, 3: 53–54; McPherson, *Reconstruction*, pp. 367–71.

20. RBH to SB, 11 Nov. 1868, in *D&L*, 3: 56; RBH to SB, 28 July, 3, 23 Aug. 1868, RBH to BAH and WCH, 4 Oct. 1868, RBH to BAH, 5 Nov. 1868, HPC; McPherson, *Reconstruction*, p. 499; C. R. Williams, *Hayes*, 1: 331–32.

21. GMB to RBH, 1 Jan. 1869, HPC; RBH to SB, 14 July 1868, RBH to GMB, 21 Jan. 1869, in *D&L*, 3: 54, 57.

22. RBH, Memorandum, "Fremont, 25 Nov. [1868]," HPC; *Ohio State Journal*, 24 Nov. 1868.

23. RBH to SB, 12 Dec. 1868, HPC; RBH to SB, 19 Dec. 1868, 7 Mar. 1869, RBH to ?, 15 Feb. 1869, in *D&L*, 3: 56–59.

24. RBH to SB, 3 Apr., 17 May 1869, in *D&L*, 3: 60, 63; RBH to John S. Newberry, 8 Nov. 1869, HPC; RBH to J. M. Comly, 23 May 1869, Ohio Historical Society, copy HPC; *DAB*, s.v. "Newberry, John Strong"; Michael C. Hansen and Horace R. Collins, "A Brief History of the Ohio Geological Survey," *Ohio Journal of Science* 79 (1979): 6, 8–10.

25. C. R. Williams, *Hayes*, 1: 334–37.

26. Ibid., 1: 338–39; RBH to WHS, 13 July 1869, in *D&L*, 3: 64.

27. RBH to SB, 9 Aug. 1869, RBH to Charles Nordhoff, 2 Nov. 1869, HPC; RBH to SB, 16 Aug. 1869, RBH to D. W. Canfield, 27 Aug. 1869, RBH to Julius O. Converse, 27 Aug. 1869, RBH to William Lawrence, 31 Dec. 1869, in *D&L*, 3: 65–66, 80.

28. W. S. Rosecrans to J. M. Comly, 11 Sept. 1869, Delaware *Gazette*, 24 Sept. 1869; Delaware *Gazette*, 8 Oct. 1869; C. R. Williams, *Hayes*, 1: 338–39.

29. RBH to Jacob Dolson Cox, 26 Sept. 1869, RBH to D. A. Higby, 3 Nov. 1869, RBH to James Scott, 4 Nov. 1869, HPC; RBH to SB, 27 Sept., 8, 13 Oct. 1869, RBH, Diary, 28 Nov. 1869, in *D&L*, 3: 66–67, 74.

30. RBH to BAH and WCH, 24, 30 Apr. 1868, RBH to BAH, 30 June 1868, 28 Jan., 28 Apr. 1869, RBH to WCH, 19 Apr. 1869, HPC; RBH to WCH, 19 Apr., 7 Nov. 1869, in *D&L*, 3: 61, 68. Jean Bernard Léon Foucault had perfected his pendulum between 1850 and 1855.

31. RBH, MS Diary, 28 Nov. 1869, RBH to SB, 27 Dec. 1869, HPC; RBH to E. Williams, 23 Dec. 1869, Ohio Governors' Letter Press Copy Book, p. 95, Ohio Historical Society, copy HPC.

32. RBH, Memorandum, 9 Apr. 1869, RBH to T. F. Nieman, 5 Nov. 1869, RBH to Benjamin Franklin Potts, 1 Dec. 1869, RBH to William H. Turner, 6 Jan. 1870, RBH to James D. Webb, 3 June 1870, HPC; RBH to Mrs. Harrison, 21 Jan. 1887, in *D&L*, 4: 306–8; Geer, *First Lady*, pp. 95–96.

33. RBH to A. Thomson, 15 Nov. 1869, RBH to Doctor [?], 10 Dec. 1869, HPC; RBH, Diary, 2 Dec. 1869, RBH to Enoch Cobb Wines, 7, 19 Dec. 1869, in *D&L*, 1: 74–78.

34. RBH to J. J. Hooker, 10 Nov. 1869, RBH to Columbus Delano, 20 Nov., 2 Dec. 1869, RBH to George S. Boutwell, 6 Jan. 1870, Letterbook, pp. 27–28, 49, 64, 116, RBH to Anne C. McMeans, 23 Nov. 1869, HPC; RBH to Jay Cooke, 24 Jan. 1870, Cooke Papers, Historical Society of Pennsylvania, copy HPC; RBH to Charles Nordhoff, 10 Nov. 1869, RBH to Lucius Fairchild, 23 Nov. 1869, RBH to D. W. C. Wilson, 11, 29 Dec. 1869, RBH to James Leroy, 11 Dec. 1869, RBH to B. W. Brice, 20 Dec. 1869, RBH to John White Geary, 29 Dec. 1869, RBH, Diary, 6 Mar. 1870, in *D&L*, 3: 70, 74, 77–80, 91.

35. RBH, MS Diary, 25 Dec. 1869, HPC; RBH, Diary, 2 Jan. 1870, in *D&L*, 3: 80–81.

36. RBH, "Governor's Message," 3 Jan. 1870, copy HPC.

Chapter 14. Second Term

1. RBH, Diary, 2 Jan. 1870, in *D&L*, 3: 81; RBH, "Inaugural Address, January 10, 1870," copy HPC.

2. RBH to Oliver P. Morton, 6, 13 Jan. 1870, in *D&L*, 3: 81–83; RBH to Schuyler Colfax, 22 Oct. 1869, RBH to Noah A. Swayne, 7 Jan. 1870, Letterbook, p. 117, HPC.

3. RBH to J. Irving Brooks, 1 Mar. 1870, RBH, Diary, 4 Apr. 1870, in *D&L*, 3: 90, 94; RBH to A. R. Keller, 25 Jan. 1870, RBH to Charles L. Frost, 17 Feb. 1870, RBH to SB, 5 Apr. 1870, HPC; C. R. Williams, *Hayes*, 1: 346.

4. RBH, Diary, 19 Apr. 1870, RBH to Robert C. Schenck, 13 June 1870, in *D&L*, 3: 101–2, 109; RBH to JS, 7 Dec. 1870, HPC.

5. RBH to John Aston Warder, 17 Feb. 1870, RBH to Scott Cook, 4 Mar. 1870, RBH to William Dennison, 22 Mar. 1870, HPC; *DAB*, s.v. "Warder, John Aston"; RBH to William Allen, 27 Oct. 1870, William Allen Papers, LC, copy HPC; *American Archivist*, 25 (July 1962): 330.

6. RBH to C. H. Booth, 19 Apr. 1870, RBH to ?, 22 Apr. 1870, in *D&L*, 3: 103, 105. Burns, no doubt, was a sound appointment, since he later served on the Board of State Managers of the Centennial. RBH, Diary, 20–23 Oct. 1874, in *D&L*, 3: 259.

7. RBH, Diary, 19 Apr. 1870, in *D&L*, 3: 101–2; C. R. Williams, *Hayes*, 1: 348.

8. RBH, Diary, 11 Apr. 1870, RBH to Clark Waggoner?, 20 Apr. 1870, in *D&L*, 3: 98–99, 103–4. In a letter to his old commander George Crook, Hayes disparaged "the men who oppose war, capital punishment, etc., etc.," although Hayes continued to drift in their direction. RBH to George Crook, 9 Nov. 1871, HPC.

9. RBH, Diary, 27 Apr. 1870, in *D&L*, 3: 105; Geer, *First Lady*, pp. 97–98.

10. RBH to Charles Nordhoff, 5 Apr. 1870, RBH to David A. Wells, 6 Apr. 1870, RBH to James D. Webb, 3 June 1870, in *D&L*, 3: 94–96, 108; RBH to SB, 2 Oct. 1870, HPC.

11. RBH to SB, 14 Jan. 1870, RBH to J. D. Sweet, 20 June 1870, RBH to MFF, 29 July 1870, HPC; RBH, Diary, 30 May 1870, in *D&L*, 3: 106–7.

12. RBH, Diary, 1 July 1870, in *D&L*, 3: 110–12.

13. RBH, Diary, 9–14 Sept. 1870, RBH to SB, 13 Sept. 1870, in *D&L*, 3: 118–19; RBH to SB, 8 Sept. 1870, HPC.

14. RBH to BAH, 4, 22, 23, 31 Oct., 2, 19 Nov. 1870, RBH to SB, 22 Dec. 1870, HPC.

15. RBH, "Governor's Message," 3 Jan. 1871, copy HPC.

16. RBH to SB, 8 Jan. 1871, in *D&L*, 3: 126–27; RBH to Jacob Dolson Cox, 12 Jan. 1871, Cox Papers, Oberlin College, copy HPC; Jacob Dolson Cox, "The Civil-Service Reform," *North American Review* 112 (Jan. 1871): 81–113.

17. RBH to O. Follett, 9 Feb. 1871, RBH to Gwynne, Johnson & Day, 2 June 1871, HPC; RBH to Stephen W. Dorsey, 17 Mar. 1871, in *D&L*, 3: 137.

18. RBH, MS Diary, 8 Feb. 1871, RBH to BAH, 8 Feb. 1871, RBH to SB, 8 Feb. 1871, HPC; RBH, Diary, 17 Feb. 1871, in *D&L*, 3: 130–31. On Roger Birchard's reclusive behavior and his death, which may have been a murder, see RBH to SB, 18 Feb. 1870, SB to RBH, 22 Feb. 1870, HPC.

19. RBH to SB, 14 Feb. 1871, RBH to Francis Amasa Walker, 25 Feb. 1871, HPC; RBH, Diary, 17 Feb. 1871, in *D&L*, 3: 130–31.

20. RBH to Charles Nordhoff, 13 Mar. 1871, RBH, Diary, 16 Mar. 1871, in *D&L*, 3: 133–36.

21. RBH, Diary, 16 Mar. 1871, RBH to LWH, 7 May 1871, in *D&L*, 3: 135, 142.

22. RBH to GMB, 29 May 1871, in *D&L*, 3: 142–43; GMB to RBH, 5 May 1871, HPC.

23. RBH to BAH and RPH, 30 July 1871, RBH to BAH, 21 Sept. 1871, GMB to RBH, 31 July, 29 Aug. 1871, RBH to GMB, 3 Aug. 1871, HPC; RBH to JS, 1 Apr. 1871, JS Papers, LC, copy HPC; RBH to WKR, 15 Sept. 1871, RBH Papers, LC, copy HPC; RBH to LWH,

12 Sept. 1871, in *D&L*, 3: 164. For Hayes's speech at Zanesville, see C. R. Williams, *Hayes*, 1: 355–61.

24. GMB to RBH, 15 Dec. 1871, HPC; RBH to GMB, 24 Dec. 1871, in *D&L*, 3: 180. The Amnesty Act passed 22 May 1872.

25. RBH to BAH, 18 Oct. 1871, RBH to The People of Ohio, 12 Oct. 1871, RBH to J. L. Keck, 17 Oct. 1871, HPC; RBH, Diary, 10–11 Oct. 1871, in *D&L*, 3: 167–68.

26. RBH, Diary, 20 Nov. 1871, in *D&L*, 3: 176; RBH and SB to Austin Birchard, 1 July 1871, RBH to WKR, 14 June, 25, 26, 31 July, 24 Sept., 24 Nov., 8 Dec. 1871, HPC.

27. RBH to BAH, 18 Oct. 1871, RBH, MS Diary, 2 Nov. 1871, HPC; RBH to SB, 3 Nov. 1871, in *D&L*, 3: 170–71.

28. JTW to BAH, 15 Dec. 1871, JTW to LWH, 19 Dec. 1871, RBH to SB, 24 Dec. 1871, BAH to SB, 31 Dec. 1871, RBH, MS Diary, 24–25 Dec. 1871, HPC. Neither Hayes nor Joe's brother-in-law Stanley Matthews had pushed for Joe's appointment at the Longview Asylum, but the presence of John W. Herron on the board of directors had no doubt helped Joe's candidacy. RBH to SB, 11 June 1871, in *D&L*, 3: 147.

29. RBH, *Governor's Message* (Columbus, 1872), pp. 3–5.

30. Ibid., pp. 5–6; RBH to A. W. Alexander, 24 Dec. 1871, RBH to JTW, 1 Jan. 1872, in *D&L*, 3: 180–81, 185–86.

31. RBH, *Governor's Message* (Columbus, 1872), pp. 7–8; RBH, Diary, 13 Feb. 1872, in *D&L*, 3: 197. Historians have read into Hayes's relationship with Jay Cooke (an old Sandusky acquaintance) a partiality for railroads that is belied by this passage in his final message to the legislature. For example, Summers, *Good Stealings*, pp. 110–11, assumes that Hayes planned to shower political favors on the Northern Pacific Railroad when he assured Cooke on 7 February 1870 that "hereafter I may be able to do more and perhaps to unite in your plans." Hayes meant that he might be able to purchase more Duluth real estate than he contemplated buying at that moment, and twelve days later he committed himself to purchase 160 acres at $8,000. Ten months later, Cooke—presuming on their friendship—asked Hayes to use his influence to get the Ohio legislature to exempt Northern Pacific bonds from taxation, but Hayes apparently ignored the request. Jay Cooke to RBH, 8 Dec. 1870, HPC; Barnard, *Hayes*, pp. 250–51.

32. RBH, *Governor's Message* (Columbus, 1872), pp. 6, 9–10.

33. RBH, Diary, 31 Dec. 1871, 3 Jan. 1872, in *D&L*, 3: 185–87; C. R. Williams, *Hayes*, 1: 362–63.

34. RBH, Diary, 9 Jan. 1872, RBH to SB, 9 Jan. 1972, in *D&L*, 3: 188, 190; RBH to John W. Herron, 8 Jan. 1872, HPC.

Chapter 15. Interlude

1. RBH to William Johnston, 9 Jan. 1872, RBH, Diary, 10 Jan. 1872, in *D&L*, 3: 191–94. Two years earlier, Hayes had told Charles Nordhoff, "John Sherman is not my sort of person but he is no 'St. Anthony' " (a saint noted for resisting temptation). RBH to Charles Nordhoff, 2 Nov. 1869, HPC. Hayes did not specify how Sherman yielded to temptation, but whatever his "sin," it was not sufficient to prevent Hayes from later naming him to his cabinet.

2. RBH, Diary, 13 Feb. 1872, RBH to SB, 1, 4 Feb. 1872, in *D&L*, 3: 196; RBH to BAH, 18 Jan. 1872, RBH to SB, 20 Jan., 1 Feb. 1872, RBH, Memorandum, 23 Jan. 1872, RBH, MS Diary, 27 Jan. 1872, HPC.

3. RBH, Diary, 11 Jan., 13–14 Feb., 15 Apr. 1872, in *D&L*, 3: 194–97, 199–201; RBH to BAH, 28 Jan. 1872, HPC.

4. RBH, Diary, 13 Feb. 1872, RBH to LWH, 1, 3 Mar. 1872, RBH to SB, 7, 17, 24 Mar.,

23 Apr., 30 June 1872, in *D&L*, 3: 197–99, 201, 205–6; RBH to WKR, 30 Mar., 19 Apr. 1872, RBH Papers, LC, copy HPC.

5. RBH to BAH, 28 Jan. 1872, RBH to LWH, 21 Feb. 1872, RBH, MS Diary, 16 July 1872, HPC.

6. RBH to BAH, 26 Apr., 28 July 1872, RBH to SB, 30 June 1872, RBH, MS Diary, 23 May, 6, 27–29 July, 10, 25, 28–29 Aug., 18 Nov. 1872, HPC.

7. RBH, Diary, 31 Dec. 1871, RBH to SB, 30 June 1872, in *D&L*, 3: 185, 205; RBH, MS Diary, 31 Dec. 1871, RBH to RPH, 8 May 1872, RBH to BAH, 9 May 1872, HPC.

8. RBH to SB, 15, 23, 30 Apr. 1872, RBH, Diary, 6 May 1872, in *D&L* 3: 201–3; RBH to RPH, 8 May 1872, RBH to BAH, 9 May 1872, HPC; RBH to WKR, 19 Apr., 9 May 1872, RBH Papers, LC, copy HPC.

9. RBH to SB, 14 May, 10 June 1872, in *D&L*, 3: 203–4; Barnard, *Hayes*, p. 259.

10. RBH, Diary, 16, 25 July, 5, 7–8 Aug. 1872, RBH to SB, 24 July 1872, RBH to Richard Smith et al., 2 Aug. 1872, RBH to MFF, 10 Aug. 1872, in *D&L*, 3: 206–10; William E. Davis to RBH, 6 Aug. 1872, RBH to William E. Davis, 6 Aug. 1872, Richard Smith to RBH, 6 Aug. 1872, RBH to Richard Smith, 6 Aug. 1872, HPC.

11. RBH to SB, 11 Aug. 1872, in *D&L*, 3: 210; RBH to B. F. Coates, 10 Aug. 1872, HPC.

12. RBH to SB, 8, 15, 18, 22, 29 Sept., 6, 9 Oct. 1872, RBH to WCH, 28 Sept. 1872, RBH, Diary, 4, 19 Oct. 1872, in *D&L*, 3: 212–16; RBH to BAH, 22 Sept. 1872, SB to RBH, 27 Sept. 1872, RBH to BAH and WCH, 22 Oct. 1872, HPC.

13. RBH to SB, 6 Nov. 1872, RBH, Diary, 7 Nov. 1872, in *D&L*, 3: 217–18.

14. RBH to BAH and WCH, 22 Nov., 1 Dec. 1872, RBH to LWH, 30 Nov. 1872, HPC; RBH, Diary, 19, 29 Nov. (misidentified Dec.), 1, 3 Dec. 1872, in *D&L*, 3: 219–22.

15. RBH, Diary, 3 Dec. 1872, in *D&L*, 3: 222–23.

16. RBH, Diary, 1, 5, 26 Dec. 1872, 28 Jan. 1873, RBH to LWH, 17 Jan. 1873, in *D&L*, 3: 221, 223–24, 226–27; RBH, MS Diary, 25 Dec. 1872, 10, 20, 23, 28, 30 Jan. 1873, RBH to LWH, 15 Jan. 1873, HPC.

17. RBH, Diary, 6, 10 Feb. 1873, RBH to LWH, 9, 23 Feb. 1873, in *D&L*, 3: 228–30; RBH, MS Diary, 10–12 Feb. 1873, HPC.

18. RBH, Diary, 10 Feb. 1873, RBH to MFF, 25 Apr. 1873, in *D&L*, 3: 229, 238–39; RBH to LWH, 14, 17, 22 Feb. 1873, RBH, MS Diary, 3 Mar. 1873, HPC.

19. RBH, Diary, 20 Mar. 1873, in *D&L*, 3: 231; RBH to LWH, 22, 24, 27 Mar., 7 Apr. 1873, HPC. Although he was prejudiced against African Americans, Sardis had traded with the Senecas and admired them; he condemned the slaughter of Native Americans in the West and praised the introduction of a humane Indian policy by Grant. RBH, Diary, 26 Dec. 1872, in *D&L*, 3: 224.

20. RBH, Diary, 26 Mar. 1873, RBH to LWH, 26, 27 Mar. 1873, in *D&L*, 3: 233–34.

21. RBH to B. R. Cowan, 29 Mar. 1873, RBH to JS, 2 Apr. 1873, in *D&L*, 3: 235–36; JS to RBH, 26 Mar. 1873, RBH to E. F. Noyes, 3 Feb. 1873, Noyes Papers, Ohio Historical Society, copy HPC. John Baldwin Neil, who was Hayes's private secretary when he was governor, was apparently referring to Garfield when he commented that Credit Mobilier was "rather tough on the 'Christian Statesmen' of the day." John B. Neil to RBH, 29 Jan. 1873, HPC.

22. RBH, Diary, 3, 6, 23 Mar., 22, 30 Apr. 1873, RBH to MFF, 25 Apr. 1873, in *D&L*, 3: 230–32, 238–39, 241.

23. RBH, Diary, 2, 4 May 1873, RBH to LWH, 27 Apr. 1873, in *D&L*, 3: 240–42; RBH to LWH, 30 Apr. 1873, RBH to BAH, 4 May 1873, HPC.

24. RBH to WCH, 11 May 1873, RBH, Diary, 2 June, 2 July 1873, in *D&L*, 3: 242–45 (part of the entry of 2 July was written by LWH); RBH to BAH, 1 June 1873, RBH, MS Diary, 21, 28 June 1873, HPC.

25. RBH to WCH, 12 June 1873, RBH, Diary, 21 June, 4 Oct. 1873, in *D&L*, 3: 244, 249; RBH, MS Diary, 21 June 1873, HPC.

26. RBH, MS Diary, 2 Aug. 1873, HPC; Geer, *First Lady*, pp. 106–7.

27. MFF to RBH, 28 Apr. 1873, RBH to Samuel A. Greene, 18 June 1873, GMB to RBH, 15 Sept. 1873, RBH and L. Leppelman, "Agreement for Purchase of Ft. Stephenson," 6 Sept. 1873, HPC; RBH to Charles J. Hoadly, 19 May, 28 Aug., 3 Sept. 1873, Hoadly Collection, Connecticut Historical Society, copies HPC; RBH to Charles Reed, 1 July 1873, Vermont Historical Society, copy HPC; RBH to MFF, 25 Apr. 1873, RBH to WCH, 6 June 1873, RBH, Diary, 13 Sept. 1873, in *D&L*, 3: 238–39, 243, 247–48.

28. RBH, Diary, 13 Sept. 1873, in *D&L*, 3: 248–49; RBH to LPM, 20 Sept. 1873, RBH to BAH and WCH, 28 Sept. 1873, WKR to RBH, 20 Sept., 26 Dec. 1873, HPC.

29. RBH to BAH, 18 Oct. 1873, HPC.

30. RBH to Austin Birchard, 21 Apr. 1874, RBH to MFF, 27 Apr. 1874, RBH to GMB, 2 Jan. 1875, in *D&L*, 3: 255, 262; Unger, *Greenback Era*, pp. 235–45.

31. RBH to BAH, 23 Jan., 18, 22 Oct. 1873, RBH to WCH, 17 Oct. 1873, RBH to BAH and WCH, 12 Oct. 1873, HPC; *DAB*, s.v. "Leggett, Mortimer Dormer." Leggett, of Zanesville, Ohio, was the commissioner of patents.

32. RBH, MS Diary, 20 Nov., 4 Dec. 1873, RBH to BAH, 30 Nov., 10 Dec. 1873, HPC.

33. RBH to Morrison R. Waite, 21 Jan. 1874, Morrison R. Waite Papers, LC, copy HPC; RBH to Austin Birchard, 21 Jan. 1874, RBH, MS Diary, 29 Jan. 1874, HPC; RBH, Diary, 29 Jan. 1874, RBH to MFF, 29 Jan. 1874, in *D&L*, 3: 250–51; *DAB*, s.v. "Waite, Morrison Remick."

34. RBH to MFF, 8 Feb., 27 Apr. 1874, RBH to WCH, 8 Mar., 19 Apr. 1874, RBH, Diary, 1 Mar., 13 Aug. 1874, in *D&L*, 3: 252–57; RBH to William F. Poole, 8 Feb., 26 June 1874, RBH to WCH, 1 Mar., 19 Apr., 3 May 1874, RBH to BAH, 13 May, 8 June 1874, RBH to BAH and WCH, 28 Apr. 1874, RBH to Jessie E. McCulloch, 1 Apr. 1874, RBH, MS Diary, 1 Mar., 10 June 1874, LWH to BAH and WCH, 28 Apr. 1874, HPC.

35. RBH to BAH and WCH, 10, 24 June 1874, RBH to WCH, 2 July 1874, HPC.

36. RBH to BAH, June 1874, HPC; RBH, Diary, 13 Aug. 1874, in *D&L*, 3: 257.

37. RBH to Mary P. Birchard, 28 Aug. 1874, RBH, MS Diary, 25, 28–29 Aug. 1874, HPC; RBH, Diary, 28–29 Aug. 1874, in *D&L*, 3: 258.

38. RBH to WCH, 13 Sept. 1874, HPC.

39. RBH to LWH, 6 Oct. 1874, RBH to WCH, 11 Oct. 1874, in *D&L*, 3: 258–59.

40. RBH to William M. Garvey, 19 Oct. 1874, RBH to LWH, 20 Oct. 1874, HPC; RBH, Diary, 1, 6, 7 Dec. 1874, 3 Jan. 1875, in *D&L*, 3: 261–63.

41. RBH to WCH, 11 Oct. 1874, 1 Mar. 1875, RBH to RPH, 26 Feb. 1875, RBH, Diary, 22, 27 Feb. 1875, in *D&L*, 3: 259, 265–67; RBH, MS Diary, 22, 27 Feb. 1875, RBH to LWH, 25 Feb. 1875, HPC.

42. RBH, *Diary,* 28 Mar. 1875, p. 2; JTW to RBH, 8 Mar. 1875, HPC.

43. RBH, Diary, 11 May 1875, in *D&L*, 3: 272.

44. GMB to RBH, 19 Dec. 1874, HPC; Foner, *Reconstruction*, pp. 549–53.

45. RBH to GMB, 2 Jan. 1875, in *D&L*, 3: 262–63. In response, Bryan denied that the South desired to reenslave the Negro, claimed that Texas was educating blacks as well as whites (although he conceded that the system was defective for both races and that the state was trying to improve it), and insisted that "it would be far better for the negroe that the intelligent tax paying citizens should govern." GMB to RBH, 8 Jan. 1875, HPC.

46. RBH, *Diary*, 28 Mar. 1875, pp. 1–2.

Chapter 16. The Campaign of 1876

1. RBH, *Diary*, 14, 18 Apr. 1875, p. 3; RBH to LPM, 1 Apr. 1875, RBH to Clark Waggoner, 17 May 1875, RBH to John Davis, 21 May 1875, RBH, MS Diary, 6, 20 May 1875,

HPC; RBH to James M. Comly, 7, 10, 17 Apr. 1875, Comly Papers, Ohio Historical Society, copies HPC; RBH to WCH, 14 Apr. 1875, RBH to W. D. Bickham, 14 Apr. 1875, in *D&L*, 3: 269–70.

2. RBH, MS Diary, 29 May 1875, HPC; RBH, Diary, 11 May 1875, in *D&L*, 3: 272; Gillette, *Retreat from Reconstruction*, pp. 196–202, 259–79 (quotation on p. 279).

3. RBH, *Diary*, 14, 18 Apr., 3 June 1875, pp. 3–4; RBH to William S. Furay, 5 June 1875, William McKinley to RBH, 8 June 1875, HPC.

4. RBH to R. M. Stimson, 6 June 1875, HPC; RBH to Morrison R. Waite, 11 June 1875, Waite Papers, LC, copy HPC; RBH, *Diary*, 3–4 June 1875, pp. 5–6, 8.

5. RBH to R. M. Stimson, 6 June 1875, William McKinley to RBH, 8 June 1875, HPC; RBH, *Diary*, 3–4 June 1875, pp. 4–6; *DAB*, s.v. "Stallo, Johann Bernhard." Apart from the school issue, Hayes was not concerned about the growing strength of the Roman Catholic Church. He was not a nativist. He contributed to the building fund of the Catholic church in Fremont and often participated in its special programs. In 1890, after speaking on religious liberty to the Ohio Council of the Catholic Knights of America, Hayes thought of a better speech that would stress that, although he could see past and present faults in the Catholic Church, he was "grateful" for its temperance work; for its care of and influence with the poor, keeping them together with the rich; for its treatment of the blacks and all unfortunate races (he noted that a black man, Daniel A. Rudd, editor of the Cincinnati *Catholic Tribune*, "sat with us at our banquet table"); and for its fidelity to the Union. RBH, Diary, 9, 11 Sept. 1890, in *D&L*, 4: 598–99; RBH, MS Diary, 9, 11 Sept. 1890, HPC. A staunch Methodist, Lucy was worried about the growth of Catholicism. See WKR to RBH, 18, 30 Jan. 1876, HPC.

6. RBH, "Campaign Notes and Speech," MS Diary, 1875, RBH to Clark Waggoner, 22 July 1875, HPC; RBH to Nash, 12 Sept. 1875, in *D&L*, 3: 293; C. R. Williams, *Hayes*, 1: 392–97, 401–3; Unger, *Greenback Era*, pp. 265–80.

7. RBH to W. D. Bickham, 8 June 1875, RBH to A. T. Wikoff, 11 Aug. 1875, RBH to LWH, 14 Aug. 1875, in *D&L*, 3: 276, 290–91.

8. RBH to W. D. Bickham, 20 July 1875, RBH to GMB, 27 July 1875, RBH to A. T. Wikoff, 8, 11 Aug. 1875, in *D&L*, 3: 286, 289–90.

9. Keith Ian Polakoff, *The Politics of Inertia: The Election of 1876 and the End of Reconstruction* (Baton Rouge: Louisiana State University Press, 1973), pp. 178–80.

10. RBH to Horace Austin, 22 Aug. 1875, Austin Papers, Minnesota Historical Society, copy HPC; C. R. Williams, *Hayes*, 1: 405–6.

11. RBH, *Diary*, 12 Oct. 1875, p. 10; RBH to LWH, 19 Sept. 1875, in C. R. Williams, *Hayes*, 1: 405–7.

12. RBH to William Johnston, 3 Nov. 1875, University of Virginia, copy HPC; RBH to B. F. Potts, 5 Nov. 1875, Breckinridge Long Papers, LC, copy HPC.

13. RBH to LWH, 17 Dec. 1875, in *D&L*, 3: 298; RBH to BAH, 16 Jan. 1876, HPC; RBH, *Inaugural Address of Governor R. B. Hayes, to the General Assembly of Ohio* (Columbus, 1876); C. R. Williams, *Hayes*, 1: 410.

14. Charles Nordhoff to RBH, 11 Jan. 1876, WHS to RBH, 26 Jan., 15, 21 Feb. 1876, JS to A. M. Burns, 21 Jan. 1876, HPC; RBH to WHS, 29 Jan. 1876, RBH to LWH, 30 Jan. 1876, in *D&L*, 3: 300–301; RBH, *Diary*, 15 Feb., 21 Mar., 11 Apr. 1876, pp. 15–19.

15. RBH to BAH, 2 Apr. 1876, RBH to GMB, 7 May 1876, RBH to W. D. Bickham, 23 May 1876, HPC; RBH to H. S. Noyes, 26 Apr. 1876, Noyes Family Collection, Oneida, N.Y., copy HPC; RBH to JAG, 7 May 1876, JAG Papers, LC, copy HPC; RBH to Eliza G. Davis, 18 Apr. 1876, in *D&L*, 3: 314; RBH, *Diary*, 2, 11 Apr. 1876, p. 18; RBH to Edwin Cowles, 6 Apr. 1876, ibid., p. 20; "Hayes of Ohio . . . ," New York *Herald*, 23 May 1876.

16. RBH to WHS, 23 Apr. 1876, RBH to James G. Blaine, 12 June 1876, RBH to Ralph P. Buckland, 14 June 1876, in *D&L*, 3: 315–16, 324–25; David M. Jordan, *Roscoe Conkling*

of New York: Voice in the Senate (Ithaca, N.Y.: Cornell University Press, 1971), p. 80. Polakoff, in *Politics of Inertia*, pp. 44–52, unravels the complicated tale of Blaine's involvement with the Union Pacific and the Little Rock & Fort Smith Railroads.

17. GWC to William M. Dickson, 17 May 1876, in RBH, *Diary*, 21 May 1876, p. 23.

18. William M. Dickson to RBH, 27 Apr. 1876, William M. Dickson to GWC, 27 Apr. 1876, HPC; RBH to William M. Dickson, 3 May 1876, in *D&L*, 3: 317.

19. RBH to William M. Dickson, 3 May 1876, in *D&L*, 3: 317–18.

20. RBH, *Diary*, 16 June 1876, p. 26; RBH to BAH, 15 June 1876, HPC.

21. RBH to BAH, 15, 16 June 1876, WHS to RBH, 21 June 1876, HPC; RBH, *Diary*, 16 June 1876, p. 26; C. R. Williams, *Hayes*, 1: 446–48.

22. RBH to BAH, 15, 16 June 1876, HPC; RBH to William A. Howard, 23 June 1876, William A. Howard Collection, University of Michigan, copy HPC; C. R. Williams, *Hayes*, 1: 448–50; Edward McPherson, *A Hand-Book of Politics for 1876* (reprint, New York: Da Capo Press, 1972), pp. 209–12. Grateful for Howard's timely support, Hayes later appointed him governor of the Dakota Territory. *DAB*, s.v. "Howard, William Alanson."

23. C. R. Williams, *Hayes*, 1: 450–52. "The Bristow men," Manning Force reported to Hayes, "became so interested in defeating Blaine that they felt sincerely your nomination was a triumph of the cause they had at heart." MFF to RBH, 16 June 1876, HPC. John M. Harlan to Benjamin H. Bristow, 19 June 1876, Bristow Papers, LC, copy HPC.

24. RBH to BAH, 15, 16 June 1876, HPC; RBH, *Diary*, 18 June 1876, pp. 26–27; RBH to James G. Blaine, 16 June 1876, Newspaper Clipping File, L. Austin to LWH, 19 June 1876, HPC; RBH to GMB, 18 June 1876, GMB Papers, University of Texas, copy HPC.

25. GWC to RBH, 22 June 1876, JS to RBH, 20 June 1876, HPC; RBH to Edwards Pierrepont, 20 June 1876, Rare Book Department, Free Library of Philadelphia, copy HPC; RBH to JS, 19 June 1876, RBH to WHS, 19 June 1876, in *D&L*, 3: 326–27.

26. McPherson, *Hand-Book for 1876*, pp. 214–17; RBH to B. F. Potts, 30 June 1876, WHS to RBH, 1 July 1876, William A. Wheeler to RBH, 1 July 1876, HPC.

27. McPherson, *Hand-Book for 1876*, pp. 212–13, 217–22; RBH to W. D. Bickham, 25 June 1876, RBH to GWC, 22, 27, 30 June, 10 July 1876, RBH to JS, 23 June 1876, JS to RBH, 26 June 1876, Charles Foster to RBH, 29 June 1876, William Dennison [quoting Bristow] to RBH, 30 June 1876, JAG to RBH, 1 July 1876, HPC; RBH to GMB, 25 June 1876, GMB Papers, University of Texas, copy HPC; CS to RBH, 21 June 1876, in Frederic Bancroft, ed., *Speeches, Correspondence and Political Papers of Carl Schurz*, 6 vols. (New York: G. P. Putnam's Sons, 1913), 3: 250–51; hereafter cited as CS, *Speeches*.

28. WHS to RBH, 1 July 1876, A. C. Botkin to WHS, Aug. 1876, Wayne MacVeagh to RBH, 10 July 1876, GWC to RBH, 13 July 1876, WKR to RBH, 18 July 1876, HPC; RBH to Ulysses S. Grant, 14 July 1876, in *D&L*, 3: 334; "The One-Term Guarantee," *Nation*, 3 Aug. 1876, p. 68.

29. Polakoff, *Politics of Inertia*, pp. 113–16; C. R. Williams, *Hayes*, 1: 470; RBH to William Dean Howells, 23 July, 5, 24 Aug. 1876, Hayes-Howells Correspondence, Harvard University, copies HPC; list of diaries, scrapbooks, letters, etc., sent to W. D. Howells [Aug. 1876], William Dean Howells to RBH, 13 Aug. 1876, HPC; RBH to JAG, 27 July 1876, in *D&L*, 3: 337. Hayes even wondered whether he should attend the Philadelphia centennial on Ohio day, since his visit would give prominence to "objectionable politicians." RBH to Ralph P. Buckland, 15 Oct. 1876, HPC.

30. RBH to Edwin D. Morgan, 30 June, 10 July 1876, Morgan Papers, New York State Library, copies HPC; William A. Wheeler to RBH, 1 July 1876, Richard C. McCormick to RBH, 26 July 1876, HPC; Polakoff, *Politics of Inertia*, pp. 94–95; C. R. Williams, *Hayes*, 1: 471.

31. C. R. Williams, *Hayes*, 1: 472; Barnard, *Hayes*, p. 308; Stanley Matthews to RBH, 24 June 1876, HPC. For perhaps the only example of Zach Chandler writing to Hayes, see Chandler to

RBH, 13 Oct. 1876, HPC. On Zach Chandler's shortcomings, see Richard C. McCormick to RBH, 28, 29 Aug., 3 Sept. 1876, HPC. On the difficulty of raising money, see RBH to JS, 24 July 1876, in *D&L*, 3: 335; Richard C. McCormick to RBH, 25, 28 Aug., 14 Sept. 1876, HPC. Years later, in 1905 and 1917, William E. Chandler estimated that the committee raised roughly the same amount in 1868, 1872, and 1876. Leon Burr Richardson, *William E. Chandler: Republican* (New York: Dodd, Mead, 1940), pp. 145, 180. On assessments, see RBH to CS, 24 July 1876, in *D&L*, 3: 335; RBH to CS, 18 Aug. 1876, RBH to WHS, 10 Aug. 1876, CS to RBH, 3, 5 Sept. 1876, RBH to Richard C. McCormick, 8 Sept. 1876, Richard C. McCormick to RBH, 11, 14 Sept., 13 Oct. 1876, HPC; CS to RBH, 14 July, 14 Aug. 1876, RBH to CS, 15 Sept. 1876, in CS, *Speeches*, 3: 260–61, 285–86, 338–39.

32. RBH to JAG, 8 July, 5, 12 Aug. 1876, RBH to JS, 7 Aug. 1876, RBH to WHS, 5, 20 Oct. 1876, RBH to Richard C. McCormick, 14 Oct. 1876, in *D&L*, 3: 333, 338–40, 343, 364–67, 369–70; RBH to CS, 15 Sept. 1876, in CS, *Speeches*, 3: 338–39.

33. RBH to JAG, 6, 12 Aug. 1876, JAG Papers, LC, copy HPC; RBH to CS, 9 Aug. 1876, in CS, *Speeches*, 3: 284–85; Charles Nordhoff to RBH, 22, 28 June 1876, RBH to JS, 2 Aug. 1876, HPC.

34. CS to RBH, 14 Aug. 1876, in CS, *Speeches*, 3: 286–87; GWC to RBH, 31 Aug. 1876, RBH to GWC, 4 Sept. 1876, HPC; Charles Eliot Norton to GWC, 3 Oct. 1876, Norton Papers, Harvard University. Among the six congressional candidates from Ohio were Joseph Warren Keifer, who later became Speaker of the House and opposed civil-service reform, and William McKinley, who, as president, restored to the spoils system a large number of civil servants whom Grover Cleveland had added to the classified list.

35. RBH to Robert G. Ingersoll, 8 Aug. 1876, letter in possession of Eva Ingersoll, Wakefield, N.Y., copy HPC; RBH to JAG, 12 Aug. 1876, JAG Papers, LC, copy HPC; RBH, *Diary*, 13 Sept. 1876, p. 35; RBH to James G. Blaine, 14 Sept. 1876, in Mary A. Dodge, *Biography of James G. Blaine* (1895), p. 422, copy HPC.

36. Alphonso Taft to RBH, 23 Aug., 12 Sept. 1876, HPC.

37. Polakoff, *Politics of Inertia*, pp. 141–42; RBH, *Diary*, 13 Aug., 18 Sept. 1876, pp. 28–29, 37–38; RBH to WHS, 9 Sept. 1876, RBH to Richard C. McCormick, 14 Oct. 1876, in RBH, *Diary*, pp. 34–35, 41–42; RBH to James P. Root, 22 Aug. 1876, in *D&L*, 3: 351.

38. Charles Nordhoff to RBH, 15 Oct. 1876, Charles Nordhoff to Charles Foster, 15 Feb. 1877, HPC; Polakoff, *Politics of Inertia*, pp. 194–95; RBH to GMB, 30 Sept., 24 Oct. 1876, GMB Papers, University of Texas, copy HPC.

39. Polakoff, *Politics of Inertia*, pp. 129–31, 157–58, 161–62, 164–67; William A. Wheeler to RBH, 16 Oct. 1876, HPC.

40. Polakoff, *Politics of Inertia*, pp. 158–62; RBH to Roscoe Conkling, 15 Aug. 1876, in *D&L*, 3: 347, CS to RBH, 22 Oct. 1876, HPC.

41. Polakoff, *Politics of Inertia*, pp. 161–63.

42. Alphonso Taft to RBH, 20 Oct. 1876, WKR to RBH, 2 Nov. 1876, HPC; Polakoff, *Politics of Inertia*, pp. 142–44. On Davenport, see ibid., pp. 168–71, which digests Albie Burke, "Federal Regulation of Congressional Elections in Northern Cities, 1871–1894" (Ph.D. diss., University of Chicago, 1968), pp. 180–89.

43. RBH, *Diary*, 22, 29 Oct., 1 Nov. 1876, pp. 44–46; Polakoff, *Politics of Inertia*, pp. 197–98.

44. RBH, *Diary*, 22 Oct., 7 Nov. 1876, pp. 44–47.

45. Ibid., 11 Nov. 1876, pp. 47–48.

Chapter 17. The Disputed Election

1. Polakoff, *Politics of Inertia*, pp. 199–202; Jerome L. Sternstein, ed., "The Sickles Memorandum: Another Look at the Hayes-Tilden Election-Night Conspiracy," *Journal of Southern History* 32, no. 3 (Aug. 1966): 342–57.

2. Sternstein, "Sickles Memorandum," pp. 342–45; Alexander Clarence Flick, *Samuel*

Jones Tilden: A Study in Political Sagacity (New York: Dodd, Mead, 1939), pp. 324–25; Polakoff, *Politics of Inertia*, pp. 202–3.

3. Polakoff, *Politics of Inertia*, pp. 202–4; William E. Chandler to RBH, 9 Nov. 1876, HPC; Flick, *Tilden*, p. 326. For Reid's story, see *New York Times*, 11, 15 June 1887. Reid disparages the role of William E. Chandler while emphasizing that of the *Times* and Zachariah Chandler.

4. RBH, *Diary*, 11 Nov., 1876, p. 48; RBH to RPH, 8 Nov. 1876, HPC.

5. RBH, *Diary*, 11 Nov. 1876, pp. 48–49.

6. William E. Chandler to RBH, 9 Nov. 1876, HPC; James Ford Rhodes, *History of the United States: From the Compromise of 1850 to the End of the Roosevelt Administration*, 9 vols. (New York: Macmillan, 1928), 7: 292, n. 2.

7. RBH, *Diary*, 11–12 Nov. 1876, pp. 49–51. In contrast to Hayes, Richard Nixon controlled his campaign and made the decision not to challenge John F. Kennedy's 1960 victory, despite irregularities at the polls in both Texas and Illinois.

8. RBH to CS, 13 Nov. 1876, in *D&L*, 3: 378–79; CS to RBH, 10, 18 Nov. 1876, WHS to RBH, 10 Nov. 1876, Jacob Dolson Cox to RBH, 14 Nov. 1876, A. G. McCook to RBH, 17 Nov. 1876, HPC; Brooks D. Simpson, "Ulysses S. Grant and the Electoral Crisis of 1876–77," *Hayes Historical Journal: A Journal of the Gilded Age*, 11, no. 2 (Winter 1992): 6.

9. James N. Tyner to James M. Comly, 14 Nov. 1876, HPC; RBH to Lew Wallace, 11 Nov. 1876, Wallace Papers, Indiana Historical Society, copy HPC; Polakoff, *Politics of Inertia*, pp. 214–19.

10. Polakoff, *Politics of Inertia*, pp. 210–12; JS to I. Scott, 12 Nov. 1876, JS to Margaret Sherman, 20, 29 Nov. 1876, JS to RBH, 23 Nov. 1876, HPC; RBH to CS, 26 Nov. 1876, RBH to JS, 27 Nov. 1876, in *D&L*, 3: 381–82.

11. Polakoff, *Politics of Inertia*, pp. 219–20.

12. Rhodes, *History of the United States*, 7: 295, 301; Polakoff, *Politics of Inertia*, pp. 210–14; JS to RBH, 23 Nov. 1876, WHS to RBH, 5 Dec. 1877, HPC; RBH, *Diary*, 30 Nov., 3, 5 Dec. 1876, pp. 52–55.

13. Polakoff, *Politics of Inertia*, pp. 216–19; RBH to CS, 6 Dec. 1876, in *D&L*, 3: 386.

14. Polakoff, *Politics of Inertia*, pp. 225–27.

15. Ibid., pp. 227–31.

16. RBH, *Diary*, 7–8 Dec. 1876, pp. 56–57; RBH, Memorandum dictated to WCH, 12 Dec. 1876, HPC; RBH to Richard Henry Dana, Jr., 18 Dec. 1876, Dana Papers, Massachusetts Historical Society, copy HPC.

17. RBH to Samuel Shellabarger, 29 Dec. 1876, in RBH, *Diary*, pp. 60–61; James N. Tyner to James M. Comly, 16 Nov. 1876, HPC.

18. CS to RBH, 5 Dec. 1876, HPC; RBH, *Diary*, 17 Dec. 1876, p. 58; Polakoff, *Politics of Inertia*, pp. 220–23, 234–41; Flick, *Tilden*, pp. 330–32, 351. Hayes later said that Tilden was "no true Democrat" in the Jackson mold, since he "had not courage if he believed he was elected." WHS, "Memoranda," 16–17 June 1883, HPC.

19. Polakoff, *Politics of Inertia*, p. 259.

20. RBH, *Diary*, 5, 17 Dec. 1876, pp. 54, 58–59; JS to RBH, 12 Dec. 1876, Albert D. Shaw to RBH, 22, 28 Dec. 1876, RBH to Albert D. Shaw, 25, 31 Dec. 1876, HPC; RBH to JS, 17 Dec. 1876, JS Papers, LC, copy HPC. On Hayes's resolution "to remain wholly uncommitted as to persons and policy," see RBH to WKR, 17 Dec. 1876, RBH Papers, LC, and RBH to Richard Henry Dana, Jr., 18 Dec. 1876, Dana Papers, Massachusetts Historical Society, copies HPC. On Hayes's belief that political rights for all were linked to prosperity, see RBH to GMB, 23 Nov. 1876, in *D&L*, 3: 380.

21. WHS to RBH, 7, 14 Dec. 1876, RBH to Ralph P. Buckland, 17 Dec. 1876, HPC; RBH to WHS, 16 Dec. 1876, in *D&L*, 3: 390. Either Smith lied to Hayes or Kellar had a change of heart, for in June, he told Smith, "We must eliminate the negro & have two par-

ties . . . again." Polakoff, *Politics of Inertia*, pp. 244–45, 248; RBH, *Diary*, 1 Dec. 1876, pp. 52–53; McPherson, *Hand-Book for 1876*, p. 213. C. Vann Woodward, *Reunion and Reaction: The Compromise of 1877 and the End of Reconstruction* (Garden City, N.Y.: Doubleday, 1956), pp. 26–27.

22. JAG to RBH, 12 Dec. 1876, William Dennison to RBH, 13 Dec. 1876, HPC; Harry James Brown and Frederick D. Williams, eds., *The Diary of James A. Garfield*, 4 vols. (East Lansing: Michigan State University Press, 1967–81), 11, 12, 13 Dec. 1876, 3: 393–95 (hereafter cited as JAG, *Diary*).

23. John A. Kasson to RBH, 17 Dec. 1876, RBH to John A. Kasson, 31 Dec. 1876, in C. R. Williams, *Hayes*, 1: 517–18.

24. JS to RBH, 9 Dec. 1876, RBH to JS, 17, 25 Dec. 1876, RBH to William Dennison, 17 Dec. 1876, RBH to John A. Kasson, 31 Dec. 1876, RBH to Edward F. Noyes, 31 Dec. 1876, RBH to William E. Chandler, 31 Dec. 1876, RBH to Albert D. Shaw, 31 Dec. 1876, in *D&L*, 3: 392–93, 396–98; RBH to WKR, 31 Dec. 1876, RBH Papers, LC, copy HPC. Hayes rigorously avoided making commitments, but fourteen years later he observed, "It is easy to commit a president, or rather, to make it appear that he has promised, or expressed an opinion, when he may have done nothing of the kind." For example, after the election, Thomas L. Young read him a dispatch from Washington that demanded a response. Hayes laughed and said, "Tom, this is a question I ought not to answer yes or no," whereupon Young telegraphed that "I would not do so and so. He thus telegraphed what he thought it ought to be or what he thought his correspondent wanted to have him say. It was a commitment to which I was not a party." Hayes preferred Comly's approach, which was to answer a dispatch on his own responsibility without showing it to Hayes. His faith in Comly was such that he knew that the reply would undoubtedly be correct. WHS, Memoranda, 8–9 Aug 1890, HPC.

25. Henry Van Ness Boynton to WHS, morning, 20 Dec. 1876, Murat Halstead to RBH, 21 Dec. 1876, HPC; JAG, *Diary*, 18, 20 Dec. 1876, 3: 397–99.

26. Henry Van Ness Boynton to WHS, evening, 20 Dec. 1876, WHS Papers, Indiana Historical Society, copy HPC; WHS to RBH, 22 Dec. 1876, HPC; JAG, *Diary*, 21, 22, 30 Dec. 1876, 3: 399–400, 404, 409; James M. Comly to RBH, 8 Jan. 1877, HPC.

27. RBH to WKR, 17 Dec. 1876, RBH Papers, LC, copy HPC; Henry Van Ness Boynton to WHS, 26 Dec. 1876, WHS Papers, Indiana Historical Society, copy HPC; RBH, *Diary*, 5 Jan. 1876, p. 68; RBH to WHS, 24 Dec. 1876, 3 Jan. 1877, in *D&L*, 3: 393, 399; RBH to CS, 4 Jan. 1877, CS, *Speeches*, 3: 355; James N. Tyner to James M. Comly, 23 Dec. 1876, WHS to RBH, 5 Jan. 1877, HPC.

28. CS to RBH, 5 Dec. 1876, HPC; RBH to CS, 6, 7 Dec. 1876, RBH to JS, 5 Jan. 1877, JS to RBH, 13 Jan. 1877, in *D&L*, 3: 386, 388, 401; RBH to WKR, 31 Dec. 1876, RBH Papers, LC, copy HPC; Richard C. McCormick to WKR, 21 Dec. 1876, James N. Tyner to James M. Comly, 23 Dec. 1876, James M. Comly to RBH, 8 Jan. 1877, Samuel Shellabarger to RBH, 8 Jan. 1877, JS to RBH, 8 Jan. 1877, William E. Chandler to RBH, 13, 16 Jan. 1877, William E. Chandler to ?, 14, 18 Jan. 1877, HPC; Allan Nevins, *Hamilton Fish: The Inner History of the Grant Administration* (New York: Dodd, Mead, 1937), p. 850; Polakoff, *Politics of Inertia*, pp. 259–69.

29. JS to RBH, 22 Dec. 1876, James M. Comly to RBH, 8 Jan. 1877, HPC; Simpson, "Grant and the Electoral Crisis," pp. 8–10. At no point had Hayes intended to appoint Bristow to his cabinet. WHS, Memoranda, 8 Aug. 1890, HPC.

30. RBH, *Diary*, 17 Jan. 1877, p. 69; JAG, *Diary*, 4, 5, 8, 14 Jan. 1877, 3: 410–13, 415; WHS to JS, 8 Dec. 1876, Richard Smith to JS, 3 Jan. 1877, JS to RBH, 3, 8 Jan. 1877, James M. Comly to RBH, 8 Jan. 1877, William A. Wheeler to RBH, 15 Jan. 1877, William E. Chandler, to ?, 20 Jan. 1877, HPC; RBH to JS, 5, 16 Jan. 1877, in *D&L*, 3: 400–402; C. R. Williams, *Hayes*, 1: 518; Polakoff, *Politics of Inertia*, pp. 268–75. Boynton maintained that,

in committee, Conkling did not go beyond the proposed compromise. Henry Van Ness Boynton to James M. Comly, 25 Jan. 1877, HPC.

31. JAG, *Diary*, 19 Jan. 1877, 3: 420; Michael Les Benedict, "Southern Democrats in the Crisis of 1876–1877: A Reconsideration of *Reunion and Reaction*," *Journal of Southern History* 46 (1980): 509–10; Simpson, "Grant and the Electoral Crisis," pp. 13–15. Dennison claimed that prominent businessmen opposed the measure, but he was probably indulging in wishful thinking. William Dennison to RBH, 22 Jan. 1877, HPC.

32. RBH, *Diary*, 21 Jan. 1877, pp. 69–70; RBH to JS, 21 Jan. 1877, in *D&L*, 3: 405–6; JAG, *Diary*, 18, 24 Jan. 1877, 3: 418–19, 423; WHS to RBH, 23 Jan. 1877, HPC; JS to RBH, 26 Jan. 1877, William Dennison to RBH, 20 Jan. 1877, in C. R. Williams, *Hayes*, 1: 526, n. 1, 529, n. 1. Although he thought that the Republicans had surrendered, Boynton recognized that their position had been weak from the start, and he had "faith" that the bill would give the election to Hayes. Henry Van Ness Boynton to James M. Comly, 25 Jan. 1877, HPC.

33. William M. Dickson to RBH, 18, 23 Jan. 1877, Charles Foster to RBH, 21 Jan. 1877, HPC; RBH, *Diary*, 26 Jan. 1877, pp. 70–71.

34. JS to RBH, 26 Jan. 1877, William E. Chandler to ?, 29 Jan. 1877, HPC; RBH, *Diary*, 31 Jan. 1877, p. 71; JAG, *Diary*, 29 Jan. 1877, 3: 426; Polakoff, *Politics of Inertia*, pp. 279–85.

35. Polakoff, *Politics of Inertia*, pp. 230–31, 286; RBH to BAH, 1 Feb. 1877, Samuel Shellabarger to RBH, 5 Feb. 1877, HPC. Rhodes, *History of the United States*, 7: 329–37, gives a full account of the commission's decision on Florida.

36. RBH to CS, 2, 4 Feb. 1877, in *D&L*, 3: 412–13; RBH, *Diary*, 8, 9 Feb. 1877, pp. 73–74; Murat Halstead to RBH, 11, 12, 13 Feb. 1877, HPC; Polakoff, *Politics of Inertia*, p. 290.

37. Polakoff, *Politics of Inertia*, pp. 290–92; Henry Van Ness Boynton to WHS, 11 Feb. 1877, WHS Papers, Indiana Historical Society, copy HPC.

38. Samuel Shellabarger to RBH, 12 Feb. 1877, HPC; RBH to Eliza Davis, 4 Feb. 1877, in *D&L*, 3: 413; JAG, *Diary*, 12–16 Feb. 1877, 3: 438–42; Rhodes, *History of the United States*, 7: 338–39; Polakoff, *Politics of Inertia*, pp. 300–301. Had David Davis been on the commission, the result might not have been different. William Henry Smith reported to Hayes from Chicago that "Judge David Davis . . . spending three days in this city . . . most heartily approves the action of Judge Bradley. He says no good lawyer, not a strict partisan, could decide otherwise." Of course, the peculiar circumstances of his election — specifically the scheme of Tilden's nephew—could have affected Davis's judgment. WHS to RBH, 17 Feb. 1877, HPC.

39. RBH, *Diary*, 17–18 Feb. 1877, pp. 74–75.

40. Andrew J. Kellar to WHS, 17 Feb. 1877, Henry Van Ness Boynton to WHS, 18 Feb. 1877, WHS Papers, Indiana Historical Society, copies HPC; RBH to CS, 4 Feb. 1877, RBH to JS, 15 Feb. 1877, RBH to Samuel Shellabarger, 18 Feb. 1877, in *D&L*, 3: 412, 415, 417; Alphonso Taft to RBH, 19 Feb. 1877, HPC; Woodward, *Reunion and Reaction*, pp. 192–93; Polakoff, *Politics of Inertia*, pp. 301–3. On delays, see JAG, *Diary*, 17 Feb. 1877, 3: 442–43.

41. Charles Nordhoff to Charles Foster, 15 Feb. 1877, enclosed in Charles Foster to RBH, 16 Feb. 1877, HPC. Nordhoff had written Hayes in a similar vein during the recent campaign. Nordhoff to RBH, 22, 28 June 1876, HPC.

42. WHS to Richard Smith, 19 Feb. 1877, Charles Foster to RBH, 16 Feb. 1877, JS to RBH, 18 Feb. 1877, HPC.

43. RBH, *Diary*, 18 Feb. 1877, p. 75; Polakoff, *Politics of Inertia*, pp. 303–4; Woodward, *Reunion and Reaction*, p. 175.

44. Andrew J. Kellar to WHS, 20 Feb. 1877, WHS Papers, Indiana Historical Society,

copy HPC; WHS to RBH, 21 Feb. 1877, Charles Foster to RBH, 21 Feb. 1877, HPC; Polakoff, *Politics of Inertia*, pp. 304–5; Woodward, *Reunion and Reaction*, pp. 194–96.

45. JAG, *Diary*, 17–23 Feb. 1877, 3: 442–47; Rhodes, *History of the United States*, 7: 350; Woodward, *Reunion and Reaction*, p. 210; Henry Van Ness Boynton to WHS, 22 Feb. 1877, WHS Papers, Indiana Historical Society, copy HPC. Hayes's old friend George Hoadly argued the Democratic case for Oregon and never got over his failure. RBH, Diary, 10 Feb. 1888, in *D&L*, 4: 370.

46. Samuel Shellabarger to RBH, 23 Feb. 1877, Stanley Matthews, Charles Foster, and William Dennison to James M. Comly, 23 Feb. 1877, HPC; Polakoff, *Politics of Inertia*, pp. 308–9; Woodward, *Reunion and Reaction*, pp. 201–5.

47. RBH, *Diary*, 25–27 Feb. 1877, pp. 76–79.

48. JAG, *Diary*, 24, 25 Feb. 1877, 3: 447–48; JS to RBH, 24, 25 Feb. 1877, HPC; Polakoff, *Politics of Inertia*, pp. 309–11; Woodward, *Reunion and Reaction*, pp. 210–15; Simpson, "Grant and the Electoral Crisis," pp. 16–18.

49. JS to RBH, 24, 25 Feb. 1877, HPC; Benedict, "Southern Democrats in the Crisis," pp. 512–18; George Rable, "Southern Interests and the Election of 1876: A Reappraisal," *Civil War History* 26 (1980): 347–61; Simpson, "Grant and the Electoral Crisis," pp. 17–19.

50. JAG, *Diary*, 27 Feb. 1877, 3: 450; Stanley Matthews and Charles Foster to John B. Gordon and John Y. Brown, 27 Feb. 1877, Hayes Scrapbook 35: 16–18, WHS, Memoranda, 8–9 Aug. 1890, HPC; Henry Van Ness Boynton to WHS, 27 Feb. 1877, WHS Papers, Indiana Historical Society, copy HPC; Barnard, *Hayes*, pp. 389–91; Woodward, *Reunion and Reaction*, pp. 213–15; Polakoff, *Politics of Inertia*, pp. 311–12.

51. JAG, *Diary*, 28 Feb., 1 Mar. 1877, 3: 451–52; Polakoff, *Politics of Inertia*, p. 312; Woodward, *Reunion and Reaction*, pp. 216–18; Barnard, *Hayes*, pp. 392–95; Simpson, "Grant and the Electoral Crisis," pp. 18–19. Hayes later said that "holding the scales even in carrying out the Electoral Commission's decision" was Randall's "greatest act." RBH, Diary, 16 May 1891, in *D&L*, 5: 6.

Chapter 18. Two New Policies

1. RBH, *Diary*, 14 Mar. 1877, pp. 79–80; Simpson, "Grant and the Electoral Crisis," p. 19. General Sherman would not have countermanded such an order without the approval of Grant and Hayes. Although Grant thought that neither the Packard nor the Chamberlain government could be upheld by federal troops, he considered it Hayes's responsibility to determine which government to support and was not perturbed by the failure to carry out his orders.

2. RBH, *Diary*, 5, 17 Jan., 17, 19, 27 Feb. 1877, pp. 68–69, 74–75, 78–79; RBH to JS, 15, 16 Feb. 1877, JS to RBH, 17, 18 Feb. 1877, RBH to WME, 19 Feb. 1877, WHS, Memoranda, 8 Aug. 1890, HPC; RBH to CS, 17, 29 Jan., 25, 27 Feb. 1877, CS to RBH, 30 Jan., 26 Feb. 1877, Murat Halstead to CS, 16, 20 Feb. 1877, in CS, *Speeches*, 3: 361–62, 376–83, 388–89, 402–6.

3. WHS to RBH, 17 Feb., [3 Mar.] 1877, WHS, "Memoranda," 16–17 June 1883, William M. Dickson to RBH, 19 Feb. 1877, Grenville M. Dodge to RBH, 15 Feb. 1877, HPC; C. R. Williams, *Hayes*, 2: 20–24; RBH, *Diary*, 27 Feb., 14 Mar. 1877, pp. 78–80; RBH, Diary, 19 Apr. 1888, in *D&L*, 4: 385; JAG, *Diary*, 4 Mar. 1877, 3: 453. Although they agreed with Conkling in public, members of the New York delegation whispered to Hayes that neither they nor New York wanted Platt appointed. WHS, "Memoranda," 16–17 June 1883, HPC.

4. WHS, Memoranda, 9 Aug. 1890, HPC; C. R. Williams, *Hayes*, 2: 22–24.

5. *The National Republican* (Washington), 6 Mar. 1877. For the inaugural address, see James D. Richardson, ed., *Messages and Papers of the Presidents*, 20 vols. (New York: Bureau of National Literature, 1897–1918), 10: 4394–99. Hayes later recalled Lucy's "angel face" on that day. RBH, Diary, 4 Mar. 1890, in *D&L*, 4: 552.

6. C. R. Williams, *Hayes*, 2: 15; CS to RBH, 25 Jan., 2 Feb. 1877, in CS, *Speeches*, 3: 366–76, 384–86. Hayes later recollected that the quotable line "occurred to me as I was walking east on the North side of Broad St. in Columbus with a small party of friends in February 1877." RBH, *Diary*, 3 Aug. 1880, p. 290. The Indianapolis *Journal* suggested that Alexander Pope's translation of Homer's *Iliad* was the source of the idea. In the tenth book, Nestor awakens Diomed, one of his captains, saying, "He serves me most who serves my country best." C. R. Williams, *Hayes*, 2: 13, n. 1.

7. JAG, *Diary*, 5 Mar. 1877, 3: 454. D. W. Middleton, clerk of the Supreme Court, presented the Bible to Lucy Hayes and said that Hayes kissed the passage that concludes, "they compassed me about, but in the name of the Lord I will destroy them" (Ps. 118:11–13). Knowing that her husband would never pick vindictive verses, Lucy "laughed gayly, and said, 'Oh, no; I guess he won't destroy anybody.'" *National Republican* (Washington), 10 Mar. 1877.

8. JAG, *Diary*, 5 Mar. 1877, 3: 454; RBH, Diary, 5 Apr. 1886, in *D&L*, 4: 279–80; Cincinnati *Commercial*, 8 Mar. 1877; Barnard, *Hayes*, p. 404; C. R. Williams, *Hayes*, 2: 5–6, n. 3.

9. C. R. Williams, *Hayes*, 2: 16–17, 25–26; RBH, *Diary*, 14 Mar. 1877, pp. 80–81; JAG, *Diary*, 7 Mar. 1877, 3: 455.

10. JS to RBH, [Mar. 1877], Edward L. Pierce to William Dennison, 10 Mar. 1877, HPC; George W. Childs, proprietor of the Philadelphia *Public Ledger*, to WME, 9, 12 Mar. 1877, Ebenezer Rockwood Hoar to WME, 12 Mar. 1877, WME Papers, HPC; JAG, *Diary*, 8 Mar. 1877, 3: 455; C. R. Williams, *Hayes*, 2: 27–29.

11. Davison, *Presidency of Rutherford B. Hayes*, pp. 97–114.

12. C. R. Williams, *Hayes*, 2: 301–2; Davison, *Presidency of Rutherford B. Hayes*, pp. 92–95; RBH, *Diary*, 17 Jan. 1877, 5 Aug. 1880, pp. 69, 81, 291; RBH, Diary, 3 Dec. 1890, in *D&L*, 4: 619; "The Men in the Executive Office Are as Follows," Memorandum, 6 Oct. 1877, HPC; RBH to James Monroe, 3 July 1877, WKR to James Monroe, 7 July 1877, Monroe Collection, Oberlin College, copies HPC.

13. On the Whig party, see Thomas Brown, *Politics and Statesmanship: Essays on the American Whig Party* (New York: Columbia University Press, 1985); on Lincoln, see David Donald, "Abraham Lincoln: Whig in the White House," in *Lincoln Reconsidered: Essays on the Civil War Era*, 2d ed. (New York: Vintage Books, 1961), pp. 187–208; on Grant, see Summers, *Good Stealings*, pp. 188, 198; on Hayes, see Harry Barnard's perceptive chapter "Un–Whiggish Old Whig" in *Hayes*, pp. 450–64. One of the few books that Hayes found time to read while president was the *Diary* of John Quincy Adams; see RBH, *Diary*, 15 Mar., 27 Dec. 1878, pp. 128, 178.

14. Samuel Ward to WME, 31 Oct. 1877, WME Papers, HPC.

15. JAG, *Diary*, 14 Mar. 1877, 3: 458.

16. RBH, *Diary*, 12 Nov. 1876, pp. 50–51.

17. Ibid., 16 Mar. 1877, p. 83; RBH, Memorandum [Mar. 1877], HPC.

18. JAG, *Diary*, 11 Mar. 1877, 3: 457; RBH, *Diary*, 14, 16 Mar. 1877, pp. 81, 83.

19. RBH, *Diary*, 20, 23 Mar. 1877, pp. 84–85.

20. William M. Dickson to RBH, 20 Mar. 1877, HPC.

21. Jacob Dolson Cox to RBH, 31 Jan. 1877, William Johnston to RBH, 19 Feb. 1877, HPC; RBH to Jacob Dolson Cox, 2 Feb. 1877, Cox Papers, Oberlin College, copy HPC; RBH, *Diary*, 4 Oct. 1876, p. 39.

22. S. Straight to Stanley Matthews, 8 Mar. 1877, C. W. McIntyre to RBH, 14 Mar. 1877, Alexander H. H. Stuart to Richard W. Thompson, 15 Mar. 1877, Benjamin H. Hill

to Richard W. Thompson, 23 Mar. 1877, WHS to RBH, 22 Mar. 1877, John J. McCook to William Dennison, 23 Mar. 1877, Robert Bolling to David M. Key, 17 Mar. 1877, Lawrence S. Marye to David M. Key, 17 Mar., 14 Apr., 1 May 1877, HPC; RBH to JAG, 10 Mar. 1877, JAG Papers, LC, copy HPC; Andrew J. Kellar to Joseph Medill, 20 Mar. 1877, Andrew J. Kellar to WHS, 29 Mar. 1877, WHS Papers, Indiana Historical Society, copies HPC.

23. L. Q. C. Lamar to RBH, 22 Mar. 1877, HPC; Gillette, *Retreat from Reconstruction*, p. 341.

24. RBH, *Diary*, 28 Mar. 1877, 11 Apr. 1880, pp. 86, 270; JAG, *Diary*, 29, 31 Mar., 4 Apr. 1877, 3: 465, 467, 469; C. R. Williams, *Hayes*, 2: 49–53; Gillette, *Retreat from Reconstruction*, pp. 340, 343–44. Chamberlain later visited South Carolina and eventually concluded that in seeking to "lift a backward or inferior race" to political equality, Reconstruction had produced "shocking and unbearable misgovernment." Foner, *Reconstruction*, p. 605. Ironically, Hayes never gave up his faith in political equality.

25. WHS to RBH, 22 Mar. 1877, HPC; RBH, *Diary*, 4 Oct. 1876, p. 39; C. R. Williams, *Hayes*, 2: 54. In editing the diary entry of 4 October 1876, T. Harry Williams incorrectly ascribes MacVeagh's and Hayes's views to Blaine.

26. WME to Charles B. Lawrence et al., 2 Apr. 1877, HPC.

27. WME to Charles B. Lawrence, "Second Instructions to Louisiana Commission, [Apr.] 1877," HPC.

28. C. R. Williams, *Hayes*, 2: 56–58; Gillette, *Retreat from Reconstruction*, p. 344.

29. John M. Harlan to Benjamin H. Bristow, 9, 13 Apr. 1877, Bristow Papers, LC, copy HPC; C. R. Williams, *Hayes*, 2: 57–59; Gillette, *Retreat from Reconstruction*, pp. 344–45.

30. Andrew J. Kellar to WHS, 12 Apr. 1877, WHS Papers, Indiana Historical Society, copy HPC; Wayne MacVeagh to WKR, 2 May 1877, Andrew J. Kellar to David M. Key, 14 Apr. 1877, Kellar to WCH, 16 Apr. 1877, HPC. Two weeks later, Kellar claimed that he had secured the "end of the Louisiana troubles . . . by peaceful, legal methods, & by consent on both sides." Andrew J. Kellar to WHS, 26 Apr. 1877, WHS Papers, Indiana Historical Society, copy HPC. Kellar did not detail how he broke the laws of Louisiana.

31. RBH to George W. McCrary, 20 Apr. 1877, George W. McCrary to W. T. Sherman, 20 Apr. 1877, HPC; C. R. Williams, *Hayes*, 2: 59–64, 312, n. 1; Gillette, *Retreat from Reconstruction*, p. 345; Barnard, *Hayes*, pp. 479–81; Davison, *Presidency of Rutherford B. Hayes*, p. 139.

32. Andrew J. Kellar to David M. Key, 19 Apr. 1877, James M. Comly to RBH, 11 May 1877, HPC; Gillette, *Retreat from Reconstruction*, pp. 345–46.

33. Gillette, *Retreat from Reconstruction*, pp. 345–46; Stanley P. Hirshson, *Farewell to the Bloody Shirt: Northern Republicans & the Southern Negro, 1877–1893* (Bloomington: Indiana University Press, 1962), pp. 33–34; C. R. Williams, *Hayes*, 2: 65; WHS to RBH, 19 Apr. 1877, HPC.

34. MFF to RBH, 10 Apr. 1877, Charles Foster to RBH, 27 Apr. 1877, HPC; Edwin L. Godkin to WME, 21 Apr. 1877, WME Papers, HPC; JAG, *Diary*, 6 Apr. 1877, 3: 471; RBH to William D. Bickham, 22 Apr. 1877, in *D&L*, 3: 431. Hirshson, in *Bloody Shirt*, pp. 34–35, says that few Republicans supported the administration. Gillette, in *Retreat from Reconstruction*, pp. 346–47, attacks Hayes's policy as appeasement.

35. Andrew J. Kellar to RBH, 20 Apr. 1877, Murat Halstead to RBH, 20 May 1877, HPC; RBH, *Diary*, 22 Apr. 1877, pp. 86–87; RBH to William M. Dickson, 22 Apr. 1877, in *D&L*, 3: 431.

36. RBH to Oliver Wendell Holmes, 2 July 1877, Holmes Papers, LC, copy HPC; *National Republican* (Washington), 26–30 June, 2 July 1877; RBH, Diary, 27 July 1890, RBH, unaddressed and undated letter, in *D&L*, 4: 590, 5: 155; C. R. Williams, *Hayes*, 2: 241–42. On this trip, Hayes was saddened to encounter Ralph Waldo Emerson, who touched his head and acknowledged that he was "losing his wits."

37. J. Madison Wells to JS, 28 June 1877, JS to RBH, 2 July 1877, HPC.

38. RBH, *Diary*, 26 Aug. 1877, pp. 94–95; C. R. Williams, *Hayes*, 2: 242–45; William A. Wheeler to RBH, 3 Sept. 1877, HPC; *National Republican* (Washington), 24 Aug. 1877.

39. C. R. Williams, *Hayes*, 2: 245–53.

40. Ibid., 2: 351ff.; RBH, *Diary*, 25 Sept., 7 Oct., 3 Nov. 1877, pp. 96–97, 101. William Henry Smith agreed that the trip south was the "greatest success." WHS to RBH, 27 Sept. 1877, HPC.

41. RBH, *Diary*, 22 Apr. 1877, p. 87; RBH to William M. Dickson, 22 Apr. 1877, in *D&L*, 3: 431.

42. William J. Hartman, "Politics and Patronage: The New York Custom House, 1852–1902" (Ph.D. diss., Columbia University, 1952), p. 202.

43. Ari Hoogenboom, "The Pendleton Act and the Civil Service," *American Historical Review* 64 (1959): 301–3.

44. On 6 February 1867, Hayes opposed the move by Thaddeus Stevens to table the Jenckes bill. *Congressional Globe*, 39th Cong., 2d sess., 1036; Hoogenboom, *Outlawing the Spoils*, pp. 13–134, passim.

45. JAG, *Diary*, 5 Apr. 1877, 3: 470. Roger Sherman of Connecticut was Evarts's grandfather.

46. Ibid., 14 Mar. 1877, 3: 458; John C. Hopper to CS, 14 Mar. 1877, William Endicott, Jr., to CS, 22 Mar. 1877, William Welsh to CS, 24 Mar. 1877, CS Papers, LC.

47. "Systematic Reform," "Civil Service Reform in England," "Blackboard Examination," *New York Times*, 21, 22, 26 Mar. 1877; William Grosvenor to CS, 26 Mar. 1877, CS Papers, LC; CS to William Grosvenor, 29 Mar. 1877, CS, *Speeches*, 3: 410. George Jones, the proprietor of the *Times*, had pledged to Jacob Dolson Cox his emphatic support of an "earnest" attempt by the administration to reform the civil service. Jacob D. Cox to RBH, 20 Feb. 1877, HPC.

48. JTW to LWH, 13 Mar. 1877, RBH to John Davis, 8 July 1877, HPC; RBH, *Diary*, 24 Mar. 1877, 28 Apr. 1880, pp. 85, 274; "The Civil Service," *New York Times*, 6 Apr. 1877; *Nation*, 12 Apr. 1877, p. 213; P. O. to editor, 9 Apr. 1877, in *New York Times*, 16 Apr. 1877; Horace White to CS, 10 Apr. 1877, CS Papers, LC. Since Dr. Joe's health was failing and he was growing more irascible, Hayes may have welcomed an excuse not to appoint him.

49. John Cochrane to CS, 16 June 1877, HPC; RBH, *Diary*, 15–16 May 1877, p. 87; *National Republican* (Washington), 15, 17 May 1877; RBH to John A. Dix, 21 May 1877, Dix Papers, Columbia University, copy HPC; GWC to WME, 28 May 1877, WME Papers, HPC. Not sufficiently wealthy to subsidize the inadequate salary of the minister to Great Britain and desirous of continuing his support of civil-service reform, Curtis remained as editor of *Harper's Weekly*.

50. WHS to RBH, 9 May 1877, RBH to WHS, 13 May, 4, 24 June 1877, in *D&L* 3: 433–34, 436, 439; WHS to RBH, 28 May 1877, HPC.

51. Harlan to Stanley Matthews, 28 May 1877, GMB to RBH, 6 June 1877, HPC; RBH to GMB, 13 June 1877, GMB Papers, University of Texas, copy HPC; RBH to William D. Bickham, 30 May 1877, RBH, Diary, 20 Apr. 1886, in *D&L*, 3: 436, 4: 281; Geer, *First Lady*, pp. 264–65; *National Republican* (Washington), 12 June 1877. Thompson, whose job Hayes helped save in 1886, apparently became a Republican.

52. "Commissions to Examine Certain Custom-Houses of the United States," *House Executive Documents*, 45th Cong., 1st sess., 1877, vol. 1, no. 8, pp. 14–16.

53. JS to RBH, 26 May 1877, HPC; RBH to JS, 26 May 1877, in *D&L*, 3: 435.

54. JS to Chester A. Arthur, 28 May 1877, in "Commissions to Examine Certain Custom-Houses," pp. 18–20; "The Prospects of Reform," *Harper's Weekly*, 7 July 1877, p. 518.

55. Horace White to CS, 14 June 1877, CS Papers, LC.

56. See CS, undated memo on the political activities of officeholders, HPC; Richardson, *Messages*, 10: 4402–3; *Nation*, 28 June 1877, p. 373; William M. Dickson to RBH, 8 July 1877, HPC.

57. JS to RBH, 5 July 1877, Charles Eliot Norton to RBH, 22 July 1877, HPC. On 15 June, Hayes saw Simmons; the New England reformers abhorred him as an "adroit knave" and an ally of Benjamin F. Butler. During Hayes's conference with him, Simmons agreed to take the Boston customhouse out of politics. Ebenezer Rockwood Hoar to WME, 31 May 1877, WME Papers, HPC; *National Republican* (Washington), 16 June 1877.

58. William Grosvenor to CS, [15 July 1877], David A. Wells to CS, 1 Sept. 1877, CS Papers, LC; *National Republican* (Washington), 18 July 1877; *Nation*, 19 July, 6, 13 Sept. 1877, pp. 33, 143, 159, 162. Arthur claimed that his removals were based on evidence collected by the Jay Commission. Hartman, "Politics and Patronage," p. 206. In the customs service, naval officers had nothing to do with the navy; they acted as a check on collectors.

59. Hoogenboom, *Outlawing the Spoils*, p. 156; JS to RBH, 8 Mar. 1881, HPC.

60. Venila Lovina Shores, *The Hayes-Conkling Controversy, 1877–1879* (Northampton, Mass.: Smith College, 1919), p. 235. The Jay Commission was possibly repeating the 25 percent estimate of loss originally made by Revenue Commissioner David A. Wells in 1866 and used by Curtis in 1871, when he was chairman of the Grant Civil Service Commission. Hoogenboom, *Outlawing the Spoils*, pp. 117–18. The Philadelphia *Press* (31 Jan. 1866) also argued that corruption and laxity in the New York customhouse made that port so attractive to importers that they ignored more honestly administered ports; in December 1877, William Henry Smith in Chicago made the same point. WHS to RBH, 13 Dec. 1877, RBH to WHS, 16 Dec. 1877, in *D&L*, 3: 454–56. These charges were probably exaggerated. New York merchants believed that they suffered rather than benefited from the spoils system; consequently, they were one of the largest and most ardent groups supporting civil-service reform.

Chapter 19. A Troubled Summer

1. Bruce, *1877*, pp. 33–34, 40–42, 47–48, 50–55.

2. Ibid., pp. 63–65, 75–85. A striker in Martinsburg was fatally wounded.

3. RBH to MFF, 22 Oct. 1871, RBH to Sheriff of Stark County, [14 Apr. 1876], Letterbook, 3: 52, RBH to Allen T. Wikoff, 16 Apr. 1876, RBH, "Governor's Proclamation," 19 Apr. 1876, RBH to GMB, 7 May 1876, HPC; RBH to JAG, 7, 17 May 1876, JAG Papers, LC, copies HPC; RBH, *Annual Message of the Governor of Ohio, to the Sixtieth General Assembly, at the Regular Session, Commencing Jan. 1, 1872* (Columbus: Nevins & Myers, 1872), pp. 7–8; C. R. Williams, *Hayes*, 1: 439–40; Bruce, *1877*, p. 87.

4. Bruce, *1877*, pp. 85–99. Earlier, General Sherman had diverted these men from New York to Washington to prevent violence over the disputed election. William T. Sherman to J. C. Audenreid, 18 Nov. 1876, William T. Sherman Papers, HPC.

5. Bruce, *1877*, pp. 100–114, 209–10; RBH, Diary, 5 Apr. 1886, in *D&L*, 4: 279–80. Hayes also had a personal reason to stay up all night on 20 July. His son Webb, on his way home from New England, was scheduled to pass through Baltimore that Friday evening but was delayed. WKR to RBH, 20 July 1877, HPC.

6. For the story of the Great Strike in Pittsburgh as given here and in the following paragraphs, see Bruce, *1877*, pp. 115–83 passim.

7. Ibid., pp. 195, 209–18; RBH, *Diary*, 24 July, 2 Aug. 1877, pp. 88, 92; *National Republican* (Washington), 23 July 1877. On the surface, it would seem that Hayes and his cabinet would be friendly to railroad management and hostile to labor. Tom Scott had lobbied for Hayes's election, Hayes occasionally used Scott's private railroad car, and mem-

bers of his cabinet were involved with railroads. Evarts's law firm did work for Vanderbilt's Lake Shore road, Thompson had asked Scott in 1873 for a job for his son, and McCrary was close to Grenville M. Dodge, who was in Scott's employ. Yet neither Hayes nor his cabinet did the bidding of railroads, although they did wish to end the riots. Hayes's hostility to railroad managers increased as he grew older, but he seemed particularly contemptuous of Scott and readily believed the story (whose truth is unknown) that, as assistant secretary of war during the Civil War, Scott had participated in a deal that "bought muskets in Vienna at two francs each and sold them to [the] Government at twelve dollars to fifteen dollars each." RBH, Diary, 10 Oct. 1888, in D&L, 4: 410; Fred Albert Shannon, *The Organization and Administration of the Union Army*, 2 vols. (Gloucester, Mass.: Peter Smith, 1965), 1: 114–22; Allan Nevins, *The War for the Union: The Improvised War, 1861–1862* (New York: Charles Scribner's Sons, 1959), pp. 352–55.

8. RBH, *Diary*, 24–27 July 1877, pp. 88–90; Bruce. *1877*, pp. 219–22.

9. Bruce, *1877*, pp. 196–208, 222–23; RBH, *Diary*, 24 July 1877, pp. 87–88.

10. Bruce, *1877*, pp. 218–19; RBH, *Diary*, 24 July 1877, p. 87. Troops were in such short supply that three naval vessels were moved up the Potomac and a "naval brigade" was organized at the Washington Naval Yard to protect the capital. *National Republican* (Washington), 9 Aug. 1877.

11. Bruce, *1877*, pp. 223–29; *National Republican* (Washington), 23 July 1877.

12. Bruce, *1877*, pp. 233–53 passim.

13. Ibid., pp. 253–60, 273–76, 281–82.

14. Ibid., pp. 270–71, 278–80; S. D. Morgan to David M. Key, 24 July 1877, HPC.

15. Bruce, *1877*, pp. 285–91.

16. Ibid., pp. 287–90, 308–9; RBH, *Diary*, 26 July 1877, pp. 89–90; Gerald G. Eggert, *Railroad Labor Disputes: The Beginnings of Federal Strike Policy* (Ann Arbor: University of Michigan Press, 1967), pp. 34–41; George W. McCrary to Winfield Scott Hancock, 27 July 1877, HPC.

17. Bruce, *1877*, pp. 310–13.

18. Ibid., pp. 310–15; RBH, *Diary*, 31 July 1877, pp. 91–92. Among Hayes's close advisers, William M. Dickson was hostile to railroad management and a strong advocate of regulation. Dickson to RBH, 29 July 1877, HPC.

19. Bruce, *1877*, pp. 300–304.

20. RBH, *Diary*, 5 Aug. 1877, p. 93; WME to RBH, 6 Aug. 1877, WHS to RBH, 8 Aug. 1877, JS to RBH, 12 Aug. 1877, RBH to WHS, 11 Aug. 1877, George W. McCrary to F. L. Wood, 13 Aug. 1877, HPC; *National Republican* (Washington), 7 May, 10 Aug. 1878; *Washington Post*, 21 June 1878; *Providence Journal*, 27 Sept. 1878.

21. Barnard, *Hayes*, pp. 443–44; C. R. Williams, *Hayes*, 2: 208–10. Much of this account is based on Claude G. Bowers and Helen Dwight Reid, "William M. Evarts," in Samuel Flagg Bemis, ed., *The American Secretaries of State and Their Diplomacy*, 10 vols. (New York: Alfred A. Knopf, 1928), 7: 239–44; Brainerd Dyer, *The Public Career of William M. Evarts* (Berkeley: University of California Press, 1933), pp. 193–203; Chester L. Barrows, *William M. Evarts: Lawyer, Diplomat, Statesman* (Chapel Hill: University of North Carolina Press, 1941), pp. 350–61.

22. William S. Rosecrans to Stanley Matthews, 13 July, 19 Oct. 1877, enclosed in Stanley Matthews to RBH, 6 Aug., 29 Oct. 1877, HPC. On Rosecrans's railroad career in Mexico, see David M. Pletcher, *Rails, Mines, and Progress: Seven American Promoters in Mexico, 1867–1911* (Ithaca, N.Y.: Cornell University Press, 1956), pp. 34–71.

23. RBH, *Diary*, 24, 31 July 1877, 25 May 1879, pp. 87, 92, 104–5, n. 5, 221; Bowers and Reid, "Evarts," 7: 239–44; Cincinnati *Commercial*, 29 June 1878; *National Republican* (Washington), 10 Aug. 1878.

24. Details on the Nez Percé war come almost entirely from Alvin M. Josephy, Jr., *The*

Nez Percé Indians and the Opening of the Northwest (New Haven, Conn.: Yale University Press, 1965), pp. 445–643.

25. Ibid., p. 491; CS to John D. Long, 9 Dec. 1880, in CS, *Speeches*, 4: 55.

26. Josephy, *Nez Percé Indians*, p. 531.

27. *National Republican* (Washington), 11, 15, 16, 29 Aug. 1877; Russell F. Weigley, *History of the United States Army* (New York: Macmillan, 1967), p. 269. The Hayes administration seemed more concerned with negotiating the return of Sitting Bull and his Sioux followers and placating the Canadians than with the Nez Percé war.

28. RBH to CS, [1877–1881], #8978, CS Papers, LC, copy HPC. These notes probably (but not positively) refer to the Nez Percé war. In any event, they reveal Hayes's attitudes.

29. Josephy, *Nez Percé Indians*, p. 630.

30. CS to RBH, 21 Feb. 1881, CS Papers, LC, copy HPC.

31. John B. Wolff to CS, 6 Aug. 1877, HPC. A Washington attorney, Wolff drafted a bill to "regulate Indian Affairs" and printed his "Thorough Digest of the Indian Question . . . ," a copy of which is in the HPC.

32. Richardson, *Messages*, 10: 4427–28; New York *Tribune*, 27 Sept. 1877; John Q. Smith to CS, 8 Jan. 1878, CS to RBH, 11 Feb. 1878, RBH to John Q. Smith, 11 Feb. 1878, HPC; Hans L. Trefousse, "Carl Schurz and the Indians," *Great Plains Quarterly* 4 (Spring 1984): 111–13; Hans L. Trefousse, *Carl Schurz: A Biography* (Knoxville: University of Tennessee Press, 1982), p. 243; *Nation*, 10, 17 Jan. 1878, pp. 18, 34. Ironically, Hayes and Schurz later removed Hayt, after hearing that his son was involved with a disreputable Indian agent.

33. Leonard D. White, *The Republican Era, 1869–1901: A Study in Administrative History* (New York: Macmillan, 1958), pp. 187–92; RBH to Robert C. Rogers, 14 Jan. 1879, HPC.

34. RBH, *Diary*, 1 July 1878, p. 149; *National Republican* (Washington), 18, 25 Dec. 1878, 25, 29 Jan., 12, 21 Apr., 22 Oct., 31 Dec. 1879, 10 Mar. 1880; *Providence Journal*, 2–3 Oct. 1878, 19 Apr., 10 Dec. 1879; Cincinnati *Commercial*, 19, 20 Apr. 1879; *Washington Evening Star*, 22 July 1879; CS to RBH, 13 Oct. 1879, HPC; Trefousse, *Schurz*, pp. 242–45.

35. William T. Hagan, *Indian Police and Judges: Experiments in Acculturation and Control* (New Haven, Conn.: Yale University Press, 1966), pp. 39–43, 69–70, 154, 169–70.

36. George W. McCrary to CS, 9 May 1879, Ezra A. Hayt to CS, 16 Aug., 23 Oct. 1879, HPC. On the persistency of the intruders, see E. J. Brooks, acting commissioner of Indian affairs, to CS, 31 Jan., 9 Feb., 9 Mar. 1880, Alexander Ramsey to CS, 14, 20 Feb., 2, 10 Mar. 1880, HPC; Richardson, *Messages*, 10: 4499–4500, 4550–51; Richard N. Ellis, *General Pope and U.S. Indian Policy* (Albuquerque: University of New Mexico Press, 1970), pp. 219–22. Oklahoma became a state in 1907.

37. *National Republican* (Washington), 27, 29 Oct., 29 Nov. 1877, 19 Apr., 13 Nov. 1878; Fremont *Journal*, 15 Mar. 1878; C. R. Williams, *Hayes*, 2: 310; Geer, *First Lady*, pp. 176–77. The piano in the Red Parlor was so out of tune that the Hutchinsons performed a cappella. Listening to music over the telephone was apparently the rage. Hayes did so earlier that summer in New Hampshire. *National Republican* (Washington), 24 Aug. 1877.

38. RBH to WME, 4 Jan. 1878, RBH to David M. Key, 9 Jan. 1878, HPC; *DAB*, s.v. "Barton, Clara"; Matthew Josephson, *Edison* (New York: McGraw–Hill, 1959), pp. 168–69.

39. RBH, *Diary*, 2 Aug. 1878, p. 156; John B. Neil to W. A. Knapp, 9 Aug., 9 Dec. 1878, John B. Neil to WKR, 16 Aug. 1878, Marian Neil to RBH, 13 Aug. 1878, John B. Neil to L. Edgerton, 15 Sept. 1878, W. A. Knapp to WKR, 16 Dec. 1878, John W. Herron to RBH, 20 Aug. 1878, John B. Neil to RBH, 20 July 1880, HPC. As executor of Edgerton's estate, Neil destroyed everything in Edgerton's papers relating to the kiss Hayes had given Marian.

40. RBH, *Diary*, 26 Dec. 1877, 11, 22 June 1878, pp. 108, 147; Nancy Wade Halsted to Mrs. A. W. Chace, 22 June 1878, copy HPC; Theodore L. Cuyler in *Evangelist*? and New York *Tribune*, 24? June 1878, RBH, Scrapbook, 45: 51, 85, HPC; *National Republican* (Washington), 24 June 1878; RBH to Murat Halstead, 13 July 1878, Halstead Papers, Cincinnati Historical Society, copy HPC.

41. RBH, *Diary*, 26, 30 Dec. 1877, pp. 108–12; JTW to RBH, 7 Dec. 1877, HPC; *National Republican* (Washington), 22 Dec. 1877; C. R. Williams, *Hayes*, 2: 318–19.

42. *National Republican* (Washington), 1, 16 Jan., 6 Feb. 1878.

43. Otto Friedrich, *Clover* (New York: Simon and Schuster, 1979), pp. 202–3.

44. *National Republican* (Washington), 5 Jan. 1878; *Graphic* (New York), 19? Mar. 1878 (dateline of correspondence is 18 Mar. 1878), HPC; LWH to William A. Wheeler, Nov. 1878, HPC; Russell Hastings, "Genealogy and Autobiography of General Russell Hastings" (typewritten bound volume, 1900), ch. 16, pp. 4–7, HPC. Clover Adams thought that Emily Platt was "unaffected" but complained that she talked "through her nose badly." Friedrich, *Clover*, p. 203.

Chapter 20. Congress Triumphant

1. "Original Draft of the Famous *Substitute Resolution . . .* ," 26 Sept. 1877, Rochester Historical Society, Rochester, N.Y., copy HPC; Jordan, *Conkling*, pp. 277–78; *Nation*, 4 Oct. 1877, p. 203.

2. Jordan, *Conkling*, pp. 278–80.

3. W. L. Sessions to Charles Foster, 29 Sept. 1877, HPC; *Nation*, 4 Oct. 1877, p. 203; Samuel Ward to WME, 28 Sept. 1877, WME Papers, HPC; WHS to Edward F. Noyes, 6 Oct. 1877, WHS, Letterbook, Ohio Historical Society, copy HPC.

4. RBH, *Diary*, 4 Oct. 1877, pp. 96–97; JAG, *Diary*, 8, 19 Oct. 1877, 3: 526–27, 532; RBH to John A. Dix, 10 Oct. 1877, Dix Papers, Columbia University, copy HPC.

5. JAG, *Diary*, 14–15 Oct. 1877, 3: 529–30; McPherson, *Hand-Book for 1878*, pp. 177–82. David M. Abshire, *The South Rejects a Prophet: The Life of Senator D. M. Key, 1824–1900* (New York: Frederick A. Praeger, 1967), pp. 160–64, claims that moderate southern Democrats did not join the Republican party because Hayes procrastinated before removing troops in support of Republican regimes in South Carolina and Louisiana.

6. RBH, *Diary*, 4, 18 Oct. 1877, pp. 96–98; Hoogenboom, *Outlawing the Spoils*, pp. 160–61; GWC to Burt, 22 Oct. 1877, Burt Collection, New-York Historical Society. Since he sought and got a report on Merritt, Hayes probably received from trusted advisers (apart from Evarts) a positive evaluation of Prince. See William A. Wheeler to RBH, 4 Sept. 1877, HPC.

7. JAG, *Diary*, 13 Oct. 1877, 3: 529; RBH, *Diary*, 24 Oct. 1877, pp. 100–101.

8. Roscoe Conkling to JS, 15 Nov. 1877, John Jay to JS, 26 Nov. 1877, HPC; *Nation*, 22 Nov. 1877, p. 309; Shores, *Hayes-Conkling Controversy*, pp. 236–37. For a critical appraisal of Arthur as collector, see Thomas C. Reeves, *Gentleman Boss: The Life of Chester Alan Arthur* (New York: Alfred A. Knopf, 1975), pp. 67–131.

9. CS to Henry Cabot Lodge, 1 Dec. 1877, CS Papers, LC; Samuel Ward to WME, 4 Nov. 1877, WME Papers, HPC; Charles Devens to J. E. Sanford, 24 Oct. 1877, RBH to A. H. Rice, 7 Nov. 1877, in *Boston Journal*, 29 Oct., 12 Nov. 1877, copies HPC.

10. Hoogenboom, *Outlawing the Spoils*, pp. 163–64; RBH, *Diary*, 10 Dec. 1884, in *D&L*, 4: 180. Under pressure from Don Cameron, the Pennsylvania delegation signed the paper supporting Simon Cameron, but by the next day, a majority of the delegation called on Hayes to say that they had "signed under constraint, that the appointment would not

be proper and was not what Pennsylvania wanted!" WHS, "Memoranda," 16–17 June 1883, in *D&L*, 3: 514–15.

11. Richardson, *Messages*, 10: 4417–18; William M. Dickson to RBH, 4 Dec. 1877 [mismarked Nov.], HPC.

12. RBH to WHS, 8 Dec. 1877, HPC; RBH, *Diary*, 9 Dec. 1877, pp. 106–7.

13. *Nation*, 13, 20 Dec. 1877, pp. 357, 373; Dana to RBH, 14 Dec. 1877, HPC. Dana was a distinguished maritime lawyer and the celebrated author of *Two Years Before the Mast*.

14. Horace White, "The Civil-Service Issue in the Senate," *Nation*, 20 Dec. 1877, p. 376; Edward L. Pierce to CS, 27 Dec. 1877, Henry Cabot Lodge to CS, 20 Jan. 1878, CS Papers, LC; "The New Year in Politics," *Harper's Weekly*, 12 Jan. 1878, p. 26.

15. RBH to Edward L. Pierce, 4 Jan. 1878, Pierce Papers, Harvard University, copy HPC; GWC to RBH, 26 Dec. 1877, HPC; RBH, *Diary*, 13 Dec. 1877, p. 107; RBH to GWC, 31 Dec. 1877, in RBH, *Diary*, p. 112. Hayes's measure of Conkling in 1877 was probably close to his final judgment of the man in 1888. RBH, Diary, 19 Apr. 1888, in *D&L*, 4: 385.

16. C. R. Williams, *Hayes*, 2: 112–13; Unger, *Greenback Era*, pp. 336–53; John Sherman, *Recollections of Forty Years in the House, Senate and Cabinet: An Autobiography*, 2 vols. (Chicago: Werner, 1895), 1: 583; Allen Weinstein, *Prelude to Populism: Origins of the Silver Issue, 1867–1878* (New Haven, Conn.: Yale University Press, 1970), pp. 205–8.

17. Unger, *Greenback Era*, pp. 353–54; McPherson, *Hand-Book for 1878*, pp. 128–29.

18. McPherson, *Hand-Book for 1878*, pp. 129, 145–47; Unger, *Greenback Era*, pp. 354–55.

19. RBH, *Diary*, 5 Nov. 1877, 1 Oct. 1878, pp. 103, 162–63; Richardson, *Messages*, 10: 4413–17, 4422–23; Weinstein, *Prelude to Populism*, pp. 239–40; William M. Dickson to RBH, 4 Dec. 1877 [mismarked Nov.], HPC.

20. Charles Conant to JS, 3 Jan. 1878, H. C. Fahnstock to JS, 1 Feb. 1878, HPC; Unger, *Greenback Era*, pp. 357–58, 360–61. Hayes later said that he had been disappointed by Matthews's lack of "political wisdom" during his short senatorial career. RBH, Diary, 23 Mar. 1889, in *D&L*, 4: 459.

21. RBH, *Diary*, 3, 6 Feb. 1878, pp. 115–16; Henry C. Lea to CS, 22 Feb. 1878, HPC.

22. Murat Halstead to RBH, 20 Feb. 1878, Murat Halstead & Co. et al. to Stanley Matthews, 25 Feb. 1878, HPC; RBH, *Diary*, 17, 23, 26 Feb. 1878, pp. 117–18, 121–22; McPherson, *Hand-Book for 1878*, pp. 129–34.

23. Richardson, *Messages*, 10: 4438–40.

24. McPherson, *Hand-Book for 1878*, p. 128; RBH, *Diary*, 1 Mar. 1878, pp. 122–23; RBH to Benjamin F. Prescott, 1 Mar. 1878, HPC.

25. Unger, *Greenback Era*, pp. 364–73; JS, *Recollections*, 1: 629–46; JS to RBH, 9 Apr. 1878, HPC; RBH, *Diary*, 13, 14 Apr. 1878, p. 139; RBH, Diary, 15 May 1891, in *D&L*, 5: 6.

26. RBH, *Diary*, 1, 12 Mar. 1878, pp. 122–23, 125–26.

27. Ibid., 12 Mar. 1878, pp. 126–27.

28. JAG, *Diary*, 3–4 Mar. 1878, 4: 32–33.

29. Reid to WHS, 7 Mar. 1878, HPC. Reid thought that Hayes was mistaken in not consulting Blaine at the beginning of his administration. WHS, Memoranda, 9 Aug. 1890, HPC. Although not duplicitous, Smith played the role of a hard–nosed, practical politician among his newspaper cronies and in March 1878 was temporarily annoyed with the administration's reaction to his charges of undervaluations of imports by the New York customhouse. RBH to WHS, 27 Mar. 1878, in *Diary*, p. 133; WHS to RBH, 31 Mar. 1878, HPC.

30. E. L. Godkin, "The Senatorial Attack on the Administration," *Nation*, 4 Apr. 1878, p. 222; *National Republican* (Washington), 28, 29 Mar. 1878; RBH, *Diary*, 25 Mar. 1878, p. 133; Hirshson, *Bloody Shirt*, pp. 41–44.

31. RBH, *Diary*, 26 Mar., 13 Apr., 1878, pp. 133, 136–39; RBH to LWH, 27 Mar. 1878,

in *D&L*, 3: 472; RBH to William A. Wheeler, 26 Mar. 1878, HPC; *Nation*, 18 Apr. 1878, p. 251; CS to Henry Cabot Lodge, 6 Apr. 1878, CS Papers, LC.

32. JAG, *Diary*, 4 Mar. 1878, 4: 33; Wayne MacVeagh to RBH, 27, 31 Mar. 1878, HPC; Wayne MacVeagh to Charles Eliot Norton, 13 Apr. 1878, Norton Papers, Harvard University.

33. *Nation*, 2 May 1878, p. 285; RBH to GWC, 2 May 1878, GWC Papers, Harvard University; GWC to Jacob Dolson Cox, 3 May 1878, Cox Papers, Oberlin College.

34. George C. Gorham to _____, 27 May 1878, GWC Papers, HPC; CS to _____, 12 June 1878, in CS, *Speeches*, 3: 420–21; *Nation*, 27 June 1878, p. 412; Charles Eliot Norton to GWC, 21 May 1878, Norton Papers, Harvard University.

35. RBH, Memorandum, 22 Feb. 1878, HPC; *National Republican* (Washington), 23 Feb., 25, 26 Apr. 1878; William A. Wheeler to LWH, 30 Apr. 1878, HPC; Geer, *First Lady*, p. 184. Apparently, all was forgiven when the Hayeses gave a reception for seventy-three delegates to the annual meeting of the national Women's Christian Temperance Union. *National Republican* (Washington), 13 Nov. 1878.

36. C. R. Williams, *Hayes*, 2: 142–48; RBH, *Diary*, 19 Jan. 1878, p. 114; McPherson, *Hand-Book for 1878*, p. 186. On assuming office, the Hayes administration wished to appoint Montgomery Blair a commissioner of the District of Columbia, but Blair did "not think a Democrat ought to accept an office from Hayes." Minna Blair to Gist Blair, Mar. 1877, Blair Family Papers, LC.

37. JS to RBH, 9 Feb. 1878, RBH to Charles Devens, 9 Feb. 1878, HPC; RBH to GMB, 27 Feb. 1878, GMB Papers, University of Texas, copy HPC; RBH, *Diary*, 15 Feb., 21 Mar. 1878, pp. 116, 132; RBH, Diary, 5 Apr. 1886, in *D&L*, 4: 280; *National Republican* (Washington), 13 Feb. 1878.

38. C. R. Williams, *Hayes*, 2: 149–50.

39. RBH, *Diary*, 14 May 1878, pp. 141–42, C. R. Williams, *Hayes*, 2: 150–51; McPherson, *Hand-Book for 1878*, pp. 186–89.

40. RBH, *Diary*, 14, 19 May 1878, pp. 141–42; WHS to RBH, 27 Sept., 5 Dec. 1877, HPC; WHS to Andrew Kellar, 3 Nov. 1877, WHS to Richard Smith, 19 Nov. 1877, WHS, Letterbook, Ohio Historical Society, copy HPC; Kellar to WHS, 8 Nov. 1877, WHS Papers, Indiana Historical Society, copy HPC; C. R. Williams, *Hayes*, 2: 152. Boynton was angry with Hayes because he did not give an appointment to the son of Boynton's boss, Richard Smith. Despite Hayes's efforts to be friendly, Boynton remained cool to him. See RBH, *Diary*, 11 Apr. 1880, pp. 269–71.

41. Gath (George Alfred Townsend), "A Talk with Hayes," *Times* (Philadelphia), 31? May 1878, RBH, Scrapbook, 49: 61, HPC; RBH, *Diary*, 19, 31 May 1878, pp. 142–43; WHS to WCH, 4 June 1878, William M. Dickson to RBH, 1 June 1878, HPC; C. R. Williams, *Hayes*, 2: 155; *National Republican* (Washington), 31 May 1878. Five years later, William Henry Smith recorded that Hayes remembered saying (in words similar to those of Dickson) that if an unconstitutional attempt were made to put Tilden in his place, "Mr. Tilden will be arrested and shot. He cannot attempt to take possession of the White House without a fight. That means Civil War, and in that event we shall whip them badly." WHS, "Memoranda," 16–17 June 1883, HPC. In the Townsend "interview," Hayes spoke of civil war but did not mention Tilden and said nothing about executing anyone.

42. RBH to LWH, 20 May 1878, in *D&L*, 3: 483; C. R. Williams, *Hayes*, 2: 153.

43. C. R. Williams, *Hayes*, 2: 157–59; Barnard, *Hayes*, pp. 465–67; RBH to Irwin B. Linton, clerk of the Committee of Investigation, 6 June 1878, in Cincinnati *Commercial*, 8 June 1878; RBH, *Diary*, 2–3 June 1878, pp. 143–46.

44. McPherson, *Hand-Book for 1878*, pp. 192–94; C. R. Williams, *Hayes*, 2: 156–59; JS to Charles F. Conant, 26 June 1878, JS Papers, HPC.

45. RBH, *Diary*, 22 June 1878, p. 147; *National Republican* (Washington), 21, 22, 26 June 1878.

46. "The Democratic Designs," *Nation*, 4 July 1878, pp. 4–5; "Illustrations of 'Reform,'" *New York Times*, 8 July 1878, *National Republican* (Washington), 29 June 1878. Hayes heard that Butler and Conkling had met with Democrats at Butler's house and that Conkling had predicted that exposure of frauds would force Hayes out of office within ninety days. WHS, "Memoranda," 16–17 June 1883, HPC. Butler was polite to Hayes in person but bitterly attacked him behind his back, leading Hayes to remark: "Gen. Butler is a curious man; in some respects a kindly man, in others an extraordinary man; in many ways a rascal." WHS, Private Memoranda, 14 Dec. 1887, HPC.

Chapter 21. Hayes Takes Charge

1. RBH to GWC, 31 July 1878, GWC Papers, Harvard University; RBH, *Diary*, 15, 19 May 1878, pp. 142–43; *National Republican* (Washington), 15 Feb., 2, 23–25 May, 4, 7, 13, 14 June 1878.

2. JS to RBH, 10 July 1878, HPC; Thurlow Weed to Henry L. Dawes, 12 Dec. 1881, Dawes Papers, LC; Charles Eliot Norton to GWC, July 1878, Norton Papers, Harvard University.

3. GWC to George Edward Hall, 17 July 1878, GWC to RBH, 17 July 1878, WME to RBH, 13 July 1878, WHS to RBH, 5 Aug. 1878, HPC; RBH, *Diary*, 27 July 1878, p. 152; RBH to James Tanner, 26 July 1878, ibid.; "The Changes in the New York Custom-House," *Nation*, 18 July 1878, pp. 36–37.

4. WME to RBH, 13 July 1878, GWC to George Edward Hall, 25 July 1878, GWC to RBH, 17 July, 20 Aug. 1878, HPC. Graham was backed by Congressman Anson G. McCook of New York, who was an old friend of Hayes's from Ohio. WCH to McCook, 19 July 1878, HPC. Whitelaw Reid, a Blaine supporter, backed William H. Robertson for surveyor. In 1881, Garfield replaced collector Merritt with Robertson. Whitelaw Reid to JS, 14, 15 July 1878, JS Papers, LC.

5. RBH to GWC, 31 July 1878, GWC Papers, Harvard University; RBH to GWC, 22 Aug. 1878, Thomas L. James to GWC, 11 July, 23 Sept. 1878, GWC to RBH, 20 Aug., 30 Sept. 1878, Anson G. McCook to RBH, 23 Aug. 1878, HPC; *National Republican* (Washington), 4 Oct. 1878. Dorman B. Eaton later used James's words to describe the reform program as "the merit system" in contrast to the spoils system.

6. RBH, *Diary*, 1, 26 Sept. 1878, pp. 161–62; RBH, Diary, 3 Feb. 1889, in *D&L*, 4: 441; LWH to FAH, 6 Sept. 1878, HPC; *National Republican* (Washington), 4–5, 7, 9, 11–12, 14 Sept. 1878; WHS to RBH, 9 July 1878, Ohio Historical Society, copy HPC; RBH to C. W. Goddard, 7 Aug. 1878, Autographs, Maine Historical Society, copy HPC.

7. *National Republican* (Washington), 20 Sept. 1878.

8. RBH, *Diary*, 1 Oct. 1878, pp. 162–63; CS to RBH, 13 Sept. 1878, GWC to RBH, 30 Sept. 1878, RBH to GWC, 4 Oct. 1878, HPC.

9. Green B. Raum to JS, 18 July 1878, HPC; RBH, *Diary*, 28, 30 July 1878, pp. 154–56. On federal enforcement of internal revenue laws, see Wilbur R. Miller, "Reconstruction and Revenue: Dilemmas of Federal Enforcement in the South, 1870–1900" (paper in possession of its author, State University of New York at Stony Brook).

10. RBH, *Diary*, 5 Oct. 1878, p. 164; *National Republican* (Washington), 15, 23, 26 Oct., 2 Nov. 1878; *Providence Journal*, 13 Nov. 1878; W. E. Burghardt Du Bois, *Black Reconstruction in America . . . , 1860–1880* (Cleveland: The World Publishing Company, 1964), p. 403.

11. Hirshson, *Bloody Shirt*, pp. 45–46. Woolsey and Henry B. Harrison to RBH, 18 Oct. 1878, HPC; RBH to Woolsey and Harrison, 21 Oct. 1878, Woolsey Papers, Yale Uni-

versity, copy HPC; *National Republican* (Washington), 25 Oct. 1878; *Providence Journal*, 2 Nov. 1878; RBH, *Diary*, 12 Nov. 1878, p. 170.

12. Charles Devens to Charles E. Mayer, 3 Oct. 1878, copy HPC; I. R. Burns (assistant U.S. attorney) to JS, 19 Nov. 1878, Key to RBH, 15 Aug. 1878, HPC; RBH, *Diary*, 6 Nov. 1878, pp. 168–69; Hirshson, *Bloody Shirt*, pp. 46–50.

13. RBH, *Diary*, 26 Oct., 25 Dec. 1878, p. 167, 178; RBH to GMB, 13 Dec. 1878, 10 Jan. 1879, GMB Papers, University of Texas, copy HPC; GMB to RBH, 23 Dec. 1878, HPC; Richardson, *Messages*, 10: 4444–47. For favorable Republican reactions to Hayes's comments on southern "outrages," see Hirshson, *Bloody Shirt*, pp. 49–54. Hayes reputedly told the *National Republican* on 13 November 1878, "*I am reluctantly forced to admit that the experiment was a failure.*" But despite his displeasure with the results of the election in the South, Hayes did not admit the failure of his southern policy in his diary. Hayes may have been influenced by Charles Nordhoff, who continued to grasp at straws and persisted in the belief that the Democratic party could be split. Nordhoff to RBH, 23 Nov. 1878, HPC.

14. RBH, *Diary*, 6, 12 Nov. 1878, pp. 168–170.

15. McCook to RBH, 28 Sept. 1878, McCook to JS, 14 Nov. 1878, HPC.

16. WHS to RBH, 27 June 1878, HPC.

17. RBH to S. W. Dorsey, 6 July 1878, HPC. Dorsey had succeeded in Arkansas politics despite Hayes's lukewarm letter of recommendation. RBH to GWC, 22 Aug. 1878, WHS to RBH, 3, 16, 30 Oct. 1878, David M. Key to RBH, 15 Aug. 1878, WHS to WCH, 17 Oct. 1878, Charles A. Boynton to WHS, 11 Nov. 1878, HPC; RBH to CS, 4 Sept. 1878, CS Papers, LC.

18. Richardson, *Messages*, 10: 4450–51; RBH, *Diary*, 4 Jan. 1879, p. 183; *National Republican* (Washington), 8, 15 Jan. 1879; RBH to JS, 7 Apr., 22 Sept. 1879, JS to RBH, 3 May, 4 Oct. 1879, HPC.

19. William M. Dickson to RBH, 25 Jan. 1879, HPC; *National Republican* (Washington), 22, 25, 27, 29 Jan. 1879; RBH to WHS, 14, 19 Dec. 1881, in *D&L*, 4: 54–56; Margaret Susan Thompson, *The "Spider Web": Congress and Lobbying in the Age of Grant* (Ithaca, N.Y.: Cornell University Press, 1985), pp. 261–62. Schurz suggested and Hayes endorsed the idea that witnesses in pension cases be cross-examined by the government to eliminate frauds, but Congress did not enact this remedy. Hayes believed that the cheating was exaggerated and obscured the good the legislation did. If he had another opportunity to sign the bill, Hayes said, "*I would do it again,*" RBH to WHS, 14 Dec. 1881, in *D&L*, 4: 55.

20. RBH, *Diary*, 8, 17 Dec. 1878, pp. 175–77.

21. Ibid., 16 Dec. 1878, pp. 176–77.

22. RBH to Thomas C. Donaldson, 6 Jan. 1879, WHS Papers, Indiana Historical Society, copy HPC; WKR to JS, 8 Jan. 1879, JS to RBH, 8 Jan. 1879, HPC; *Nation*, 23 Jan. 1879, p. 60; Horace White, "Reform Within the Party," ibid., 30 Jan. 1879, p. 78; Reeves, *Arthur*, pp. 140–47; Jordan, *Conkling*, pp. 297–98; RBH to the Senate of the United States, 31 Jan. 1879, in Richardson, *Messages*, 10: 4463–64.

23. *Journal of the Executive Proceedings of the Senate of the United States of America* (Washington, 1828–1948), 21: 501–4; RBH to GWC, 5 Feb. 1879, E. Dunbar Lockwood to CS, 4 Feb. 1879, HPC; *New York Times*, 4 Feb. 1879; *Nation*, 6 Feb. 1879, p. 93; "Who Is Responsible for the Custom-House?" *Nation*, 6 Feb. 1879, pp. 96–97; Reeves, *Arthur*, pp. 146–47.

24. *Nation*, 12 Sept. 1878, p. 154; RBH to CS, 4 Sept. 1878, CS Papers, LC; CS to RBH, 13 Sept. 1878, RBH to JS, 4 Dec. 1878, D. M. Key to RBH, 4 Jan. 1879, HPC.

25. RBH to Edwin A. Merritt, 4 Feb. 1879, GWC to RBH, 13 Feb. 1879, HPC; RBH to Silas W. Burt, 6 Feb. 1879, RBH to C. K. Graham, 6 Feb. 1879, in RBH, *Diary*, p. 186.

26. *Nation*, 20 Feb., 13 Mar. 1879, pp. 127, 174; "The Civil Service Reform in the Custom-House," *New York Times*, 9 July 1879; Silas Wright Burt, "A Brief History of the Civil

Service Reform Movement in the United States," pp. K–L, Burt Writings, New York Public Library. Internal evidence suggests that this manuscript was written in 1906 and revised in 1908. S. W. Burt to RBH, 4 Apr. 1879, GWC to RBH, 28 June 1879, HPC; Edwin A. Merritt to GWC, 13 June 1879, GWC Collection, Staten Island Institute of Arts and Sciences; GWC to Silas W. Burt, 18 Aug. 1879, Burt Collection, New-York Historical Society.

27. C. R. Williams, *Hayes*, 2: 160–69. Years later, Hamilton Fish possibly revealed more about Republican partisanship than about Tilden's ethics when he assured Hayes that those who knew Tilden's "methods and character" did not doubt "his knowledge and connection" with the cipher dispatches. RBH, Diary, 7 Oct. 1885, in *D&L*, 4: 241.

28. *Providence Press*, 16 Apr., 12 Aug. 1878; *National Republican* (Washington), 20 Dec. 1877. As governor, Hayes pardoned "320 convicted criminals, including a dozen murderers, a score of forgers, and . . . two cases of abortion."

29. *DAB*, s.v. "Heywood, Ezra Hervey"; Martin Henry Blatt, *Free Love and Anarchism: The Biography of Ezra Heywood* (Urbana: University of Illinois Press, 1989), pp. 100–132; RBH, *Diary*, 10 Jan. 1879, pp. 183–84; RBH to Rev. Dr. R. M. Hatfield, 21 Feb. 1879, ibid., p. 188; Lyman Abbott to RBH, 25 Jan. 1879, Abbott to W. Claflin, 24 Feb. 1879, HPC; *Providence Journal*, 6 Jan. 1879.

30. Barnard, *Hayes*, pp. 135, 169, 504; RBH to Oliver Wendell Holmes, 21 Nov. 1885, Holmes Papers, LC, copy HPC.

31. Barnard, *Hayes*, pp. 480–81; RBH, *Diary*, 26, 28 Feb. 1879, 15 Feb. 1881, pp. 190–92, 310–11.

32. C. R. Williams, *Hayes*, 2: 312–15; RBH, Diary, 10 Jan. 1887, in *D&L*, 4: 304; *National Republican* (Washington), 26 Feb. 1879.

33. Blatt, *Free Love and Anarchism*, pp. 118–33; *DAB*, s.v. "Bennett, De Robigne Mortimer;" RBH, *Diary*, 10, 19 July 1879, pp. 237, 240; RBH, Diary, 27 Mar. 1892, in *D&L*, 5: 67–68. Hayes met Anthony Comstock when he came to Fremont in 1892 to preach at the Presbyterian church. He did not mention the Heywood pardon and praised Hayes for his Bennett decision. RBH, Diary, 17 July 1892, in *D&L*, 5: 97. In the 1990s, Americans are still groping for a pornography policy.

34. Alexander Saxton, *The Indispensable Enemy: Labor and the Anti-Chinese Movement in California* (Berkeley: University of California Press, 1971), pp. 5–7, 76–77.

35. Ibid., pp. 104–5, 109–10.

36. Ibid., pp. 118–20, 128–29, 132–33; McPherson, *Hand-Book for 1880*, pp. 39–41.

37. Saxton, *Indispensable Enemy*, pp. 134–35; GWC to RBH, 21 Feb. 1879, HPC; Henry Ward Beecher to WME, Feb., 26 Feb. 1879, WME Papers, HPC.

38. Saxton, *Indispensable Enemy*, pp. 136–37; RBH, *Diary*, 23 Feb. 1879, p. 190; Joaquin Miller to RBH, 26 Feb. 1879, HPC.

39. RBH, *Diary*, 23, 28 Feb. 1878, pp. 189–90, 192; RBH, Diary, 20 Dec. 1885, in *D&L*, 4: 257; C. R. Williams, *Hayes*, 2: 214–15; Barrows, *Evarts*, pp. 383–84; Richardson, *Messages*, 10: 4466–72. When suggestions were made in 1882 that Hayes regretted this veto, he wrote emphatically to Congressman William S. Rosecrans of California, "I certainly never expressed or entertained any doubt about the rightfulness of the veto." RBH to William S. Rosecrans, 17 Mar. 1882, in *D&L*, 4: 71.

40. RBH, *Diary*, 20, 23, 28 Feb. 1879, pp. 187–88, 190, 192; RBH to Henry Ward Beecher, 1 Mar. 1879, HPC.

41. *Congressional Record*, 45th Cong., 3d sess., 1770, 2141, 2384–85, 46th Cong., 1st sess., 1774–75; *DAB*, s.v. "Seward, George Frederick"; Barrows, *Evarts*, pp. 384–85.

42. Bowers and Reid, "Evarts," 7: 254–55; George F. Seward, "Memorandum on the Chinese Question Handed by Minister Seward to Mr. Evarts," 25 Mar. 1879, HPC. George F. Kennan flatly states that Hay "knew little if anything about China" and that the open door, though an old British policy, "was not an American policy." George F. Kennan, *American Diplomacy, 1900–1950* (Chicago: University of Chicago Press, 1951), pp. 27, 36.

Foster Rhea Dulles, however, observes that the roots of the open-door notes extend back to the mid-nineteenth century, though the notes themselves reflected America's expansion into east Asia. Foster Rhea Dulles, *America's Rise to World Power, 1898–1954* (New York: Harper & Row, 1955), pp. 62–63.

43. *National Republican* (Washington), 10 Jan. 1881; *DAB*, s.vv. "Angell, James Burrill," "Swift, John Franklin," "Trescott, William Henry"; Bowers and Reid, "Evarts," 7: 255–56; Charles I. Bevans, ed., *Treaties and Other International Agreements of the United States of America, 1776–1949*, 13 vols. (Washington, D.C.: Government Printing Office, 1968–76), 6: 685–90. President Chester Arthur vetoed the twenty-year suspension as an "unreasonable" restriction.

Chapter 22. Riders, Politics, and Reform

1. Trefousse, *Radical Republicans*, pp. 433–35; McPherson, *Reconstruction*, pp. 546–50; McPherson, *Hand-Book for 1872*, pp. 3–8, 85–87; McPherson, *Hand-Book for 1880*, pp. 55–64; Anson G. McCook to RBH, 11 July 1878, HPC; RBH to William Dean Howells, 9 Mar. 1879, Hayes-Howells Correspondence, Harvard University, copy HPC; *National Republican* (Washington), 7 Mar. 1879.

2. William Johnston to RBH, 15 May 1879, in C. R. Williams, *Hayes*, 2: 172, n. 1. In 1868, Grant lost New York by 10,000 out of 850,000 votes cast. Republicans, including Hayes, believed that frauds in New York City were responsible for the loss. RBH, *Diary*, 23 Mar. 1879, p. 199.

3. RBH, *Diary*, 9 Mar. 1879, p. 192; Richardson, *Messages*, 10: 4472–73.

4. C. R. Williams, *Hayes*, 2: 178–79; RBH, *Diary*, 18, 21, 22 Mar. 1879, pp. 193–94, 196–98.

5. RBH, *Diary*, 22, 23 Mar. 1879, pp. 198–202; William O. Stoddard to RBH, 23 Mar. 1879, HPC. Stoddard, a journalist and an author, later wrote a sketch of Hayes for his *Lives of the Presidents* (10 vols., 1886–89).

6. RBH, *Diary*, 18, 23 Mar. 1879, pp. 193, 201.

7. RBH, *Diary*, 23, 28 Mar. 1879, pp. 201, 205–6; RBH to WHS, 27 Mar. 1879, in C. R. Williams, *Hayes*, 2: 179.

8. RBH, *Diary*, 29–31 Mar. 1879, pp. 206–10; William Johnston to RBH, 29 Mar. 1879, RBH to William Johnston, 31 Mar. 1879, HPC. Ironically, a rider had authorized the creation of the Grant Civil Service Commission, and since it was important legislation, it infuriated spoilsmen such as John A. Logan of Illinois. Hoogenboom, *Outlawing the Spoils*, p. 87.

9. J. H. Jordan, M.D., to JS, 25 Mar. 1879, HPC; RBH to Murat Halstead, 31 Mar. 1879, in "Recollections and Letters of President Hayes," *Independent*, 16 Feb. 1899, copy HPC.

10. On the Porter case, see Kenneth P. Williams, *Lincoln Finds a General: A Military Study of the Civil War*, 5 vols. (New York: Macmillan, 1950–59), 1: 328–30, 2: 785–89. The board's report convinced Grant; in 1882, he wrote "An Undeserved Stigma" for the *North American Review* in Porter's behalf. K. P. Williams, *Lincoln Finds a General*, 2: 787. Choate was a partner in Evarts's law firm.

11. RBH, *Diary*, 13 Apr. 1879, p. 216.

12. Ibid., 18 Mar., 14 Dec. 1880, pp. 267, 302; MFF to RBH, 9 Nov. 1877, 22 Apr. 1879, 1 Dec. 1880, RBH to MFF, 26 Apr. 1879, JAG to Jacob Dolson Cox, 18 Feb. 1880, HPC. Hayes acknowledged the aid of Hancock—a Democratic general he trusted—in the Porter case. RBH, Diary, 5 Apr. 1886, in *D&L*, 4: 280.

13. RBH, *Diary*, 26–28 Apr. 1879, pp. 216–17.

14. For Hayes's veto message, see Richardson, *Messages*, 10: 4475–84; McPherson, *Hand-Book for 1880*, p. 107. Judge William Johnston of Cincinnati influenced this veto message. Johnston to RBH, 29 Mar. 1879, RBH to Johnston, 31 Mar. 1879, HPC.

15. JS to RBH, 3 May 1879, WHS to RBH, 10 May 1879, HPC; Cincinnati *Commercial*, 5 May 1879. See also William A. Wheeler to RBH, 5 May 1879, HPC.

16. RBH, *Diary*, 1, 11 May 1879, pp. 218–19; McPherson, *Hand-Book for 1880*, pp. 107–9.

17. RBH to E. D. Morgan, 15 May 1879, HPC. For Hayes's veto message, see Richardson, *Messages*, 10: 4484–88. The opinion of Samuel Shellabarger helped Hayes shape his veto message. Shellabarger to RBH, [May 1879], HPC.

18. JAG to RBH, 12 May 1879, Whitelaw Reid to RBH, 13 May 1879, HPC.

19. RBH, *Diary*, 15 May 1879, pp. 219–20; William M. Dickson to RBH, 20 May 1879, HPC.

20. Richardson, *Messages*, 10: 4488–93; McPherson, *Hand-Book for 1880*, p. 121; RBH, *Diary*, 25 May 1879, p. 221. "My habit is, if time permits," Hayes indicated, "to write my documents, to print and then, having them before me in satisfactory shape, to make the final additions and corrections." Ibid. Sherman and Schurz appreciated the clarity of Hayes's vetoes and, on one occasion, advised him not to allow Evarts, a master of obfuscation, to prepare a veto. WHS, Personal, 9 Sept. 1891, HPC.

21. C. R. Williams, *Hayes*, 2: 181, n. 1.

22. WHS, "Personal Memoranda," 25 May 1879, HPC; JAG, *Diary*, 25 May 1879, 4: 239–40.

23. RBH, *Diary*, 2, 4, 20 June 1879, pp. 224–26, 230–31; C. R. Williams, *Hayes*, 2: 199–200.

24. Richardson, *Messages*, 10: 4493–96; McPherson, *Hand–Book for 1880*, p. 128.

25. RBH, *Diary*, 25 June 1879, p. 232.

26. Ibid., 27 June 1879, pp. 232–33; Richardson, *Messages*, 10: 4497–99; McPherson, *Hand–Book for 1880*, p. 130.

27. RBH, *Diary*, 3 July 1879, pp. 233–34; Murat Halstead to RBH, 3 June 1879, HPC; RBH to L. Clarke Davis, 5 June 1879, in *D&L*, 5: 50–51.

28. WHS, "Personal Memoranda," 25 May 1879, HPC.

29. Ibid., 25, 26 May 1879; RBH, *Diary*, 6 June 1879, pp. 226–27.

30. GWC to RBH, 21 Apr. 1879, WKR to WHS, 23 Apr. 1879, WKR to Dear Sir, 1 Nov. 1879, WKR Papers, HPC.

31. WHS to WKR, 26 Apr. 1879, WKR Papers, HPC; WHS to RBH, 9 July, 7 Nov. 1879, WHS, "Personal Memoranda," 11 Sept. 1879, D. V. Bell to Sherman, 5, 13, 24 May 1879, HPC. Postmaster George C. Codd of Detroit reiterated Bell's argument that the rules were admirable for a large office but not for his office with its forty clerks. Codd to Key, 27 June 1879, HPC. For an example of modifying the rules out of existence, see T. B. Shannon to Sherman, 26 Nov. 1879, HPC.

32. Tyler to JS, 17 May, 25 June 1879, Tobey to Key, 19 May 1879, GWC to RBH, 30 Sept., 2 Dec. 1878, HPC.

33. Hilan H. Husted to RBH, 18 Apr. 1879, James N. Tyner to RBH, 29 Apr. 1879, HPC. Hayes may have paid more attention to Husted and his plea to be reinstated because he, like Hayes, had ties to "old Delaware." Having associated with Brady and others involved in the star-route frauds, Tyner resigned his post in 1881 at President Chester A. Arthur's request. Reeves, *Arthur*, p. 300.

34. James N. Tyner to David M. Key, 26 May 1879, HPC.

35. Richard W. Thompson to RBH, 22 Sept. 1879, HPC.

36. RBH, *Diary*, 7, 13 July, 8, 10, 15 Aug. 1879, pp. 238–39, 242–43.

37. Grace had been pardoned and had seen Sherman and Hayes in a successful attempt

to collect his back pay. *New York Times*, 21 July, 14, 21, 22, 25 Sept., 29 Nov., 18, 19 Dec. 1877; GWC to RBH, 28 June 1879, RBH to JS, 30 June 1879, HPC.

38. On Baltimore, see JS to RBH, 13 June 1879, C. Irvin Ditty to JS, 11 July 1879, HPC. On Cincinnati, see CS to RBH, 22 Aug. 1879, HPC; RBH to Thomas L. Young, 13 Aug. 1879, in *D&L*, 3: 570. On New York, see GWC to RBH, 8 Aug. 1879, WME to RBH, 10 Aug. 1879, HPC; GWC to WME, 8, 10 Aug. 1879, WME Papers, HPC; WME to GWC, 12 Aug. 1879, GWC Papers, Harvard University.

39. RBH, *Diary*, 14 Aug. 1879, pp. 243, 248.

40. GWC to RBH, 24 Aug. 1879, WHS, "Personal Memoranda," 11 Sept. 1879, HPC.

41. RBH to WME, 22 Aug. 1879, RBH to GWC, 30 Aug. 1879, HPC.

42. WHS, "Personal Memoranda," 11 Sept. 1879, GWC to RBH, 5 Sept. 1879, HPC. Recognizing that this very frank letter was atypical, Curtis asked Hayes to destroy it. Ibid. By 1 July 1881 (four months into the Garfield administration), Charles A. Gould had replaced Tyler as Buffalo collector, and Daniels had replaced Seth P. Remington as Ogdensburg collector.

43. WHS, "Personal Memoranda," 11 Sept. 1879, HPC.

44. RBH, *Diary*, 26 July 1879, p. 241; A. M. Stem to JS, 5 Sept. 1879, JS to A. M. Stem, 9 Sept. 1879, James N. Tyner to RBH, 8, 12 Sept. 1879, HPC. Assistant Treasurer Stem, with whose family Hayes had been intimate for years, held the position Grant had offered Hayes in 1873.

45. RBH, *Diary*, 5, 8, 21 Sept., 5 Oct. 1879, pp. 245–48; RBH to WME, 22 Sept. 1879, RBH to JS, 22 Sept. 1879, HPC; Cincinnati *Commercial*, 23–30 Sept. 1879; *National Republican* (Washington), 1–3 Oct. 1879.

46. JS to RBH, 4 Oct. 1879, HPC.

47. WHS, "Private Memoranda," 7 Oct. 1879, HPC.

48. RBH, *Diary*, 15 Oct. 1879, pp. 250–51.

49. WHS, "Private Memoranda," 7 Oct. 1879, JS to RBH, 4 Oct. 1879, CS to RBH, 25 Oct. 1879, HPC.

50. RBH, *Diary*, 5 Nov. 1879, p. 252.

51. Wayne MacVeagh to RBH, 29 Oct., 10 Nov. 1879, HPC; RBH to Wayne MacVeagh, 30 Oct. 1879, MacVeagh Papers, Historical Society of Pennsylvania, copy HPC; Wendell Phillips Garrison, "Disappearance of the Reform Administration," *Nation*, 20 Nov. 1879, pp. 339–40; Edward Cary to Silas W. Burt, 3 Dec. 1879, Burt Collection, New-York Historical Society. MacVeagh, who was also spoilsman Simon Cameron's son-in-law, was more in touch with political realities than the average reformer.

Chapter 23. The Succession

1. WHS, "Personal Memoranda," 23 Nov. 1879, HPC; RBH, *Diary*, 26 Nov. 1879, p. 253.

2. Richardson, *Messages*, 10: 4510–11, 4525–27; Unger, *Greenback Era*, pp. 372–73; Edward C. Kirkland, *Industry Comes of Age: Business, Labor, and Public Policy, 1860–1897* (New York: Holt, Rinehart & Winston, 1961), pp. 279–80; Joseph Wharton to Wayne MacVeagh, 24 Nov. 1879, HPC; RBH to Wayne MacVeagh, 25 Nov. 1879, MacVeagh Papers, Historical Society of Pennsylvania, copy HPC.

3. Richardson, *Messages*, 10: 4513–18.

4. RBH to William Walter Phelps, 7 Dec. 1879, in RBH, *Diary*, p. 255; RBH to Murat Halstead, 30 Nov. 1879, Halstead Papers, Cincinnati Historical Society, copy HPC.

5. WHS, Private Memoranda, 22 Nov. 1879, HPC; RBH, *Diary*, 18 Dec. 1879, pp. 256–57; JS to R. M. Stimson, 27 Dec. 1879, JS Papers, HPC. Hayes left no record of the

conversation with Grant beyond that they "had a quiet nice time" and that Grant "looks well and is in excellent spirits." RBH to LWH, 27 Dec. 1879, in *D&L*, 3: 583. Grant apparently asked Comly to arrange the interview. WHS, Private Memoranda, 14 Dec. 1887, HPC.

6. Jose S. Decond to WME, 1 Aug. 1879, HPC.

7. David McCullough, *The Path Between the Seas: The Creation of the Panama Canal, 1870–1914* (New York: Simon and Schuster, 1977), pp. 70–86, 104. Hayes had insisted that the American delegation be in full accord with his friend Ammen. RBH to Richard W. Thompson, 26 Mar. 1879, George N. Meissner Collection, Washington University, copy HPC.

8. Richardson, *Messages*, 10: 4521–22; "Message Recommending . . . Naval Stations on the American Isthmus," 2 Feb. 1881, RBH, Scrapbook, 85: 19, HPC; Dexter Perkins, *The Monroe Doctrine: 1867–1907* (Baltimore: Johns Hopkins University Press, 1937), pp. 74–75; RBH, *Diary*, 13 Jan. 1880, p. 258. On 11 September 1862, the Lincoln administration and Ambrose W. Thompson of Philadelphia approved a contract providing for a colony of freed slaves to mine coal and to establish a naval coaling station on lands owned by his Chiriqui Improvement Company. Because the coal was inferior and free blacks did not want to be colonized, the project failed, but the contract remained. On the Chiriqui grant, see Lincoln, *Collected Works*, 4: 561–62, 5: 414, 418–19, 434, 561–62; J. G. Randall, *Lincoln the President: Springfield to Gettysburg*, 2 vols. (New York: Dodd, Mead, 1946), 2: 137–40; John G. Nicolay and John Hay, *Abraham Lincoln: A History*, 10 vols. (New York: Century, 1890), 6: 357–59.

9. RBH, *Diary*, 7 Feb. 1880, pp. 261–62.

10. Ibid., 8 Feb. 1880, pp. 262–63.

11. Ibid., 11, 17, 20 Feb. 1880, pp. 263–65.

12. GWC, "M. Lesseps and the Monroe Doctrine," and Theodore Salisbury Woolsey, "The United States and the Lesseps Canal," *Harper's Weekly*, 28 Feb., 27 Mar. 1880, pp. 131, 195; Perkins, *Monroe Doctrine*, pp. 86–88.

13. WKR to GWC, 23 Feb. 1880, WKR Papers, HPC; GWC, "M. Lesseps and the Monroe Doctrine," *Harper's Weekly*, 13 Mar. 1880, pp. 162–63; RBH, *Diary*, 11 Apr. 1880, p. 273.

14. Richardson, *Messages*, 10: 4537–38; McCullough, *Path Between the Seas*, pp. 118–22; Perkins, *Monroe Doctrine*, pp. 71–77, 86–88.

15. McCullough, *Path Between the Seas*, pp. 122–27; Perkins, *Monroe Doctrine*, pp. 86–88; Richard W. Thompson to RBH, 18, 26 Aug. 1880, Richard W. Thompson to John Sherman, 10 Dec. 1880, JS to Richard W. Thompson, 10 Dec. 1880, HPC; RBH to Richard W. Thompson, 28 Aug. 1880, Lincoln National Life Foundation, copy HPC; C. R. Williams, *Hayes*, 2: 223–24.

16. Perkins, *Monroe Doctrine*, pp. 78–86.

17. Stanley P. Hirshson, *The Lion of the Lord: A Biography of Brigham Young* (New York: Alfred A. Knopf, 1969), pp. 189–90, 323–25.

18. Hayes's resolution was strengthened after consulting with William S. Godbe, leader of the schismatic "Godbe movement" in the Mormon Church and an opponent of Brigham Young. Hirshson, *Lion of the Lord*, pp. 304–7, 313; *National Republican* (Washington), 10 Jan. 1880; Thomas W. Ferry to RBH, 18 Jan. 1880, RBH to Thomas W. Ferry, 18 Jan. 1880, Ferry Papers, University of Michigan, copy HPC; J. B. Neil to RBH (introducing Godbe), 31 Dec. 1879, J. B. Neil to [John M.?] Morton, 13 Feb. 1880, HPC; RBH, *Diary*, 13 Jan. 1880, pp. 258–59; RBH to CS, 19 Feb. 1880, CS Papers, LC, copy HPC.

19. Richardson, *Messages*, 10: 4511–12, 4557–58; E. H. Murray to John M. Harlan, 18 Mar. 1880, HPC.

20. RBH to GMB, 28 Mar. 1880, GMB Papers, University of Texas, copy HPC; *Providence Journal*, 2 Jan. 1880; *National Republican* (Washington), 2, 14 Jan., 11 Feb. 1880.

21. *National Republican* (Washington), 30 Mar. 1880; RBH, *Diary*, 11 May 1880, p. 276; Menu, John Jacob Astor, 30 Mar. 1880, HPC; Elinor Mead Howells to Winifred Howells, 9 May 1880, in Ginette de B. Merrill and George Arms, eds., *If Not Literature: Letters of Elinor Mead Howells* (Columbus: Ohio State University Press, 1987), pp. 226–27.

22. Elinor Mead Howells to Winifred Howells, 9 May 1880, in Merrill and Arms, *If Not Literature*, pp. 226–27; RBH, *Diary*, 28 Apr. 1880, pp. 273–75.

23. *National Republican* (Washington), 6, 10 Mar. 1880.

24. An excellent, sympathetic, brief account of the Whittaker case is John F. Marszalek, Jr., "A Black Cadet at West Point," *American Heritage*, August 1971, pp. 30–37, 104–6; for the detailed story, see Marszalek's *Court-Martial: A Black Man in America* (New York: Charles Scribner's Sons, 1972). For an account that is skeptical of Whittaker's story, see Stephen E. Ambrose, *Duty, Honor, Country: A History of West Point* (Baltimore: Johns Hopkins University Press, 1966), pp. 234–37.

25. *National Republican* (Washington), 14, 17 Apr. 1880; RBH to John M. Schofield, 9 July 1880, in *D&L*, 3: 608; RBH, notes, 18 July 1880, HPC.

26. RBH, *Diary*, 12 July 1880, p. 283; RBH to MFF, 18 July 1880, in *D&L*, 3: 613–14; *National Republican* (Washington), 10, 24 Feb. 1881. Accused of "habitually" reversing courts-martial, restoring officers to the army, and demoralizing the service, Hayes responded that he and the secretary of war carefully examined all cases and that if mistakes were made, they "were, I hope, in all cases on the side of mercy and never on the side of severity." Hayes also doubted that these decisions, which usually involved young officers accused of "excesses" that their superiors indulged in themselves, demoralized the army. RBH, Diary, 9 Apr. 1884, 31 May 1887, RBH to Henry W. Slocum, 23 Jan. 1884, in *D&L*, 4: 138–39, 145, 327; RBH, MS Diary, 23 Jan., 13 June, 24 July 1884, George W. McCrary to RBH, 14 July 1887, HPC.

27. RBH to MFF, 18 July 1880, in *D&L*, 3: 613–14; MFF to RBH, 21 July 1880, HPC.

28. RBH to MFF, 28 July 1880, in *D&L*, 3: 616; MFF to RBH, 12 Aug. 1880, HPC; Marszalek, *Court-Martial*, pp. 142–45.

29. Ambrose, *Duty, Honor, Country*, p. 235; Marszalek, "Black Cadet," p. 37. In January 1884, Hayes, with no mention of the Whittaker case, attempted to restore cordial relations with Schofield. In August 1885, Schofield called on Hayes in New York on the occasion of Grant's funeral and told a moving story about Grant. RBH to John M. Schofield, 30 Jan. 1884, RBH, Diary, 7 Aug. 1885, in *D&L*, 4: 140, 229–30.

30. *National Republican* (Washington), 29, 30 Dec. 1880; Ambrose, *Duty, Honor, Country*, p. 236.

31. Marszalek, "Black Cadet," p. 106.

32. S. Peyton to JS, 3 Jan. 1880, WHS to JS, 9 Feb. 1880, WHS to WCH, 17 Feb. 1880, HPC.

33. RBH to GWC, 15 Jan. 1880, GWC to RBH, 20 Jan. 1880, HPC.

34. GWC to RBH, 20 Jan. 1880, HPC.

35. RBH, *Diary*, 20 Mar., 8 May 1880, pp. 267–68, 276; Richardson, *Messages*, 10: 4512–13, 4525–26, 4543–44.

36. McPherson, *Hand-Book for 1880*, pp. 135–40, 143–45; Richardson, *Messages*, 10: 4544–50.

37. WHS to RBH, 5, 15 May 1880, HPC; JS to C. W. Moulton, 21 May 1880, JS Papers, HPC. On the desperate mood of Grant's supporters, see Robert D. Marcus, *Grand Old Party: Political Structure in the Gilded Age, 1880–1896* (New York: Oxford University Press, 1971), pp. 29–36.

38. McPherson, *Hand-Book for 1880*, pp. 188–92; Marcus, *Grand Old Party*, pp. 30, 34–35; Peskin, *Garfield*, pp. 480–81; RBH, *Diary*, 5 June 1880, pp. 277–78; BAH to LWH, 13 June 1880, HPC.

39. RBH, *Diary*, 11 June 1880, pp. 278–79. Evidence that Hayes included Blaine among

those who were bitter against him may be found in Lucy Hayes's comment, "We are happy in the general's [Garfield's] nomination, and the escape from James G. B[laine]." LWH to Elinor Mead Howells, quoted without place or date in *D&L*, 3: 606, n.

40. JS to C. W. Moulton, 9, 13 June 1880, JS Papers, HPC; Charles Foster to S. T. Everett, 12 June 1880, Charles Foster to JS, 23 June, 7 July 1880, Letterbook 1880–82, pp. 237–38, 240–41, 247–54, 266–68, Foster Papers, Ohio Historical Society, copies HPC; RBH, *Diary*, 15 June 1880, p. 279; WHS, Memoranda, 9 Aug. 1890, HPC.

41. RBH, *Diary*, 15 June 1880, p. 279; RBH, "*The issues*: Notes by Pres. Hayes June 16, 1880," JAG Papers, LC, copy HPC.

Chapter 24. The Garfield Campaign

1. E. L. Applegate to JAG, 16 June 1880, JAG to RBH, 30 June 1880, Richard W. Thompson to CS, 30 June 1880, RBH to Richard W. Thompson, 7 July 1880, HPC.

2. JAG to RBH, 21 June, 5, 19 July 1880, WHS Papers, Indiana Historical Society, copy HPC; RBH to JAG, 8 July 1880, JAG Papers, LC, copy HPC.

3. RBH to JAG, 23 July 1880, JAG Papers, LC, copy HPC; Richard W. Thompson to RBH, 27 July, 18 Aug. 1880, HPC. Hayes wanted Huidekoper to "understand that no commendation by me of any applicant for place is to override your judgment as to what the good of the service requires." RBH to Henry S. Huidekoper, 18 Nov. 1880, HPC.

4. McPherson, *Hand-Book for 1880*, pp. 192–94; Peskin, *Garfield*, p. 484; GWC to Silas W. Burt, 22 July 1880, Burt Collection, New-York Historical Society; RBH, *Diary*, 13, 14, 19 July 1880, pp. 285–88. Evarts, however, thought that Garfield's letter was "very well done." WME to Thurlow Weed, 15 July 1880, WME Papers, HPC.

5. RBH to JAG, 26 July 1880, JAG Papers, LC, copy HPC. Peskin, *Garfield*, p. 484, clearly explains the "simple arithmetic" that compelled Garfield to appease the stalwarts.

6. JAG to RBH, 31 July 1880, WHS Papers, Indiana Historical Society, copy HPC; JS to C. W. Moulton, 2 Aug. 1880, JS Papers, HPC; RBH, *Diary*, 5, 8 Aug. 1880, pp. 290–91; RBH to JAG, 5 Aug. 1880, JAG Papers, LC, copy HPC; Peskin, *Garfield*, pp. 487–91.

7. JAG to RBH, 18 Aug. 1880, WHS Papers, Indiana Historical Society, copy HPC.

8. RBH, *Diary*, 21 July 1880, pp. 288–89; McPherson, *Hand-Book for 1880*, p. 195.

9. C. R. Williams, *Hayes*, 2: 290–92; RBH, *Diary*, 26 June, 5 July, 5 Aug. 1880, pp. 280, 282, 291.

10. RBH to Frank Hatton, 24 Aug. 1880, in C. R. Williams, *Hayes*, 2: 292–93.

11. After Hayes's administration, Republican apathy over the civil rights of blacks increased. In 1894, under Grover Cleveland, the Democrats swept away the Enforcement Acts, disfranchising virtually all southern blacks. McPherson, *Hand-Book for 1894*, pp. 131–142; Hirshson, *Bloody Shirt*, pp. 192–200.

12. RBH, *Diary*, 14 Aug. 1880, p. 293; RBH to JAG, 16 Aug. 1880, JAG Papers, LC, copy HPC. For example, Walker's expert in charge of collecting social statistics about cities was George E. Waring, the most outstanding sanitary engineer of his generation. For Walker's work on the ninth and tenth census, see *DAB*, s.vv. "Walker, Francis Amasa," "Waring, George Edwin"; White, *Republican Era*, pp. 193–94; Trefousse, *Schurz*, p. 247.

13. Geer, *First Lady*, p. 159; Richardson, *Messages*, 10: 4430; *National Republican* (Washington), 6 Aug. 1877; RBH to J. Edwards Clarke, 24 Dec. 1886, in C. R. Williams, *Hayes*, 2: 225–26; *DAB*, s.vv. "Mills, Robert," "Corcoran, William Wilson," "Marsh, George Perkins."

14. RBH, *Diary*, 14 June 1879, p. 230; Washington Metropolitan Chapter of the American Institute of Architects, *A Guide to the Architecture of Washington, D.C.* (New York: Frederick A. Praeger, 1965), pp. 39–40; Richardson, *Messages*, 10: 4533.

15. RBH, *Diary*, 8 Aug. 1880, p. 291; Peskin, *Garfield*, pp. 495–96; JAG to Jay Hubbell, 22 Aug. 1880, JAG Papers, LC, copy HPC; Edw. M. Johnson to S. B. Curtis, 23 Oct. 1880, John Cessna to [officeholder], 25 Oct. 1880, GWC Papers, HPC.

16. RBH, Diary, 28 Apr., 3 May 1881, in *D&L*, 4: 10–14; *Nation*, 28 Apr. 1881, p. 287; Ellis Paxson Oberholtzer, *A History of the United States Since the Civil War*, 5 vols. (New York: Macmillan, 1917–37), 4: 116–17; White, *Republican Era*, pp. 376–77. Tyner was subsequently (1893–1903) involved in defrauding the Post Office Department. Ibid., pp. 271–74.

17. Anson G. McCook to RBH, 7 May 1880, HPC.

18. RBH, *Diary*, 8 July 1880, p. 282; RBH to William Dean Howells, 4 Aug. 1880, Hayes-Howells Correspondence, Harvard University, copy HPC; RBH to W. D. Bickham, 19 Aug. 1880, HPC.

19. RBH, *Diary*, 19, 24, 28 Aug. 1880, pp. 293–95. An excellent account of this western trip is in Davison, *Presidency of Rutherford B. Hayes*, pp. 213–23.

20. C. R. Williams, *Hayes*, 2: 293–94; RBH to FAH, 18 Sept. 1880, HPC; RBH to JAG, 13 Sept. 1880, JAG Papers, LC, copy HPC; *National Republican* (Washington), 3–4, 6–8, 10, 13 Sept. 1880; *Daily Evening Post* (Monterey), 17 Sept. 1880.

21. C. R. Williams, *Hayes*, 2: 295–96.

22. *Oregon Sentinel* (Jacksonville), 29 Sept., 6 Oct. 1880, 15 Jan. 1881; *Democratic Times* (Jacksonville), 15 Oct. 1880; *National Republican* (Washington), 4 Oct. 1880; LWH to FAH, 3 Oct. 1880, HPC; RBH, *Diary*, 7 Nov. 1880, p. 297; Geer, *First Lady*, pp. 225–27; Davison, *Presidency of Rutherford B. Hayes*, pp. 218–19. Referring to Madame Holt's complaint, Hayes maintained that "nothing to injure her was ever done by me or any of the party." *Oregon Sentinel* (Jacksonville), 15 Jan. 1881.

23. *Daily Oregonian* (Portland), 5–8 Oct. 1880; *National Republican* (Washington), 6, 7 Oct. 1880; RBH to FAH, 3, 6, 17 Oct. 1880, LWH to FAH, 3 Oct. 1880, Programme, First U. S. Cavalry Band, 5 Oct. 1880, CS to RBH, 2 Oct. 1883, HPC; Geer, *First Lady*, pp. 213–14, 227–29; Davison, *Presidency of Rutherford B. Hayes*, pp. 219–20; *NAW*, s.v. "Winnemucca, Sarah."

24. RBH, *Diary*, 7 Nov. 1880, p. 297; RBH, Scrapbooks, 78: 140, RBH to FAH, 17 Oct. 1880, RBH to Eliza Davis, 1 Dec. 1880, MFF to RBH, 2 Nov. 1880, HPC; *National Republican* (Washington), 19, 21, 23, 25, 26, 30 Oct., 1 Nov. 1880; J. K. Shiskin, "The Wonderful Year of 1880," *La Gaceta: El Boletin del Corral de Santa Fe Westerners* 5 (1970): 14–17; Davison, *Presidency of Rutherford B. Hayes*, pp. 220–23.

25. *Oregonian* (Portland), 26? Oct. 1880; *National Republican* (Washington), 2 Nov. 1880; C. R. Williams, *Hayes*, 2: 297; RBH to JAG, 22 Aug. 1880, JAG Papers, LC, copy HPC; JS to RBH, 1 Nov. 1880, HPC. See also Charles Francis Adams, Jr., to CS, 3 Nov. 1880, WHS to RBH, 8 Nov. 1880, HPC.

26. C. R. Williams, *Hayes*, 2: 297–98.

Chapter 25. Lame Duck

1. RBH to JAG, 30 Oct. 1880, JAG Papers, LC, copy HPC; RBH, *Diary*, 14 Nov. 1880, p. 299.

2. Richardson, *Messages*, 10: 4553–58.

3. Ibid., 10: 4561–63, 4565–66, 4573; Charles S. Campbell, *The Transformation of American Foreign Relations, 1865–1900* (New York: Harper & Row, 1976), pp. 87–91.

4. The chief sources of revenue were tariffs ($186.5 million) and excise taxes ($124 million). The major expenditures were for interest on the public debt ($95.8 million); for pensions ($56.8 million); for the army, including river and harbor projects by army engineers

($38.1 million); for public buildings, collecting the revenue, and miscellaneous expenses ($34.5 million); for civil expenses ($15.7 million); for the navy ($13.5 million); and for Native Americans ($5.9 million). Richardson, *Messages*, 10: 4566–69.

5. Ibid., 10: 4569–75.

6. Ibid., 10: 4577; A. Hunter Dupree, *Science in the Federal Government: A History of Policies and Activities to 1940* (Cambridge: Harvard University Press, 1957), pp. 195–210.

7. Richardson, *Messages*, 10: 4575–77.

8. RBH, *Diary*, 8 Dec. 1880, p. 301; George F. Hoar to RBH, 20 Nov. 1880, RBH to George F. Hoar, 24 Nov. 1880, RBH to Henry L. Dawes, 27 Nov. 1880, in *D&L*, 3: 626.

9. *National Republican* (Washington), 10 Nov. 1877; Cincinnati *Commercial*, 10 Nov. 1877; CS to John D. Long, 9 Dec. 1880, in CS, *Speeches*, 4: 50–57.

10. CS to John D. Long, 9 Dec. 1880, in CS, *Speeches*, 4: 57–70; Trefousse, *Schurz*, pp. 245–46; Richardson, *Messages*, 10: 4582–84.

11. *DAB*, s.v. "Bright Eyes"; Trefousse, *Schurz*, p. 246; Richardson, *Messages*, 10: 4584.

12. Richardson, *Messages*, 10: 4582, 4585; Trefousse, *Schurz*, pp. 246–47. Hayes urged Hoar to persuade Congress to provide Garfield with a contingency fund, declaring, "With ten thousand dollars each year I could have done a great deal of good." RBH to George F. Hoar, 16 Dec. 1880, in *D&L*, 3: 631. In his methodical way, Hayes had already made inquiries about Allen. RBH to William Dean Howells, 8 Aug. 1879, Hayes-Howells Correspondence, Harvard University, copy HPC. Hayes rejected a candidate named by the Boston committee because he was "bitterly hostile" to the Interior Department. RBH to Walter Allen, 18 Dec. 1880, HPC.

13. CS, "Report of the Secretary of the Interior," *House Executive Documents*, 46th Cong., 3d sess., 1880, no. 1, pt. 5, Interior, 1: 3–4; CS, "Draft of a Message on the Ponca Commission," Jan. 1881, HPC; Richardson, *Messages*, 10: 4585–86.

14. Richardson, *Messages*, 10: 4585–86; Henry L. Dawes to RBH, 1 Feb. 1881, in *D&L*, 3: 629 n.; Trefousse, *Schurz*, p. 247; RBH, Memorandum, 21 Jan. 1887, Collection of Joseph Rubinfine, Pleasantville, N.J., copy HPC.

15. RBH to WHS, 3 Jan. 1881, *D&L*, 3: 634; Davison, *Presidency of Rutherford B. Hayes*, p. 132; *DAB*, s.v. "Woods, William Burnham."

16. RBH to Dorman B. Eaton, 3 Dec. 1880, in Dorman B. Eaton, *The "Spoils" System and Civil Service Reform in the Custom-House and Post-Office at New York* (New York: G. P. Putnam's Sons, 1881), pp. vi, 62–69, 71–77; Committee on Civil Service and Retrenchment, "Report [to accompany Bill S.133]," *Senate Reports*, 47th Cong., 1st sess., 3, no. 576, p. 57. Schurz stimulated workers in the Pension Office to do their utmost by adjusting their salaries every three months on the basis of efficiency reports. CS to Edwin L. Godkin, 7 Dec. 1879, CS Papers, LC.

17. RBH to JAG, 29 Nov. 1880, 28 Jan. 1881, JAG Papers, LC, copies HPC. For decades, Hayes had thought highly of Pease. RBH to GMB, 9 Feb. 1854, HPC; RBH to GMB, 22 Jan. 1855, in *D&L*, 1: 478.

18. RBH to JAG, 4 Dec. 1880, 8, 28 Jan. 1881, JAG to RBH, 17 Feb. 1881, JAG Papers, LC, copies HPC; JAG, *Diary*, 16 Nov. 1880, 4: 487–89.

19. JAG to RBH, 14 Jan. 1881, JAG Papers, LC, copy HPC; JAG to RBH, 1 Dec. 1880, WHS Papers, Indiana Historical Society, copy HPC; Peskin, *Garfield*, pp. 146, 305–6, 488.

20. JAG to RBH, 14 Jan. 1881, JAG Papers, LC, copy HPC; Collis P. Huntington to JS, 6 July 1880, personal file of Gen. E. O. C. Ord, National Archives, copy HPC; Thomas A. Scott to JAG, 29 Nov. 1880, copy HPC; Wayne MacVeagh to WKR, 4 Nov. 1880, HPC; JAG to RBH, 1 Dec. 1880, WHS Papers, Indiana Historical Society, copy HPC.

21. RBH, *Diary*, 23 Jan. 1881, p. 307. William T. Sherman to JS, 31 Jan. 1881, William T. Sherman Papers, HPC; *DAB*, s.vv. "Miles, Nelson Appleton," "Hazen, William Babcock"; Robert Wooster, *Nelson A. Miles and the Twilight of the Frontier Army* (Lincoln: University of Nebraska Press, 1993), pp. 129–31.

22. RBH to JAG, 16 Dec. 1880, 8 Jan. 1881, JAG to RBH, 14 Jan. 1881, JAG Papers, LC, copies HPC.

23. J. D. Cameron to Stanley Matthews, 29 Jan. 1881, Stanley Matthews to RBH, 31 Jan., 5, 8 Feb. 1881, RBH to WKR, 5 Feb. 1881, HPC; RBH to JAG, 11 Feb. 1881, JAG Papers, LC, copy HPC; *Journal of the Executive Proceedings of the Senate . . . ,* 23: 75–76 (12 May 1881), copy HPC; *DAB,* s.v. "Matthews, Stanley"; United States, *Register of Officers,* 1881.

24. JAG to RBH, 7 Feb. 1881, RBH to JAG, 11 Feb. 1881, JAG Papers, LC, copy HPC; *Fremont Journal,* 11 Mar. 1881. For an example of Conkling's efforts to frustrate Hayes, see *National Republican* (Washington), 15 Jan. 1881.

25. RBH to JAG, 28 Jan., 11 Feb. 1881, JAG to RBH, 7, 17 Feb., 4 May 1881, JAG Papers, LC, copies HPC; RBH, *Diary,* 14 Dec. 1880, 16 Jan. 1881, pp. 302, 305–6. Hayes liked the phrase "amiable obstinacy" but later preferred "good-humored inflexibility," which he discovered in Emerson's "Self Reliance." RBH, Diary, 29 Mar. 1890, in *D&L,* 4: 560.

26. RBH, Memorandum for Garfield, 17 Jan. 1881, in *D&L,* 3: 639–40; JAG, *Diary,* 8 Jan. 1880, 4: 348.

27. Geer, *First Lady,* pp. 220–24; RBH to Frederick Merrick, 15 Jan. 1881, RBH, Letter Draft, [15 Jan. 1881], RBH to Daniel Huntington, 12 Mar. 1881, HPC; RBH, *Diary,* 9 Feb. 1881, p. 308. Also, as long as he was president, Hayes did not want circulars of the Woman's Home Missionary Society of the Methodist Episcopal church to be sent out over Lucy's signature, even though he had encouraged her to accept the titular presidency of that organization. In January 1881, he thought that he had made a mistake and wondered if there were a graceful way for her to resign, but upon returning to Fremont, Hayes wanted Lucy to retain her office. RBH to Eliza Davis, 14, 19 Jan. 1881, HPC; Geer, *First Lady,* pp. 224, 254–60.

28. RBH to Frederick T. Frelinghuysen, 2 Apr. 1877, HPC; RBH, *Diary,* 4, 17 Dec. 1880, 11, 15 Feb. 1881, pp. 300, 302–3, 308–10; *National Republican* (Washington), 15 Dec. 1880.

29. RBH, *Diary,* 2, 9 Jan. 1881, pp. 304–5; *National Republican* (Washington), 2, 17, 31 Jan., 28 Feb. 1881. John A. Logan often opposed Hayes, but he was always ready to mend political fences, and neither Hayes nor Lucy harbored grudges. As far as pushing their husbands' political careers, Mary Logan was far more involved than Lucy was. Edith King Davis was the daughter of Thomas Starr King, the Unitarian clergyman who ardently defended the Union in California.

30. *National Republican* (Washington), 12 Jan., 23, 25 Feb. 1881; RBH, *Diary,* 25 Feb. 1881, pp. 311–12; RBH to James M. Comly, 24 Feb. 1881, Comly Papers, Ohio Historical Society, copy HPC.

31. RBH, *Diary,* 15, 16 Dec. 1880, p. 302; *National Republican* (Washington), 5 July, 15, 30 Dec. 1880, 14 Jan., 4, 18 Feb. 1881; LWH to Mrs. L. Austin, 13 July 1880, Whitelaw Reid to RBH, 2 Apr. 1881, HPC; Geer, *First Lady,* pp. 219–20; Friedrich, *Clover,* p. 262. Lizzie Reid inherited half of her father's fortune and became a distinguished philanthropist. *NAW,* s.v. "Reid, Elizabeth Mills."

32. RBH, *Diary,* 28 May 1879, p. 222; C. R. Williams, *Hayes,* 1: 82, 2: 299–301; Barnard, *Hayes,* p. 404.

33. RBH, *Diary,* 8 Feb. 1878, 13 June, 25 Dec. 1879, 13 Mar., 25 Dec. 1880, pp. 116, 230, 257–58, 266–67, 303.

34. RBH, *Diary,* 1 Jan., 4 Oct. 1877, 21, 31 Mar., 14 June 1879, pp. 65, 96, 196, 208, 230; "Guests at the Last Family Dinner . . . 2 Mar. 1881," HPC.

35. RBH to Murat Halstead, 26 Nov. 1880, Halstead Papers, Cincinnati Historical Society, copy HPC; RBH to WHS, 3 Jan. 1881, in *D&L,* 3: 635; RBH to JS, 3 May 1881, HPC; New York *Tribune,* 15 Dec. 1880. Ten years later, Hayes claimed that his expenditures out-

ran his income in the White House and that the reduction of his debts came from real-estate sales. RBH to Thomas Donaldson, 10 Mar. 1891, in *D&L*, 4: 640–41. Since Hayes paid little attention to his expenditures while president or in retirement, either story could be true, or the truth might lie between. In 1881, he was trying to assure Garfield that his salary would more than cover his expenses, and in 1891, he was trying to counter stories that parsimony had motivated his ban on alcoholic beverages and enabled him to save $20,000 annually.

36. Richardson, *Messages*, 10: 4589–91; McPherson, *Hand-Book for 1882*, pp. 10–12; RBH, *Diary*, 3 Mar. 1881, p. 313; Thurlow Weed to WME, 26 Feb. 1881, WME Papers, HPC.

37. Barnard, *Hayes*, p. 500; Peskin, *Garfield*, p. 540; JAG, *Diary*, 3, 4 Mar. 1881, 4: 552–53; *National Republican* (Washington), 5 Mar. 1881.

Chapter 26. Spiegel Grove

1. RBH, *Diary*, 9 Mar. 1881, pp. 313–14; RBH to JS, 6 Mar. 1881, HPC; RBH to JAG, 6 Mar. 1881, JAG Papers, LC, copy HPC; *Fremont Journal*, 11 Mar. 1881.

2. RBH, *Diary*, 9 Mar. 1881, p. 314; C. R. Williams, *Hayes*, 2: 335–36.

3. RBH, *Diary*, 10 Mar. 1881, p. 315; GWC to RBH, 4 Mar. 1881, CS to RBH, 6 Mar. 1881, Silas W. Burt to RBH, 7 Mar. 1881, HPC.

4. JS to RBH, 8 Mar. 1881, RBH to WME, 16 Mar. 1881, WME to RBH, 29 Mar. 1881, WHS, Private Memoranda, 14 Dec. 1887, HPC; RBH, Diary, 11 Mar. 1881, RBH to WHS, 29 Mar. 1881, in *D&L*, 4: 3, 6.

5. Lyman Abbott to RBH, 8 Mar. 1881, S. C. Armstrong et al. to RBH, 7 Mar. 1881, HPC; RBH to S. C. Armstrong, 27 Aug. 1877, Massachusetts Historical Society, copy HPC; RBH to S. C. Armstrong, 16 Mar. 1881, *Southern Workman* (Hampton Institute) 10, no. 4 (Apr. 1881): 41, copy HPC.

6. LWH to William A. Wheeler, c. 15 Apr. 1881, HPC.

7. RBH, Diary, 12 Apr., 3, 6, 9, 12 May, 27 July, 10 Sept. 1881, 1 Jan. 1882, 13 Feb., 27 Mar. 1883, RBH to MFF, 10 May 1881, 11 Jan., 26 July 1882, in *D&L*, 4: 7, 11–12, 15–17, 27, 35, 59–60, 62, 83–84, 107, 113–14; C. R. Williams *Hayes*, 2: 355.

8. RBH, *Diary*, 16 Jan. 1881, pp. 306–7; John D. Defrees to RBH, 26 Mar., 10 Apr. 1881, HPC.

9. William A. Wheeler to LWH, 10 Apr. 1881, JS to RBH, 12 May 1881, HPC; RBH to JAG, no day or month 1881, 14 May 1881, JAG to RBH, 22 May 1881, JAG Papers, LC, copies HPC; RBH to John Hay, 16 May 1881, Hay Papers, Brown University, copy HPC; RBH to MFF, 21 May 1881, in *D&L*, 4: 19.

10. RBH, Diary, 18 May 1881, RBH to Austine Snead, 25 Apr. 1881, in *D&L*, 4: 10, 19.

11. *Nation*, 24 Feb., 28 Apr. 1881, pp. 122, 287; Peskin, *Garfield*, pp. 504, 579. Peskin estimates Republican expenditures in Indiana at $70,000. Ibid., p. 504. In 1871, Dorsey was incensed with Hayes, who refused to write a laudatory letter of introduction for him before his departure to Arkansas. RBH to S. W. Dorsey, 17 Mar. 1871, in *D&L*, 3: 137.

12. RBH, Diary, 28 Apr., 3 May 1881, RBH to unidentified, 3 May 1881, in *D&L*, 4: 10–14.

13. RBH, MS Diary, 3 July 1881, HPC; RBH, Diary, 3 July 1881, RBH to JS, 7 July 1881, RBH to John Hay, 8 July 1881, in *D&L*, 4: 23–25.

14. RBH to H. C. Corbin, 11 July 1881, RBH to Lucretia Garfield, 26 July 1881, RBH to D. C. Swaim and H. C. Corbin, 28 Aug. 1881, RBH, Diary, 27, 30 Aug., 19 Sept. 1881, in *D&L*, 4: 25–27, 32–36.

15. RBH to Silas W. Burt, 8 Aug. 1881, Burt Papers, New-York Historical Society, copy

HPC; Silas W. Burt to RBH, 13 Sept. 1881, HPC; RBH, Diary, 28–29 Sept. 1881, RBH to Emile Kahn (editor, *Fair Journal of the Jewish Orphan Asylum*, Cincinnati), 1 Oct. 1881, in *D&L*, 4: 37. When in Washington, Hayes called at the White House but was so depressed by the thought of Garfield suffering "two long months in the room we occupied as our sleeping room" that "it was a relief to get away." RBH to Martha Porter, 15 Nov. 1881, Yale University, copy HPC.

16. RBH, Diary, 7–13, 20 Oct. 1881, 17 May 1882, RBH to WCH, 6, 12 Oct. 1881, RBH to FAH, 7, 9, 11 Oct. 1881, RBH to GMB, 8 Oct. 1881, in *D&L*, 4: 38–48, 76.

17. RBH, Diary, 9 Oct. 1881, in *D&L*, 4: 42. On the establishment of the Slater Fund, see "Introduction" and the correspondence primarily between Hayes and Leonard W. Bacon from 10 Oct. to 4 May 1882, in Rubin, *Teach the Freeman*, 1: xiv–xvii, xx, 3–36.

18. "Introduction," RBH to Leonard W. Bacon, 1 Dec. 1881, Leonard W. Bacon to RBH, 26 Dec. 1881, 4 May 1882, in Rubin, *Teach the Freeman*, 1: xvii–xx, 19–20, 25–26, 35–36; RBH, Diary, 18 May 1882, in *D&L*, 4: 76–77.

19. "Introduction," Leonard W. Bacon to RBH, 6 Feb., 27 Mar., 5 May, 17 Sept. 1882, RBH to JLMC, 15 July 1882, JLMC to RBH, 17 July 1882, James P. Boyce to RBH, 31 July 1882, William E. Dodge to RBH, 8 Aug. 1882, RBH to DCG, 14 Aug., 14 Oct. 1882, DCG to RBH, 16 Aug. 1882, AGH to RBH, 11 Oct., 13 Nov. 1882, in Rubin, *Teach the Freeman*, 1: xxi–xxiii, 30, 32, 36–41, 49–51, 55–59, 65–66, 70–74.

20. RBH, Diary, 9 Oct. 1881, in *D&L*, 4: 42; Leonard W. Bacon to RBH, 27 Mar., 21 July 1882, JLMC to RBH, 8 July 1882, RBH to JLMC, 15 July 1882, in Rubin, *Teach the Freeman*, 1: 31–32; 47–48, 50, 52–53.

21. Leonard W. Bacon to RBH, 5 May 1882, in Rubin, *Teach the Freeman*, 1: 40; RBH to Edward Daniels, 10 July 1882, RBH, Diary, 7 May, 27 Aug., 4 Oct. 1882, in *D&L*, 4: 76, 83, 85, 88; Geer, *First Lady*, p. 268.

22. Leonard W. Bacon to RBH, 4 May 1882, RBH to Morris K. Jesup, 23 Nov. 1882, in Rubin, *Teach the Freeman*, 1: 36, 75–76; RBH, Diary, 6 Oct. 1882, in *D&L*, 4: 89.

23. RBH, Diary, 6 Oct., 18 Dec. 1882, in *D&L*, 4: 89, 98–99; RBH, MS Diary, 18 Dec. 1882, HPC.

24. RBH, Diary, 17 Feb. 1882, in *D&L*, 4: 68.

25. RBH to B. T. Tanner, 20 Feb. 1883, in *D&L*, 4: 109. Tanner, who later became an African Methodist Episcopal bishop, was the father of the distinguished painter Henry Ossawa Tanner. *DAB*, s.vv. "Tanner, Benjamin Tucker," "Tanner, Henry Ossawa."

26. RBH, Diary, 5 Sept. 1882, RBH to Alfred T. Waite, 28 Mar. 1883, in *D&L*, 4: 85–86, 114; RBH, MS Diary, 5 Jan. 1882, HPC.

27. RBH, Diary, 3 May 1881, RBH to WHS, 26 Oct. 1881, RBH to David M. Key, 5 Nov. 1881, in *D&L*, 4: 13, 49–51; WHS to RBH, 23 Oct., 12 Dec 1881, David M. Key to RBH, 2 Nov. 1881, HPC; RBH to David M. Key, 27 Oct. 1881, Collection of Sarah Key Patten, copy HPC.

28. RBH, Diary, 10 Dec. 1881, RBH to WHS, 14 Dec. 1881, in *D&L*, 4: 52–54. In Aesop's fable, Jupiter made a log king for the frogs, but when they complained that it was too inert, he replaced it with a stork, which ate them.

29. RBH to JS, 5 July 1882, in *D&L*, 4: 81–82; JS to RBH, 2 July, 3 Aug. 1882, D. M. Key to RBH, 31 Dec. 1882, HPC. A few years later, when Logan died leaving no appreciable estate, Hayes, who thought him "the most . . . distinguished of the volunteer soldiers" in the Civil War, pledged $250 to a fund for Mary Logan. RBH, Diary, 27–28 Dec. 1886, in *D&L*, 4: 302–3. On 31 May 1882, Hayes anticipated that he would be able to pay off his "floating debts" and also hoped to reduce by $3,000 his "funded debt of about thirty thousand dollars." RBH, Diary, 31 May 1882, in *D&L*, 4: 79. Hayes had borrowed $7,000 from the Adams Express Company of Baltimore, Maryland, through his friend S. M. Shoemaker and had apparently increased that debt to $30,000. RBH, MS Diary, 20 Dec. 1881, 22 Mar. 1887, HPC.

30. RBH to D. M. Key, 4 Jan. 1883, RBH, Diary, 21 Feb. 1883, in *D&L*, 4: 100–101, 110; Silas W. Burt to RBH, 10 Jan. 1883, HPC. In fairness to Garfield, he had only four months, rather than four years, to develop his reputation as an executive.

31. RBH, MS Diary, 1 Jan., 9, 11, 14 Feb., 8, 21 Mar., 3 Apr., 27 July, 4 Aug. 1882, 20 May, 11–12 Oct. 1883, HPC; RBH to CS, 9 Feb. 1882, CS Papers, LC, copy HPC. Sugar of lead is lead acetate.

32. RBH, MS Diary, 5 Jan., 15 Mar. 1882, 13 May, 22 June, 15 Aug., 29 Nov. 1883, HPC; RBH to Miss Mittleberger, 12 Nov. 1882, RBH to FAH, 1 June, 11 Dec. 1883, RBH, Diary, 17 Feb., 23 May 1882, 7 May, 30 Nov. 1883, in *D&L*, 4: 68, 78, 91, 117, 119, 130–32; Geer, *First Lady*, pp. 266–68.

33. RBH, MS Diary, 20 Mar., 16–17 Apr. 1882, HPC; RBH, Diary, 25 Mar. 1882, in *D&L*, 4: 73.

34. RBH, MS Diary, 22, 26 Dec. 1882, HPC; RBH, Diary, 26, 30 Dec. 1882, in *D&L*, 4: 99–100.

Chapter 27. Popular Education

1. RBH, Diary, 11 Jan. 1883, RBH to FAH, 13 Jan. 1883, RBH to MFF, 26 Jan. 1883, RBH to James M. Comly, 23 Feb. 1883, in *D&L*, 4: 102–3, 110; RBH, MS Diary, 1, 13, 20, 21 Jan., 13–15 Mar., 27 Apr., 14–15, 20 May, 8 Sept. 1883, HPC. The attacks in early January occurred almost daily and lasted from one to three hours. Lucy's illness was also described and diagnosed at various times as "too frequent colics," "indigestion or dyspepsia," and neuralgia. Dr. John B. Rice was also a congressman.

2. RBH, Diary, 11 Jan., 4–5 Feb., 2 Apr. 1883, RBH to FAH, 7 July 1883, in *D&L*, 4: 102, 104–5, 115, 121; RBH, MS Diary, 14 Feb., 8 Sept. 1883, HPC. Bowen was the publisher of the *Independent*, one of the leading religious periodicals of the Gilded Age. *DAB*, s.v. "Bowen, Henry Chandler."

3. RBH to Whitelaw Reid, 2 Dec. 1883, in *D&L*, 4: 130–31; RBH, MS Diary, 22 June 1883, Whitelaw Reid to RBH, 21 Dec. 1883, HPC.

4. AGH to RBH, 23 May, 30 June, 6 Nov. 1883, RBH to DCG, 14 Nov. 1883, in Rubin, *Teach the Freeman*, 1: 91–93, 101–2.

5. RBH, MS Diary, 14 Jan. 1883, HPC; *Fremont Journal*, 2 Mar. 1883; *Messenger* (Fremont), 24 Jan. 1884; RBH, Diary, 18, 27 Mar., 21–22 May, 26 Sept., 1 Oct. 1883, 14, 16 Sept. 1884, RBH to Randolph Foster, 28 Sept. 1883, RBH to James M. Comly, 19 Dec. 1883, 31 Jan. 1884, in *D&L*, 4: 111, 113–14, 118, 124–25, 133, 140–41, 160–61.

6. RBH, Diary, 7 Jan., 27 Oct., 21, 23 Dec. 1883, in *D&L*, 4: 102, 128, 133–35.

7. RBH to FAH, 1 Nov. 1885, RBH, Diary, 6, 19–20, 23 Feb., 4 Apr., 7 May, 24 Aug., 12 Sept., 4 Nov. 1884, 10 May 1891, in *D&L*, 4: 141–43, 145, 148, 158, 160, 172, 247, 5: 4; RBH, MS Diary, 5 Jan. 1884, HPC.

8. RBH, Diary, 26 May 1884, in *D&L*, 4: 151; John Marshall Harlan to RBH, 30 Nov. 1883, HPC. So that Hayes would understand the majority's position, Harlan sent him Joseph P. Bradley's majority opinion and self-deprecatingly and humorously added: "It may be that when you read the opinion of the court any doubt you have on the merely legal question will be removed. Not long since one of my brethren paid me the compliment of saying that an opinion of mine *satisfied* him that my views were unsound on the question discussed in it!"

9. RBH to GMB, 29 Oct. 1883, in *D&L*, 4: 128–29.

10. Despite the circumstances of Payne's election, Hayes thought that he was "able, conservative, well-meaning." RBH, Diary, 9 Jan. 1884, in *D&L*, 4: 135–36; *DAB*, s.v. "Payne, Henry B."

11. RBH, Diary, 19 Apr., 8 June 1884, RBH to C. H. Grosvenor, 13 June 1884, in *D&L*, 4: 146, 152–53.

12. RBH to WHS, 12 June 1884, RBH to LWH, 5 Nov. 1884, RBH to GMB, 13 Nov. 1884, RBH, Diary, 12, 21 July, 4, 9, 11 Nov. 1884, in *D&L*, 4: 153, 156–57, 172–76.

13. RBH to LWH, 5 Nov. 1884, RBH to GMB, 13 Nov. 1884, RBH, Diary, 11 Nov., 10 Dec. 1884, in *D&L*, 4: 173, 175–76, 179–80; RBH to CS, 28 Nov. 1884, CS Papers, LC, copy HPC.

14. RBH, Diary, 29 Apr., 18 May, 30–31 Dec. 1884, 4 Jan. 1885, RBH to GMB, 13 Nov. 1884, in *D&L*, 4: 148, 150, 176, 181; RBH, MS Diary, 2 June 1884, HPC.

15. RBH, Diary, 2, 3 Oct. 1884, RBH to LWH, 2 Oct. 1884, in *D&L*, 4: 164–65.

16. RBH, Diary, 3, 4 Oct. 1884, in *D&L*, 4: 165–66; AGH to RBH, 14 Jan., 18 June, 29 Aug., 19 Sept., 3 Nov., 22 Dec. 1884, RBH to DCG, 31 Oct., 11 Nov. 1884, William E. Dodge, Jr., to RBH, 17 Nov. 1884, in Rubin, *Teach the Freeman*, 1: 103–5, 108–9, 112–13, 116–18, 121–25, 129–31.

17. RBH to DCG, 3 Apr. 1885, DCG to RBH, 15 Apr. 1885, AGH to RBH, 4 May 1885, in Rubin, *Teach the Freeman*, 1: 141, 143–48; RBH, Diary, 20 May 1885, in *D&L*, 4: 211.

18. RBH, Diary, 22 Jan., 20 May 1885, RBH to Andrew J. Kellar, 28 Nov. 1885, in *D&L*, 4: 187–88, 211, 252; AGH to RBH, 12 June, 18 Aug., 12 Oct. 1885, in Rubin, *Teach the Freeman*, 1: 149–52, 154–57.

19. RBH, Diary, 27 Feb., 20 Mar., 4, 14, 15, 27 Apr. 1884, in *D&L*, 4: 143–48. Hayes correctly guessed that Hay had written the anonymously published novel *The Bread Winners*.

20. RBH, Diary, 4 Oct. 1883, in *D&L*, 4: 126; RBH, MS Diary, 17 Nov. 1883, HPC; Edmund Morris, *The Rise of Theodore Roosevelt* (New York: Coward, McCann & Geoghegan, 1979), p. 201.

21. RBH, Diary, 12 Sept. 1884, 17–18, 29 Oct. 1885, in *D&L*, 4: 160, 242–43, 246; RBH, MS Diary, 30 Apr. 1885, HPC. The interconnections among reform movements is illustrated by the fact that Eugene Smith's "intelligent and bright" wife Katharine happened to be Leonard W. Bacon's sister.

22. RBH, Diary, 15 Oct. 1884, 2 Apr., 9 Nov. 1885, 27 Mar. 1887, in *D&L*, 4: 168, 200–202, 247–48, 315; RBH, MS Diary, 17 Mar., 19 Oct. 1884, HPC. Hayes was critical of missionaries even in his own family. Mary Fitch, the "bright" daughter of Hayes's cousin Belinda Elliot McLelland, and her husband, John Fitch, were Presbyterian missionaries in China. John Fitch particularly offended Hayes with his "monstrous" idea that a million Chinese were perishing monthly without salvation—doomed "to eternal torment"—causing Hayes to explode: "He to bring a new religion to a polite and cultured people!" RBH, Diary, 31 Aug. 1891, 4, 9 Sept. 1892, in *D&L*, 5: 21, 102, 104.

23. RBH, Diary, 17, 21–23 Oct. 1884, 2 Apr. 1885, in *D&L*, 4: 168–69, 200; RBH, MS Diary, 6, 7 Jan., 17 Feb., 2, 6, 10 Mar., 16 Nov., 16, 21–22 Dec. 1884, 13 Jan. 1885, HPC.

24. RBH, Diary, 23 Mar. 1885, RBH to GWC?, 31 Aug. 1885, in *D&L*, 4: 198, 234–35; RBH to CS, 31 Aug. 1885, CS Papers, LC, copy HPC. Schurz believed that George William Curtis's speech at the recent annual meeting of the league had been critical of Democratic spoils practices. CS to RBH, 6 Sept. 1885, HPC.

25. RBH to GWC, 5 Jan. 1885, RBH, Diary, 20 Dec. 1885, RBH to JS, 21 Dec. 1885, in *D&L*, 4: 182, 256–57.

26. RBH to LWH, 16 Jan., 25 Oct. 1885, RBH to JS, 25 Oct. 1885, RBH, Diary, 18 Jan., 11 Sept., 13–14, 25 Oct., 9 Nov. 1885, in *D&L*, 4: 184–86, 236, 242–45, 247–48; Philip D. Jordan, *Ohio Comes of Age* (Columbus: Ohio State Archaeological and Historical Society, 1943), pp. 176–77.

27. RBH to W. D. Bickham, 24 Mar. 1883, RBH, Diary, 25–26, 28 May, 11 June 1885, RBH to W. H. H. Bartraus, 26 May 1885, RBH to Charles F. Manderson, 27 May 1885, in *D&L*, 4: 113, 212–14, 217; RBH to Anson G. McCook, 28 Aug. 1883, McCook Papers, LC, copy HPC.

28. RBH, Diary, 9 Oct. 1883, RBH to Mrs. N. B. Gates, 11 Oct. 1883, RBH to Frances E.

Willard, 13 Oct., 14 Nov. 1833, RBH to LWH, 13 Dec. 1883, RBH to James M. Monroe, 26 Dec. 1885, in *D&L*, 4: 126–29, 133, 257–58; RBH, MS Diary, 26 Dec. 1885, HPC.

29. RBH, Diary, 19 Jan., 20 May, 9 Aug. 1885, 19, 21 Nov. 1886, RBH to James M. Comly, 21 Jan. 1885, in *D&L*, 4: 186–87, 211–12, 230–32, 294–95. Hayes urged that the GAR immediately raise funds for a national monument to Grant in New York. RBH, Diary, 24, 26 July 1885, RBH to S. S. Burdette, 29 July, 15 Aug. 1885, in *D&L*, 4: 224–26, 232–33.

30. RBH to MFF, 7 July 1885, RBH, Diary, 26–27, 29 Nov., 7 Dec. 1885, in *D&L*, 4: 221, 251–53.

31. RBH, Diary, 7, 22 Feb. 1885, RBH to JS, 10, 16 Feb. 1885, RBH to J. M. Comly, 10 Feb. 1885, RBH to GMB, 16 Feb., 3 Mar. 1885, in *D&L*, 4: 188–93, 195–96. Hayes may have gone to the dedication ceremony if he had been invited and informed about the proceedings earlier than 10 February 1885. This neglect combined with serious financial problems kept him close to Fremont.

32. RBH, Diary, 31 May 1882, 23–24 Feb. 1885, RBH to GMB, 3 Mar. 1885, RBH to Eliza G. Davis, 23 May 1885, in *D&L*, 4: 79, 194–96, 212; RBH, MS Diary, 23 Feb. 1885, HPC. Although the Fremont Savings Bank was well run, Hayes never became reconciled to the management of the First National Bank, whose mindless lending and heartless labor policies disgusted him. It had increased its loan to the Malt Works and unjustly fired without notice two of its own employees. In March 1887, Hayes sold $20,000 of his bank stock for $30,000 and paid off his debt of that amount to the Adams Express Company. RBH, Diary, 30–31 Mar. 1887, in *D&L*, 4: 316; RBH, MS Diary, 15–16 Feb., 15, 21–22 Mar. 1887, HPC.

33. RBH, Diary, 20, 26 Mar. 1885, RBH to JS, 11, 26, 27, 31 Mar. 1885, in *D&L*, 4: 197–99; JS to RBH, 5 Mar. 1885, HPC; *Washington Evening Star*, 6 Mar. 1885. To meet the Louisiana commission expenses, Hayes had borrowed through Sherman from the First National Bank of New York, which had agreed to waive interest charges and to wait for a federal appropriation. Four years later, the bank asked for its money, and Hayes evidently repaid the loan, with Sherman advancing $1,000. On hearing of the appropriation, the bank demanded $800 in interest but backed off when Sherman reminded it of the original interest-free arrangement and that Congress had included no interest in its appropriation.

34. RBH, MS Diary, 4 Mar. 1885, LWH to Linus Austin, 10 Mar. 1885, HPC; RBH to FAH, 5 Mar. 1885, RBH, Diary, 14–16 Apr. 1885, in *D&L*, 4: 196–97, 205–7.

35. RBH, Diary, 9 Dec. 1885, 2 Feb., 13 May 1886, 28 Oct. 1891, RBH to Fred D. Grant, 10 Dec. 1885, in *D&L*, 4: 253–54, 264–65, 286–88, 5: 31–32.

36. RBH to James M. Comly, 9 Nov. 1885, 20 Feb. 1886, in *D&L*, 4: 248, 268–69.

37. RBH, Diary, 11 Mar. 1886, 11 Nov. 1890, in *D&L*, 4: 273–74, 614; Lucy M. Salmon, "History of the Appointing Power of the President," *Papers of the American Historical Association* 1 (1886): 291–419.

38. RBH, Diary, 20 Apr. 1886, in *D&L*, 4: 281; Geer, *First Lady*, pp. 264–65. Despite an overall commitment to equal rights, Hayes did not become a feminist. He realized that "the work, and the influence of women grow wider and wider"; although he believed that influence to be elevating and inspiring, he did not favor women's suffrage. RBH to unaddressed, 10 Nov. 1890, in *D&L*, 4: 614.

Chapter 28. Social Justice

1. RBH, Diary, 22, 24 Jan., 6 Apr. 1886, in *D&L*, 4: 261–62, 280.

2. RBH, Diary, 17–20, 26 Mar. 1886, in *D&L*, 4: 277–78; RBH, MS Diary, 25 Mar. 1886, HPC.

3. RBH, Diary, 2 May 1886, in *D&L*, 4: 282; RBH, MS Diary, 18 Apr., 10 May 1886, HPC; Toledo *Commercial*, 1 May 1886.

4. RBH, Diary, 12 May 1886, RBH to GMB, 12 May 1886, in *D&L*, 4: 285–86.

5. RBH to William E. Dodge, 1 Feb. 1887, RBH, Diary, 6 Nov., 4, 10 Dec. 1887, 11 Mar. 1888, in *D&L*, 4: 309, 348, 354–56, 374; RBH, MS Diary, 22 July 1887, WHS, Private Memoranda, 14 Dec. 1887, HPC.

6. RBH, Diary, 4, 10 Dec. 1887, in *D&L*, 4: 354–56; WHS, Private Memoranda, 14 Dec. 1887, HPC. In 1886, Hayes discovered that when Henry George was running for mayor of New York, he had considerable support among respectable conservatives, who also were disturbed by the growing power of wealth. Ibid.

7. RBH to WHS, 22 June 1885, RBH to Leland Stanford, 12 Dec. 1885, RBH to George R. Morse, 24 Feb. 1887, RBH, Diary, 11 Dec. 1885, in *D&L*, 4: 218–19, 254–55, 312; RBH, MS Diary, memoranda following 26 Jan. 1888 at the end of vol. 20, HPC.

8. RBH, Diary, 5 Sept. 1888, 13 Jan. 1889, in *D&L*, 4: 405, 434–35.

9. RBH to Isaac H. Taylor, 9 Mar. 1886, RBH to James M. Comly, 27 Mar. 1886, in *D&L*, 4: 272–73, 278; RBH to DCG, 31 Mar. 1886, DCG to RBH, 17 Apr. 1886, Robert C. Winthrop to RBH, 8 May 1886, in Rubin, *Teach the Freeman*, 1: 33 n., 177, 179–81.

10. RBH to WHS, 1 Nov. 1886, RBH to LWH, 7, 12 Nov. 1886, RBH to FAH, 19 Nov. 1886, RBH, Diary, 18 Nov. 1886, in *D&L*, 4: 291–94; Rufus B. Bullock to RBH, 3 Dec. 1886, 30 July 1891, HPC; AGH to RBH, 29 Sept. 1886, in Rubin, *Teach the Freeman*, 1: 184–85; *Fremont Journal*, 15 July, 12 Nov. 1886. Despite Haygood's optimism, the convict lease system remained until 1907. Rubin, *Teach the Freeman*, 1: 184–85.

11. RBH, Diary, 10 June, 4–5, 12, 15, 17, 22 July 1888, RBH to LWH, 14–15 July 1888, in *D&L*, 4: 391, 397–400; RBH, MS Diary, memoranda entered following 31 Aug. 1888, HPC; *Fremont Courier*, 19 July 1888.

12. RBH, Diary, 5–7 Sept. 1888, in *D&L*, 4: 405–6. Prior to 1885, counties were responsible for executions.

13. RBH, Diary, 4 Mar. 1886, 22 Jan. 1887, RBH to FAH, 27 Feb., 15 Mar. 1886, RBH to GMB, 12 May, 23 Dec. 1886, RBH to H. M. Rawson, 19 Dec. 1886, in *D&L*, 4: 271–72, 276, 285, 299–300, 308; RBH, MS Diary, 26–27 Feb. 1886, 6 Feb. 1887, Linus Austin to RBH, 23 Apr. 1886, HPC. Webb served with the Cleveland Troop in the Spanish-American War and subsequently in the Philippines, where he was awarded the Congressional Medal of Honor for gallantry. Troop Veteran Association, "First Cleveland Troop," HPC; typescript service record, "Major Webb C. Hayes 1st. Ohio Vol. Cavalry," HPC. One of Webb's associates in the National Carbon Company was Myron T. Herrick, who would become a successful banker and an outstanding ambassador to France. *DAB*, s.v. "Herrick, Myron Timothy."

14. RBH, Diary, 30–31 Dec. 1886, 5, 7 Jan. 1887, RBH to GMB, 23 Dec. 1886, in *D&L*, 4: 300, 303–4; RBH, MS Diary, 26 Apr. 1887, HPC.

15. RBH, Diary, 10 May 1886, 9–10, 14, 28 Jan., 7 Feb., 28–29 May 1887, in *D&L*, 4: 285, 304–5, 308, 310, 327; RBH, marked copy of Lyof N. Tolstoi, *Anna Karenina*, trans. Nathan Haskell Dole (New York: Thomas Y. Crowell, 1886), HPC.

16. RBH to William E. Dodge, 1 Feb. 1887, RBH, Diary, 23 Jan., 9 Apr., 3 July 1887, 2, 5 Dec. 1888, in *D&L*, 4: 308–9, 317, 330, 425–26. Benton was also the grandfather of Thomas Hart Benton (1889–1975), a distinguished American artist.

17. RBH to WHS, 27 Nov. 1887, RBH, Diary, 3 Feb., 12–13 May, 25, 27 Nov., 10 Dec. 1887, in *D&L*, 4: 309–10, 325–26, 351–52, 355.

18. *Democratic Messenger* (Fremont), 5 Jan. 1888; RBH, Diary, 17 May 1888, in *D&L*, 4: 390. Butler's school was chartered in 1889 as New York College for the Training of Teachers and was known as Teachers College after 1892. Butler later served as president of Columbia University from 1901 to 1945.

19. RBH, Diary, 7 Sept., 17 Dec. 1888, in *D&L*, 4: 406, 429–30; RBH, MS Diary, 16 May 1888, HPC; RBH to Morris K. Jesup, 17 Nov. 1886, RBH to DCG, 20 Jan. 1887, AGH to RBH, 12 Jan., 3 Feb., 7, 21 Nov. 1887, 17, 26 Jan. 1888, 1 Jan., 20 May, 8 June

1889, in Rubin, *Teach the Freeman*, 1: 185–86, 189–96, 223–24, 235–36, 2: 6–7, 42, 66–69, 71–73.

20. RBH to FAH, 19 Mar. 1888, in *D&L*, 4: 376; RBH, MS Diary, 3 Dec. 1887, HPC.

21. RBH to FAH, 19, 27 Feb. 1888, RBH, Diary, 26 Feb., 1, 8 Mar. 1888, in *D&L*, 4: 371–74.

22. RBH, Diary, 24 Mar., 22 June, 20 Sept., 11 Nov. 1888, 19 Feb., 28 Mar. 1889, in *D&L*, 4: 381, 392, 408, 422, 444, 461. Hayes also did not appreciate President Scott's opposition to the appointment of a German-American professor on the grounds that it would promote beer drinking and discourage Sunday observance. RBH, Diary, 2 Aug. 1888, in *D&L*, 4: 401.

23. RBH, Diary, 3 Oct. 1887, in *D&L*, 4: 342–43; RBH, MS Diary, 13, 26 Oct. 1887, HPC.

24. RBH, Diary, 18 Nov., 2 Dec. 1887, 30 June 1888, in *D&L*, 4: 349, 353, 397; RBH, MS Diary, 2 Dec. 1887, HPC.

25. RBH, Diary, 3 Sept. 1887, RBH to FAH, 18 Dec. 1887, RBH to J. M. Sturtevant, 21 Mar. 1888, in *D&L*, 4: 337, 358–59, 377–78.

26. RBH, Diary, 8, 22, 24–26, 29 June, 26 July 1888, RBH to WHS, 11 June 1888, RBH to William McKinley, 27 June 1888, in *D&L*, 4: 391–96, 400.

27. RBH, Diary, 26 Aug., 6, 9 Nov., 1, 21 Dec. 1888, RBH to Benjamin Harrison, 31 Dec. 1888, RBH to WCH, 31 Dec. 1888, in *D&L*, 4: 402, 420–23, 425, 430–32; LWH to Caroline Harrison, [1889], HPC. Annoyed by James Bryce's claim in his chapter, "Presidential Powers and Duties," in *The American Commonwealth* (2 vols. [New York: Macmillan, 1888]) that "Cleveland *gained* by his numerous vetoes," Hayes believed that they offended veterans and their friends and contributed to his defeat in 1888. RBH, Diary, 31 Jan. 1889, in *D&L*, 4: 439–40.

28. RBH, Diary, 23–25 Jan., 2, 10, 28 Feb. 1889, RBH to James Tanner, 25 Jan. 1889, RBH to JS, 26 Feb., 16 Mar. 1889, RBH to Benjamin Harrison, 5 Mar. 1889, in *D&L*, 4: 437–41, 444, 447–48, 455; RBH, MS Diary, 12 Feb. 1889, HPC. Hayes later asked Gov. William McKinley to give Camp a job. RBH to McKinley, 30 Apr. 1892, in *D&L*, 5: 79. Goodloe died later that year in a spectacular shoot-out with a Republican rival in the Lexington post office, leading Hayes to condemn "Kentucky public sentiment," which promoted such violence. RBH, Diary, 10 Nov. 1889, in *D&L*, 4: 523–24.

29. RBH, Diary, 5–6, 13, 28 Mar. 1889, RBH to Benjamin Harrison, 5 Mar. 1889, RBH to JS, 15 Jan., 20 Feb., 10 [11], 15 Mar., 8 Apr. 1890, in *D&L*, 4: 450–51, 453, 461, 538, 547, 553–55, 562; John Marshall Harlan to RBH, 1, 10 Apr., 15 May 1889, Benjamin Harrison to RBH, 14 Apr. 1890, HPC.

30. *Fremont Journal*, 6 Jan. 1888; RBH, Diary, 25, 27 Apr., 5 May, 18 Oct. 1888, RBH to LWH, 17 Oct. 1888, in *D&L*, 4: 387–88, 410–13.

31. RBH, Diary, 12 Mar. 1889, RBH to Oliver Downing, 15 Mar. 1889, in *D&L*, 4: 453–55.

32. RBH to GMB, 3 Jan. 1888, RBH, Diary, 17 Dec. 1887, 22 June 1888, 31 Jan. 1889, in *D&L*, 4: 357, 363, 392, 440; RBH, MS Diary, 11, 22 Jan., 6, 17–18 May, 23 July 1888, 5, 15 Apr. 1889, HPC. Fanny and Birch's loss of hearing may have been a congenital problem. Hayes's uncle Austin Birchard was deaf, and his grandniece Lily Mitchell was mute.

33. RBH, Diary, 19 Apr., 3–4 June, 8, 24–25, 28 July, 21 Aug. 1887, 29 Mar. 1889, in *D&L*, 4: 321–22, 327–28, 330, 333, 337, 462. Force improved after a trip abroad, and Hayes engineered his appointment to head the Soldiers' Home in Sandusky. RBH to MFF, 28 Apr. 1888, in *D&L*, 4: 387; RBH, MS Diary, 13 Aug. 1889, 25 July 1891, HPC.

34. RBH, Diary, 23–24 Mar. 1888, 23–25, 28–30 Mar. 1889, RBH to GMB, 25 Mar. 1889, in *D&L*, 4: 380–81, 458–62; RBH, MS Diary, 15 Feb. 1888, HPC. Hayes and Matthews also shared Dr. Joseph Webb as a brother-in-law.

35. RBH, Diary, 27, 29–30 Nov. 1888, in *D&L*, 4: 424–25; RBH, MS Diary, 29 Nov. 1888, HPC.

36. RBH, Diary, 8–11 Feb., 13 Apr., 28 Aug., 17 Sept., 15–16 Dec. 1888, 12, 16–18 Mar., 25 May 1889, in *D&L*, 4: 369–70, 382–83, 403, 408, 429, 452–53, 455–56, 469; RBH, MS Diary, 2 July, 28 Oct. 1887, 20 May 1888, HPC. Hayes, who regularly participated in Roman Catholic fund-raising and other affairs, noted that "Dick Tobin, Irish Catholic drayman, paid over the first cash—one dollar" for the Methodist church rebuilding fund. RBH, Diary, 8, 13 Feb. 1888, in *D&L*, 4: 370–71.

37. RBH, Diary, 27 Apr., 3–4, 8–9 May 1889, in *D&L*, 4: 466–68; RBH, MS Diary, 3 May 1889, HPC. Shepard's home was one of the famous Vanderbilt houses on Fifty-second Street, just off Fifth Avenue.

38. RBH, Diary, 22 June 1889, in *D&L*, 4: 471.

39. RBH to Anson G. McCook, 12 July 1889, McCook Papers, LC, copy HPC; WHS, Memoranda, 9 Aug. 1890, HPC.

40. RBH, Diary, 22–25 June 1889, in *D&L*, 4: 471–74; RBH, MS Diary, 23–24 June 1889, Lucy Elliot Keeler, Diary, 22–23, 26 June 1889, HPC. Lucy died at 6:30 A.M., Tuesday, 25 June 1889.

Chapter 29. Without Lucy

1. RBH, Diary, 26 June 1889, RBH to WHS, 27 June 1889, in *D&L*, 4: 474–75.

2. RBH, Diary, 29 June, 1, 2, 7, 21 July 1889, RBH to GMB, 6 July 1889, in *D&L*, 4: 475–80, 483–84, 491. Winnie Monroe, as bored at Spiegel Grove as Lucy was taxed by her mercurial temper, had returned to Washington, where she died in 1886; Hayes paid her funeral expenses. Geer, *First Lady*, p. 246.

3. Hayes hoped that William Dean Howells or William Henry Smith would write Lucy's memorial, but it was done by Eliza G. Davis. RBH, Diary, 9, 11, 13, 18–19, 23, 25 July, 1–2 Aug., 13 Sept. 1889, 1, 29 Jan. 1890, RBH to Eliza G. Davis, 12 July, 9 Dec. 1889, 1 Mar. 1890, RBH to William Dean Howells, 14, 30 Sept. 1889, RBH to WHS, 9 Dec. 1889, in *D&L*, 4: 485–87, 490–91, 493, 495–96, 509–10, 512–13, 529–30, 535, 541, 551; RBH, MS Diary, 4 July, 29–31 Dec. 1889, HPC.

4. RBH, Diary, 2, 4–7, 10, 18, 20–22 Aug. 1889, RBH to Harriet C. Herron, 28 Aug. 1889, in *D&L*, 4: 496–99, 502–4.

5. RBH, Diary, 1–5, 13, 17–18, 23 Sept. 1889, 11, 22, 29 June 1890, in *D&L*, 4: 506–7, 509–11, 580–81, 583.

6. RBH, Diary, 28–30 Sept., 3–4 Oct. 1889, in *D&L*, 4: 512–13; RBH, MS Diary, 16 May 1890, HPC; Larry E. Burgess, *The Smileys: A Commemorative Edition* (Redlands, Calif.: Moore Historical Foundation, 1991), pp. 31, 37.

7. RBH, MS Diary, 7 Oct. 1889, HPC; RBH, Diary, 4–6, 8 Oct. 1889, in *D&L*, 4: 513–14.

8. RBH, Diary, 13–14, 17, 19 Oct. 1889, in *D&L*, 4: 515–16; DCG to RBH, 10, 19 Oct. 1889, AGH to RBH, 4 Nov. 1889, in Rubin, *Teach the Freeman*, 2: 77, 79, 81–82.

9. RBH, Diary, 19 Oct. 1889, in *D&L*, 4: 516; RBH, MS Diary, 20, 22 Oct., 23 Dec. 1889, 23 Jan. 1890, HPC.

10. RBH, Diary, 4, 20 July, 18 Aug., 28 Oct. 1889, RBH to Harriet C. Herron, 29 Oct., 5 Dec. 1889, 21 May 1890, in *D&L*, 4: 480, 491, 502, 517–19, 527–28, 577; RBH, MS Diary, 29 Nov. 1889, HPC. The Chautauqua Literary & Scientific Circle, established in 1878, sponsored a program of college-level studies in the home and at summer assemblies at Lake Chautauqua, N.Y. At the close of his seventieth year, Hayes joined the Chautauqua class of 1896 with the words, "Let education continue to the end of life"; he then earnestly

began reading his assignment on the topic of Greece. RBH, Diary, 4 Sept., 1–2 Oct. 1892, in *D&L*, 5: 102, 108–9.

11. RBH, Diary, 17–18, 24 Nov. 1889, 8 Oct. 1890, in *D&L*, 4: 524–25, 601; RBH, MS Diary, 24 Nov., 4 Dec. 1889, HPC.

12. RBH, Diary, 24 Dec. 1889, 14, 16 Jan., 14, 27 Feb., 1, 18 Mar. 1890, RBH to GMB, 5 Dec. 1889, RBH to Harriet C. Herron, 26 Dec. 1889, in *D&L*, 4: 528, 532–33, 537, 539, 546, 550–51, 556; RBH, MS Diary, 25 Dec. 1889, HPC. Like his better-known sociologist brother Lester Frank Ward, Cyrenus Osborne Ward, a labor organizer and social reformer, was a federal civil servant. *DAB*, s.v. "Ward, Cyrenus Osborne."

13. RBH, Diary, 26 Feb., 19, 31 Mar. 1890, 15 Dec. 1891, RBH to WCH, 20 Mar. 1890, in *D&L*, 4: 550, 556–57, 560, 5: 39.

14. RBH, Diary, 4–7, 10, 21–24 Mar., 5, 15 Apr. 1890, in *D&L*, 4: 552–53, 557–58, 561, 564; RBH, MS Diary, 4–7 Mar., 4–5 Apr. 1890, HPC.

15. RBH, Diary, 17–18, 20–30 Apr., 11 May 1890, in *D&L*, 4: 565–70, 573; RBH, MS Diary, 30 Apr. 1890, HPC.

16. RBH, Diary, 5–6, 8 May 1890, in *D&L*, 4: 571–73; RBH, MS Diary, 6–7 May 1890, HPC.

17. RBH, Diary, 8, 11, 14 May 1890, in *D&L*, 4: 573–74 RBH, MS Diary, 16, 18 May 1890, HPC. Covert apparently toned down his paper and gave it at the conference. RBH, Diary, 4 June 1890, in *D&L*, 4: 578. Influenced by Atticus Haygood, Hayes made it a prime goal to avoid breeding hostility between southern whites and blacks .

18. RBH, Diary, 2–6 June 1890, in *D&L*, 4: 578–79; C. R. Williams, *Hayes*, 2: 354–55; Glenn C. Altschuler, *Andrew D. White: Educator, Historian, Diplomat* (Ithaca, N.Y.: Cornell University Press, 1979), p. 184. Two years later, Hayes thought that Tourgee's anti-plutocratic novel *Murvale Eastman: Christian Socialist* (1890), stressing the achievement of social justice by applying the Golden Rule, "puts the question of our time admirably." RBH, MS Diary, 15 June 1892, HPC; Otto H. Olsen, *Carpetbagger's Crusade: The Life of Albion Winegar Tourgee* (Baltimore: Johns Hopkins University Press, 1965), pp. 276, 289–92.

19. RBH, Diary, 10, 17–18 June, 23 July 1890, in *D&L*, 4: 580–81, 589; RBH, MS Diary, 14 June 1890, HPC.

20. RBH, Diary, 19 June, 7 July, 7 Aug. 1890, in *D&L*, 4: 581, 585, 591; RBH, MS Diary, 11 July, 9 Aug. 1890, WHS, Memoranda, 8–9 Aug. 1890, HPC.

21. RBH, Diary, 24 Aug., 12 Sept. 1890, in *D&L*, 4: 595, 600; RBH, MS Diary, 14, 24 Aug., 3, 14 Sept. 1890. HPC.

22. RBH, Diary, 25, 29 Aug., 6, 9, 11 Sept., 8, 19 Oct. 1890, RBH to Eliza G. Davis, 27 Oct. 1890, in *D&L*, 4: 595–96, 598–99, 601–3, 606–7, 610. In his Loyal Legion speech, Hayes planned to stress "equality of opportunity for happiness; that is, of education, wealth, power."

23. RBH, Diary, 27, 29–31 Oct. 1890, in *D&L*, 4: 610–11; W. E. B. Du Bois to RBH, 4 Nov. 1890, in Rubin, *Teach the Freeman*, 2: 158–61. Hayes's idea about the success of Ohio blacks was confirmed when on a train from Cincinnati to Columbus he "met a couple of young colored men who were returning" to their homes in Ohio from Troy, Missouri, where they had taught "public colored schools" during the eight-month school year. RBH, MS Diary, 6 May 1892, HPC.

24. RBH, Diary, 5–6, 9 Nov. 1889, 4–5 Nov. 1890, in *D&L*, 4: 521–23, 611–13.

25. RBH, Diary, 23 Oct., 5, 17 Nov. 1890, in *D&L*, 4: 608, 613–15. Hayes elaborated on justice and equality on Thanksgiving Day and the weeks following. RBH, Diary, 27 Nov., 15 Dec. 1890, in *D&L*, 4: 616, 623.

26. RBH, Diary, 7 Jan., 2, 10, 12 Dec. 1890, in *D&L*, 4: 536, 619, 621–22.

27. RBH, Diary, 17, 19 Dec. 1890, RBH to JLMC, 26 Dec. 1890, in *D&L*, 4: 624, 626; RBH, MS Diary, 19, 23 Dec. 1890, HPC.

28. RBH, Diary, 25–28, 30 Dec. 1890, in *D&L*, 4: 625–27; RBH, MS Diary, 25, 30 Dec. 1890, HPC.

Chapter 30. Joining Lucy

1. RBH, Diary, 1 Jan. 1891, in *D&L*, 4: 627–28.
2. RBH, MS Diary, 27 Apr. 1891, HPC; RBH, Diary, 1–2 May 1891, in *D&L*, 5: 1–2.
3. RBH, Diary, 28 May, 9 June 1891, 2 Feb. 1892, in *D&L*, 5: 8–9, 53.
4. JLMC to RBH, 8 Apr., 27 Nov., 23 Dec. 1891, in Rubin, *Teach the Freeman*, 2: 192–93, 220–23, 238–39; RBH, Diary, 21, 26 Nov. 1891, 13 Apr. 1892, in *D&L*, 5: 33–36, 75.
5. W. E. B. Du Bois to RBH, 19 Apr., 6, 25 May 1891, Nathaniel Southgate Shaler to RBH, 2 Mar. 1891, JLMC to RBH, 8 Apr. 1891, in Rubin, *Teach the Freeman*, 2: 189–90, 192, 194–95, 198, 203–5.
6. W. E. B. Du Bois to RBH, 3 Apr. 1892, Albert Bushnell Hart to DCG, 14 Apr. 1892, RBH to DCG, 17 May 1892, DCG to Du Bois, 23 May 1892, in Rubin, *Teach the Freeman*, 2: 245–48, 251–52; RBH, Diary, 13, 15 Apr. 1892, in *D&L*, 5: 75–76; RBH, MS Diary, 12 Apr. 1892, HPC.
7. RBH, Diary, 3, 31 Mar., 4–5 Apr., 5 May 1891, 17, 26 Feb. 1892, RBH to Samuel M. Taylor, 30 Jan. 1891, RBH to S. T. Mitchell, 23 Feb. 1886, 1 Apr. 1891, in *D&L*, 4: 270, 635–36, 639, 643–45, 5: 2, 59, 61.
8. RBH, Diary, 26 June, 23, 29 July, 21 Nov. 1891, 3 May, 1 June, 23 Nov. 1892, in *D&L*, 5: 11, 15–16, 34–35, 79–80, 87, 125, 200; James E. Pollard, *History of the Ohio State University* (Columbus: Ohio State University Press, 1952), pp. 112–13.
9. RBH, Diary, 3 Jan., 12 Oct. 1891, 8, 13 Sept. 1892, in *D&L*, 4: 629, 5: 28, 103–4. Despite the growing disparity between wealth and poverty, Hayes believed that there was less fighting and fewer riots in the large cities than there had been fifty years earlier because of the increased number of arrests and convictions for misdemeanors, which paradoxically gave the opposite impression. RBH, Diary, 30 Nov. 1891, in *D&L*, 5: 36–37.
10. RBH, Diary, 16 Sept., 4, 13 Oct. 1892, in *D&L*, 5: 105, 110–12, 115. The exact quote from *Hamlet* (3.4.168) is: "For use almost can change the stamp of nature." RBH, Diary, 16 Sept. 1892, in *D&L*, 5: 105.
11. RBH, Diary, 11 May 1891, 29 Jan. 1892, in *D&L*, 5: 4–5, 51. Approximately forty years earlier, Hayes wrote approvingly of vigilantism. RBH, Diary, 23 July 1851, in *D&L*, 1: 373.
12. RBH, Diary, 30 July, 27 Oct. 1891, 7 Jan., 8–11 June 1892, in *D&L*, 5: 16, 31, 47, 90–92.
13. RBH, Diary, 15 Oct., 8–9 Nov. 1892, in *D&L*, 5: 115, 122–23.
14. RBH, Diary, 11, 14–16, 19, 21, 23 Feb., 8 May 1891, in *D&L*, 4: 638–39, 5: 3–4.
15. RBH, MS Diary, 17, 20, 24, 27 Jan., 1 Feb., 23 Mar., 2, 21–22, 26 Apr., 6, 16 May, 15, 21–22 Oct. 1891, HPC.
16. RBH, MS Diary, 8–11, 15, 16, 19, 24 Apr. 1892, HPC; RBH, Diary, 4–6, 13–23 Apr. 1892, in *D&L*, 5: 71–72, 75–77.
17. RBH, MS Diary, 22 June, 9 July 1892, HPC; RBH, Diary, 22–23 June 1892, RBH to Scott Hayes, 19 Apr. 1892, in *D&L*, 5: 93–94, 136.
18. RBH, Diary, 8 Sept., 31 Dec. 1891, in *D&L*, 5: 22–23, 43.
19. RBH, MS Diary, 22 Sept. 1892, HPC; RBH, Diary, 2, 15–22 Sept. 1892, RBH to Henry C. Corbin, 2 Oct. 1892, in *D&L*, 5: 101, 104–10.
20. RBH, Diary, 4, 6–16 Oct. 1892, in *D&L*, 5: 110–16.
21. RBH, MS Diary, 17–18 Oct. 1892, HPC; RBH, Diary, 23 Mar. 1891, 17–21, 23 Oct.

1892, RBH to Louise C. Austin, 19 Oct. 1892, in *D&L*, 4: 642, 5: 116–18; Robert Muccigrosso, *Celebrating the New World: Chicago's Columbian Exposition of 1893* (Chicago: Ivan R. Dee, 1993), pp. 74–77. The exception was a "noble" address in the evening by Archbishop John Ireland of St. Paul, advocating "congresses for moral, educational, and religious" concerns.

22. RBH, Diary, 25–26 Nov. 1892, in *D&L*, 5: 125–26; RBH, MS Diary, 24–26 Nov., 11 Dec. 1892, HPC. Severance Hall, the home of the Cleveland Orchestra, is named for Julia Millikin's family.

23. RBH, Diary, 27 Nov., 25 Dec. 1892, in *D&L*, 5: 126, 130; RBH, MS Diary, 25 Dec 1892, HPC.

24. RBH, Diary, 26–28 Dec. 1892, in *D&L*, 5: 130–31. Wilbur H. Siebert later published *The Underground Railroad from Slavery to Freedom* (1898).

25. RBH, Diary, 30 Dec. 1892, 1, 5–6, 8 Jan. 1893, in *D&L*, 5: 132, 143; RBH, MS Diary, 30–31 Dec. 1892, 1–8 Jan. 1893, HPC. William K. Rogers and Laura Platt Mitchell also were alive.

26. RBH, Diary, 9–13 Jan. 1893, in *D&L*, 5: 143–44; Lucy Elliot Keeler, "Rutherford Birchard Hayes," *Fremont Journal*, 20 Jan. 1893.

27. RBH to William G. Lane, 22 Sept. 1845, Yale University, copy HPC; C. R. Williams, note following 13 Jan. 1893, Appendix B, in *D&L*, 5: 144–45, 158–59; Keeler, "Hayes," 20 Jan. 1893; Lucy Elliot Keeler, Diary, 15–16, 18 Jan. 1893, HPC.

28. C. R. Williams, Appendix B, in *D&L*, 5: 159–60; Lucy Elliot Keeler, "The Funeral of General Hayes," *Fremont Journal*, 27 Jan. 1893; Fremont *Daily News*, 21 Jan. 1893; John W. Herron to BAH, 18 Jan. 1893, Lucy Elliot Keeler, Diary, 19–20 Jan. 1893, HPC.

29. C. R. Williams, Appendix B, in *D&L*, 5: 161–269; W. E. B. Du Bois to DCG, no date, in Rubin, *Teach the Freeman*, 2: 281.

Afterword

1. RBH to CS, 26 Feb. 1883, CS Papers, LC, copy HPC.

2. RBH, Diary, 29 Dec. 1881, RBH to Alexander Johns[t]on, 6 June 1882, in *D&L*, 4: 58, 80; Henry Adams to Charles Milnes Gaskell, 14 June 1876, Henry Adams to Henry Cabot Lodge, 13 May 1880, in Levenson, *Letters of Henry Adams*, 2: 276, 400.

3. Samuel Langhorne Clemens to RBH, 10 Apr. 1882, HPC. As a brash young man, I thought Hayes inconsistent as a civil-service reformer. See Hoogenboom, *Outlawing the Spoils*, pp. 135–78.

4. RBH, Diary, 5 Dec. 1888, in *D&L*, 4: 426.

5. RBH, Diary, 12 Dec. 1890, in *D&L*, 4: 622.

INDEX